ECONOMICS
of EDUCATION

Michael Lovenheim
Cornell University

Sarah Turner
University of Virginia

worth publishers
Macmillan Learning
New York

Vice President, Social Science and High School: Charles Linsmeier
Director of Content and Assessment: Shani Fisher
Program Manager: Tom Digiano
Marketing Manager: Andrew Zierman
Marketing Assistant: Morgan Ratner
Editorial Assistant: Courtney Lindwall
Executive Development Editor: Sharon Balbos
Development Editor: Lukia Kliossis
Associate Development Editor: Sarah Nguyen
Director, Content Management Enhancement: Tracey Kuehn
Managing Editor: Lisa Kinne
Director of Design, Content Management: Diana Blume
Senior Content Project Manager: Edgar Doolan
Senior Workflow Supervisor: Susan Wein
Senior Design Manager: Vicki Tomaselli
Interior Designer: Patrice Sheridan
Cover Designer: Joseph DePinho
Photo Editor: Jennifer MacMillan
Composition: codeMantra
Illustration Coordinator: Janice Donnola
Illustrations: Network Graphics
Printing and Binding: King Printing Co., Inc.
Cover and Title Page Image: 3DDock/Shutterstock

Library of Congress Control Number: 2017937836

ISBN-13: 978-1-319-28220-2
ISBN-10: 1-319-28220-2

Printed in the United States of America

First printing

Worth Publishers
One New York Plaza
Suite 4500
New York, NY 10004-1562
www.macmillanlearning.com

Michael Lovenheim is an Associate Professor in the Department of Policy Analysis and Management at Cornell University and is a Faculty Research Fellow at the National Bureau of Economic Research in the Economics of Education and Public Economics working groups. He joined the Cornell faculty in 2009 after receiving his BA in Economics from Amherst College in 2000 and his PhD in Economics from the University of Michigan in 2007. From 2007 to 2009, Professor Lovenheim was a Searle Freedom Trust Postdoctoral Fellow at the Stanford Institute for Economic Policy Research. He received both a Spencer Foundation Dissertation Fellowship in 2006 and a postdoctoral fellowship from the Spencer Foundation and the National Academy of Education in 2011. Professor Lovenheim's research focuses on the economics of higher education as well as on teacher labor markets, and he has published widely in top economics, policy, and education journals. He currently sits on the editorial board of *Journal of Human Resources* and *Demography* and is a co-editor at *Journal of Policy Analysis and Management*.

Sarah Turner is a University Professor of Economics & Education and the Souder Family Professor at the University of Virginia, where she holds appointments in the Department of Economics, the Curry School of Education, and the Batten School of Leadership and Public Policy. She is also a Faculty Research Associate of the National Bureau of Economics Research. Turner received her PhD in economics from the University of Michigan and her undergraduate degree from Princeton University. Professor Turner's research focuses on how students make choices about college going, the impact of financial aid, and the determinants of postsecondary degree attainment. Turner's research also examines global education markets and the role of high-skill immigration in labor market outcomes. Turner is a co–principal investigator (with Caroline Hoxby) of the *Expanding College Opportunities* project, a randomized controlled trial that had a substantial impact on college choice for high-achieving low-income students. Professor Turner's research has received funding from federal agencies and private foundations including the Institute for Education Sciences, the Bill & Melinda Gates Foundation, the Spencer Foundation, and the Smith Richardson Foundation.

BRIEF CONTENTS

CONTENTS

Part II. The Foundations of Education Production and Investment

Part III. Elementary and Secondary Education Policy

Part IV. Higher Education Policy

Defining the Economics of Education

The importance of education as a driver of economic gains for individuals and productivity growth for society has likely never been as high as it is today. Increasingly, one's success in the labor market is determined by one's skills and abilities, otherwise known as human capital. Arguments that education can produce a more productive, healthy, and socially involved citizenry have been around at least since Aristotle and are echoed repeatedly by politicians, educators, business leaders, and parents today. Indeed, the United States spends over 7% of its gross domestic product (GDP) on education, amounting to $1.2 trillion per year. By any measure, education is critically important to the U.S. economy, and we invest heavily in formal educational institutions as a society.

While there tends to be broad agreement that investments in education can have high individual and social returns, there is much less agreement about what types of education policies and systems generate the skills that are valued in the labor market and by society more generally. A pioneer of the economics of education, William Bowen, wrote more than 50 years ago:

> As more money is spent on education, the old undocumented assertions that "we know" or "we believe" that "education pays," will prove less and less satisfactory to the private and public groups that have to pay the mounting bills.—*Economic Aspects of Education*, 1964

The goal of this book is to provide students with the tools to use an economic lens to analyze fundamental issues in education: how and why people make decisions to invest in education, the effect of education on long-term social and economic outcomes, the behavior of the institutions that "produce" education, and how best to design and implement public policies affecting the level and distribution of education resources.

Why We Wrote This Book

This book is an outgrowth of Economics of Education courses we have taught at the University of Virginia and Cornell University for many years. In turn, these courses build on the insights and research innovations from our colleagues throughout the world.

- Analytical tools used in the subfield of economics of education come from a combination of microeconomic theory, public economics, labor economics, and industrial organization. Along with ideas unique to the subfield, such as human capital, we wanted to collect the common ideas from often disparate subfields into one place and show how they can be applied to the study of education.

- Education is different from other commodities and services in fundamental respects, which makes it important to analyze separately. For one, education is embodied and therefore cannot be traded in the same way that we trade commodities or buy and sell capital goods like automobiles. For this reason, it is difficult to collateralize an investment in education. The resulting credit constraints, combined with the positive externalities associated with education, lead to circumstances in which a private market would likely generate too low a level of educational attainment among the population. This forms the basis of the large role played by the government in U.S. education markets.

- Distinctive features on the production side of the market differentiate education from other commodities. How "knowledge" and "skills" are produced by formal education institutions often defies easy quantification. Peers—the other consumers—may contribute to the learning of classmates, and educational outcomes also depend on individual effort. These features combine to make the study of the economics of education both fascinating and complex.

- Education markets in the United States are composed of a complex set of institutions and regulations. Providers of education include federal, state, and local governments; private nonprofit firms; and private for-profit firms. Federal, state, and local governments also fund education at all levels, whether the providers are public or not. The mix of education providers and funders can differ according to the level of education, with higher education markets including a large role for the private sector while the market for primary and secondary education is dominated by the public sector. To analyze U.S. education policy, it is critical to understand how various education markets are structured and how these markets operate. Describing U.S. education markets is a core focus of this book.

- Economists studying the economics of education have been leaders in developing and applying powerful empirical tools that provide important evidence on the causal effects of various education policies and of how individual education investment decisions affect short-run and long-run outcomes. A focus of this book is on providing a guide to the ways economists have approached empirical analyses and what the empirical research has found with respect to each topic we consider. Comprehensive and technical literature reviews in economics can be found in the *Handbook of the Economics of Education*, the *Handbook of Labor Economics*, and the *Journal of Economic Literature*. Primary source research outlets, including general interest journals like the *American Economic Review* and the *Quarterly Journal of Economics* and more specialized journals like the *Economics of Education Review* and the *Journal of Labor Economics*, provide frontier technical analyses on questions in the domain of the economics of education. Our goal is not to duplicate these comprehensive and technical publications but rather to provide an overview of empirical approaches and findings from economics of education research that is accessible to those without a PhD in economics. Rather than forcing instructors to teach solely using published research papers that often are too technical for undergraduate or master's degree students, we provide an overview and assessment of economics of education research in one place.

Goals of This Book

What economists do best is to provide theoretical models and empirical methods that allow for careful analysis of the costs and benefits of alternative policies. Yet, reasonable economists disagree. Critically, economics is a positive, not a normative, science. Economists (or at least the economists writing this book) do not have an advantage in determining what our society's values or goals should be. Rather, we focus on how to best achieve these goals with the resources available. This book will not adjudicate between different political viewpoints or debates about education policy; advocating for (or against) particular policies is not our aim. The goal instead is to lay out the evidence as clearly as possible; to note the agreements, disagreements, and unresolved points in the research literature; and to provide students with the empirical and theoretical tools necessary to draw their own conclusions. Students reading this book will develop the skills needed to apply economic ideas and principles to core questions and problems in education.

We also hope that students will come away from the experience of working through this textbook with an excitement about the prospects of applying economic models to fundamental questions of education policy. From the start, our goal has been to convey a clear understanding of educational institutions and policies, an appreciation for the problems of measuring how education policies affect outcomes, and a clear grasp of how economic models can help explain educational outcomes.

Organization and Objectives of Text

This book has four major parts:

Part I (Chapters 1–3) defines the subject matter, setting forth the basic tools and the institutional structure of the U.S. education system that will be used throughout the book.

Part II (Chapters 4–7) covers the broad models explaining investment in education and the measurement of the returns to education.

Part III (Chapters 8–12) and Part IV (Chapters 13–15) cover major topics in primary–secondary education policy and higher education policy, respectively, and include specific chapters on accountability programs, school finance, and financing education at the collegiate level.

Part I: Introduction and Background

Chapter 1, Why Do Economists Study Education Policy? addresses the most obvious question: What is the economics of education? We begin by relating the study of the economics to education: How is education "produced"? What types of education should be produced? For whom should it be produced? Central to this section is the presentation of the distinguishing features of education as an economic activity and the reasons why market failures such as credit constraints and potential externalities motivate public policies related to education. We also cover how the models from specific fields in economics—labor, public, industrial organization—shape our understanding of individual investments in education and the provision of education. Like all subsequent chapters, this chapter reinforces the understanding of basic economic ideas, with examples and exercises that illustrate concepts and tools like opportunity cost, comparative advantage, the production possibilities frontier, and budget constraints.

Chapter 2, The Structure and History of Education Markets in the United States, links together education, economic growth, and income inequality in the context of the institutional history of schooling at the elementary, secondary, and collegiate levels. Students will have a clear understanding of the link between the education market and the labor market after reading this chapter. We provide a detailed overview of the structure of education markets in the United States as well as a brief history of the development of current education institutions. The content illustrates the broad trends in educational attainment over the course of the past two centuries. It also addresses institutional movements, such as the development of common schools in the nineteenth century, the high school movement at the start of the twentieth century, and the growth of mass higher education. Tied to changes in educational attainment are changes in the structure of wages in recent decades, with the decline in the college wage premium during the 1970s followed by persistent increases in the return to schooling in the most recent decades. Research covered in this chapter includes articles from researchers Richard Freeman, Kevin Murphy, Finis Welch, Lawrence Katz, David Autor, and Alan Krueger. They explore the determinants of wages in the context of changes in the supply of college-educated workers, shifts in labor demand, and technological change.

Chapter 3, Empirical Tools of Education Economics, outlines the basic empirical methods used by economists who study education. Faulty inferences about education policies follow from the confounding of correlation and causation and from the failure to consider whether differences between schools or groups of students may result from choices parents and students make about their education environment. Many important empirical questions, such as how reductions in class size affect student learning or whether increases in the availability of financial aid affect collegiate attainment, can be understood and discussed with a relatively modest level of training in econometrics. Our aim is to introduce and apply basic methodologies such as experimental design, basic multivariate linear regression, instrumental variables, regression discontinuity, and the difference-in-differences approach in a way that undergraduate students and graduate students with limited economics preparation can understand in an applied context.

Part II: The Foundations of Education Production and Investment

Chapter 4, The Human Capital Model, describes the core concept of human capital, the ways in which it differs from physical capital, and the implications of these differences for education markets. The human capital investment model, which has roots in the writing of Adam Smith and was formalized by economist and Nobel laureate Gary Becker (and others) presents the decision to go to school in terms of a discounted stream of costs (tuition costs and forgone earnings) as well as benefits (e.g., wage increases). This basic model provides students with a range of computational problems as well as opportunities to show how changes in tuition, the college wage premium, and the cost of capital potentially affect educational attainment. After setting forth the basic model, we ask students to consider the implications of violations of standard assumptions such as limitations in borrowing or uncertainty in the outcomes for education choices. More generally, the chapter examines the very different implications of credit constraints and variation in ability in the explanation of observed educational attainment differences across individuals and the consequent implications for public policy. This chapter forms the basis for thinking about the decision to invest in education, which we return to throughout the book.

Chapter 5, The Signaling Model: An Alternative to the Human Capital Framework, poses an important challenge to the notion that educational investment generates human capital or productive skills. Is it true that added skills explain the gains in earnings associated with greater educational attainment? The classic exposition of the signaling model is found in the work of Michael Spence (*Job Market Signaling*, 1973), which considers how asymmetric information may affect incentives to invest in education. The chapter starts with a basic model in which employers are limited in their capacity to assess worker skills at the point of hiring. In this context, education may provide information about individual ability and productivity. While education can serve a private investment function in both human capital and signaling models, the social returns are likely to be different across models, with significant implications for policy design.

Chapter 6, The Returns to Education Investment, emphasizes empirical studies of the returns to schooling. A starting point is the Mincer earnings equation and the interpretation of the observed relationship between educational attainment and earnings. Estimating the return to education is the bread and butter of labor economics; yet, a simple relationship between earnings and education is likely to misrepresent the causal effect of education on earnings. There are a number of examples in the research literature of innovative attempts to overcome this bias to measure whether educational attainment causes an increase in earnings: controlling directly for student ability, examining identical twins who share the same genetics and home environment, and using natural variation from policies such as compulsory schooling age or distance to a university.

Chapter 7, How Knowledge Is Produced: The Education Production Function, turns to an examination of how educational inputs link to outcomes in terms of measured gains in achievement or skills. Just as we can think of a manufacturing firm combining inputs like raw materials, capital equipment, and labor to produce goods, schools can be thought of as engaging in the production of student learning. In doing so, educational institutions must choose how intensively to employ inputs like teachers, books, facilities, and computers as well as the mode of "production" that combines all of these inputs to produce education outputs. While there are parallels with the theory of the firm that is the staple of any course in microeconomics, the production function for education is replete with additional challenges tied to incomplete information about how students learn, the role of peers, and the considerable difficulty in measuring the full set of inputs and outcomes to the education process.

Part III: Elementary and Secondary Education Policy

Chapter 8, The Financing of Local Public Schools, grounds the institutional evolution of elementary and secondary education in the United States in economic theory. Local control in the provision of K–12 education historically has been a defining feature of schooling in the United States. The Tiebout model outlines how families "vote with their feet" to get their preferred level of spending on education and local public goods. This model helps us understand how local control serves to capitalize school quality in housing prices while allowing for variation across communities in the demand for public schooling. Yet, there are good reasons to think that the central assumptions of the Tiebout model (no economies of scale, perfect information about choices, a large range of options) may not hold in practice. Purely local funding leaves unaddressed the difficulties that low-income families may face in buying into high-quality school districts, as well as the potential that low levels of school funding in some districts may have negative effects on society more broadly as students enter adult life poorly prepared for employment and civic responsibilities. These market failures provide scope for centralization of funding at the state and federal level as well as regulation from state and federal agencies. We discuss the school finance reform movement with a focus on the economics behind the different funding mechanisms, recognizing that the success of reform policies in raising funding or reducing inequality ultimately depends on the economic incentives provided to different constituencies. The chapter concludes with an examination of the empirical research on how school finance reform affects spending inequality.

Chapter 9, Does Money Matter? The Relationship Between Education Inputs and Educational Outcomes, focuses on how added resources affect outcomes in the context of the education production function. The starting point is the empirical observation that aggregate increases in educational spending are not always associated with gains in measured student achievement. This association leads some researchers to ask if it is productive inefficiency in the schools, not the absence of resources, which generates disappointing educational outcomes. We critically examine the data underlying this critique as well as the alternative evidence. We then turn to an analysis of the two most studied education inputs: class size and teacher quality. The conclusion from this chapter is nuanced: schools may not function in ways that are productively efficient; at the same time, there is substantial evidence that increases in certain types of resources have a positive effect on student achievement.

Chapter 10, School Choice: A Market-Based Approach to Education Reform, examines how competition among public schools and between public and private schools affects the efficiency and the distribution of schooling. At issue is whether the "production" of education by local districts is efficient. Are local districts bureaucratically inefficient local monopolies? Would initiatives such as voucher programs and charter schools increase the capacity of families to exercise choice, rewarding schools with high performance? Does injecting competition into local schooling markets by inducing schools to compete over students raise the productivity of all schools? The argument for school choice is not new, dating as far back as Friedman's *The Role of Government in Education* (1955). Policies such as charter schools and intradistrict open enrollment have grown to change the market options faced by families, particularly those who are constrained in their ability to afford housing in a high-quality school district. We identify the economic context of the various choice policies in the United States and examine the empirical research on how these policies affect students and schools.

Chapter 11, Test-Based Accountability Programs, looks to both economic theory and empirical evidence to assess a range of accountability programs. State-level initiatives and the federal No Child Left Behind Act of 2002 imposed rewards and sanctions based on test performance. This chapter presents models of why such rewards and sanctions may change the behavior of both teachers and students and lead to improvements in test scores. We then examine the limited empirical evidence on the effects of accountability systems on student achievement. In addition, the text considers some of the potential unintended consequences of high-stakes testing, such as cheating and gaming the system.

Chapter 12, Teacher Labor Markets, begins with a detailed analysis of the determinants of supply and demand in the labor market for teachers. We introduce the Roy model, which provides a theoretical framework for understanding the decision to become a teacher and how changes in alternative wages and the return to skill outside of teaching affect this decision. With salaries determined by a rigid scale and substantial licensure requirements, critics have charged that teacher pay is poorly aligned with teaching performance and, over time, improvements in the labor market opportunities for women have pulled many of the ablest teachers from the profession. These changes in the composition of teachers are captured well by a simple Roy model. The chapter then turns to the consideration of the role of teachers unions. We provide a brief history of the teachers union movement, present a theoretical discussion of how unions may affect educational resource allocation and outcomes, and discuss research that empirically estimates union effects. The final section of this chapter discusses teacher incentive (or merit) pay, which provides a way to introduce a return to skill in teacher salaries by tying monetary bonuses to observed productivity. We discuss the different types of incentive pay designs as well as findings from recent research on how incentive pay affects student achievement.

Part IV: Higher Education

Chapter 13, Market Dimensions of Higher Education in the United States, outlines how colleges and universities form a complex market for higher education in the United States. Competition in this market is undeniable, with institutions vying for students, faculty, and even success on the athletic field. Yet, the marketplace for higher education is far from perfectly competitive given substantial public subsidies and the presence of economies of scale. The aim in this chapter is to outline the nature of competition in higher education markets and the factors driving both the costs of provision and the prices faced by students.

Chapter 14, Paying for College: Student Financial Aid Policies and Collegiate Enrollment, considers the structure of financial aid in the United States and how the availability of grants and loans affects decisions to enroll in college as well as collegiate attainment. The mechanics of student aid allocation, particularly the determination of need-based awards, are described in detail. Beyond understanding the determination of aid eligibility, the bulk of this chapter focuses on how aid affects enrollment and attainment in theory and practice. Given the widespread attention to rising student debt levels in recent years, we focus particular attention on student loans and consider how the structure of repayment options affects incentives.

Chapter 15, The Economics of College Life: Admissions, Peer Effects, and Graduation, addresses the economics of college choice and college life. "Where to apply?" and in turn, "Whom to admit?" are fundamentally economic questions involving the allocation of a scarce resource. We present evidence on the functioning of this market, as well as circumstances where students' limited information may impede optimal matching. In turn, colleges' and universities' aims in "crafting a class" pose some genuine challenges that entail costs and benefits, such as the consideration of race in admissions decisions. Moving from admissions to the critical years of college enrollment, we present models and evidence on how peers may impact college student outcomes and factors that affect the ability of students to graduate once they enroll.

Over the course of the development of this book, which was initiated more than a decade ago, we have benefited enormously from constructive guidance and thoughtful debate with our peers, colleagues, and mentors. Turner's start on this book dates to 2005, and she never would have gone beyond the initial chapters without the determination of Lovenheim. The project has benefited enormously from our (usually productive) exchanges over the past several years and is a clear example of the returns to collaboration.

A number of people have offered (or been drafted) to provide direct assistance with the preparation of this book. At Cornell, Rebecca Lovenheim provided extraordinary research and editorial assistance, while Alexander Willén also supplied outstanding research assistance in drafting many of the Deep Dives. At Virginia, the list of people who have helped with the preparation of this book is longer than space will permit, although Amanda Pallais' work on this project as an undergraduate merits special mention.

Our biggest debts are intellectual, and we are exceedingly fortunate to come from the same doctorate program in economics at the University of Michigan where John Bound, Charlie Brown, Paul Courant, Joel Slemrod, and Jeffrey Smith have pushed for careful empirical analysis, methodological rigor, and well-framed exposition. Much of our approach to thinking about the economics of education, not to mention our own research, is deeply influenced by their mentorship and example. We have benefited enormously from participation in the NBER Program on the Economics of Education, led by Caroline Hoxby; it has served as a forum for frontier scholarship. Senior scholars including Bill Bowen, Sue Dynarski, Ron Ehrenberg, Charlie Clotfelter, David Figlio, Eric Hanushek, Caroline Hoxby, Alan Krueger, Michael McPherson, Richard Murnane, Steve Rivkin, and John Shoven have not only helped to change how the economics discipline approaches education but also increased the impact of economic thinking on the design and implementation of education policies. Some of their influence is reflected in this book. We have benefitted greatly from the input of our peers, junior colleagues, and graduate students, and we are grateful to a number of people who were exceedingly generous in reading early drafts, sharing data, or providing feedback, including Jessica Howell, Maria Fitzpatrick, Scott Imberman, David Deming, Kirabo Jackson, and Rucker Johnson. Finally, we would be remiss if we did not mention how important our own students at the undergraduate and graduate levels at both Cornell University and the University of Virginia have been in pushing us to focus on interesting questions and improve explanations. We expect that this ongoing process of teaching and learning will only improve the *Economics of Education* in the years to come.

On a personal note, Michael Lovenheim would like to express his profound gratitude toward his wife, Rebecca, for her consistent patience and support in writing this book. Without her patience with phone calls at inopportune times, working late at night to meet deadlines, and the general stress that writing a book like this entails, this textbook could not have been completed. Lovenheim also would like to thank his parents, John and Barbara, for their commitment to education and learning, which helped inspire his academic career. He additionally is indebted to his first economics teacher, Michael Noto, who provided early inspiration for studying economics and is a clear example of the value of a high-quality teacher. Lovenheim dedicates this book to his children, Julia and Natalie, with the hope that it will in some small way improve the education system they experience.

For Sarah Turner, a significant debt of gratitude is owed to parents James and Susan Turner, who made extraordinary efforts to provide access to wonderful educational opportunities from preschool to college and beyond. A word of admiration goes to grandmother Margie Shriver, who was ahead of her time in taking economics classes at the University of Iowa in the 1930s. And, looking forward, one hopes that efforts to use the best of economics to design better education policies will strengthen the opportunities for Sophia, Paul, and George Turner, along with many other young people, in the coming generations.

We must also thank the academic reviewers who encouraged us and provided incredibly thoughtful feedback that, as they will see, has been applied in our revisions. Many thanks to

Rodney Andrews, *University of Texas at Dallas*
Peter Bergman, *Columbia University*
Sean Corcoran, *New York University*
Timothy Diette, *Washington and Lee University*
Mike Kofoed, *United States Military Academy*
Andrew Hill, *University of South Carolina*
Scott Imberman, *Michigan State University*
Karthik Muralidharan, *University of California, San Diego*

Michael Podgursky, *University of Missouri*
Randall Reback, *Columbia University*
Jessica Simon, *Babson College*
Judith Scott-Clayton, *Columbia University*
Leanna Stiefel, *New York University*
Cecilia Suarez, *University of Illinois*
Patrick Walsh, *St. Michael's College*

Extraordinary thanks must be extended to Sean Corcoran, New York University, for his close and thoughtful reading of first-pass pages and for his many excellent suggestions. We look forward to working with him again.

We are also grateful to the editorial and production teams at Macmillan Learning: Tom Digiano, who ably saw this book through manuscript turnover to publication; Shani Fisher, for her guidance; Edgar Doolan, our Content Project Manager, who has done a masterly job keeping manuscript, pages, and us on track and moving; Sharon Balbos, Lukia Kliossis, and Sarah Nguyen for their help with manuscript and art development; Courtney Lindwall and Carlise Stembridge for their valuable contributions; and Diana Blume and Vicki Tomaselli for the stunning interior and cover designs. And to those of you working behind the scenes and who will be out on campus selling our book: our heartfelt thanks!

Why Do Economists Study Education Policy?

The U.S. Educational Attainment Gap

Education matters. How do we know? One answer is in the numbers: In 2013 the United States spent nearly $1.2 trillion on education, amounting to 7.1% of the economy. The United States is not alone. Throughout the world, governments spend considerable resources on the financing and operation of schools. They make these investments in education because it is widely believed that the strength of the overall economy depends on the knowledge and skills of the workers in that economy. Nearly 70% of economic output in the United States comes from labor, and schools are seen as a central way for individuals to acquire the skills that are rewarded in the labor market. Workers with more education earn more, which reflects their higher level of productivity: By some estimates, those with a college degree earn twice as much as those without a college degree. These earnings have to be balanced with the costs to taxpayers who foot the bill for public education and to families who make sacrifices to pay escalating tuition costs.

Historically, the United States has been a world leader in education. In the first half of the twentieth century, the United States far outpaced other countries in educational attainment because of large expansions that gave all children access to a publicly provided high school education. Similar investments in public higher education after World War II led to the development of big and diverse colleges and universities, and so the majority of Americans had some opportunity for collegiate attainment. At the same time, many U.S. universities became research hubs, producing innovations ranging from hybrid corn to GPS and email that touch all aspects of our lives. The rise in the educational attainment of U.S. workers over the twentieth century positioned them to make use of new technologies and to adapt quickly to new innovations. These dramatic increases in educational attainment have been widely recognized as an important driver behind economic growth over the last century.[1]

Yet in recent decades, growth in educational attainment has stagnated in the United States while it has accelerated in many European and Asian countries. As a result, these countries went from lagging behind to leading the United States in education at the dawn of the twenty-first century. What's more, the

---

[1] See Goldin and Katz (2008).

3DDock/Shutterstock

"Big deal, an A in math. That would be a D in any other country."

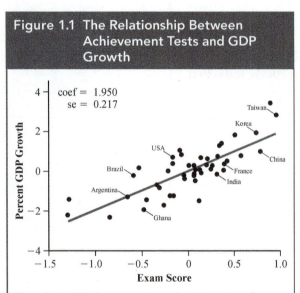

Figure 1.1 The Relationship Between Achievement Tests and GDP Growth

The relationship between 1 standard deviation change in the PISA test score and growth in real per-capita GDP between 1960 and 2000 after controlling for initial GDP level and average years of education in each country. A 1 standard deviation increase in test scores across countries is associated with a 2% higher rate of GDP growth. *Data from:* Hanushek and Woessman (2008).

challenges in U.S. education run deeper than indicated by raw measures of the number of years spent in school. There is increasing evidence of a knowledge gap between U.S. students and those in many other industrialized nations. For example, just under one-third of U.S. tenth-grade students achieve a score of *proficient* on the international mathematics exam called the PISA (Program for International Student Assessment). When the scores of U.S. students are compared with those of children from other countries, it becomes clear that 32% is not very good. In South Korea, 58% of students achieve proficiency on this exam. In Finland, 56% do. And just to our north, in Canada, 50% of students are proficient in math according to this measure.[2]

Why might these international comparisons be cause for concern? The correlation between international test scores and the overall growth rate of the economy as measured by *gross domestic product (GDP)*—the sum total of all goods and services produced—is very high. Figure 1.1 shows the relationship between a 1 standard deviation change in PISA exam scores and growth in real per-capita GDP between 1960 and 2000 for several countries. After accounting for initial GDP level and average years of education in each country, a 1 standard deviation increase in test scores is associated with a 2% higher rate of GDP growth. Of course, this correlation does not necessarily mean that the higher math test scores cause the higher GDP growth rates—correlation does not necessarily indicate causation—but it does suggest the need for a closer look at how the United States can better use its educational institutions to produce the knowledge and skills demanded by employers in our increasingly high-skilled economy.

To design education policies that produce skills valued by individuals and society and that are rewarded in the labor market, we need to understand how the organization of schooling, along with incentives faced by students, teachers, and parents, affect learning. To be sure, educational psychologists and experts in human development have much to contribute in explaining how students learn. Economists, however, are uniquely positioned to frame trade-offs and model how different incentives affect educational outcomes.

Economics offers a unique set of models and methods that allow us to better understand how and why people make decisions to invest in education, the effect of education on long-term social and economic outcomes, and the behavior of those institutions that produce education. With an understanding of these behaviors, economic models

---

[2] Detailed international and U.S. state PISA comparisons and their relationship to economic growth can be found in Hanushek, Peterson, and Woessmann (2013). These statistics are taken from that analysis.

also provide insights into how public policies affect the level and distribution of education resources. This book emphasizes how the models and methods of economics help us to understand education markets and in turn how public policies can improve schools and increase student achievement at all levels.

What insights and techniques does economics bring to the analysis and formulation of education policy that can be useful in helping to solve some of the most pressing policy issues of our time?

1. Economics provides comprehensive models of human behavior that can help us understand how individuals make decisions about how much and what type of education to obtain and about how schools produce knowledge and skills.
2. Economic models of behavior capture how individuals will react to changes in costs and benefits. In other words, these models predict how people will respond to changes in incentives. Since public policies are just a set of incentives, the tools of economic theory can provide powerful insights into the design and analysis of education policy interventions.
3. Economists have been leaders in the development of the empirical tools of causal analysis. In analyzing public policies, correlation is not sufficient. We need to know the causal effect of a given policy on individual behavior and on outcomes of interest. The techniques of causal analysis are highly prevalent in economics research, and as a result, a large portion (but by no means all) of what we know about the effects of various education policies comes from economics researchers.

Economists are increasingly leaders in efforts to improve schools and raise student achievement at all levels. A central goal of this book is to provide you with these tools and to give you a facility with the techniques necessary to approach education policy questions from the perspective of an economist.

In this chapter, we provide an overview of the economics of education. We begin by discussing what education is and provide an overview of economics and how economists approach problems. Next, we discuss the ways economists study education and elaborate on the role of economics in analyzing education decisions and policies. Finally, we provide a roadmap for the remainder of this book that offers some guidance to its organization.

1.1 Defining the Economics of Education

To ground our discussion of what the economics of education is all about, let's take a moment to consider the definitions of both *education* and *economics*. These most likely are terms you have heard before, but they often are used in very different ways that can cause confusion. It therefore is helpful to formalize what we mean by them. We then will discuss how economics as a social science contributes to understanding the choices that individuals and governments make concerning education.

What Is Education?

A simple starting point for defining education is the dictionary definition: education is defined as the "process of training and developing knowledge, skill, mind, character, etc. especially by formal schooling…" (*Webster's New World Dictionary*). This definition is instructive because it highlights two important characteristics of education:

1. Education can occur both formally in schools and informally in other settings, such as at home or at work.
2. Education has many outcomes, such as knowledge, skills, and character; some of these outcomes are difficult to measure.

In this text, we focus largely on the provision of education through formal institutions, such as elementary schools, high schools, and colleges. We are interested in how the formal schooling system and education policies can support the development of knowledge and skills among participants. This focus is driven by the fact that education policies are predominantly (although not exclusively) aimed at the formal institutions of education rather than at home or early childhood educational environments, in which much skill development takes place.

We also tend to focus on specific, measurable outcomes of education, such as test scores, the number of years of education obtained, and labor market earnings. As illustrated by the definition of education, there are many other outcomes that the education system seeks to generate, such as creativity, moral character, civic responsibility, and interpersonal skills. These outcomes are difficult to measure, which is an important challenge faced by education researchers that we highlight throughout the book. For good or for ill, the outcomes used by academic researchers tend to be those that we can measure.

The definition of education highlights that education is a *process* of training and developing student knowledge. Specifically, education combines teachers, books, fellow students, a curriculum, and other factors to produce student knowledge and skill. The terms *knowledge* and *skill* are intentionally vague, as one can think of an increase in any type of knowledge or specific skill as an example of education. For instance, an individual learning to drive a truck for a career and a student learning how to solve differential equations both fall under our definition of education. Teachers, books, and so forth are **inputs into education**, while student learning is an **outcome of education**. While learning may have intrinsic value for individuals, knowledge and skills learned in school may increase an individual's productivity in the labor market, in turn increasing wages.

The sum total of an individual's knowledge, skills, and abilities comes from many sources, only a small part of which is formal schooling. It would be far too narrow to claim that enrollment in schools is the only way to acquire skills or to learn. Many other institutions contribute to skill development. Employment and military service, for example, may include components of education. Family background and one's home environment also can greatly influence the development of knowledge and other skills. In addition, many people acquire education as adults, past the traditional time when schooling ends. With vocational programs ranging from cosmetology to truck driving and recreational courses from cooking to whale watching, education is unlikely to end when one exits school in young adulthood.

How educational institutions generate skills is a central question on which we focus throughout this book. Because the outcomes of education are varied and often are hard to measure, we need to pay particular attention to what types of skills and knowledge educational institutions are producing. Education may generate gains in understanding that are general, helping individuals to read, reason, and problem solve analytically; these skills will apply to a broad range of circumstances later in life. In the United

inputs into education
Any factors or resources that contribute to building an individual's ability or knowledge.

outcome of education
Any knowledge, skill, or attribute that is a result of participation in the education process.

States, the education system tends to focus on such general skills among younger children in particular. Alternatively, education may generate specific skills, which increase the capacity of individuals to do a particular task, such as typing or fixing a computer.

The study of how schools generate knowledge is made considerably more complex by the fact that we have incomplete information about the inputs to education, what the relevant outcomes are, and how to combine the inputs to produce the outputs. A little honesty and humility are in order: No one, not economists nor education specialists nor cognitive scientists, knows exactly how people learn. In this regard, education is more complicated than processes in engineering or cooking that can be described quite precisely with blueprints, formulas, and recipes. That we lack a full understanding of how knowledge is generated makes it difficult to formulate policies to increase learning. The problem we face is analogous to that of a chef who wants to make her food taste better but who does not know what the raw ingredients are or what recipe to use.

A chef in this situation likely would employ her knowledge or theory about how ingredients interact and experiment with trial and error until she found the right recipe. With education, experiments are costly, and we must be very careful when conducting experiments that could negatively affect children. One can view education policies as informal, or natural, experiments that can give us much insight into the ways in which knowledge is produced. We will spend a good bit of time in the coming pages discussing how variations in the inputs to education and the way education systems are organized affect how much and what students learn.

Participating in school (enrollment) or completing a particular level of school (e.g., finishing the sixth grade or graduating from high school) does not mean that the schooling produced particular skills. For example, if a student is a capable reader before entering first grade, we would not want to conclude that the student learned to read through first grade attendance. A central question therefore concerns how (or whether) schooling produces gains in students' achievement and other skills and how we can go about measuring such gains.

The fact that schools are responsible for only a part of the production of knowledge and skills makes it very hard to disentangle whether an individual's skills were acquired in school or through other experiences, such as at home. This question is not easy to answer in practice, particularly if the amount of time spent in school and the amount of schooling inputs mirror other differences across individuals, such as resources available at home. We thus will focus considerable attention on the difficulty of causal estimation in evaluating education policies.

What Is Economics?

Economics is the study of how scarce resources are used to satisfy unlimited human wants. That resources are limited implies **scarcity**, which means that there are too few resources to fully satisfy peoples' unlimited desire to consume goods and services. That resources are not infinite necessitates choice: We need to determine how to allocate scarce resources across individuals in a way that best meets our individual goals or our interests as a society. Economics provides little guidance as to what these individual or social goals should be. As economists, we cannot tell you whether you should like broccoli or whether opera is better than rap music. What we can tell you is how to allocate food in a way that best meets the goals of society, depending on how much people in the society like broccoli (and other foods).

economics The study of how limited resources are allocated to help satisfy unlimited human wants.

scarcity Having too few resources to satisfy individuals' unlimited desire to consume goods and services.

Think for a moment about what is meant by the scarcity of resources. There are only 24 hours in a day, so even if you would like to spend 25 hours a day studying for this class, it just is not possible. Time is a scarce resource. Spending another hour a day studying for this class implies giving up doing something else for an hour, such as sleeping or studying for another class. The best alternative use of your time that is given up is the **opportunity cost** of another hour of studying. For example, the opportunity cost of studying for this class is the value to you of the other activity you gave up, which could be studying for other classes, sleeping, working, or hanging out with your friends.

Opportunity cost is a fundamental concept in economics because it defines what is given up with each choice we make. All choices have costs, since time and money are both scarce resources. When you commit time to one activity, such as going to graduate school, you are forgoing another choice, like getting a job. The opportunity cost of graduate school attendance includes both the tuition payment, which you might have used instead to buy a car, and the forgone wages and experience you would have obtained if you were not sitting in class.

Opportunity cost also applies to choices made by administrators in schools and universities. Because the budget of any administrator is limited, an objective like reducing class size necessarily implies some costs or trade-offs. For example, smaller classes might require reduced expenditures on computers or the substitution of graduate students or teacher aides for faculty.

Your instructor also faces scarcity in time—she might like to cover many more topics or spend several weeks discussing financial aid or local school finance. Because she is likely to have only 20–30 lectures, she must choose among many important topics in organizing the class schedule. She also must determine how much of her time to devote to teaching this class versus teaching other classes, engaging in research, and doing nonacademic activities. The opportunity cost of her time for an additional hour planning a lecture for this class is the value of whatever other activity she would have done with this hour of time if she did not have to write the lecture.

To produce skills, schools must make decisions about how to allocate financial resources. For example, the principal of your elementary school had to figure out how to balance the purchase of textbooks, the acquisition of new computers, and the hiring of teachers. Similarly, the administrators of your college ultimately face choices about how many faculty members to hire and in which disciplines. Because scarcity of money and time necessitates these choices, we want to think about the alternative to each choice and the costs and benefits of making a given choice. Determining what combinations of curriculum, faculty, and peers lead to the most learning or skill acquisition, subject to the limits on total financial resources, is a central policy challenge at all levels.

Examining Trade-Offs: The Budget Constraint   Resource allocation necessitates trade-offs across resources. How best to allocate scarce resources is the motivating problem of all economics. Resource allocation is made considerably easier by prices, which is why economists talk so much about them. If a market is functioning correctly, prices are set so that the demand for a given good or service equals supply. Put differently, prices help us determine how to trade off different goods by showing what the opportunity cost of one good is in terms of another. For example, if computers cost $500 and a book costs $100, the opportunity cost of buying one computer is five books.

opportunity cost The value of the other goods or activities you have to give up to engage in an activity or purchase a given good. For example, the opportunity cost of studying for this class is the value to you of studying for other classes, or of sleeping, working, or spending time with your friends.

The main way economists think about resource trade-offs is in terms of a **budget constraint**. A budget constraint shows all of the attainable combinations of schooling inputs, such as books, computers, and teachers. If a school district spends more money on teachers, there will be less money to spend on computers. Consider the problem faced by a university that is thinking about hiring additional faculty in either economics or English. Suppose economics professors make twice as much as English professors. Coming back to the notion of opportunity cost, this means that the opportunity cost of hiring one economics professor is two English professors.

This trade-off is represented in the budget constraint shown in Figure 1.2, where the number of English professors is shown on the vertical (Y) axis and the number of economics professors is shown on the horizontal (X) axis. The slope of the budget constraint is the relative prices of the two goods. Since economics professors are twice as expensive as English professors, the slope of this line is -2. The slope of the budget constraint represents the opportunity cost of purchasing one good over the other, and this opportunity cost is the relative price of the goods.

The *y*-intercept in the graph, with coordinates (0, 10), shows the point at which only English professors are hired. Conversely, the university can hire all economics professors and no English professors, which is the *x*-intercept with coordinates (5, 0). Between these extremes is the option of hiring a mix of economists and English faculty. For example, the university can afford to have 8 English professors and 1 economics professor, or it can have 4 English professors and 3 economics professors. Now, imagine the college receives a donation from a wealthy alumnus. What will happen? The budget constraint will shift out. Although the relative price of each type of professor has not changed, the college can now hire more of both. Alternatively, one can imagine that the price of economists rises relative to the price of English professors. In this case, the budget constraint will rotate to become steeper: The opportunity cost of hiring an economist has now increased.

Typically, we consider allocations of financial resources that are on the budget constraint. Why? Clearly, the university in this scenario would like to hire more of both economics and English faculty, but it cannot afford to do so. Any point to the right (i.e., outside) of the budget constraint is not feasible: It would cost more than the sum total of the budget available to the college. It also is unlikely that the university will choose an allocation to the left (i.e., inside) of the budget constraint. At these points, the college can afford to hire more faculty members, which would make it better off. Another way of saying this is that individuals and institutions typically spend all of their available budget on goods and services. This makes the relevant choice set all of the points on the budget constraint.

Examining Trade-Offs: The Production Possibilities Frontier In addition to trade-offs among inputs to education, we can frame choices in terms of outcomes. That is, schools and individuals face choices about what types of

budget constraint The trade-off between inputs given input prices. The slope of the budget constraint is given by the relative prices of inputs, and the location of the constraint is determined by the overall amount of money that is available to spend.

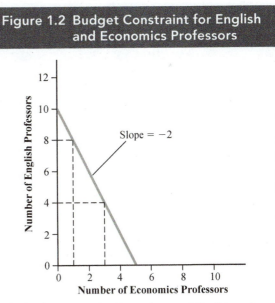

Figure 1.2 Budget Constraint for English and Economics Professors

The budget constraint shows the set of English and economics professors the university can afford to hire. The slope is determined by the relative prices of the two goods, or the opportunity cost of purchasing one good rather than the other. Since economics professors are twice as expensive as English professors, the slope of this *budget constraint* is −2.

production possibilities frontier (PPF) The combinations of outcomes that are feasible when all available resources are employed efficiently.

diminishing marginal returns Productivity of a given input declines as additional units of the input are added, holding all other inputs fixed. Adding additional units of an input, holding other inputs fixed, will eventually make each of those units less important for production.

outcomes to produce. You might have seen the classic trade-off between guns and butter in an introductory economics class. The same idea applies in the production of educational outcomes. A **production possibilities frontier (PPF)** shows the combinations of outcomes that are feasible when all available resources are employed.

As an example of a production possibilities frontier, consider how different allocations of study time will affect your outcomes in English and economics. This trade-off is presented in Figure 1.3, which shows a *PPF* for this scenario and demonstrates the trade-off you face in terms of grades in each subject when you shift an hour of study time between English and economics. If you spend all of your time studying for English, you will produce a high grade in English, but your performance in economics will be poor and your grade will be correspondingly low. At the other extreme, if you spend all of your time studying for economics, you will expect to perform poorly in your English classes.

Starting from the point where you are spending all of your time studying for economics (the *x*-intercept), reallocating a little time from economics to English is likely to lead to quite a large improvement in your English grade (i.e., turning in the paper or reading the assignments). But, one might suspect that the increments in your English grade that can be expected from another hour of studying will become smaller with each additional hour of English study time. This is an example of **diminishing marginal returns**: the productivity of a given input declines as additional units of the input are added, holding all other inputs fixed. Holding constant the number of hours you study for English, each additional hour of studying for economics should increase your grade by a smaller amount. The existence of diminishing marginal returns gives the *PPF* its bowed (or concave) shape.

What is important in thinking about the choice along the frontier is that no time is wasted; you are not surfing the Internet during part of the time that you are supposed to be studying. If time is wasted, you are at a point inside the *PPF*, where your grade in one course could be improved without sacrificing your grade in the other course. When you are using all of the designated study time on course work, you are on the frontier. At any point on the *PPF*, it is impossible to get a higher grade in English without sacrificing some attainment in economics. No point outside of the *PPF* is attainable at the total allocation of study time. If you increase the total amount of study time (say, if you decide to spend less time socializing or if you quit your job), then the *PPF* will shift out, as you now can attain a higher grade in both subjects by studying more. As with the budget constraint, the shape of the curve tells us about the trade-offs across these outcomes, while the location of the curve tells us about the total amount of resources available.

Figure 1.3 Production Possibilities Frontier for Grades in English and Economics

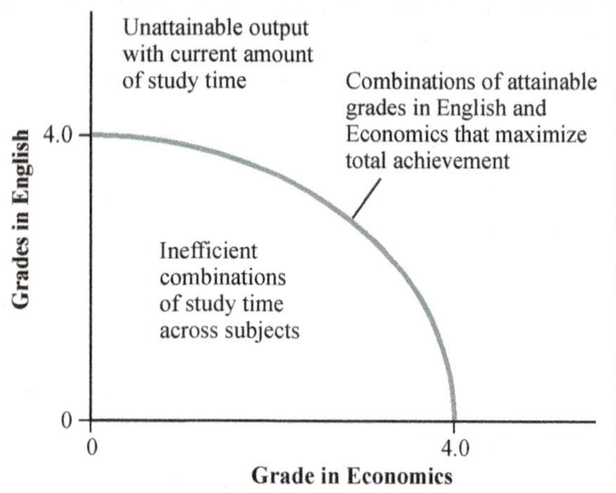

The production possibilities frontier shows the trade-off between grades in economics and grades in English when the student shifts study time between these subjects; the shape is determined by the diminishing marginal returns to studying each subject. Spending more time on English means spending less time on economics, and so English performance improves at the expense of economics performance.

1.2 Studying the Economics of Education

The tools of economics can be used in a range of contexts related to education policy, from classroom-level decisions to national issues related to the impact of federal spending or regulations. Put simply, problems related to resource allocation when overall resources are limited affect every aspect of our education system and every type of education policy. This is a main reason economics has come to play such a large role in the analysis and development of education policy in the United States and throughout the world. In applying economics to analyzing education systems and policies, we want to think carefully about how the basic tools of the discipline apply to choices made in education.

Scientific Method and the Economics of Education

Economics is a social science. Like other scientists, such as physicists and chemists, economists are devotees of the scientific method. This means that inquiry starts with a theory; a theoretical model leads to a hypothesis; observation or empirical work leads to a test of the hypothesis; and it ends with conclusions or revision of the theory.

There are more details about the process of causal estimation in Chapter 3, where we discuss the challenging problem of measuring how changes in education policies affect outcomes. We want to be able both to explain choices and events that have occurred and to predict future outcomes. For example, economists studying education not only hope to assess whether a reduction in class size last year in a given school district increased learning, but they also want to predict whether a reduction in class size next year or in another district would similarly increase achievement. This is commonly referred to as the *generalizability* of a study's results: the extent to which the findings from a given study can be applied more broadly to people in other locations or times.

Economics covers a wide array of questions and consists of a number of fields or particular areas of specialization, including labor economics, industrial organization, macroeconomics, international trade, and public finance. You will find economists in many fields and professions, ranging from the study of the environment to the analysis of tax policies and health care. Economists even study a wide range of topics you might not naturally think of as part of the discipline, such as crime and religion. The study of the economics of education is increasingly common, with many researchers focusing on issues related to the education system in the United States and throughout the world. The economics of education brings together ideas from diverse fields like public finance, labor economics, and industrial organization, but it is its own subdiscipline of economics that addresses a unique set of problems in markets dominated by an assortment of institutions not found in other settings. These institutions and the structure of these markets are discussed in Chapters 2 and 13.

Questions for the Economics of Education

Economics in general is concerned with three broad questions:

1. What should be produced?
2. How should it be produced?
3. For whom should it be produced?

These basic questions apply directly to the study of choices and markets in education. They relate to issues about what types of education services should be produced (the what), how to structure the delivery of education services (the how), and how to allocate resources across students and schools (the for whom). Consider some specific examples of these questions for the economics of education:

What Should Be Produced?

- Should we train more lawyers or doctors?
- Should we teach students to excel at standardized tests in math and English, or should we focus on a broader set of skills like creativity and teamwork?
- Should schooling be focused on more traditional academic skills or have a vocational component?

How Should It Be Produced?

- Should we have policies that mandate small class sizes of, say, 16 students?
- To what extent should we allow elementary and secondary students (or their parents) to select the schools they attend regardless of where they live?
- Do we want a large set of government-run schools or more privatized provision of education?
- Should we pay teachers more and/or pay them for achieving measurable education outcomes (like test score gains)?

For Whom Should It Be Produced?

- Should all 4-year-olds attend preschool?
- How extensive should financial aid policies be? More generally, who should go to college?
- What effects do race-based college admissions (i.e., affirmative action) have on student postsecondary enrollment patterns and outcomes?
- Do we want most of the resources in higher education to be concentrated in a small set of elite universities, or should we seek to have a more even distribution of funding across schools?
- Should we fund elementary and secondary schools equally or allow funding levels to reflect the wealth and preferences of the local community?

All of these questions are about the allocation of education resources. How they are answered depends on individual choices, individuals' incentives to make various education decisions, and the rules and education policies of governments.

Markets in Education

Are there markets in education? Absolutely. Markets are just the connection between consumers and producers, where students and their parents are the buyers and schools, colleges, and universities are the producers. Consider two features of the market for education.

The first is the level of competition. To what extent are education institutions in competition with each other? A core tenet of economic theory is that perfect competition leads to an allocation of resources that maximizes the well-being of members of society. In education, competition works through student choice: If students can make free choices about which schools to attend, schools will have to compete for them. Schools may compete over students because enrolling more students means more revenue and higher prestige. In no education market is there *perfect competition*, which exists when it is costless to enter and exit an industry and all firms are price takers in the sense that they can alter the quantity sold without affecting the market price. In some instances there is more competition than in others. For example, elementary and secondary schools in rural markets often face little competition over students. In contrast, the market for higher education, and in particular the market for highly selective postsecondary schools, is very competitive. The different levels of competition in these markets have important implications for education policy that we will explore throughout this book. For competition to work, students must have accurate information about the relevant characteristics of different schools. The lack of complete information among students and their families likely hampers competitiveness in education markets.

The second feature to consider is who are the participants in the education market. Students and their parents constitute the demand side of the market. They are the ones who "purchase" education services, and we should think of them as the consumers in this market. Colleges, schools, and universities form the supply side of the market, bringing together teachers, books, curriculum, and the various inputs to education to produce the educational services demanded by students and parents. The education market, then, represents exchanges between those who produce education services and those who wish to acquire those services. In addition, the production of education relies on the labor markets for teachers and university faculty, as each of these inputs has quite specialized knowledge.

1.3 What Can Economics Teach Us About Education Policies?

Now that we have discussed the basics of economics and education, we can think about why the tools of economics are useful in studying education policy.

The Different Types of Education Policies

Education policies fall into three broad groups:

1. *Total resource policies* increase the total amount of funding to a school or to individuals making education decisions.
2. *Input-based policies* are targeted at specific inputs to the education process, such as class sizes, teachers, or the offering of certain educational programs.
3. *Output-based policies* alter the incentives schools, teachers, and students face, with the objective or promoting certain educational outcomes.

In addition to the type of policy, there is the critical question of how the policy should be targeted to various members of society. We could have a broad-based policy that affects all students. An example of such a policy is the federal No Child Left Behind (NCLB) Act (described in detail in Chapter 11), which pertained to all public elementary and secondary school students in the United States. Alternatively, policies can be targeted at specific groups. An example of a targeted education policy is financial aid for college. Eligibility for federal aid, which makes up most financial aid disbursements in this country, is aimed at students from low-income backgrounds. Students from higher-income backgrounds typically are not eligible for financial aid, which makes this a highly targeted policy. Many education policies are aimed at reducing income- and race-based inequalities in school funding and in student educational outcomes. Typically, these are more targeted programs.

To demonstrate the value of approaching the analysis of these policies with the tools of economics, let's now look more closely at an example of each type of policy. One prominent example of a total resource policy is increasing the total amount of funding available to schools. This could be done across the board or for specific types of schools to reduce cross-school spending inequality. Another example of a resource-based policy is giving money to parents or students, which would increase the amount they could spend on all goods, including education. Many government transfer programs provide assistance for low-income children and families, such as the Earned Income Tax Credit and Temporary Aid for Needy Families (i.e., "welfare").[3] These can be thought of as total resource policies.

What do we expect a total resource policy to do? In the last section, we reviewed the concepts of the budget constraint and the production possibilities frontier. When total budgetary resources increase, the *PPF* and the budget constraint shift out. The relative allocation of resources does not change, but the total amount of money does. These core economics concepts give us a framework for thinking about what this type of education policy might do. We predict that total resource policies will increase education outputs. Indeed, this is a core argument made by proponents of these policies.

Why do we need education policies other than total resource ones? It seems intuitive that giving people or institutions more money would increase learning. The problem with this argument comes from the particular way that education markets are structured: in general, education markets are characterized by a lack of full competition. Furthermore, the market is dominated by public and private nonprofit institutions. While there are many arguments for this public and private nonprofit role, there also is no strong profit motive, and it is likely that schools lack the incentives to allocate resources in the most effective way possible. This problem is compounded by the fact that resource allocations in schooling can be highly political, which may further reduce the degree to which resources are being put to the best uses. In short, schools or individuals may be operating inside their *PPF*s, which indicates a misallocation of resources. As a result, simply providing more money may not be sufficient.

If we do not believe that money will be used to purchase the most important inputs, we can use input-based policies to directly alter the amount of certain inputs used in the production of education. For instance, we can mandate smaller classes or that all teachers (or professors) have a minimum level of education or obtain a professional certification. Distributing computers to all schools or requiring the school day to contain a minimum number of instructional hours are other examples of input-based policies. These policies can work through government mandates (such as smaller classes), or they can work by explicitly altering prices through subsidies and taxes. For example, the government could provide a subsidy for every highly qualified teacher hired by a school. Financial aid is a key way that the government changes the trade-off between enrolling in college and doing something else (like working), which makes financial aid a very prominent example of an input-based policy. One thus can think of input-based polices as altering the trade-off across goods. In other words, it changes the slope of the budget constraint. As with resource-based policies, input-based policies can be broad-based or can be targeted at certain types of students or individuals.

The final type of policy focuses on outputs rather than inputs. Like with input-based policies, the underlying arguments for this type of policy stem from the limited

---

[3] A more detailed discussion of these policies can be found in the excellent textbook *Public Finance and Public Policy*, 5th ed., by economist Jonathan Gruber (2016).

amount of competition in the education market that can preclude resources from being allocated effectively. Rather than promoting specific inputs directly, output-based policies alter the incentives faced by individuals and schools. If the main problem we face is that the incentives are not properly structured in education, then altering those incentives directly could allow the resources that do exist to be used more effectively in generating student outcomes.

Education economists have played a large role in the development of output-based policies, and we will spend much time in this book examining such policies and the evidence of their effect on student outcomes. School choice is a prominent example of an output-based policy. School choice policies increase competition for students by allowing them to choose which local school to attend without forcing their parents to move. Another example is teacher merit pay (or incentive pay), which ties teacher compensation directly to measured education outcomes. *Test-based accountability* policies (such as No Child Left Behind) that provide sanctions for schools failing to meet certain measured objectives also are an important example of output-based policies. If you have been enrolled in elementary or secondary schooling in the past 15 years, chances are high that you have experienced one or more of these output-based policies. This reflects a large change in education policy in the United States, as these types of programs have gained favor only recently. They are increasingly popular with both Democrats and Republicans, making up important components of both President George W. Bush's and President Obama's education policy initiatives. They therefore are likely to be an important aspect of education policy in the future, and a core focus in this book is on understanding these policies and their effects on educational outcomes.

Policies as a Set of Incentives

At base, any policy is simply a set of incentives. For example, with teacher merit pay, the incentive of cash payments leads teachers to make efforts to increase certain outcomes, such as test scores. Mandating lower class sizes provides a strong incentive for schools to hire more teachers, as failing to meet these class size limits may trigger fines or sanctions. An underlying goal of economics is to understand how individuals and institutions react to incentives, so the tools of economics are powerful for analyzing education policy.

Issues of scarcity, choice, and opportunity cost are central to education policy at the local, state, and national levels. Often, these policies will alter incentives in ways that are not intended by the law. These unintended consequences of education reform can be dramatic and can alter the desirability of the entire policy. A poorly designed program can produce poor outcomes even if the underlying idea of the policy is sound. Thus, we do not want to ask, "Does school choice work?" but rather we want to focus on the more relevant policy question: "Does a specific school choice policy alter incentives in such a way as to improve student outcomes?" Furthermore, it is not enough to know whether a given policy will improve some outcome; we also want to know whether it does so relative to any alternative use of those resources. We need to know the opportunity cost of a given policy in terms of other potential uses of the resources employed to implement the policy.

For example, school accountability systems mandated under NCLB provide strong incentives for schools to meet proficiency targets, meaning that a certain percentage of students have to score at a proficient level on state standardized exams. As pointed out in the excellent analysis by Neal and Schanzenbach (2010), this produces incentives for schools to focus on students who are close to the proficient threshold. It is more costly to get those who are far below the threshold to be proficient, and very high achieving students are not in danger of scoring below proficiency. Although it was not an intention of the law, the incentives generated by NCLB led to a focus on a specific set of students and caused others to be "left behind by design," as the title of their paper highlights. Furthermore, this policy contains incentives for schools to improve performance in tested areas, like math and English. This may lead to reductions in instruction in other areas, and the focus of the instruction is now more likely to be on passing the exam. Whether this change in focus is helpful or harmful for students is an open question, but to assess the desirability of these policies, it is critical to understand the myriad ways they can alter incentives. These types of issues are central to the way economists approach problems, which is why this discipline provides a powerful lens through which to analyze education policy.

To take another example, in 1996 California passed a law that required all kindergarten through third-grade classes to be smaller than 21 students. The policy was motivated by the evidence that small classes increase students' test scores. But the policy also had a large unintended consequence: In the first two years, schools had to hire 25,000 new teachers, and many of these teachers were inexperienced. The fact that so many new teachers had to be hired significantly reduced the effectiveness of the class-size reductions, at least in the short run. It also was very expensive, and a central question is whether the money put toward these class-size reductions could have been better spent on other policy interventions inside or outside of education.

Every education policy choice affects the distribution of resources to segments of the population. For instance, if your governor chooses to budget more money for higher education, it may come at the expense of kindergarten to 12th-grade (K–12) spending. Higher allocations to children with disabilities may come at the expense of funding for class-size reduction, and raising college tuition may hinder the ability of students from low-income backgrounds to finance postsecondary education. Additional resources for education also may require either reduced spending on other public services, such as road construction and police protection, or higher taxes. Such costs are critical to consider along with any benefits of the policies to students and to society at large.

1.4 The Road Ahead: Objectives and Organization of the Book

We have three goals in the remainder of the book:

1. Provide an overview of the structure of education markets and institutions in the United States
2. Present the core theoretical models used to analyze and understand how individuals, schools, and governments make education and resource allocation decisions
3. Build a firm understanding of the way economists approach the evaluation of education policies and the research evidence on the determinants of educational attainment and the effect of education-related policies

After reading this book, you should be able to apply the theoretical and empirical tools of economics, combined with your institutional knowledge of the education system in the United States, to think rigorously about how a specific type of policy will affect students, schools, and society more broadly. Our goal also is to teach you the empirical tools to be able to understand education policy research, the limits of our ability to analyze certain questions, and how to translate empirical research findings into lessons for education policy.

The tools of economics provide a rich framework to use in evaluating education policies. What economists do best is provide clear analysis of the trade-offs that come with alternative policies. Reasonable economists may (and often do) disagree about models, the importance of various hypotheses, and the interpretation of the evidence that is brought to bear to test hypotheses. Advocating for or against particular policies is not the aim of this book. The goal of this text is to lay out the evidence as clearly as possible and to note the agreements, disagreements, and unresolved points in the research literature.

Toward these ends, the next chapter of this book provides an overview of education markets in the United States. We focus almost exclusively on U.S. education policy and institutions, although we will note international differences in many places as well. There is a large body of research focusing on education systems throughout the world; an analysis of these other systems would be far too lengthy to include here. Chapter 2 details U.S. education markets, along with the players in these markets and economic arguments for the large role played by the public sector (i.e., government) in providing and financing education services. We also examine the history of education in this country to explain why education markets today look the way that they do.

Chapter 3 gives you an overview of the empirical techniques used by researchers in the economics of education. We will come back to these techniques and illustrate their use throughout the book. A main emphasis of this chapter is on how to establish causality. It is not enough to know that a certain outcome is positively or negatively correlated with a policy; we need to know whether the policy *causes* a change in the outcome. As we discuss, causal estimation is very challenging in education. How economists seek to overcome this challenge, along with the extent to which they are successful in doing so, is a major theme of this book.

In Chapters 4 to 7, we present the foundational models for production of and investment in education. We first focus on the two core theoretical models that economists use as a framework to think about education choices: the human capital model (Chapter 4) and the signaling model (Chapter 5). These models will give us the theoretical tools to analyze individual behavior and government policies, and they form the backbone of economic analysis of education. Both models emphasize the importance of education in increasing future earnings as a driver of decisions about how and what types of education to invest in. In Chapter 6, we turn to the research that seeks to estimate the effects of educational attainment on labor market earnings and on social outcomes like crime, civic engagement, and growth. The final foundation of education we discuss is the way knowledge is produced in the education system. This is called the education production function, and it is the focus of Chapter 7.

The next section of the book focuses on K–12 education policy. We begin in Chapter 8 by detailing the way schools are financed in the United States, why government intervention in these markets may or may not be desirable, and the reform movement that has led to a radical change over time in how schools are financed to be more equitable across students. In Chapter 9, we take a close look at school resources and inputs. In particular, we ask whether it is sufficient to simply increase school funding or whether other policies might be necessary. We then examine the relationship between two particularly important inputs and outputs: class sizes and quality of teachers. In Chapters 10 and 11, we focus on two output-based policies that have grown dramatically in importance over the past several decades: school choice and test-based accountability. Our analysis of K–12 education concludes with an examination of teacher labor markets, including an analysis of who becomes a teacher, the role of teachers' unions in K–12 education, and teacher incentive pay policies.

The last section of this book studies higher education in the United States. Chapter 13 describes this sector in detail and highlights its history as well as the varied nature of postsecondary institutions and the increasing stratification of resources in higher education across schools. Chapter 14 focuses on financial aid policies: We detail the sources of financial aid and how it is determined and discuss the research that examines how financial aid policies affect students' enrollment decisions. We also provide an overview of trends in student debt levels in this chapter. The final chapter in the book deals with the economics of college life: we examine the economics of college admissions, peer effects, student labor supply, and affirmative action.

1.5 Conclusion

Economics provides a very valuable lens through which to view and analyze education policy. There is little disagreement that there is ample room for improving student achievement and educational attainment in the United States. There is much disagreement, however, about the appropriate policy responses to address this challenge. The stakes are high: Economic growth and, in turn, the prospects for future generations depends on the capacity of the education system to meet the needs of an increasingly skill-based economy. Economics can provide much insight into the types of policies that might be most effective in reforming our education system.

Highlights

- **Economics** offers an important lens through which education policy can be viewed. By providing comprehensive models that describe how people make decisions when faced with **input** resource constraints, economic theory offers a framework that allows us to analyze how people make education decisions and how schools and governments make resource allocation decisions that affect educational **outcomes**, the amount of knowledge and skills individuals obtain.

- Economic researchers have been leaders in the development of tools of causal analysis, which are critical to the study and design of education policies.

- Education can occur formally and informally and has many outcomes. This text focuses on the provision of education through formal institutions and on the measurable outcomes produced by these institutions.

- Education markets in the United States are distinct from other more traditional markets for consumer goods. They are characterized by a large role for public and private nonprofit institutions and by imperfect competition.

- Economics is the study of how resources are used to satisfy unlimited human wants when there is **scarcity**. **Opportunity cost** is a core economic concept that describes the cost of spending resources on one input or activity in terms of not being able to spend those resources on any other

input or activity. Opportunity costs thus tell us the trade-off between uses of different resources. This trade-off is represented by the **budget constraint**, which shows the trade-off between inputs as a function of the relative price of those inputs. The **production possibilities frontier** shows the trade-off among outcomes that are attainable when all available resources are employed.

- Core economics questions concern what should be produced, how it should be produced, and for whom it should be produced.

- A central focus in economics is how individuals and institutions react to incentives. Education policies are simply sets of incentives. They may be in the form of total resources, input-based, or output-based policies. Total resource policies shift the budget constraint out; input-based policies change the slope of the budget constraint; and output-based policies alter incentives for schools, students, and teachers. This text examines each kind of policy and shows how economics can help inform future policy decisions and designs.

- Education spending in the Unites States is in the trillions of dollars. The lower measured educational attainment in the U.S. relative to countries that spend less per student suggests there may be opportunities to strengthen outcomes through improved policy design.

Problems

1. What does economics bring to the study of education policy?

2. Discuss some ways education can occur outside of schools. How does the fact that the development of knowledge can occur in and out of schools complicate our ability to determine whether schools are successful at educating students?

3. List three inputs to and three outputs of the production of knowledge. Are all outputs of education easy to measure? How might the fact that some outputs are easy to measure and some are difficult to measure influence the skills on which schools focus?

4. On any given Saturday night, you have the option of going to a party or studying. Studying for an hour will increase your grade by 0.1 percentage point (out of 100). Clearly, partying will not help your grades. If the average length of a party is four hours, what is the opportunity cost of attending a party in terms of your grade?

5. An undergraduate has a weekly budget of $20. The only two goods that the student consumes (not covered by the meal plan) are coffee and beer. The price of coffee (at Starbucks) is $2 and the price of a beer is also $2.
   a. On a graph, plot the potential combinations of beer and coffee the student may consume. Be sure to label your axes carefully. Write down the equation for the line describing this budget constraint.
   b. What is the opportunity cost of consuming one more beer?
   c. Is it feasible for the student to consume 8 beers and 4 cups of coffee? Explain.
   d. Explain (and illustrate graphically) the change in the choice set if the student's allowance is increased to $30 per week.
   e. Explain (and illustrate graphically) the change in the choice set if the price of beer increases to $3 per mug with the allowance held constant at $30 per week.

6. The test scores of U.S. children are low in comparison to other countries with similar levels of wealth and development. This cannot be explained by spending, as the United States spends more per child than most other countries. What are two explanations for the lagging achievement of U.S. students?

7. As the principal of a school, you can produce some combination of two outputs: math test scores and writing skills.
   a. Draw a production possibilities curve for these two outputs with math test scores on the *x*-axis. (*Hint:* The shape should closely resemble the *PPF* in Figure 1.3.)
   b. Starting from the *y*-intercept, why is the slope of the *PPF* relatively flat at first?
   c. Explain why points inside the *PPF* curve are inefficient.
   d. Show what happens to the *PPF* if the school receives more resources to spend on both math and writing.
   e. Show what happens to the *PPF* if a new math curriculum is developed that makes teachers more effective at math instruction.

8. What are the three broad questions on which economists focus? Give an example of each type of policy question that is different from the examples in the chapter.

9. What is an education market? Who constitutes the demand side of the market? Who constitutes the supply side?

10. What are the three types of education policies? Give an example of each type of education policy that is different from the examples listed in the chapter.

11. Medicaid is a large federal program that provides health insurance to low-income children and families. Although many Medicaid rules are federal, states are responsible for financing most of the program. In 2012, total Medicaid spending by the states was $415 billion. Let's say the federal government passes a law that requires states to cover more children, which will cost more money. Can this policy negatively affect children's educational outcomes? Can it positively affect their educational outcomes? Explain.

12. *Teacher merit pay* describes a set of policies that tie monetary bonuses for teachers to their students' performance on exams. If the State of Virginia decides to implement a merit pay system based on standardized math test scores, what do you think will happen to student achievement in English?

The Structure and History of Education Markets in the United States

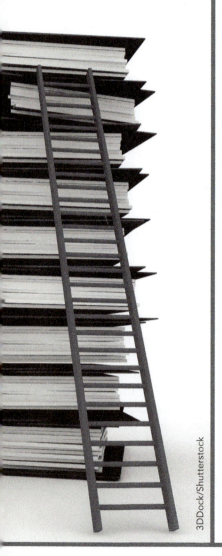

3DDock/Shutterstock

The Education of Benjamin Franklin

Benjamin Franklin was born in Boston, Massachusetts, in 1706, and he became one of the founding fathers of the United States; he was also a celebrated states-man and a known scientist. The New England area was one of the most progres-sive in terms of education policy in Colonial America, with laws stating that all children must receive some education. A small set of public grammar schools in Boston that educated children free of charge was also unique for that period. There were eight "writing schools," two of which were publicly financed and the rest private. These schools bear little resemblance to the schools educating young children today; they focused on Latin, rote memorization, and religious instruc-tion. Despite having only two years of formal schooling, which ended when he was 10 years old, Franklin was one of the most learned men of his generation and made seminal contributions to our understanding of electricity, demography, and oceanography.

Consider the differences that a modern-day Benjamin Franklin, born in Boston, might experience in terms of his education. The Boston public school system includes 128 publicly financed schools that span all grade ranges, from prekindergarten to twelfth grade. In contrast to the educational choices in the early eighteenth century, the types of schools in a metropolitan area like Boston are incredibly varied. Some schools are traditional public schools that teach all students who live in the local area. Others are publicly financed but privately managed charter schools; space permitting, they can enroll any student who wishes to attend. Boston also is home to several "exam schools" that are publicly run and financed but that admit only the most academically advanced students in the area. In addition, there are over 20 private schools in Boston that range from religious to secular in focus.

Once graduated from high school, today's Franklin would have access to a system of higher education that was unfathomable in the 1700s. In the greater Boston area alone there are 135 postsecondary institutions, with large differ-ences among them. Some are two-year community colleges and some are four-year public colleges and universities. The Boston area has a large number of private colleges and universities that range dramatically in their selectivity, from Harvard University, with an admissions rate of 6%, to schools that admit virtually all applicants. In short, the market for education is extremely diverse at all levels of education, mixing private and public financing and control of schools.

Education markets today also differ markedly from those in Franklin's time because of the widespread increase in access to educational institutions that has occurred over the past three centuries. In the early eighteenth century, access to a publicly provided form of education was uncommon, and higher education was extremely rare. Today, virtually all U.S. students have a primary school education, and about 90% complete high school.[1] Furthermore, about 32% have obtained a four-year college degree. It is extremely unlikely that anyone, much less an accomplished scientist, diplomat, and thinker such as Benjamin Franklin, would have only two years of formal schooling. In fact, it is very likely his modern-day equivalent would have a college degree if not a graduate degree as well.

A simple comparison of the early American education system with today's system highlights the large changes in the structure of education that have taken place since the founding of our country. In this chapter, we will focus on understanding how the markets for education work in the United States and on the evolution of today's education markets from a time when education options were less prevalent and attainment was much lower. This historical perspective is important for understanding why many aspects of the U.S. education system look like they do.

This chapter starts by describing the organization of educational offerings at different levels. We introduce the agents in the marketplace for education and discuss the provision of education by schools, colleges, and universities under private and public control. Then we consider how changes in educational institutions and public policies over the past century have affected educational attainment in the U.S. population. The next section examines how rising educational attainment affects economic growth to highlight the importance of these changes in education markets and the associated growth in attainment among U.S. workers. Finally, we discuss policy implications of these markets as they relate to the design of many of the K–12 and higher education policies we focus on throughout the rest of the book.

2.1 Defining Education Markets

Economists often refer to the **market for education (education market)**. To understand what is meant by *education markets*, it is easiest to think in terms of the supply and demand for education services. Families and individual students desire the provision of education services that will lead to the development of knowledge and skills. This is the demand side of the education market. The demand here is not for education per se; rather, what students and families want is the ability to learn skills that will lead to higher long-run well-being. Someone must supply these services. The supply side of the education market refers to the institutions that provide the services demanded by students and families. We will focus on schools as the primary supplier of education

market for education or **education market** The mechanism through which education services are exchanged.

---

[1] This tabulation comes from the *Digest of Education Statistics*, Table 104.20. In careful empirical work on high school graduation rates in the United States, Heckman and LaFontaine (2010) put the graduation rate somewhat lower, at about 80%.

services, although other providers of these services (such as private tutors) can and do exist. As with the market for any other good, the market for education refers to the mechanisms through which buyers (demand) and sellers (supply) interact to exchange services.

It is important to highlight some ways education markets are distinctive. Consider the difference between the market for education and the market for some commodity, such as pencils. Education services are distinctive in ways that affect how the market functions:

perfectly competitive market (perfect competition) A market in which it is easy to enter and exit and all firms are price takers in the sense that the quantity they sell does not affect the market price.

spillovers or **externalities** Occur when an individual's market transaction affects other members of the economy.

- Education markets typically are not **perfectly competitive markets (perfect competition)** as there are barriers to entry and exit of schools and colleges.
- Education can have **spillovers (externalities)** to other people in the society through the benefits (or costs) that accrue to a society with well-educated citizens.
- Education is a highly differentiated good: There is not just one type of education but considerable differences in what schools and colleges teach, how material is taught and the level of resources devoted to production.
- The supply of education services is often local: usually one must be close to a school to take advantage of its offerings.
- Education services may be subject to asymmetric information, as students and parents may have a difficult time assessing the quality of educational offerings.
- The quality of education one receives can be influenced by the characteristics of other consumers—*peer effects.*
- Education is a *customer input technology*: the amount of effort students exert affects learning.

The importance of these differences cannot be overstated: they impact virtually every aspect of education markets and education policy. Think about a perfectly competitive market for pencils. By definition, in a perfectly competitive market, *firms* are price takers, and no one firm can alter the price of the good. Critical to the idea of perfect competition is the notion of free entry and exit of firms. If some firms are inefficient at producing pencils, they will go out of business. However, if the market price is too high, it will induce entry, thus increasing supply and driving prices down. Local schools tend to face very little competition. Until very recently, with the rise of school choice policies, students either had to attend their local public school, attend a (typically expensive) private school, or move to another area associated with a different public school.

Quick Hint: A firm is an organization that produces a good or service, usually with the intent of making profits. Firms may be large corporations owned by a group of shareholders, such as Google or Microsoft, or they may be enterprises owned by a few individuals, such as the small businesses in your neighborhood. Economic theory provides clear models of how profit-maximizing firms choose what and how to produce given prevailing prices of inputs and the price likely to be received on the market for the final good or service.

Public schools typically may not close in the way an inefficient pencil producer might go out of business. When a firm fails to cover its costs of continued production, the owners choose to close down and employ their capital in alternative, profit-generating activities. The absence of a direct pricing structure for public education combined with public administrative control without clear shareholders complicates the closing or restructuring of public schools. In general, it is rare for public schools to shut down.

Setting up a school also requires significant capital investments that restrict entry of new schools into areas. That is, schooling exhibits **economies of scale**, which means that the average cost of operating a school declines as more students enter at typical enrollment levels. This characteristic implies that it will be cheaper to produce a given amount of education in fewer schools with more students than with many small schools. Restricted entry and exit in the supply side of the education market results in students having little choice in education providers and in schools facing less than perfect competition. As argued by Nobel laureate Milton Friedman (1955), the lack of competition in schooling has generated a government natural monopoly in education in the United States because governments are the ones who have incurred the large fixed costs of setting up schools and can take advantage of the increasing returns to scale. This also imposes a burden on the government to regulate this large natural monopoly. A significant part of education policy is concerned with understanding the best way to structure these regulations as well as how to reduce government's monopolistic control over education to increase competition.

In contrast to the consumption of typical commodities, the consumption of education services is likely to impact other members of society. That one individual's market transaction can affect others in the economy is what economists term spillovers, or externalities. While these spillovers can be positive or negative, typically in education we think they are positive. For example, education can increase civic participation, reduce crime, and lead to economic growth. We will discuss the evidence on externalities associated with education in Chapter 6, but the fact that each individual's decisions about education can have implications for the well-being of society at large makes the market for education services very different from the market for normal commodities.

Education is not a single, homogeneous commodity but an umbrella term applied to an array of differentiated offerings. Education services can take many forms, all of which we call education. It is distinguished by both the level and the quality of services provided. Preschool and after-school programs, truck-driving academies, and theological seminaries all provide education services, although the specific services offered are quite different. There also are large differences in the quality of education services at a given level of education. For example, some elementary schools excel at teaching mathematics to third-graders, and some teach third-graders very little math. While students attending the two schools are enrolled in the same level (third grade), they receive vastly different education services from their school. It is this difference that forms the basis for much of the education policy initiatives in this country and throughout the world.

Although education markets are characterized by less-than-perfect competition, there are many choices families can make regarding the types of education services they receive. For preschool education, parents often have choices in the type of instruction, including the Montessori model, which emphasizes self-directed learning, and the Waldorf model, which emphasizes imitation. Parents make choices based on their preferences for types of programs, willingness and ability to pay, and their proximity to types of education offerings. In addition to the quality of education services, parents and students can make choices about the quantity purchased. With after-school programs, private tutors, and private schooling more generally, there is ample opportunity to purchase a higher quantity of education services than is offered by the local public school alone.

economies of scale Refers to a situation in which the average costs of operation decline with the scale of the operation. In terms of schooling, this means the average operating cost of a school or district is declining with the number of kids enrolled. Economies of scale occur in firms in which there are large fixed costs of operation: As scale increases, fixed costs are spread over a larger number of outputs, which leads to declining average costs.

Related to education markets operating as natural monopolies is the importance of location. Having a high-quality option 100 miles away does a student little good; unless families can move easily, one's education choices are restricted to *local* options. This is very different from the way the market for commodities like pencils works. With low transportation costs, a pencil can be produced anywhere. You do not have to travel to the pencil plant to buy one. For education, one must generally attend the school to be able to take advantage of its services. For many (but not all) types of education, commuting distance or the local area defines the market. When choosing a preschool or elementary school, parents are limited by commuting distance. Working adults are limited by proximity to place of work and home in choosing whether and how to continue their education. This further serves to reduce competition in education markets, as most competition must be local.

Not all education is so geographically constrained. The most selective institutions in higher education participate in an international market, drawing students from all over the world. Stanford University and Yale University compete to attract many of the same students, with some high school students from Connecticut going to college in California and some high school students from California going to college in Connecticut. In this sense, the market for the most selective colleges is national (and international, since students from China and other countries also attend Stanford and Yale). The growth of online education programs also has reduced the local nature of education, but most education markets, particularly for elementary and secondary education, remain local. That the amount of geographic competition varies by the level and the quality of schooling adds even more differentiation to education markets.

The characteristics of other pencil purchasers do not affect how well a pencil works for me. Some firms may have consumers who have better handwriting or make fewer spelling mistakes, but selling to different types of consumers does not affect the quality of the pencil I purchase. The same is not true in education: One's learning can be affected by the academic ability and the characteristics of one's peers. Having lower-ability peers may reduce the amount of education one receives from a given school. This possibility is not lost on parents, and the desirability of schools seems to be driven at least in part by the characteristics of the students who attend these schools.[2] These peer effects make education markets operate differently from the market for typical consumer goods.

The Levels of Education in the United States

In the United States, education is organized around four basic stages:

1. Early childhood education: typically ages 0–4. About 52% of 3- and 4-year-olds are enrolled in a school
2. Elementary and secondary education (grades kindergarten through 12): typically ages 5–18
3. Postsecondary undergraduate: two-year and four-year collegiate training
4. Graduate education

---

[2] For a more detailed look at what parents value in terms of the characteristics of schools, see Black (1999), Bayer, Ferreira, and McMillan (2007), and Imberman and Lovenheim (2015).

Figure 2.1 shows the configuration of these stages of education, along with the general age of students at each level. Students typically begin in prekindergarten programs at age 3 or 4 and then progress to elementary and secondary education for grades kindergarten through 12. Many elementary schools today offer kindergarten programs that are available to all students and that are a full day, so for a sizable proportion of students in the United States, elementary schooling begins in kindergarten. After twelfth grade, students can attend a range of postsecondary schools for undergraduate collegiate training. Education beyond the undergraduate years has become increasingly important as well.

Here are brief descriptions of each level of schooling:

- *Early childhood education:* Early childhood education focuses on the first four to five years of a child's life and often is thought of as the period before formal schooling begins. Early childhood programs range considerably, from different day care options to more academically oriented programs. Many of these programs are private, particularly for younger children, and many children do not attend any early childhood education programs but instead remain at home during these early years. Figure 2.2 shows the proportion of 3-, 4-, and 5-year-olds enrolled in any early childhood education program and the proportion in public versus private programs. The prevalence of private programs can make access to high-quality early childhood education difficult for low-income families. *Head Start*, a large government-funded program that provides free prekindergarten programs as well as parenting help

Figure 2.1 The Structure of Education in the United States

Grade		Age
	Graduate School	22+
16		21
15	Four-Year College	20
14	Vocational/Technical Community *or* University	19
13	College College	18
12		17
11	High School	16
10		15
9		14
8		13
7	Middle School	12
6		11
5	Combined Elementary	10
4	and Middle School	9
3	Elementary School	8
2		7
1		6
K		5
		4
		3
	Early Childhood and Preschool	2
		1
		0

The education system in the United States is hierarchical, with compulsory schooling beginning in elementary school and ending in high school. Many children begin school prior to elementary school, and a large proportion continue their studies in the postsecondary education system after high school.

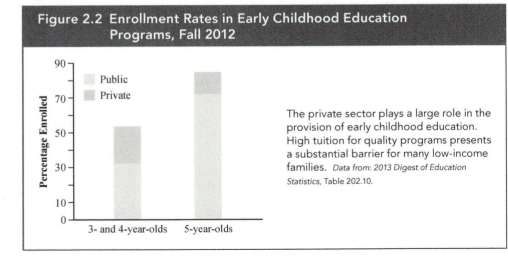

Figure 2.2 Enrollment Rates in Early Childhood Education Programs, Fall 2012

The private sector plays a large role in the provision of early childhood education. High tuition for quality programs presents a substantial barrier for many low-income families. *Data from: 2013 Digest of Education Statistics, Table 202.10.*

and health care for children from low-income backgrounds, is one important enrollment path for early childhood education programs. Universal pre-K programs are increasingly common in the United States as well. Recent research has emphasized the role of early childhood education in preparing young children to take full advantage of the learning experiences later in life (Heckman, 2006).[3]

- *Elementary and secondary education:* Kindergarten plus the 12 years of graded schooling—often referred to as elementary and secondary education—are generally completed before age 18. Early years (K–6) are referred to as elementary and later years as secondary, though there is considerable variation among localities in how the "middle grades" (typically 6, 7, 8) are organized (see Figure 2.1).

- *Postsecondary education:* Beyond high school there are many education options. Both two- and four-year institutions are categorized as postsecondary education providers. Colleges and universities differ markedly in specialization: Cal Tech specializes in the sciences and Juilliard in music and the arts, for example. They also differ in the types of degrees offered, with some institutions awarding associate degrees and others awarding baccalaureate (BA)[4] degrees as well as many professional and graduate degrees. Additionally, they differ in terms of the level of resources employed in the production of education. The structure of the higher education market is discussed in detail in Chapter 13.

- *Graduate education:* After finishing undergraduate education, people may either enter the labor force or go to graduate school, which typically is more specialized than undergraduate training. These programs are quite varied, from academic masters programs (e.g., master of arts in history) and professional masters programs (e.g., masters of public policy) to law (JD) and medical degrees (MD) as well as PhDs.

This book focuses on the formal schooling years that begin with kindergarten and continue through postsecondary education. In Figure 2.1, we denote 5 as the age at which formal schooling usually starts. However, an increasing phenomenon in education is what is termed *academic red-shirting*, whereby parents hold students back an extra year so that they begin kindergarten at age 6.[5] Thus, it is becoming more common for students to graduate high school at 19 years old. Red-shirting is particularly prevalent for boys.

Quick Hint: The term *red-shirting* comes from intercollegiate athletics to refer to an athlete who purposefully does not play his or her first year of college to retain an extra year of eligibility to play.

---

[3] For research on how Head Start affects children's outcomes, see research by Currie and Thomas (1995), Garces, Thomas, and Currie (2002), and Ludwig and Miller (2007); and see Fitzpatrick (2008) for an analysis of universal pre-K programs.

[4] Baccalaureate degrees usually take the form of a Bachelor of Arts (BA) or a Bachelor of Science (BS). Education researchers typically use the term BA as a shortcut to refer to all baccalaureate degrees. We maintain this terminology throughout the book.

[5] Deming and Dynarski (2008) and Elder and Lubotsky (2009) provide in-depth analyses of academic red-shirting.

In the early grades, the U.S. education system is not specialized and tends not to make strong distinctions among students. Although there are special education programs and gifted and talented programs, most students in the United States through high school are on an academic track. Specialization increases as one advances in the education system; this can be observed in vocational and technical high schools, which are focused on preparing students for the labor force. In addition, **academic tracking** tends to increase with grade for middle and high school students according to prior academic performance. Colleges, particularly graduate schools, are much more specialized in terms of the students they serve because of differing admissions criteria as well as the breadth and depth of skills taught to students. The lack of tracking in early grades and the broad focus on an academic rather than a vocational course of study for the vast majority of students is not universal throughout the world. For example, the German system entails significant tracking at early ages, separating students into those who will be trained for vocational careers and those who will receive a more academically oriented education that will prepare them for college.

At the postsecondary level, colleges and universities in the United States are distinguished by large variation in types and quality of schools as well as the significant role played by the private sector. In most other countries, higher education is almost exclusively public. Even in countries with private colleges and universities, such as Canada and England, they are a small part of the postsecondary system. The same is not true in the United States, where private colleges and universities actually outnumber public ones, even though enrollment in public postsecondary schools is larger. Furthermore, the private sector makes up a large percentage of elite colleges and universities in the United States, which is not the case in most other countries.

academic tracking
Separating students by academic ability groups.

DEEP DIVE: International Schooling Comparisons

While there are many similarities between the K–12 education system in the United States and those in other parts of the world, there also are substantial differences. An in-depth analysis of the various education systems across the globe is outside the scope of this book, but here we highlight some of the key differences between the American K–12 education system and those in other countries.

In **Germany**, children generally start school at age 6 and are required to complete nine years of education. For children attending public schools, education is free at all levels except university. As in the United States, education policy is primarily the responsibility of the states (*Länder*); they determine the curriculum, recommend teaching methods, and approve textbooks.

The main difference between the U.S. and German systems arises during secondary school, with Germany's extensive tracking system. Having completed primary education (age 10 to 12), the parents—through discussions with their children and their teachers—have to decide between four kinds of secondary schools: *Gesamtschule, Gymnasium,*

Hauptschule, and Realschule. Gymnasium is reserved for the most academically skilled children and is the sole path to university. *Hauptschule* provides the same basic secondary education at a slower pace, with more hands-on experience, and is reserved for the manually inclined. *Realschule* is focused on more extensive vocational training. Following the completion of *Realschule*, the children can decide to engage in additional vocational training through *Berfusschule*, switch to *Gymnasium* if their grades are satisfactory, or enter the labor force. *Gesamtschule* is a combination of *Haupschule* and *Realschule*, and depending on how long the child remains in *Gesamtschule*, he or she will either receive a *Hauptschule* or a *Realschule* certificate. Vocational training is greatly emphasized in Germany and is organized for some 360 professions. Following the completion of mandatory education, individuals are free to decide whether they want to join the labor force, obtain further vocational training, or enroll in preparatory classes for university or college.

In **Malawi**, schooling is separated into three levels: primary school (8 years), secondary school (4 years), and tertiary schooling (4 years). The official language of schooling in Malawi is English, although students in early primary grades can receive instruction in any of the main local languages. Primary school is compulsory for all eight years and is provided by a mix of government and private sources. Since 1994, universal and free primary school has been offered throughout Malawi. However, students are expected to purchase their own uniforms and supplies, which can be a large burden in a country with extremely high poverty rates. Primary schools often lack sufficient space for students or access to basic resources such as electricity. Particularly in rural areas, dropout rates can be extremely high because of early marriage, employment, and sickness.

Secondary schooling is provided by the government and privately, but school fees and low rates of primary school completion make secondary schooling much rarer than in industrialized countries such as the United States. Fewer than 15% of appropriate-age children enroll in secondary school. Students take the Junior Certificate of Education exam in their second year of secondary schooling and to go on must pass six of the exams in English, math, agriculture, physics, biology, geography, history, Bible knowledge, social studies, and Chichewa. To graduate, students must pass six of these subjects on the Malawi Secondary Certificate of Education exam in their fourth year.

Tertiary, or university, education is quite uncommon in Malawi in part because of the small proportion of children who make it through the secondary system; only about 1% of the college-age population is enrolled in college. Unlike in the United States, all university education in Malawi is public and run by the University of Malawi.

In **England**, the education system is overseen by the Department for Education and the Department for Business, Innovation and Skills. While there is a national curriculum and standards that determine what students in each grade should be taught, just as in the United States, local authorities are responsible for determining how to teach the curriculum and for implementing policies for public education. Children begin school at age five, and compulsory education extends from age 5 to 17. Unlike in the United States, students do not repeat years if they do not make sufficient progress. Students take standardized assessments in years 2 (age 7), 6 (age 11), 11 (age 16), and 13 (age 18). At the end of compulsory education, students take the GCSE examinations, a battery of tests in mathematics, English literature, English composition, chemistry, biology, physics, history or the classics, one modern language, and one other subject, such as art or computer studies.

Following the completion of compulsory education, students can choose to pursue secondary education for an additional two years (sixth form) to obtain A-level subject qualifications that enable them to apply to university. During sixth form there is more focus on subject depth than breadth, and normally a student takes only three or four A-level subjects. This stands in stark contrast to U.S. high schools, which generally require a broader range of subjects.

State schools and sixth form are funded through taxes, and most students enroll in public schools: in 2012, fewer than 10% of students aged 3–18 attended private schools. This is slightly lower than the proportion of U.S. children who enroll in private schools. In the United Kingdom, private schools are not required to follow the national curriculum, and their teachers are not regulated by the official teaching qualification laws.

China has the largest education system in the world, and the state invests approximately 4% of its GDP in education each year. It is a completely state-run system under the control of the Ministry of Education.

Children normally begin school at age 6 or 7 and are required by law to complete at least nine years. For most provinces, this entails six years of primary education and three years of junior middle school. After this, children have the option to enroll in a three-year senior high school or vocational high school or to end their formal schooling. Admission to the senior high school programs are granted through *Zhongkao* (the Senior High School Entrance Examination), a series of exams in a broad set of subjects. Cutoff levels for the most elite high schools are set by the level of demand, which ensures that the top students sort into the most elite schools. There typically are enough spaces in the less selective senior high schools to accommodate all students who wish to enroll. Attending an academic senior high school is a necessary condition for enrolling in a postsecondary school. Admission to postsecondary schools also is based on national exams, called *Gaokao*, which students take in their last year of senior high school.

Canada has a universal publicly funded K–12 education system, with compulsory education extending from age 7 to 16 (with the exception of Manitoba, Ontario, and New Brunswick, where education is mandatory from age 7 to 18). Education in English and in French is available in most provinces. Throughout most of Canada, secondary schooling ends in twelfth grade. In Quebec, secondary schooling ends at eleventh grade, and students then can attend a two-year junior college called *Cégep* (Collège d'enseignement général et professionnel). *Cégep* programs range from an academic focus to a vocational focus. Students intending to enroll in a BA program first attend an academic *Cégep* and then apply to a university. Universities in Quebec have three-year BA programs, so the total number of years of schooling leading to a BA degree is the same in Quebec as in the rest of Canada and in the United States.

Canadian education policy falls within the jurisdiction of its provinces. The provinces are divided into school districts, and all publicly funded schools are under the authority of their local district boards. The one exception to this is Alberta, which allows public charter schools to operate independently of the school boards. Canada does not have a national department of education.

Providers in Education Markets

There are many types of producers, or sellers, of education services in U.S. education markets, and they vary considerably across the levels of education. The three main types of education producers are:

1. Public, usually state or local governments
2. Private *not-for-profit*
3. Private for-profit

These three types of education providers exist at all levels of education but in different proportions. Private schools are most common in early childhood education, while public schools dominate the elementary and secondary school market. Private not-for-profit schools also are very prevalent in the postsecondary market, although recent years have seen growth in for-profit private schools as well in this sector.

> **Quick Hint:** A not-for-profit, or nonprofit, is recognized under section 501(c)(3) of the U.S. tax code. In exchange for providing services that are broadly defined as charitable or in the public interest, such as education, not-for-profits are exempt from taxes, and individuals can receive tax deductions for donations to them.

The providers of education services often are distinct from those who pay for education services. Government support of higher education is pervasive, and even private schools receive substantial funding from the government. Therefore, it is important to distinguish **publicly funded education** from **publicly provided education**. *Publicly funded* means simply that government resources subsidize the provision of education services, with funds awarded either to schools or to students; *publicly provided* means that the government is charged with resource allocation decisions and the management and delivery of the education services themselves. When we refer to private or public institutions, we are describing the governance of the institution rather than the way in which it is funded.

publicly funded education Education that is paid for by government revenues. Education that is publicly financed does not need to be publicly provided.

publicly provided education Education that is operated and controlled by a public entity.

Public Education Providers Public providers of education services range from public elementary and secondary schools to public two-year and four-year colleges and universities. Examples of public universities operated by the Commonwealth of Virginia include the University of Virginia, the College of William and Mary, Virginia Commonwealth University, and Virginia Tech. Public high schools, such as George Washington Senior High School in Cedar Rapids, Iowa, and elementary schools, such as French Road Elementary School in Rochester, New York, are examples of K–12 education suppliers operated by local governments.

As shown in Table 2.1, 84.1% of students enrolled at the elementary and secondary levels attend public schools. All public elementary and secondary schools are operated by local governments; while states can provide considerable funding for K–12 education, they typically do not operate any schools. Public K–12 schools also are funded by the locality, usually through property taxes, and many schools receive funds from the federal government as well. When students attend public schools, they do not pay tuition directly but must simply be a resident in the locality. While there are no posted prices, this does not mean that the price mechanism is absent from parental decision making. All else equal, housing is more expensive in neighborhoods with higher-quality public schools (Black, 1999). School districts, which are extensions of local governments, hire teachers, build and maintain schools, and make some choices about curriculum. Local public schools are not completely autonomous, though, as they are subject to regulations and requirements (mandates) from state and federal governments.

As Table 2.1 shows, most students in higher education also are enrolled in public sector institutions: over 72% of students enrolled in higher education attend a public college or university. State governments have some oversight of nearly all public universities, although a modest number of community colleges are under the control of local governments. While students overwhelmingly enroll in public postsecondary

Table 2.1 Distribution of Enrollment and Institutions by Sector and Level

Elementary & Secondary	Enrollment (× 1,000) Fall 2012	Number of Institutions Fall 2011
Public	47,714	92,632
Private	5,181	30,861
Charter	2,057	5,696
Homeschooled	1,773	N/A
Public	84.1%	71.7%
Charter	9.1%	4.4%
Homeschooled	3.1%	
Postsecondary	**Enrollment (× 1,000) Fall 2012**	**Number of Institutions Fall 2011**
Public	14,880	2,011
Private	5,762	5,223
Not-for-profit	3,954	1,830
For-profit	1,809	3,393
Public share	72.1%	27.8%

Data from: 2013 Digest of Education Statistics, Tables 105.30, 105.50, 206.10, 216.90, 303.10.
The number of public school students and schools is calculated by subtracting charter counts from total public counts.

schools, there are many more private than public institutions. An implication of these differences is that the public universities are much larger than the private ones. The private sector's relatively large role in higher education distinguishes the U.S. system from other systems around the world that are much more reliant on the public sector.

Private Nonprofit Providers Nonprofit institutions are private organizations chartered by the state and recognized under section 501(c)(3) of the tax code. The presence of a **nondistribution constraint** produces the structural distinction between a for-profit and not-for-profit (or nonprofit) firm. In nonprofits, there are no residual shareholders. In turn, there are no owners of nonprofit organizations that earn money from profits, unlike the case of private for-profit companies like Apple or Amazon. In nonprofits, all revenues that exceed operating costs (including worker wages) must be spent on future activities of the nonprofit firm. Private colleges and universities, such as Princeton University or Oberlin College, as well as a number of independent secondary schools such as the Collegiate School in New York City or Phillips Exeter Academy in New Hampshire, are organized as nonprofits. Many *charter schools*, privately run but publicly funded elementary and secondary schools, are also not-for-profit. Charter schools differ considerably from more traditional private schools in that they are almost completely publicly financed, have no tuition, and do not have selective admissions. While many consider charter schools to be part of the public system of higher education because of the fact that they are publicly financed and cannot choose their students, these schools are privately operated. Charter schools quite clearly illustrate the distinction between who provides education services and who funds education services. Table 2.1 shows that about 9% of elementary and secondary students are enrolled in charter schools.

A wide array of other entities are organized as nonprofits, including zoos, museums, soup kitchens, and environmental preservation groups. You should not think of this organizational structure as exclusive to education. Because the activities performed by nonprofits (including education institutions) benefit society, they receive tax privileges. Nonprofits do not pay taxes on either property or income. Particularly for many private colleges and universities that sit on considerable amounts of land in expensive areas, such as Columbia University in New York City and Stanford University in the San Francisco Bay Area, the savings from not having to pay property taxes are considerable. In addition, individuals making contributions to nonprofits can deduct those contributions from their income taxes as charitable donations. These tax preferences are implicit public subsidies that can be quite large.

Private nonprofit schools offer an alternative to local public schools. Students (or their families) can choose to forgo local public schools and attend private schools. Aside from charter schools, the distinctive features of privately operated schools are that they charge tuition and can select which students they will serve. There is much variation across areas in the availability of private alternatives to public schooling, and it is commonly argued that areas with more private school options have more competition in their education markets.

One reason parents send their children to private schools is the belief that private schools offer a higher quality of education than the available local public option. A second explanation is that parents want their children to have a philosophically or culturally different type of education from that offered by the local public schools. The most common example of this preference is when parents want religion integrated with education and hence choose to send their children to a parochial school specific to a

nondistribution constraint Because there are no residual shareholders in a nonprofit, those who exercise control over the organization cannot receive residual earnings. In theory, this should reduce incentives to take advantage of consumers and ensure that donations are used for their intended purposes.

faith. Regardless of motivation, sending children to private schools means often a willingness to pay tuition and forgoing opportunities at the local public schools.

Higher education has a long history of nonprofit involvement. According to Table 2.1, a simple count of college campuses shows that private not-for-profits are the single most prevalent type of college, even though they do not constitute the bulk of student enrollments. Many of these entities trace their origins to a time before the start of the twentieth century, when they were founded either by religious institutions or wealthy individuals concerned with providing opportunities for the training of teachers, preachers, and professionals.

For-Profit Providers For-profit providers are by no means absent in the production of education. Profit-making firms have long been in the business of providing services to education, such as textbooks, cafeteria services, and construction. What is relatively new is the involvement of for-profit providers directly in education. The expansion of for-profit firms at all levels of education has been notable in recent years. In elementary and secondary education, private education companies like Advantage Schools and Edison Schools have contracted to manage public schools and entire districts. Also, many charter schools, such as National Heritage Academies, are run by for-profit companies.

In higher education, for-profit schools existed as far back as the eighteenth century, although they were very small and offered specialized business and technical training. There has been a sharp increase in the importance of for-profit schools in the past decade. Schools like the University of Phoenix, which is run by the Apollo Corporation, now offers undergraduate and graduate degrees in a number of states as well as online. Enrollment in for-profit postsecondary programs increased by over 9,700% between 1970 and 2012. As a share of total undergraduate enrollment, this was an increase in the proportion of total college students from 0.2% to 6.9%. The implications of the rise in for-profit education are poorly understood and are an ongoing topic of study among education researchers.

Arguments for the Role of Government and Nonprofits in Education

The dominance of service providers that are not profit-seeking is a unique aspect of education markets. Education is not the only market in which governments are involved in production, though. Other examples include police protection, air traffic control, roads, and national parks. Education is not entirely unique in the mix of public, nonprofit, and for-profit providers, either. The closest parallel to education's mix of public, nonprofit, and for-profit providers is health care: Hospitals and other medical service providers may be operated by large corporations, nonprofits, or local governments. When education—or any other service—is not provided by a for-profit firm, it is important to consider the economic reasons. Why might we expect to see a large public and nonprofit presence in education markets when most other markets, such as personal computers and automobiles, are comprised of only for-profit firms? One explanation is that the quality of education provided by private firms would not necessarily be high. Education markets are characterized by **asymmetric information**: consumers—students and their parents—have a hard time observing the quality of an educational product, which they purchase infrequently and at great expense. As a result, they have less information about a school's quality than those who run the school. Because it may be difficult to write a contract that fully specifies all of the dimensions of an education and

asymmetric information Arises when one individual or group in a market transaction has more information about the product or good being sold than another individual or group in the transaction.

because students may have a hard time observing the product, there are opportunities for seller opportunism. In this type of trust market, nonprofit and public entities may be preferred because their agents are not positioned to profit from diverting resources from the provision of education.[6]

A second type of argument for a government role in education markets is that the efficient production of education requires economies of scale and scope that are difficult to realize with for-profit provision. Government provision of schooling can be justified by the natural monopoly argument explained previously as well. Schools have large fixed costs that considerably raise the cost of entry. This generates increasing returns to scale that reduce the supply of schools in a local area and thus competition. As well, there are some areas in which no private school would want to locate and others in which private schools would want to close. Since all students need to be assigned to a local school, there is a large role for government provision of education services. A related argument is that the nonprofit and public sectors may provide types of education that are valued by individuals and society but could not be produced at a profit—examples include training in art, history, or sciences that require considerable access to laboratory equipment.

Spillover benefits—or positive externalities to education—can generate underprovision of education. When I make my choice about how much education to get, I will not pay attention to the fact that if I get more education, it may make others better off. Both government and nonprofit provision of education are ways to subsidize education services, thereby lowering the price and increasing the amount of education people will obtain. Alternatively, the government could choose to subsidize private or nonprofit providers directly or could provide resources for education to individuals in the form of vouchers or grants. These subsidies do exist and form the basis for many school choice policies, discussed in Chapter 10.

A related concern that can justify government intervention in education markets is that people may face *credit constraints* that inhibit their ability to purchase an optimal level of education. Credit constraints arise when individuals lack sufficient access to credit, which precludes them from making an educational investment that would yield a positive return. For example, a student may not have sufficient cash on hand to fund tuition expenditures for college, even when the student could be expected to repay a loan for college with earnings gains. Alternatively, even when a family recognizes that the long-term gains from sending children to better schools may far exceed the additional cost of buying (or renting) a house in a neighborhood with better schools, it may be limited by income and assets and unable to locate in areas with better schools. Costs of education services may be too high for some families, which can generate inequality in access to education services and can result in too few education services being purchased by society at large. By providing education at a price below what would be charged in the market, government intervention can help alleviate these credit constraints. An important question is whether the best way for government to address this challenge is through provision of education at a public institution or through funding to individuals.

---

[6] Winston (1999) and Hansmann (1980) outline these ideas in more detail. Winston asks, "Did the CARE package get delivered to Somalia?" to illustrate the type of services where individuals may be particularly poorly positioned to monitor outcomes. In such cases, nonprofits may be best positioned to deliver in these markets. Other parallels include nursing homes and day care.

2.2 The Roles of Government in Education

The roles of government in the market for education are threefold:

1. Local and state governments participate in the production of education. They provide education services directly.
2. Governments, including legislatures and the judiciary, set the rules of the market through regulations. These regulations can specify the type of education that will be provided, the method of production, prices associated with education services, funding levels, and resource allocation.
3. The government provides public funding or subsidies to virtually all education markets in the United States.

Regulations and Mandates in Education

In addition to directly providing education services, governments set regulations that can impact both public and private education institutions. Regulations can be set by federal, state, or local authorities, and they can place limitations or provide guidance on how any aspect of the education service is produced and for whom it is produced. One salient example of an education regulation that has influenced education provision at all levels is the Individuals with Disabilities Education Act (IDEA), passed in 1975 and subsequently reauthorized. IDEA mandates a free and appropriate education for children with special needs (both learning disabilities and physical handicaps), requiring that states and school districts provide special education to eligible children with disabilities.

Since 2002, the passage of the federal No Child Left Behind Act mandates, or requires, that all states must establish performance standards in specific subjects, test the progress of children in meeting these objectives, and provide public reports on performance at the level of local public schools. The No Child Left Behind Act is a prime example of an *unfunded mandate*, as it laid out rules and a system of rewards and punishments without substantively altering the resources available to schools to meet the terms of the mandate.

States are also important players in setting standards and regulations for education. Examples of state-level regulatory policies include ages of compulsory attendance, the training required of teachers for licensure, and the length of the school term. For example, in Virginia, schools must provide at least 180 teaching days per student, with a calendar day defined to consist of 5.5 hours of instructional time, excluding breaks for meals and recess.

The influence of the government on education is not limited to the legislative process: the judiciary has played a large role in setting education policy throughout U.S. history. Education policies often are examined by the judiciary for consistency with state and federal constitutions. A number of important court rulings at the state and federal level have had substantial effects on the market for education through their effects on the allocation of educational resources.

Perhaps the most widely known Supreme Court case related to education is the 1954 decision in *Brown vs. Board of Education*, which held that racially segregated systems of public education were inherently unequal, violating the Fourteenth Amendment. While the school resources available to students by race did not adjust sharply with the Brown decision (and de facto segregation persists in many cities), the ruling symbolized the start of federal efforts to end discrimination in education at the local level.

State judicial action also affects education policy and the distribution of resources to schools. In the early 1970s, a California State Supreme Court case, *Serrano vs. Priest*, led to a ruling that the unequal level of funding for public schools across districts was a violation of the equal protection clause of the state constitution. The result was a complete revamping of the way schools in California were financed. There have been dozens of school finance cases since *Serrano*, which, combined with legislative action, have generated large changes in schools' finance systems in the United States. These changes are discussed in Chapter 8.

Public Funding for Education

In the United States, direct funding of education at all levels of government is substantial. In the 2012–2013 school year, direct outlays for education among state and local governments was almost $880 billion, about 65% of which was for K–12 education. The federal government spent $190 billion in direct outlays for education in that year as well, which was about evenly split between support for higher education and for elementary and secondary education. Another $109 billion in federal outlays could be found in off-budget programs, including student loans. Total public outlays for education were $1.2 trillion in the 2012–2013 school year.

Over the past century, the balance between state and local governments in funding elementary and secondary schools has changed significantly. There has been a move to a greater reliance on *centralized* or state funding of public schooling provided at the local level. In 1930, localities provided nearly 85% of school resources, with much of the remainder coming from the states and virtually no support from the federal government. In more recent years, the balance has shifted dramatically, with state and local governments providing roughly equal shares of funding and the federal government providing about 10% of total funds. Some of the impetus for this shift has come from litigation (starting with the *Serrano* case in California), arguing that substantial disparities of funding among local school districts violated state constitutions.

When it comes to higher education, state governments are not just important funders of education but also manage many higher education systems. Professors at most public universities are state employees. By providing direct funding to public colleges and universities, states are able to offer residents access to college education for tuition charges that are well below the cost of educating a student, with in-state tuition and fees often more than $20,000 less per year than the price charged to out-of-state students.

Ultimately, the level of educational attainment we observe for different groups is the outcome of market conditions. Government policies—including legislative regulations, public subsidies, and judicial rulings—affect the structure of education markets and therefore influence the ways education services are produced and purchased.

2.3 Development of Education Institutions and Attainment in the United States

Now that we have set forth the contemporary structure of education markets in the United States, it is instructive to examine the history of educational institutions and attainment to develop an understanding of how these markets came to be. As the opening to this chapter highlights, the structure of education and its importance to our

Figure 2.3 Enrollment Rates for Ages 5–19, 1850–2000

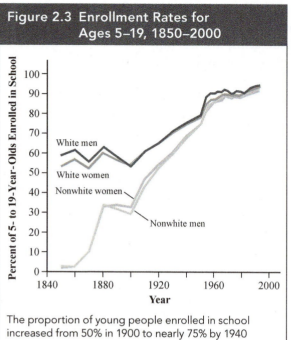

The proportion of young people enrolled in school increased from 50% in 1900 to nearly 75% by 1940 before reaching a plateau near 90% in 1970. Included in this increase is the nearly universal enrollment rate of those under 14 by 1970. These increases occurred equally for men and women and were particularly large for Black, whose enrollment rates in the early twentieth century were very low. *Data from:* Goldin (2005).

society were vastly different several hundred years ago than they are today. Why has educational attainment increased so much, and how did the modern system of education grow to meet this demand for education? These questions are the focus of this section.[7]

Through much of the twentieth century, education has been a growth industry in the United States. One illustration of this point is the rising enrollment rates of young people in the 5 to 19 age range shown in Figure 2.3; overall, the proportion of young people enrolled in school increased from about 50% in 1900 to nearly 75% by 1940 before reaching a plateau of about 90% in 1970. Included in this increase is the near-universal enrollment rate of those under 14 by 1970. Increases in enrollment translate to higher levels of educational attainment measured by years of completed education, the proportion of the population with high school degrees, and the proportion of the population with any collegiate attainment.

Greater educational attainment may benefit individuals through higher earnings while also generating some community-level benefits, to the extent that better-educated individuals are more likely to participate in civic institutions and are less likely to be involved in criminal activity. Expansion in educational attainment is hierarchical—college participation requires high school completion, which requires the basic skills from primary education. It should be no surprise that educational attainment proceeded in phases of development, moving from the widespread availability of elementary education in the mid-nineteenth century to the high school movement in the early part of the twentieth century. After World War II (which ended in 1945), education increases mostly have come through higher collegiate and graduate attainment.

The history of educational attainment and education markets presents particularly stark differences in education outcomes by race, generated by the legacy of discrimination and segregation in education institutions at all levels. The persistence of slavery into the mid-nineteenth century followed by de jure and de facto segregation of schooling in many areas excluded Black from many of the educational opportunities available to Whites. Figure 2.3 shows these large differences in enrollment rates by race that were present at the start of the twentieth century. While the racial gap in educational attainment has narrowed considerably over the past century, from about 3.6 years to about 0.6 years, a persistent difference has remained rather constant in recent decades. In addition to Black–White differences in the quantity of education, there are large historic differences in the quality of education services provided to White and Black students. Particularly in the U.S. South in the early part of the century, schools serving Black students had many fewer resources as measured by teachers and expenditures per student than those serving White students. As with the quantity of education, racial differences in education quality have narrowed over time, but the gap has not fully closed yet either.

---

[7] This section follows the excellent narrative presented by Claudia Goldin and Lawrence Katz (2008) in their monograph, *The Race Between Education and Technology*.

In reviewing the history of education in the United States, we follow Goldin and Katz (2008), who split the growth in educational attainment into three periods, and we add a fourth period that extends their historical analysis to today:

1. The common school movement (mid-nineteenth century)
2. The high school movement (1910–1940)
3. Expansion at the postsecondary level (1940–1975)
4. The growth in demand for skills and the shift to market-based schooling policies (1975–today)

Mid-Nineteenth Century: The Common School Movement

Publicly provided primary education goes back to the colonial years in the United States. Colonial statesmen such as Thomas Jefferson, John Adams, Benjamin Rush, and Benjamin Franklin argued that the stability of a democracy depends on educated and informed citizens (Goldin and Katz, 2008). To this end, these men advocated for the availability of at least a basic education, including literacy and numeracy, for all citizens. In many areas, local or community schools—often called common schools—were established to accomplish this basic purpose. Today, we refer to this level of education as elementary or primary education. While most communities operated schools and provided at least some days of schooling free of charge, communities charged for additional days of attendance (known as rate bills). The effect was to inhibit school attendance for students from the least affluent families.

The mid-nineteenth century brought a strong movement, led by reformers like Horace Mann, to provide public schooling without direct charge for all children. Massachusetts (1826) and Maine (1820) were early in passing laws eliminating rate bills or direct fees for publicly provided schools, while rate bills persisted into the latter half of the nineteenth century in communities in the South and Midwest. State laws eliminating rate bills led to local-level changes in the financing of schools, with communities generally financing schools out of local property tax revenues. In addition to providing primary education at no direct charge, states and localities often went further, to institute laws requiring attendance until a minimum school-leaving age was reached, as well as passing laws that restricted work among children to help induce school attendance. By the end of the nineteenth century, mass primary education had arrived in the United States.

1910–1940: The High School Movement

The next chapter in the transformation of U.S. educational attainment arrived at the start of the twentieth century with the proliferation of public secondary education.[8] While fewer than 10% of youth graduated from high school at the start of the century, nearly 75% of youth had enrolled in high school and about 50% of youth completed high school by 1940. These trends are shown in Figure 2.4.

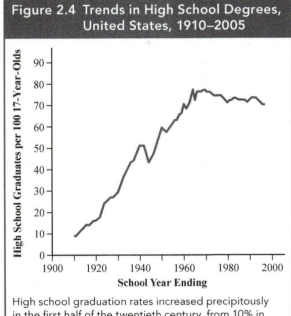

Figure 2.4 Trends in High School Degrees, United States, 1910–2005

High school graduation rates increased precipitously in the first half of the twentieth century, from 10% in 1910 to about 60% in 1950. They continued to increase until the mid-1960s, when they reached a plateau of 80%. *Data from:* Goldin (2005).

---

[8] The rise of public high schools was preceded by the growth of private academies in the late nineteenth century.

Changes in the economy in the early twentieth century brought new rewards to basic knowledge of the applied sciences, including chemistry and the capacity to read mechanical drawings. Because young people found that they benefited substantially from education beyond the primary years and obtaining a high school diploma, availability of a high school education proved to be important in attracting families to communities. In her analysis of the spread of secondary schooling in the United States, Goldin (1998) emphasized the decentralized nature of the rise of high schools in the early twentieth century. She argued that the combination of high labor market returns to a high school degree and interdistrict competition driven by the large number of school districts in the United States at the time led to dramatic increases in secondary school attainment.

By 1955, the proportion of young people in the United States graduating from high school, which neared 80%, was well above educational attainment in European countries, where high school graduation rates were often about 20%. This U.S. educational advantage has not been permanent. Many countries had caught up and in some cases surpassed the United States in high school attainment by the end of the twentieth century (Goldin, 2005). At mid-century, the European systems of secondary education were structurally different from those found in the United States in two main regards. First, schooling in European countries tended to be centrally controlled, with national governments providing funding and setting regulations. Second, the templates for secondary training differed appreciably between the United States and European countries. Secondary systems in European countries did not offer general skill development but emphasized separating students at early ages between vocational apprenticeships and, for a few, classical training in preparation for civil service or advanced study at universities. In contrast, high schools in the United States combined academic and vocational training, representing a portfolio of skills that could be used either in employment or in college-level work.

1940–1975: Expansion at the Postsecondary Level

Expansion of college-level opportunities—what some have called the introduction of mass higher education—is a major development of the last century. Figure 2.5 shows the trend in the number of BA degrees awarded to men and women from the late nineteenth century to the current millennium. The rate of change in the first part of the century is extraordinary, with the total number of undergraduate degrees awarded increasing by a factor of about 4.5, from 27,410 in 1900 to 122,488 by 1930. Much of this change occurred in the public universities, which dramatically expanded in scale and scope.

The G.I. Bill, formally known as the Serviceman's Readjustment Act (1944), provided unprecedented subsidies to men returning from military service in World War II. The impact on collegiate attainment was significant, as seen in the large spike in degree attainment for men in the late 1940s. Concurrently, a commission appointed by President Truman in 1946 to evaluate postsecondary opportunities issued a report under the general title *Higher Education for American Democracy* (more commonly known as the Truman Commission Report). A central conclusion of the report was that there were many more Americans prepared to benefit from higher education than were afforded the opportunity to attend, and it recommended significant expansion of the community college system as well as increases in student aid. As a result, the number of community

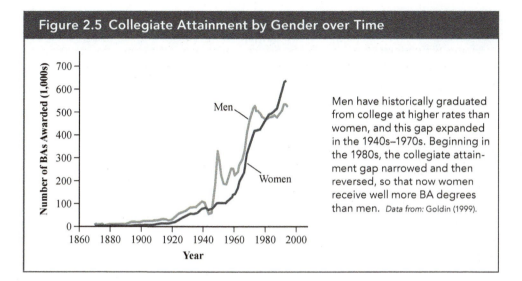

Figure 2.5 Collegiate Attainment by Gender over Time

Men have historically graduated from college at higher rates than women, and this gap expanded in the 1940s–1970s. Beginning in the 1980s, the collegiate attainment gap narrowed and then reversed, so that now women receive well more BA degrees than men. *Data from:* Goldin (1999).

colleges increased substantially in the 1950s and 1960s. The modern student financial aid system also began to be developed in the 1960s and 1970s. A number of writers have referred to the period from the late 1950s through the 1960s as the golden years of higher education. Not only did the number of undergraduate degrees continue to rise, but doctorate and professional education expanded as well.

Part of the story in Figure 2.5 is the striking change in college graduation rates of women relative to men. While the G.I. Bill and the associated economic changes served to widen the difference in attainment in the immediate postwar years, the past two decades have brought not only convergence but a sizable advantage to women in undergraduate degree attainment. This is a dramatic turn of events given that women accounted for only about 33% of undergraduate degree recipients in 1955.

Despite the reversal of the gender gap in many measures of educational attainment, such as college completion, women remain significantly underrepresented in some professional fields and in many science and engineering disciplines. A challenge for social scientists is to understand the extent to which persistent differences in specialization reflect preferences, opportunities in school, or differences in labor market incentives.

1975–Today: The Growth in Demand for Skills and the Shift to Market-Based Schooling Policies

Throughout most of the 1970s, the college wage premium, defined as the difference in earnings between those with a high school degree and a college degree, declined. The low returns to college led many to argue that people were obtaining too much education. A highly influential book by economist Richard Freeman (1976), *The Overeducated American*, asked whether a saturation of the labor market with new college graduates had produced a circumstance in which college graduates would struggle for economic success. With a rapid expansion of the supply of collegiate opportunities in the late 1960s, it appeared that Americans in this period were overinvesting in higher education. This argument may seem foreign today given the strong policy focus on

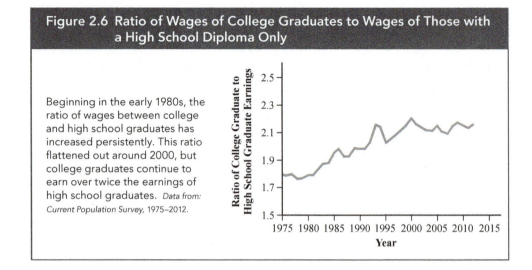

Figure 2.6 Ratio of Wages of College Graduates to Wages of Those with a High School Diploma Only

Beginning in the early 1980s, the ratio of wages between college and high school graduates has increased persistently. This ratio flattened out around 2000, but college graduates continue to earn over twice the earnings of high school graduates. *Data from: Current Population Survey, 1975–2012.*

increasing higher education attainment. But in the 1970s, it is clear, many had the opposite concern.

What can account for this change? As argued in careful empirical work by Murphy and Welch (1989), the decline in the earnings return to a college education was a temporary phenomenon driven by a supply shock. The 1970s saw a large increase in the number of college graduates that largely reflected the unusually large cohort sizes associated with the postwar baby boom years. As the supply of college-educated workers expanded, their wages declined.

Murphy and Welch go on to document a precipitous rise in the college wage premium that began around 1980. As many other researchers have documented, this premium has continued to grow or remained at a stable high level since that time. Figure 2.6 shows the ratio of wages among workers with a college education relative to a high school education between 1975 and 2012. Beginning in the early 1980s, the wage ratio increases persistently until about 2000, where it has remained since that time. Since the early 1980s, the earnings difference between a high school and a college worker has diverged considerably, and the wage premium associated with a college education has never been higher than at present.

What led to this increase in the relative wages of college-trained workers? A series of papers in economics have argued that since the mid-1970s changes to the U.S. economy have led to higher demand for skilled labor.[9] After World War II, manufacturing played a large role in the U.S. economy, and relatively high-paying jobs that required little post-secondary education were common. In recent decades, the importance of manufacturing has declined, and there has been a rise in high-skilled service industries such as finance and health care. Technological changes in industries such as manufacturing, which used to employ large numbers of lower-skilled workers, have replaced routine, manual tasks with automated processes, thereby lowering demand for such workers. Both within and across industries, demand for high-skilled labor has increased while demand for low-skilled labor has declined.

---

[9] See Murphy and Welch (1989), Autor, Katz, and Kearney (2008), DeLong, Goldin, and Katz (2003), and Autor (2014).

A central prediction of economic theory is that when the return to a given activity increases, more people should engage in that activity. Looking at Figure 2.6, one might predict that college completion has increased alongside the economic benefits of a college degree; however, such is not the case. Particularly for men, collegiate attainment has changed little since 1980. While it has increased for women, this is a continuation of a longtime trend discussed in the previous section. The data therefore point to barriers that are preventing the education system from producing a sufficient number of college-educated workers. Some of the most likely constraints facing the production of more college degrees are:

1. Insufficient academic preparation for college in K–12 school
2. Reduced funding for higher education that exposes many students to low resource levels, making it difficult for them to complete college
3. Financial and information barriers that preclude students from making optimal choices about whether and where to go to college

Concerns about the stagnation in the growth of college degrees earned by U.S. students has led to many of the education policies that we will study in this book.

One of the dominant trends in education policy over the past several decades is a shift from a focus on total school resources and input-based policies to using market-based approaches to enact education reform. This shift is motivated by the evidence that there is at best a weak relationship between the amount of money schools spend on students and their academic success; in short, simply giving schools more money does not seem to improve educational outcomes. As a result, education policy initiatives have moved much more in the direction of altering the incentives faced by schools and students. Examples of this shift include school choice (discussed in Chapter 10), accountability policies (Chapter 11) that generate a system of rewards and punishments for schools based on their students' academic performance, and teacher incentive pay (Chapter 12), which provides monetary rewards to teachers for their students' performance.

In addition to increasing the demand for college-educated labor, the rise of the computer and information technologies such as the Internet have begun to transform the provision of education services. Recent years have seen a proliferation of universities offering online courses and online degrees. Much of the increase in online postsecondary education services has been coincident with the expansion of the for-profit higher education sector, which has eschewed typical brick and mortar campuses for online degree programs. Universities also have begun to offer massive open online courses (MOOCs), free online courses that seek to disseminate knowledge and skills across the globe.

2.4 Conclusion

We have looked at the basic dimensions of education markets and sketched the big picture of how educational attainment has evolved in the United States. The agents include students, their families, schools, colleges, and various levels of government. Government policies have a substantial effect on outcomes in education through funding, regulations, and judicial decisions. In addition, the government is a major provider of education, with nearly 90% of students in the elementary and secondary levels attending public schools. At all levels, education is provided by public, nonprofit, and for-profit institutions. These dimensions of the education market will serve as important fundamentals in subsequent chapters as we consider how economic theory and evidence apply to the evaluation of education policies.

The next chapter introduces the difficult questions of evaluation of education policies. To understand how policies as diverse as class size reduction, the provision of school vouchers, and increases in tuition affect educational outcomes, it is imperative to have a measurement strategy. While discussions of ideas for education reform are common, evidence of how policies work that distinguishes causation from correlation is needed to solve the most challenging problems facing students, teachers, and schools.

Highlights

- A market for education is defined by the exchange of education services between the demand and supply sides of the market. The demand side is composed of families and individual students who want education services, while the supply side is made up of institutions that provide those services.
- Education markets are characterized by major distinctions from other commodity markets, such as not being perfectly competitive, the existence of spillovers (externalities), the differentiated nature of the good, local production, asymmetric information, peer effects, and the fact that education is a customer input technology. These differences influence almost all education policies at the local, state, and federal levels.
- Education in the United States can be divided into four levels: early childhood education, elementary and secondary education (K–12 schooling), postsecondary education (two- and four-year colleges and universities), and graduate education. Early grades are not specialized, while higher grades tend to include academic tracking, which makes them more specialized for students of different achievement levels.
- Provision of education (who supplies the services) is distinct from its funding (who finances the provision of services). Providers and funders may be public, private and not-for-profit, or private and for-profit. Publicly provided education can be distinct from publicly funded education, as many private-sector providers receive substantial government funding.
- The majority of elementary, secondary, and postsecondary education is publicly provided in the United States. The government plays a significant role by providing education services directly and by regulating education. Private not-for-profit institutions, which are defined by having a nondistribution constraint, also provide a significant proportion of education services in the United States. A much smaller but growing role is played by private for-profit institutions.

- The economic arguments for the large role played by the public sector in education revolve around the potentially large spillovers of education to society at large, the high fixed costs of school operation that generate economies of scale and make local schools operate like natural monopolies, and the difficulty in assuring and monitoring the quality of educational outputs.
- The twentieth century saw enormous growth in educational attainment in the United States and the consequent rise in the number of schools providing education services at all levels. Increased educational attainment measured by years of education, proportion of the population with a high school diploma, and proportion of the population with a college degree all rose over the past century. Because education is a hierarchical system, the history of education in the United States reflects the system's growth as stepwise progress, with variations in the rate of growth for various subgroups of the population including race and gender.
- The history of education can be split into four general periods of growth: the common school movement (mid-nineteenth century), the high school movement (1910–1940), the expansion of postsecondary education (1940–1975), and the most recent and ongoing growth in demand for skills and the shift to market-based schooling policies (1975–present).
- In recent years, the rate of growth of educational attainment has slowed, even though the labor market returns to education are growing. In particular, economists and policy makers are interested in understanding why changes in college completion rates have not matched the increasing financial returns to a college degree. This change in educational attainment is a critical motivation for recent efforts to reform the education system.

Problems

1. What do economists mean by education markets, and how they differ from the market for a more traditional commodity such as cars or books?

2. Briefly discuss how education markets today differ from those in Benjamin Franklin's time.

3. What is the difference between publicly provided education and publicly supported education? Can privately provided education be publicly funded?

4. Who are the different providers of education in the market? Give an example of each one.

5. What are the roles of government in the market for education?

6. Briefly describe the four periods of the history of education in the United States.

7. What evidence would support the contention that the supply of college-educated workers is inefficient?

8. Draw a supply and demand curve for education services.
   a. What is on each axis?
   b. What does the intersection of the supply and demand curve represent?
   c. Show what will happen to the supply and demand curves if more schools are built.
   d. Show what will happen to the supply and demand curves if the wage returns to schooling increase.

9. What is meant by an economy of scale in the production of education? When would a local school have a natural monopoly in education production?

10. Assume that education leads to more civic participation and lower crime. Do these positive externalities of education mean that people will tend to get too little, just the right amount, or too much education without government intervention in these markets?

11. Consider the market for after-school programs, which are claimed to foster achievement and discourage undesirable activities like teen smoking. Suppose the demand for after-school programs is described by: $E_D = 200 - \frac{T}{3}$ where T is the posted tuition per month and E is enrollment. The supply of these programs is described by the function: $E_S = \frac{T}{2}$.
    a. Plot the relationship between the demand for after-school programs and the tuition price. Plot the relationship between the quantity of after-school openings supplied and tuition. Label the axes and the demand and supply curves carefully. What is the equilibrium price and quantity?
    b. Suppose that the program prevents 1 in 10 enrollees from smoking, reducing future public health costs. How does the equilibrium enrollment level differ from an efficient outcome that incorporates the public benefit to the reduction in smoking? Comment on how this illustrates the nature of an externality.

Empirical Tools of Education Economics

Why Does College Enrollment Differ by Family Income?

If you compared students from wealthier family backgrounds with those from poorer ones, you would see a rather unsurprising pattern: Students from higher-resource households are far more likely to go to college than their less-advantaged counterparts. These differences are large. Among students graduating from high school in the late 1990s and early 2000s, 29% from the lowest family income quartile went to college, while 80% from the top quartile did so[1]—a 51 percentage point gap.

Before we design a policy response to address this inequality in outcomes, it is important to understand *why* it exists. One prominent explanation is the role of costs. College is expensive in the United States, with tuition, fees, and room and board averaging more than $19,500 per year for a public four-year school and $43,900 for a private four-year school for academic year 2015–16. Even for two year colleges, which are considerably less expensive, costs could be expected to exceed $11,400.[2] Even for two-year colleges, which are considerably less expensive, costs exceed $11,000 per year on average. If the high price of a college education drives some of the enrollment gaps by family income, providing financial aid for low-income students may be a useful policy. Indeed, the federal government distributed more than $161 billion in financial aid in academic year 2014–15, and the core argument for offering such aid is to support the ability of students to pay for college.

Given the large differences in enrollment patterns by family income and the high cost of college, it is natural to ask whether financial aid would increase college enrollment among lower income students. However, we need to be extremely careful about drawing such a conclusion from the negative correlation between family resources and college enrollment. For financial aid to increase college enrollment, it must be the case that a lack of financial resources among students at the time of the enrollment decision *causes* them not to enroll in college.

3DDock/Shutterstock

---

[1] These tabulations come from the NLSY97 as reported in Bailey and Dynarski (2011). See Appendix A for an overview of the NLSY97.

[2] College cost information comes from the College Board publication *2014 Trends in College Pricing*, and financial aid information comes from the publication *2015 Trends in Student Aid*.

To see the potential problem with the causal interpretation of the data in this setting, consider the other ways students from low-resource backgrounds may differ from more advantaged students. Students whose parents have more money tend to have more education. Such parents may understand how to navigate the college enrollment process better, which could lead to higher attendance. Kids whose parents have fewer resources when they are of college age tend to have had fewer resources throughout their childhood. This can translate into lower levels of academic achievement by the time the students reach high school. Family resources thus are correlated with academic preparation for college, which should affect enrollment decisions. Isn't it possible that the differences in college attendance rates across students from lower- versus higher-income households are due to these other differences rather than the ability to pay for a college education? The short answer is yes; this is entirely possible.

As this example demonstrates, we need to find ways to establish the difference between two variables being correlated and an outcome being causally determined or impacted by another variable. If the inability to pay college tuition is a main driver of the gap in college enrollment by family income, financial aid should be an effective policy tool to increase enrollment among low-income students. If these gaps largely reflect differences in parental education or early life educational investment, then financial aid will do little to address college enrollment gaps by family socioeconomic status. In effect, we would be deploying our resources in the wrong place because we misinterpreted the data. To justify a policy that provides financial support to low-income students for college enrollment, we need a way to disentangle the causal effect of the family's ability to finance tuition expenses on college enrollment from the other factors that may reduce collegiate investments for low-income students.

The empirical tools economists use to separate causation from correlation to inform education policy are the focus of this chapter. One of the core contributions of the social science of economics to the evaluation of education policies is the combination of *models* of behavior and *methods* for evaluating how education policies affect outcomes. These models and methods are not distinct: the models of behavior give us important predictions of the ways we expect individuals to react to specific policies and incentives.

This chapter discusses several of the tools economists and other social scientists use to determine whether a given policy causes education outcomes rather than simply being correlated with those outcomes.[3] Our objective is to be able to answer questions like these:

- Do smaller classes lead to improvements in student achievement?
- Does providing more money to schools improve students' outcomes?
- Does completing a college degree lead to higher earnings?
- Do charter schools lead to gains in student achievement over regular public schools?
- How does teacher quality affect student academic outcomes?
- Does incentive pay for teachers improve students' academic achievement?

First, we consider what we can learn from descriptive measures as well as their fundamental limitations. Next, we introduce experiments in education as the basic

---

[3] This chapter is meant to provide a broad overview of the ways in which researchers approach causal analysis in the economics of education. We point interested students who want more details to the excellent methods books *Mostly Harmless Econometrics* by Joshua Angrist and Jörn-Steffen Pischcke (2009) and *Methods Matter: Improving Causal Inference in Educational and Social Science Research* by Richard Murnane and John Willett (2011). The econometrics textbook *Introductory Econometrics: A Modern Approach* by Jeffrey Wooldridge (2009) also provides a clear and detailed introduction to the econometric techniques used in this book.

scientific framework for understanding how education policies affect outcomes. While experiments in economics are relatively rare, they form a useful baseline with which to analyze policies in a nonexperimental setting. Then, we turn to the question of how we can estimate the impact of policies without the benefit of full experiments using **econometrics**. The concepts of **selection bias** and **omitted variables bias** are introduced; they are the fundamental problems to overcome when doing causal analysis. Finally, we discuss three nonexperimental methods that are most commonly used by economists to overcome the biases associated with selection: difference-in-difference, instrumental variables, and regression discontinuity.

For policymakers to make good decisions about how to allocate resources, such as spending more (or less) money on particular policies, they must have a way to assess the causal effect of a given policy on outcomes of interest. Generating measurements and methods to assess these causal relationships is often quite difficult. A central focus of the rest of this book is on providing an understanding of the ways economists have approached and attempted to solve these problems. The methods we describe in this chapter will be referenced with regularity throughout the rest of the book.

econometrics The use of statistical techniques to measure relationships among variables in data.

selection bias The bias that occurs because individuals choose whether they are part of the treatment or control group based on characteristics or preferences related to an outcome. This can lead to the characteristics of those in the treatment group being systematically different from those in the control group.

omitted variables bias The bias that occurs when a variable is correlated with both the treatment and the outcome but is not included in the regression. This creates a bias in the estimate of the causal effect of the treatment, the sign of which depends on how the omitted variable is correlated with the treatment and with the outcome.

3.1 Descriptive Evidence and the Distinction Between Correlation and Causation

Researchers and policymakers have access to a wide array of data on the financing of education, the inputs to the education process, student achievement, and levels of educational attainment. Local, state, and federal governments collect a range of measures about schools, colleges, and students. Appendix A details many of the most widely used data sources in the economics of education.

One important use of these data is to *describe* outcomes. For example, we can record spending per student across districts in a state, the level of educational attainment among adults, or the distribution of test scores at a school. Typical descriptive measures include the mean, median, and percentiles of the distribution. The statistics provided in Chapters 1 and 2 are all examples of descriptive statistics. See the accompanying Toolbox for more details on descriptive statistics. Basic familiarity with descriptive statistics will help you read articles related to education policy and approach this work as a critical consumer. Descriptive measures are important for accounting purposes—they tell us what the outcome is—but they don't tell us what the outcome would be if we changed policies.

TOOLBOX: Descriptive Statistics

Suppose we observe an educational outcome such as test scores for sixth-grade students in a particular school district. The test score for each individual (i) in the district is t_i. Assume there are N students in the district. The first and most common descriptive measure is the mean or expected value—$E(t)$, which is the sum of all individual values divided by the number of observations:

$$\mu_t = E(t) = \sum_{i=1}^{N} \frac{t_i}{N}$$

Without any other information, the mean of the test score distribution is the best estimate of any individual's test score. We can compute the mean for subgroups of students, and we describe these measures as the conditional expectation. For example, we might be interested in the mean for girls or the mean at a particular elementary school and denote these conditional expectations $E[t \mid sex = girl]$ or $E[t \mid school = Lansing\ Elementary\ School]$.

Another measure of interest in describing the distribution of education data is the variance, or the spread of a distribution. A distribution with a large variance is going to take on a much wider range of values than a distribution with a smaller variance. The variance of a distribution, often denoted var(t) or σ^2, is measured as the expected value of the square of the deviation of a variable from its mean. It is denoted as:

$$\text{var}(t) = \sigma^2 = E[(t - \mu_t)^2] = \frac{\sum_i (t_i - \mu_t)^2}{N - 1}$$

Other measures, such as percentile ranks and the median, are indicators of the dispersion of a distribution. The median is the value at which half of the cases are above it and half of the cases are below it.

When we have two or more variables of interest—such as class size (S) and test scores (t) or educational attainment (Ed) and earnings (Y)—we will often want to describe the extent to which these variables move together or in different directions. The covariance between variables S and t is defined as:

$$\text{cov}(S, t) = \sigma_{S,t} = E[(t - \mu_t)(S - \mu_S)] = \frac{\sum_i (t_i - \mu_t)(S_i - \mu_S)}{N - 1}$$

Quick Hint: We divide by $N - 1$ in the variance and covariance formulas to adjust for degrees of freedom. The idea is that one must first use up one observation to calculate the mean before calculating the variance. There are $N - 1$ free observations once one calculates the mean. To calculate the covariance, one must first calculate the mean, which also uses up one observation. So there are only $N - 1$ free observations. See Wooldridge (2009) for a more detailed discussion of degrees of freedom adjustments.

Intuitively, the covariance will be positive in cases where observing t greater than the mean of t is accompanied by observing a value of S greater than the mean of S. If on average t is greater than the mean when S is less than the mean, there is a negative covariance between the two variables. When knowing that one variable is greater than (or less than) its mean on average provides no systematic information about the likelihood that another variable is greater than (or less than) its mean, and the associated covariance is zero.

Given that covariance measures are dependent on the units of observation (multiplying a variable by 100 will change the measure of the covariance), it is common to use the measure of correlation as a standardized description of the association between two variables. The **correlation** measure, which will always have values between -1 and 1, is defined as:

correlation The extent to which variables move together in the data.

$$\rho_{S,t} = \frac{\text{cov}(S, t)}{\sqrt{\text{var}(S)\,\text{var}(t)}} = \frac{\sigma_{S,t}}{\sigma_S \sigma_t}$$

Descriptively, we can measure how variables move together, the degree of correlation. For example, we can measure the association between finishing college and earnings. On average, college graduates have higher earnings than those who stop formal schooling at high school, so education and earnings are positively correlated.

Similarly, we would likely find that educational attainment and arrest rates are negatively correlated.

The most important point to take from the observation of the relationship between two variables such as education and earnings is that a correlation does not necessarily imply a **causal link**.[4] The observation of a positive link between education and earnings need not imply that increasing an individual's educational attainment would lead to an increase in earnings. It is often the case that we can describe the relationship between two variables (the correlation between X and Y) without demonstrating a causal relationship (the effect of changing X on outcome Y).

Knowing that two measures are correlated tells us little about the causal effect of changing one policy variable on an educational outcome. Suppose we are interested in the link between class size and student achievement. Looking across students, we may see that those in smaller classes have higher achievement. Such a descriptive result does not reveal how changing class size would affect achievement because we don't know *why* class size differs among students. It may be that students with higher (or lower) achievement are systematically assigned to smaller classes. Alternatively, it may be that schools with more resources across a number of dimensions, including teacher quality, also have relatively small classes, so it is not class size per se but some other third factor that is causing the higher achievement in schools with smaller classes.

For the purposes of education policy, we need to answer causal questions, such as how changing an individual's educational attainment would affect earnings or how reducing class size would affect a student's achievement. Suppose we want to know whether completing another year of high school is likely to make *any given student* earn more than if he were to drop out. Imagine a hypothetical situation in which we can "treat" an individual with more schooling or not. We want to know how the treatment will affect earnings. The earnings outcome is designated as Y, and we use the subscript T (the "treatment") for an additional year of schooling and C (the "control") for unchanged schooling. To answer this question for a single student, whom we will call Larry, we would like to know:

$Y_T(Larry)$ = Larry's wage if he finishes one more year of high school
$Y_C(Larry)$ = Larry's wage if he doesn't finish another year of high school

We want to measure the earnings gain from attending another year of high school which is in Larry's earnings in these two states:

$$\textbf{Treatment effect} = Y_T(Larry) - Y_C(Larry)$$

You may have noticed that we have a big problem in performing this calculation: there is only one Larry. He could not have concurrently finished another year of high school and not done so. Put another way, the problem is that we observe only one outcome for each person. We do not observe the **counterfactual**, or what would have

causal link between two variables; altering one variable leads directly to a change in the other variable. That is, a change in one variable results in a change in another.

treatment effect The causal effect of the treatment on a specific outcome.

counterfactual What would have happened to an individual in the absence of the treatment.

---

[4] When variables like education and earnings are positively correlated, it does not mean that all college graduates earn more than all high school graduates. Indeed, one can think of a number of examples of college dropouts who are very high earners—take, for example, Mark Zuckerberg, who started Facebook. A positive correlation means that *on average* two variables move together.

DEEP DIVE: Why Is It Important to Distinguish Correlation from Causation?

The distinction between causation and correlation is fundamental in the design of policy. To illustrate how correlations fail to inform policy, it is instructive to consider some examples that border on the absurd.

1. *Does weight gain reduce your intelligence?*

   A study done in France on 2,200 adults examines how changes in weight gain are associated with changes in performance on a cognitive ability test. They find that those who gain weight have reduced cognitive ability, which they interpret as a causal effect of weight gain on intelligence (Goswami, 2006). If true, this would seem to argue for policies that lead to weight loss among adults, because the costs of lowered intelligence are high. But we need to be very careful in assessing the claims of causality in this study. One way to think about this problem is to ask, 'Why do people gain weight?' It could be that an adverse life event makes them less motivated, which would also show up on a test score. A similar story holds for any adverse health shock. Alternatively, what if those who lose intelligence gain weight? While the correlations found in this research are valid, the causal claims likely are not.

2. *Does reading* 50 Shades of Grey *make you less healthy?*

   The novel *50 Shades of Grey* was a bestselling erotic romance novel. In a research study comparing outcomes among young women ages 18–24 who read the novel to those who did not, Bonomi et al. (2014) found evidence that those who read this book were more likely to binge drink, to be in abusive relationships, and to have more sexual partners. Is the conclusion that there would be benefits from banning this book? This depends on whether these outcomes are caused by reading *50 Shades of Grey*. Rather than being causal, it is highly likely that women who drink more, who have more sexual partners, and who are in abusive relationships are more likely to read this book, in which these behaviors all are prevalent.

3. *Does smoking pot lead to less domestic violence?*

   Researchers at the University of Buffalo found evidence that couples who smoke marijuana had fewer incidences of domestic violence (Smith et al., 2014). It could

be that smoking pot leads to less domestic violence, which might argue in favor of relaxing restrictions on this drug. An alternative and highly plausible explanation for these findings is that couples who smoke pot are less likely to engage in domestic violence in the first place. That is, selection into smoking pot drives this correlation. In such a case, legalizing marijuana would have little effect on domestic violence rates.

4. *Do big weddings lead to stable marriages?*

   The Relationship Development Study, conducted by psychology researchers at the University of Denver, tracks 418 initially single people between the ages of 18 and 40 over time. When these individuals got married, the researchers found that the marriages were more likely to last if the wedding had at least 150 people in attendance (Kaplan, 2014). Does this mean you should spend the money for a big wedding? You may want to do so for the fun of it, but you should be careful in using these findings to justify such an expense. It is probable that couples with large weddings have larger support networks, higher incomes, and stronger family bonds. These are more likely to be the mechanisms through which marriages remain more stable. Big weddings are a result of these mechanisms, so increasing the size of your wedding is not likely to lead to a better marriage.

5. *Does drinking coffee while pregnant lead to miscarriage?*

   Researchers at Kaiser Permanente examined the caffeine intake of 1,063 pregnant Kaiser patients in the San Francisco Bay Area (Wang, Odouli, & Li, 2008). They found that women who consumed over 200 mg of caffeine per day (about 2 cups of coffee) had twice the risk of miscarriage as those who consumed none. It is tempting to conclude from this study that one should not consume caffeine while pregnant. Although many women do make this choice, the findings of this study do not support such a policy. We must ask why some women consume more coffee than others while pregnant. It is highly likely that coffee consumption patterns are related to outside stress from family pressures or work. It thus is quite plausible that these stress factors drive the miscarriage result, not the amount of coffee one drinks.

happened in the absence of the additional educational attainment. In the absence of observing Larry in both education states, we would like to observe someone who is identical to Larry in every way *except* that he took a different schooling path. We thus want to use another similar individual to measure Larry's counterfactual earnings outcome.

Our challenge is to find a valid counterfactual. This is very difficult because we can't observe the same individual in different states of the world. One approach is to use random assignment to generate comparison groups that are similar on average. We also consider other ways in which the nature of policy design may generate similar groups that did and did not receive the education intervention. If we can measure average outcomes for groups that are identical in all respects except for receipt of an education intervention, we can capture an estimate of the causal effect of the treatment. This is our challenge.

3.2 Randomized Control Trials: The Experimental Ideal

randomized controlled trial (RCT) An experiment in which people are randomly assigned to the treatment and control groups. On average, this makes the two groups identical but for receiving the treatment.

Experiments, or **randomized control trials (RCTs)**, are often viewed as the gold standard for measuring causal effects. In a randomized control trial or experimental design, one group of individuals (or other units, like classrooms or schools) is assigned to a treatment status to receive some intervention, while others are assigned to control status and are not subject to the intervention. The idea in an experiment is to separate participants into a treatment group and a control group, using random assignment. The treatment might be receiving a new medication in the medical sciences or, in our context, participating in additional schooling. The key to the design is that individuals are randomly assigned to the treatment status. This ensures that, on average, outcomes would be identical in the two groups in the absence of the treatment.

Participants in the experiment are necessarily not perfectly identical, but because we have randomly assigned participants to treatment and control groups, there should be no differences, on average, in baseline characteristics between the two groups. Any differences between the outcomes of the treatment and control groups at the end of the experiment must be due to the treatment: The control group is an accurate measure of the counterfactual outcome for the treated group.

Let's think for a moment about what random assignment implies about treatment and control groups. We would expect those assigned to the treatment and control groups to have similar observable characteristics. If we started with 100 students and randomly assigned those students to be in the treatment group or control group, we would expect that the proportion female, average prior test scores, and average family income would be similar across treatment and control groups. We can observe whether this condition holds, and we would expect these measures to be more similar as we increased the total number of students in our study. Importantly, with random assignment we also expect treatment and control groups to be similar on average in dimensions that are difficult to measure, such as motivation or determination.

The measurement of the causal effect in the context of a randomized control experiment is straightforward: One need only compare outcomes for the individuals in the treatment group to the outcomes of individuals in the control group. If our outcome is a measure of student achievement, the causal effect of an RCT intervention like class size

Table 3.1 Measuring Treatment Effects in an Experimental Context

Group (randomly assigned)	Mean Outcome
Treatment	A
Control	B
Treatment effect	A − B

In an experimental setting, the treatment effect can be calculated as the difference in outcomes across those randomly assigned to the treatment versus those randomly assigned to the control group (A − B).

reduction is simply the difference in average test scores between the treatment group and the control group. Table 3.1 illustrates the simple comparison needed to measure a treatment effect with a random assignment experiment.

Randomized trials have long been used in medicine to test the effectiveness of new treatments and as a tool for discovery in the life sciences and the physical sciences. Historically, experiments have been far less common in education, though certainly not unheard of. Perhaps the most widely cited experiment in education is the 1962 Perry preschool project involving the random assignment of low-income children from Ypsilanti, Michigan, to a treatment that included intensive preschool and home visits. This study found generally positive long-term gains associated with early education intervention. Until recently, experiments like this in education have been few and far between. Indeed, in 2000 only one of the 84 projects that were part of the Department of Education's annual plan involved a randomized trial (Angrist, 2004), but the standards of evidence have changed dramatically in education research in recent years. One factor in this shift is the 2002 Education Sciences Reform Act, which emphasizes "scientifically based research" and explicitly identifies randomized control trials as the gold standard in research design.

Table 3.2 describes some of the most widely known experiments related to education policy. We will discuss the results of many of these experiments in later chapters in the context of particular policy questions. While some of these experiments have been conducted by economists, others have been designed by psychologists and social scientists from other disciplines. Education experiments include random assignment to various preschool settings, vouchers for elementary schooling, particular pedagogical tools such as computer-based instruction, and access to assistance with completion of financial aid forms and college application information.

The reason well-designed experiments are so persuasive is that they address the fundamental problem of selection. In a nonrandomized setting, agents are allowed to choose a treatment, such as whether to get another year of education or whether to pursue an intensive math curriculum. Economic theory tells us that individuals will choose the activity that will maximize their utility—that is, choose the activity that will make them the best off. As a result, those who take the treatment are likely to be systematically different from those who do not. So at the end of the day, differences associated with the program or intervention also would capture systematic differences in individual characteristics correlated with the outcome. When an estimation method produces a result that differs systematically from the causal effect of interest, we say that method is a **biased estimator**. *Selection bias* is a particular form of bias driven by that fact

biased estimator A method of estimating causal effects is biased if, on average, the resulting estimate differs from the true causal effect.

Table 3.2 Examples of Random Assignment Experiments in Education

Experiment	Basic Strategy
Project Star	Random assignment of students in Tennessee to small and large classes in grades K–3
Perry preschool	Random assignment of poor children to an intensive preschool program
Computer instruction: Fast ForWord	Evaluation of program designed to improve language and reading skills
H&R Block financial aid information	Random assignment of low-income students and parents to receive information about financial aid and assistance with financial aid forms
Private school tuition vouchers	Experiments in Milwaukee and New York City that provide vouchers to low-income youth to attend private schools
Expanding College Opportunities Project	Provided information about college application strategies, college quality, and application fee vouchers to a randomly selected set of low-income, high-achieving high school students

that individuals can choose whether they are in the treatment or not. Since economists tend to focus on how people make choices when resources are limited, selection bias is the most prevalent problem addressed by economists engaging in causal analysis. The beauty of random assignment in the RCT is that selection bias should be zero by design.

The ideal experimental design that forms the basis for most laboratory and pharmaceutical experiments not only employs random assignment of the treatment but is also *double blind*—neither the participants nor those running the experiment know which group is treated. It is very difficult in education to conduct experiments that use this ideal design because both the researchers and participants often know who is receiving the treatment. As a result, randomized field experiments in education are often more challenging to design and study than typical laboratory experiments.

We say a research design has **internal validity** if the estimated causal effect of the treatment is unbiased. Threats to internal validity can come from several sources:

internal validity The extent to which the estimated causal effect of the treatment is unbiased.

- Differential attrition between treatment and control groups
- Sampling error[5]
- Knowledge of the treatment (or control) status, which independently affects behavior

Typically, a treatment is an intervention that is desired by potential participants. For example, a class size reduction experiment involves a treatment—smaller classes—that is likely to be of value to children and parents. As a result, parents assigned to the control group may get angry and leave the school. In this setting, parents know whether their child is in a smaller class, which can lead to differential attrition. If the highest-achieving students in the control group (or, more generally, students with different

---

[5] As the number of cases assigned to treatment and control groups gets large, sampling variation should approach zero owing to the law of large numbers.

achievement levels) drop out of the sample, the estimate of the causal effect of the program will be biased. This occurs because the control group is now lower-achieving than the treated group: The higher-achieving control group students left the school. In social sciences, we cannot compel people to comply with their assigned treatment status or to stay in an experiment, which can cause many problems for estimating causal relationships.

Another problem is sampling error: If the experiment has few people in it, the treatment and control groups may differ for random reasons. That is, the groups differ by accident. Including a larger number of people in the experiment reduces this problem, although it also increases costs.

The inability to perform double-blind experiments in education policy also leads to the possibility that the treatment assignment itself could independently affect participants' behavior. One example of this problem is called the **Hawthorne effect**, which refers to the phenomenon that when people know they are in an experiment to demonstrate a particular effect, they are likely to behave in a way to make that effect occur. For example, teachers who know they are in a class size experiment may behave in accordance with the study's hypothesis: teachers of small classes will perform better than those with larger classes. This response is not due to the effects of class size per se but is due to the knowledge of being in the experiment.

A final concern with randomized controlled trials is that even when they lead to internally valid results, the estimated effects may lack **external validity**. External validity pertains to whether we can generalize the results to other settings. For example, results from a study in Iowa may not necessarily apply in California if students' and institutions' characteristics are vastly different. RCTs with very small samples also make the results unlikely to be externally valid, as the small group of people studied are unlikely to be representative of state or national populations.

External validity can be a particular concern with many education interventions because RCTs often are conducted among a group of participants who volunteer for the experiment. RCTs can tell us what the effect of an education treatment is among those who sign up for the experiment, but strong assumptions are needed to apply this estimate to those who do not sign up.[6] If we want to scale up an intervention to a broader population, it is critical to understand its effect on those who chose not to be a part of the experiment. External validity therefore is a critical issue to consider when using results from RCTs to design education policies.

Hawthorne effect What happens when people know they are part of an experiment and behave in a way that is more likely to make the hypothesis being tested seem true.

external validity The extent to which we can generalize results from an empirical study to other settings.

3.3 Nonexperimental Methods

Many important questions in education policy cannot be examined with randomized controlled trials. Substantial time lags to observe results combined with high costs are one deterrent to the randomized control approach. In addition, in a number of circumstances it may not be logistically or ethically feasible to employ a random assignment design. For example, assigning students at random to receive admission to selective universities might result in considerable objections to implementation. Even the proposed

---

[6] Heckman and Smith (1995) term this problem randomization bias to reflect the fact that there likely are differences between those who receive the treatment in the experiment and those who would select the treatment in the absence of the experiment.

experiment with Larry to assign him an extra year of education is unlikely to be logistically feasible because it is not possible to "force" completion of a year of school, not to mention morally acceptable. While experiments that are short-term and do not involve large time commitments are straightforward, very resource-intensive experiments are typically extremely expensive while also raising ethical questions when children are participants. As a result, economists have turned to nonexperimental methods that in some circumstances can also overcome selection biases. These methods use observed variation in outcomes that is plausibly unrelated to both observed and unobserved individual characteristics to estimate causation. In short, economists must mimic experiments by using naturally occurring variation.

To solve vexing questions like estimating the causal effect of education on earnings, we must build a rich methodological toolkit and think creatively about how to use the data at hand to statistically isolate causal effects when we cannot conduct an RCT. The main workhorse of nonexperimental economics is *multivariate regression*. This is the tool most used to estimate causal effects, but as we shall see, using multivariate regression is *not* sufficient for isolating causality. Multivariate regression is a tool, and like all tools, it must be used correctly to get the desired result. While we will leave many of the more advanced methodological tools to a course in econometrics, it is useful for every student to have a baseline understanding of regression analysis and statistical inference.

> Quick Hint: By *desired result*, we do not mean the specific result of the study. Rather, the desired result is the causal estimate that overcomes the problem of selection bias, regardless of whether this is the result any constituency would "like" to see.

Regression Analysis

If we want to know how another year of education affects earnings, we might start with a simple plot with observed education on the horizontal axis and observed earnings on the vertical axis. What would we expect? We would likely expect to find that individuals with higher levels of education had, on average, higher levels of earnings. We would not expect to see a perfect correlation, with all combinations of education and earnings on a single line, as there are many determinants of earnings beyond education. Figure 3.1 shows this type of positive relationship between observed educational attainment and earnings.

independent variable (explanatory variable) The variable in a regression used to describe the dependent variable or outcome of interest.

dependent variable In a regression, the variable we are seeking to explain with the independent or explanatory variables. It is the outcome of interest in a regression.

To fix terms, we call education (*Ed*) the **independent variable (explanatory variable)** and earnings (*Y*) the **dependent variable**, or outcome variable. With a positive relationship between education and earnings, knowing an individual's level of education is going to help predict that person's earnings. Assuming that the link between education and earnings is linear in the sense that each year of education predicts a constant increase in earnings, we could describe the data as:

$$Y_i = \alpha + \beta Ed_i + \varepsilon_i$$

where the subscript i designates individual observations; α is the intercept, or the amount a person with zero years of education could expect to earn; β is the slope; and ε represents other determinants of individual earnings. Regression analysis is a statistical technique to pick the α and β that best fit the data; it is common to designate estimates of these parameters as $\hat{\alpha}$ and $\hat{\beta}$. We can describe the relationship between education and earnings predicted by a regression as the line $Y = \hat{\alpha} + \hat{\beta}Ed$, as shown by the red line in Figure 3.1, where $\hat{\beta}$ is the slope of the line and $\hat{\alpha}$ is the *y-intercept*. This is an example of a *bivariate regression*, because there are only two variables, earnings (dependent variable) and *Ed* (independent variable).

> **Quick Hint:** In statistics, we distinguish between the true values of the parameter that we can never observe and our estimates of those parameters that we generate using data. The true, unobserved parameters are the population parameters, and one can think of regressions as trying to estimate these unknown population parameters.

Suppose that we had randomly assigned a large number of individuals to different levels of education. Our estimate of $\hat{\beta}$ would be equal to the experimental estimate, and comparing the earnings expected with $Ed = 1$ and $Ed = 0$, produces:

$$E[Y_i \mid Ed = 1] - E[Y_i \mid Ed = 0] = \hat{\alpha} + \hat{\beta} - \hat{\alpha} = \hat{\beta}$$

In this context, a regression estimate is just a particular way of presenting an experimental result.

> **Quick Hint:** $E[Y|X]$ is called a conditional expectation function. It shows the expected value (i.e., average) of Y for each value of X. In this setting, $E[Y|Ed]$ shows average earnings for each level of education. The parameter $\hat{\beta}$ therefore shows how average wages change when education changes by one year, which is the slope of the line shown in Figure 3.1.

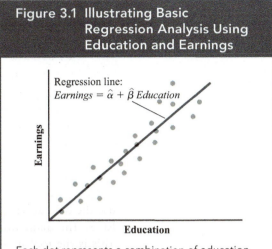

Figure 3.1 Illustrating Basic Regression Analysis Using Education and Earnings

Each dot represents a combination of education and earnings for a different individual. The regression line is the line that best fits these data: The slope of the regression line is the regression coefficient on education in the bivariate regression of earnings on education, $\hat{\beta}$.

Now, what if we can't run an experiment but are able to observe a large number of people with different levels of education? We still can compute an estimate of $\hat{\beta}$, but we should be very cautious about interpreting this measure of the association between education and earnings as the causal impact of education on earnings. The problem is that individuals who choose to get more education are likely to differ from those who choose lower levels in ways that are also related to earnings. The counterfactual earnings for the high-education group is unlikely to be the earnings that we observe for the low-education group. Suppose that individuals with higher underlying earning potential tend to choose higher levels of educational attainment. The bivariate correlation between earnings and education then will reflect this ability difference as well as the effect of education on earnings.

Figure 3.2 illustrates this problem, which is a canonical example of selection bias. We have plotted education attainment and earnings for high- and low-ability students. Students' ability is measured by SAT scores in this example, which we do for illustrative purposes. As the figure shows, it is true that those with more education earn more, but they also have higher SAT scores on average. If there is an independent return to this ability in the labor market, the bivariate regression will not allow us to separate the effect of SAT scores from the effect of education on earnings. As panel A of the figure shows, the differences in earnings by education capture both the causal effect of education and the differences generated by selection of higher-ability people into receiving more education.

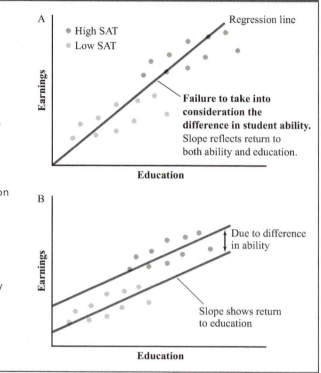

Figure 3.2 Ability Bias in Regression Analysis

Both panels show a plot of education attainment and earnings for high- and low-ability students, with students' ability measured by SAT scores. **A.** Differences in individual ability correlated with education. We do not control for ability, and as a result the estimated regression line reflects both the return to ability and the return to education. **B.** Including an ability measure in the regression. After we control for ability, the regression slopes become flatter, as they now reflect only the return to education.

Quick Hint: The SAT is a college entrance examination that is accepted by most schools in the United States. Alternatively (or additionally), many students take the ACT. The ACT is another widely used college entrance examination that is most popular in noncoastal states.

omitted variables In a regression, any variables that are correlated with both the treatment and the outcome that are not included in the estimation.

From an econometric standpoint, ability here is an **omitted variable**, which leads to an omitted variable bias. An omitted variable bias occurs when a variable is not included in the regression but is correlated *both* with the treatment and the outcome. The Toolbox has a more detailed derivation and discussion of omitted variables bias in regression models. Omitted variables bias and selection bias are basically the same thing: There is some reason why the treated group is systematically different from the control group. In essence, selection causes omitted variables bias. In our example of education and earnings, the omitted variable bias is caused by the selection of higher-achieving students into receiving more education.

TOOLBOX: Omitted Variables Bias

In this toolbox, we derive the formula for omitted variables bias and discuss how one can sign this bias when thinking about the influence of a potentially omitted variable in an empirical study. Let's begin by considering a general regression with two independent variables:

$$Y = \beta_0 + \beta_1 X_1 + \beta_2 X_2 + \varepsilon$$

where Y is the dependent variable, X_1 and X_2 are the independent variables, and ε is the error term. Assume that this model is the true (i.e., population) model; it correctly describes the relationship among the three variables. Consider what happens if we have a data set that does not include X_2. We thus estimate a bivariate regression of Y on X_1:

$$Y = \gamma_0 + \gamma_1 X_1 + \mu$$

Recall that the definition of bias is that our estimate must on average differ from the truth. This means that, on average, our estimate $\hat{\gamma}_1$ must equal β_1 if our estimate is to be unbiased. Under what conditions will this occur? The expected value of the bivariate linear regression estimator can be written as:

$$E(\hat{\gamma}_1) = \frac{\text{cov}(Y, X_1)}{\text{var}(X_1)}$$

where $\text{cov}(Y, X_1)$ is the covariance between Y and X_1 and $\text{var}(X_1)$ is the variance of X_1. If we substitute $\beta_0 + \beta_1 X_1 + \beta_2 X_2 + \varepsilon$ for Y in this expression, since by assumption this equality holds, we get:

$$E(\hat{\gamma}_1) = \frac{\text{cov}(\beta_0 + \beta_1 X_1 + \beta_2 X_2 + \varepsilon, X_1)}{\text{var}(X_1)}$$

$$= \frac{\text{cov}(\beta_0, X_1)}{\text{var}(X_1)} + \beta_1 \frac{\text{cov}(X_1, X_1)}{\text{var}(X_1)} + \beta_2 \frac{\text{cov}(X_1, X_2)}{\text{var}(X_1)} + \frac{\text{cov}(\varepsilon, X_1)}{\text{var}(X_1)}$$

In the expression on the second line, the first piece is zero, since β_0 is a constant and the covariance between any variable and a constant is zero. The second piece reduces to β_1, as $\text{cov}(X_1, X_1) = \text{var}(X_1)$ by definition. The final piece is also zero, since by assumption of the linear regression model, the error term is uncorrelated with each independent variable. We are left with the following expression for the expected value of $\hat{\beta}_1$:

$$E(\hat{\gamma}_1) = \beta_1 + \beta_2 \frac{\text{cov}(X_1, X_2)}{\text{var}(X_1)} \equiv \beta_1 + \beta_2 \delta$$

The bias in this formula is given by $\beta_2 \delta$. This bias has two parts. The first part is the coefficient from the true model on X_2. The sign of the bias therefore depends on how X_2 and Y are correlated. The second piece $\delta\beta$ is the regression coefficient from a bivariate regression of X_2 on X_1. We cannot actually estimate this regression, since our data do not include X_2, but the sign of this coefficient is driven by the correlation between X_2 and X_1. This is a very useful piece of information.

The sign of the bias when we cannot control for X_2 depends on the signs of β_2 and δ. When they have the same sign, the bias is positive, and when they have different signs, the bias is negative. Let's think through a couple of examples. First, imagine Y is yearly earnings, X_1 is education, and X_2 is ability. If we estimate a regression of earnings on education (omitting ability), what will be the sign of the omitted variables bias? The sign of β_2 is determined by the correlation between ability and earnings, which almost certainly is positive: All else equal (including educational attainment), higher-ability people earn more. The sign of δ is determined by the correlation between education and ability, which also is likely to be positive: Higher-ability people get more education—see Chapters 4 and 6. The omitted variables bias will be positive: Education will look more important than it is in determining earnings because we have not controlled for ability.

Consider the potential for bias if we estimated a bivariate regression of test scores at the school level on average class size in the school. Depending on the circumstances, the bias could go either direction. On one hand, suppose students in schools with higher-income parents are in schools with smaller class sizes. It is likely that parental income is positively correlated with test scores ($\beta_2 > 0$). Since parents with more income tend to sort into schools with higher resources, we would expect parental education to be negatively correlated with class sizes ($\delta < 0$). The omitted variables bias therefore is negative: Class sizes look as if they have a larger negative effect on test scores in the bivariate regression than they actually do because we have failed to account for the confounding influence of parental education.

On the other hand, resource distribution may be *compensatory*, such that more educational resources are given to more disadvantaged students. In such a circumstance, parental income would positively covary with class size ($\delta > 0$). While we expect the true effect of class size on achievement to be negative ($\beta_1 < 0$), the omission of parental resources in the compensatory case will bias the estimated effect upward or toward zero as ($\beta_2 > 0$, $\delta > 0$). This makes class sizes appear less linked to test scores than they actually are. To predict the sign of the omitted variable bias, we need to know something about why different students experience different class sizes.

The omitted variables bias formula gives us a framework for thinking about what belongs in a regression. If what we care about is estimating the causal effect of X_1 on Y, then we need to control for all variables that are correlated with *both* X_1 and Y. In the education–earnings regression, we need to control for all variables that are correlated with both education and earnings; a variable that is correlated with only one of these will not produce a bias. Similarly, for the test score–class size regression we need to control for all variables correlated both with class sizes and with test scores.

Since in both of these examples the set of variables that are correlated with the treatment and outcome is large and because many of them are hard to measure (e.g., motivation and preferences for education), it is rare that a study can credibly overcome problems associated with omitted variables bias simply by controlling for observable characteristics of students and/or schools. Rather, to avoid biases from omitted variables, we typically look for sources of variation in the treatment that will be uncorrelated with these characteristics.

What can we do to address selection bias? There are two main solutions, each of which can be implemented in several ways:

1. Include in the regression control variables that account for the ways in which the treatment and control groups are different.
2. Find a source of variation in the treatment variable that is unrelated to underlying differences between those who are treated and untreated. We need variation in the treatment that is generated by luck or randomness, not by individual preferences and abilities.

Every nonexperimental paper we will discuss in this book uses one of these two methods to establish causality.

The first approach can be thought of as attempting to address the selection problem by making comparisons among treated and untreated individuals who are similar in all observable dimensions that might also affect our outcome. For example, rather than comparing individuals with different levels of high school achievement, we might make our comparison among individuals with the same level of high school achievement. Among individuals with the same level of high school achievement, we may be able to assume that differences in educational attainment are plausibly just random, or unrelated to eventual outcomes. If this assumption is correct, then we can measure the effect of our education variable on our outcome of interest by controlling for the observed characteristics of students that make treatment and control students different.

Returning to the regression framework for our education and earnings example, we could control or condition on high school achievement (SAT scores). In essence, we would measure the causal effect as the difference in outcomes for groups with the same level of achievement:

$$E[Y_i \mid Ed = 1, SAT = High] - E[Y \mid Ed = 0, SAT = High] \text{ or}$$

$$E[Y_i \mid Ed = 1, SAT = Low] - E[Y \mid Ed = 0, SAT = Low].$$

We also could use a regression framework to specify this relationship. If the education treatment has the same effect on low-achieving and high-achieving students, we can specify the relationship as

$$Y_i = \alpha + \beta Ed_i + \delta Ability_i + \varepsilon_i$$

and estimate the parameters $\hat{\alpha}$, $\hat{\beta}$, and $\hat{\delta}$. This is an example of a *multivariate regression*, as there are multiple independent variables in the model. What we have done is to specify a different intercept in earnings for high-ability students relative to low-ability students, which leads to an unbiased estimate of $\hat{\beta}$ so long as there are no other omitted determinants of education that also affect earnings. This scenario is shown in panel B of Figure 3.2. The relationship between education and earnings now is much smaller, although it still is positive. Because we did not control for ability in panel A, our estimate of the effect of education on earnings was biased upward: Education looked more important for earnings than it actually is because we were conflating the effects of education and ability.

In panel B of Figure 3.2, the effect of education on earnings is the same for the high- and low-SAT groups. This need not be the case. In general, we do not require that treatment effects are the same for individuals with different characteristics. Variation in treatment effects with individual characteristics is called **heterogeneous treatment effects**. Multiple regression techniques can handle these cases simply by including interactions between the treatment and the relevant characteristic.

Multivariate regression analysis can be a very important and powerful tool. It allows analysts to control for observed differences among individuals and schools when trying to ascertain how education policies or interventions affect student outcomes. When using these methods, it is critical to recognize that the set of characteristics we can control for is limited by the data. We are able to condition only on the *observed* differences that may be related to the intervention and the outcome. To the extent that there are important *unobserved* differences among individuals or schools that are related to both the policy and the outcome, the regression estimates will be biased. Since many aspects of education decisions are based on factors we do not observe, like motivation and preferences, it is rare that simply controlling for observed differences across individuals or schools is sufficient to establish causality.

Because of these limitations, most economics research in education seeks to use the second method: Find a source of variation in the treatment that is uncorrelated

heterogeneous treatment effects When the treatment has different effects on those with different background characteristics. For example, financial aid policies likely have heterogeneous effects on low- versus high-income students.

with differences across individuals or institutions. This is much easier said than done. Economists have developed a number of tools and strategies to make comparisons in ways that focus on differences in education treatments generated only by processes that are, in effect, similar to random assignment. For this reason, we often refer to these approaches as **natural experiments (quasi-experimental designs)** to capture the point that we are trying to think as if we could run an experiment. Knowledge of policy changes and how rules for determining education requirements work are the main ways in which economists approximate experiments using observational data.

natural experiments (quasi-experimental designs) Use of variation in treatment exposure determined by nature or changes in policy that are outside the control of the researcher but nevertheless approximate random assignment.

Policy Changes and the Difference-in-Difference Approach

The Difference-in-Difference Approach When governments change policies related to funding for education or requirements for participation in schooling, they create opportunities to evaluate the effects of these policies. Particularly when policy changes are not fully anticipated by students, parents, and schools, the measurement of outcomes before and after the policy change can be a powerful way to assess a program's effects. Examples include the imposition of compulsory attendance laws, which make some students stay in school longer than they otherwise would, or the introduction of a financial aid program that reduces the price of college.

The easiest way to proceed in such situations is to look at how students' outcomes change after the policy is implemented relative to before. For example, if a state increases its compulsory schooling age from 16 to 17, we can see how the educational attainment of 16-year-olds changes over time in the state. We would expect the pool of 16-year-olds in a given state in two consecutive years to be very similar along observed dimensions (e.g., test scores, gender, race) as well as along unobserved dimensions (e.g., motivation, unmeasured skills), which satisfies one requirement for unbiased estimation of our policy effect. With this change in the compulsory attendance law observed at the state level, comparisons of attainment and earnings before and after the change provide a measure of the policy effect.

Looking at outcomes before and after may still leave some concerns about whether the before and after cohorts would have had the same outcomes in the absence of the policy change: Is the before cohort an accurate counterfactual for the after cohort? In many ways we should think so. However, what if there is an economic shock (such as a recession) in the same year as the law change? What if educational attainment among 16-year-olds is increasing over time for reasons having nothing to do with the law change? In both cases, we will be unable to disentangle these unobserved shocks and secular trends from the effect of the policy itself.

To account for these other factors, we can look at outcomes over this period for a group that is otherwise similar but that was not subjected to the policy change. As long as the national economic shock or the trends in 16-year-olds' enrollment are similar in the unaffected and affected areas, we can use changes among those in the unaffected areas to control for these confounding factors. In effect, we can "difference" or subtract the change among the untreated or control group from the change observed among the treated group. This is the idea of the *difference-in-difference* approach to causal estimation.

What we need to do is to establish a measure of the counterfactual change in the absence of the policy shift. Let's make the difference-in-difference approach concrete with an example. In 1993, the state of Georgia instituted a merit aid program, called HOPE, providing essentially free tuition at Georgia public postsecondary schools to Georgia high school graduates with a high school GPA above 3.5. Our policy question: Did this program increase college enrollment among Georgia high school graduates? We observe that enrollment rates in public universities among Georgia high school graduates increased, but a careful analyst would question whether this result was caused by the introduction of the scholarship program. College enrollment rates at these schools might have increased in the absence of this aid program, as this was a period of relatively robust economic growth in Georgia and other states in the southern United States.

We can address this concern by thinking about the enrollment change in states that border Georgia as providing our counterfactual change in enrollment. Figure 3.3 illustrates the observed trend in Georgia as well as the observed trend in bordering states. As you can see, there is a level difference between the two: Enrollment in the bordering states is higher in both periods. This alone is not a problem, as the difference-in-difference method controls for fixed differences across treatment and control individuals, states, or schools. The difference-in-difference estimate, then, is the posttreatment difference between Georgia and the bordering states minus the pretreatment difference between the two groups. This is shown in the figure as $(D - B) - (C - A)$. Alternatively, one can calculate this as the change in Georgia minus the change outside of Georgia, which is $(D - C) - (B - A)$.

To estimate the causal effect of the introduction of merit aid on college enrollment among high school graduates in Georgia, we calculate the change, or difference in enrollment in Georgia before and after the program introduction minus the difference in enrollment over this period in the bordering states. This *difference-in-difference estimator* takes this form:

$$\{E[Enr_{it} \mid i = GA, t = Post] - E[Enr_{it} \mid i = GA, t = Pre]\} -$$

$$\{E[Enr_{it} \mid i = Other, t = Post] - E[Enr_{it} \mid i = Other, t = Pre]\}.$$

Table 3.3 (panel A) presents this calculation schematically, which subtracts the pretreatment difference in enrollment across the treatment and control groups from the posttreatment difference.

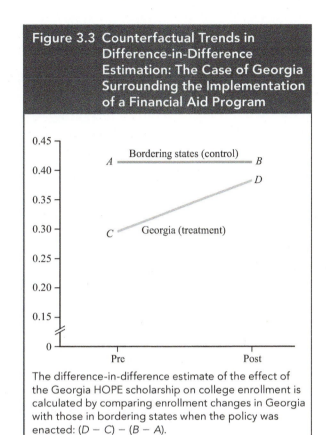

Figure 3.3 Counterfactual Trends in Difference-in-Difference Estimation: The Case of Georgia Surrounding the Implementation of a Financial Aid Program

The difference-in-difference estimate of the effect of the Georgia HOPE scholarship on college enrollment is calculated by comparing enrollment changes in Georgia with those in bordering states when the policy was enacted: $(D - C) - (B - A)$.

Table 3.3 The Difference-in-Difference Approach

	Treatment	Control	Difference
Pre	Enr_t^1	Enr_t^2	$Enr_t^1 - Enr_t^2$
Post	Enr_{t+1}^1	Enr_{t+1}^2	$Enr_{t+1}^1 - Enr_{t+1}^2$
Difference	$Enr_{t+1}^1 - Enr_t^1$	$Enr_{t+1}^2 - Enr_t^2$	$(Enr_{t+1}^1 - Enr_t^1) - (Enr_{t+1}^2 - Enr_t^2)$

A.

In panel B we show these calculations from the analysis in Dynarski (2000) for the case of the introduction of the Georgia HOPE program:

	Before 1993	1993 and after	Difference
Georgia	0.300	0.378	0.078
Rest of southern states	0.415	0.414	−0.001
Difference	0.115	0.036	**0.079**

B.

Data from: Dynarski (2000).

College enrollment grows by 7.8 percentage points in Georgia, while the change over this interval in the comparison states is slightly negative. The result is an estimated increase in college enrollment attributable to the HOPE program (i.e., a difference-in-difference estimate) of about 7.9 percentage points.

Difference-in-difference estimators have significant appeal for education analysts and have been used widely in a number of research settings. The validity of these estimates rests on the assumption that the policy change of interest is the only reason why outcomes among the treated group change relative to outcomes among the control group.

Difference-in-Difference in Regression Form   While difference-in-difference models can be represented simply in tabular form, as shown in Table 3.3, the most common way to estimate a difference-in-difference model is using regression analysis. Let's say we have data on college enrollment for each year and state in the South from 1990–1998. For the Georgia merit aid analysis, we can represent the model as follows:

$$Enroll_{it} = \alpha + \gamma Georgia_{it} + \vartheta Post_t + \delta Georgia_{it} \times Post_t + \varepsilon_{it}$$

where i indexes the state and t indexes the year.[7]

dummy variable A binary variable that takes on a value of 1 if a condition is met and zero if not. For example, the variable *Georgia* takes on a value of 1 if the observation is for Georgia and a value of zero if the observation is for any other state.

The variable *Georgia* is an indicator, or **dummy variable**, that is equal to 1 if the state is Georgia and is equal to zero otherwise. It controls for any fixed, unchanging differences between Georgia and the control states. The *Post* variable is a dummy equal to 1 after the implementation of the merit aid program (in 1993) and equal to zero before. It controls for any systematic changes occurring across all states after 1993 that have nothing to do with the Georgia program (like an economic shock). *Post* does not vary across states: It refers to whether the year is 1993 (the first year of the Georgia program)

[7] Examples of research on the George HOPE program that use a version of this method are Dynarski (2000) and Cornwell, Mustard, and Sridhar (2006).

or later. The interaction of *Georgia* and *Post* gives the difference-in-difference estimate, which is δ in this model. It shows how enrollment changes in Georgia relative to other southern states when the program is implemented. In its current form, δ will be *identical* to the estimate in panel B of Table 3.3. It is easy to adapt this model to control for time-varying observable characteristics (such as student income and racial composition) of each state as well as in the regression. This will cause the estimate of δ to diverge from the estimate in Table 3.3.

Fixed Effects It is common that we observe individuals, schools, or states at multiple points in time in a given dataset. Such datasets are examples of *panel data*, which are defined by multiple observations of the same unit over time. With panel data, we can account for fixed differences between individuals, states or other units of observation that relate to outcomes. Florida and Virginia differ in a number of dimensions that are unlikely to change much over time, like climate and demographics; Mike and Sarah differ in lots of ways, such as height, hometown, and favorite TV shows. But, we need not observe or quantify all of these fixed differences between states or people to control for these factors in a regression context. Instead, we can simply include a dummy variable or a *fixed effect* for each unit in our regression. This approach allows each unit to have its own intercept, which means that it accounts for all characteristics of the unit, both observed and unobserved, that are unchanging over time.

> **Quick Hint:** When we have a panel data set with many units (such as people or schools), it is possible that there will be thousands of fixed effects. A nice statistical result is that instead of controlling for lots of unit fixed effects, one can instead control for fixed differences across units of observation by subtracting out the unit-specific mean of each variable for every observation. De-meaning the data in this way can reduce computational complexity significantly.

A model that includes fixed effects is called a **fixed effects estimator.** It provides a more general way to estimate the difference-in-difference effect of the Georgia merit aid scholarship on enrollment than the approach discussed previously. In this case, the unit of analysis is the state, and there are multiple observations of each state over time. By controlling for a set of state and year fixed effects, which entails including in the model a dummy variable for each state and each year, we can account for fixed differences over the period of our sample across each state and for fixed differences across states in each year. The variation that remains to estimate the difference-in-difference coefficient is within-state over time. This model can be written in the following form:

$$Enroll_{it} = \alpha + \beta Georgia_{it} \times Post_t + \gamma_i + \vartheta_t + \varepsilon_{it}$$

In this model, δ still is the difference-in-difference estimate, while now we have a set of state fixed effects (γ_i) and a set of year fixed effects (ϑ_t). This is a more general model than the one we presented previously, because now we control for fixed differences across each state, not just across Georgia and the rest of the South. We also control for fixed characteristics of each year, not just the way in which the post period differs on average from the pre period.

While we motivated fixed effects analyses using state year data, the use of fixed effects to estimate difference-in-difference models is pervasive. One example is the use of individual student fixed effects to estimate the effect of charter schools on educational achievement (see Chapter 10). In these models, the student fixed effects control

fixed effects estimator Fixed effects control for fixed differences across units of observation and across different units of time with a series of indicator variables for each unit of analysis and each unit of time. For example, a fixed effects estimator with observations of students in each year would include an indicator variable for each student and an indicator variable for each year.

for average fixed differences across individual students. As a result, they tell us how achievement *changes* for students who enter a charter school relative to students who remain in their traditional public school. The idea is that the students who do not change schools tell us about the counterfactual change in outcomes among students who do change schools.

Instrumental Variables

Sometimes, life events are shaped by random events: whether or not young men were drafted to serve in the Vietnam war was directly related to lottery numbers. The enrollment of a student in a charter school that is oversubscribed also depends on the outcome of a random lottery. These lotteries produce **instruments** or **instrumental variables** that can be used to disentangle the causal effects of activities like military service or charter school enrollment on outcomes like long-term earnings or academic achievement. Because winning or losing the lottery is random, comparing outcomes of winners versus losers essentially mimics a randomized controlled trial.

In a seminal paper on the effect of education on earnings, Angrist and Krueger (1991) use quarter of birth as an instrument for educational attainment. We discuss this paper at length in Chapter 6, but the idea is that states have school starting ages that historically have mandated that students must be 6 in January of the year in which they enter school. This is combined with compulsory schooling laws that mandate a student must be enrolled until he or she is a certain age. As a result, a student born on January 1 will start school a year later than a student who is born the day before, on December 31. The January 1 child will therefore be a year behind in school when he reaches the compulsory schooling age. Angrist and Krueger show that, indeed, those born in the first two quarters of the year get less education than those born later in the year.

> **Quick Hint:** Historically in the United States, schools had January 1 cutoff dates for ages of entry. In the older cohorts of the Angrist and Krueger study, this cutoff was common across states. Since that time, school age cutoff dates have changed considerably and now vary across states.

Quarter of birth acts as an instrument for education because it isolates the variation in educational attainment that is as good as random: The variation in education because of quarter of birth is assumed to be unrelated to underlying characteristics of those who obtain more versus less education. If quarter of birth is essentially randomly assigned, we can compare differences in earnings across people whose education levels differ only because they have different quarters of birth. This will isolate the causal effect of education on earnings. In essence, an instrument pulls out the part of the variation that is akin to a randomized controlled trial.

Instrumental variables (or IV) estimation in this setting works by isolating the variation in education *that is only due to when in the year you were born* to estimate the effect of schooling on earnings. This works under two assumptions:

1. The instrument must be correlated with treatment: Quarter of birth must actually affect educational attainment.
2. The *only* reason the instrument and the outcome are correlated is because the instrument affects the treatment. This means that the only reason quarter of birth is related to earnings is because it affects educational attainment.

instrument (instrumental variable) A variable that isolates variation in the treatment that is uncorrelated with underlying characteristics of those who are treated or untreated.

The nice aspect of IV is that the first assumption can be tested with the data very easily. The drawback is that the second assumption cannot be tested. This is the major source of controversy surrounding the use of instruments: It often is hard to know whether there are other reasons that the instrument is correlated with the outcome of interest.

In the education–earnings example, the question is whether there is *any* other mechanism through which quarter of birth can influence earnings. What if people born earlier in the year are in families with lower income or have parents with less education? What if there is an effect of being older in one's class (as the early-quarter children are) on educational attainment? These are all threats to this type of design. When you see an instrumental variables strategy, it is useful to go through ways it would fail to help determine whether the assumptions underlying the instrument are plausible or not.

Many government policy changes can be used as instruments. As long as the policy change is random with respect to unobserved changes in a school or state, these policy changes can induce quasi-random variation that can be used to estimate causal effects. When we see a paper that uses quasi-experimental variation, we should subject it to the same type of scrutiny as an instrumental variables model. We will get much practice at this throughout the book as we discuss empirical results from economics research.

Regression Discontinuity: Examining Sharp Breaks

Policies that generate sharp breaks in eligibility for a treatment get a lot of use and attention among education researchers. Consider some policy rules that may generate sharp breaks, or discontinuities, in eligibility for education programs and resources:

- Rules that mandate maximum class size at a fixed cutoff, say 30 students
- Regulations stipulating the minimum age of school entry at a specific date, such as age 5 by September 1
- Policies that designate eligibility for financial aid at a particular achievement score cutoff or income threshold
- University admission policies that admit all students with an SAT score above a certain mark

If we are willing to assume that students or schools just above and below the cutoff in these cases are nearly identical in observed and unobserved characteristics, then the comparison of student or school outcomes just above and below the threshold provides a good measure of the causal impact of the education policy on such outcomes. This sharp break can be thought of as an instrumental variable: It generates variation in the treatment that is unrelated to underlying characteristics of students or schools.

Suppose there is a $5,000 college scholarship with a strict test score threshold for qualification. Because there is some random noise in test scores, we would not expect to see a difference in collegiate outcomes (such as enrollment or completion) across those right above versus right below the threshold absent the scholarship rule. The cutoff (or discontinuity) for scholarship eligibility provides an opportunity to estimate the causal effect of the scholarship on collegiate attainment. If no one below the cutoff received the scholarship and everyone above the cutoff received the scholarship, the causal effect of the scholarship on graduation can be estimated by comparing graduation rates right above the cutoff to those right below the cutoff. The main assumption with this approach is that students are unable to manipulate their test performance to place themselves over the cutoff. That is, those just above and just below the treatment threshold are essentially the same on average.

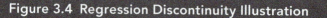

Figure 3.4 Regression Discontinuity Illustration

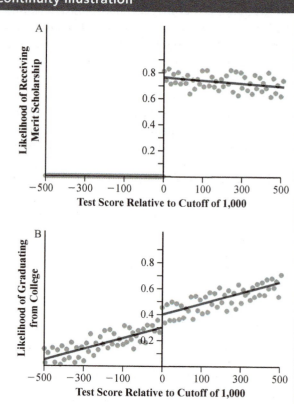

A. The effect of the merit aid eligibility rule on receipt of scholarships. There is a discontinuity in the likelihood of receiving a merit scholarship at a test score of 1,000. This is a fuzzy regression discontinuity because the likelihood of receiving the scholarship increases by less than 1 at the cutoff; some students who are eligible do not attend college in-state. The discontinuity increases the likelihood that one receives a merit scholarship by 75 percentage points. **B.** The effect of the merit aid eligibility rule on college graduation. The likelihood of college graduation jumps by 10 percentage points at the cutoff. If we assume that this increase is completely driven by the 75% of people who receive the scholarship, the effect of receiving a scholarship on college completion is 13.3 percentage points (0.1/0.75).

running variable (forcing variable) The variable that describes how close an individual is to a treatment threshold in a regression discontinuity design.

fuzzy regression discontinuity design A regression discontinuity design in which the likelihood of treatment changes by less than 1 at the threshold.

Often, there is incomplete take-up or there are other eligibility criteria that determine treatment. The top panel of Figure 3.4 shows such a scenario. Test scores are shown relative to the test score cutoff on the x-axis; they are referred to in this scenario as the **running variable (forcing variable)**. The y-axis shows whether an individual received the scholarship: Some below the cutoff receive the scholarship and some above do not accept it. Nevertheless, there is a clear discontinuity around the cutoff of 75 percentage points. This is an example of a **fuzzy regression discontinuity design**, which occurs when the likelihood of treatment changes by less than 100 percentage points at the threshold.

In the bottom panel of Figure 3.4, there is a corresponding jump in the likelihood of college completion at the cutoff of 10 percentage points. If this increase is determined by the increase in scholarship receipt, the effect of receiving a scholarship on college completion is 13.3 percentage points (0.1/0.75). The discontinuity in the assignment rule thus acts as an instrument for scholarship receipt: The instrumental variable estimate of the effect of scholarship receipt on graduation is 13.3 percentage points.[8]

The main assumption underlying this method is that the students just above and just below the break are very similar. One way to think about this condition is that there must be some randomness in test outcomes, such that one cannot determine on which side of the discontinuity one locates. As long as this randomness exists in an

---

[8] For a more detailed discussion of the properties of regression discontinuity estimators and their link to instrumental variables methods, see Hahn, Todd, and Van der Klaauw (2001).

area local to the cutoff, then those just above and below the cutoff will be the same on average (since they are allocated by the random test outcomes). Running variables that have randomness associated with them, like test scores, are often used in these settings. Forcing variables without this property, like income, can cause more problems, as people typically can bunch right above the cutoff. Thus, either it must be difficult to adjust around a known cutoff (the case of birthdays or test scores) or the cutoff must be unknown to individuals. As long as one cannot choose what side of the discontinuity to be on, we can interpret the magnitude of the change around this break as a causal estimate of the effect of financial aid on college completion.

Regression discontinuity estimates of program effects are specific to the region of the cutoff—what economists refer to as local treatment effects. Regression discontinuity designs can tell us about causal treatment effects for those who are right next to the cutoff. It cannot tell us how those far away from the cutoff are affected. This is an important caveat to these studies, as often we use test scores to determine eligibility. We cannot learn how very high- or very low-achieving students are affected by the treatment using regression discontinuity methods; we only know the impact among those whose test scores place them right near a cutoff. This is a key limitation of regression discontinuity studies that affects the external validity of the findings.

3.4 Conclusion

How we establish a causal relationship between a treatment and an outcome is a core question in the economics of education. Economic theory is critically important in generating hypotheses about how policy innovations ranging from class size reduction to changing the age of compulsory school attendance to increasing financial aid affect outcomes. To inform policy, it is imperative to test the predictions of theory and evaluate education policies. Evaluating education policies is challenging because we need to move beyond correlational measures to capture the causal impact of education on student and school outcomes. In the next chapters, we present both theoretical models of how we expect education policies to affect these outcomes and empirical evidence on the causal effects of education-related policies.

Highlights

- To study the effectiveness of an education policy, it is essential to estimate a **causal link**, or the **treatment effect** of the policy, not just a **correlation** among variables. There also can be **heterogeneous treatment effects**, whereby the treatment effect differs across different types of individuals. We use the tools of **econometrics** to help us determine whether (and for whom) a given policy is causing a specific outcome or whether it is simply correlated with that outcome.

- The idea of the **counterfactual** is essential to assessing causation. The counterfactual is the outcome that would have occurred absent the treatment. Because we see people in only one state of the world (treated or untreated) at any given time, the counterfactual is never observed. We must find other groups—control groups—that allow us to measure the counterfactual.

- Obtaining an accurate measure of the counterfactual is complicated by **selection**: People can choose whether to receive the treatment, so those who select into the treatment will be systematically different from those who do not. Comparisons among the treated and untreated groups will reflect both the difference in their characteristics and the effect of the treatment.

- Empirical results have **internal validity** if the estimated causal effect is unbiased, that is, if we are not using a **biased estimator**. They have **external validity** if the results can be generalized to other individuals or settings.

- **Randomized controlled trials (RCTs)** are the most straightforward way to estimate the counterfactual in a manner that overcomes selection bias. Because people are randomly assigned to receive the treatment or not, the treatment and control groups are, on average, identical. RCTs are the gold standard for policy analysis, as the randomization overcomes any selection bias and the treatment effect is easily calculated by comparing differences in mean outcomes across the treated and untreated groups.

- Experiments in education are difficult to conduct. Such experiments face several obstacles, including **Hawthorne effects**, necessary time lags to observe outcomes of interest, high costs, the inability to compel people to comply with their assignment, and ethical boundaries. As a result, we need to develop nonexperimental methods that allow us to overcome *selection bias*.

- Economists studying education often rely upon quasi-experimental methods, which mimic experiments by using naturally occurring variation in treatments.

- Multivariate regression, which entails one **dependent variable** and multiple **independent (explanatory) variables**, is a powerful tool that economists can use to overcome selection bias in many circumstances. We can include control variables in a regression that account for differences between the treatment and control group, but we are limited by the variables in the data. If there are **omitted variables** in the regression model that are correlated both with the treatment and with the outcome, it will create **omitted variables bias** in the estimates. A **natural experiment (quasi-experiment)** that generates variation in the treatment unrelated to differences between the treated and untreated groups also can be used to address selection bias. All nonexperimental papers discussed in this text use one of these methods to estimate causal effects.

- When there are changes in education policies or laws, one often can overcome **selection bias** by comparing changes in outcomes among the treated group to changes among the control (or unaffected) group. This difference-in-difference method often is implemented using a **fixed effects estimator** that entails controlling for a series of **dummy variables** that account for fixed differences across groups.

- **Instrumental variables (IV)** can be used to isolate variation in the treatment assignment that is uncorrelated with the underlying characteristics of those who are at risk of treatment. The main assumptions underlying instrumental variables are that the **instrument** is strongly correlated with the treatment and that the *only* reason the instrument is related to the outcome is because of its relationship with the treatment. While a powerful tool, the second assumption cannot be tested, which leads to much controversy and discussion related to instrumental variables studies.

- Regression discontinuity methods also are widely employed in economics. This method is used when treatment status changes abruptly (i.e., discontinuously) based on some characteristic of an individual or school. A **fuzzy regression discontinuity design** is one in which the likelihood of treatment changes by less than 1 at the cutoff. Rules that determine college admissions or eligibility for a gifted and talented program based on test score cutoffs, for example, allow for a regression discontinuity analysis. This method works as long as people cannot choose which side of the discontinuity to be on, which usually requires some randomness in the **running variable (forcing variable)** that assigns treatment. In such cases, we can estimate the causal effect of a program by comparing people just above with those just below the cutoff.

Problems

1. What is selection? Why does self-selection make it difficult to measure the effect of education policies?
2. Consider the following scenarios and explain why the correlation described need not imply that one factor causes the other. Be explicit about the other factors that might be at play.
   a. Students in charter schools have higher test scores than their counterparts in nearby public schools.
   b. A negative correlation between maternal smoking and their children's birth weight.
   c. On average, students with relatively large student loans are less likely to default.
   d. Within a school, students in smaller classes have lower end of year test scores.
   e. Children in families that spend more time on educational activities do not have better educational outcomes than children in families who spend less time on educational activities.
3. Explain how randomized controlled trials overcome selection bias.

4. What is the difference between internal validity and external validity? Does the fact that a study is internally valid mean it is externally valid?

5. What problems arise in Randomized Control Trials (RCTs) in which treatment assignment is not double-blind? How might these problems bias the estimates of an experiment that randomly assigns some schools in a city to receive more financial resources?

6. Some financial aid such as the Pell grant is assigned on the basis of financial need. Suppose you examine the relationship between college completion and financial aid receipt by running a regression of college completion on aid receipt. Why might it be incorrect to interpret the coefficient on financial aid eligibility as the causal effect of aid on college completion?

7. In 2001, the federal government enacted a law that forbade any student with a drug offense from receiving financial aid. Lovenheim and Owens (2014) study the effect of this law on college enrollment behavior by examining how enrollment among those with convictions changes relative to those without convictions in a difference-in-difference analysis. A difference-in-difference analysis takes two successive differences. The first difference is the difference between the pre and post treatment values of a group that underwent treatment and the difference between the pre and post treatment values of area group that did not undergo treatment. Once these two values are calculated, the difference between these differences is computed.

   a. Using the provided information, calculate the difference-in-difference estimate.

	No Conviction	Conviction
Pre-change	0.623	0.358
Post-change	0.652	0.269

   b. Does the fact that college enrollment was rising throughout the United States for all students over the period cause a problem for their study?

   c. Write the regression formula that will allow you to estimate the difference-in-difference treatment effect.

   d. How might selection bias the results?

8. Regression discontinuity can be a useful strategy for estimating the causal effect of a policy with a sharp break in eligibility for treatment. What are the two main considerations of this approach?

9. Gifted and talented programs provide extra services for academically high-performing students. Eligibility for these programs is typically based on having a test score above a threshold. A study by Bui, Craig, and Imberman (2014) estimate the effect on achievement of participating in a gifted and talented program using a regression discontinuity design.

   a. Explain in words how the regression discontinuity method leads to a valid estimate of the causal effect of being in a gifted and talented program on educational outcomes.

   b. Can this method tell us how very high-achieving students are affected by the gifted and talented program?

   c. Would it be a problem for this approach if not all students who were eligible for the program decided to enroll in it?

3DDock/Shutterstock

The Human Capital Model

The Education Investment Decisions of Morgan and Stanley

Morgan and Stanley are analysts at one of the top financial firms in the world. After graduating from a prestigious college several years ago with degrees in economics and mathematics, they each weighed several lucrative job offers and settled on joining their current firm. Now that they have worked at this firm for a couple of years, each is considering his next career move. Stanley loves finance and wants to spend his career working in the financial sector, while Morgan is more academically inclined and believes he would be happiest doing research and teaching finance at the collegiate level.

Both Morgan and Stanley realize that they may benefit from obtaining further education by attending graduate school; however, leaving their job to enroll in graduate school has costs. For Stanley, who is considering MBA programs, the costs of enrollment are considerable. Not only does he have to pay a sizable amount of tuition, but he is working at a high-salaried position and would have to give up this salary to enroll in graduate school. Morgan is considering a PhD program in finance, which is considerably less expensive in terms of tuition, as most PhD students pay their tuition through teaching and research positions. However, PhD programs are long and intensive, and they entail a large amount of risk because success is not assured.

Being good financial analysts, Morgan and Stanley realize that the decision they face is a classic investment problem, similar in many ways to a firm's decision to invest in physical capital. They are both considering giving up some earnings today to produce higher earnings (or happiness) in the future. This is an investment decision with respect to **human capital**, the attributes of an individual worker that have value in the labor market. How do Morgan and Stanley make these human capital investment decisions? Our intuition likely tells us that each of them should weigh the costs and benefits and make the investment choice that has the highest expected return. Stanley faces very high costs in terms of tuition and foregone wages while enrolled. He would need a large rise in future wages to make such an investment worthwhile. Morgan faces high costs of a different form: Because it will take him longer to earn a degree, he is forgoing more years of income while he is enrolled in graduate school. Additionally, Morgan enjoys research and working with students. Since he needs a PhD to become a professor, these nonwage benefits to him of obtaining a PhD may help offset some of the costs of investing in this degree.

The investment decisions being made by Morgan and Stanley are examples of the **human capital model** of education investment. The human capital model explains the decision to invest in human capital (i.e., skills) that is rewarded with higher future earnings. This is the core model that guides how economists think about the decision to invest in obtaining a given level of education. We can view every potential student who is deciding how much education to obtain and when to obtain it as going through cost–benefit calculations similar to those of Morgan and Stanley. The human capital model is general enough to provide a framework for thinking about virtually all educational investment decisions. It is the foundation of how economists think about the forces that drive individual investment decisions and how those decisions might respond to government policy changes related to education as well as by changes in the labor market.

In this chapter, we develop a human capital model that will help us to analyze formally how individuals make decisions to invest in education. We will return to this model throughout the book, as it allows us to predict how decisions to pursue education would change in response to adjustments in prices, such as college tuition, or individual circumstances, such as family resources. The model also will help us to generate predictions about how changes in the structure of wages, in particular the growing demand for skilled labor, will affect individuals' decisions to invest in more education.

human capital The skills, knowledge, and attributes of a worker that have value in the labor market.

human capital model This model, pioneered by Gary Becker, explains the decision to invest in human capital (such as education) that is rewarded with higher future earnings.

4.1 What Is Human Capital?

Human capital is the term economists use to describe the attributes and skills an individual possesses that have productive value in the labor market. This terminology does not refer to humans *as* capital. Rather, it is a way to conceptualize the fact that each individual has a set of skills and attributes that cannot be separated from them and that have value in the labor market.

Often, we refer to human capital synonymously with education, but the two are conceptually distinct. Human capital is much broader than just formal education. Gary Becker, one of the economists who first formalized the idea of human capital in the 1960s,[1] writes: "Human capital refers to the knowledge, information, ideas, skills and health of individuals. This is the 'age of human capital' in the sense that human capital is by far the most important form of capital in modern economies" (2002, p. 3).

Human capital is essential to our understanding of how various economies have developed over time, since physical capital and the stock of land are insufficient to explain the economic growth of nations. In particular for the United States, the GDP growth experienced in the twentieth century was much larger than would be predicted by the stock of land and growth in physical capital. A main reason the U.S. economy grew so dramatically over this period is that the twentieth century witnessed an historic rise in the education level and skills of the U.S. workforce. The quotation by Gary Becker reflects the view that human capital today is more important for economic growth than physical capital, which is consistent with the evidence on the high and growing demand for skill in the labor market.

Becker also highlights the fact that human capital is much more than education. Any personal attribute that increases your productivity is part of your human capital. Human capital comes from several sources, such as the health care system, family

---

[1] See Becker (1962, 1964) for original work on this subject.

environment, and genetic makeup. In fact, some of those with the highest levels of human capital—professional athletes—do not have much formal schooling at all. Lebron James, a forward for the Cleveland Cavaliers and multiple NBA champion as well as league MVP, has only a high school diploma. However, he has an immense amount of human capital, since his athletic skills are highly rewarded by the labor market. These skills cannot be separated from him: The only way Lebron James can realize a return on his human capital is to use his skills himself in the labor market.

For those of us who may not have the talent to be a professional athlete, formal schooling is a core pathway through which we can invest in increasing our human capital. We therefore focus on the formation of human capital through schooling for the remainder of this book. Before we proceed to a formal model of human capital investment, it is helpful to highlight the similarities and differences between investments in human and physical capital. This comparison helps in understanding how much of our intuition about investment in physical capital that we learned in other economics courses can be applied to the human capital context.

Writing in 1776, Adam Smith drew the direct parallel between investments in physical capital and investments in education, which yield skills that enhance productivity in the workplace:

> When any expensive machine is erected, the extraordinary work to be performed by it before it is worn out, it must be expected, will replace the capital laid out upon it, with at least the ordinary profits. A man educated at the expense of much labour and time to any of those employments which require extraordinary dexterity and skill, may be compared to one of those expensive machines. The work which he learns to perform, it must be expected, over and above the usual wages of common labour, will replace to him the whole expense of his education, with at least the ordinary profits of an equally valuable capital. It must do this, too, in a reasonable time, regard being had to the very uncertain duration of human life, in the same manner as to the more certain duration of the machine. The difference between the wages of skilled labour and those of common labour is founded upon this principle. (Smith, 1776, Book 1, Chapter 10)

market rate of return The financial return an individual can expect from investing money in typical financial vehicles, like stocks or bonds.

collateralized loan A loan in which there is a physical asset (such as a house or car) that the lender can seize if the loan is not paid back. The existence of a physical asset significantly reduces the financial risk to the lender, as the asset can be sold to recoup at least some of the lender's money if the borrower defaults.

The point is that if people are to acquire skills through a costly learning process, they must find rewards in the labor market sufficient to repay the costs of their education. Smith's analogy to physical capital is significant because it provides a benchmark: Investments in physical capital and skills produced through education should produce ordinary profits. These are rewards over and above the **market rate of return**, the financial return an individual can expect from investing money in typical financial vehicles like stocks or bonds.

Despite these similarities, there are two main differences between physical and human capital that have profound implications for education policy:

1. Human capital cannot be **collateralized**, meaning that it is not a physical asset that can be seized by a lender if a loan is not paid back.
2. Human capital cannot be owned by anyone other than the individual and cannot be sold.

These may seem like trivial differences, but they affect virtually every aspect of the market for education. Both of these differences stem from the fact that in most modern economies, slavery and indentured servitude are illegal (and rightly so!). Because of this prohibition, one cannot collateralize one's human capital for the purposes of a loan the same way one can for a house or a car. When you take out a home loan, your house is put up as collateral; if you default, the lender can seize the house. This collateral significantly reduces the risk to the lender. Thus, it reduces interest rates as well. Imagine what such a situation would look like in a human capital context: You would take out an education loan, and if you defaulted, the bank could compel you to work to repay the loan. Such a contract is thankfully illegal, but the fact that one cannot collateralize an education loan makes those loans more risky for lenders and creates potential market failures in terms of binding credit constraints faced by students.

The second difference between physical and human capital means that the only way to realize the return on an investment in human capital is through your own work in the labor market. Unlike a machine, you cannot sell human capital to another except through the labor market. The only way to sell your human capital would be to sell yourself into slavery or indentured servitude, but such a transaction is not legal in most areas of the world. An important implication of this attribute of human capital is that the returns on a given investment should decline with age, since the time span over which one can accrue any benefits from the investment will be smaller.

4.2 The Costs and Benefits of an Education

Now that we have defined human capital and examined some of the ways it is similar to and different from physical capital, we are going to turn to a model of human capital investment through formal schooling. As illustrated by the decisions faced by Morgan and Stanley at the beginning of the chapter, the starting point for such a model is an understanding of the costs and benefits associated with a given investment in education.

When individuals decide whether to attend school, we expect them to evaluate both the benefits and the costs. A primary benefit of an investment in education is the higher earnings that can be expected to accrue over a long working life. As with the decision facing Morgan, some of the benefits of investing in a specific type or level of schooling may be nonpecuniary. These benefits may include, for example, access to a given career that has high personal value to an individual (like being a college professor) or greater appreciation of art and literature. In economics, we tend to focus on the expected monetary gains from an investment in education, but we stress that these other benefits are important for many students and that the human capital model can easily be adapted to include such benefits. Because they are hard to measure, researchers tend to focus more on the labor market returns to education investments, and we follow that convention here.

The costs of education are twofold. First, it is likely that you will have to pay tuition or incur other expenses (such as buying books) that you would not otherwise face. Such expenses are often called the *direct* costs of education. Second, education takes time, which means part of the cost of attending school comes in the form of lost wages, or **foregone earnings**. These foregone wages are the indirect costs of education. Both Morgan and Stanley face considerable costs in terms of foregone earnings, as they are employed in high-wage jobs. High school graduates deciding whether or not to go to college likely face much lower foregone earnings. Given that full-time school attendance limits employment, foregone wages will be a nontrivial component of the cost of education for all students who are old enough to work, however.

foregone earnings The earnings one would have received in the labor market during the period of enrollment in school if he or she had not been in school.

The outline of the human capital model is simple: Individuals compare benefits in terms of higher wages that accompany greater skills to the costs of educational attainment to determine how much (and what type of) schooling to pursue. In practice, people choose from a range of educational options that differ in curricular focus (arts versus math) and skills taught (architecture versus medicine). Some choices are clearly sequential (second grade is a prerequisite for third grade), while other choices may be mutually exclusive (the decision to go to graduate school for law or medicine). To simplify our analysis, we put aside these multiple dimensions of education and think only in terms of individuals choosing a simple number of units or years of education.[2]

As with most models of individual behavior, it is not necessary for people to go through the exact calculations of the model. What is important is that they make choices *as if* they had followed the path of the model; the model is a success if it predicts outcomes on average. Our goal in the coming pages is to explore the basic predictions about how individuals decide to invest in education.

4.3 Basic Setup of the Human Capital Model

A useful starting point for conceptualizing how people decide to acquire more education is the decision a firm faces when deciding whether to purchase physical capital, such as a piece of manufacturing equipment. The firm's decision to purchase the machine is an investment; the initial cost produces a stream of benefits in the form of production in future years. In the same sense, an individual's decision to invest in education has an initial cost, while also producing a stream of benefits in the form of higher earnings in future years.

To model an investment in education, we need to know what an individual would earn without more schooling (Y_0) and what the individual will earn with more schooling (Y_S). To start, let's assume that these amounts stay constant over the period of work and that we know the number of years of expected labor force participation (K), the tuition and fees that will be charged (F), and the rate at which the individual can borrow and lend (r). Another assumption of the model is that all of these parameters are known at the time the individual makes the schooling choice. We will for now assume that credit markets function perfectly, which means all individuals are able to borrow to finance their education. Later in the chapter, we will examine how educational attainment is likely to change if individuals cannot borrow.

Figure 4.1 outlines the parameters of the problem: The squares show the pattern of earnings an individual would

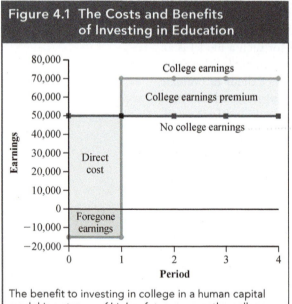

Figure 4.1 The Costs and Benefits of Investing in Education

The benefit to investing in college in a human capital model is a stream of higher future wages: the college wage premium. The cost of obtaining this premium is in the form of direct costs (tuition) and foregone earnings (indirect costs) that are paid early in one's life.

---

[2] For a long time, *years of education* was the standard unit for measuring schooling outcomes. As part-time enrollments evolved, however, it has become increasingly difficult for researchers to know the "quantity" of education associated with responses to questions about years of attainment. In 1993, the *Current Population Survey* (see Appendix A) shifted from a question based on years of attainment to a question based on the highest completed degree. As a result, researchers increasingly focus on highest degree completed rather than on years of education completed.

expect if she invests in college, while the circles illustrate the earnings path if she does not invest in a year of schooling. After the first period, the *college earnings premium* causes earnings with a college degree to be higher than earnings without a college degree; the squares are above the circles. For periods 2–4, the individual is receiving positive benefits of education in terms of higher earnings. In period 1, the individual is forgoing earnings she could have obtained had she not invested in college and has to pay direct education costs such as tuition.

From the point of view of the individual, education is a good investment if benefits exceed costs. In Figure 4.1, the earnings pathway that comes with investing in additional schooling has *direct costs* in the initial period, followed by earnings higher than those the individual would have received without additional education in the later periods. To compare benefits with costs meaningfully, we need to take into consideration that the higher earnings that come with additional schooling occur in later years, while the costs are incurred initially.

> **Quick Hint:** In deciding what belongs in *direct costs*, we include only expenses specific to a particular course of education. For example, if you would not have purchased this textbook if you weren't enrolled in this course, the cost of the book and other materials are direct costs. Computation of direct costs can be particularly tricky for room and board expenses. Subsistence expenses—outlays for food and clothing that would have been incurred in any event—should not be included, while additional expenses should be counted.

Because the benefits and costs of an education occur at different times, we need to adjust the stream of payments illustrated in Figure 4.1 to reflect the value at a particular point in time. We suspect that you would prefer $100 today to $100 five years from now. If you had $100 today, you could put it in the bank or in some other investment and it would yield more than $100 in five years. In thinking about the expected future stream of payments, consider the **present value**—the value today of earnings received in the future.

To receive a payment of $100 one year from now rather than today, you would have to put only $97.08 in the bank today if the annual interest rate (r) is 3%. This is because $97.08 $\times$ (1.03) equals $100. What this means is that if the interest rate is positive, receiving money today is more valuable than receiving the same amount at a future date. The toolbox provides a more detailed discussion of present value calculations.

present value The value today of inflows of cash (e.g., wages) that will be earned sometime in the future.

🧰 TOOLBOX: Present Value and Compound Interest

Present value is a key concept for thinking about investing in education or any other decision that involves multiple points in time (what economists call intertemporal choice). Why would I rather have $100 today than $100 in a year? If I have $100 today, I can deposit that money in the bank and it will earn interest at a rate of r. Hence, $100 today will be worth $100(1 + r)$ in a year if I put it in the bank. I may be indifferent between $100 today and $100(1 + r)$ at the end of the year, but I clearly prefer $100 today to $100 at the end of the year. The cost of deferring payment to the end of the year therefore is $100r$.

If I left the sum of $100 in the bank for two years, it would be worth $100(1 + r)(1 + r)$, or $100(1 + r)^2$ at the end of two years. Another year, or three years total, would yield $100(1 + r)(1 + r)(1 + r)$ or $100(1 + r)^3$, and so on, with the value after N years being $100(1 + r)^N$.

A related question: How much would I give up today for $100 at the end of the year? The answer is that I would give up $100/(1 + r) today to get $100 a year from now. For $100 at the end of two years I would give up somewhat less, or $100/(1 + r)^2, as I would be giving up two years of interest accumulation. More generally, $100 N years from now would have a present value today of $100/(1 + r)^N.

With an understanding of present value for a single payment, it is worth contemplating a series of payments, which could be a stream of earnings or interest payments on a bond. Suppose I offer to pay you $100 at the end of each year for the next N years. How much should you value this series of payments? Mechanically, we can write down the present values of each of these payments and add them up:

$$\text{Present value} = \frac{\$100}{1 + r} + \frac{\$100}{(1 + r)^2} + \frac{\$100}{(1 + r)^3} + \cdots + \frac{\$100}{(1 + r)^N}$$

$$\text{Present value} = \sum_{t=1}^{N} \frac{\$100}{(1 + r)^t}$$

We could compute the value of each of these terms and sum, but this process is time-intensive if N is large. This stream of payments is identical in form to what is called an annuity in the finance world, a series of payments recurring over a fixed period. With a little bit of rearrangement in steps *i–iv*, we have an equation that is easy to work with:

(*i*) PV annuity stream $= A = \dfrac{Y}{(1 + r)} + \dfrac{Y}{(1 + r)^2} + \cdots + \dfrac{Y}{(1 + r)^N}$

(*ii*) Multiply both sides by $(1 + r)$: $A(1 + r) = Y + \dfrac{Y}{(1 + r)} + \cdots + \dfrac{Y}{(1 + r)^{N-1}}$

(*iii*) Subtract (*ii*) − (*i*): $Ar = Y - \dfrac{Y}{(1 + r)^N}$

(*iv*) Divide both sides by *r*: $A = \dfrac{Y}{r}\left[1 - \dfrac{1}{(1 + r)^N}\right]$

If N goes to infinity, we have a perpetuity (a series of payments recurring forever), and the formula simplifies to $A = Y/r$.

As an example, suppose that a worker with a college degree earns $60,000 per year for a working life of 40 years. With an interest rate of 5%, the present value of this annuity stream is

$$PV = \sum_{t=1}^{40} \frac{\$60,000}{(1 + 0.05)^t} = \frac{\$60,000}{0.05}\left[1 - \frac{1}{1.05^{40}}\right] = \$1,029,545$$

The same principle applies when we think about how to value the stream of earnings expected from any investment in schooling. To make this more tangible, think about cardiac surgeons, who have high annual earnings—say $500,000 per year. While this annual income may seem attractive, remember that it is realized only upon completing a long course of undergraduate education, medical school (which costs an average of $50,000 per year), internships, and residencies. Hence, such an impressive level of earnings may follow only after more than 19 years of school, low-paid apprenticeships, and internships. The amount of time a surgeon will spend in the workforce earning this salary also has been reduced by this lengthy training period.

4.4 Present Value Formulation and Educational Investments

To value an education investment option, we want to determine the value today of the stream of future benefits and the value today of the stream of costs required for the investment. We want to know the present value of both benefits and costs. To make things easy (at least initially), start with a case of four periods corresponding to Figure 4.1. Consider the present value of the stream of costs and benefits generated by the option of working full-time in all four periods versus the option of attending school in the first period and then working full-time in the remaining three periods. Working full-time brings four wage payments, which are received at the end of each period. The present value of this stream is:

$$PV_0 = \frac{Y_0}{(1+r)} + \frac{Y_0}{(1+r)^2} + \frac{Y_0}{(1+r)^3} + \frac{Y_0}{(1+r)^4} = \sum_{t=1}^{4} \frac{Y_0}{(1+r)^t}$$

The alternative, identified with the subscript S, is attending school in the first period and then working in subsequent periods. This alternative has a present value of:

$$PV_S = -F + \frac{Y_S}{(1+r)^2} + \frac{Y_S}{(1+r)^3} + \frac{Y_S}{(1+r)^4} = -F + \sum_{t=2}^{4} \frac{Y_S}{(1+r)^t}$$

Education is a worthwhile investment for the individual if the present value of attending school for a year and then working (PV_S) is greater than the present value of working full time for all four periods (PV_0); in short, $PV_S > PV_0$. Taking the difference between PV_S and PV_0 yields the **net present value** of the investment in education:

$$NPV_S = PV_S - PV_0$$

$$= -F + \frac{Y_S}{(1+r)^2} + \frac{Y_S}{(1+r)^3} + \frac{Y_S}{(1+r)^4}$$

$$- \frac{Y_0}{(1+r)} - \frac{Y_0}{(1+r)^2} - \frac{Y_0}{(1+r)^3} - \frac{Y_0}{(1+r)^4}$$

By rearranging the terms, we can highlight the benefits and costs associated with the investment in education:

$$NPV_S = PV_S - PV_0 = -F - \frac{Y_0}{(1+r)} + \frac{Y_S - Y_0}{(1+r)^2} + \frac{Y_S - Y_0}{(1+r)^3} + \frac{Y_S - Y_0}{(1+r)^4}$$

$$NPV_S = PV_S - PV_0 = -F - \frac{Y_0}{(1+r)} + \sum_{t=2}^{4} \frac{Y_S - Y_0}{(1+r)^t}$$

The first two terms of the final equation capture costs, which include foregone earnings ($\frac{Y_0}{1+r}$) and the direct tuition cost (F). The summation term reflects the benefits of having higher earnings in the final three periods because of the higher level of education ($Y_S - Y_0$). If this net present value is positive ($PV_S > PV_0$), then the investment in education is worthwhile, and if it is negative, it is not optimal for the individual to invest in schooling level S.

net present value The value today of a stream of current and future inflows and outflows of cash. In education, the net present value of a schooling investment is the value today of the change in wages that will be earned sometime in the future because of the increase in education net of the cost of investing in an education today.

4.5 Predictions from the Investment Model of Education

Now that we understand the basic setup of the model, we can make some predictions about behavior and how changes in various policies will affect educational attainment.

Changes in Direct Costs

Increases in tuition and other direct costs of education (such as books and supplies) reduce the net present value and hence the attractiveness of any given educational choice. The demand for education declines with an increase in schooling costs. Research has shown that college enrollment is somewhat sensitive to tuition price, which is consistent with this prediction. For example, a $1,000 increase in tuition at community colleges is associated with a 4.5 percentage point decrease in enrollment rates (Kane, 2010).

Changes in Indirect Costs

By requiring time out of the labor market, educational investments involve the indirect cost of foregone earnings. Foregone earnings differ considerably across individuals depending on their preinvestment skills. For example, an outstanding basketball player faces large costs in foregone earnings for remaining in college for another year, since his current skills are highly valued by the labor market. A high school graduate who can work in a family business without a college degree also can face a large indirect cost of investing in further schooling.

Because education tends to increase earnings, the indirect costs of education rise with more education. A student faces little in the way of foregone earnings by investing in third grade, while both Morgan and Stanley from the beginning of the chapter will forgo considerable earnings as part of the costs of enrolling in graduate school. Furthermore, the longer you live and work, the more years you will have to reap the rewards of an early investment in education. As discussed earlier in the chapter, this feature of human capital gives it some properties that are distinct from those of physical capital. The model predicts that people will be more likely to invest in education when they are relatively young because they will have more time to accrue the benefits of schooling.

In general, the data support the proposition that most investment in education should occur when people are relatively young, with many people following a path from high school graduation to college. This pattern is by no means universal, and in recent decades there have been increases in college enrollment among students well beyond traditional college-going age. The percentage of 25–29-year-olds enrolled in college increased from 2.8% in 1980 to 12.1% in 2013, while the percentage of 30–35-year-olds enrolled in college increased from 1.2% to 5.9%. In addition, the time it takes students to finish college has increased substantially: The average time to degree among college graduates now is over 5 years, and the evidence does not suggest that this additional time is being spent accumulating more human capital through additional coursework.

The basic human capital model shows that elongating time to degree and/or enrolling in college later in one's life reduces the net present value of the investment. It is important for making education policy that we understand what is at the root of these changes and what policies could be used to address them.

Changes in Benefits

A change in the structure of the economy that leads to higher demand for skilled labor will increase the wages of those with more education relative to the wages of those with less education. This has been happening in the U.S. economy over the past several decades. The sources of this shift in demand for skilled labor are twofold. First, the U.S. economy has undergone a decline in industries that require low-skilled workers (like manufacturing) and a rise in industries that need higher-skilled workers (like finance).

Second, even within industries there has been a long-run increase in the demand for more highly skilled workers. Much of this has been driven by the rise of computers and machinery that can do the routine tasks historically done by low-skilled laborers. For example, complex machines now can do a lot of the assembly line work in manufacturing that used to be done by people. Consequently, there has been a rise in demand for the highly skilled workers in manufacturing who can design and operate these machines. This is what economists call **skill-biased technological change (SBTC)**: Changes in the economy favor skilled over unskilled workers more. There is ample evidence to suggest SBTC is responsible for the large growth in earnings of highly educated workers relative to less educated workers over the past several decades in the United States.[3]

When the wages for more-educated relative to less-educated workers rise, the return on investment in the human capital model rises. This situation should lead to an increase in educational investment among workers, because the economic benefits have increased but not the costs. In contrast, when the relative benefits to education shrink, fewer people will attend college.

This model does a reasonably good job of predicting changes in the skill level of the workforce over time. In an influential paper, Kevin Murphy and Finis Welch (1989) show that when the value of a college degree fell relative to the value of a high school degree in the 1970s, college participation rates declined. In the terminology of the model, $(Y_S - Y_0)$, declined. College enrollment rates then rose in the 1980s as the wage premium for skilled workers increased (that is, $Y_S - Y_0$ increased), reflecting demand induced by skill-biased technological change. In recent decades, the demand for skilled workers has increased faster than the growth in supply, which has placed upward pressure on this wage premium.

Increases in the demand for workers in occupations that do not require a college education (but may require other skills) can lead to reduction or deferral in educational investments as well. Consider what would happen if there was a boom in the local oil and gas industry—the opening up of many more drilling rigs. The oil and gas industry employs a lot of workers in manual labor; therefore, increasing production of oil and

skill-biased technological change (SBTC) Growth or changes in the economy that favor higher-skilled workers over lower-skilled workers. An example of SBTC is the introduction of computers, which made higher-skilled workers who knew how to use computers more productive and replaced many low-skilled jobs.

---

[3] For a detailed treatment of SBTC, see Katz and Murphy (1992); Autor, Levy, and Murnane (2003); Autor, Katz, and Kearney (2008); and Goldin and Katz (2009).

gas should increase labor demand. This will drive up wages of workers without college degrees—including high school graduates and high school dropouts—relative to those of college graduates. The human capital model predicts that this will reduce educational investments among younger workers. This prediction is supported by empirical evidence showing that the expansion of the fracking industry produced relatively high wages for those with just secondary education and reduced high school completion rates (Cascio & Narayan, 2015).

Enrollment in specific types of occupational training also varies with labor market conditions. When the real estate market was booming before 2008, the real estate education industry expanded at a rapid clip. A 2005 *New York Times* article noted: "Hundreds of thousands of people have entered real estate in the last four years, hoping to grab a share of the big money moving in the industry. All of them had to take real estate courses to obtain state licenses."[4] Yet as home prices dropped by as much as 30% in some areas just a few years later, real estate agents were no longer assured high earnings. Not unexpectedly, the number of people enrolling in real estate courses has fallen precipitously.

4.6 Continuous Schooling Choices

The question of educational attainment is not just, "Should I go to school or not go to school?" but, "*How much* school should I complete?" as well as "What course of study should I pursue?" We can extend the basic model to a framework with continuous schooling decisions. Similar to the model presented earlier, the decision rule is based on finding the incremental benefit and cost associated with another year of schooling and using these incremental changes to find the best choice from a range of schooling options.

For each choice of schooling, there is an expected level of earnings. The expected annual earnings associated with each level of education is called the *earnings–schooling locus*. An example of an earnings–schooling locus is shown in Figure 4.2. This curve increases steeply at first, and then the rate of increase slows appreciably: There are *diminishing marginal returns* to education, which means that wages increase at a decreasing rate as one obtains more education. The eventual slowing of growth in the increments in earnings with each additional year of schooling is represented by the concave shape of the curve. This shape matches the reality of the labor market. After a point, there is likely to be little reward to obtaining more formal schooling.

For a given schooling–earnings locus, how much education is optimal? At what point does the return on investment become negative? Similar to the human capital investment model presented previously, the answer depends on the costs

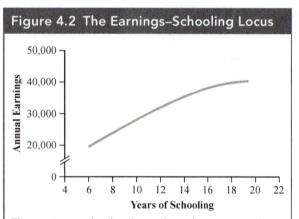

Figure 4.2 The Earnings–Schooling Locus

The earnings–schooling locus shows how expected annual earnings change with years of schooling. It is upward sloping, reflecting the fact that human capital obtained through schooling increases earnings. But it is increasing at a decreasing rate because of the diminishing marginal returns to schooling.

---

[4] Louise Story, *New York Times*, July 2, 2005, Saturday Personal Business. Schools that train real estate agents are booming, too.

in terms of foregone earnings and tuition. What matters in making this choice is the **marginal rate of return**, or the percentage net gain from an additional unit of educational investment. Because the gains in earnings for different levels of education vary over time and across geography, it is typical in empirical research on the returns to education to think in terms of rate of return or percentage change. The Toolbox shows a straightforward derivation for the marginal rate of return in a simplified version of the human capital model.

marginal rate of return
The percentage gain in earnings, net of costs, from purchasing an additional unit of the investment. With respect to schooling, it is the percentage change in earnings, net of costs, to obtaining an extra year of education.

🧰 TOOLBOX: Calculating Marginal Rates of Return: The Mincer Formulation

A simplified version of the education investment model, introduced by Jacob Mincer in 1974,[5] is a particularly clear representation of the model that is used extensively in empirical work. (See Chapter 6.) Mincer makes the following assumptions:

- Direct costs of schooling are zero.
- Years in the labor force are the same for all workers. For example, if there are two workers, one who has 12 years of education and one who has 14, the one with 12 years will stop working two years before the one with 14 years of education.

Let Y_S be the earnings of an individual with S years of education. Thus, Y_{12} is the earnings of someone with 12 years of education. The variables $Y_1, Y_2, Y_3, \ldots Y_S$ define the earnings–schooling locus for a representative individual.

We want to calculate the marginal rate of return for another year of schooling. This is the rate of return that equates the present value of expected earnings at two levels of education. Put differently, this is the return that one would need on any nonschooling investment to be just indifferent between this investment opportunity and pursuing another year of education.

Let PV_S be the present value of schooling level S. Because we assume direct costs of schooling are zero, the present value equals the net present value in this setup. The marginal rate of return is found by setting the PV of schooling level S equal to the PV of schooling level $S + 1$ (i.e., one more year of schooling). We assume all individuals will work for K years, so by the second assumption, one who obtains $S + 1$ years of schooling will work from period 2 to period $K + 1$ (which is K years). Algebraically,

$$PV_S = PV_{S+1}$$

$$\sum_{t=1}^{K} \frac{Y_S}{(1 + r)^t} = \sum_{t=2}^{K+1} \frac{Y_{S+1}}{(1 + r)^t}$$

$$\frac{Y_S}{r}\left[1 - \frac{1}{(1 + r)^K}\right] = \frac{Y_{S+1}}{r}\left[1 - \frac{1}{(1 + r)^K}\right]\frac{1}{(1 + r)}$$

$$Y_{S+1} = Y_S(1 + r)$$

$$\frac{Y_{S+1}}{Y_S} = (1 + r)$$

In this case, the percentage difference in earnings associated with another year of schooling is approximately equal to the discount rate. If the rate of return to the investment in $S + 1$ years of schooling is at least $1 + r$, then the investment is worthwhile. If not, one could earn a higher return on the alternative use of the money.

---

[5] Mincer, J. *Schooling, Experience, and Earnings*, New York: NBER, 1974.

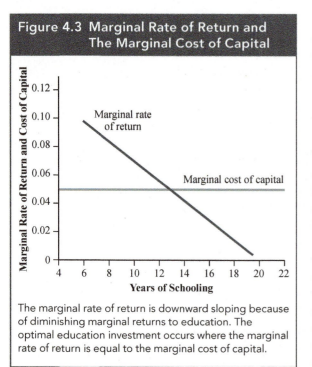

Figure 4.3 Marginal Rate of Return and The Marginal Cost of Capital

The marginal rate of return is downward sloping because of diminishing marginal returns to education. The optimal education investment occurs where the marginal rate of return is equal to the marginal cost of capital.

The marginal rate of return for each additional unit of education is likely to decrease with additional education for two reasons:

1. As shown by the shape of the earnings–schooling locus, there are diminishing returns to education.
2. There is a trade-off between years spent in school and time in the labor force.

While more years of education may produce higher absolute earnings in a year, additional schooling comes at the cost of having fewer years over which to accrue these benefits. This downward-sloping marginal rate of return function is shown in Figure 4.3.

The fact that the marginal return gets somewhat smaller with each additional unit of education does not mean that more education is necessarily a bad idea. What matters is whether the marginal rate of return to schooling is greater than the return from the best alternative (nonschool) investment. Let's define this alternative benchmark as the *marginal cost of capital*, the rate at which an individual is able to borrow money. We will think of this as a fixed rate (say, 5%) at all levels of education. This assumption is appropriate for the market as a whole, although individuals may face different and increasing capital costs.

Suppose the marginal rate of return of going from the eleventh grade to the twelfth grade is 10%, while the cost of capital is 5%. Should you complete twelfth grade? Absolutely. Even if the marginal rate of return drops from 10% to, say, 8% between the twelfth and thirteenth years of schooling, going to school still yields a higher return than the outside option. Borrowing money from the bank at 5% and earning a yield of 8% from a further investment in education clearly leaves you better off. It is only when the marginal rate of return to education fails to exceed the marginal cost of capital that an individual should stop investing in education. This condition defines the individual's decision about optimal investment in education: Invest until the marginal rate of return equals the cost of capital. In other words, invest in more education if the return on that investment is larger than the return expected from the best alternative investment option.

4.7 Why Does Educational Attainment Differ Among Individuals?

There are significant differences among individuals in the level of educational attainment. Table 4.1 shows the distribution of education in the United States in 2012 for those aged 25–54, overall and by race, ethnicity, and gender. Over 30% of those between 25 and 54 hold at least a four-year baccalaureate (BA) degree, with almost 11% having an advanced degree such as a PhD or MD. All but 12% of Americans have a high school degree, illustrating the rather high level of educational attainment in this country.

We observe substantial variation in educational attainment by race and ethnicity. Blacks, for instance, are about 17 percentage points less likely to hold at least a college degree than Whites, and Asians and are less than half as likely to have a graduate degree. Hispanics have a much higher high school dropout rate than Whites, Asians, or Blacks,

Table 4.1 Educational Attainment of 25- to 54-Year-Olds in the United States, Overall and by Race, Ethnicity, and Gender

Highest Attained Education Level	All Workers	White or Asian	Black	Hispanic	Male	Female
High school dropout	12.08%	6.67%	12.39%	33.13%	13.58%	10.60%
High school degree	25.99%	24.61%	30.90%	27.46%	28.66%	23.35%
Some college	30.81%	31.22%	36.28%	24.80%	28.99%	32.62%
BA degree	20.21%	24.12%	13.53%	10.20%	18.77%	21.64%
Graduate school	10.91%	13.38%	6.89%	4.41%	10.01%	11.80%

Data from: 2012 American Community Survey.

and they also have much lower levels of college and graduate school completion than these other ethnic groups. Table 4.1 also shows a sizable gender gap in education, with men obtaining less education than women. What insights can the human capital model give us regarding some of the causes of these differences?

People Differ in Their Ability to Finance Direct Costs

We have considered the case in which the cost of capital was constant across levels of education and was the same for all individuals. The horizontal representation of the marginal cost of capital in Figure 4.3 ignores the fact that many people must borrow to finance the direct costs associated with education, such as tuition. The cost of obtaining the requisite funds to finance an educational investment is the interest rate at which a family can borrow. In the U.S. education system, the need to borrow typically increases when a student enrolls in college, as most students attend public K–12 schools that do not charge tuition. As the amount of education increases, the need to borrow to finance additional years of education also increases. This results in an upward-sloping marginal cost of capital curve.

Figure 4.4 depicts such an upward-sloping curve. The upward slope indicates that the cost of funds increases as the level of educational attainment paid for by borrowing goes up. We would expect individuals to borrow first from low-cost sources of funds such as federally sponsored student loans or home equity before turning to sources of funds that are far more expensive, such as private loans and credit cards.

College students typically face an interest rate of about 18% on credit card borrowing, which is well above rates charged in the federal student loan programs. We would only expect college students to accumulate credit card debt if federal loans are insufficient to cover their costs. In 2010, over 25% of college students had credit card debt, and the average

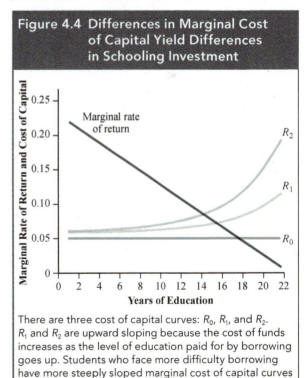

Figure 4.4 Differences in Marginal Cost of Capital Yield Differences in Schooling Investment

There are three cost of capital curves: R_0, R_1, and R_2. R_1 and R_2 are upward sloping because the cost of funds increases as the level of education paid for by borrowing goes up. Students who face more difficulty borrowing have more steeply sloped marginal cost of capital curves and as a result obtain fewer years of education.

credit card debt among college students was $304. However, among students with any credit card debt, the average balance was over $2,300. Credit card debt among students has declined substantially since the early 2000s, when 40% of students had credit card debt and the average student with debt had a balance of over $4,300.[6] Despite the decline in credit card debt, this evidence makes clear that many college students either are unable to borrow from lower-cost sources of capital or are very poorly informed about the credit market (carrying balances at unnecessarily high costs).

When borrowing costs rise sufficiently, such that they dissuade students from investing in an education level that would have been worth it had they been able to borrow at the market rate of return, they are **credit-constrained**. For example, take a student who has a rate of return to an educational investment of 8% and faces a rate of return of 5% to a capital investment. Assume he can only borrow at 10%. He is credit-constrained, because he lacks access to sufficiently inexpensive capital to finance his investment. If he could collateralize his human capital and thus borrow at the market rate of return, this constraint would disappear. Parental wealth levels are a main source of variation in the marginal cost of capital students face, as higher-wealth families have access to cheaper forms of credit. Students from lower-wealth families typically face a higher cost of capital, which is driven by their lower access to equity. Differential access to credit across the wealth distribution therefore can lead to lower educational investment among students from lower-wealth families. That is, students from low-resource backgrounds may invest in less education because they face binding credit constraints.

credit constraint Limitation that arises when an individual cannot borrow money or cannot borrow money at a sufficiently low interest rate to finance an educational investment that would have a positive rate of return if the individual could borrow at the market rate.

Credit constraints produce inefficient allocations in attainment along two dimensions. First, the number of individuals obtaining a given level of education is too low, and second, the wrong distribution of people is obtaining an education. These inefficiencies are driven by the fact that individuals with the same capacity to benefit from education, as represented by the same marginal rate of return schedule, end up with different levels of education.

People Differ in the Benefits They Receive from Education

People differ in personality and in innate ability. Some people learn a great deal in high school calculus, while others do not. Therefore, individuals are likely to differ in underlying characteristics that will affect the benefits of schooling. Figure 4.2 (along with the associated marginal returns schedule in Figure 4.3) describes the relationship between earnings and education for one individual (or for an average individual), not for the population as a whole.

Figure 4.5 shows the marginal rates of return for two very different individuals, Ana and Felix. Ana is more able than Felix, so her return to an additional year of schooling is above Felix's at every level of schooling. In this case, both Ana

Figure 4.5 Marginal Rates of Return for Workers of Different Ability Levels

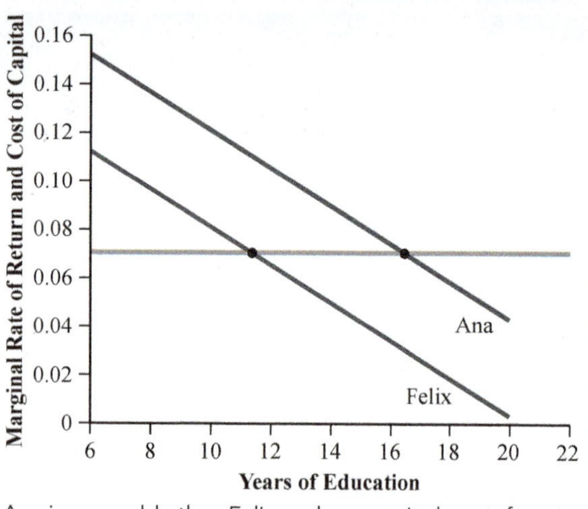

Ana is more able than Felix, so her marginal rate of return schedule is above Felix's at every level of schooling. Both Ana and Felix invest in the efficient level of schooling—the point where their marginal rate of return intersects with the marginal cost of capital. Ana obtains more education than Felix because she is of higher ability.

---

[6] These tabulations come from the *Survey of Consumer Finances*. They are calculated using all 18- to 22-year-olds who report having at least some college education.

and Felix are investing in the efficient level of schooling because the marginal rate of return is just equal to the marginal cost of capital (which is assumed to be the same for Ana and Felix). Ana obtains more education than Felix because she is of higher ability.

What would happen if we introduced a policy such as a subsidy for education that went to Felix to encourage him to get the same level of education as Ana? As illustrated in Figure 4.5, the associated marginal return for Felix would be below both the marginal discount rate and the marginal rate of return received by Ana. Felix would be better off in the sense of higher lifetime earnings if he were given a cash transfer, which he could invest at the market rate of return rather than a subsidy restricted to education.

Another feature of this illustration is that we cannot determine the rate of return to education from the *observed* earnings of people on different education–earnings loci. The rate of return to Ana per year for an investment in schooling that moves her from 12 to 14 years of completed education is clearly greater than the rate of return that Felix would receive for this increase in schooling. If we used the difference in earnings between Ana and Felix to calculate the rate of return to education, we would likely overestimate the benefits of education. This estimate would be biased upward because Ana's characteristics (such as ability) that lead to the higher earnings–education profile are also related to her level of educational attainment. The result of this mismeasurement is what economists call **ability bias**. A formal representation of this argument is presented in Chapter 6. When the divergence in earnings–schooling loci is driven by one attribute, such as a single measure of ability that is positively related to productivity, it is straightforward to identify the direction of the bias.[7]

Thus far we have presented the model with individuals making choices about schooling attainment based on expected earnings. One doesn't need to believe that only money matters to see that the basic model provides important predictions. Still, some variation in schooling choices will follow from different tastes for schooling. We can predict that people who very much enjoy education (who receive what might be called a consumption benefit) will elect more schooling than those who dislike going to school, holding all else equal.

ability bias The bias that occurs when differences in underlying labor market productivity or ability lead people to obtain different levels of education. In such a case, comparing earnings across workers with different education levels will provide a biased estimate of the returns to education, as these workers also differ in terms of their underlying productivity.

Policy Implications of Differences in Attainment

The robust and growing demand for high-skilled labor and the evidence suggesting that obtaining more education brings large wage returns underscore the policy importance of addressing cross-group differences in attainment. Policies that can support higher educational attainment among disadvantaged groups, such as racial and ethnic minorities and low-income students, have the potential to reduce inequality and increase socioeconomic mobility.

These examples make clear that understanding *why* individuals differ in educational attainment is critical for designing appropriate public policy responses. In the case of credit constraints, there are clear benefits to innovations in financial aid and credit markets that would equalize the marginal cost of capital among individuals. Such policies yield potential gains in both equity and efficiency.

---

[7] For a more formal treatment see Griliches (1977). Griliches sets out the case where schooling (*S*) and ability (*A*) are related and have independent effects on earnings. Others, such as Willis and Rosen (1979) and Heckman and Honore (1990) have expanded the problem to consider the link between multiple attributes, education choice, and earnings. These are classic applications of the Roy model to education investment decisions. We discuss the Roy model in terms of selection of workers into the teaching profession in Chapter 12.

If differences in attainment are driven by differences in the marginal return to education or by differences in preferences, public policy interventions designed to boost schooling are inefficient. Consider the role of financial aid for college. If credit constraints are the main reason that students from low-income backgrounds invest less in college than do students from wealthier families, financial aid can enhance efficiency by overcoming a market failure (the inability to borrow or borrow at a sufficiently low rate). If the reason these students are less likely to go to college is that they are less academically prepared because of long-run differences in the quality of schooling they receive, financial aid can reduce efficiency. This is because it would induce individuals to attend college who are not academically qualified to do so. In such a case, interventions at younger ages to increase marginal returns to education when the children are older might be more effective.

4.8 Conclusion

We now have in place a basic framework to model education as an investment. Comparing the values of discounted streams of payments yields predictions about educational choices and also shows how these choices are likely to be affected by changes in market conditions. To summarize:

- Increased direct costs (such as tuition) reduce the attractiveness of investing in further schooling.
- Increased earnings associated with additional schooling (or decreased earnings associated with less schooling) increase the attractiveness of further education.
- A longer expected period of labor force participation increases the number of years over which a worker can enjoy the benefits of education and thus increases the attractiveness of further schooling.
- Increasing the rate at which an individual can borrow or lend reduces the present value of future benefits relative to near-term costs, thus decreasing the attractiveness of schooling.

Not everyone makes the same schooling choices. One reason people make different choices is that they face different costs of education. An alternative explanation for their choices is that people differ in ability or in other characteristics that affect the benefits they will receive from additional education. Understanding the determinants of educational attainment thus is a key question for research and policy. We are going to pursue this in more depth in subsequent chapters. The basic model for investing in education that we have developed in this chapter can be modified to accommodate complexities that are likely to surface in practice, such as uncertainty and the specialization of education outcomes.

Our model of individual choice in investing in education also does not address the social returns to education. Because the positive benefits to others of education are not incorporated in individual choices, the social return from further schooling may exceed the private return. This can provide some motivation for public policies.

In the next chapters, we put the human capital interpretation of investments in education that we covered in this chapter to theoretical and empirical tests. The first challenge is to examine whether increased schooling actually generates greater skills and, in turn, higher earnings. An alternative interpretation described in Chapter 5 is that schooling may not change skills but may instead only serve as a mechanism to identify individuals who are more productive to begin with. Thus, measuring the effect of education on skills and earnings is an important challenge.

Highlights

- The **human capital model** provides the foundation for economic thinking about an individual's decision to invest in a given level of education and about the way individuals will respond to the costs and benefits associated with an investment in education. Changes in these costs and benefits can come from education policy as well as independent changes in the labor market, such as **skill-biased technological change (SBTC)**.

- **Human capital** and physical capital are similar in that we expect investments in both to generate profits over and above the **market rate of return**. They are distinct in that human capital cannot be **collateralized** and it cannot be owned by anyone other than the individual. These differences affect all aspects of education markets.

- The decision to invest in education must take present and future costs and benefits into consideration. Education costs entail both direct costs, such as books and tuition, and indirect costs in the form of **foregone earnings**. The value today of a stream of benefits accruing in the future

is called the **present value**, while the **net present value** is the present value of benefits from an investment net of the costs of the investment.

- The percentage gain in earnings, net of costs, from investing in an additional year of schooling is the **marginal rate of return**. There are diminishing returns to education, as each year of investment leads to a successively smaller increase in earnings. This means there is an optimal amount of education each person should obtain, characterized by the education level at which the marginal rate of return equals the cost of capital.

- Observed earnings differences across individuals with different years of schooling likely do not tell us the causal effect of schooling on earnings because of **ability bias**. Individuals also invest differently in education because they have different costs, such as **credit constraints**, which increase the cost of capital. To properly design education policies to address different investment behaviors, it is essential to pay attention to their underlying causes.

Problems

1. What are the similarities between physical and human capital? In what ways do physical and human capital differ?

2. Human capital cannot be pledged as an asset that can be seized by a lender in the event that the borrower defaults on a loan; in other words, human capital cannot be used as "collateral." Does the observation that human capital cannot be collateralized mean that in the absence of government-provided loans interest rates on student loans would be too high, just about right, or too low?

3. Walter is a chemistry teacher who earns $50,000 per year, while Jesse is unemployed. Both Walter and Jesse want to go back to school to earn a business degree to help them operate their new business. The tuition each one would have to pay is the same, and they have agreed each to pay half of the tuition regardless of which one attends. Assume they cannot attend part-time. Do they indeed face the same cost of enrolling in this program? Why or why not?

4. Suppose you have two friends who have the same underlying ability, took the same courses in college, and have the same GPA. One of them decides to go to a business school for an MBA, while the

other one chooses to pursue a PhD in English literature. Given that the expected earnings of an MBA are much higher than the expected earnings of an English PhD, is one of your friends being irrational?

5. Congratulations! You have just won the lottery, which will pay you an annuity of $50,000 per year for the rest of your life. If you are 21 today and will die with certainty at 90, this means you will receive 70 payments of $50,000. Let's say someone offers to give you $1,000,000 today in exchange for this annuity. If the interest rate is 5%, should you take this deal? Why or why not?

6. After defeating the Dark Lord, Ron's brother offers him a job at Weasleys' Wizard Wheezes. If Ron takes this job, his annual income will be 1 million galleons. Alternatively, Ron can return to Hogwarts to finish school, but then he must give up the job with his brother. Graduating will take him a year and it will cost 10,000 galleons in direct costs. He knows for sure he can become an Auror after finishing his education, at a yearly salary of 500,000 galleons. He thinks that the probability that he becomes Minister of Magic 25 years after graduating is 25%, and the minister's

salary is 5 million galleons per year. Regardless of his choice, he wants to retire in 30 years. Assume the interest rate is 5%.

a. If Ron is only concerned with the monetary rewards, will he go back to Hogwarts?

b. What probability of becoming Minister of Magic would make him indifferent between going back to school and going to work for his brother?

7. Miss Piggy, trying to prove that she is not just a pretty face, urged all of the Muppets to apply to law school at Sock Puppet University. In preparation for their law school applications, each Muppet took the LSAT and received scores uniformly distributed from Animal's score of 10 to Kermit the Frog's score of 180. The total cost (in present value) of attending Sock Puppet University Law School is $136,000. The Muppets' earnings are directly related to their performance on the LSAT, regardless of whether they go to law school. Those who do not go to law school will earn a present value of $Y_{NL} = 100 \times \text{LSAT}$, while those who do attend law school earn $Y_L = 1{,}000 + 1{,}000 \times \text{LSAT}$.

a. Above what LSAT level will attending law school increase the Muppets' net earnings?

b. What is the average earnings of the Muppets who do not attend law school?

c. What is the average earnings of the Muppets who do attend law school?

d. If we compare the average earnings of the Muppets with and without a law degree, is it correct to interpret this as the causal effect of law school on earnings? Why or why not?

e. What earnings level would the person with the average LSAT score have with education and without education?

8. Why is it more likely that people will invest in education when they are relatively young?

9. Doogie lives for four periods. He has just completed the first period of his life (by getting his high school diploma). Doogie is trying to decide on his future career path. He's very good at opening things up and fixing them, so he has narrowed his options to two possible paths. He will either become an auto mechanic or a brain surgeon.

- If Doogie becomes an auto mechanic, he will earn $25,000 as an apprentice in period 2, $50,000 as a solo mechanic in period 3, and $75,000 as a master mechanic (with apprentice) in period 4.

- If Doogie becomes a brain surgeon, he will pay $50,000 to attend college in period 2, another $75,000 to attend medical school in period 3, and will earn $300,000 in period 4.

Doogie must make all tuition payments at the beginning of each period, he is paid at the end of every period, and he can borrow and lend at a rate of 8% per period.

a. What is the present discounted value (PDV) of Doogie's possible career paths? If Doogie wants to maximize the PDV of his lifetime earnings, which career should he choose?

b. Would Doogie's choice change if he was making his decision at birth? Would the PDV of his earnings streams be different at birth? Would Doogie's evaluation of this investment change if he started life with a trust fund of $1 million? Explain. (Assume that Doogie's high school education in period 1 is necessary for both career paths and is costless.)

c. How would your answer change if Doogie could work for an additional 10 periods after period 4? How would your answer change if the discount rate decreased? (Answer intuitively in terms of whether the surgery track becomes relatively more or less attractive).

d. The actual lifetime earnings of brain surgeons are much higher than those of auto mechanics, yet we observe that the number of auto mechanics is much greater than the number of brain surgeons. How can the human capital model explain these patterns?

10. In the most recent recession, the earnings of college-educated workers declined. This caused many policy makers and those in the press to claim that college was no longer worth it for students. Does this conclusion necessarily follow from the observed changes in college-educated workers' earnings?

CHAPTER 5

The Signaling Model: An Alternative to the Human Capital Framework

How Would You Hire the Best Workers?

After years of toil on your new software, you have successfully obtained seed funding from a venture capital firm and are now in the process of setting up your own company. Although you have a great product, it is imperative to hire the best employees you can to staff your nascent company to help ensure its success. You go out and advertise jobs, receive résumés, and then face a problem common to all employers: How do you use the information on the résumés to find the most productive workers?

Thinking about this problem, it is clear you face a large information barrier. As an employer you lack the detailed information about each applicant's actual productivity, and so you likely will look for markers, or *signals*, of that productivity. For example, you might think that an applicant who has a computer science degree will be a more productive employee in your software firm than one who does not. You also might infer that someone who attended a more elite postsecondary school is more qualified for a position with your firm than someone who attended a lower-ranked institution. In such cases, the type of education and/or the observed quality of that education act as *signals*: you are using these observed characteristics of applicants to proxy for the unobserved skills of individual workers. These credentials communicate something about an applicant's productivity to an employer because many people would find it difficult to obtain them.

Consider the problem faced by an applicant to this firm. Workers have private knowledge about their own productivity, but it is very difficult to convey this information to an employer credibly. For example, if an employer were to ask a job candidate if he is persistent in solving complex problems, it is unlikely that any prospect who wanted the job would respond in anything but the affirmative. Less-productive workers can simply lie about these dimensions of productivity in an interview. The most productive workers want to find a way to signal credibly to an employer that they have productive characteristics that are difficult to observe. Recall that you, as an employer, have given potential workers a way to signal such productivity: invest in a computer science degree. For a productive individual, this is a particularly attractive signal in which to invest: the costs of majoring in computer science are arguably lower for those who are tenacious in solving complex programming challenges. Importantly, formal course work in college may not have generated this skill.

Now you as the employer have decided to interpret a candidate having a computer science degree as a signal of high productivity, and thus you will pay higher wages to such workers. More-productive workers will invest in obtaining a computer science degree because of the higher pay associated with this degree, and the costs of doing so are lower for them than for less productive workers. Lo and behold, your initial beliefs about these workers will turn out to be true: They are more productive in your firm than those without a computer science degree.

This is an example of a *signaling model*, following along the lines of the pioneering work of Michael Spence. Spence won the 2001 Nobel Prize in Economics for setting forth a model in which firms had difficulty observing (and thus lacked information about) the productive characteristics of workers. In his Nobel lecture, Spence recounted the query of a reporter who asked "whether it was true that you could be awarded the Nobel Prize in Economics for simply noticing that there are markets in which certain participants don't know certain things that others in the market do know." Spence and his cowinners, George Akerlof and Joseph Stiglitz, developed economic models in which participants in a market have incomplete information, allowing them to examine the ways in which agents in these markets adapt to information asymmetries. An important contribution of Spence's signaling model is that it demonstrates how educational attainment may provide information to employers—and in turn higher wages to individuals with more education—when no productive skills (human capital) are acquired in school. At the extreme, education simply acts as a mechanism to identify more-productive and less-productive workers. Unlike the human capital model, it need not be the case that the educational experience makes workers more productive. Taking computer science courses does not necessarily have to improve problem-solving skills or build skills that employers value.

In this chapter, we introduce a simplified version of the basic signaling model. Then, we discuss policy implications; whether the human capital or signaling model more accurately characterizes the relationship between education and productivity is a critical question for educators and policy makers. The answer has a substantial impact on the desirability of investment in education and public subsidies for education. We also consider some of the challenges associated with empirically testing which model is more relevant for education policy as well as some of the empirical evidence on the signaling value of degrees.

5.1 The Motivation for the Signaling Model

Why might education contain information about an individual's characteristics? We start with a very basic proposition that was highlighted in the previous example: It may be very difficult for employers to infer an individual's full set of skills from an interview. Some skills, such as whether you type more than 40 words per minute or whether you have mastered basic math, can be measured through simple testing. But other skills, such as the capacity to work well with others, task commitment, attention to detail, creativity, and work ethic, may be difficult to observe directly. While employers might ask during an interview about punctuality or creativity, there is little incentive for a candidate to respond truthfully. Would you volunteer that you perpetually hit the snooze button on your alarm or that you are not very creative? Eventually, an employer will figure out who is strong and who is weak on these dimensions, but this will take time and implies substantial costs in terms of large turnover among employees and the persistence of less-productive workers on staff. Just as you seek to staff your software firm, all employers want to find a way to avoid the aforementioned costs and hire the most productive workers upfront.

A core motivation for the signaling model is that employers have imperfect information about the true skills of a potential employee, and potential employees face serious hurdles in their ability to convey their true productivity to employers. We call this situation asymmetric information, as workers have information about their own productivity and skills that potential employers do not have. The problem faced by workers is to find some way to convey truthfully and credibly this private information to employers.

The insight of the signaling model is that workers can engage in specific behaviors that under certain conditions can signal their productivity to an employer and thus can resolve this uncertainty. For example, wearing a suit to an interview, wearing nice shoes, and having a professional-looking résumé all are potential signals to employers. Employers might believe from previous experiences that applicants who wear a nice suit or who have résumés that are free of typos are more likely to pay attention to details or to write effectively. Applicants with these attributes are more likely to be hired and/or to command higher wages.

The education system can be used to help resolve information asymmetry in hiring through the provision of signals. This is the core example that Spence uses in his Nobel Prize–winning 1973 paper, which introduces the concept of signaling. Imagine there was a way to structure the education system such that only highly productive people received a high school diploma. Then, the diploma could be used as a **signal**, or proxy, for a worker's productivity. Employers could see whether or not a worker had a high school degree and infer from this whether the worker was highly productive or not. The signaling model shows the exact assumptions and the structure of the education system needed to allow education to be used as a signal in this way.

> **signal** A malleable characteristic of a worker that can provide information to employers about the worker's underlying productivity.

5.2 Setup of the Signaling Model

The setup of the model we use here follows Spence's original model closely. We refer students interested in more details on this model to his original paper (Spence, 1973).[1] There are two central agents in a signaling model:

1. Workers, who differ in their underlying productivity levels
2. Employers, who cannot perfectly observe worker productivity at the time of hire but have *beliefs* about how productive workers are based on their observed characteristics

Let's first think about the incentives employers and workers face. Employers want to know how productive the workers are that they are hiring. But, only some of their skills are observed at the time of hire—for example, how fast a worker can type or some communication skills. Many of the important skills that lead workers to have different productivity levels are unobserved to employers when they are interviewing candidates: punctuality, problem-solving skills, the ability to lead and/or work in teams, writing skills,

---

[1] A difference between the signaling model described here and the original Spence (1973) model is that we consider the range of signaling costs that would generate an equilibrium for a specific education level. For example, what range of costs would support a college degree as being an effective signal in a signaling equilibrium? In Spence's original model, he analyzed what range of education levels could act as a signal for a given signaling cost. The formulation of the model given here more closely aligns with the current structure of education in the United States, but the predictions and implications of the model are the same as in Spence's original version.

and attention to detail. Since employers may find it difficult to observe these skills directly, they generate beliefs about how these characteristics of workers map into productivity.

In a perfectly competitive labor market in which workers differ in productivity, employers need to pay workers different amounts based on their productivity. Employers' beliefs therefore lead to wage differences across workers with different attributes. For example, if an employer believes that those with a college degree are more productive, she will pay a higher wage to college-educated workers. In such a case, what will workers do? Clearly, all workers will want to get a college education, as it increases their wages. If the cost of investing in college is the same regardless of one's productivity, then workers of all productivity levels will obtain a college degree. The employer then will observe that her beliefs are incorrect: College-educated workers are not more productive than less educated workers, and she will have to revise her beliefs about the relationship between college degree and worker productivity.

Imagine instead that more productive workers have lower costs of obtaining a college degree. This might arise because they face lower costs of studying or because they find course work to be easier. Since the high-ability workers face lower costs of collegiate attainment, it is possible that only higher-ability workers find it worthwhile to invest in a college degree. In such a case, the initial beliefs of the employer that workers with a college degree are more productive will be confirmed. A college degree here is acting as a signal to separate higher-productivity workers from lower-productivity workers.

Now that we have discussed the intuition for how the signaling model works, we will more formally lay out the setup. For simplicity, assume that there are two types of workers, who differ in terms of their skills as well as in their costs of obtaining additional education: high (H) and low (L) type workers. Type H workers have skills that make them more productive in the workplace, and type L workers are less productive. For any amount of time spent working, type H workers are able to generate more output than type L workers. If type H workers could credibly convey to employers that they are of this type, they should earn more than type L workers. The problem is that a type L worker would like to masquerade as a type H worker to be considered more productive and thus earn higher wages. This is the source of the information asymmetry.

Table 5.1 summarizes the characteristics of type L and type H workers. Type L workers have a productivity level of 1, while type H workers have a productivity level of 2. The productivity levels here can be thought of as each worker's **marginal product of labor**, which is his or her contribution to overall firm profits or output. As is typical in economic models of labor markets, we will assume that workers will be paid according to their marginal product, because this is the value of what the worker produces. This assumption means that if employers can tell a type L worker from a type H worker, they will pay type L workers a wage of 1 and type H workers a wage of 2. When the

marginal product of labor A worker's contribution to overall firm profits or output.

Table 5.1 Characteristics of Type *L* and Type *H* Workers

Worker	Productivity	Cost of Education (e)	Proportion of the Population
Type L	1	c	p
Type H	2	$\dfrac{c}{2}$	$(1 - p)$

worker types can be distinguished, each worker needs to be paid her marginal product. Paying type L workers more than one would cause the firm to lose money. Paying type H workers less than two would lead there to be no type H workers at the firm, as they all would choose to work at another firm that pays their marginal product. If employers cannot tell the worker types apart, wages will be set equal to the average marginal product across workers. According to Table 5.1, the proportion of type L workers is p (where $0 \leq p \leq 1$), so the average marginal product across workers is:

$$1 \times p + 2 \times (1 - p) = p + 2 - 2p = 2 - p$$

Quick Hint: If the firm wants to pay workers a wage of 2, it needs to be able to distinguish between type L and type H workers. The reason is that if they offered a wage of 2 to all workers, the firm would go out of business because the marginal product of workers would be lower than the amount they were getting paid, thus generating negative profits.

Think about who would be happy with such a situation. If all workers get paid $2 - p$, then type L workers will earn more than their marginal product and type H workers will earn less. Type H workers thus will be displeased with this state of affairs: They are being paid less than what their labor is worth to the firm because the firm cannot tell who is a high-skilled employee and who is a low-skilled employee. Type H workers will want to find a way to convince employers that they are high-productivity types.

Type H workers will want to invest in a signal, such as education, to convey their productivity to employers. Assume that workers can decide to invest in a given level of education, e. You can think of this as workers deciding whether to get a high school diploma, a bachelor's degree, or any other degree or certification. Any level of education that is observable to employers could act as a signal of productivity, and since degrees are more easily observed than years of education, we typically think of the signaling value of specific educational degrees or credentials.

The core assumption of this model also is shown in Table 5.1: The cost of obtaining education level e is inversely related to a worker's productivity. This is a reasonable assumption, as more productive workers are likely to be able to complete schoolwork more easily, may have better study skills, and tend to be more interested in academic learning. Additional schooling therefore is less costly for them than for less productive workers because of these differences in implicit costs, even though the direct tuition cost does not vary across worker types. More specifically, in this model, type L workers face a cost c of obtaining degree e, while type H workers face cost $\frac{c}{2}$ of obtaining the same degree. These cost differences are important because the lower cost faced by the higher-productivity worker can generate circumstances in which *only* type H workers will invest in e. In such a case, degree e will act as a signal through which employers can distinguish between type L and type H workers.

5.3 Signaling Model Equilibrium

How can educational degrees be used by employers to tell who is a highly productive worker and who is a less productive worker? To answer this question, we introduce the concept of a **signaling equilibrium**. Figure 5.1 illustrates the components of a signaling equilibrium. This can be thought of as a set of employer beliefs about how productivity and e are related that are reinforced through the wage structure the employer sets as a result of these beliefs and through the resulting investment decisions made by workers.

signaling equilibrium When employers' beliefs about the relationship between worker productivity and a signal are true. In turn, wages reflect the expected value of productivity among workers who invest in the signal. A signaling equilibrium exists when the productivity of workers who invest in a given signal matches the initial beliefs of the employer about the productivity of these employees.

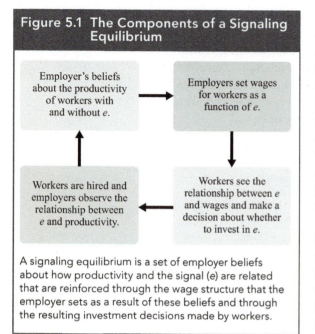

Figure 5.1 The Components of a Signaling Equilibrium

Employer's beliefs about the productivity of workers with and without e.

Employers set wages for workers as a function of e.

Workers see the relationship between e and wages and make a decision about whether to invest in e.

Workers are hired and employers observe the relationship between e and productivity.

A signaling equilibrium is a set of employer beliefs about how productivity and the signal (e) are related that are reinforced through the wage structure that the employer sets as a result of these beliefs and through the resulting investment decisions made by workers.

Let us start with employer's beliefs: Employers begin with some belief about the productivity of workers with and without e. In this model, it does not matter where these beliefs come from, but they likely are informed by employers' past experiences in the labor market. Once the employer has these beliefs, she uses them to set wages that can differ as a function of e. For example, if the employer believes that all workers with degree e are type H and all workers without e are type L, she will set wages equal to 2 for those with e and to 1 for those without. Alternatively, the employer may believe that e is unrelated to productivity, in which case she will set wages equal to $2 - p$ for all workers regardless of whether they have this degree.

The wage structure, combined with the cost of investing in e, will drive workers' decisions about whether or not to obtain this degree. The beliefs of the employer set the returns to the investment in degree attainment, and a worker will compare these returns with the cost and invest in e if the benefit exceeds the cost. The worker's decision is identical to the decision in the human capital model: invest in education if the benefit exceeds the cost. From a worker's perspective, it is not clear that education is acting only as a signal of productivity. All the worker sees is that there is some wage return to obtaining education credential e, and he compares this return with the cost of the investment. To the worker, investment decisions in the human capital and signaling models are virtually identical.

The final step is that workers are hired at the wage rates the employer sets, and now the employer gets to observe the relationship between e and the productivity of workers. The underpinning of the signaling equilibrium is that employers must never observe a relationship between e and productivity that deviates from their beliefs. If they believe all workers who obtain education level e are highly productive and thus offer them a wage of 2, workers must make investment decisions based on this such that only type H workers obtain e. The employer then will observe that workers with e are indeed more productive, which confirms her initial beliefs. This is very similar to the situation described at the beginning of this chapter. When you were hiring workers for your firm, you believed that college graduates were more productive and so paid them more. This wage structure, combined with the cost of education, induced only more productive workers to invest in college, and your beliefs turned out to be self-reinforcing. These self-reinforcing beliefs are the defining characteristics of a signaling equilibrium.

Conversely, if the employer believes that all workers with e are type H, but type L workers also invest in e, then the average productivity of those with e will be less than 2. The employer will see this and her initial beliefs thus will not be confirmed. This is an example of employer beliefs that do not generate a signaling equilibrium.

Separating Equilibrium

Now that we have a definition of a signaling equilibrium, we want to know under what conditions education can be used as a mechanism for employers to distinguish between type L and type H workers. We want to know when e can be used as a signal of productivity that will allow employers and workers to overcome the information asymmetry in this labor market. We are looking for a **separating equilibrium**, in which type L and type H workers can be correctly distinguished from one another by employers.

In a separating equilibrium, e acts as a signal of productivity that allows employers to tell the worker types apart. We need to find a set of employer beliefs and education costs such that only type H workers and no type L workers will obtain e. Recall that in any signaling equilibrium, employer beliefs must be self-reinforcing. In a separating equilibrium, employers must believe that workers with education level e are type H with probability 1 and that workers without education level e are type L with probability 1. With these beliefs, employers will pay workers with e a wage of 2 and will pay workers without e a wage of 1.

For these beliefs to be self-reinforcing, only type H workers should obtain e. Type H workers will invest in e when the benefits of doing so outweigh the costs. The cost of obtaining e is $\frac{c}{2}$, and the benefit is 2. If the worker does not invest in e, he gets a wage of 1. This setup leads to a series of **incentive compatibility constraints** that ensure workers will not invest in the signal unless the benefit outweighs the cost. Type H workers will invest in e when:

$$1 < 2 - \frac{c}{2} \Rightarrow c < 2$$

This equation states that type H workers will invest in e if the net return $\left(2 - \frac{c}{2}\right)$ is larger than the wage he would have received without the signal (1). The algebra shows that as long as the cost is less than 2, type H workers will find it beneficial to obtain education level e.

Type L workers will not invest in e when the cost of investment is sufficiently large to make them better off without the degree. In this case, a type L worker will not obtain e as long as:

$$1 > 2 - c \Rightarrow c > 1$$

As with the decision of type H workers, this equation states that type L workers will not invest in e if the net cost of obtaining e $(2 - c)$ is larger than the wage the worker receives without e. As long as $c > 1$, this is the case and type L workers will not invest in e.

Combining these two equations, we see that type L workers will not obtain e when $c > 1$ and type H workers will invest in e as long as $c < 2$. For any c between 1 and 2, type L workers will not obtain e and type H workers will obtain e. If c is in this range, employers will see that workers with e have a productivity level of 2 and workers without e have a productivity level of 1, which reinforces their initial beliefs. These costs and employer beliefs therefore support a separating equilibrium.

The separating equilibrium is shown in Figure 5.2, where wages below education level e are 1, and wages for education levels above e are 2. The cost of education for type L workers is higher than for type H workers, represented by a steeper slope of the cost curve. Figure 5.2 shows the same outcome as the algebra: for c between 1 and 2, education level e will be too costly for type L workers but will pass a cost benefit test

separating equilibrium A signaling equilibrium in which workers of different productivity levels obtain different schooling amounts and thus get paid different wages.

incentive compatibility constraints A set of conditions that ensure workers will only behave in such a way that maximizes their net benefit. In terms of the signaling model, this means they will not invest in a signal unless the benefit of the investment outweighs the cost.

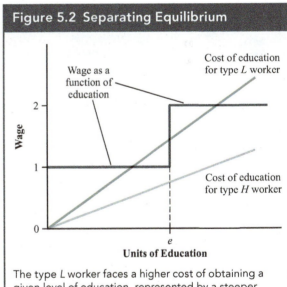

Figure 5.2 Separating Equilibrium

Cost of education for type L worker

Wage as a function of education

Cost of education for type H worker

Wage

2

1

0

e

Units of Education

The type L worker faces a higher cost of obtaining a given level of education, represented by a steeper slope of the cost curve. For c between 1 and 2, education level e will be too costly for type L workers but will be cost-beneficial for type H workers. Type L workers will not obtain e but type H workers will, thus generating a separating equilibrium.

for type H workers. As a result, type L workers will not obtain e and type H workers will, thus generating a separating equilibrium.

Pooling Equilibrium

pooling equilibrium A signaling equilibrium in which all workers invest identically in the signal and therefore are paid identical wages.

The other type of equilibrium that can come out of a signaling model is one in which all workers obtain the same level of education. This is called a **pooling equilibrium**, because unlike with the separating equilibrium, the workers are pooled together.

> **Quick Hint:** Sometimes, people use the terms "separating equilibrium" and "signaling equilibrium" interchangeably. This can be confusing, because technically a pooling equilibrium also is a type of a signaling equilibrium. We will maintain the distinction between these two types of signaling equilibria throughout this book.

There are two types of pooling equilibria: one in which all workers obtain e and one in which no worker obtains e. Let us consider the former first. If employers believe that workers without e are of type L with probability 1 and that workers who obtain e are type L with probability p and are type H with probability $1 - p$, then they will pay $1 \times p + 2 \times (1 - p) = 2 - p$ to those with e and will pay a wage of 1 to workers without e. Type L workers will invest in e if:

$$2 - p - c > 1 \Rightarrow c < 1 - p$$

Type H workers will invest in e if:

$$2 - p - \frac{c}{2} > 1 \Rightarrow c < 2(1 - p) < 1 - p$$

Figure 5.3 Pooling Equilibrium in Which Everyone Obtains the Signal

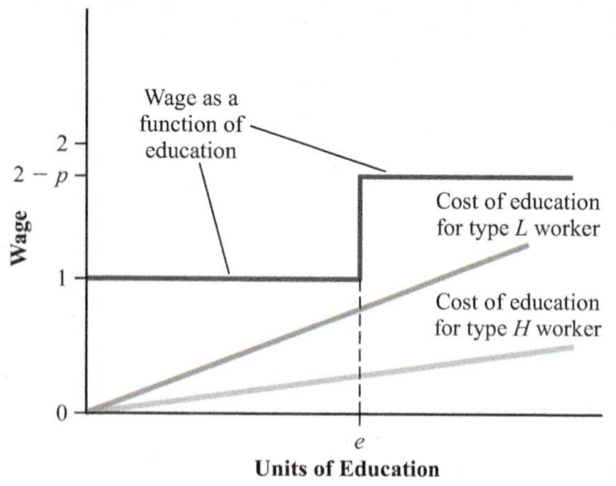

The type L worker faces a higher cost of obtaining a given level of education, represented by a steeper slope of the cost curve. For $c < 1 - p$, the cost of the signal is sufficiently low that both types will invest in education level e, generating a pooling equilibrium.

As long as $c < 1 - p$, both type L and type H workers will obtain education level e. This is shown in Figure 5.3: The cost of obtaining e is sufficiently low for both workers relative to the payoff that both workers find it cost-beneficial to obtain e. As p is the proportion of the population that is a type L worker, this means that the cost needed to support a pooling equilibrium in which all workers obtain the degree is falling with respect to the low-productivity proportion of the workforce. If most of the workforce is composed of less productive types, there will be a pooling equilibrium only if the degree is very inexpensive.

This type of pooling equilibrium may seem odd, but there are some real-world situations that this model can describe well. One example is master's degrees (MA) among K–12 teachers. Most teacher contracts include a salary increase for those with an MA degree. This has led to a rise in low-cost MA degrees for teachers, and a large portion of teachers obtain these degrees. The evidence to date (covered in Chapter 9) suggests there is no correlation between having a master's degree and teacher productivity, which is consistent with a pooling equilibrium model in which virtually all employees obtain the signal.

There also can be a pooling equilibrium in which no one invests in the degree. If employers believe workers with e are type H with probability 1 and that those without e are type L with probability p and are type H with probability $(1 - p)$, then they will pay $2 - p$ to those without e and will pay a wage of 2 to workers with e. Type L workers will not invest in e if:

$$2 - c < 2 - p \Rightarrow c > p$$

Type H workers will not obtain e as long as:

$$2 - \frac{c}{2} < 2 - p \Rightarrow c > 2p$$

As long as $c > 2p$, no one will obtain e and the employer will never observe information to overturn his initial beliefs. This is a pooling equilibrium in which no one obtains the degree because it is too expensive. From a policy perspective, this pooling equilibrium is important because it highlights the potential problems caused by high costs of obtaining the signal. If costs rise sufficiently, neither type of worker finds it beneficial to invest in e, which renders the degree an ineffective signal with which to separate high- and low-productivity workers.

5.4 Signals and Indices

Spence's original formulation of the signaling model highlights the critical distinction between signals and indices. As discussed earlier, a signal is a malleable characteristic that workers can choose to invest in or not, such as education or wearing a suit to an interview. In contrast, an **index** is a characteristic of workers that is immutable. The prime examples of indices are gender and race. These are extremely difficult, if impossible, for workers to change, and they thus cannot act as signals.[2]

This does not mean that factors like race, ethnicity, and gender are not important worker characteristics for labor market outcomes. In fact, the large literature on and policy responses to male–female as well as Black–White and Hispanic–White pay gaps suggest quite the opposite. An important insight of the Spence signaling model is that employers can have different beliefs about the relationship between a signal and worker productivity conditional on an index. That is, employer beliefs can differ by gender, race, ethnicity, eye color, height, or any other immutable worker attribute.

To see why this is important, consider a situation in which all workers are from either group A or group B, where the group type is an index. Within each group, type L and type H workers are represented in the same proportion. One might think that since the workers are of identical productivity in the two groups, they will have the same wage structure. This will not be true if employers do not have similar beliefs for group A and B workers.

index A worker characteristic that cannot be changed, such as race/ethnicity or gender. An index is distinguished from a signal by the fact that workers can obtain a given signal by investing in it, while an index cannot be changed.

[2] The potential correlation of index characteristics with individual characteristics that are difficult to observe is a particular challenge for employers. A concern is that employers may use group membership or the index characteristics to make inferences about individual productivity. This problem of asymmetric information generates statistical discrimination in which an employer infers something about an individual's productivity based on the average productivity of the group to which the employee belongs.

As an example, consider that for group A workers, employers believe that a worker with signal e is type H with probability 1 and without e is type L with probability 1. For group B workers, employers believe that those without e are type L with probability p and type H with probability $(1 - p)$. These sets of beliefs about group A and group B correspond to the separating equilibrium and the pooling equilibrium in which no worker obtains the signal, respectively. If $c > 2p$ and $1 < c < 2$, group B workers will get less education and will have lower wages than group A workers. Even though the groups are identical in terms of average skills and the costs of education they face, different employer beliefs change their return to investing in the signal. Such beliefs can generate low investments in education for different groups that will lead to lower wages for a given educational credential even as the average wages for group A and group B are the same. If a signal provides different information to employers for various groups (such as by race), there will be differences across groups in the incentives to invest in degree attainment.

5.5 The Importance of Distinguishing Between the Human Capital and Signaling Models

Now that you have been introduced to the signaling and human capital models, it is important to consider whether the distinctions between these models matter for policy as well as how one might tell from the data which model is a more accurate description of how the returns to education operate. We emphasize the fact that these models are not mutually exclusive: There can be aspects of education that accord more closely with the signaling model and features that are better described by human capital theory. For education policy, the distinction between these models and their applications is critical, as they have vastly different implications for the benefits of education to society and for the public investment in educational institutions.

There are two main reasons why distinguishing between the human capital and signaling models is important for education policy:

1. In the signaling model, all returns are private. In the human capital model, some of the returns to education can be experienced by society at large.
2. Under the human capital model, it matters how we produce knowledge and skills through education, while under the signaling model it does not.

The Private and Social Returns to Education

Externalities in Education Thus far in this book, we have focused exclusively on the **private return to education**. As suggested by the name, the private returns are the benefits of investment in education that flow only to the individuals making the investment. In economics, we typically measure the private returns to education through subsequent labor market wages or earnings, although there likely are other private returns not captured by wages (such as individual fulfillment from learning). While from the point of view of the individual the private returns are the most important to consider when making an educational investment, there may be other important outcomes that accrue to society at large from having a more educated citizenry. These are termed the **social returns to education**.

private return to education The return on an education investment that accrues only to the individual.

social returns to education The returns on an individual's education investment that go to society at large rather than to the individual herself.

The social benefits of education stem from the fact that education can produce spillovers, or externalities. Externalities describe a situation in which individual decisions indirectly affect the well-being of other people in the economy. A classic example of an externality is pollution. When you decide to turn on a light switch or drive a car, the energy used generates pollution. This pollution affects other people in the society who did not benefit from the light or from the car travel. Pollution is an example of a negative externality, but externalities can be positive as well. Planting a tree can generate positive externalities: The benefits of the tree are felt among many more agents than the planter.

Externalities can lead to market inefficiencies because the public costs or benefits are not accounted for when individuals make decisions. In terms of pollution, the cost of a unit of energy, say the price of a gallon of gas, typically does not include the negative externality associated with the harm that burning that gasoline will cause to others. Thus, the private cost of gasoline is lower than the social cost, and as a result people consume too much gasoline. Society could be made better off if the price was raised and gasoline consumption was reduced. This creates scope for government intervention in the form of taxes to lower consumption of a good that has a negative externality associated with it. Conversely, the government should subsidize goods that create a positive externality, as people will consume too little of it at prevailing market prices.

> **Quick Hint:** A tax or subsidy that alters prices to undo an externality is said to be a Pigouvian tax or subsidy, after the English economist Arthur Pigou, who developed the theoretical basis for such government interventions.

It is often argued, even as evidence is limited, that education creates positive externalities by supporting a better-functioning democracy, lowering crime rates, and producing a healthier populace. In addition, education can lead to more innovation and economic growth, which can generate higher levels of productivity and a higher standard of living nationwide. The claims that education has broad benefits to society are widespread and have been made over many years by philosophers and presidents alike:

All who have meditated on the art of governing mankind have been convinced that the fate of empires depends on the education of youth.—Aristotle

Whenever the people are well informed, they can be trusted with their own government; that whenever things get so far wrong as to attract their notice, they may be relied on to set them to rights.—Thomas Jefferson

A popular Government without popular information or the means of acquiring it, is but a Prologue to a Farce or a Tragedy; or, perhaps both. Knowledge will forever govern ignorance: And a people who mean to be their own Governors, must arm themselves with the power which knowledge gives.—James Madison

Let us think of education as the means of developing our greatest abilities, because in each of us there is a private hope and dream which, fulfilled, can be translated into benefit for everyone and greater strength for our nation. —John F. Kennedy

Figure 5.4 The Marginal Private and Social Benefit to Education

The marginal social rate of return (MSRR) is higher at all education levels than the marginal private rate of return (MPRR) because of positive spillovers of education. Individuals will invest in education until the private marginal benefit equals the marginal cost (e_p^*). This will produce too little education, as the amount of education that maximizes social welfare is e_s^*.

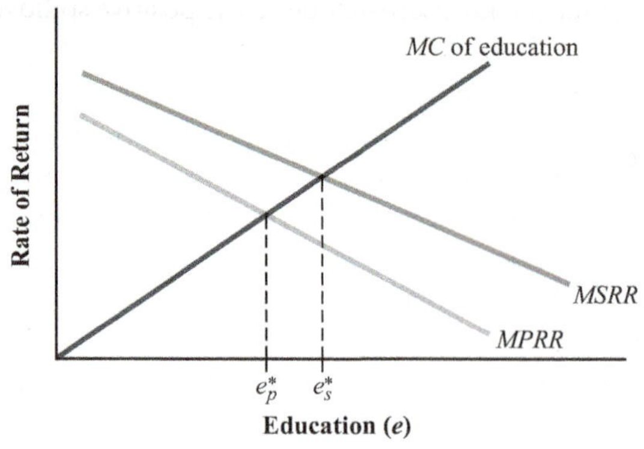

marginal social rate of return (MSRR) The rate of return to an individual's education investment that accrues to society at large. The MSRR depends on both the private and social returns to education.

An individual's decision to invest in education may confer benefits (or costs) on others not involved in the schooling decision. The return for society of an individual making an education investment is the **marginal social rate of return (MSRR)**. The MSRR depends on both the private and the social returns to education. Figure 5.4 shows an *MSRR* curve—it has a downward slope that reflects the diminishing marginal returns to expenditures on education. It is located above the private rate of return schedule; at any education level, the marginal social rate of return is at least as large as the private rate of return. With government education subsidies, the reverse could be true and the private rate of return would be larger than the social rate of return. This results when the government provides too large a subsidy to the education system, which makes education too inexpensive and causes individuals to overinvest.

An important implication of Figure 5.4 is that when there are positive social returns to education, the competitive marketplace will not yield the socially efficient outcome. The marginal social benefit will not be equal to the marginal social cost. This inefficiency occurs because individuals make schooling decisions without considering the marginal social returns; they consider only the private returns. As a result, individuals will obtain too little education on average, and the aggregate well-being of the society will be lower than if e_s^* were achieved. If the social returns to education are large, meaning if education produces large positive spillovers to society, classical economic theory suggests a potentially important role for public policy and government intervention to raise schooling to the level that equates the marginal social cost to the marginal social benefit.

The Social Returns to Education in the Human Capital and Signaling Models Why are the social returns to education important for detailing the differences between the human capital and signaling models? First, both models have the same implications for private returns to students. In each model, students invest in more education if the private benefits exceed the cost, and those who obtain more education earn more in the labor market. The same is not true for the social returns: A core distinction between the human capital and signaling models is that *all* of the returns in the signaling model are private, while in the human capital model there can be both private and social returns to education.

In the human capital model, education can have potentially large social benefits that stem from the fact that schooling increases an individual's skills and talents. The social benefits of education are due to the positive spillovers of those skills and talents to society at large. For example, learning computer skills might lead to technological innovations (such as the Internet) that increase the productivity and welfare of many members of society. Human capital acquired through schooling also may help individuals stay healthier throughout their lives, which both raises their productive capacity and reduces strain on the health care system. Additionally, the knowledge learned through the education system may lead citizens to be more civically involved and to elect representatives that produce more effective public policies. These outcomes all benefit society at large, not just the individuals making the given education decision. The human capital model suggests there could be large positive externalities from education, which would support government interventions in education to help generate socially optimal education investment.

In contrast, under the signaling model there need not be any social benefit to education at all. In fact, education is socially *inefficient* in the signaling model: It imposes costs on those who obtain an education credential to achieve a separating equilibrium. Unlike in the human capital model, schooling does not alter one's productive capacity. Degree attainment only provides information about productivity; it does not make anyone more productive.[3] To see the social inefficiency in the signaling model, consider the costs that support a separating equilibrium. As shown in Section 5.3, there is a separating equilibrium if $1 < c < 2$, so any cost between 1 and 2 will generate this equilibrium.

Now consider the well-being of type H individuals (i.e., those investing in e) within the signaling model. As c increases from 1 to 2, their behavior does not change, nor does their wage. The only thing that changes is that their net payoff to education, $2 - \frac{c}{2}$, declines. One can think of this as a tax paid by type H workers to achieve the separating equilibrium. It is privately worth it for them to obtain e, but as c rises between 1 and 2, they become worse and worse off because of this tax. However, no one in this model reaps the benefit of this tax. Unlike normal taxes, such as sales taxes or income taxes, this tax is not acting as a transfer to other people; these resources are just thrown away. This is the source of the inefficiency. If we had a benevolent and omniscient dictator, she could tell the employers who the type L and type H workers were, each would earn wages equal to their marginal products as in the separating equilibrium, and each type H worker would save $\frac{c}{2}$. We have no such ruler, of course, and because in the signaling model education does not influence an individual's productivity and acts only as a cost, it is socially inefficient.

Quick Hint: Economists term the resources lost from inefficiencies brought about by the tax system "deadweight loss."

---

[3] As discussed in an influential paper by Joseph Stiglitz (1975), if there are multiple types of worker skill, then, even in a signaling model, education could be socially beneficial by providing information to workers about what skills they possess. For example, someone may learn she has good problem-solving skills or is a good writer by investing more in education, even if the education does not build these skills. This can help better match the worker to a job, making her more productive and raising aggregate productivity. A distinction between *screening* and *signaling* is that in the former case it is the student (worker) who lacks information about his or her true productivity, while in the latter case it is the employer (firm) that has incomplete information.

The differences between these models in terms of total social well-being is illustrated in Figure 5.5. The figure shows the aggregate well-being (i.e., total utility of all members of society) with and without an education system under both models. The left two columns show the effect of the education system on well-being under the human capital model. Education increases well-being, which is a combination of the private and social returns to education. Consistent with the evidence, the private returns are larger than the social returns. The right two bars show the same comparison under the signaling model with a separating equilibrium. Here, there are no social returns, and the cost of the education investment leads to lower well-being than if there were no education system at all. The reason is that under the separating equilibrium, the same total amount of wages are earned—$N \times (2 - p)$, where N is the total number of workers—as under the pooling equilibrium without any education system. Now, the type H workers need to pay the signaling cost, making the total net wages earned equal to:

$$N \times \left[1 \times p + \left(2 - \frac{c}{2} \right) \times (1 - p) \right] = N \times \left[(2 - p) - \frac{c}{2} \times (1 - p) \right]$$

The first piece of the right-hand side of this equation is the total amount of wages under the pooling equilibrium $(2 - p)$, but now we must subtract the signal cost $\left(\frac{c}{2} \right)$ for the type H workers, who are the $(1 - p)$ proportion of the population. The difference in the height of the bars for the separating equilibrium in Figure 5.5 reflects the total amount spent on education $\left[N \times (1 - p) \times \left(\frac{c}{2} \right) \right]$. While type H workers are better off under a separating equilibrium, they are worse off than if they could achieve a wage of 2 without having to pay the signaling cost. The result is lower aggregate well-being from the education system in this model.

The human capital and signaling models have different implications for the marginal social benefit of education as well as the level and type of government intervention in education markets. When there may be positive spillovers to education that lead individuals to choose less than the socially optimal level of education, there is a role for public policy to increase education investment. When education serves a signaling role, in contrast, there is no efficiency gain from government efforts to increase educational attainment. Innovations from either the public or private sector that increase social welfare in a signaling model are those that reduce the cost of conveying information about individual skills. It also is possible that improved information about workers' skills can lead to better matching of workers to jobs based on their skill type, however. This can raise aggregate productivity (and thus social welfare) in the economy under both models.

One prominent example of an education policy designed to convey information about individual skills is the *General Education Diploma* (*GED*). The GED is an exam that was first introduced during World War II to provide those veterans who began service before the receipt of a high school degree the opportunity to demonstrate knowledge at the high school level. Veterans could use this certification in the labor market or for enrollment in postsecondary education, avoiding costly

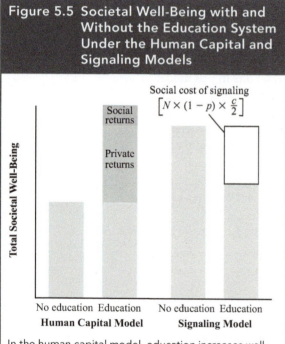

Figure 5.5 Societal Well-Being with and Without the Education System Under the Human Capital and Signaling Models

In the human capital model, education increases well-being as a result of a combination of private and social returns to education; the private returns are larger than the social returns. Under the signaling model with a separating equilibrium, there are no social returns, and the costs of the educational investment lead to lower well-being than if there were no education system at all.

time spent in a high school classroom after military service. Today, the GED has evolved to certify a level of academic achievement intended to parallel that need for high school graduation. Another example is *competency-based learning*, which substitutes skill-based testing for time spent in classes and being enrolled in school. Alternatively, policies might be aimed at reducing signaling costs within the range of costs that generate a separating equilibrium.

Despite the importance of understanding whether there are social returns to education over and above the private returns, much research remains to be done on this topic. A well-established empirical fact is that people with more years of education are healthier, more likely to vote, and less likely to commit crimes. These correlations are hardly proof that schooling itself *causes* these improved civic outcomes. It may well be that other factors, including family resources and personal character traits, also determine these outcomes. The research that does exist on the social returns to schooling as well as the problems associated with isolating the causal role of education on society are discussed in Chapter 6.

The Importance of Education Production As a society, we spend a lot of resources trying to understand how best to support student learning and what public policy interventions might be most effective in generating learning outcomes. Under the human capital model, the time and money spent studying these questions are worthwhile investments. While we cover the production of cognitive skills through education in Chapter 7, these questions are irrelevant under the signaling model. For the signaling model to work, education does not necessarily alter one's productivity; rather, it provides information about one's underlying productivity. Much of education policy—and more specifically, economics of education—implicitly assumes that education increases human capital. If not, the resources spent on "bettering" the education process are largely wasted.

As an example of this distinction, consider the instruction you are receiving for this class. It is likely you expended effort to select and enroll in this class based on your interests and the skills you are interested in learning, as well as your perceived quality of the instructor. According to human capital theory, the time and effort you spent on this selection process are well-justified. If your postsecondary degree is simply acting as a signal of your underlying productivity, however, it matters little how proficient your professor is at teaching the class or the specific skills introduced in this class. What matters is the information conveyed to future employers by your very enrollment in and completion of this class as well as the ensuing degree you will earn. To the extent employers believe such information tells them about your capacity as a worker, it will affect the wage the firm offers you.

An important policy implication that comes out of this difference between the two models is that under the signaling model, it would be highly beneficial to develop tests and assessments that provide information to the market. After all, if certain degrees, like an MBA or a high school diploma, are just signals, would it not be better to develop a way to convince the market of your attributes at a lower cost? The human capital model suggests that such tests would do little, since they would not impart skills and knowledge on those who take them. One could interpret the lack of such tests in areas that are most likely to have signaling content as an argument for human capital. That markets have not provided these types of assessments suggests that something about the education system is important for driving productivity differences across workers, and human capital is a natural explanation for these differences.

This discussion further illustrates that the human capital and signaling models are both relevant but for different aspects of the education system. The question should not be, "Which model is correct?", but rather, "Which model is more relevant for understanding a specific part of the education system?" For example, completing early grades in which core skills are taught probably increases students' human capital. Professional degrees, like medical school and law school, probably also increase human capital by teaching specific skills and knowledge that have value in the labor market. However, the actual receipt of education credentials, such as a high school diploma or a bachelor's degree, may have considerable signaling value that is unrelated to any human capital acquired during the course of one's education. The relevance of both of these models for our education system is, at base, an empirical question. We now turn to a discussion of the difficulties of distinguishing between these models in the data as well as what current research says about human capital versus signaling.

5.6 Empirical Evidence on Signaling Models

Distinguishing Between Human Capital and Signaling Models

Despite its importance, distinguishing between human capital and signaling models is very difficult. To date, only a small amount of research has attempted to address this question, which underscores the difficulties involved. Think for a moment about how you might disentangle these models. A starting point is to consider the different predictions they make. One problem that arises when undertaking this comparison is that the majority of the predictions these models make are very similar. In particular, both predict that there will be positive wage and earnings returns to obtaining a given degree. Even if we could credibly demonstrate that educational degrees have a positive causal effect on earnings later in life, it does not help us to distinguish between the two models.

As discussed previously, one difference in predictions between the models is in the existence of positive spillovers from more education. Positive spillovers suggest that some human capital acquisition has positive externalities, and existing studies on this question focusing on high school attainment indicates that this is the case (Chapter 6). However, a large caveat is needed for this interpretation. Because education increases earnings in both models, it could be the higher earnings themselves that are generating some of the perceived social returns, such as increased civic participation and lower crime rates. Even this evidence could be consistent with either model.

The most starkly different prediction between the two models is that we should observe students' skills increasing with enrollment under the human capital model but not under the signaling model. This is a difficult prediction to test in the data, especially for postsecondary students, because typically datasets do not contain cognitive test scores for people who are enrolled in college. We do have many datasets that contain such tests for younger students, but it is challenging to isolate the role of the school from the role of students' other background characteristics. Existing evidence suggests that some aspects of schools, in particular teachers, have large effects on student achievement. This is consistent with there being an important human capital component to K–12 schooling. No such evidence exists for postsecondary education, largely because of data constraints.

Empirical Evidence

The research to date that can speak directly to the relative importance of the human capital versus signaling models takes two forms. The first is a set of studies that examines the returns to a high school degree, measured both by high school diplomas and by GED credentials. These papers estimate the signaling value of a high school degree by examining differences in earnings among students with similar levels of human capital but who do and do not earn these degrees. Human capital is ostensibly held constant, so any difference in earnings reflects the signaling value of the degree. Although this strategy is compelling, only a few papers use it because of the difficulty of finding any variation in degree receipt that is unrelated to students' underlying abilities.

DEEP DIVE: Estimating the Labor Market Signaling Value of a GED

To determine whether there is signaling value to a given education credential, it is necessary to find variation in receipt of the credential that is unrelated to variation in human capital. This is an extremely difficult endeavor because students who have different levels of educational attainment usually differ in terms of their underlying skill levels. A seminal economics of education paper that investigates the labor market signaling hypothesis and attempts to overcome this problem is by Tyler, Murnane, and Willet (2000). They examine the signaling value of the GED credential—a comprehensive test that enables high school dropouts to obtain an education credential that is intended to be equivalent to a traditional high school diploma.

The insight of Tyler, Murnane, and Willet is to exploit the fact that although the GED Testing Service sets a national minimum passing score, each state is allowed to impose higher standards than this minimum. The GED consists of a battery of subject-specific tests, and passing is determined by both the minimum score and the average score across subjects. These differences across states generate variation in GED receipt between students who obtained the same GED test score.

The empirical method consists of comparing the labor market earnings of individuals who attempted the GED in states with low passing requirements to individuals *with the same GED score* in states with more stringent passing requirements. Although these individuals have identical skills as measured by the GED score, individuals from states with high passing standards (the control group) will not receive the GED credential, while those from states with less stringent passing requirements (the treatment group) will receive it. By exploiting the structure of the GED in an innovative way, the authors are able to net out any potential human capital effects associated with the GED and isolate the signaling effect of the GED credential.

Another problem facing this study is that there may be permanent earnings differences across states that are correlated with passing standards. For example, it may be the case that earnings are higher in more stringent states than in less stringent states, which would bias the cross-state comparison. To overcome this concern, the study employs a difference-in-differences approach, where the earnings of those with test scores above the threshold in even the most stringent state are used as a control group. The authors estimate how the difference in earnings between high- and medium-scoring students varies across states according to whether the medium-scoring students would pass the GED threshold in their state. By taking the difference of these differences, the authors can eliminate the bias induced by permanent earnings differences between the two groups. The central assumption underlying this analysis is that earnings for high-scoring students accurately characterize fixed labor market differences across states faced by lower-scoring students.

To perform this analysis, the authors rely on administrative data from the GED Testing Service and the state education agencies from 1990, as well as taxable earnings data from the Social Security Administration between 1988 and 1995. They find that the labor market signal induced by the GED credential raises the earnings of White dropouts by 10–19% but does not affect the earnings of minority populations. The authors speculate that the latter result could be driven by the fact that a significantly larger proportion of the minority dropouts that attempted the GED did so while being incarcerated, something that may depress the earnings of minority GED recipients. At least for White students, the results from this study suggest a sizable signaling value to the GED.

The value of the GED estimated by Tyler, Murnane, and Willett is measured relative to students with no GED and no high school diploma. Evidence on the relative earnings value of the GED versus a traditional high school diploma suggests traditional high school diplomas have much larger impacts on subsequent wages (Cameron & Heckman, 1993; Heckman & LaFontaine, 2006). The difference in returns to a GED versus a traditional diploma could itself be interpreted as evidence for the human capital model, which may be one reason high schools have not been completely replaced by GED exams.

DEEP DIVE: Estimating the Labor Market Signaling Value of a High School Diploma

The signaling value of obtaining a high school credential has received much attention by researchers. As with all signaling studies, the main difficulty is in disentangling the signaling value from any human capital accumulation that occurs in high school. One particularly clever study that attempts to solve this problem was completed by economists Damon Clark and Paco Martorell (2014). They implement a regression discontinuity approach induced by high school exit exams, which compares students with the same level of human capital but who differ in terms of whether they receive a high school diploma.

As the name suggests, high school exit exams are high-stakes tests that students must pass to obtain a high school diploma. This study focuses on exams given in eleventh grade in Texas. Clark and Martorell's empirical strategy consists of comparing the earnings of individuals who narrowly pass the exam and obtain a high school diploma with the earnings of students who narrowly fail

the exam and thus do not obtain a diploma. The rationale is that students who narrowly fail the exam should, on average, possess productivity and ability levels identical to those of students who narrowly pass the exam. That they are on either side of the cutoff is driven by randomness in exam outcomes, not underlying differences in human capital. The authors show extensive evidence of this by demonstrating that there are no differences in student characteristics across the exam's passing threshold.

To perform this analysis the authors rely on rich administrative student-level data from Texas (1991–1995) and link this to labor market data on earnings after the high school exit exam. The paper first shows that there is a large effect of exam passage on whether one obtains a high school diploma. Despite the large jump in degree receipt, their analysis shows no change over this threshold in earnings. This finding, illustrated in Figure 5.6, suggests

Figure 5.6 The Signaling Value of a High School Diploma

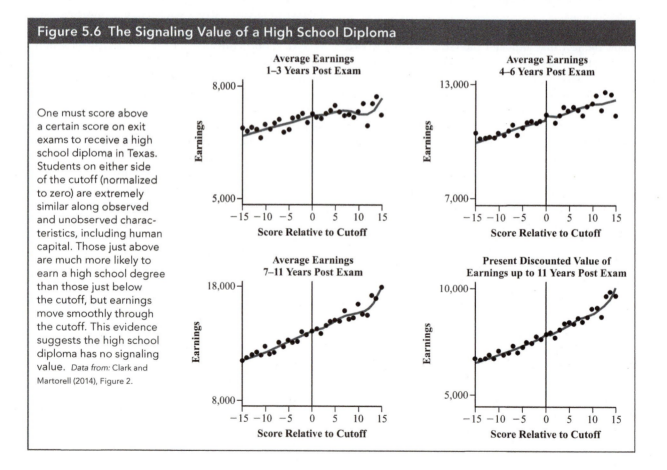

One must score above a certain score on exit exams to receive a high school diploma in Texas. Students on either side of the cutoff (normalized to zero) are extremely similar along observed and unobserved characteristics, including human capital. Those just above are much more likely to earn a high school degree than those just below the cutoff, but earnings move smoothly through the cutoff. This evidence suggests the high school diploma has no signaling value. *Data from:* Clark and Martorell (2014), Figure 2.

that the signaling value of a high school diploma is small at best: There is no jump in earnings across the passing threshold even though there is a jump in diploma receipt. This result stands in contrast to earlier studies that investigated the signaling value of education credentials. These earlier studies may have been unsuccessful in separating the signaling value of education credentials from the productivity differential between individuals with and without a diploma. Although these results suggest that there is no signaling value of a high school diploma, it still is possible that other education credentials (e.g., a bachelor's degree) have signaling value.

See Appendix A for an overview of the Texas administrative data.

Another way researchers have attempted to disentangle the signaling and human capital models is by examining **sheepskin effects**. Sheepskin effects are so named because diplomas were historically printed on sheepskin, and this research examines whether there are larger jumps in earnings for obtaining another year of education that includes a degree than for obtaining another year of education that does not include a degree. For example, sheepskin effects would arise if the wage increase going from completion of one's eleventh to twelfth year of education was much larger than going from completion of one's tenth to eleventh year of education. These nonlinear increases in the relationship between earnings and education for the degree-receipt years are what characterize sheepskin effects.

sheepskin effect The phenomenon that the return to a year of education is higher when that year includes the awarding of a degree or education credential.

It is important to highlight the problems with causality in such research. In their purest form, sheepskin effects are estimated by comparing those who do and do not complete an education credential but who have the same level of human capital. This means, for example, comparing those who take the same number of courses in college, but one student does not "turn in the form" for graduation and the other one does. In practice, there are very few students who do not turn in forms conditional on obtaining all of the credits for graduation.

Sheepskin effects therefore reflect the comparison of earnings among individuals with and without a degree with the same years of educational attainment. We must then consider what type of student drops out so close to graduating, especially if there is a positive return to the degree. Such students might be less productive, they may experience personal shocks that affect their likelihood of completing (such as pregnancy or a sick parent), or they may be less motivated. Furthermore, the differences across such students who do and do not graduate may reflect actual human capital differences: the ability to follow the rules to obtain the correct distributional requirements for graduation, attention to detail, and perseverance. These human capital differences could be what is driving some of the earnings differences across these students, not the signaling value of the degree. Concerns that these differences across students exert an independent influence on earnings underscores the difficulties in establishing causality in this literature.

The preponderance of evidence to date suggests that the earnings jumps after the twelfth and sixteenth years of education are much larger than the increases in any other year (Hungerford & Solon, 1987; Jaeger & Page, 1996). This finding is consistent with the existence of sheepskin effects for high school and college graduation. These findings also suggest some signaling value to these degrees, since one typically does not acquire more human capital in the twelfth and sixteenth years than in other years of education.

DEEP DIVE: Sheepskin Effects in the Returns to Education

One of the first papers to explicitly examine sheepskin effects in the returns to education is by Hungerford and Solon (1987). To investigate whether there are sheepskin effects associated with returns to education, the authors use data on 25- to 64-year-old males from the May 1978 Current Population Survey (CPS). They looked for jumps in returns to education following the school years associated with receiving a credential—years 8, 12, and 16. If individuals are rewarded not only for the human capital gain associated with schooling but also for obtaining the diplomas that come with certain levels of schooling, the economic return associated with completing these diploma years should be higher than that of other years.

Their empirical strategy consists of first estimating the return to each additional year of education by comparing the labor market earnings of individuals with a given amount of education to individuals that left school one year earlier. They then investigate whether the economic return to education associated with going from a prediploma year to a diploma year (e.g., from 11 to 12 years of education) is different from the economic return associated with an additional year of education that does not lead to a diploma (e.g., from 10 to 11 years of education).

This estimation method hinges on the assumption that differences in years of schooling across men in their sample are unrelated to other determinants of labor market earnings. This is a very strong assumption, as individuals with fewer years of schooling may be of lower productivity and/or may be less motivated. If this assumption does not hold, then any observed jump in the return to education at the diploma years may simply reflect a productivity difference between those who chose to drop out and those who graduated.

Another problem encountered by the authors is that they lack information about degree completion, so they are forced to use information on self-reported years of schooling to infer the education credentials of the individuals in the sample. For example, if an individual has completed 12 years of education, the authors treat this individual as a high school graduate. Because degree times may differ across students, the inability to measure degree receipt causes them to understate any sheepskin effects, as shown by a subsequent analysis by Jaeger and Page (1996).

The 1996 study by Jaeger and Page demonstrates that the main diploma years are associated with substantially larger earnings increases than other years. This is illustrated in Figure 5.7, which shows the estimated relationship between each additional year of schooling and earnings changes in percent terms. For example, students who obtain their sixteenth year of schooling earn 33% more than those who only obtain 15 years of schooling. Only the jump in the return to education at year 16 is statistically significantly different from zero. This finding suggests a sizable sheepskin effect of graduating from college.

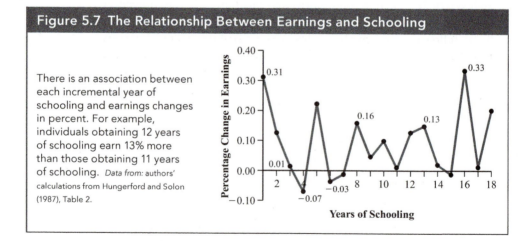

Figure 5.7 The Relationship Between Earnings and Schooling

There is an association between each incremental year of schooling and earnings changes in percent. For example, individuals obtaining 12 years of schooling earn 13% more than those obtaining 11 years of schooling. *Data from:* authors' calculations from Hungerford and Solon (1987), Table 2.

5.7 Conclusion

The signaling model offers an alternative explanation, relative to the human capital model, for how education affects workers' earnings. In the signaling model, employers generate beliefs about how a given level of education (or signal) relates to a worker's productivity, which leads to different wages being offered based on whether a worker has obtained the signal. Of particular interest is the existence of a separating equilibrium, in which high-ability workers obtain the signal and are paid higher wages, while lower-productivity workers do not obtain the signal and are paid lower wages. Unlike the human capital model, in which education makes workers more productive, under the signaling model it simply acts to separate high- and low-productivity workers.

The signaling and human capital models differ markedly in terms of the role of the education system in driving future earnings. In both models, there is a private return to investing in schooling, and indeed a worker cannot tell whether the return is due to learning more skills that are valued by the labor market or whether she is simply signaling productivity. From a policy perspective, this difference is very important because of the possibility of social returns to education as well as the amount of resources spent on developing effective teaching practices.

The human capital and signaling models are not mutually exclusive: Both models likely have some truth to them that operates with varying importance over the different levels of education. In the next chapter, we turn to the evidence on the returns to education, examining it from both a private and a social perspective. This research will shed important light on the relevance of these two models as well as on the private return an individual can expect from making a given education investment.

Highlights

- Labor markets are characterized by **asymmetric information**, as employers have imperfect information about the **marginal product of labor** (productivity) of potential hires. The signaling model explains how education attainment can act as a **signal** and provide information about worker productivity to employers, regardless of the specific knowledge or training acquired during schooling.
- In both the human capital model and signaling model, workers follow their **incentive compatibility constraints** and invest in education if the individual benefit exceeds the cost.
- In the signaling model, a **signaling equilibrium** is characterized by an employer's self-reinforcing beliefs about the relationship between worker productivity and whether the worker has a given signal (e.g., diploma or degree) or not.
- Two kinds of signaling equilibria exist: a **separating equilibrium** and a **pooling equilibrium**. In a separating equilibrium, the higher-productivity worker obtains the education signal and is paid more, while the

lower-productivity worker does not obtain the signal and is paid less. This equilibrium is driven by the fact that the cost of obtaining the signal for the high-productivity worker is lower than the cost for the lower-productivity worker.
- A signal can be altered by workers, while an **index** is a fixed characteristic that cannot be changed, such as race/ethnicity. Employers can have different beliefs about how the productivity of those with and without a signal differs across those with different index characteristics.
- There are important distinctions between the human capital model and the signaling model. Primary among those differences is that the signaling model results in a **private return to education**, whereas the human capital model also allows for **social returns to education**, which are enjoyed by society at large. The social returns are due to **spillovers (externalities)**, and they lead the **marginal social rate of return (MSRR)** from investing in education to be larger than the private rate of return. If there are social returns to education, people will underinvest in

education, which leaves scope for government intervention in education markets.

- While most education policy functions under the assumptions of the human capital model, the signaling model has relevance for various aspects of the education system. Distinguishing which model best explains behaviors in the education system is a critical step in understanding how best to design education policies and institutions. Researchers have attempted to disentangle these models using variations in degree receipt unrelated to human capital and have looked for evidence of **sheepskin effects** that are consistent with a signaling value of educational attainment.

Problems

1. Discuss whether the human capital and signaling models have different implications for each of the following education policies:
   a. Providing financial aid to students for college.
   b. Introducing a test that high school students could take to provide reliable measures of task commitment and capacity to work effectively in teams.
   c. Increasing the age at which students can drop out of high school from 16 to 17.
2. Define the following concepts:
   a. Signaling equilibrium
   b. Separating equilibrium
   c. Pooling equilibrium
   d. Index
3. Explain what the asymmetric information problem is with respect to the hiring of workers. What are *signals*, and how can they help solve this problem?
4. State whether each of the following characteristics is a signal or an index.
   a. Ethnicity
   b. Economics Degree
   c. Wearing a tie to an interview
   d. Height
5. Explain the difference between the private and social returns to schooling. Give two examples of each type of return.
6. In 2014, the federal government spent $30.3 billion on Pell grants. The federal government gives large amounts of financial aid to students to help them afford the cost of a college education. Can this lead to the marginal social rate of return to be below the private rate of return? Explain.
7. The Iron Throne is in debt and lacks the ability to provide subsidies to the residents of Westeros to attend the only college on the continent, the Citadel. Therefore, the people of Westeros have to pay the full tuition cost for enrollment without any type of government support.
   a. The Citadel is the only way to receive medical training in Westeros. Draw the marginal cost curve and the marginal social and private benefit curves for education in this scenario. What is the education market equilibrium, and how does it differ from the socially optimal amount of education?
   b. Many argue that the Citadel does not actually provide valuable medical knowledge and produces few benefits to society. How does this change whether the equilibrium is socially optimal or not?
8. Clark and Martorell (2014) use a regression discontinuity approach to compare students scoring just below the passing score on the high school exit exam to students scoring just above the passing score. They find that students who barely pass the exam are, indeed, much more likely to receive a high school degree, but that the students who "barely pass" the exam do not earn appreciably more than students who "barely fail" the exam.
   a. Why do researchers like Clark and Martorell look at this kind of comparison as a way to measure the signaling role in education?
   b. What are the limitations to this research approach? Should we infer that a high school degree does not have any signaling role?
9. Elves are a mixed bunch—some are inherently good (born on the North Pole) and some are evil (born on the South Pole). The archenemy of Santa Claus, Anti Claus, lives in the South Pole and trains a community of evil elves, helping them procure jobs in Santa's workshop and ruin Christmas. All elves have the reservation option of posing in a

display at the local department store for $25,000 per season.

a. Santa cannot tell the difference between North and South Pole elves when he is hiring them each year because Anti Claus teaches the evil elves to act just like North Pole elves in the interview. To get a job in Santa's workshop, elves must attend a training class for a certain number of weeks (W) prior to the Christmas season. Suppose it costs $10,000 per week for the North Pole elves to attend the class, while the burden of attending class for the South Pole elves is twice as high, owing to the stress and added expense of living a double life. The North Pole elves can make toys valued at $75,000 per season, while the South Pole elves destroy all of the toys they produce. What is the range of weeks of training Santa can require so that the only elves working in his shop are good elves (and thus he would pay them $75,000)?

b. If *all* we observed is that all South Pole elves did not get training and did not work for Santa while all of the North Pole elves were trained and worked for Santa, is this consistent with a human capital story as well? Describe one such human capital story that could produce this outcome.

10. Some dimension of university policy prohibits faculty from charging higher prices to eliminate excess demand for popular courses. Since faculty can't maximize profits, many choose instead to maximize student engagement (E), as there is utility that follows from students who don't snore and laugh at jokes (however bad). Of course, there is a good bit of variation across students in E and faculty can't determine high E students by name, picture or year.

a. Suppose the instructor of an economics of education class wishes to maximize E. Use an economic model to explain why the professor chooses to restrict access to the class based on instructor permission and asks interested students to write an essay rather than allocating spaces on a first come, first serve basis.

b. What would happen if, rather than asking for an essay, students were asked to write 200 pages of publishable research? More generally, write down a model in which the essay requirement was sufficiently onerous to leave unfilled chairs.

11. Suppose that there are two types of employees: Narutos and Sasukes. Employers cannot distinguish between the two types during a job interview, but they value Narutos more because everyone is more productive around them. Assume that the value of a Sasuke-type employee is $10 and the value of a Naruto type is $20. Also assume that the cost of education for a Sasuke is 2.5y and the cost of education for a Naruto is 2y, where y is years of education. If Narutos make up 25% of the population:

a. What is the pooling equilibrium wage?

b. What values of y will lead to a separating equilibrium?

The Returns to Education Investment

Is Investing in Education "Worth It"?

A fundamental concern facing every high school student is the economic return to investing in a college education. Few students likely undertake an explicit analysis of the net present value of attending college, but most students have a sense that there is a positive return to such an investment. If not, they could use their time or money on more productive endeavors. As with all education, the returns to college can be both monetary and nonmonetary. The monetary return typically comes in the form of higher wages throughout one's life, while the nonmonetary returns include the enjoyment of the college experience itself as well as individual enrichment. Just thinking about your own decision, if you knew that the overall return to enrolling in your undergraduate program would be negative, it is doubtful you would have done so.

As college costs have risen steadily for most U.S. households over the past several decades, it has given rise to much policy debate and many opinion articles in newspapers, often focusing on, "Is college worth it?" An online search for this phrase yields hundreds of stories and opinion pieces addressing this question. An article in *The Economist* sums up the focus of these stories well:

> ...there is no simple answer to the question "Is college worth it?" Some degrees pay for themselves; others don't. American schoolkids pondering whether to take on huge student loans are constantly told that college is the gateway to the middle class. The truth is more nuanced...
> *The Economist*, 2014

The concerns many have about the value of a college education surround rising tuition costs and debt faced by college attendees and college graduates. Figure 6.1 shows trends in average tuition among public four-year, private four-year, and public two-year institutions. In all sectors and types of schools, tuition has risen markedly. All four tuition measures have increased by between 270% and 300% between 1980 and 2012 in constant dollars. While such numbers can be misleading because they ignore how financial aid changes the actual amount of tuition that students pay, they highlight the growing cost of college attendance, particularly for those students who do not receive financial aid.

Commensurate with the rise in tuition has been a growth in student debt that has received a great deal of policy attention. Trends in undergraduate student debt are shown in Figure 6.2. Panel A presents trends in accumulated student debt among college graduates per borrower, while panel B shows debt per graduate. Approximately 55% of public university graduates and 65% of private university students have student loan debt. Since data on student debt became available in 1999, there has been about a 30% increase in debt per degree recipient and about a 20–25% increase in debt per borrower. These increases are smaller than the 50–80% rise in tuition over this period, which suggests grant aid and out-of-pocket tuition expenditures also likely have risen in the past decade and a half.

Examining tuition and debt levels among U.S. undergraduates, it is hard not to be concerned that investing in college may no longer be "worth it" for many students. This is indeed a growing focus among policy makers and journalists. In fact, an initiative launched in 2013 by billionaire Peter Thiel provides grants of $100,000 to promising high school students to skip college, with the idea that their time and energy are best spent on other endeavors. The title of a recent book by former U.S. Secretary of Education William Bennett (with David Wilezol), *Is College Worth It? A Former United States Secretary of Education and a Liberal Arts Graduate Expose the Broken Promise of Higher Education*, illustrates clearly the concerns many have over the rising cost of college and growing student debt.

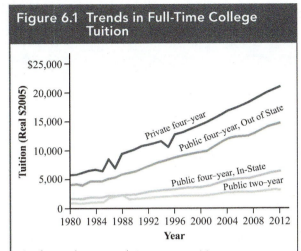

Figure 6.1 Trends in Full-Time College Tuition

The figure shows trends in average tuition among public four-year, private four-year, and public two-year institutions in real 2005 dollars. Tuition has risen in all sectors and types of schools. Four-year school tuition increased by 270–300% between 1980 and 2012 in real dollars, while tuition in two-year schools increased by 271% over this period. Such numbers can be misleading because they ignore financial aid, but they highlight the growing cost of college attendance for students who do not receive financial aid. *Data from: 1980–2012 IPEDS.*

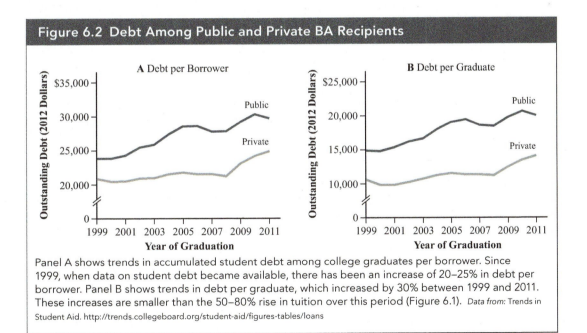

Figure 6.2 Debt Among Public and Private BA Recipients

Panel A shows trends in accumulated student debt among college graduates per borrower. Since 1999, when data on student debt became available, there has been an increase of 20–25% in debt per borrower. Panel B shows trends in debt per graduate, which increased by 30% between 1999 and 2011. These increases are smaller than the 50–80% rise in tuition over this period (Figure 6.1). *Data from: Trends in Student Aid. http://trends.collegeboard.org/student-aid/figures-tables/loans*

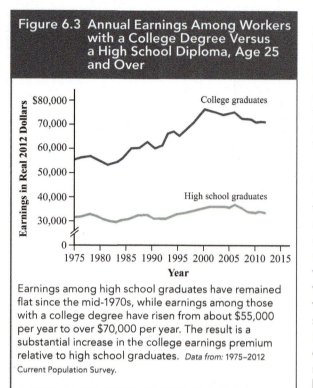

Figure 6.3 Annual Earnings Among Workers with a College Degree Versus a High School Diploma, Age 25 and Over

Earnings among high school graduates have remained flat since the mid-1970s, while earnings among those with a college degree have risen from about $55,000 per year to over $70,000 per year. The result is a substantial increase in the college earnings premium relative to high school graduates. *Data from: 1975–2012 Current Population Survey.*

The claim that the growing cost of college has made it a poor investment decision for students ignores half of the equation: Rising costs of college attendance are only a problem if the returns are not rising as well. In both the human capital and signaling models, students balance the costs and benefits of a given investment in education, and they invest if the marginal benefit is at least as large as the marginal cost. Discussing the cost of higher education without discussing the benefits can be deeply misleading.

Existing evidence suggests that the wage premium associated with college completion is persistently large and growing. Figure 6.3 shows yearly earnings among workers who have a high school diploma only and workers who have a BA. These data clearly indicate that more educated workers earn considerably more in the labor market and that the difference in earnings across workers with different education levels has grown over time. Both the human capital and the signaling model would predict this relationship, but to justify large expenditures on postsecondary training, this relationship must be *causal*. That is, the higher education levels need to cause workers to earn more, either because they are more productive as a result of the education (as in the human capital model) or because education separates the more productive from the less productive workers (as in the signaling model).

The earnings differences in Figure 6.3 pay no attention to education quality, but several studies have shown that wages among workers who attended or graduated from more selective and resource-intensive colleges are much larger than wages among those who attend or graduate from a less selective school.[1] In addition, students who attend primary and secondary schools with higher resource levels tend both to obtain more education and to earn more in the labor market. Not only is the level of educational attainment correlated with earnings, but the quality of that education is as well.

Are these correlations reflective of a causal relationship between education and future earnings? Put differently, is the correlation between education and wages evidence of a positive return to investment in education? The answer is surprisingly tricky to figure out. A serious problem in trying to assess the causal impact of a given educational investment on earnings is that education is not assigned randomly across workers. The human capital and signaling models both make clear that students will choose how much education to obtain based on their perceived returns. This typically leads to the prediction that students who obtain more education are systematically different from those who obtain less education in ways that also should influence earnings. The same argument holds true for education quality: Students who attend higher-quality schools are from backgrounds that suggest they will have higher wages independent of the education they receive.

In the presence of such omitted variables, how can we isolate the causal effect of an educational investment on earnings? Much attention has been paid to this

---

[1] Examples of such studies are Brewer, Eide, and Ehrenberg (1999), Dale and Krueger (2002), Black and Smith (2004), Long (2010), and Andrews, Li, and Lovenheim (2016).

problem among social scientists generally and among economists specifically. Solutions to this problem generally take two forms:

1. Observing sufficient information about students' backgrounds to control for the nonrandom sorting of students to different education levels and schools
2. Finding a natural experiment that generates differences in schooling across individuals that are uncorrelated with students' background characteristics

In this chapter, we first provide an overview of the challenges associated with establishing a causal link between schooling and earnings. While this problem and the associated solutions can become quite technical, the underlying problem is not. How do we account for the fact that students who obtain different levels of education are systematically different from one another? This is one of the fundamental problems faced by economists studying education, going back to the first studies on the returns to education.[2]

After we discuss the challenges to generating causal estimates of education on future earnings, we review the literature on the returns to educational attainment. Our primary focus will be on the private returns (i.e., earnings and wages), but we also discuss research related to the social returns to education that can lend direct insight to the human capital and signaling models. The chapter concludes with a focus on the private returns to college quality as further evidence of the importance of schooling to labor market outcomes.

6.1 The Difficulty of Estimating the Causal Effect of Education on Earnings

Both the human capital and signaling models imply that students choose different education levels based on background characteristics that are likely to be independently valued by the labor market. This selection problem raises serious concerns about whether we can interpret as causal the correlation between education and wages or earnings. We begin with a discussion of how students select different education levels in the human capital model when there is a one-dimensional measure of "ability." When there is a single measure of underlying productivity that differs across students and affects their wages and their education investment decisions, what are the challenges in estimating the returns to schooling? We then turn to a more complicated (and more realistic) scenario in which multiple dimensions of ability make some students more suited for jobs that require schooling and some students more suited for jobs that require less schooling.

Selection When Ability Is One-Dimensional

In Chapter 4, we considered the predictions of the human capital model for Ana and Felix. Ana has more underlying ability than Felix, by which we mean that Ana has skills and abilities that make her a more productive worker. We presented graphical arguments suggesting that Ana will invest in more education than Felix. Here, we formalize this argument to show the biases associated with ability in the human capital model.

---

[2] For early research on the returns to education, see Grilliches (1977) and Willis and Rosen (1979).

Assume that wages are determined only by education (E) and ability (A) and that wages increase with both education and ability. More educated workers earn higher wages, as do higher-ability workers. A serious problem in estimating the returns to education arises when workers of different abilities obtain different education levels. To see this problem, consider again the educational investment decisions of Ana and Felix. Ana has ability A_{Ana}, and Felix has ability A_{Felix}. As discussed previously, $A_{Ana} > A_{Felix}$. Figure 6.4 depicts an example of the optimal education decisions of both Ana and Felix under the assumption that they face the same cost of investing; the formal mathematical solution is shown in the accompanying Toolbox. In the figure, Ana's marginal benefit curve is shifted out relative to Felix's because of her higher ability level. This leads her to obtain more education. In the bottom panel, we see that Ana's wage curve is above Felix's because her higher ability is also valued by the labor market. Ana earns more than Felix *both* because she has higher ability and because she obtains more education.

What is the implication of this scenario for studying the returns to education? Ana has higher wages than Felix, but we cannot interpret this difference as being solely due to differences in education levels between the two. Some of this wage difference reflects their differences in ability as well. This is an example of *ability bias*, as the wage differences across individuals reflect *both* differences in educational investments and differences in underlying ability. In this case, the ability bias will be positive because the higher-ability worker gets more education: The wage difference across the two is larger than the wage difference that would be caused by schooling alone. As a result of this type of selection bias, wage differentials by education level, as in Figure 6.3, may reflect differences in ability across workers that are correlated with education rather than demonstrate the causal effect of education on wages itself. The Toolbox provides a more formal treatment of ability bias.

TOOLBOX: Ability Bias in Estimating the Returns to Education

To obtain a mathematical representation of the ability bias inherent in estimating the returns to education, we first specify a wage equation that shows how wages are related to both education and ability: $W = f(E, A)$. It is highly likely that wages increase both with education and ability, so $f'(E) > 0$ and $f'(A) > 0$. Thus, $f'(E)$ shows the marginal benefit of an extra year of education in terms of wages. To make this example more concrete, assume $W = A\ln(E)$, so the marginal benefit of schooling is $\frac{A}{E}$.

> **Quick Hint:** $f'(E)$ and $f'(A)$ represent the change (or slope) of earnings with respect to education and ability, respectively. Technically, these are the first derivatives of the wage function with respect to education and ability, which is a way of expressing with calculus how one variable changes in terms of another. These expressions thus show how wages change when either education or ability change by a small amount, holding the other fixed. That they are both positive indicates that wages increase with both ability and education.

Now, consider the cost of obtaining an education. For each year of schooling, one must pay a cost (T). This cost includes tuition as well as forgone earnings from enrolling in school rather than being in the labor force. Let's assume that the cost of obtaining schooling level E is given by $C = TE^2$. Education is squared to account for the fact that forgone earnings rise at an increasing rate because remaining out of the labor force is increasingly costly. With this cost function, the marginal cost of an additional year of schooling is $C' = 2TE$.

In economic analyses of consumption, individuals consume optimally when they choose a level of a good that equates the marginal benefit of the good to the marginal cost. The condition for the optimal level of education is set similarly here, so that the optimal level of education, E^*, is determined by setting the marginal benefit equal to the marginal cost of an additional year of schooling:

$$\frac{A}{E} = 2TE$$

$$E^* = \sqrt{\frac{A}{2T}}$$

E^* is found by solving the first row of the equation for E. This equation shows the intuitive finding that optimal education investment should increase with ability and decrease with tuition.

To see the importance of ability bias in estimating the returns to education, consider the case of Ana and Felix. Assuming Ana and Felix face the same education cost:

$$E^*_{Ana} = \sqrt{\frac{A_{Ana}}{2T}} > \sqrt{\frac{A_{Felix}}{2T}} = E^*_{Felix}$$

In other words, Ana will get more education than Felix because she has more ability. The wages of Ana and Felix are:

$$W_{Ana} = f(A_{Ana}, E^*_{Ana}) > f(A_{Felix}, E^*_{Felix}) = W_{Felix}$$

Ana will have higher wages than Felix. Some of this wage difference will reflect their difference in ability and some will reflect their difference in education. This is the scenario shown in Figure 6.4. It demonstrates that raw wage differences across individuals with different levels of education are likely to be biased measures of the causal effect of education on wages.

It is possible for ability bias to be negative as well, which is likely to be the case if the cost of forgone earnings is sufficiently high. To see this result, let's alter the cost function to be $C = TE^2A^2$. Here, costs increase with education, and the cost increases are higher for higher-ability students. The marginal cost curve is $C' = 2TEA^2$. Setting marginal cost equal to marginal benefit, we get the following expression for E^*:

$$\frac{A}{E} = 2TEA^2$$

$$E^* = \sqrt{\frac{1}{2TA}}$$

Comparing the two equations we derived for E^*, we can see that the optimal education level now is decreasing in A.

While Ana and Felix provide a specific example, the fact that ability, education, and earnings are correlated with one another is a feature of virtually all human capital

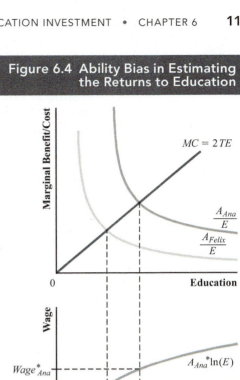

Figure 6.4 Ability Bias in Estimating the Returns to Education

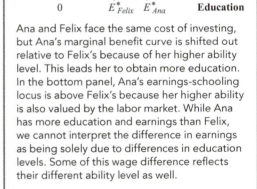

Ana and Felix face the same cost of investing, but Ana's marginal benefit curve is shifted out relative to Felix's because of her higher ability level. This leads her to obtain more education. In the bottom panel, Ana's earnings-schooling locus is above Felix's because her higher ability is also valued by the labor market. While Ana has more education and earnings than Felix, we cannot interpret the difference in earnings as being solely due to differences in education levels. Some of this wage difference reflects their different ability level as well.

models in which individuals face similar costs but in which ability is independently valued by the labor market. As illustrated in the toolbox, the bias from ability can be negative as well. One reason this can happen is forgone earnings. We thus far have assumed that the cost of a year of education did not vary with ability. But, if forgone earnings are higher for high-ability workers, as the wages they are giving up are higher, then ability and education can be negatively correlated.

With negative ability bias, we can no longer predict the difference in wages across workers just from knowing their education and ability levels, since it depends on whether the education differences are large enough to overcome the ability differences. Interpreting such wage differentials as a reflection of education will understate the return to education, as one is comparing a high-ability, less educated person to a low-ability, highly educated person. Especially because ability bias can bias estimates of the return to education in either direction, it is very important to develop empirical strategies that are not prone to such problems.

Selection When Ability Is Multidimensional

Using a single measure of ability is a helpful shortcut that provides much of the intuition behind the difficulty in establishing a causal link between schooling and earnings. However, it clearly is an oversimplification. People differ markedly in their skills, talents, and interests, and these differences might lead them to make different schooling decisions. Consider two people, Anita and Tara. Anita is extremely well suited to academia because she is studious and is interested in focusing for long periods on very specific problems. However, she has poor interpersonal skills and communication skills that would make her a bad fit for other high-skilled professions, such as consulting or management. Tara has strong interpersonal skills, enjoys interacting and working with others, and is a strong communicator, but she does not enjoy focusing on specific tasks and projects for long periods. As a result, Tara obtains a BA and goes into consulting, while Anita earns a PhD and becomes an academic researcher.

Let's think about what we learn from comparing Tara and Anita's earnings. Their education levels are different—Anita has a PhD, while Tara only has a BA—but their interests and skills also differ. Tara and Anita both sort into the education levels and professions that suit their individual talents. Neither has *higher* "ability." Rather, they have *different* abilities. Anita could not earn what Tara does if she went into consulting (as she would not be a good consultant), and Tara would not be a very productive researcher. Comparing their earnings and calling this the return to a PhD would be highly misleading.

That individuals have different skills and talents which can lead them to make different decisions about their education and professions was first discussed by Roy (1951) and is commonly referred to as the Roy model. We discuss the Roy model in more detail in Chapter 12, when we examine the decision to become a teacher, but the insights of this model are very important in considering how to interpret wage differences across workers. If workers sort into different occupations that require different education levels based on their individual abilities, then wage differences will reflect both these abilities and the education differences. This type of multidimensional ability bias typically will lead education to appear more important than it actually is in driving wage differences across workers, since much of the differences will reflect the fact that workers are sorting into the jobs that they are best suited for.

6.2 Empirical Evidence on the Private Returns to Educational Attainment

The Mincer Equation

One of the first and most important contributions to how economists think about the returns to schooling comes from economist Jacob Mincer (1958, 1974). Mincer derived his estimating equation of the relationship between wages and schooling by considering the optimal investment in schooling. Individuals invest in education early in their lives and then reap the benefits of this investment throughout their working careers; this observation is reflected in Becker's human capital model (1964) and in Mincer's work.[3] The core difference between these models is that in Mincer's model, individuals can continue to invest in human capital after formal schooling ends. This investment is called **on-the-job training**. Mincer's theoretical model yields a very simple estimating equation for the relationship between schooling, earnings, and work experience, which often is called the **human capital earnings function**:

$$Ln(Y) = \beta_0 + \beta_1 S + \beta_2 Exp + \beta_3 Exp^2 + U$$

In this equation, Y is earnings, S is years of education, Exp is the number of years since completion of formal schooling, and finally, U is a statistical error term. The Exp term often is referred to as *potential experience* because it measures the number of postschooling years a person could be working. This is a log-linear model that can be simply estimated using linear regression techniques.

> **Quick Hint:** The function $Ln()$ is the natural logarithm (or natural log), which is the inverse of the exponential function (e). Thus, if $x = e^z$, then $ln(x) = z$.

on-the-job training Employer-provided training that occurs while workers are employed and that increases worker skills.

human capital earnings function An equation that relates how earnings change with respect to years of schooling and work experience.

The *Mincer model* predicts that log earnings should increase linearly with education, which is akin to assuming that years of education have a linear effect on the percentage change in wages. This is represented by the parameter β_1, which shows the returns to another year of education. Since its inception, literally thousands of "Mincer regressions" have been estimated on data in almost every country throughout the world. Despite its simplicity, the Mincer regression remains the benchmark for how economists approach the economic returns to schooling. Estimation of Mincer regressions on U.S. Census data for Whites produces estimates of β_1 between 10% and 12%, depending on the census year. For Blacks, the estimates range from 9–15% and have grown dramatically over time.[4]

Two main issues arise in the Mincer model. The first is that it assumes a linear relationship between schooling and log earnings. As we saw in Chapter 5, this assumption may not fit very well with the data. With sheepskin effects, earnings tend to increase more when the year of education obtained includes a degree (such as a high school diploma or a BA). Hence, an additional year of education has different effects on earnings depending on the education level. This problem is present

---

[3] Also see Ben-Porath (1967) for a dynamic human capital investment model in which individuals make repeated schooling decisions throughout multiple periods of their life.

[4] Heckman, Lochner, and Todd (2006) and Lemieux (2006) provide detailed reviews of Mincer earnings functions.

in all estimates of the return to education that do not allow the effect of schooling to differ by the level of schooling obtained.

The second important issue with the Mincer equation is the extent to which we can interpret β_1 as a causal estimate of education on earnings. Does the estimate of β_1 show us how increasing education by one year will lead to a change in wages, or does it just reflect a correlation between education and wages that is influenced by other, unobserved, factors (like ability)? Estimates of β_1 from the Mincer model only isolate the causal effect of education on earnings if there are no other variables correlated with both schooling and earnings.[5] In the prior section, we discussed how student ability probably is correlated with both outcomes. It is likely β_1 is going to be biased if student ability is not accounted for, and this bias can be in either direction. The modern approaches to estimating the causal effect of education on earnings are highly focused on overcoming this concern.

Modern Approaches to Estimating the Private Returns to Schooling

A large body of research in economics has focused on trying to isolate the causal effect of education on earnings in a way that attempts to overcome ability bias or selection bias more generally. This research has varied widely in the methods used, the time periods studied, and the level of education analyzed. Most studies find that a year of schooling increases yearly wages or earnings by 6–12%. These estimates are surprisingly similar to those from the Mincer model.

To estimate the causal effect of education on earnings, it would be ideal to run an experiment in which we randomly assign some people to receive more education and assign some to receive less. This is likely to be highly morally objectionable, and it would be almost impossible to implement unless one could compel those in the control group not to invest in more education. As a result, we cannot rely on randomized experiments to estimate how education affects earnings.

Moving away from the experimental ideal, three main methods have been used to estimate the causal effect of education on wages or earnings:[6]

1. Use a dataset with detailed information on student background characteristics that can potentially control for underlying ability
2. Use differences in education and earnings across identical twins to account for common genetic and family background characteristics
3. Find quasi-experiments that provide a source of variation in educational attainment uncorrelated with students' ability and backgrounds

---

[5] These important insights were first discussed in the seminal contributions of Grilliches (1977) and Willis and Rosen (1979).

[6] A fourth method is to use economic theory to explicitly model the relationship between student ability and earnings. This approach is called structural estimation, as it comes from researchers first laying out the underlying theoretical structure of students' behavior. Studies that use this technique are very technical, and thus we do not focus on them here. Estimates of the returns to schooling using structural methods tend to be slightly smaller than those using selection-on-observables methods, at around 4–7% per year of education. Examples of studies that use this technique are Willis and Rosen (1979), Keane and Wolpin (1997), and Belzil and Hansen (2002). See Belzil (2007) for a review of this literature. Card (2001), Heckman and Urzua (2010), and Carneiro, Heckman, and Vytlacil (2011) also provide in-depth discussions of the relative merits of structural estimates of the returns to education.

Studies Controlling for Observed Differences Across Students A large set of studies in the literature on returns to education uses students' observed characteristics to try to control for the confounding role of underlying ability. If the ability of students can be perfectly accounted for using what we can observe in the data, then simple multivariate regression techniques will allow us to isolate the causal effect of another year of education on earnings. The estimates from these papers, most of which use the National Longitudinal Survey (NLS)—Young Men,[7] find returns to a year of schooling between 7% and 12%.[8]

The controls used in these studies include some combination of age, race/ethnicity, geographic location, and parental education and income. In some cases, direct ability measures like IQ scores also are included in the model (Grilliches, 1977). These controls are all designed to capture dimensions of student ability that likely correlate with labor market success. Although these variables are undoubtedly important to include in the estimating equation, it is instructive to think about how the returns to education are estimated when we account for them. Recall from Chapter 3 that controls in a multivariate model "hold these variables constant." Say we control for parental education and income as well as race/ethnicity, gender, state of residence, and IQ score. You can think of this as comparing the earnings between two people whose parents had the same income and education, who are of the same gender and race/ethnicity, who live in the same state, and who have the same measured IQ but who obtained different levels of education.

Why might such observationally similar people obtain different levels of education? Many of the reasons cast doubt on whether these controls are sufficient to account for the ability bias discussed previously. For one, these students may have other characteristics, such as motivation and work ethic, which lead to differences in educational attainment. More motivated students are likely to obtain more education, and motivation is highly rewarded in the labor market. For this method to estimate the causal effect of education on earnings, the controls used must account for differences across students in motivation as well as in underlying productivity. Motivation is extremely hard to measure, and the types of variables available in most datasets therefore are unlikely to be sufficient for this purpose.

A second concern is that these students may have different types of abilities that are not well measured by IQ scores and other background characteristics. Ability has many dimensions to it, and any one proxy (such as IQ scores) is likely to pick up only part of a student's underlying productive capacity. If so, the wage differences across these workers will reflect their ability differences as well as their education differences.

Twins Studies The central concern with studies that attempt to control for differences in student abilities with observable characteristics is that many aspects of one's genetic makeup and family background are impossible to measure with available data. What if one could find a way to account for genetics as well as for the family environment in which each person grew up? This is exactly what is done in a large strand of the returns

---

[7] The NLS was a nationally representative survey of young men that began in 1966 and followed men for several decades thereafter. It has detailed information on earnings and schooling as well as IQ test scores.

[8] Representative papers that use this technique are Grilliches (1977), Card (1995), Ashenfelter and Zimmerman (1997), and Card (1999).

to education research that compares differences across twins in their earnings and educational attainment.

Typically, these studies examine monozygotic twins who are identical in terms of both family background and genetics. The idea is to relate the differences in earnings across twins to the differences in the amount of education they have. The underlying assumption that supports this strategy is that educational differences across twins are unrelated to any of their characteristics that also correlate with labor market earnings.

Much of our knowledge about the returns to education come from data that several researchers have collected from participants at the Twins Day Festival, which is held every year in Twinsburg, Ohio. This festival hosts the largest collection of twins, both identical and fraternal, anywhere in the country. In the early 1990s, economists Orley Ashenfelter and Alan Krueger began attending this festival to collect firsthand data from pairs of twins on their educational attainment as well as on their earnings. These data provide extremely rich information about twin pairs that can be used to estimate the returns to schooling while accounting for both genetics and family backgrounds.

The other large twin dataset comes from the National Research Council twins sample of veterans born between 1917 and 1927. The estimates from these two datasets

---

DEEP DIVE: Estimating the Returns to Education Using Data on Identical Twins

A core problem faced by researchers who want to estimate the returns to education is that unobserved differences across students, such as ability, are correlated with both educational attainment and earnings. What if we could find pairs of students who are identical with respect to their underlying characteristics? In a novel and creative analysis, Ashenfelter and Krueger (1994) do just this by estimating the returns to education using a sample of identical (monozygotic) twins. Since, by definition, identical twins share the same genetic code and family background, many of the unobserved characteristics that can bias the estimates of the returns to education should be identical across pairs of twins.

To perform their analysis, Ashenfelter and Krueger collected data on monozygotic twins by interviewing pairs of twins at the Annual Twins Days Festival in Twinsburg, Ohio. By relating intrapair differences in wages to intrapair differences in schooling, the authors can estimate the returns to schooling. An important caveat to their results is that twins attending a twins festival might be different from twins more broadly or from nontwins. However, the value of being able to control for unobserved differences across individuals still makes such estimates highly informative about the causal effect of education on earnings.

They find that an additional year of schooling leads to 9% higher earnings. This is remarkably close to other

estimates in the literature, and the authors show that adjusting for ability bias by examining within-twin differences has almost no effect on the estimates. In other words, ability bias appears to be unimportant in their results, which is a very surprising finding.

Another novel contribution of this paper is that it can address problems associated with measurement error in reported levels of education. Ashenfelter and Krueger had the foresight to ask each twin about his or her own completed education as well as on the twin's level of completed education. The results are striking in showing that these estimates do not line up! In fact, they disagree 8–12% of the time. This also is extremely surprising, since both twins knew their sibling was being asked the same questions. It suggests that there are important errors in individual reports about their own completed level of schooling, and the likely effect of this measurement error is to understate the effect of education on earnings. Ashenfelter and Krueger show just that. Once they adjust for measurement error, they obtain a return to a year of education of 12–17%. This estimate is 50% larger than earlier estimates of the return to education. Their results suggest that a failure to correct for measurement error in reported schooling may lead to a sizable underestimation of the effect of education on earnings. Even without this correction, however, the returns to education they estimate are large and suffer little from ability bias.

are remarkably similar to each other and to the papers using student observable characteristics discussed previously, typically finding that a year of schooling increases earnings by between 8% and 11%.[9] It is reassuring that these estimates are all so close to one another, and it suggests that the methods that use observed student characteristics do not suffer from large problems because they cannot perfectly control for family background and genetics.

While a compelling and fascinating set of studies, the assumption underlying twin comparisons can be very difficult to justify. In the words of Bound and Solon (1999), "… if monozygotic twins are perfectly identical, why do they ever display any schooling difference at all? By the same token, why do monozygotic twins with the same schooling show any difference in wages?" The answer, as discussed in this important paper, is that monozygotic twins are not identical. They can differ in terms of temperament, preferences, abilities, and health. For example, most monozygotic twins differ in their birth weight, and these differences in birth weight have been shown to translate into longer-run differences in educational outcomes across twins.[10] Given the similarities of monozygotic twins, it is likely that such small differences play an outsized role in generating any intrapair education and earnings differences. If twins studies are *more* reliant on unobserved ability differences to generate variation in education than the nontwin studies discussed previously, they can be more biased. We are not guaranteed that twins studies will produce more accurate estimates of the causal effect of education on earnings than studies that control for observed student characteristics and ability measures.

Another reason why education might differ across identical twins is that twins may seek to differentiate themselves from each other. One way they may do this is by focusing on academics versus other endeavors (such as athletics). Parents also may treat twins differently, which would lead to an important difference in their home environments that could have long-run impacts on labor market outcomes. The way in which parents treat different twins likely exacerbates the behaviors twins engage in to differentiate themselves from each other. Many of the reasons twins vary in their educational attainment may therefore be related to factors that should be independently correlated with labor market outcomes. The difficulties in understanding exactly why education varies across identical twins have made this approach to estimating the returns to education somewhat controversial. Undoubtedly, however, these studies provide useful information about how education and earnings relate to each other when one accounts for the role of genetic makeup and common environmental components during childhood.

Quasi-Experimental Studies The third, and by far the most prevalent, set of studies relies on using *quasi-experiments*, which also are called *natural experiments*, to produce variation in education across individuals that is unrelated to their ability and family background. The way to think about these natural experiments is that they reproduce the experimental ideal by accident. A policy or event occurs that has the effect of randomly increasing or decreasing educational attainment among a group of people, even though this was not the intent. These quasi-experiments then are used to produce variation in education that is effectively random and uncorrelated with underlying student abilities, which are also known as instrumental variables. (See Chapter 3.)

---

[9] See Ashenfelter and Krueger (1994), Ashenfelter and Rouse (1998), Rouse (1999), Behrman, Rosenzweig, and Taubman (1994), and Behrman and Rosenzweig (1999).

[10] This result is taken from Figlio, Guryan, Karbownik, and Roth (2014).

An instrument for education needs to be strongly correlated with the amount of education individuals obtain and should affect earnings only because of its impact on education. The latter requirement is the exclusion restriction discussed in Chapter 3, and finding an instrument that satisfies this condition is very difficult. If there is any other reason why the instrument is correlated with earnings other than through educational attainment, the instrument is invalid.

The most common instruments in the literature are based on state and local policies regarding ages of school entry and exit and on the location of schools of different types. Here we list some instruments that have been discussed in the literature or that researchers have used to estimate the causal effect of education on earnings:

- Quarter of birth: Because of the interaction between school age of entry laws and mandatory schooling ages, children born earlier in the year have obtained less schooling when they reached the compulsory schooling age than their peers born later in the year (Angrist & Kruger, 1991).
- Proximity to a college: Those who live closer to colleges are more likely to attend college (Card, 1995).
- Compulsory schooling laws: States and countries change their rules about how old a child can be before he or she drops out of school. Variation in these laws can generate changes in the amount of schooling students receive (Acemoglu & Angrist, 2001; Oreopoulos, 2006).
- College tuition: States differ a lot in the tuition they charge for enrollment at public colleges and universities. Differences across states and regions in the structure of tuition charges may affect college enrollment and attainment.

DEEP DIVE: Estimating the Returns to Education Using "Random" Variation in Education from Quarter of Birth

One of the most influential studies on the returns to schooling that attempts to overcome ability bias using a natural experiment is Angrist and Krueger (1991). They use an instrumental variable strategy, which isolates variation in education that is plausibly unrelated to underlying student ability. Their method builds on two fundamental aspects of the structure of the education system in the United States. First, children born in different months of the year start school at different ages. This seasonality in school start age arises because, historically, most school districts in the United States would not allow children to enroll in school unless they would be at least six years old by January 1 of the academic year. As a consequence of this rule, children born in the beginning of the calendar year are older when they first enter school. The second feature the researchers exploit is the compulsory schooling laws that require children to remain in school until they have reached a certain age, generally between 16 and 18. Together, these rules should generate seasonality in

educational attainment: Children born in the beginning of the year will start school when they are older, and when they reach the compulsory schooling age, they will have had fewer years of schooling.

Angrist and Kruger (1991) use data from the 1970 and 1980 U.S. Census, focusing on birth cohorts born between 1920 and 1949. They first show that quarter of birth is indeed related to educational attainment: Those born in the first quarter of the year obtain 0.1 fewer years of education and are 2 percentage points less likely to graduate from high school. This relationship is shown in top curve of Figure 6.5, which is reproduced from their paper. Those born in the first two quarters tend to have less education than those born in the last two quarters of each year. Because of the focus of compulsory schooling laws, we would expect this variation across quarters of birth to reflect differences in high school rather than collegiate attainment. The paper shows this to be the case, as there are no seasonal patterns to college enrollment or completion.

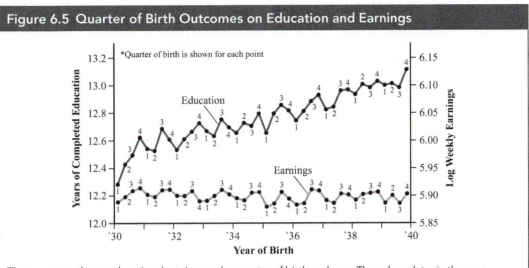

Figure 6.5 Quarter of Birth Outcomes on Education and Earnings

The top curve shows educational attainment by quarter of birth and year. Those born later in the year—quarters 3 and 4—have higher educational attainment than those born earlier in the year. The authors argue this pattern is driven by the school entry rule that students must be 6 years of age by January 1 of the year in which they enter kindergarten. Those born earlier in the year start school a year later and as a result will reach the compulsory schooling age with fewer years of education. The bottom curve shows a similar pattern for earnings: Those born earlier in the year tend to earn less than those born later in the year. Assuming that these earnings differences are driven solely by the education differences shown by the top curve, quarter of birth is a valid instrument for education. *Data from:* Figure I, Angrist and Krueger (1991) and Figure V, Angrist and Krueger (1991).

How do the seasonal education patterns shown by the top curve in Figure 6.5 translate into earnings? The bottom curve in Figure 6.5, reproduced from their paper as well, shows the variation in earnings across quarters of birth. On the whole, it appears that men born earlier in the year (in quarters 1 and 2) earn less than those born later in the year (in quarters 3 and 4). The use of quarter of birth as an instrument for education hinges on the assumption that the *only* reason for income to vary across season of birth is the differences in education caused by the interaction of school start age and compulsory schooling laws. In other words, quarter of birth should be uncorrelated with other attributes of students that are valued in the labor market, such as innate ability and motivation.

Their findings point to a large effect of additional education on wages, on the order of about a 6–10% increase for each year of schooling. One of their most striking findings (and one that is similar to the results in Ashenfelter & Krueger [1994]) is that the instrumental variables models produce estimates very similar to results from simple regression models that do not account for ability differences across students. In fact, the regression estimates tend to be smaller than the instrumental variables estimates, although the differences are not large. This finding could mean that ability bias is small (and perhaps negative) or that those who are induced to stay in school by compulsory schooling laws have particularly high returns to schooling relative to the average student.

It is important to highlight that each of these instruments estimates a **local average treatment effect (LATE)**. The LATE refers to the fact that instrumental variables estimate a treatment effect only among those whose behaviors are influenced by the instrument. For example, in the Angrist and Krueger analysis, the return to schooling is estimated from students who obtained less high school education because they were born earlier in the year and thus could drop out when they had completed less schooling. It cannot tell us much of anything about the returns to college training or to schooling below the high school level. It also tells us little about the returns to schooling among students who would never drop out regardless of the compulsory schooling laws.

local average treatment effect (LATE) The treatment effect among those individuals who are induced to change their behavior because of an intervention or natural experiment. In an instrumental variables setting, the LATE refers to the group whose behavior is impacted by the instrument. The effect estimated is therefore local to this group.

This is important in interpreting the instrumental variables estimates across studies, as they often estimate effects related to different levels of schooling and among different populations. This makes these results difficult to compare with the studies discussed earlier. For example, the quarter of birth and compulsory schooling instrument affects the amount of high school attainment individuals obtain, not collegiate attainment. Proximity to college and college tuition influence college enrollment rather than high school completion. Tuition policies are likely to impact middle class and less affluent students, while college proximity likely affects higher-income students more (as they are more likely to live closer to colleges). These differences in the level of schooling and in the treated populations make comparisons across studies very challenging.

Each of these quasi-experimental studies has generated a large body of research focused on whether the instrumental variables can successfully isolate the causal effect of education on earnings. This literature has rendered the studies that use these techniques rather controversial, and their findings are not universally accepted as true. Because of its large influence, the quarter of birth instrument has received the most attention among subsequent researchers. Although the Angrist and Krueger (1991) paper makes a persuasive and compelling argument for the value of using quarter of birth, some more recent research suggest that quarter of birth is not random with respect to earnings. The composition of births varies in ways that makes birth quarter independently correlated with earnings. Bound and Jaeger (2000) present evidence that quarter of birth and earnings are correlated even in cohorts that were not impacted by compulsory schooling laws. And as the association between quarter of birth and education has weakened over time (because fewer students drop out of high school), the correlation between quarter of birth and earnings has not weakened. These findings suggest that the birth quarter–earnings correlation is driven in part by factors other than educational attainment. Furthermore, Cascio and Lewis (2006) document a strong correlation between children's cognitive test scores and quarter of birth, and Buckles and Hungerman (2013) show that lower socioeconomic–status mothers are more likely to give birth earlier in the year. These studies cast more doubt on the validity of the quarter of birth instrument.

The proximity to college instrument also is controversial. The central concern with this approach is thinking about why certain families live closer to colleges than others. If proximity to a college is correlated with unobserved factors such as preferences for education, parental occupation, and household resources, then this instrument will provide misleading information on the effect of schooling on earnings. To justify this instrument, one must argue that the only reason children who live closer to colleges get more education is because of this proximity and not because of any other differences that are correlated with their family's location choice. This assumption is very difficult, if impossible to test.

Because compulsory schooling laws are set by state policy makers, changes to these policies are more likely to satisfy the exclusion restriction. At least in recent years, compulsory schooling laws have not changed much in the United States. Historical circumstances that make tuition at public colleges and universities in some states higher than in others might affect enrollment in ways that are unrelated to underlying student characteristics. Yet, cross-state variation in tuition is not strongly tied to enrollment, while changes in tuition levels within states might also be related to the returns to education. These limitations have precluded tuition from being used more widely as an instrument for collegiate attainment.

6.3 Empirical Evidence on the Social Returns to Educational Attainment

Thus far, we have examined only the effect of education on labor market earnings. This is the primary measure of the private return to schooling used by economists. As discussed in Chapter 5, there also might be social returns to schooling driven by positive externalities of education that lead to benefits to society at large. Education may have effects on a broad range of outcomes that benefit society, such as lowering crime rates, spurring economic growth, and increasing civic participation. Although it is generally accepted that people with more education are more civically involved and commit fewer crimes, this is not evidence of the causal effect of education on these outcomes. Isolating causal effects of education on outcomes that broadly benefit society is made very difficult by the fact that those who attain more education differ in a whole host of ways that are independently correlated with these outcomes. This problem is very similar to the ability bias that is endemic to the estimation of the private returns to schooling.

Researchers have tried to overcome this problem in several ways. In a very influential study, Lochner and Moretti (2004) use changes in compulsory schooling laws as natural experiments that should affect education. These laws differ in whether they allow students to drop out in the eighth, ninth, tenth, or eleventh grade; and states changed their rules substantially over the course of the 1960s and 1970s (the focus of their study). The authors link changes in compulsory schooling laws to crime data from the U.S. Census and FBI reports, and they examine how changes in schooling because of changes in compulsory schooling laws affect changes in criminal activity. They find that compulsory schooling laws induce education to increase and incarcer-

ation to decline significantly. The effects are greater for Blacks than for Whites. The variation in schooling in this paper all comes from increased high school completion, and the findings suggest that compelling students to remain in high school leads to long-run reductions in their criminal activity.

Dee (2004) examines a related question: Does education increase civic engagement later in life? He uses two instruments for education. The first is the availability of local community colleges. If a student happens to live in an area with a greater concentration of these intuitions, he or she is more likely to obtain at least some college training. A key issue with this instrument is the concern that the availability of community colleges is correlated with unobserved attributes of students who are themselves positively correlated with civic engagement. Because of the potentially strong assumption underlying this instrument, Dee (2004) also uses restrictive state child labor laws as an instrument for education. The idea here is that more restrictive laws will induce children to stay in school for more time.

"If I had a better education, I wouldn't have guessed wrong when the judge asked 'how do you plead?'"

J.P. Rini The New Yorker Collection/The Cartoon Bank

He finds that both instruments have large effects on education and that both lead to increases in civic engagement. Students induced to obtain more education because they live near a community college or because they live in a state with restrictive child labor laws are more likely to vote when they are older and to support free speech, and their civic knowledge is substantially higher. These results strongly suggest that education leads to higher civic engagement, which has potentially large returns to society at large.

In addition to the effect of education on civic participation and crime, a large body of research examines whether education affects overall growth of the economy. This research is motivated by the fact that over the past century, as the education level of U.S. workers has risen, real per capita income in the United States also has increased from about $5,000 at the start of the twentieth century to nearly $35,000 at the end of the twentieth century (in real dollars). Increasing income per capita in an economy—economic growth—raises the standard of living because people are able to buy more goods and services. How closely are the substantial increases in educational attainment over this period linked to this economic growth?

When thinking about the total output in an economy, it is common to use a basic aggregate production function that relates the inputs of production to the outputs at an economy-wide level. We want to relate output (Y), or national income, to the level of physical capital (K), the inputs provided by workers through their time and skills (L), and the state of technology (A) over some time interval (t) such as a year. The aggregate production function can be written as:

$$Y(t) = f[A(t), K(t), L(t)]$$

In this setup, increasing education may work through multiple channels to increase output. If people learn productive skills in school, then a more educated workforce should be able to produce more, and the level of effective labor inputs (L) increases. Moreover, if more highly educated workers aid the development and implementation of new technologies that increase output, education also contributes to the level of technology (A).

> **Quick Hint:** Other determinants of technology employed in the economy, which often is called total factor productivity (TFP), include the regulatory environment and the security of property rights.

As discussed in Chapter 2, educational attainment among U.S. workers rose consistently throughout much of the twentieth century. Because young cohorts with higher levels of education were replacing retiring cohorts with lower levels of education, the stock of education in the labor force expanded. Such a pattern was particularly evident in the post–World War II period: In successive 10-year periods of observation, the share of workers with a college education increased, while the share never completing college declined. In recent decades, the pace of this change has slowed.

Of prime interest is understanding how these changes in the educational attainment level of U.S. workers affected total output. This is an important question in its own right, but it also relates directly to the implications of the more recent slowdowns in the growth in educational attainment. DeLong, Goldin, and Katz (2003) assembled data from the twentieth century to answer this question. They calculate that labor represents about 70% of aggregate production; that is, about 70% of the production of all goods and services in the United States is attributable to labor. Consistent with the estimates on the private return to education, they also estimate that more educated workers are more productive. One therefore can think of the growth in educational attainment of workers as a growth in the amount of productive labor in the economy. They calculate that increases of about 5.7 years in average educational attainment between 1915 and 2000 led to a growth in annual labor productivity of 0.5 percentage points.

How large is this growth effect? Multiplying the growth in labor productivity because of education (0.5) by the total contribution of labor to output (0.7) leads to the conclusion that increases in education attainment over the twentieth century contributed about 0.35 percentage points to the annual growth in productivity. This increase represents about 22% of the overall growth in labor productivity over this period, and as the authors emphasize, it underestimates the importance of education to growth because it ignores the effect of education on technological innovation (A).

Further evidence on the role of education in spurring economic growth comes from cross-country comparisons. Much research has focused on estimating cross-country regressions, which compare differences in education to differences in worker output, or gross domestic product, across countries. These studies tend to find a strong cross-country correlation between overall output and education. Figure 6.6, reproduced from Acemoglu and Angrist (2001), shows that across countries, years of schooling are strongly positively tied to per-worker output.

Careful empirical work combining several decades of international test scores and GDP growth underscores how the education system can have a large impact on growth. Hanushek and Woessman (2008) estimate regressions of annual GDP growth rate on both test scores and years of education. They show evidence that growth is much higher in countries with higher average test scores. But conditional on test scores, years of education have little relation to economic growth. In other words, growth is not generated by years of schooling itself but rather by what one learns while in school. These results suggest that school quality could be an important driver of economic growth.

One of the main problems associated with cross-country regressions is the concern that other country characteristics are driving the education–growth relationship. For example, the United States has much higher education and GDP than Mexico. Can we truly believe that the GDP difference between the United States and Mexico can be fully attributed to the education difference across the two countries? It is doubtful this is the case, which makes it difficult to interpret cross-country evidence as reflective of the causal effect of education on economic growth.[11] As Hanushek and Woessman point out, despite low achievement test scores, economic growth in the United States has been robust in recent decades. This suggests that cross-country regressions

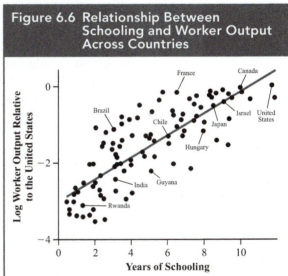

Figure 6.6 Relationship Between Schooling and Worker Output Across Countries

Across countries, there is a strong positive relationship between average years of schooling and log output per worker relative to the United States. The slope of the line is 0.29, suggesting another year of schooling is associated with about 30% higher per capita output relative to that in the United States. However, we should be wary of interpreting this relationship as causal, since many omitted factors are likely to be correlated both with per capita output and with years of schooling across countries. *Data from:* Figure I, Acemoglu and Angrist (2000).

---

[11] See Brock and Durlauf (2001) for a detailed discussion of issues pertaining to cross-country growth regressions and a review of that literature.

may mischaracterize the contribution of education to economic growth. Alternatively, it could be the case that other factors in the United States, such as a stable labor market, government institutions, and relatively open markets are substituting for our lackluster test scores.

The problems with interpreting cross-country growth regressions have led researchers to find ways to use quasi-experiments to estimate the effect of schooling on overall economic activity in the United States. Acemoglu and Angrist (2001) provide a primary example of this line of research applied to U.S. states. They use changes in compulsory schooling and limited child labor laws as instrumental variables for education. They also are able to control for the private returns to schooling using the quarter of birth method pioneered by Angrist and Krueger (1991). The approach in this study is to examine how average wages within a state and across birth cohorts change when compulsory schooling laws change, holding constant the private returns to education. Because the private returns are being held constant, the average wage changes driven by changes in the compulsory schooling law reflect the effect of educational attainment on overall state economic growth. They find modest but statistically significant growth effects of education, on the order of 1–3% higher wage growth for a one-year average increase in education in a state and birth cohort. While much smaller than the private returns, these results suggest that there are positive growth externalities associated with education.

A very innovative paper by economist Enrico Moretti (2004) also examines whether there are positive growth effects of education. He analyzes whether workers in cities with more college-educated citizens are more productive as measured by their wages. Similar to Dee (2004), he uses the proximity of a four-year college as an instrument for education, which he shows is highly positively related to the number of college-educated workers in a city. He finds that cities with more college-educated workers have more productive workers: a 1% increase in the number of college graduates in a city raises the wages of workers without a high school degree by 1.9%, raises high school graduates' wages by 1.6%, and increases college graduates' wages by 0.4%. These estimates, similar to those in Acemoglu and Angrist (2001), point to sizable social spillovers of college education in terms of fostering higher productivity among workers, which leads to higher economic growth.

6.4 Empirical Evidence on the Private Returns to Education Quality

Overall, the studies in Section 6.2 suggest that the private returns to education as measured by individual earnings that have been estimated, using several methods across different time periods, range from 6–12%. Higher educational attainment also appears to increase overall economic growth, on the order of 1–3% for each average year of education increase in the United States. One limitation of these studies is that they treat education as a single good, without making distinctions regarding the quality of that education. Ignoring the quality of education received may miss an important aspect of how schooling operates. Is the return to a year of schooling at an elite private university the same as the return to a year of schooling at a community college? Are earnings similarly affected by a year spent in a low-performing public high school as in a well-funded private school? These core questions in the economics of education provide insight into what types of schools students should attend and what the returns may be to subsidizing different types of schools with public funds. In this section, we provide an overview of the evidence on the returns to college quality, as this is the question that has received the most attention among economists. We discuss the research on the returns to K–12 quality in Chapter 9.

Defining College Quality

The first question you may ask when thinking about the returns to college quality is, "What is quality?" Schools differ in their focus and in their strengths and weaknesses, so how can we characterize one educational environment as being higher quality than another? One approach is to use variation in education inputs as measures of quality, while a second approach distinguishes among institutions by organizational structure. Using observed resource levels, we can characterize schools with lower student–faculty ratios as being of higher quality. Alternatively, we can use average SAT/ACT scores that measure the average pre-collegiate academic ability of students at each institution, instructional expenditures per student, or the selectivity of undergraduate admissions as proxies for quality. Since these measures all tend to be highly correlated with each other, some researchers even have combined them into a single index of quality.[12]

Another approach is to split schools according to their institutional control (public vs. private) as well as by the degrees offered (two-year vs. four-year). In addition, many studies break up the four-year public sector into *flagship* schools and all other schools. (See Chapter 13 for a more detailed discussion of the structure of the higher education sector.) Flagship universities are the public schools designated as the most selective and elite in each state. Examples of state flagship universities include University of Michigan–Ann Arbor; University of Virginia–Charlottesville; University of Colorado–Boulder; and University of Minnesota–Twin Cities.

Table 6.1 presents quality characteristics of institutions by different higher education tiers. Here, we also have split the private sector into highly selective and less selective groups based on *U.S. News and World Report* rankings.[13] We consider several direct quality measures, including expenditures per student, average graduation rates, student–faculty ratios, and SAT/ACT scores. The table demonstrates that the college quality tiers we use are highly correlated with these observed quality measures. The flagship public and selective private schools have much higher graduation rates and expenditures per student and have lower student–faculty ratios than their less selective counterparts. Additionally, the four-year schools as a whole have more resources than two-year schools. The value of using college quality tiers is that they are straightforward to measure, do not change much over time, and characterize the choice set faced by most undergraduate students in terms of deciding what type of school to attend. Still, direct resource or quality measures capture the considerable variation within these tiers.

---

[12] See Black and Smith (2006) for a detailed discussion of this method.

[13] The highly selective private schools are the top 65 private universities and colleges according to the 2012 *U.S. News and World Report* rankings as well as the top 50 liberal arts schools.

Table 6.1 Quality Measures of Colleges and Universities Across Sectors in 2012						
School Characteristic	Public Flagship	Public, Not Flagship	Highly Selective Private	Less Selective Private	Public Two-Year	Private Two-Year
Expenditures per Student	$43,897	$28,047	$78,373	$20,545	$6,225	$8,769
Instructional Expenditures per Student	$13,873	$7,978	$23,894	$5,982	$3,690	$3,532
Student–Faculty Ratio	15.1	22.3	9.3	18.7	29.0	27.8
25th Percentile Math SAT Score	549.8	462.0	625.0	462.4		
75th Percentile Math SAT Score	663.7	569.3	720.7	575.1		
25th Percentile ACT Score	23.6	19.3	27.7	19.8		
75th Percentile ACT Score	28.7	24.1	31.6	25.1		
Graduation Rate	71%	43%	86%	45%		

ACT scores are composite scores, while SAT scores are for mathematics only. All per-student measures are relative to all enrolled students, graduate and undergraduate. SAT/ACT data are not reported for two-year schools because very few students who attend these schools take these college admissions exams.

Data from: 2012 IPEDS.

Estimating the Causal Effect of College Quality on Earnings

In addition to concerns about how to measure college quality, the potential for ability bias in these studies is significant. As all undergraduates who have gone through the grueling college application process can relate to, students are not sorted randomly into schools. Students select the schools they want to attend, and the schools select the students they want. This two-sided selection process presents many problems for causal analysis. Students choose schools based on many factors: academics, social life, proximity to home, athletics, and specific program strength, to name a few. Comparing earnings among even observationally similar students who attend schools of differing quality necessarily means we are comparing students who differ in their preferences for these attributes. If such preferences are related to labor market outcomes, it will cause a bias in our estimates.

To take an example that illustrates the problem, consider the college choices made by Seth and Evan. They went to the same high school, are from similar backgrounds, and both performed well in high school. Evan is highly academically motivated, while Seth is more interested in the social life of college. Evan enrolls in an academically elite school with high per-student spending, while Seth attends a large university where spending per student is much more modest. Comparing Seth's and Evan's earnings post-college, it would be a mistake to attribute all of the difference to the quality of school they attended. They differ in their preferences and motivation, which can independently influence earnings. These are the types of biases that research on the returns to college quality have sought to overcome. Three main strategies have been used:

1. Controlling directly for student academic preparation for college (usually high school test scores) as well as student background characteristics
2. Regression discontinuity designs using admission cutoffs in test scores
3. Comparisons of earnings among students who applied to and got into the same set of schools but who attended schools of differing quality levels

Each of these methods has its benefits and drawbacks. On the whole, none of the estimates of the returns to college quality is perfect, but together they paint a rather clear picture in pointing to sizable earnings returns to enrolling in a higher-resource and more selective college or university. This is true particularly for students from disadvantaged backgrounds.

Studies That Control for Student Academic Preparation for College The largest set of studies that examines the earnings returns to college quality uses a strategy that attempts to control for student academic ability with precollegiate test scores. Typically, these studies use nationally representative longitudinal datasets, such as the NLS72, HSB, NELS:88, ELS:2002, and NLSY,[14] which allow one to control extensively for student background characteristics as well as for precollegiate cognitive outcomes as measured by test scores during high school. These test scores are useful controls, because they are direct (if imperfect) measures of student academic preparation for college. These studies also include controls for parental income, parental education, household composition, and in some cases geographic differences across students. This is a rich set of controls, as much of the nonrandom sorting of students across different school types is likely to be correlated with this battery of characteristics.

An early and representative example of this research strategy is Brewer, Eide, and Ehrenberg (1999). They use the NLS72 and HSB to examine how wages and earnings differ across quality tiers, conditional on the large set of academic and student background controls in these datasets. They find that students who attend a top-ranked private or public school have earnings 20–25% higher than those of students who attend a bottom-ranked public school. This method has been used repeatedly with different datasets and across different time periods, and the results from these studies tell a remarkably similar story about the large earnings returns to enrolling in a higher-quality postsecondary school.[15]

A similar set of studies examines the returns to attending a two-year community college versus a four-year school. As shown in Table 6.1, community colleges have much lower per-student resources, but they also are less expensive to attend. Many policy makers and politicians have argued that students could dramatically reduce their college costs by enrolling in a two-year school for several years and then transferring to a more expensive four-year school. Given the lower resources at those schools, an important policy question is whether enrolling in a community college has a negative

---

[14] See Appendix A for a description of each of these datasets.
[15] For other selection-on-observables studies of the returns to higher education quality, see Black and Smith (2004, 2006), Long (2010), and Andrews, Li, and Lovenheim (2016).

effect on earnings relative to attending a four-year school. The answer, on average, is yes. Using NELS:88 data, Reynolds (2012) controls for a rich set of background characteristics of students and finds students enrolling in a community college earn about 7% less in the future than those beginning college at a four-year school. Andrews, Li, and Lovenheim (2016) find a similar effect in Texas, although they also show that the difference in earnings disappears at the top of the earnings distribution. On average, the returns to a community college are lower, but for higher-earning students the returns are similar. This finding suggests that for some students, a community college may be a lucrative investment.

DEEP DIVE: The Returns to Two- and Four-Year Colleges

One of the first papers that examines the differential wage effects of two- and four-year colleges is Kane and Rouse (1995). This novel paper compares workers based on how many college credits and the degrees they have received at two- and four-year colleges. The variation that the authors rely on to estimate the wage impacts that stem from different types of collegiate attainment comes from differences in course credits and college degrees across the individuals. This research strategy allows the authors to more accurately distinguish between human capital effects (driven by college credits) and sheepskin effects (driven by degrees completed). Using variation in college credits further enables the authors to more precisely estimate the returns to education among individuals who attended college but did not complete a degree, something earlier studies have struggled to do.

To perform this analysis, Kane and Rouse rely on two datasets: NLS72 and NLSY79. (See Appendix A.) A novel feature of these datasets is that they follow individuals for a long time and are linked to detailed college enrollment information as well as, for NLS72 respondents, college transcripts. The core problems associated with this analysis pertain to the now-familiar notion of ability bias—the differential education decisions of workers may be correlated with unobserved characteristics that independently affect earnings. The datasets used by the authors enable them to at least partially address this issue. First, the data contain detailed information on a battery of standardized tests and family background characteristics. These variables measure differences in students' academic preparation for college as well as underlying ability, and the study argues that these controls therefore eliminate ability bias. However, it is unclear why some students drop out of college when

they are close to graduating and whether such decisions are driven by factors that will influence subsequent earnings (such as health).

The results differ for men and women. Among men, the results point to significantly higher returns to a two-year credit than a four-year credit for those not graduating. However, there is a large sheepskin effect for males who obtain a four-year degree: their wages increase by 23% and are much larger than what would be predicted from accumulating four years of college credits without obtaining a degree.

In contrast, for women Kane and Rouse (1995) find that the economic return to an additional year of education (30 credits) at a community college is very similar to that of an additional year at a four-year institution, approximately 6–10%. Remarkably, the statistical tests used by the authors fail to reject the hypothesis that the economic return to a credit at a two-year college is the same as that at a four-year college. The implication is that the higher earnings enjoyed by four-year female students is due to the fact they earn more credits, not the fact that their education is more valuable on a per-credit basis. In addition, the results suggest that students who have completed a two- or four-year college education in general only earn marginally higher wages than students with the same number of course credits but no degree. These results suggest little sheepskin effect of college diplomas for women and that the return to college education is primarily driven by increases in human capital accumulation. It is interesting that these results differ so much by gender; why this is so remains an open question among researchers.

To reinforce their results, the authors extend the analysis by exploiting an alternative source of variation to measure the impact of college credits on the economic return to education. First, they note that enrollment in two- and four-year colleges has varied dramatically across states. Provided that this variation is not driven by unobserved state-specific characteristics that also affect earnings, the authors can obtain a measure of the economic return to a two-year college education by comparing the returns to education in states with more versus fewer two-year college students. If two-year colleges are associated with a smaller economic return than four-year colleges, then states with a greater proportion of students enrolled in two-year colleges should have smaller average returns to education. The results suggest that there are no significant differences in the returns to education based on the

fraction of two-year college enrollees, which reinforces the results stated earlier.

Given these sizable returns, is attending a community college worth it even if one does not finish? The findings from this analysis suggest that the answer is yes. Their estimates indicate that two-year college degree holders earn 15–25% more than those with only a high school diploma. Accounting for the earnings that these students have to give up while studying as well as tuition costs, the authors calculate that even if an individual only completes one year at a two-year college, the return to that education will more than compensate for the cost of the schooling.

Quick Hint: It is important to distinguish between gross returns, which do not include tuition and forgone wages, and net returns, which do account for these costs. Since community colleges are cheaper to attend, gross returns that are similar between two- and four-year students translate into higher net returns for two-year students. All returns discussed in this chapter are gross returns, which have been the focus in the economics literature.

Regression Discontinuity Studies Although the selection-on-observables studies contain detailed measures of student demographic and academic backgrounds, there still is much concern that they are insufficient to account for unobserved student differences across schools that are correlated with earnings potential. Returning to Seth and Evan, even the rich set of controls in the datasets used are unlikely to be able to fully control for their differences in preferences. Other empirical methodologies are needed to generate differences in college quality across students who are otherwise identical with respect to all of their characteristics, whether they are observed or not.

One such promising method is a regression discontinuity design based on admissions cutoffs for colleges. The idea behind these studies is that certain schools have admissions rules such that students with above a minimum SAT score or GPA will automatically be admitted if they apply, and those below the threshold are unlikely to be admitted. The threshold does not perfectly describe enrollment at the school: Some students below the cutoff, such as exceptional athletes, still can get in, and many above the cutoff will go elsewhere. However, as long as students cannot choose which side of the cutoff they are on, students just above and just below the cutoff will be identical in all of their characteristics on average. Because it is very hard to target a specific SAT score due to randomness in the test, it is plausible that students just above and just below the admissions threshold will be the same on average. If so, comparing earnings just above and below the cutoff and relating the comparison to the change in enrollment at the school will show the effect on earnings of enrolling in the specific school. The papers using this method show substantial earnings returns to being just above the threshold, which gives the students access to the higher-quality school.[16] The consensus estimate from the research using this approach is that attending the higher-quality school increases earnings by about 20%.

[16] Hoekstra (2009) and Zimmerman (2014) are the two main papers that employ this method.

DEEP DIVE: Estimating the Return to College Quality Using a Regression Discontinuity Design

The major threat to uncovering the causal effect on earnings of attending a more elite university is ability bias: Admission to high-quality universities is likely correlated with unobserved individual characteristics that independently affect labor market earnings. To overcome this problem, one needs to find academically equivalent students who enroll in schools of differing quality. The difficulty of finding such variation is underscored by the fact that students value education quality, and so one always must worry about why seemingly equivalent students are attending different schools.

One of the most credible and influential papers that tries to overcome this selection problem is by Mark Hoekstra (2009). The contribution of his paper is to compare nearly identical students who, because of university admissions rules, attend schools of differing quality. The institutional background of this study is that admission to the unnamed state flagship university he studies is determined by a combination of the applicant's GPA and SAT score. For each GPA level, there is an SAT score cutoff

above which students are admitted and below which students are unlikely to be admitted. He therefore employs a regression discontinuity method that exploits this college admission rule to compare the labor market earnings of individuals narrowly above the cutoff (who were admitted to the flagship state university) with those who were narrowly below the cutoff (and not admitted). Because of randomness in SAT scores and GPAs and because the thresholds were not made public, it would be extremely difficult for students to perfectly target where they are in relation to the cutoff. This randomness leads to those just above and below the cutoff being identical, on average, in terms of their observed and unobserved characteristics.

To perform this analysis, Hoekstra relies on confidential administrative admissions data from the flagship state university between 1986 and 1989 and labor market earnings data from 1998 to 2005 obtained from unemployment insurance tax reports. He first demonstrates that the admission rule indeed generates a discontinuity (jump) in enrollment: The jump at the cutoff

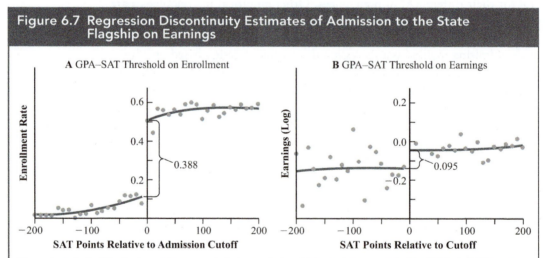

Figure 6.7 Regression Discontinuity Estimates of Admission to the State Flagship on Earnings

A GPA–SAT Threshold on Enrollment

B GPA–SAT Threshold on Earnings

The university in this study employs an admissions rule in which students are admitted if their SAT scores are above a GPA-specific cutoff. Panel A shows the likelihood of enrollment as a function of how far a student is from the SAT admissions cutoff. At the cutoff, the likelihood of enrolling in the flagship university increases by 39%. This is an example of a fuzzy regression discontinuity, as the likelihood of enrolling does not change by 1 at the cutoff. The discontinuity is fuzzy because not all admitted students enroll, and some students below the cutoff are admitted (such as those who are good at football). Panel B shows the associated jump in earnings at the cutoff. Earnings increase by 9.5%. Assuming that the earnings increase is due solely to the jump in enrolling in the flagship university, the instrumental variables estimate of the effect on earnings of enrolling in the flagship university is 24% (0.095/0.39). *Data from:* Figures 1 and 2, Hoekstra (2009).

is approximately 39%. This is illustrated in panel A of Figure 6.7, which plots the probability of enrollment by how far a student is from the admission cutoff.

If attendance at the flagship state university contributes to an increase in the individual's earnings, one would expect this cutoff to cause a discontinuity in labor market earnings as well. The author shows that this indeed is the case: The discontinuity in earnings at the cutoff is 9.5%, as shown in panel B of Figure 6.7.

Assuming the jump in earnings is due to the 39% increase in the likelihood of attendance, Hoekstra's results suggest that individuals attending the flagship state university have approximately 24% higher earnings when they are between 28 and 33 years old compared with those who narrowly missed the admission cutoff. This result suggests that college quality may have substantial effects on later-in-life earnings.

While the magnitude of the estimates from these studies matches closely with the findings from the research method in which student academic ability is controlled for directly, comparing the results from these analyses is difficult. First, the regression discontinuity results only apply to students who are affected by the cutoff. If the effect of college quality differs across students of differing academic ability, then regression discontinuity estimates cannot tell us how more academically qualified students are affected by attending the more selective school. As well, the regression discontinuity studies are unable to observe where students went who were below the threshold. Without a strong understanding of what the comparison group did, it is difficult to interpret the resulting estimates. Despite these drawbacks, the credibility of the regression discontinuity design makes these studies some of the most trusted and important in this literature. That the results match closely with the results from other methods helps to affirm the results from both types of research.

Comparisons Using Observed Applications and Admissions Outcomes A third approach that has been used to estimate the returns to college quality was pioneered by Dale and Krueger (2002).[17] This novel research argues that unobserved attributes of students, such as motivation and preferences, are reflected in where students apply to college and where they get in. Comparing Seth and Evan, their different preferences for college attributes are reflected in the fact that they applied to and were admitted to different schools. The research strategy employed in this paper is to compare Seth to other students who applied to and were admitted to the same school as him but who went to a school of differing quality. The same comparison would be made for Evan, but with an "Evan-specific" control group. The insight that underlies this approach is that preferences and unobserved student attributes are expressed more in the application–admission stage than in the matriculation stage.

They estimate their model using College & Beyond data, which contain information on the schools to which students applied and were admitted. Their results that simply control for students' observed characteristics show estimates that are similar to the rest of the literature discussed earlier, much of which uses the same dataset. However, their main results run contrary to the prior research. Once they compare students at different-quality schools who applied and got into the same set of schools, there is no difference in earnings overall. Interestingly, there still is a sizable earnings effect for Black students and for students from low-income backgrounds.

---

[17] See also the update to this paper in Dale and Krueger (2014), which uses administrative earnings records.

This study casts some doubt on the existence of an effect of college quality on earnings. But this approach has been criticized for many of the same reasons as the studies that rely on direct measures of student ability.[18] The crux of this criticism is that it is unclear why two students who have the exact same choice set would choose schools of differing quality. As in the twins studies, many of the explanations suggest that the reasons could be correlated with future earnings. These include preferences for different academic majors, preferences for proximity to home, and information differences that lead some types of students to choose lower-quality schools. In addition, the college quality differences among most students in an application–admission group are small. There may be little return to small differences in college quality, especially given the fact that quality is measured with error. Large differences in quality, such as occur across sectors as shown in Table 6.1, may produce much larger effects on earnings.

Why Is There a Return to College Quality?

On the whole, the research on the returns to college quality indicates a substantial earnings premium to enrolling in a more resource intensive school. Why might this be? One of the main hypothesized pathways through which college quality might affect student earnings is by supporting college completion. There are large differences in the likelihood of graduating across higher education quality tiers, and measured college resources strongly predict graduation rates of students even when one controls for background characteristics and test scores. Using data from the NELS:88 longitudinal dataset, Bound, Lovenheim, and Turner (2010) analyze *college completion rates*, defined as the proportion of students who obtain a degree among those who enroll. They show that among the high school class of 1992, completion rates are 26 percentage points higher for students at elite public schools relative to students at less elite public universities. In addition, students enrolling in a community college are 46 percentage points less likely to obtain a BA than four-year public university students.[19] If employers place a value on workers having a BA degree, then the differences in completion across schools of differing quality could generate post-college earnings differences.

It also is the case that students at more elite schools may obtain more human capital. At higher-quality colleges and universities, faculty may be more effective teachers, students may experience smaller class sizes and higher per-student expenditure, and there is more exposure to research. If these resource differences translate into more skill development, one would expect students attending such schools to earn more subsequently. Unfortunately, little research has been done that can shed light on this critically important question.

Student networks and peer effects also might be important in generating a return to college quality. Evidence from random assignments to roommates at several elite colleges, such as Dartmouth and Williams, as well as at the less elite Berea College, suggests that college students are influenced by their peers.[20] Since the academic quality of

---

[18] Hoxby (2009) provides a useful discussion of the relative merits of the different studies on the returns to college quality.

[19] For evidence of the effect of enrolling in a community college on four-year degree receipt, see Rouse (1995), Leigh and Gill (2003), Sandy, Gonzalez, and Hilmer (2006), Long and Kurlaender (2009), and Reynolds (2012).

[20] Sacerdote (2001) studies peer effects from randomly assigned roommates at Dartmouth. Zimmerman (2003) studies Williams College. Carell, Fullerton, and West (2009) examine random assignment to dorm groups at the Air Force Academy. Estimates from Berea College are in Stinebrickner and Stinebrickner (2006). See Chapter 15 for a more detailed discussion of this research.

peers is higher at high-quality universities, interactions with such peers could contribute to more skill acquisition among students at those institutions. Additionally, it could be the case that formal job recruiting efforts targeted at more elite schools, alumni networks that are active in career placement of graduates, and informal networks that operate through peers' parents could lead to higher earnings among graduates of more elite postsecondary schools.

6.5 Conclusion

Despite the concerns surrounding ability bias, most of the research that examines the returns to schooling points to a large effect of an additional year of schooling on subsequent earning. Most studies indicate an effect of 7–10% for each additional year of education. The evidence also suggests that the returns are higher for higher-quality schooling environments for postsecondary education. School quality seems particularly important for students from low-income and minority backgrounds as well. In addition to the evidence suggesting large private returns to schooling, there also appear to be social returns. This evidence suggests that the signaling model alone is insufficient to explain the importance of education, since there should be no social benefits to the education system under this model.

That there are substantial private and social returns to education highlights the importance of understanding how education is produced and what the technology is that relates the inputs of the education process to the desired outputs. Simply put, if it matters what students learn in school, as suggested by the human capital model, we want to know how best to use the education system to produce knowledge and skills. In the next chapter, we will develop our understanding of how knowledge is produced through the schooling system. We then focus on the efficacy of education policies that are designed to alter this schooling process to generate higher levels of student learning.

Highlights

- When using a single measure of ability, wage differentials by education level may reflect differences in ability that are correlated with education rather than be causally related to education. This *ability bias* may be positive or negative.
- The Roy model provides a framework for thinking about how selection into different levels of education occurs when ability is multidimensional. The sign of the ability bias in this model is very difficult to determine, as students who attain different education levels have different strengths that make them suited for very different professions.
- The Mincer model is a **human capital earnings function** that provides a benchmark for estimating the returns to schooling and predicts a linear increasing relationship between years of education and percent change in wages. In the Mincer model, individuals can invest both in formal schooling and in **on-the-job-training** while working.

- Despite its wide use, the model is limited by its inability to overcome ability bias.
- A body of research exists that attempts to estimate the causal effect of education on earnings. Typically, they employ one of three techniques: control for student ability using observed characteristics in the data, control for unobserved family and genetic factors using identical twins, and exploit quasi-, or natural, experiments generating variation in education that is unrelated to student ability.
- Natural experiments are useful in estimating the returns to education because they take advantage of "random" sources of variation in educational attainment. There is a trade-off because these approaches estimate a **local average treatment effect (LATE)**, which is relevant only for the set of individuals whose education decisions are affected by the natural experiment.

- In addition to the private benefits of education, which economists typically measure using wages or earnings, there is evidence of substantial social returns to education. Researchers have found evidence that education reduces crime, increases civic engagement, and helps spur economic growth. These social returns indicate that the signaling model is insufficient to explain all of the ways in which education impacts individuals and society.
- The returns to a year of education might vary depending on the "quality" of the educational experience.

Economists have spent considerable effort to understand the returns to education quality, in particular for higher education. Despite the difficulties associated with measuring college quality and in estimating the causal effect of college quality on earnings, a variety of evidence from different data sources and empirical approaches suggests that higher-quality schools, however defined, lead students to have higher subsequent earnings in the labor market.

Problems

1. Is a positive correlation between education and wages evidence of a positive return to education? Why or why not?

2. Between 1980 and 2012, tuition increased by 270–300% in real dollars. Does this mean college is now a worse investment than it was in 1980?

3. The government of Tuvalu has hired you to estimate the returns to schooling among its citizens. You have administrative data on the amount of education for each person's mother (*mothed*) and father (*fathed*), parental income when children in elementary school (*income*), IQ score (*IQ*), and completed education (*education*). You estimate a regression of wages at age 30 on these variables. Can you interpret the coefficient on completed education as the causal effect of education on wages? Why or why not?

4. Concerned over the potential problems with the regression from problem 3, you have decided to look only at identical twins. How would you use twins to estimate the returns to schooling? What problems might there be in interpreting the resulting estimate as the causal effect of schooling on wages?

5. In the paper "Does compulsory school attendance affect schooling and earnings?" by Angrist and Krueger (1991), differences in quarter of birth are shown to be correlated with educational attainment and, in turn, future earnings. Why is there a relationship between quarter of birth and educational attainment? Under what assumptions can we use comparisons of earnings among individuals born in different months of the year to measure the causal effect of education on wages?

6. Anna and Elsa are sisters with very similar genetics and home environments. With her magical ice powers, Elsa decides to go into the ice sculpture business, which requires only a high school education. Anna, however, is more interested in working with people and decides to go into politics. This requires a college education. Why is it problematic to use the comparison of Anna's and Elsa's wages as an estimate of the return to college?

7. While having lunch with his friend *Mr.* Howard Joel Wolowitz (Howie), *Dr.* Sheldon Cooper decided to explain to him that he makes more money not only because he has a PhD. but also because he is a "master." Sheldon estimates that wages at the university can be approximated by $W = A\ln(E)$, where E is years of education and A is ability. Sheldon's ability is 4,200 and Howie's ability is 3,600. Furthermore, Sheldon calculates that the cost of obtaining schooling level E is given by $C = 200E$. Assuming that Sheldon's estimation of the cost and benefit functions are correct, answer the following questions:
   a. Calculate Sheldon's and Howie's years of education assuming Sheldon and Howie choose the level of education that makes them best off.
   b. Calculate Sheldon's and Howie's wages when they obtain the level of education found in part a.
   c. Calculate Sheldon's wage if he had Howie's education.

d. Explain why it is not optimal for Howie to get more education than he did.

e. Is it incorrect to interpret the difference in Howie's and Sheldon's wages as the return to education?

8. What is the implication of sheepskin effects for the Mincer model?

9. In what ways do colleges differ that may affect future earnings of graduates? Explain how economists measure the return to college quality and the arguments for and against using each type of measure.

10. In a paper published in the *Journal of Human Resources* (2016), Andrews, Li and Lovenheim find that at the top of the earnings distribution, community college and non-flagship four-year graduates earn the same amount. Lower in the earnings distribution, community college graduates earn much less than non-flagship four-year graduates. Is this pattern consistent with a human capital model, a signaling model in which one's highest degree attained is the only signal, or both? Explain.

11. The government of Tuvalu wants you to expand your study of the returns to education by examining the returns to college quality (see questions 3 and 4). In Tuvalu, there are three types of public colleges (and no private colleges): an elite public flagship school (University of Tuvalu—Funafuti), three less selective public schools (Tuvalu State University, Northern Tuvalu University, and Southern Tuvalu University), and a set of two-year colleges.

You have all of the data described in question 3 plus information on where each student went to college.

a. Using the sample of those who attend college, you estimate a regression of wages at age 30 on all control variables (except *education*) and include indicator variables for whether someone attended the flagship or not and whether someone attended one of the less selective public four-year schools or not. What might be the problem with interpreting the resulting estimates as the causal effect of attending each college type on wages?

b. To overcome some of these problems, you now compare students who applied to and got into both the flagship school and one of the non-flagship four-year schools but who made different enrollment decisions. Does this comparison allow you to accurately estimate the causal effect on wages of attending Tuvalu University—Funafuti? Why or why not?

12. Suppose a selective state flagship university employs a cutoff in test scores, which is not known at the point of application, to determine admission. How might this administrative rule, combined with the observation of earnings a decade later, be used to estimate the return to attending the state flagship university? Why would the publication of the admissions cutoff to students and families before application likely invalidate this estimation approach?

inputs Factors used in the process of production. With respect to education, any factors or resources that contribute to building an individual's cognitive ability or knowledge.

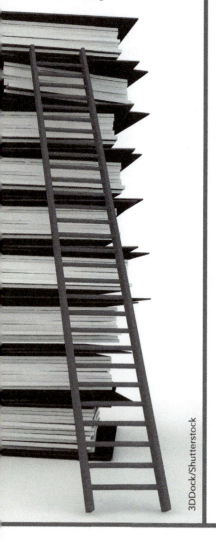

3DDock/Shutterstock

How Knowledge Is Produced: The Education Production Function

Knowledge Production Versus the Production of Computers

How are the skills, knowledge, and cognitive abilities of students produced? This is the central question that surrounds education policy, since the core goal of the education system is to help in the building of such skills. Put differently, we want to know how to combine various factors, or **inputs**, to increase student cognitive ability and knowledge.

As a reference point, imagine you are the manager of a plant that produces computers. You understand what raw materials are needed to produce the computer—screen, keyboard, hard drive, memory—and the plant provides the production process whereby the inputs are combined to produce the computer. This production process is straightforward precisely because both the inputs and the process are known, and the outcome of the process—computers—is known and simple to observe. As a plant manager, you can improve profits either by producing the same number of computers at a lower cost or by producing higher-quality (and thus higher price) computers with the same inputs. Both changes would involve altering the production process to make it more effective, and it is simple to know whether any such changes work because the quality of computers and the costs of production can be observed.

Now consider how this straightforward production process relates to the production of knowledge and skills. Principals and administrators face a similar problem to that of the computer plant manager—namely, they seek to combine education inputs to produce student learning. However, the challenge faced by the principal is considerably harder than that of the computer plant manager. One main difference between the two is that the principal does not have a full understanding of what all of the relevant inputs are or, more precisely, each input's degree of relevance. Exactly how important are education inputs such as teacher quality, availability of computers, textbooks, class size, and peer quality to the production of knowledge? As we will discuss throughout this book, the evidence on the importance of those various inputs is mixed, leading to much uncertainty about which inputs are most important and how best to combine these inputs to produce knowledge.

Many education inputs cannot be purchased in the market and are hard to quantify. For example, the quality of one's peers is both difficult to measure and cannot be purchased in the same way that a computer or textbook can. Similarly, education is what we call a **customer input technology**. This term refers to the fact that what a student gets out of the education system depends on the effort he or she puts in. If a student puts in no effort, the education system is unlikely to produce any knowledge in that student, while the same education system may have large impacts on a student who puts forth lots of effort. This is in stark contrast to the production of the computer, the quality of which is unrelated to the characteristics of the customer who buys it.

A final difference between computer production and education production is that in the former we can measure the outputs directly, but in the latter the full range of outputs from education is often difficult to measure and may include outcomes that occur many years in the future, like earnings or citizenship. Some cognitive ability also is "innate" or is produced in nonschooling environments such as the home. Thus, unlike the production of a computer, a principal only has control over some part of the production technology. How do we measure students' cognitive abilities, skills, and knowledge? How do principals know they are producing the "right" outcomes when those outcomes are very hard to measure, and how can we isolate the school's role in knowledge production from what students learn outside of school?

The focus of this chapter is on understanding the **education production function**, the process by which the outcomes of education, such as cognitive ability and knowledge, are produced from the "raw" inputs. The terminology and concept of the education production function borrow heavily from the standard analysis of production in microeconomics, in which firms choose inputs such as capital and labor to maximize profits, given a production function and prices of inputs and outputs. As the prior example illustrates, issues surrounding the uncertainty about the inputs to the production function, the form of the production function itself, and how to measure outcomes make education a far more difficult process to understand and to manipulate with policy than a typical production setting.

We focus in particular in this chapter on theoretical issues surrounding the education production function. This theoretical model will be used throughout the book as a framework to think about how various education policies might influence student achievement. We begin by presenting a simple two-input education production function to demonstrate the economic intuition that comes from this model. We then will extend the model to include multiple inputs, and we provide a discussion of the role of the education production function in guiding education policy. The chapter will conclude with a discussion of the empirical issues faced by researchers who want to use data to understand aspects of the education production function. These issues will surface throughout the later chapters of the book when we discuss empirical research related to education production.

customer input technology A production technology in which those who purchase the outputs are also inputs. In terms of education, student effort is an important input into the production of the knowledge and skills that form the output of the education process. This is in contrast to the production of a typical commodity, in which the quality of the final product is unrelated to which consumers purchase it.

education production function The process by which the outcomes of education, such as cognitive ability and knowledge, are produced from the "raw" inputs.

7.1 Microeconomics of Production Functions

The foundation for assessing how student knowledge and skills are produced is the education production function. In general, a **production function** measures the link between inputs and outputs. Production functions in education parallel the more general concepts that you may have seen in other economics classes: Schools combine inputs, such as teachers and computers, to produce educational outputs.

production function Specifies the way in which a set of inputs are combined to produce a final product.

Uncertainties about which inputs matter, what the production process is, and what is the "right" output measure can make analyses of education production functions very complex. We thus will start with a basic model with two inputs—teachers (T) and computers (C)—and consider the predictions from economic theory about the level of student achievement (A) produced by schools. This is akin to a standard production function in economics, with labor and capital as inputs and with a single, well-measured output. We then will provide extensions of the model that help account for some of the complexities in understanding the education production process.

The Production Function

Let's start by thinking about a school that faces a production function in which teachers and computers are combined to produce student achievement (A): $A = f(T, C)$. The function $f(.)$ represents the education production function and shows how teachers and computers are combined to produce student achievement. In the current notation, we have left this function general. A considerable body of research that will be discussed in the ensuing chapters is devoted to understanding what the function $f(.)$ looks like. All production functions, including education production functions, are expected to have some basic properties that are critical to understand:

- Positive **marginal product (MP)** of inputs: increasing an input generally will have a positive effect on student achievement if we hold the other inputs constant.
- **Diminishing marginal product**: adding additional units of one input while holding other inputs fixed will increase output by successively smaller amounts. That is, marginal product of a given input declines as you add more of the input without altering other inputs.
- **Returns to scale**: increasing all inputs simultaneously will increase total output. **Increasing returns to scale** occur when doubling all inputs more than doubles output. A production function exhibits **decreasing returns to scale** when output less than doubles when all inputs are doubled, and **constant returns to scale** refers to the case when doubling all inputs exactly doubles output.
- Short run versus long run: Whether or not some factors can be added or subtracted depends on the time frame considered. Some factors are fixed in the short run, such as the number of classrooms and the quality of the school's facilities. In the long run, all factors can be altered.

> **Quick Hint:** In more technical terms, marginal product is the first partial derivative of the production function with respect to the given input, and diminishing marginal product means that the second partial derivative of the production function with respect to the given input is negative.

In terms of the education production function with two inputs, these properties tell us that adding another teacher (or computer), holding the level of the other input fixed, will increase educational output but will do so at a declining rate. We will use the notation MP_T and MP_C to describe the marginal products of teachers and computers, respectively. We expect both MP_T and MP_C to be positive but to get smaller as we add more teachers and computers, respectively.

marginal product (MP) The change in output generated by employing one more unit of a particular input, holding all other inputs fixed.

diminishing marginal product The marginal product of a given input declines as additional units of the input are added, holding all other inputs fixed. Adding additional units of an input, holding other inputs fixed, eventually will make each of those units less and less important for production.

return to scale The rate of increase in output in relation to an increase in the inputs.

increasing returns to scale Doubling all inputs more than doubles output.

decreasing returns to scale Doubling all inputs less than doubles output.

constant returns to scale Doubling all inputs exactly doubles output.

Diminishing marginal product, or the law of diminishing returns, as it often is called, is a particularly important property of production functions. To understand the intuition, consider a classroom with 1 teacher and 15 computers and compare it to a classroom with 1 teacher and 0 computers. The effect of adding one additional computer to the first classroom will be smaller than the effect of adding a single computer to the second classroom. The impact on both classrooms might be positive, but adding a computer in a classroom that previously had none has a larger marginal impact than adding one in a classroom with many. At some point, there will be 0 marginal return to adding computers, likely around the point at which there is one computer per student.

Choosing Input Levels

How should schools make decisions about the choice of inputs? In our example, how does the principal decide whether to hire more teachers or to buy more computers? Because the marginal product of inputs is increasing, principals clearly would like to have as much of all inputs as possible. However, they face a **budget constraint**, which shows the trade-offs they have to make among the various inputs at the level of total resources available to them. In other words, the budget constraint shows the combination of inputs that the school can afford to purchase at prevailing prices. Because resources are not infinite, principals have to choose how to allocate their total budget across inputs, and the relative prices of the inputs determine the cost of such trade-offs.

Figure 7.1 shows a budget constraint for our two-input example of computers and teachers, where p_T and p_C represent the prices of teachers and computers, respectively. The slope of this line is determined by the relative prices of the two goods, and the position of the budget constraint is set by the total revenue of the school. Increases in revenues produce an outward parallel shift in the budget constraint, while input price changes rotate the budget constraint. For example, the two right lines in Figure 7.1 show that an increase in total revenue shifts out the budget constraint, while the left line shows what happens when the price of computers rises relative to the price of teachers, holding the total resource level constant.

Given total school resources and input prices, how do schools choose the best mix of inputs? In the context of for-profit firms, the answer is to choose inputs to maximize profits. Schools, however, typically do not operate as for-profit firms. So what are they trying to maximize if not profits? An equivalent way to think about the production problem of a firm is **cost minimization**. From the perspective of the computer manufacturer, for example, this means producing a target number of computers at the minimum cost. While schools are not attempting to maximize profits, they do face resource limitations that make cost minimization a useful framework for thinking about their decision problem. At base, they are trying to produce a specific level of an education outcome (be it test scores, grade completion, or understanding of particular

budget constraint Shows the trade-off between various inputs given input prices. The slope of the budget constraint is given by the relative prices of inputs, and the location of the constraint is determined by the overall amount of money the school has to spend.

cost minimization The objective of a firm that is analogous to profit maximization. The firm's goal is to produce a given output at the minimum possible cost. This will lead to the same input allocation as trying to maximize profits.

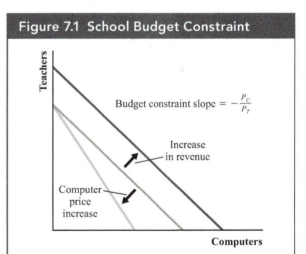

Figure 7.1 School Budget Constraint

$$\text{Budget constraint slope} = -\frac{p_C}{p_T}$$

Increase in revenue

Computer price increase

The school budget constraint for the two-input model shows all combinations of computers and teachers the school can afford. The budget constraint is given by $R = p_T \times T + p_C \times C$, where R is total school revenues and p_T and p_C represent the prices of teachers and computers, respectively. The slope of this line is determined by the relative prices of the two goods, and the position is set by the total revenue of the school. Increases in revenues produce an outward parallel shift in the budget constraint, while input price changes rotate the budget constraint.

concepts) at the minimum cost. Like the manager of the computer plant, a school principal must decide how to combine the various inputs at her disposal to produce those educational outcomes at the lowest cost.

To solve this cost minimization problem for the school, we need to know how much student achievement will increase by spending another dollar on a given input. As discussed previously, the marginal product gives us the effect of adding an additional input on the output of interest. Thus, the amount of output we can expect from purchasing an additional dollar of an input is the marginal product of the input divided by its price: $\frac{MP}{p}$.

The ratio $\frac{MP}{p}$ is extremely important in the cost minimization problem because it allows us to express the contribution of each input to producing the output on the same scale: dollars. Hiring an additional teacher is different from purchasing a computer because one teacher is much more expensive than one computer. We therefore would not expect the marginal product of a teacher to be the same as the marginal product of a computer. Dividing each marginal product by the price of the input allows us to compare the marginal product per dollar of each input so that we can determine whether spending an additional dollar on teachers will raise output more than spending an additional dollar on computers. If spending another dollar on computers leads to large gains in student achievement, while spending another dollar on teachers leads to only modest gains in achievement, a school should spend more of its budget on computers and less on teachers. A gain in achievement could be achieved by reallocating inputs without changing total spending.

efficient in production
Refers to the case of when there is no way to combine the school's resources to produce a higher level of outputs.

We say a school is **efficient in production** if there is no way to combine resources to produce a higher level of student achievement. Using this logic, productive efficiency occurs when the marginal product per dollar of each input is equalized. In terms of our two-input example, the school is efficient in production when:

$$\frac{MP_T}{p_T} = \frac{MP_C}{p_C}.$$

The intuition for this result is that if the last dollar spent on each input is not equalized, it is possible to generate achievement gains by reallocating expenditures among inputs without increasing total spending on education. For example, if the marginal product per dollar for teachers is 3 and the marginal product per dollar for computers is 2, reallocating one dollar from computers to teachers produces a productivity increase of 1. This reallocation will produce output gains until the marginal product per dollar is the same across the inputs. At that point, we can no longer shift resources around at the same overall expenditure level to increase total output; the school is efficient in production. The Toolbox shows a graphical derivation of this result and presents a mathematical example of how to calculate optimal input allocations.

TOOLBOX: The Efficient Allocation of Inputs

To derive the expression for the efficient allocation of inputs graphically, we begin with a school budget constraint. Assuming schools spend all of their revenues, total expenditures equal total revenues. The formula for the budget constraint shown in Figure 7.1 is:

$$R = p_T \times T + p_C \times C$$

The left-hand side of this equation is total revenues (R), and the right-hand side is total expenditures. Total expenditures here are on teachers and computers only, as this is a two-input model.

Expanding the set of inputs means the right-hand side would include more inputs multiplied by their respective prices. The slope of the budget constraint is equal to the negative of the price ratio:

$$Budget\ constraint\ slope = -\frac{p_C}{p_T}.$$

Quick Hint: To derive this result, solve the budget constraint formula for T: $T = \frac{R}{p_T} - \frac{p_C}{p_T}C$. Here, $\frac{R}{p_T}$ is the y-intercept and $-\frac{p_C}{p_T}$ is the slope of the budget constraint.

Schools may be able to produce the same level of learning with different combinations of teachers and computers—lots of computers and a few teachers may produce the same outcome as many teachers and few computers. An **isoquant** shows different combinations of inputs that produce the same amount of an output. Figure 7.2 shows an example of isoquants for the production function, with teachers and computers as the inputs. Movements along each isoquant produce the same level of A (the output), while an outward shift represents an increase in A.

> **isoquant** Shows combinations of inputs that can be combined to produce the same amount of an output.

The slope of the isoquant in Figure 7.2 is given by the ratio of the marginal products of the inputs:

$$Isoquant\ slope = -\frac{MP_C}{MP_T}$$

Quick Hint: In terms of calculus, the marginal product with respect to computers is $\frac{\partial f(C, T)}{\partial C}$ and the marginal product with respect to teachers is $\frac{\partial f(C, T)}{\partial T}$. These are the partial derivatives of the production function with respect to each input.

The diminishing marginal productivity of each input gives the isoquant its shape. As we move leftward along the isoquant, adding more teachers and reducing the number of computers, the marginal product of each teacher declines and the marginal product of each computer increases. Thus, the slope becomes steeper. As we move rightward along the isoquant, the reverse situation occurs: The marginal product of computers declines and the marginal product of teachers increases. As a result, the slope flattens.

Graphically, the efficient allocation of inputs occurs when the school is on the highest isoquant that it can afford. This is shown in Figure 7.3. The right isoquant is the highest affordable isoquant,

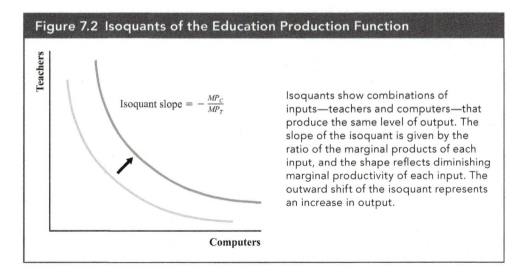

Figure 7.2 Isoquants of the Education Production Function

Teachers

Isoquant slope $= -\frac{MP_C}{MP_T}$

Computers

Isoquants show combinations of inputs—teachers and computers—that produce the same level of output. The slope of the isoquant is given by the ratio of the marginal products of each input, and the shape reflects diminishing marginal productivity of each input. The outward shift of the isoquant represents an increase in output.

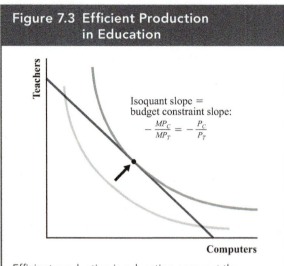

Figure 7.3 Efficient Production in Education

Efficient production in education occurs at the tangency between the isoquant and the budget constraint. At this point the marginal product per dollar of each input is equalized: $\frac{MP_C}{P_C} = \frac{MP_T}{P_T}$. It is not possible to alter the allocation of resources to increase output.

as it is just touching the school's budget constraint. Any higher isoquant (and thus higher level of *A*) would require more revenue than the school has, and a lower isoquant, such as the left isoquant, does not maximize output given available resources. The point shown in Figure 7.3 is the highest level of output the school can produce with the given resources and production technology. This tangency point therefore is the point at which resources are being allocated efficiently; any reallocation of resources will reduce output. At this tangency point, the slope of the budget constraint equals the slope of the isoquant. That is, the ratio of the marginal products equals the price ratio of the inputs. Rearranging this formula, we see that setting the ratio of the marginal utilities equal to the price ratio is the same as equalizing the marginal product per dollar of each input:

$$-\frac{P_C}{p_T} = -\frac{MP_C}{MP_T} \Rightarrow \frac{MP_T}{p_T} = \frac{MP_C}{p_C}$$

This is the condition that characterizes productive efficiency.

We now show an example of how to calculate the efficient resource allocation in practice. First, we need to know input prices as well as the total resources available to the school, then we need to specify a production function that tells us how inputs relate to outputs. Assume the budget constraint for a school is given by:

$$500 = 10T + 2C$$

and that the education production function is of the Cobb–Douglas form:

$$A = 2C^{\frac{1}{2}}T^{\frac{1}{2}}$$

By taking the first derivative of the production function with respect to both *C* and *T*, we can calculate the marginal product of each input:

$$MP_C = C^{-\frac{1}{2}}T^{\frac{1}{2}}$$

$$MP_T = C^{\frac{1}{2}}T^{-\frac{1}{2}}$$

The ratio of the marginal products is:

$$\frac{MP_C}{MP_T} = \frac{C^{-\frac{1}{2}}T^{\frac{1}{2}}}{C^{\frac{1}{2}}T^{-\frac{1}{2}}} = \frac{T}{C}$$

The optimal allocation of inputs occurs when the ratio of marginal products equals the price ratio, which in this example leads to:

$$\frac{T}{C} = \frac{2}{10} \Rightarrow 10T = 2C \Rightarrow C = 5T$$

This expression tells us how *C* and *T* are related when inputs are optimally allocated: There will be 5 computers per teacher. To find the allocation that is achievable under the resources available, we plug this expression into the budget constraint:

$$500 = 10T + 2(5T) = 10T + 10T = 20T$$
$$T^* = 25$$
$$C^* = 5 \times 25 = 125$$

The optimal input allocation is achieved with 25 teachers and 125 computers.

The equation characterizing the optimal allocation of inputs highlights the importance of input prices in driving resource allocation decisions. Suppose that in our two-input model, a school is at an efficient allocation point, such that the marginal product per dollar of each input is equalized. Now, consider what happens when the price of teachers rises: The marginal product per dollar for teachers will be lower than that for computers, leading to a substitution away from teachers and toward computers. Intuitively, as teachers become more expensive relative to computers, we should use more computers and fewer teachers. Thus, as relative prices change, the efficient mix of inputs also changes.

Substitution across inputs because of price changes can lead otherwise similar schools to have different optimal resource allocations. For example, in New York City, where labor costs (and thus teacher salaries) are high, it will be optimal for schools to use relatively more nonteacher inputs (such as computers). In contrast, in Ithaca, New York, where labor costs are much lower, schools should use relatively more teachers. That schools in New York City and Ithaca allocate resources differently therefore may reflect the different input prices they face rather than inefficient resource allocation decisions.

DEEP DIVE: Technology in the Classroom: Changing Input Prices and Education Production

Input price changes driven by technological change in the economy can affect the education production process. The proliferation of computers and information technology is a stark example of this phenomenon. Since the 1970s, computer processing speed has increased at an exponential rate (in accordance with Moore's law[1]), which has led to a dramatic increase in computer processing power and a reduction in the cost of computers. Coupled with the rise of the Internet over the past three decades, access to information and our ability to analyze it have never been easier and cheaper in human history. One can think of these changes as reducing the prices of key inputs to the education production process. How have these changes affected education production?

The answer to this question varies somewhat depending on what level of education one examines. In the K–12 system, there is mixed evidence on the role of computers in the development of human capital. One of the most influential studies on this question was done by economists Ofer Malamud and Cristian Pop-Eleches (2011), who examined a computer subsidy program for low-income children in Romania. Using a regression discontinuity approach surrounding eligibility for the program, they found that receiving a subsidy increased the likelihood of getting a personal computer, led to better computing skills, but also lead to worse grades in school. They also found some evidence of test score increases from the computer subsidy program.

While Malamud and Pop-Eleches focused on home computers, computer use in the classroom also can affect learning. Of course, computers tend not to be randomly assigned to classrooms, so a mere association between computer access and student outcomes does not tell us the causal effect. Joshua Angrist and Victor Lavy (2002) overcame this problem using the expansion of computers in classrooms in the mid-1990s in Israel, which was driven by lottery proceeds. They found that the expansions greatly increased computer use but had no effect on test scores. Together with the Malamud and Pop-Eleches findings, these results suggest that computers have a limited effect on measured outcomes among K–12 students.

The effects of computer and information technology have been somewhat different in the higher education sector. Here, computers and the Internet have changed the way some students interact with the postsecondary system through the proliferation of online courses and degree programs. In the 2011–2012 school year, 32% of students enrolled in the U.S. higher education system took an online class. In addition, 6.5% were enrolled in a degree program that was entirely

---

[1] Moore's law refers to the observation made by Gordon Moore that the number of transistors per integrated circuit doubles every two years.

online.[2] Many of these online degree programs and courses are offered by the for-profit sector, but online classes also offer a relatively low-cost way for all colleges and universities to meet enrollment demands. These courses allow as well for much more flexibility among students in terms of the time demands of taking college credits. Thus, the ability to take courses online may make it easier for students to balance the demands of working while enrolled.

Computing technology has changed the day-to-day operation of more traditional postsecondary classroom environments, too. Instructors can disseminate information more easily, students can access readings from the comfort of their rooms without going to the library, and students can engage with each other and the instructor through online discussion tools. That computers and the Internet have altered the way in which higher education services are delivered is apparent by examining how reliant both students and instructors are on their computers and access to the Internet. What remains to be studied, however, is the effect these large changes in higher education service delivery have on postsecondary outcomes and the cost of higher education.

---

[2] These tabulations come from the 2013 *Digest of Education Statistics*, Table 311.20.

The Education Production Function with Many Inputs

Although we introduced the production function by thinking about a production process with two inputs, in actuality there are many inputs to the education process that schools and local education policy makers control. Examples of such inputs include school facilities, textbooks, teachers' aides, and the composition of one's peers within a school. It is straightforward to extend this model to accommodate a production function with many inputs.

Let $X_1, X_2, ..., X_N$ denote N potential inputs to the education production function. The production function that translates these inputs into some educational output, A, is given by $A = f(X_1, X_2, ..., X_N)$. Each input also has a price associated with it: $p_1, p_2, ..., p_N$. Similar to the two-input model, the optimal allocation of funds requires that the effect of an extra dollar spent on each of the N inputs be the same:

$$\frac{MP_1}{p_1} = \frac{MP_2}{p_2} = \cdots = \frac{MP_N}{p_N}.$$

The intuition for this result is the same as in the two-input model. If an extra dollar spent on any one input produced a larger effect on A than a dollar spent on the others, one could reallocate spending to increase output, holding the total amount of expenditure fixed.

The model presented thus far has not made any distinction about the quality of the inputs. For example, we have considered teachers all to be the same in terms of their effect on educational outcomes. This simplification has obvious limitations: Some teachers are more effective than others, and other inputs like computers, textbooks, and school facilities all can differ dramatically in terms of their quality. In theory, the education production function can handle quality differences among similar inputs very simply.

In terms of teachers, we can define teachers of differing quality as different inputs. The price of a teacher of a given quality then would be the "quality-adjusted" price. Such a price typically requires that higher-productivity teachers cost more than lower-productivity teachers, and so while they have a higher marginal product, they also come with a higher price. Hence, many of the goods in the N-input production function might be different quality levels of the same good. Principals then must decide both how to allocate funds across broad groups of inputs (e.g., teachers, computers, facilities) and how to allocate resources across the different types of each input (e.g., how many old versus new computers to purchase). While more complex, an education production function with inputs that vary by quality has the same optimality condition: The effect of a dollar spent on each input must be the same across all inputs. However, quality differences in inputs often are hard to observe, which makes the resource allocation problem faced by policy makers considerably more difficult. This is particularly an issue for teacher quality, which is a point to which we will return at length in Chapter 9.

7.2 Implications for Education Policy

Different Types of Education Policies

The basic education production function model produces powerful predictions about how different types of education policies should affect student achievement. There are three broad types of policies that education policy makers typically consider:

- *Total resource policies* increase or decrease total school revenues. In theory, schools then may alter their expenditures so that the effect of spending an additional dollar on each input is equalized.
- *Input policies* alter a particular input, such as class sizes, the qualification level of teachers, or school facilities.
- *Output policies* provide incentives for schools and teachers to increase output by tying some monetary reward to measured outcomes like student test scores.

Total resource policies shift out the budget constraint. As shown in Figure 7.4, increasing revenues moves the budget constraint to the right. In effect, the school now can increase both inputs, and we would expect the principal to choose a new combination so that:

$$\frac{MP_T}{p_T} = \frac{MP_C}{p_C}$$

In the figure, this is represented by going from point *A* to point *B*. Adding inputs increases output, so as a result of shifting out the budget constraint, achievement should increase.

If policy makers at the school district, state, or federal level have a better understanding of the need for specific inputs than principals do, input-based policies may be desirable. Input-based policies typically take the form of a government mandate that requires schools to have certain levels of a given input. Examples include maximum class size rules, a requirement that all teachers earn a certification before teaching, and a law mandating that there be a minimum number of computers per student in each classroom.

Figure 7.5 shows how a policy requiring that each school have a minimum number of teachers $(\underline{T})$ affects the budget constraint and therefore the allocation of school resources. The solid line shows the original budget constraint. The minimum teacher mandate cuts off the bottom part of the budget constraint, as now schools

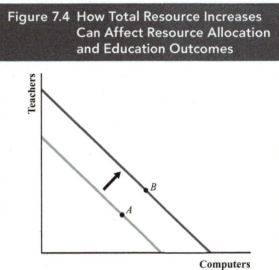

Figure 7.4 How Total Resource Increases Can Affect Resource Allocation and Education Outcomes

Total resource policies shift out the budget constraint by increasing school revenues. The school moves from the left to the right. The principal now can choose a new combination of inputs, going from point A to point B. Adding inputs increases output, so achievement should increase because of an increase in total resources.

Figure 7.5 How Input Policies Can Affect Resource Allocation and Education Outcomes

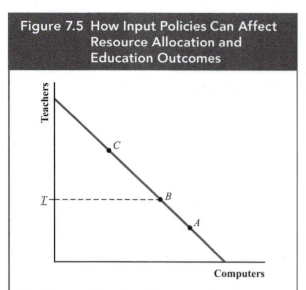

A policy mandating the minimum number of teachers ($\underline{T}$) or the maximum class size in each school changes the applicable part of the budget constraint. The solid line shows the original budget constraint. Imposing a rule specifying the minimum number of teachers, means that the school must choose a number of teachers at or above point B. If the school was at point C prior to the policy, it will have no effect on resource allocation. If it was at point A prior to passage of the rule, the policy will force the school to purchase fewer computers and to hire more teachers, up until it has $\underline{T}$ of them, at which point it will be at point B.

cannot have below $\underline{T}$ teachers. The feasible part of the budget constraint is the segment above the dashed line. The effect of school resource allocation varies by how many teachers were employed by the school prior to the policy. If the school was at point C, where they were employing more than $\underline{T}$ teachers, the policy will have no effect on resource allocation. However, if it was at point A, the policy will force the school to hire more teachers, up until it has $\underline{T}$ of them, at which time it will be at point B.

The resulting impact on student achievement is difficult to predict. If the school is initially at point C, achievement will be unaffected by the policy. If the school is initially at point A, the teacher mandate forces it to substitute teachers for computers. Depending on the marginal product per dollar of each input at points A and B, this could lead to either an increase or a decrease in efficiency (and thus achievement).

The policies discussed thus far are focused on inputs. If the goal is to increase student achievement, it may be possible to reach it by providing incentives for schools to increase specific achievement measures. These types of policies are termed output-based policies because they are focused directly on increasing student outcome measures rather than on inputs that policy makers believe will increase achievement. Examples of such a policy are teacher incentive pay, which provides monetary rewards to teachers for meeting specified performance levels, and school choice, which allows students to attend schools other than their zoned local public school and thus creates competition among schools for student enrollment.

The argument advocated by proponents of output-based policies is that these policies tie performance to compensation by linking measured outcomes, such as test scores or graduation rates, to money or other rewards such as public recognition. One of the desirable characteristics of output-based policies is that they usually do not require a lot more resources other than the monetary reward. Instead, they provide incentives to use preexisting resources more efficiently, thus increasing student achievement. Output-based policies also have the potential to provide insight into the education production function. By providing incentives for school districts to innovate and experiment with different ways to raise student achievement, they can produce new information on how knowledge is produced.

> **Quick Hint:** The lack of a profit motive also can support input policies. If principals allocate too few resources to a given input because of the absence of a motivation to use resources efficiently, targeting that input through an input-based policy could help fix this problem.

At the same time, output policies can be problematic because they, by design, favor some types of outputs over others. The outputs of the education system are multifaceted, including measured test scores but also creativity, the ability to work in teams, civic engagement, and self-esteem. Aside from test scores, these outputs are very difficult to measure systematically. Output-based policies typically focus on test scores because they are straightforward to measure and are standardized. If policies that produce higher test scores also produce these other, difficult-to-measure outcomes, then focusing policy on improving test scores should produce better student outcomes across the board. However, if policies that increase test scores have no effect, or even a negative effect, on these other outputs, output-based policies can cause distortions in the education process that may not be intended.[3] We will discuss this issue more in Chapter 11 when we discuss school accountability and in Chapter 12 when we examine teacher incentive pay.

Theoretical Arguments for Different Education Policies

From a theoretical perspective, total resource policies are very appealing. As shown in Figure 7.4, giving schools more money shifts out the budget constraint, which should lead to higher achievement levels. Why, then, do we need other types of policies? After all, wouldn't the simplest policy be to give schools money and allow them to spend it in a manner that maximizes student achievement?

The central challenge facing total resource policies is that schools may not be allocating resources efficiently: They may not equalize the marginal product per dollar of each input. This inefficiency can come about for two reasons:

1. The production function is not known. While administrators may have ideas about how to produce knowledge, we have yet to uncover the magic formula that tells us how to transform inputs into education outputs consistently.
2. Schools face insufficient competitive pressures to induce them to allocate resources efficiently.

Lack of knowledge of the production function is an important hurdle to implementing sound education policy. Despite their best intentions, administrators and teachers may misallocate resources because they do not know what the efficient allocation mix is. In such cases, simply giving schools more money may do little to raise achievement, as this money will not be used efficiently. Input-based policies provide a potential remedy to this problem when some schools are purchasing too little of an input. However, such policies require that some policy makers understand the production function sufficiently well to determine the minimum input amount needed to raise achievement.

The second challenge faced by total resource policies is that public schools do not face the same types of competitive pressures as private firms. The owner of a private firm has incentives to maximize profits because he or she is the owner of those profits. Failure to maximize profits typically will lead the firm to go out of business as well. Conversely, consider a principal, superintendent, or school board member. Public schools are not profit driven, and aside from the very real motivation to educate students, there often is little external incentive placed on these policy makers to increase educational achievement. That public schools are unlikely to close due to poor performance further reduces outside incentives to raise achievement.

---

[3] See Holmstrom and Milgrom (1991) for a detailed discussion of production with multiple outputs, some of which are difficult to measure.

As a result of the lack of incentives to maximize achievement, schools may allocate resources inefficiently. Furthermore, administrators may be responding to political pressures—for example, from teachers' unions or parents—when allocating inputs, which could lead to an inefficient allocation. Output-based policies can help solve the problem by providing monetary incentives to allocate resources more efficiently, which can increase student achievement. Input-based policies also can help remedy this problem, especially when political pressures on administrators lead to an allocation in which too little of a given input is used.

7.3 Challenges to Estimating Education Production Functions

Thus far in this chapter, we have covered the basics of production function theory as it relates to education, and we have examined the importance of production function analysis for education policy. As our discussion has highlighted, a serious problem facing education policy makers is the lack of information about the form of the education production function. As our access to education data has grown along with the computing power necessary to analyze these data, economists have learned a lot about the education production function, which has been highly informative for policy. In this section, we discuss the challenges inherent in estimating an education production function.

Given the importance of the education production function for guiding education policy, why is there still so much uncertainty about what this function looks like? After all, academic researchers have been exploring this question for decades. How can there still be so much ambiguity about how to produce knowledge? The answer is that establishing causal relationships between the relevant inputs and the relevant outputs of education is extremely difficult. The production function, by definition, tells us how inputs are translated into outputs, so estimating a production function requires us to estimate these causal links. Because school inputs typically are not randomly assigned to schools, this is not a simple task. So while the theory underlying education production functions is straightforward, there are substantial challenges to applying this framework in an empirical setting.

There are a number of complications in empirically estimating an education production function. These complications come in four basic forms:

- *Measuring inputs.* What are the relevant inputs to student learning? There are many potential determinants of learning, some of which are under the control of the school (such as the number of teachers) and some of which are not (such as parent and community resources). Many inputs, like teacher quality, are also very hard to measure.
- *Measuring outputs.* While it is convenient to think about a single composite measure of student achievement such as a standardized test score, the outcomes of education are likely to be multidimensional and are often difficult to measure in the short run.
- *Specifying the production process.* Knowing the exact "technology" that leads to student learning is extremely difficult, and it is likely that best practices vary among students with different needs and different background characteristics.

- *Choosing the unit of analysis.* Input allocation decisions in education are made by many actors, such as the federal government, state government, school district, principal, and individual teachers. To estimate how specific inputs translate to educational outputs, we must determine which of these units are relevant for the input allocation decisions under consideration.

Measuring Inputs

As discussed in section 7.1 under the heading "The Education Production Function with Many Inputs," there are many potential inputs to the education production function. Thus far, we have focused mainly on the inputs that schools can control, such as teachers, classroom technology, and school facilities. But in thinking about what factors drive learning, it is apparent that children's knowledge and skills come from several sources that often are outside of the control of the school:

- *Family background.* There are enormous differences across children in the amount that their parents are able to invest in their education. For example, compare a child who grows up in a family with one illiterate parent to a child who grows up in a family with two college-educated parents. The latter child has parents who can provide far more resources in terms of time and individual knowledge to facilitate the production of knowledge. Furthermore, factors like child health and parental income have been shown to be important inputs to the development of knowledge and skills.
- *Peers.* Inputs to a student's learning include fellow students, and thus the learning and behavior of one student can affect outcomes for other students. The presence of peer effects may impact the optimal assignment of students to classrooms— do students learn more when students in a grade differ in ability or when there is tracking? One might also think about how one particularly disruptive student may adversely affect the learning of other students in a classroom. Peer effects create a peculiar challenge for modeling education production, as each student's learning is an input to the education of other students as well as the outcome we are interested in measuring for that student.
- *Community inputs.* Factors such as the crime rate of the neighborhood one lives in and the ability to observe first-hand information about the value of an education from highly educated adults in one's local area can affect educational outcomes.

The central problem in estimating education production functions is that school-based inputs are highly correlated with these nonschooling inputs. For example, let's say we are interested in estimating the effect of class sizes on student outcomes. One way we could proceed would be to relate differences across schools in their average class sizes to differences across schools in their average test scores. This is an example of a cross-sectional comparison. If we saw that those schools with smaller classes had higher test scores, is this evidence that smaller classes cause the higher test scores? The answer is no for several reasons:

- Schools with different class sizes differ in terms of other school-based inputs, such as teacher quality and per-student spending. It could be that schools with smaller classes have more overall resources with which to purchase other inputs, which makes class size look more important for education production than it actually is.

- Schools with different class sizes have different types of students. If students with wealthier, more educated parents sort into schools that have smaller classes, we will overstate the role of class sizes in producing student test scores.
- Schools with smaller classes may be in lower-crime neighborhoods and can have higher peer quality.

The main problem we face in making these cross-sectional comparisons is that class sizes are not randomly assigned across schools. As a result, schools that differ in terms of class sizes are likely to differ along a number of other dimensions that independently relate to student outcomes. This is a classic example of an omitted variables bias, and even with a very detailed dataset, we are unlikely to be able to control for all of these confounding factors.

One potential solution to this problem is to use repeated observations of schools over time. With panel data on schools, we can compare *within-school* changes in class sizes to *within-school* changes in test scores (or some other student outcome of interest). As long as the composition of the student body and the neighborhoods from which the school's students are drawn do not change much over time, such within-school comparisons can handle many of the problems that arise with cross-sectional estimates.

However, examining within-school changes over time does not necessarily solve the problem because it usually is unclear why class sizes in a school are changing. What if classes are getting smaller because school district revenues are growing? In this case, class size reductions are positively correlated with increases in other school resources. This is a case of **complementary resource allocation**, and it will bias class size estimates away from zero. Conversely, imagine that a school is experiencing declines in test scores and reduces class sizes to try to reverse this trend. Class size changes would be an example of **compensatory resource allocation**, as they are compensating for other educational deficiencies. If class size changes are compensatory, it will bias the estimates toward zero because class sizes are declining more in schools in which test scores also are declining the most for other reasons.

A final approach to solving the omitted variables bias problem would be to relate outcomes in a class to the size of the class within a school, year, and grade. While this comparison may seem like it can control for the most confounding factors, as it is making comparisons across children within the same school, grade, and year, it actually is subject to the same problems as the other approaches. Complications again arise because neither students nor teachers are randomly assigned to classes. Principals could assign the lowest-performing students to the smallest classes (a compensatory policy), or they could assign the best students to the smallest classes (a complementary policy). They have similar leeway to make teacher assignments to different class sizes, which also can be either complementary or compensatory. Because this allocation process is hard to observe, the existence of student outcome differences across different-sized classes within the same school, grade, and year does not necessarily provide us with evidence of a causal effect of class size on student outcomes.

While this discussion focused on class size, similar difficulties arise with trying to estimate the causal role of any school-based input on student outcomes. At base,

complementary resource allocation Provides more resources to students who have access to higher levels of resources outside of the schooling environment.

compensatory resource allocation Provides more resources to students from disadvantaged back-grounds whose families have fewer nonschool resources.

because schools have control over a small number of inputs to the development of cognitive ability and because these inputs are not allocated randomly across students, it is not straightforward to ascertain which inputs are the most important for education production and which schools are the best at producing knowledge. This dimension of the production function makes the production of education very different from the production of physical goods, like cars. Being a principal is a little like being the manager of a single automobile plant within a large corporation in which the quality of the raw materials differs dramatically across plants and is largely outside of the manager's control. Building cars that are of consistently high quality when one is allocated lower-quality inputs is extremely challenging.

Given these difficulties, how can we estimate education production functions? In general, researchers have taken three approaches:

- Use the small number of randomized controlled trials that have been done to assess the role of specific inputs
- Find natural experiments that generate as-good-as-random variation in specific inputs
- Use rich administrative and survey data to attempt to control for confounding factors such as student background characteristics, neighborhood and peer quality, and other school-based inputs

We cover these approaches in more detail in Chapter 9 in the context of class sizes and teacher quality, which are the two education inputs that have received the most attention in the empirical literature.

Measuring Outputs

While the designation of the outcome from schooling as student achievement (A) is straightforward in theory, it is hardly transparent in practice. One complication is that there are many desired outcomes of education. In each grade, schools teach a number of subjects, including math, reading, writing, social studies, and so forth. Beyond the problem of multiple subjects, many of the skills that schools aim to teach are not easily captured by standard tests. For example, it is hard to measure commitment to citizenship, artistic ability, creativity, and self-esteem on most tests, but most teachers would likely argue that these are important skills to impart to students.

The fact that some outputs are easier to measure than others is a problem for education policy if the inputs that produce measured outcomes (like test scores) are less effective at producing difficult-to-measure outcomes (like creativity). Thus, the difficulties associated with estimating education production functions with multiple educational outcomes are directly tied to how correlated these outcomes are with one another and the extent to which they are similarly impacted by the same inputs (Holmstrom & Milgrom, 1991). Moreover, one might ask whether the outcome of interest to policy makers or parents is total student learning (the sum of learning across all students) or a measure that incorporates distributional considerations, such as maximizing the share of students who achieve at some minimal level.

Not only is there an absence of consensus about what the outcome of interest is for schools (i.e., what should administrators maximize), but the technology for measuring what schools teach is far from complete. In particular, there is considerable concern that many of the objectives of school-based learning affect long-term outcomes, like earnings or civic participation. These outcomes are difficult to assess with short-term testing instruments, and they make policy analysis challenging because of the need to wait many years before assessing whether a given policy is effective.

With the growing availability of large administrative datasets that permit researchers to link policy interventions among students to their long-run outcomes, like educational attainment and labor market earnings, there is a mounting body of evidence that short-run outcomes may be insufficient to understand the effect of education policies. A core finding is that effects on standardized test scores of a number of different interventions, from reduced class sizes to teacher and classroom quality, tend to fade out after the intervention ends and then reappear later in life in the form of better long-run outcomes of affected students. These studies call into question whether short-run achievement measures are sufficient for understanding the effects of education policies on students.

Specifying the Production Process

In many manufacturing or engineering processes, it is possible to describe a production function with great precision. In essence, one could look at a setup of blueprints or manuals that specify quite precisely the raw materials and the process of assembly. The understanding of how students learn and how different inputs affect learning is an area of inquiry in its own right. Indeed, one of the reasons economists and other social scientists are so focused on education production functions is that testing different models is a way to learn about the underlying nature of the production function for student learning.

There are two main concerns in thinking about how to specify the production process: (1) differences across students in how they learn and (2) interactions of school and home inputs. The first concern is simply the fact that students learn in different ways and often have very different educational needs. Because students learn in different ways, inputs may have different effects on different students. Although the production function can be specified to handle some heterogeneity across students, we are always limited by sample sizes and our ability to measure the factors that predict this heterogeneity. The education production functions estimated by economists tend to focus on averages, but these averages may mask important differences across students.

The second concern relates to the fact that the impact of school inputs may be different depending on parental inputs. This problem also works in reverse: parents may compensate for a deficiency in school inputs, and their ability to do so may differ markedly according to their own educational background as well as their preferences for their children's education.[4] For example, it may appear in some environments that teacher quality is unimportant, but this could be because parents are compensating for low-quality teachers in a way that hides their effect on student outcomes. Because parent inputs are rarely observed, this makes it very hard to assess the causal impact of a given school input on student outcomes.

---

[4] Put differently, parental inputs may be complements or substitutes for schooling inputs. A related concern highlighted by economists Flavio Cunha and James Heckman (2007) is that inputs may exhibit dynamic complementarities in which education investments at a young age make later-in-life education investments more productive.

Choosing the Unit of Analysis

Input allocation decisions are made at many levels, from the federal government to individual teachers. These are the most important factors to consider when thinking about the appropriate unit of analysis:

- *The federal government* provides specific types of aid to schools, typically focused on low-income students and students with disabilities. Many education regulations that have important implications for resource allocation decisions also come from the federal government.
- *The state government* accounts for a significant proportion of resources for most schools. States can allocate aid equally to all districts or can give more aid to lower-income districts to help equalize spending in the state.
- *The school district* takes the total amount of resources from the federal and state government as well as from local taxes and decides how to allocate these resources to individual schools in the district. The school district also makes important staffing decisions, such as assigning principals to schools, and creates school attendance zones that allocate students to specific schools.
- *The principal* decides which teachers to hire, how to allocate them to different classes, and which students to assign to which teachers.
- *The teacher* makes decisions about how much time to spend on each subject, how to divide time among different types of instruction (for example, individual versus group), and on which students to expend more instructional effort.

Importantly, the resource allocation decisions made by one unit can affect decisions made by all of the others. For example, a state regulation that ties teacher pay to test scores can affect how principals allocate teachers to different students and how much time teachers spend on specific subjects and preparing for exams. Paying attention to the unit of analysis is important, particularly if we want to understand the mechanisms through which resource policies at the state and federal level affect student outcomes through their impact on the school district's, principal's, and teachers' reactions to these policies.

7.4 Conclusion

How schools use resources can have a substantial impact on student achievement. At each level of academic leadership—superintendents, principals, and teachers—there are key questions to answer about how resources are allocated between different potential inputs. Economic theory in the form of a production function motivates optimal input choices, given prices, to maximize student achievement.

Looking forward, we will focus on the structure of the K–12 and higher education systems and discuss specific policies that are being used to increase the quality of education in the United States. In Chapter 8, we discuss how total resources are determined at the district level, and in Chapter 9 we present the evidence on whether school resources and specific inputs affect educational and labor market outcomes as predicted by the education production function. Chapters 10–12 explore important questions concerning what types of output-based incentives and policies can lead to improved use of existing resources.

Highlights

- Schools typically behave as **cost minimizers**. They attempt to produce outputs at the lowest possible cost, given their total level of resources and the prices of education **inputs**.
- A school is **efficient in production** when it equalizes the **marginal product** per dollar of each input. If this condition holds, it is not possible to alter resources in a way that will increase output. Graphically, the efficient point occurs where the **isoquant** is tangent to the school **budget constraint**.
- All **production functions** have some basic properties: positive marginal product, **diminishing marginal product**, either **increasing**, **decreasing**, or **constant returns to scale**, and the extent to which inputs are fixed in the short versus the long run.
- The **education production function** specifies how one takes the various inputs to education and combines them to produce the outputs of education. The production of education differs in important ways from the production of normal consumer goods: We have incomplete knowledge of what the relevant inputs are; there are multiple outputs to education, many of which are difficult to measure; there is little understanding of the technology that

produces those outputs from the inputs; and there are complications related to the multiple units of analysis.

- There are three types of resource-based policies that policy makers can use: total resource policies, input policies, and output policies. The desirability of these policies is based on whether schools allocate resources efficiently or whether changes in incentives or specific inputs are needed.
- Estimating education production functions is difficult because resources and inputs are not randomly assigned to different schools or to different students within a school. Comparisons both across schools and within schools over time are problematic for uncovering the causal effect of inputs on educational outcomes, and the bias can go in either direction, depending on whether there is **compensatory resource allocation** or **complementary resource allocation**.
- Education production function estimation is further complicated by the fact that many outcomes of the education process are difficult to observe. If these outcomes respond differently to a given input than do observable outcomes, our production function estimates will not provide a complete picture of the effect of the input.

Problems

1. Rhonda is the manager of a plant that produces cars, while Sofia is the principal of a local elementary school.
   a. What is Rhonda's main objective as the manager of the car plant?
   b. Assuming Rhonda has full knowledge of the production function for cars, what will she do to meet this objective?
   c. How is Sofia's objective as principal similar to or different from Rhonda's objective as a plant manager?
   d. Explain the differences in the way knowledge relative to cars is produced that make it more challenging for Sofia to meet her objectives.
2. Consider an education production function with two inputs: teachers, and books.
   a. Draw the budget constraint associated with these two inputs, with books on the *x*-axis. What determines the slope of the budget constraint?
   b. Draw the isoquant that shows the efficient allocation. What is the slope of the isoquant? What

property of production functions gives it its shape?
   c. Why can't the school achieve a point above the budget constraint?
   d. Show what happens to the efficient allocation if the school district gets more overall resources. What if the price of books rises?
3. Define the term "education production function."
   a. Name three potential inputs to the education production function that come from schools.
   b. Name three potential inputs to the education production function that come from outside of school.
   c. How does the fact that inputs come from the schooling environment and from other areas of children's lives complicate the study of how school-based inputs impact educational outcomes?
4. Why do we call education a customer input technology? Is the same true of the production of a normal commodity good, like automobiles?

5. Consider the various outputs of the education process.
   a. List three outputs that are easy to measure.
   b. List three outputs that are difficult to measure.
   c. How does the existence of the difficult-to-measure outputs complicate our understanding of the education production function?

6. Explain the difference between a total resource policy, an input policy, and an output policy. Give an example of one of each type of policy.

7. In terms of the education production function, what are the potential costs and benefits of giving principals more flexibility in determining how resources should be allocated? How do these costs and benefits relate to the relative desirability of resource-, input-, and output-based policies?

8. Suppose a school's total revenue is $10 million per year. The cost of hiring a teacher for a year is $50,000, and the cost of leasing a computer for a year is $5,000.
   a. Write the equation for the budget constraint.
   b. Draw the budget constraint.
   c. What is the price of teachers in terms of computers? How does the budget constraint show these relative prices?
   d. Can the school afford to hire 200 teachers and lease 10 computers?

9. Imagine you have been made the superintendent of a school district. As part of your job, you need to allocate resources among four inputs: teachers, books, pencils, and smart boards. Each one of these inputs has a price associated with it, denoted P_t, P_b, P_p, and P_s, respectively.
   a. Explain what the marginal product of books is.
   b. Holding the number of teachers, pencils, and smart boards constant, will the marginal product of books increase or decrease as you add more books? Explain.

c. Write the formula that shows how marginal product and prices will be related among all four inputs when allocation is efficient. Describe in words what this efficiency condition means.
   d. Is providing the best teachers to the weakest students an example of a complementary or a compensatory policy?

10. Consider the problem of how teachers can allocate their time between group instruction (G) and individual instruction (I). The number of students in the class (N) is 30. The class time is 300 minutes per week. Assume that each student gets the same amount of time of individual instruction (I).
    a. What is the budget constraint faced by the teachers?
    b. What happens to the budget constraint if we increase total instruction time by 50 minutes?
    c. What happens to the budget constraint if we decrease class size to 20 students?

11. Explain what peer effects are. Give an example of a positive and a negative peer effect. Why does the existence of peer effects make it difficult to model the education production function?

12. The Hogwarts School of Witchcraft and Wizardry has three inputs: wands (w), potions (p), and broomsticks (b). Wands cost 2 galleons, potions cost 10 galleons, and broomsticks cost 20 galleons. Assume the total budget of the school is 1,000 galleons. The production function is given by $A = w^{\frac{1}{4}} p^{\frac{1}{2}} b^{\frac{1}{4}}$.
    a. Calculate the marginal product of each input.
    b. What is the relationship between wands, potions, and broomsticks that characterizes an efficient allocation?
    c. Calculate the efficient allocation.
    d. What happens to the efficient allocation if the price of wands doubles? What happens if there is a tax increase in the wizarding world that leads revenues to increase to 1,500 galleons?

CHAPTER 8

The Financing of Local Public Schools

3DDock/Shutterstock

Serrano v. Priest

In 1968, John Serrano found himself concerned over the quality of the public schools in Los Angeles, of which his son was a student. He did not believe his son was receiving an adequate education, and when he approached local education leaders to ask about what could be done to increase the quality of the education his son was receiving, he was told that his best option was to enroll him in another district that had more money. Frustrated that he needed to move to a different school district to provide his son with an adequate education, he joined a class action lawsuit against the State of California. The lawsuit claimed that the existing system of school financing violated the state's equal protection provision, based on the fact that school district revenues were raised almost fully by local property taxes. Low-income areas faced many difficulties in raising sufficient revenue for local schools because property values often were lower than in high-income areas. This led to lower tax revenues and hence lower school spending. Since many parents place considerable value on school quality when making decisions about where to live, the lower levels of funding in lower-income districts can feed back into property values, which further depresses tax revenues and funding for schools.

The class action lawsuit argued that this system of funding necessarily led to funding disparities across school districts that put districts serving low-income students at a disadvantage. In 1971, the California Supreme Court issued an historic ruling, *Serrano v. Priest*, which was a sweeping victory for the plaintiffs. The ruling stated:

> We have determined that this funding scheme invidiously discriminates against the poor because it makes the quality of a child's [public] education a function of the wealth of his parents and his neighbors. Recognizing, as we must, that the right to an education in our public schools is a fundamental interest which cannot be conditioned on [individual] wealth, we can discern no compelling state purpose necessitating the present method of financing. We have concluded, therefore, that such a system cannot withstand constitutional challenge and must fall before the equal protection clause.

While the California Supreme Court ruled that complete local financing of public schools violates the equal protection clause of the California State Constitution, it had nothing to say about how to fix this problem.

How can we fund public schools in a way that provides equality of educational opportunity when localities may have very different resources? In particular, how can this be done without ceding local control to a central authority like the state or federal governments? People in different localities vary in their preferences for funding education; to what degree should we respect the preferences and priorities of local residents over and above the need to educate all children adequately? Furthermore, government interventions to reduce funding disparities across districts can result in distortions that yield an inefficient allocation of resources for education. How can we balance equity versus efficiency in the financing of public schools? These are the fundamental questions of **school finance**, which is concerned with the level and distribution of funding available to schools. As we will see, states and education policy makers have been struggling with these issues ever since *Serrano*.

Serrano v. Priest was a landmark ruling that highlighted the need for more equity in school financing across schools serving students of different socioeconomic backgrounds. It no longer was legal in California for wealth differences across school districts to drive funding differences across those same districts. The ruling unleashed a torrent of lawsuits and legislative reforms that continue to this day. Changes to the way in which schools are financed, often in response to legal and political pressure, are referred to as **school finance reform**. Since *Serrano*, virtually every state has altered its school financing system in response to either court or legislative action. The result has been a large decline in the inequality in funding across school districts within states: One highly influential research paper estimates that court-mandated school finance reforms reduced within-state inequality in spending across schools by upward of 34% (Murray, Evans, & Schwab, 1998).[1]

In this chapter, we examine where schools districts get their money and how funding sources and the forms of taxation affect spending on education. Do different funding schemes have implications for **allocative efficiency** and **productive efficiency** as well as for equity in the provision of education? Keep in mind that equalizing funding across districts does not guarantee equalizing educational outcomes across districts. This occurs because out-of-school inputs vary across schools and because schools may differ in how productively they use inputs. What is more, it is unlikely that equality in funding is efficient for two reasons: Different students have different educational needs and costs, and families may differ in their desire to devote resources to education.

The source of funds and the mechanism of taxation used to finance schools potentially has a large impact on the level and distribution of resources for elementary and secondary education. It is too simplistic to assert that equalization or redistributing resources through centralized policies will necessarily make students better off. Indeed, a key lesson that economics brings to school finance is that we need to think about *why* there are differences in funding across districts and how people will respond to changes in taxes and subsidies as we design school finance systems. Ignoring behavioral responses to tax and funding changes can cause unintended consequences that can lead to worse outcomes than before the reform, which is one of the cautionary lessons of the school finance reform movement.

school finance The revenue sources that fund schooling. We are interested in the source of these funds, the level of funds, and the distribution of funds across schools.

school finance reform The set of legal and legislative changes designed to decouple the link between property values and education spending and to increase equity in per-pupil spending across schools within a state, as well as the adequacy of education services.

allocative efficiency When there is no reorganization of resources across schools or students that could improve outcomes for at least some students without making any worse off.

productive efficiency (efficiency in production) When a school is distributing inputs in such a way as to maximize total output.

---

[1] The evidence on whether these reductions in funding disparities have led to reductions in achievement disparities within states is mixed. We discuss this research in Chapter 9.

This chapter begins with an overview of trends and levels of school financing in the United States. We then consider the economic model for local provision and public control of education. This basic model, known as the Tiebout model, helps us to think about the determinants of efficiency in the production of education. Families' choices about where to live reveal preferences for educational provision, while competition among districts can help to foster productive and allocative efficiency. In the third section, we evaluate the economic arguments for a greater degree of centralization in school finance and present some of the judicial history and precedents that have generated the wide range of school finance systems in place in the United States. In the final section, we consider how different school finance systems affect the level and distribution of funding for schools and then turn to the assessment of school finance reforms.

<u>8.1</u> School Financing in the United States: Trends and Levels

In the United States, there is a long tradition of local control and of predominantly local financing of schools. Local control has the advantage of allowing people to match their preferences for education with the characteristics of local schools. At the same time, the significant differences in wealth across districts often lead to substantial inequality in spending on schools. The local control of schools historically is highly valued in the United States, and federal and state efforts to local control typically are met with vigorous opposition.

Despite the high level of decentralization and local control in the United States, the dominant trend over the past half century has been toward more centralization. Figure 8.1 shows the number of public school districts in the United States from 1940 through 2010. Even though the population of the United States grew dramatically over this period, there has been a marked consolidation of school districts. In 1940, there were over 117,000 separate school districts, while by 2010 the number had shrunk to 13,625. The large reduction in the number of school districts was driven by the elimination of single-room schools in rural areas rather than the merging of school districts in more urban areas (Fischel, 2009). Much of this consolidation occurred in the two decades

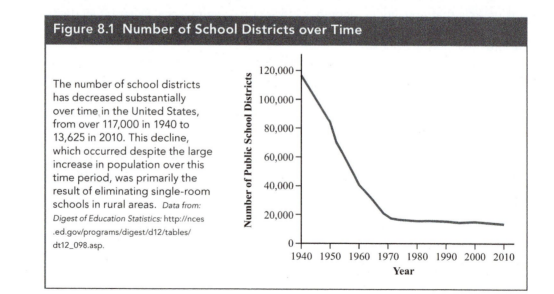

Figure 8.1 Number of School Districts over Time

The number of school districts has decreased substantially over time in the United States, from over 117,000 in 1940 to 13,625 in 2010. This decline, which occurred despite the large increase in population over this time period, was primarily the result of eliminating single-room schools in rural areas. *Data from: Digest of Education Statistics:* http://nces.ed.gov/programs/digest/d12/tables/dt12_098.asp.

after World War II, such that since the 1970s the number of districts has shrunk only slightly.

A related trend, shown in Figure 8.2, is a move away from local financing of public schools to more state and federal support. In 1940, 68% of school revenues came from local sources, while only 30% came from the state and less than 1% came from the federal government. By 1970, right before *Serrano v. Priest* was decided, the state and federal share of revenues had grown to 40% and 8%, respectively. Thus, the shift to more centralized forms of financing was occurring even before the school finance reform movement took off. By 2010, state and local sources accounted for roughly equal shares of revenues, at 47% and 44%, respectively, and federal contributions had grown to almost 10% of total revenues. Together, Figures 8.1 and 8.2 demonstrate that education provision in the United States is much more centralized today than it was a century ago, both in terms of the share of resources that come from state and federal sources and in terms of the number of independent school districts.

A final important trend in school financing that has occurred over the past 70 years is a dramatic rise in the *level* of funding. Figure 8.3 shows total expenditures per student in constant 2011 dollars from 1940–2010. In real terms, per-student expenditures increased from $1,447 to $12,756 over this period, an increase of 782%! Other than a flattening of expenditure growth in the early 1990s, this increase has occurred at a steady pace since 1940. In the next chapter we will discuss the evidence on what, if anything, these additional expenditures have achieved in terms of students' academic outcomes.

To fund increasingly large expenditures on public schools, state and local governments must levy taxes on their citizens. Policy makers have many types of taxes

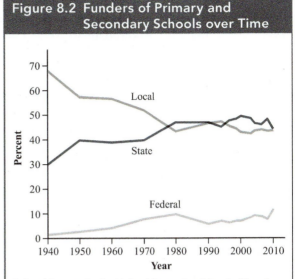

Figure 8.2 Funders of Primary and Secondary Schools over Time

School finance in the United States is a blend of local, state, and federal resources. In the early twentieth century, schools were funded predominantly with local resources obtained through property taxes. Since the 1930s, there has been increasing centralization of school finance. While federal funds remain about 10% of schools' resources, the share of state and local funds is now nearly equal. *Data from: Digest of Education Statistics:* http://nces.ed.gov/programs/digest/d12/tables/dt12_202.asp.

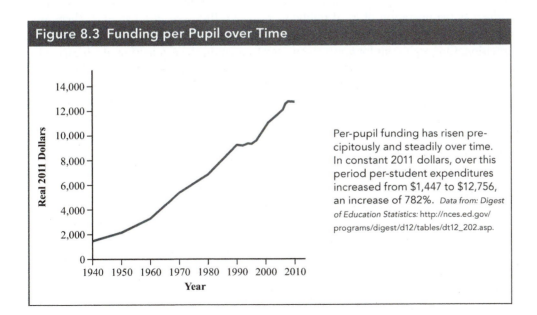

Figure 8.3 Funding per Pupil over Time

Per-pupil funding has risen precipitously and steadily over time. In constant 2011 dollars, over this period per-student expenditures increased from $1,447 to $12,756, an increase of 782%. *Data from: Digest of Education Statistics:* http://nces.ed.gov/programs/digest/d12/tables/dt12_202.asp.

available to them. At the local level, most schooling revenue comes from property taxes on school district residents. State governments have many more tax instruments at their disposal:

- Income taxes
- Sales taxes
- Statewide property taxes
- Excise taxes, levied on particular commodities like cigarettes, alcohol, and gasoline
- Revenues from lotteries, gambling, and casinos
- Tobacco litigation settlement revenues

Some local governments also can levy income, sales, and excise taxes. In addition, certain areas have taxes on restaurants and hotels that can be used to finance education. Centralization of school financing often implies a shift in the types of taxes that are used to fund public schools, which can have important implications for the tax burden borne by different types of people in the economy.

8.2 Local School Choice: Voting with Your Feet

What are the costs and benefits of local control of school finance? How does a shift to more centralized finance affect the level and distribution of schooling resources students receive as well as where families choose to live? This section presents arguments for government intervention in education markets and provides a theoretical framework that will help us think about what is the "right" mix of local versus state and federal funding in public education finance. As we will see, economic theory identifies circumstances in which local control leads to efficiency in the provision of public education. However, these circumstances are unrealistic in practice, which allows for a potentially important role to be played by higher levels of government.

Localities provide a range of community services, such as road maintenance, police protection, and utilities like sewage and water. But the largest single item on most local budgets is the operation of local public schools. As discussed in Chapter 2, there are several reasons why it might be desirable for governments to be involved in schooling provision. One argument for government involvement in the production of education is that school districts are able to benefit from **economies of scale**. Local school districts are able to coordinate provision of education across grade levels, arrange for student transportation, and provide services like special education for students with disabilities and athletic facilities that individual families would find it difficult to finance independently. By spreading out the fixed costs of schooling to a larger set of students, government provision of education therefore can reduce the overall cost of provision.

Additionally, families may lack the resources to invest in the optimal amount of education, a circumstance that economists term **credit constraints**. Credit constraints arise when there is a mismatch between families' ability to pay and what they would like to spend on education. They arise in part because parents with young children are often early in their own careers, with levels of income far below later career earnings. Some children also are born into low-income families with limited capacity to pay for education. If these families cannot borrow to finance their desired level of education investment in their children, they will underinvest in education.

economies of scale When average costs are declining with additional students; in this sense, it will cost less per student to operate one relatively large high school than multiple small high schools in a local area. Large fixed costs of school district operation can generate economies of scale.

credit constraint Arises when an individual cannot borrow money or cannot borrow money at a sufficiently low interest rate to finance an educational investment that would have a positive rate of return if the individual could borrow at the market rate.

Government financing of education can help overcome these credit constraints by increasing the ability of students from low-income backgrounds to invest in human capital.[2] It also is the case that there may be a public interest in funding education, to the extent that there are substantial positive externalities and spillovers from education that benefit society at large, such as higher economic growth, a more informed and engaged electorate, and lower crime.

These reasons for possible government intervention in schooling say little about whether any public provision should be done by local versus state or federal governments. Why might local provision be preferred to more centralized government control? The core economic argument for more local control is that people have different preferences. Some want to live in areas that provide certain types of education environments and some would rather spend money on other local goods, such as parks and roads, than on schools. Others still may prefer low taxes and a small amount of local service provision. Put simply, the more localized the control of public services, the more people can move to an area with a local government that matches their preferences.

The Free Rider Problem

How does a local government decide on the total level of resources to devote to public education? One—albeit naïve—approach would be to ask each resident to record his or her preferences for education and to tax them accordingly. It is easy to imagine that such a system would quickly unravel, as individuals would not have any incentives to reveal their preferences truthfully. When there is a large number of individuals in the community, each person's contribution to government finances is small. Thus, even when residents have a high private valuation of education services, they might lie about their true preferences to avoid paying more in taxes. Since each individual's contribution is a small proportion of the total, the effect of any one person underpaying on total provision will be small. This is called the **free rider problem** in public economics.[3] The free rider problem leads to too little being spent on education, as residents will systematically underreport their preferences for education services. As a result of the free rider problem, reliance on people to volunteer their willingness to pay for education is unlikely to produce sufficient resources to operate a school system. To this end, a key problem in the provision of local services is the challenge of **preference revelation**: how localities can learn the preferences of residents to achieve the efficient provision of local services.

The Tiebout Model

In an ingenious paper published in 1956, Charles Tiebout suggested that with a sufficiently large number of localities for residents to choose from, the market mechanism would reveal people's preferences and in the process lead to an efficient provision of

free rider problem A situation that occurs when people can benefit from goods and services without paying for them, often resulting in underprovision of collective and public goods. Because each person's contribution is a small part of the total and as all members of the community receive these goods and services, individuals will find it in their best interest to spend little and free-ride on the donations of others. This leads to underprovision of the good or service.

preference revelation How localities can learn the true preferences of residents to be able to tax them in accordance with their desired level of the public good or service.

---

[2] Financing schools through local property taxes also is a way for the government to alleviate credit constraints (Hoxby, 1996). Schooling investments are made when children (and thus parents) are younger and tend to have fewer resources. Instead of having to pay for the full cost of educating their children up front, property taxes allow parents to spread out education costs over a longer period, as one must continue to pay property taxes even when one's children are no longer enrolled in the local schools.

[3] For a more detailed treatment of the free rider problem, see the discussion of public goods in Gruber (2012), *Public Finance and Public Policy*.

public services. Tiebout's insight was essentially that people make comparisons among communities, such that the difference in housing prices between localities captures the valuation at the margin for local services. In essence, this is a model of voting with your feet: if you don't like the public services in one community, then move to another town where the public goods and services better match up with your preferences. Thus, there is no need to ask people how much they want to spend on public schools, as the choices they make will reveal their demand.

In the Tiebout model, the capacity of consumers to exercise choice and the resulting competition among localities lead to an efficient allocation, with housing prices acting as the driving force for clearing the market. This mechanism can induce efficiency in the provision and allocation of services produced at the local level, such as education. If there is a large number of communities available, a local school district that is using resources unwisely or inefficiently will find families moving to districts that make better use of resources. In this sense, competition among localities leads to productive efficiency. In addition, the presence of a number of localities providing different levels or quality of resources per student gives families choice, which allows for the matching of preferences to educational offerings. This generates allocative efficiency.

For example, let's say there are two families, the Griffins and the Quagmires, who have similar levels of income and wealth. The Griffins have three children and highly value education. They therefore have a high willingness to pay to live in an area with a lot of quality school services. The Quagmires, on the other hand, have no children and do not value school services. If, on the margin, people place a high value on school services, then the areas with more such services will be more expensive to live in. This will lead to the Griffins expressing their preferences by purchasing a more expensive home in a school district with higher levels of education services. The Quagmires can purchase a similar home for less in a district that offers fewer education services. The two families have sorted according to their preferences for education, with relative home prices acting as the force that allows them to express those preferences in a truthful manner. This sorting of families according to preferences for local public goods and other amenities is termed **Tiebout sorting**. As a result of this sorting process, property values in areas with more (or better) schooling services will tend to be higher because families like the Griffins outnumber families like the Quagmires.

Efficiency with Tiebout sorting follows for two reasons. First, as illustrated by the example of the Griffins and Quagmires, families will sort across school districts such that their preferences for schooling match the amount of schooling services provided by the local government. This generates allocative efficiency. Second, each district has the incentive to allocate education resources to achieve productive efficiency. Districts with the same spending would be expected to have the same outcomes, otherwise people would vote with their feet and move to obtain the better value in schooling.

Challenges for the Tiebout Model

The theoretical version of the Tiebout model of local provision of education can lead to schooling outcomes that are efficient in production and efficient in allocation. Yet there are good reasons to believe that the full set of assumptions necessary to achieve this outcome are not satisfied in practice. Let's focus on the specific assumptions that

Tiebout sorting The process by which families will sort across localities to find the locality that has the right mix of taxes and public services to match their preferences.

are implicit in the Tiebout model and consider what might happen if these assumptions do not hold:

- *Mobility.* Families must be able to vote with their feet—mobility costs cannot deter moving. *Problem:* Families are likely to face large direct costs to moving, and employment commitments may limit their capacity to move to a location with better schools. This is a particular issue for low-income families that may not be able to afford moving costs.

- *Full information.* Families must have full information to evaluate the quality of schools in a particular area as well as the benefits that their children would receive from attending particular schools. *Problem:* It may be very hard for parents to know whether a particular school is "high quality," as inputs like teacher quality and long-term outcomes may be difficult to observe. It also is difficult for families (and researchers) to establish causality: How certain can they be that schools are causing the educational outcomes they observe?

- *Many options.* If families differ in their taste for education, there must be a large number of options to match each family's taste for educational services. *Problem:* Outside of very large metropolitan areas, it may be impossible to have a large number of districts without having districts that are too small to provide economies of scale in the provision of education.

- *Absence of spillovers or externalities.* The setup does not allow for benefits of education provision to the nation or to neighboring communities. *Problem:* With population mobility, poorly educated students from one community may generate negative externalities through crime and dependence on social services in another community, while highly educated citizens may generate positive externalities through invention and civic contributions.

- *No resource constraints.* The model holds that families will be able to afford to live in in the communities with educational services that best meet the needs of their children. *Problem:* Many low-income families likely face considerable resource constraints in their ability to afford to live in a school district that satisfies their preferences for education. Thus, many families may be forced to live in areas that underprovide educational services.

Because each of these assumptions is likely violated to some degree in practice, pure local school finance in which all school resources are raised through local taxes is unlikely to achieve either allocative or productive efficiency. Consider, for example, why educational expenditures historically were lower in school districts serving low-income populations; it is far more likely that resource constraints and lack of mobility and information are more common among low-income populations than that these families place a very low value on education. Indeed, this is the rationale for the school finance reform movement.

Empirical Evidence on Tiebout Sorting

How well does the Tiebout model do in explaining how families make locational decisions? There is ample evidence that the Tiebout model can describe several phenomena related to local housing prices and the location decisions of different families. A key feature of Tiebout sorting is that home values (prices) will contain information about the quality of the local public schools and families' demand for school quality. Think specifically about how school quality is then **capitalized** into home prices. Consider

capitalization (of school quality into home prices) The extent to which quality differences across schools are reflected in price differences across houses in different school attendance zones.

two homes that are identical in every way—number of bedrooms, number of baths, and so on. One home is in a district that is widely recognized as having exemplary schools; the other is in a district known for having weak schools. We would expect the difference in the prices of the homes to reflect the amount that parents are willing to pay for high-quality schools.

As this example illustrates, evidence that local school quality affects home prices is consistent with the Tiebout model. In fact, it is the differences in home prices across areas with different local amenities (such as education) that allow parents to vote with their feet to express their preferences for the given amenity. Importantly, all local amenities, such as parks, road quality, and neighborhood safety, should be capitalized into the price of housing. One of the central tests of the Tiebout model, therefore, has been to see if local property values do indeed respond to variation in local amenities. Because of the dominance of school spending in local budgets, capitalization of education quality is the amenity that has received the most attention in the empirical literature.

What we want to measure is whether there is a strong link between the quality of the public schools in an area and parents' willingness to pay for housing. There is a problem, however: Differences in school quality across areas typically are correlated with differences in the quality of the housing stock, other local amenities, and neighborhood characteristics. If we were just to compare the selling prices of homes to some measure of school quality at public schools nearby these homes, we would get a biased measure of how parents value school quality because it is likely that such a measure will confound housing characteristics (number of bedrooms, number of baths) and neighborhood characteristics (proximity to parks and public transportation) with school characteristics.

Researchers have taken several approaches to try to solve this empirical problem. In one of the most influential studies to address this question, Sandra Black (1999) examines differences in the prices of houses in close proximity that are assigned to different schools on either side of an attendance zone boundary within a school district.[4] Attendance zones are areas within a district in which all of the families send their child to the same school. Black has detailed data on home sale prices and school characteristics in the Boston suburbs, using information on 22,679 single residence homes, 39 school districts, and 181 attendance zones.

Figure 8.4 shows attendance zones from a school district to illustrate the kind of comparison that Black makes in her analysis. Consider the prices of similar houses in the same neighborhood (as defined by the circled areas) that happen to fall on opposite sides of an attendance zone

Figure 8.4 Measuring How School Quality Is Capitalized into Housing Prices

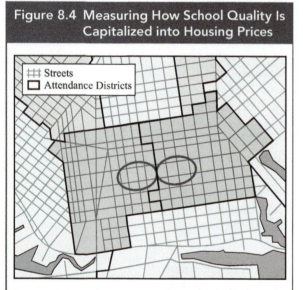

Streets
Attendance Districts

One testable implication of the Tiebout sorting model is that the quality of public education is capitalized into housing prices. It is difficult to test this hypothesis because houses differ in many ways aside from the schools to which they are zoned. Sandra Black devised a method of testing the hypothesis by comparing the prices of houses that were in close geographic proximity—and also had similar characteristics—but were zoned to different schools that had different performance levels. For example, Black compared the price of houses in one circled area to those in the other, adjacent circled area. *Data from:* Black (1999), Figure I.

---

[4] Black's analysis examines how quality differences across schools within a district are capitalized into property values. This may be different from how quality differences across districts are capitalized because all schools in the same district face the same tax level and are controlled in part by a similar central administration.

boundary (as defined by the thick lines). Black compares price differences across attendance zones within the same neighborhood as they relate to school quality measures. She uses student average performance on a standardized test as her measure of school quality and finds that homes within a neighborhood are worth about $4,000 more on the high test score side of the attendance zone border than on the low test score side: The test score differs by 5%. Because the composition of residents and houses within a neighborhood is very similar, it is likely the price difference is due to the school quality difference and not some other characteristic of these various attendance zones within a neighborhood. This evidence points to the conclusion that home buyers highly value school quality.[5]

A second approach has been to study shocks to local residents' information about school quality. In an innovative study, Figlio and Lucas (2004) examine the effect on property values of Florida releasing "school report cards" that provide information on local schools' test scores. The report card information most likely increased local residents' knowledge of school quality, and Figlio and Lucas show that receiving higher grades led to large increases in property values. Interestingly, these effects were relatively short-lived, fading out after the first year. Their study therefore provides further evidence that parents value school quality. It also suggests that parents do not have perfect information about the quality of local schools, because if they were fully informed, the information would not have affected home prices.

Another implication of the Tiebout model is that in areas with more schooling options, productive efficiency should be higher. This is the case because parents can move across schools more easily when there are more choices, which induces competition among these schools. Of course, it would be highly problematic to compare student outcomes across different cities with different numbers of school districts and attribute all of the difference to competition. We also would worry about using changes within a city over time in the level of local competition, since these changes could be correlated with unobserved trends in student achievement.

A way around this problem is to compare outcomes across metropolitan areas that have more choice among different school districts for reasons that might be thought of as an historical accident. In a creative approach to this problem, Caroline Hoxby (2000) uses the fact that the number of districts relative to students is higher in areas where there are more natural boundaries, such as rivers. The idea behind her approach is that school districts historically did not jump these natural boundaries, and so areas with more such boundaries have more school districts and thus more school choice. She then compares academic outcomes in places that have more local competition to those that have less because of the prevalence of these boundaries. Her findings indicate that areas with more competition because there are more natural boundaries have better-performing school districts. In short, it appears as though competition increases productive efficiency.[6] This finding is consistent with the Tiebout model, as the mobility of residents in areas with more school districts generates competition that raises the quality of the schools.

[5] A similar study in San Francisco that has even more detailed information about the demographic composition of neighborhoods finds similar effects (Bayer, Ferreira, & McMillan, 2007). See Black and Machin (2011) for a detailed literature review of school quality capitalization research.

[6] This result has generated much discussion in the literature about the validity of the instrumental variables strategy and about the correct interpretation of the results. See the comment by Rothstein (2007) as well as Hoxby's (2007) reply for a detailed discussion of these issues.

Although the Tiebout model makes several strong assumptions, it is useful to see the model as a theoretical framework that provides broad predictions about capitalization of school quality and the effects of interdistrict competition on education provision. Tiebout sorting predicts the main findings discussed previously: School quality is capitalized into home prices, and areas with more interdistrict competition are more efficient at producing education. Two propositions follow from these results. First, an increase in school quality within a district, holding what families pay in taxes constant, should lead to an increase in housing prices. Think about this type of change as the result of an extraordinary school superintendent or a policy adjustment that produces an improvement in student achievement. More families would want to move to the district, leading to upward pressure on home prices.

Second, any policy that shifts resources from one district to another in turn affects relative demand for locations and home prices. This is particularly important for school finance reforms that can involve redistribution across districts. For example, consider a policy that fully centralizes and equalizes school financing across all districts in the state. The Tiebout model predicts that this will lead to some equalization of property values, with home prices rising in previously low-spending districts and with prices falling in previously high-spending districts. Families now cannot express their preferences for local schooling services through their location decisions, so any prior differences in prices that were due to the capitalization of schooling services across districts will disappear.

8.3 The School Finance Reform Movement

Local Versus Centralized Financing

One of the central implications of the Tiebout model is that there are potentially large benefits of local financing of education. At base, if the assumptions of the model hold, the only reason why localities will differ in education spending is the preferences of the residents. In such a case, disparities across school districts in per-student spending would be efficient. However, as discussed in Section 8.2, many of the assumptions of the Tiebout model are implausible, and at least some of the cross-district inequities in spending are likely to be inefficient. If, for example, schools serving low-income populations do not have high spending because their property tax revenues are low and because local residents are financially constrained from moving to a district where more resources are spent on public schools, it might be beneficial to society to have some centralized (i.e., state or federal) school financing that allows these poor districts to spend a socially optimal amount on education.[7]

---

[7] In the original Tiebout (1956) model, there were no property taxes. Instead, there was a per-resident head tax equal to the amount per resident that was needed to fund the level of public good provision. In reality, such a head tax is not feasible, and the basic intuition and predictions of the Tiebout model are borne out when public goods are financed through property taxes instead.

What is the correct mix of local versus centralized funding? To understand the trade-off between local school finance and a more centralized finance system at the state level, for example, it is useful to think about the polar cases (that rarely occur in practice in the United States) of complete local financing and complete state financing.

In both cases, the preferences of the voters determine the level of spending and taxation. First, consider a state financing system in which all school districts spend an identical amount per student. The amount spent on education will reflect the preferences of the median resident in the state. In a state with widely different preferences across localities, many areas will have either stronger or weaker preferences for education than what the state uniformly provides to all school districts. Thus, many individuals in this state will be off their demand curve for education. This problem is increasing with the diversity of preferences for education across areas within a state: If a state has citizens with uniform preferences for education, central financing should produce an efficient amount of education spending.

Contrast this scenario with complete local financing. The preferences of the community *in each district* now will determine the local level of school funding. Under the conditions of the Tiebout model, Tiebout sorting will generate cross-district differences in funding that are allocatively efficient, as they reflect only the preferences of the local community members for education. In practice, the question is not whether school finance should be completely local or completely centralized; rather the salient questions concern how much centralization or redistribution is optimal and how to achieve these funding levels efficiently through the tax system.

Looking back to Figure 8.1, funding for schools in the United States has a long tradition of including some funding from the state and federal governments, generating more centralization than would occur under a system of pure local finance. However, the mix between local, state, and federal funds has changed markedly over time. The overwhelming trend since the mid-twentieth century has been an increase of the role of state and federal governments in both financing public schools and in setting education policy more broadly. A large contributor to the move toward greater centralization has been the school finance reform movement. We now turn to a brief discussion of the history of this movement as well as a detailed examination of the changes it has led to in the way schools are financed in the United States.

Judicial Action and Legislative Response

School finance reform was initiated by the *Serrano* decision in 1971, in which the California Supreme Court ruled that the existing funding of schools by local property taxes was unconstitutional. The state was required to develop an alternative funding scheme. Further challenges followed in 1976, resulting in a court ruling that required per-pupil spending across districts to be equalized to within $100 by 1980. These reforms dramatically changed incentives for localities to raise funds from local property taxes, as additional taxes at the local level produced minuscule changes in the resources available for education. In turn, these shifts fueled taxpayer revolt in the form of the passage of Proposition 13, which limited property taxes to 1% of assessed value. Over time, California has fallen precipitously in rank in spending per student, from eleventh in 1970 to twenty-ninth in 2006, leading many analysts to question whether the equalization policies imposed after *Serrano* may have reduced the public's willingness to pay for traditional public education (Silva & Sonstelie, 1995).

How could this drop in funding in California occur? California did succeed in achieving more statutory equality in school finance across districts, but this was achieved by effectively reducing the overall level of spending on education. Many families objected to taxation when additional dollars paid in taxes for schools produced little or no change in spending for their students' local school. The result was that a well-intentioned effort to increase the degree of equality across districts actually produced reductions in real spending for some students. California's experience with school finance reform highlights that sometimes adverse unintended consequences of school finance equalization policies can undermine the goals of the reforms.

Throughout the 1970s and early 1980s, school finance litigation was launched in many states, which resulted in rulings in nine states that found the existing school finance rules to violate the state constitution. The decisions relied on arguments for "equity" under the equal protection language in state constitutions. Beginning in the mid-1980s, however, arguments for educational "adequacy" began to appear, based on language in state constitutions that require the adequate provision of educational services.[8] Essentially, adequacy litigation requires courts or legislatures to determine the basic level of educational services needed to meet constitutional standards. The first adequacy ruling was issued by the Kentucky Supreme Court in the case *Rose v. Council for a Better Education* (1989). The decision stated that Kentucky did not "provide an efficient system of common [public] schools throughout the state." The *Rose* case marked a shift in the school finance reform movement from calls for absolute equity to appeals for adequate spending for all students. Adequacy arguments generally allowed for some differences across districts, so long as increases in funding for the lowest-wealth districts were achieved.

> **Quick Hint:** The U.S. Supreme Court ruled in *San Antonio Independent Schools v. Rodriguez* (1973) that school funding disparities did not violate the equal protection clause of the U.S. Constitution. Hence, school finance litigation has remained at the state rather than at the federal level.

In the four decades since the *Serrano* case, nearly every state has faced some form of litigation about its school finance policies.[9] When a state court rules that an existing system of school finance is unconstitutional, it generally falls to the legislative branch to craft an alternative that meets the criteria set forth by the courts. In many cases, legislatures also have acted to revise school finance policies without a court mandate. Table 8.1 lists the dates of each state's first court-ordered reform and each state's first legislative reform if it had not faced prior court-ordered reform.

---

[8] Hanushek and Lindseth (2009) note the very general language, ranging from "free common schools" (New York) to "make suitable provision for finance of the educational interests of the state" (Kansas) to a "thorough and efficient system of public schools" (Wyoming).

[9] Although one may think of courts as the purview of lawyers, economists have played substantial roles in providing expert testimony in these cases. Well-qualified economists often disagree and can be found on both sides of school finance litigation.

Table 8.1 School Finance Reforms by State

First Court-Ordered Reform

State	Year	State	Year	State	Year
Alabama	1993	Massachusetts	2003	Oregon	2009
Alaska	1999	Michigan	1997	South Carolina	2005
Arizona	1994	Missouri	1993	Tennessee	1993
Arkansas	1983	Montana	1989	Texas	1989
California	1971	New Hampshire	1993	Washington	1977
Connecticut	1978	New Jersey	1973	West Virginia	1979
Idaho	1998	New Mexico	1998	Wisconsin	1976
Kansas	1972	New York	2003	Wyoming	1980
Kentucky	1989	North Carolina	1997		
Maryland	2005	Ohio	1997		

First Legislative Reform Without Preceding Court-Ordered Reform

State	Year	State	Year	State	Year
Arizona	1980	Michigan	1973	Oregon	1978
Colorado	1994	Minnesota	1973	Pennsylvania	1991
Florida	1973	Mississippi	1997	Rhode Island	1985
Georgia	1986	Missouri	1977	South Carolina	1977
Illinois	1973	Nebraska	1967	South Dakota	1986
Indiana	1993	New Hampshire	1985	Tennessee	1977
Iowa	1972	New Mexico	1974	Texas	1986
Louisiana	1992	North Carolina	1997	Utah	1973
Maine	1978	North Dakota	2007	Vermont	1969
Maryland	1987	Ohio	1975	Virginia	1972
Massachusetts	1993	Oklahoma	1981	Wisconsin	1973

No Reforms Before 2010

Delaware		Hawaii		Nevada	

Data from: Jackson, Johnson, and Persico (2014) and Murray, Evans, and Schwab (1998).

Currently, 28 states have had their school finance systems ruled unconstitutional by state courts, and 33 states have enacted legislative reforms to change their school finance system. Note that some of the court cases were a result of previous legislative actions. As of 2010, only three states had not reformed their school finance system, which illustrates the pervasiveness of school finance reform.

8.4 Forms of School Finance Centralization and Aid

The economics of school finance centralization involves both raising resources through taxes and distributing resources to districts and students. How resources are collected through taxes and how they are distributed through different types of funding mechanisms will have a substantial impact on the benefits and costs of different equalization plans. Indeed, a central point to take away from this section is that the design of school finance plans may have very different effects on the distribution of resources across districts. Furthermore, state aid formulas can alter the incentives for districts to raise revenues through local property taxes, leading to potentially large (and often unintended) impacts on total district spending.

School finance plans take many forms. One important distinction concerns whether aid is allocated on the basis of student characteristics, which is called categorical aid, or district characteristics, which is called equalization aid. **Categorical aid** is revenue that is directed to students who fit into a defined category, such as being of low-income status or having special learning needs. Programs that distribute aid on a categorical basis include Title I funds from the federal government targeted to low-income students and funds for special education and gifted and talented programs that in many states are distributed in accordance with the number of students in a district meeting specified criteria. **Equalization aid** is money that is distributed based on the socioeconomic or financial characteristics of entire districts, with the intent of equalizing per-pupil expenditures across districts. What is important to keep in focus—and why we spend so much time studying the optimal design of school finance policies—is that the structure of any equalization policy will generate a response from parents and local officials in terms of how much they wish to support their local public schools financially.

In this section, we start by describing the basic mechanisms for distributing resources under centralized school finance schemes and consider how these designs differentially affect local incentives. Then, we turn to the equally important consideration of the tax mechanism used to raise resources to accomplish the objectives of school finance equalization. Finally, we consider empirical evidence on how differential forms of centralization policies instituted across states have affected the level and distribution of funding.

categorical aid Revenue that is directed to students who fit into a defined category, such as being from a low-income family or having a learning disability.

equalization aid Revenue that is distributed based on the socioeconomic or financial characteristics of the school district, with the intent of equalizing per-pupil expenditures across districts.

The Community Budget Constraint

Before discussing how state revenues might be used to equalize funding among districts, it is useful to think about why funding differs among districts. Let's start with a very simple model of how local policy makers decide how much money to spend per student without centralized finance. The resources used for schools will have to come from the local community through tax revenue. Every dollar spent on schools is a dollar not available for spending on other goods, both public and private. We can capture this trade-off in a *community budget constraint* with school spending on the *horizontal axis* and spending on all other goods on the *vertical axis*, as shown in the left panel of Figure 8.5. The intercepts represent the total amount of income from tax revenue in the community, and the slope of the *budget constraint* is −1. If R is school spending, X is spending on all other goods, and B is the total revenue available to the district, then the equation for the budget line is:

$$X + R = B$$

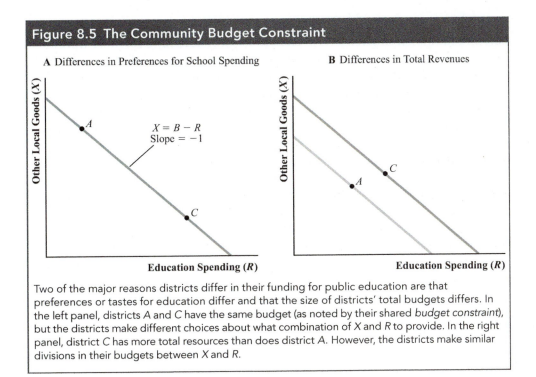

Figure 8.5 The Community Budget Constraint

A Differences in Preferences for School Spending

B Differences in Total Revenues

Two of the major reasons districts differ in their funding for public education are that preferences or tastes for education differ and that the size of districts' total budgets differs. In the left panel, districts A and C have the same budget (as noted by their shared *budget constraint*), but the districts make different choices about what combination of X and R to provide. In the right panel, district C has more total resources than does district A. However, the districts make similar divisions in their budgets between X and R.

This budget constraint simply means that all revenue must be spent either on schools or on other goods. Assuming that the number of students in a district is fixed at n, per-pupil expenditure is $\frac{R}{n}$.

How does the community decide which point on its budget constraint to choose? That is, how much should it spend on schools and other goods? We can simplify this analysis tremendously by assuming that the community behaves just like a single person confronting a budget constraint.[10] For any district, we expect one point along this budget constraint will be preferred to all others.

This simple framework of a budget constraint and each district's preferred combination of R and X helps us to understand why spending on schooling differs across districts. One reason is that different districts may simply have different preferences for schooling and other goods. In districts where families place a high emphasis on education, R will be high relative to X. Such a district is represented by point C in the left panel of Figure 8.5. In districts where private consumption or other public goods such as parks are highly valued, there will be low values of R relative to X. Point A shows this type of district. These differences reflect different *preferences* for spending on education across districts.

The second reason that spending on schools may differ across districts is that districts differ in wealth. A district with a higher level of B, such as the outer budget constraint in the right panel of Figure 8.5, will have more dollars to spend on both education and other goods. We have every reason to think that for most, if not all, communities, schooling is a **normal good**, one you spend more on when you are

normal good A good for which consumption increases when income increases. That is, when people have more money, they purchase more of a normal good.

---

[10] More generally, we can think about the residents of the community as voting; it will be the preferences of the median voter that determine the level of spending.

richer. Thus, wealthier communities—those with higher property values—will spend more on education for a given level of preferences for education versus other amenities.

Since differences both in tastes and in revenues generate differences in school spending, it is clear that an outside observer needs to know more than just the level of schooling expenditures to address the question of why we observe substantial differences in school funding across districts. If there are sufficient differences in the demands for education among families, we would expect considerable sorting of households along preference lines, as predicted in the Tiebout model. That is, families with very high tastes for education would live in districts with other families who have similar tastes, and likewise for those who care little about education. In short, differences in spending on education observed across districts might be due to differences in the preferences of families rather than differences in income or wealth.

Fundamentally, school finance equalization policies that increase resources in some districts and either hold constant or decrease resources in others operate by changing the budget constraint—shifting the total amount a district can spend, changing the relative prices of spending on education versus other goods, or adjusting both total resources and prices. In turn, how much a district spends on education depends on *both* preferences for education and the specific form of the budget constraint.

Block and Matching Grants

Now, let's think about how the state or federal government might provide equalization aid to increase school spending. Funding from the state or federal government to local school districts can have two broad types of impacts. First, a grant that comes as a fixed sum, called a block grant, can change the total budget available for education spending. Block grants shift out the budget constraint in a parallel manner. Second, a grant can supplement each dollar of school spending—a matching grant. By changing the price associated with education spending, matching grants alter the slope of the budget constraint.

As a starting point, consider an unrestricted block grant of size G to the community. There are no strings attached to this grant; it can be spent on anything. In this instance, the budget constraint of the district becomes:

$$X + R = B + G$$

It is as though the community received G dollars more in tax income, and the effect on schooling is the same as if overall income increased in the district: Education spending increases. Unrestricted block grants therefore increase spending on all government services in proportion to local residents' preferences for those services. Figure 8.6 (panel A) shows an example of an unrestricted block grant.

What if the donor government restricted the use of the grant money to education spending? Would that mean that all of the G dollars end up as extra spending on schooling? The simple answer is no. The effect on the budget constraint of giving G dollars that must be spent on education is shown in panel B of Figure 8.6. The community faces a budget constraint exactly like the one it faced in panel A of Figure 8.6, except that it cannot spend less than G on schooling. But as long as G is less than the amount the community would have spent on education in the absence of the grant, the effect of giving a restricted grant of G dollars is exactly the same as giving an unrestricted grant. The G dollars of grant money just substitute for G dollars of community income that would

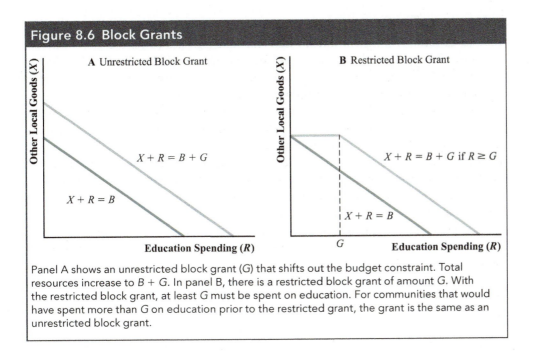

Figure 8.6 Block Grants

A Unrestricted Block Grant

$X + R = B + G$

$X + R = B$

B Restricted Block Grant

$X + R = B + G$ if $R \geq G$

$X + R = B$

Panel A shows an unrestricted block grant (G) that shifts out the budget constraint. Total resources increase to B + G. In panel B, there is a restricted block grant of amount G. With the restricted block grant, at least G must be spent on education. For communities that would have spent more than G on education prior to the restricted grant, the grant is the same as an unrestricted block grant.

have been spent on schooling. The effect of the grant is not zero, but it is no greater than giving G dollars in unrestricted funds. That giving targeted grants typically is equivalent to giving unrestricted grants is an important insight of public economics that tends not to be well understood by policy makers. This result indicates that to target funds to a specific service, like education, mechanisms other than lump-sum grants are needed.

One such type of grant that is very commonly used is a matching grant, in which the amount of the grant depends on the amount of its own money that the community spends for a particular purpose. In the simplest form of a matching grant, the grant amount is just a proportion of the community's spending on a particular good. If the ratio is 1 to 3, for example, then for each $3 that the community spends on the specific good, such as schooling, the state or federal government will give $1 to be spent on schools.

The effect of a matching grant on the community's budget constraint can be seen in Figure 8.7. The grant amount is the horizontal distance between the *original budget constraint* and the *matching budget constraint*. At the vertical intercept, where spending on schools is zero, the grant amount is also zero. The effect of the matching grant is to rotate the budget constraint counterclockwise, making it flatter. In the case of the matching grant, the budget constraint for the district will be:

$$X + R = B + mR$$

$$X + (1 - m)R = B$$

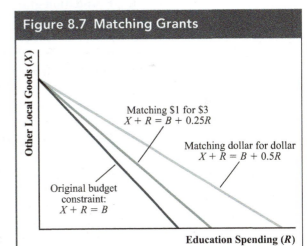

Figure 8.7 Matching Grants

Matching $1 for $3
$X + R = B + 0.25R$

Matching dollar for dollar
$X + R = B + 0.5R$

Original budget constraint:
$X + R = B$

When a district is given a matching grant for education, the state or federal government agrees to award the district a set amount of money for each dollar that the district spends on education. The matching grant changes the effective price of education spending. Without aid, the district traded spending on education dollar for dollar for spending on other goods—the slope of the budget constraint was −1. With a matching grant of $1 for each $3 the community spends on education, the district gives up only 75 cents of other goods to spend another dollar on education—the slope of the budget constraint is −0.75.

where m is the share of each dollar spent that comes from state or central sources. In the case of the 1 to 3 match, which means the state provides \$1 for every \$3 from local funds that are spent on education, the budget constraint would be $X + R = B + \left(\frac{1}{1+3}\right)$ $R = B + 0.75R$. This will have two effects on the community's spending decision, which economists refer to as the income and substitution effects. The income effect of the grant comes from the fact that the grant makes the community richer, and richer communities spend more on schooling (as well as on other goods). This effect is similar to the effect of a lump sum grant G. The substitution effect follows from the change in the slope of the budget constraint, reflecting a change in the relative price of spending on R versus X. In effect, the cost of spending on schools relative to spending on other things is reduced. In this example, to get an extra dollar spent on schools, the community only has to give up 75 cents of spending on other goods, since the grant will rise by 25 cents for each 75 cents more spent on schools. In other words, to get a dollar of education spending, the community now will only have to sacrifice 75 cents of spending on the other good. The total effect of the matching grant on spending depends on the community's preferences, but the substitution effect generally leads to increases in spending on education relative to other goods.

Actual State Aid Formulas

State aid formulas come in many different forms. Here, we go over several of the differences across school finance reform plans. We also pay particular attention to how these formulas affect the tax system. School finance equalization plans can be categorized into several different types:

1. **Foundation grant.** States provide assurance of a minimum level of funding. These plans designate a minimum foundation level of spending and then provide block grants to districts based on the difference between the foundation level and the district's expected contribution to expenditures.
2. **Power equalization grant.** States provide a subsidy to tax revenue at a given property tax rate that is based on the difference between actual property wealth in the district and a common minimum property wealth level across districts. This is a form of a matching grant.
3. **Equalization grant.** States provide aid to districts based on wealth and income levels in the district. This is a form of a block grant.
4. **Centralization.** States completely centralize school financing, such that they assess taxes for education and then distribute the money to school districts directly. Centralization plans are block grants, because states provide a set amount of spending per student across all districts.

While the features of a foundation grant system, a power equalization mechanism, or both appear in most state equalization policies, there is a great deal of variation among states in what mechanisms are used and the extent to which the distribution of funding for schools is controlled at the state versus the local level. We start by describing the distribution of resources under different equalization plans and considering how such revenues are likely to change the behavior of recipient districts.

Each of the four main types of aid systems is intended to narrow the differences in spending between rich and poor districts. As a starting point to understand how they affect district revenues, consider the revenue formula for district d in the case of full local financing from property taxes: $B_d = W_d \tau_d$. In this formula, B_d is the total revenues per student from property taxes collected by district d, W_d is the per-student property tax base (i.e., the average property wealth per student), and τ_d is the tax rate. With pure local financing through property taxes, the district's only way to increase revenues is to raise the tax rate. The other school finance reform systems, which we discuss in turn later in the chapter, all provide alternative ways for low-income districts in particular to increase their expenditures on schooling.

Foundation Grants The goal of a foundation program is to ensure that each district can attain some standard level, the foundation level, of spending with the same tax rate. The foundation program sets a level of spending, F, and a tax rate, τ^f, and then gives localities a grant sufficient to achieve spending level F if it were to tax at rate τ^f. The grant to district d, G_d, is given by the following formula:

$$G_d = \max(0, F - \tau^f \times W_d)$$

The max function is used to ensure that the foundation grant cannot be negative. That is, these programs typically do not punish high-wealth districts by taking away local property tax revenues above the foundation level. This is not always true in practice, as some states have allowed for negative foundation grants. These cases are rare, however, and we do not focus on them here.

Total revenues in a foundation grant plan are equal to:

$$B_d = W_d \tau_d \text{ if } F < \tau^f \times W_d$$

$$B_d = W_d \tau_d + F - \tau^f \times W_d = F + W_d(\tau_d - \tau^f) \text{ if } F \geq \tau^f \times W_d.$$

This formula states that if the district has a high property tax base such that revenues at the foundation tax rate are greater than F, it funds its schools fully through local property taxes. If not, then it receives a block grant equal to the foundation aid amount. The grant is larger for poorer districts (those with lower W_d), but it does not depend on how much a district actually spends. So this is an example of a restricted block grant, as the foundation grant must be spent on education.

How will foundation grants affect the distribution of spending? It will not fully equalize spending across districts. This is demonstrated in Figure 8.8. The budget constraint for district A shows a wealthy district that is unaffected by the foundation grant, and the budget constraint for district B shows a lower-income district that receives the foundation grant. The grant ensures that the district now spends *at least F* on schooling, but the district can spend more than that as well. The district with the higher tax base is likely to spend more on education than the lower tax base district because it continues to have higher total government revenues. However, school spending in each district still depends on how residents value R versus other local public goods. By increasing all district spending levels to *at least F* and by leaving high-spending districts unchanged, foundation grants are likely to reduce inequality in spending. Foundation grants also tend to increase total spending on education.

Power Equalization The goal of a power equalization program is to ensure that if two districts have the same tax rate (effort), they can spend the same amount per pupil, even if they differ in terms of the taxable wealth in their district. One way to think of this is to imagine that the state ensures that each locality can spend an amount equal to its tax rate times some guaranteed per-pupil taxable wealth, W^{pe}.

In such a system, the grant per pupil must make up the difference between the district's actual revenue per pupil, $W_d \tau_d$, and the amount it would raise under the

Figure 8.8 Foundation Grants

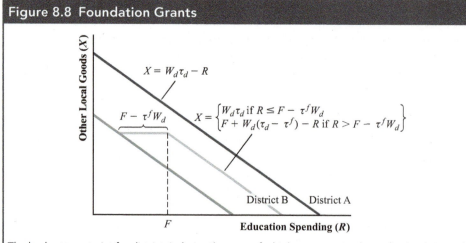

The budget constraint for district A shows the case of a high property tax base district that would not be eligible for a positive foundation grant. Districts with relatively high property tax bases are likely to spend more on education because residents typically have greater income/wealth and/or have greater preferences for education that may be capitalized in property values. The budget constraint for district B illustrates how a foundation grant of $F - \tau^f W_d$ with the requirement of spending F on education shifts out the budget constraint beyond expenditures of F. This greater income would likely lead to more spending on education in district B, resulting in a reduction of the inequality between district A and district B in school spending.

Figure 8.9 Power Equalization Grants and Capitalized School Quality

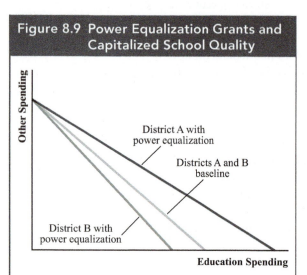

Assume residents of districts A and B have the same income and assets, while residents of district B prefer to spend more on education than on other goods and services. The resulting differences in school quality are capitalized in housing prices: $W_B > W_A$. Suppose a revenue neutral power equalization grant is introduced such that $W_B > W^{pe} > W_A$. The tax price of schooling in district A falls, as illustrated by the flatter budget line, while the tax price rises for district B as indicated by the increased slope.

guaranteed property wealth base at the district's chosen tax rate, $W^{pe}\tau_d$. The grant formula under power equalization is:

$$G_d = \tau_d W^{pe} - \tau_d W_d = \tau_d(W^{pe} - W_d)$$

As the name suggests, power equalization plans ensure a common taxing power across districts for education, and then the districts are free to set tax rates according to local preferences. The grant amount depends negatively on district wealth and positively on district effort (its tax rate).

If education were the only good on which the district spent money, then total education spending would be:

$$R_d = \tau_d W_d + G_d = \tau_d W_d + \tau_d(W^{pe} - W_d) = \tau_d W^{pe}$$

Let's think about the tax price of spending another dollar on schooling or the amount of revenue the district needs to generate to spend another dollar on education. When $W_d < W^{pe}$, a district's choice to increase its tax rate, say raising τ_d from 1% to 2%, would require district residents to pay more (an additional $0.01 \times W_d$) while they would receive a grant of $0.01 \times W^{pe}$. Consider the case of a district with a local property tax base of W_d that is half of W^{pe}. For each additional dollar raised by increasing taxes, the district would receive a grant for education of $2. This yields a matching relationship as discussed earlier in the chapter and illustrated in Figure 8.7.

But not all districts have a property tax base less than the guaranteed tax base. For districts with a high taxable property base, it may be the case that $W_d > W^{pe}$. To achieve budget balance for school finance equalization, states often allow for negative grants in power equalization plans. In such a case, the tax price for spending on education will be negative and each dollar the district raises in additional tax revenue will produce less than a dollar of funding for education. Figure 8.9 presents an example with negative power equalization grants. Note that variation across districts in property tax bases (W_d) reflects both differences in capacity to pay – the income and assets of district residents, including physical housing stock – and differences in residents' preferences for education when school quality is capitalized in property values.

Power equalization plans are likely to reduce inequality in spending across districts, as high property-value districts will spend less and lower property value districts will increase spending. This is the case even if power equalization grants are constrained not to be negative, such that wealthier districts or those with higher property values are not penalized. Because districts still are able to set local tax rates, spending will not fully equalize across districts, but the differences are likely to be more a reflection of local preferences for education than an expression of wealth levels.

> **Quick Hint:** Hoxby (2001) calls the amount of money from local sources that is necessary to generate a dollar of education revenue the inverted tax price. An inverted tax price of less than 1 means that districts must raise more than $1 to spend an extra dollar on education. A tax price of greater than 1 means a district must raise less than $1 to raise $1 of revenue for local education spending. ▪

Equalization Grants Equalization grants are block grants that are a function of district income or wealth levels. Unlike foundation grants, they are not designed to top up all districts to a minimum funding level. Instead, such grants are made in proportion to some observable characteristic of the district, such as the income level of residents. Denoting the grant level EG_d, total revenues are given by:

$$B_d = W_d \tau_d + EG_d$$

As with foundation grants, equalization grants are restricted block grants. The critical difference is that equalization grants are not explicitly a function of local revenues raised through property taxes. They are designed to give more money to lower-income districts; however, the exact formula for the distribution varies considerably across states. Because equalization grants provide more money for lower-income (and thus lower-spending) districts, they should reduce spending inequality across districts and raise total education spending.

Centralized Spending Some states have fully centralized school spending. The most prominent example of such a system is Michigan. School finance reform in Michigan began in the summer of 1993 with the decision by the state legislature to eliminate the reliance on the property tax as the primary source of revenue to fund schools in the state. The resulting finance plan shifted the source of funding from the property tax to three other taxes: a sales tax, a tax on so-called sin products like cigarettes, and a tax on other communication services. The law also capped assessed property values for tax purposes at 1% per year. It almost completely decoupled local property tax revenues and school financing, with all funding coming from the state. High-spending districts were held harmless against spending reductions by allowing them to raise a small amount of local property tax revenues. Gradually, state financing was raised to equalize spending across all districts for all but the highest-spending districts in the state. The result is a school finance mechanism with reduced inequality and higher overall levels of spending. School funding increased from $9.3 billion in 1993 to $14.5 billion in 2003. This increase outpaced Michigan's inflation. In 1993, the 10 highest-revenue school districts outspent the 10 lowest-revenue districts per pupil by a ratio of 3 : 1. In 2003, the ratio was less than 2 : 1.

Paying for School Finance Equalization

A central balancing principle in public finance is that expenditures must be offset by revenues. Neither the state nor the federal government can provide localities with aid or grants for education without imposing taxes. By definition, if state taxes simply returned to districts the revenues generated locally, state financing would not achieve any meaningful goals of equalization. Thus, equalization aid requires taking tax revenues garnered from families in some districts and transferring these resources to other districts. Differences in how revenues are raised to support equalization can have substantial consequences for the efficiency of the school finance system and the outcomes of equalization efforts.

Many of the school finance reform systems we discussed previously lead to increases in the total amount of education spending. In such cases, states have to raise the needed revenues from some combination of tax increases using the tax instruments listed earlier. Another mechanism for funding many of these plans is to make them revenue-neutral in the sense that negative grants from districts with high property values are used to provide funding for districts with lower property values. Such policies can be attractive because they do not require new taxes, but they can generate substantial distortions by inducing high-wealth districts to reduce property taxes. These property tax changes can have negative effects on property values through the capitalization mechanism. Alternatively, states can use other tax mechanisms, such as income and sales taxes, to fund power equalization plans. Power equalization and foundation grants both can have redistributive elements to them, while equalization grants do not take money away from wealthy districts and thus cannot be revenue-neutral. Instead, these grants are funded out of other state revenue sources.

Economists have given considerable attention to the potential distortions that redistributive school finance systems can generate. The central insight is that altering the price of a unit of education revenues can have unintended consequences in terms of both demand for education services and property values. Recall that in the Tiebout model, property taxes are an efficient tool for financing community services, such as education, because they reflect local preferences. Yet when some districts face very high tax prices in a school finance system, economic theory makes clear that residents will reduce their demand for education spending. If the resulting reduced spending is capitalized into housing prices, then property wealth will decline in the district. This wealth reduction can have negative consequences for families beyond education, as housing wealth is an important component of total household wealth portfolios among U.S. families.

To take an extreme example, imagine a state changes its financing formula such that all revenues above a foundation threshold, F, are collected by the state to be given to lower-wealth districts. For local residents, the incentive is to set the local property tax rate such that the district raises exactly F. The tax price above that amount is infinite, meaning that every dollar raised above F goes in total to other residents in the state. Parents in this district pay a premium to live in a high-spending school district. Now that spending

DEEP DIVE: "Robin Hood and His Not So Merry Plan"

One particularly clear example of a school finance plan that had large unintended consequences due to its redistributive components is Texas's reform in the 1990s. School finance litigation was initiated in Texas in 1984 and led to a string of court-ordered reforms culminating in a plan, known as Robin Hood, implemented in the 1993–94 school year. As the name suggests, the goal of this plan was to redistribute property tax revenues from wealthy to poor districts. Specifically, it included a baseline foundation grant that was funded largely through a recapture mechanism. Taxes on all property above a specific threshold were designated for the state equalization program and "recaptured" from the district, flowing directly to the state.

The recapture of local revenues above a certain threshold basically sets a cap on spending in each district. Any revenue collected over the cap is sent to the state to be used for foundation aid to poorer districts. Since parents in high-spending districts likely value education a lot, as revealed by their willingness to pay more to live in a high-spending district, economic theory predicts that capping per-student expenditures should reduce property values. Thus, the redistributive elements of this finance scheme could lead to lower overall spending and potentially large reductions in family wealth levels.

Hoxby and Kuziemko (2004) study the effect of this program on property values and show evidence that this is exactly what happened in Texas. Districts subject to the recapture provision saw a sharp reduction in property values, as taxes paid on wealth above the threshold held no benefits for local students. The problem compounded itself because as property values fell in high-wealth areas, state policy makers were forced to lower the recapture threshold to fund the system. This further reduced property values in affected areas.

Hoxby and Kuziemko estimate that the plan led to a relatively modest reduction in inequality: about $500 per student between the poorest and richest districts. This inequality reduction, however, came at the expense of nearly $27,000 per student in the aggregate value of housing. The researchers make a dramatic calculation: If the state invested $27,000 per student, it could have endowed a school spending fund that would have allowed every district to spend per student what the top 5% of districts spend. Thus, the main outcome of this plan seems to have been to significantly reduce property wealth, an unintended consequence of the reform that ultimately reduced its effectiveness. In the end, the negative capitalization of the taxes in home prices made this financing approach unsustainable. As Hoxby and Kuziemko argue, if policy makers had paid closer attention to economic theory at the outset, they would have been able to predict the adverse effects of this type of plan.

has declined, demand to live in the school district also declines, lowering property values. Thus, residents are harmed both because they cannot spend as much as they desire on education and because the funding restriction has lowered the value of their house. While school expenditures will become more equal across districts, this is an example of leveling down, as total expenditures on education likely will decrease.

This is admittedly an extreme scenario, but many school finance systems have such redistributive elements. There is a delicate balance in school finance reforms between the need to generate equity and the desire to reduce distortions that cause students living in more affluent districts to be worse off. This problem is endemic to the tax system more generally and often is referred to as the **equity–efficiency trade-off**. Depending on the design of a school finance system, the distortions created by the financing mechanism may be sufficiently large to offset the benefits of equalization aid.

equity–efficiency trade-off To make allocations more equal, distortionary taxes are needed that make production less efficient.

School Finance Reform in Practice

School finance in each state is a function of both legislative and judicial decision making. As a result, each state in the United States has its own unique mechanism of school finance and employs a different balance between local decision making about taxing and spending for schools and the mechanism used for distributing state resources. States differ in the combination of tax tools and their choice of power equalization or foundation grants in school finance equalization. As a result, there is also a great deal of variation among states in the level of inequality in spending on schools.

Over the course of the past four decades, states have differed in the extent to which they have faced judicial mandates to equalize funding. Many states also have enacted legislative reforms without judicial pressure (or in anticipation of judicial mandates). Table 8.1 shows the distribution of different types of reforms. Economists have looked carefully at the incentives of these reforms and the associated changes in the distribution of resources, which has led to a sizable body of research on the effectiveness of these reforms in equalizing school spending.

In one of the earlier and most influential studies of the effect of school finance reform on the distribution of school resources, Murray, Evans, and Schwab (1998) examined the impact of court-ordered school finance reforms in 16 states between 1971 and 1996. They exploit the difference in the timing of these judicial rulings to estimate difference-in-difference models that compare changes in spending in states that have a judicial ruling to changes in states that do not. Using several measures of cross-district inequality in per-student expenditures, the paper shows that court-ordered reforms lead to large and statistically significant reductions in education expenditure inequality. On the whole, their results are suggestive of a leveling-up effect: Spending in the higher-wealth districts remains unchanged and spending in lower-wealth districts increases. Thus, these court-ordered reforms led to higher overall spending and faster spending growth in poorer districts, which significantly reduced cross-district spending inequality.

In a complementary analysis, Card and Payne (2002) look at the effect of school finance reforms in the 1980s on school spending inequality. They show that in states in which the courts ruled the finance system unconstitutional, state aid to low-income districts rose faster, on the order of about $300 per student. However, state aid rose even in the states in which the finance systems were upheld or not challenged, suggesting a general trend toward more equalizing aid over this period. The increased aid to these lower-income districts caused spending in these districts to rise relative to wealthier areas.

Much of the prior research on school finance reforms focuses on court-ordered reforms, as such reforms are the most likely to be unrelated to the underlying demand for education. But, school finance reform rulings and the legislative reforms are much more complicated than a dichotomous "yes/no" variable! In a research paper titled "All School Finance Equalizations Are Not Created Equal," Hoxby (2001) recognizes that this classification misses a lot of important differences in the specific components of court-ordered reform plans.[11] Instead, she advocates for directly examining the effects of several important aspects of school finance reform systems. This is necessary because different school finance reform systems embed incentives in them that would predict opposite effects on spending. Lumping all court-ordered reforms together yields a misleading result.

To measure the response of individuals and districts to school finance reform, a key question is how a policy change affects the price of increasing funding for schools; in a system with taxes and subsidies it may cost more or less than a dollar of tax revenue to increase school spending by a dollar. Hoxby (2001) estimates how overall spending on education and spending inequality respond to the inverted tax price (i.e., how much money a district would have to raise to increase spending by $1), the foundation tax rate (τ^f), income and sales tax rates in support of school spending, and flat grants. She finds that higher inverted tax prices, which make raising local revenue more costly, reduce

---

[11] Card and Payne (2002) also make this point.

education spending, as do higher foundation tax rates. However, flat grants and income and sales taxes have large positive effects on overall spending. The inverted tax price and foundation tax rate effects operate at least partially through changing property values, which underscores the distortive nature of these tax changes. While all of the financing reforms studied by Hoxby (2001) reduce cross-district spending inequality, the paper demonstrates that the specific rules have profound impacts on overall expenditures. Some of the reforms level up and some level down, depending on the amount of distortions in property values and the local property tax rates they induce. Hence, the mechanisms used to generate more spending equality matter, which means the equity–efficiency trade-off should be taken seriously by policy makers.

The evidence from nearly four decades of judicial and legislative reform since the *Serrano* decision points to the effectiveness of school finance reforms in reducing education spending inequality across the United States. However, many of the school finance reforms enacted show an absence of an understanding of economic theory, imposing high tax rates that reduce the willingness to spend on education. As a result, the overall impact of these reforms on student performance is unclear. In the next chapter, we turn to a formal examination of the evidence of the impacts of school finance reform legislation on student academic achievement.

8.5 Conclusion

Economic theory provides clear predictions about how equalization aid and the associated tax changes will affect the distribution of educational resources and the willingness of families to support expenditures on public education. The evidence of school finance reform in response to litigation and legislative reform reflects that not all policy makers have learned these important lessons in economics. Local school finance has many desirable properties generated by competition and choice, which leads to increased efficiency in production and allocation. Some centralization—funded at either the federal or state level—is certainly desirable to address the economic challenges of credit constraints and spillovers (externalities).

Yet it seems unlikely that school finance reform alone, in moving to reduce inequalities in expenditures across districts, will be sufficient to reduce the sizable inequality in student achievement persisting across schools in the United States. Other types of systematic reform, including increased school choice (Chapter 10) and greater accountability (Chapter 11) might be promising additional policies to help address these challenges.

Highlights

- While decentralization is a hallmark of the U.S. education system, there has been a steady and significant increase in state and federal funding over the past half century as well as a large amount of consolidation of school districts.

- The **free rider problem** leads to too little being spent on education, as residents will systematically underreport their preferences for education services. This is a problem of **preference revelation**: Localities cannot determine residents' preferences for education spending simply by asking them.

- **Tiebout sorting** is a solution to the problem of how to provide local public goods such as schooling. According to the Tiebout model, people will vote with their feet and move to an area in which the local amenities, including school quality and tax levels, match their preferences. This allows them to truthfully reveal their preferences for spending on schooling.

- There is empirical evidence that supports the Tiebout model: Housing prices **capitalize** the quality of local schools. However, the assumptions of perfect mobility, full information, a large number of local options, the lack of spillovers, and the presence of **credit constraints** make it unlikely that **Tiebout sorting** will lead to an efficient allocation of spending across districts.

- Concerns over the inequality in spending that arises across schools serving children from lower- versus higher-income families have led to a series of court challenges and legislative changes. This **school finance reform** movement has altered the funding system in virtually every state and has decoupled the traditional link between local property values and school spending. This increase in funding, fueled largely by litigation, is being used to equalize spending and thus, theoretically, provide more equal educational opportunities.

- Given district budget constraints, the state and federal government can attempt to equalize funding across districts by shifting the budget constraint out (via a block grant) or by changing the slope of the budget constraint (via a matching grant). These grants can be in the form of **categorical aid**, revenue directed to students who fit into a defined category, or **equalization aid**, which is distributed according to the socioeconomic characteristics of entire districts.

- School finance reform plans can take many forms. They differ in their use of foundation grants, power equalization grants, equalization grants, and centralization of financing at the state level. The way in which each of these funding mechanisms is used to help equalize spending across districts can have large impacts on **allocative efficiency**, **productive efficiency**, the degree to which funding is equalized, and the overall level of education spending.

- Some school finance reforms reduce spending gaps across districts by leveling up spending. In other words, they provide more funding for poorer districts and allow wealthy districts to maintain their preferred (higher) level of spending. Other plans equalize spending by leveling down, which reduces the gap between the districts' budgets but also reduces the total amount spent on education.

- Economists and policy makers must pay close attention to the potential distortions that the redistributions of school finance systems can generate. In any scenario that alters local funding policies, parents and local officials will react to the new set of incentives. These reactions can have unintended consequences that policy makers need to take into account when designing school finance reforms.

Problems

1. What was the 1971 *Serrano v. Priest* California Supreme Court decision? What method of financing local public schools did it rule to be unconstitutional?

2. Between 1940 and 2010, the number of school districts in the United States declined from 117,000 to 13,625 even though the U.S. population increased from 132 million to 317 million. Under what conditions will this consolidation increase efficiency in schooling provision? Under what conditions will it reduce efficiency?

3. Historically, the operation and financing of public schools has been left up to states and local governments. What are the benefits of allowing local communities to finance and operate their own schools? What are the benefits that come from a fully centralized system in which the federal government operates and finances all schools (such as in France)?

4. Briefly explain the free rider problem with respect to the funding of local public schools. How does the Tiebout model propose to solve this problem?

5. What are the main assumptions necessary in the Tiebout model to achieve an outcome that is efficient in production and allocation? How do these assumptions relate to the question of whether we might want a less centralized versus a more centralized funding system for schools?

6. What is the capitalization of school quality? How can we use home prices in adjacent districts or attendance zones to measure the capitalization of school quality?

7. Explain the differences between categorical aid and equalization aid. Give an example of each type of aid.

8. What are the four types of state aid formulas that have been used to enact school finance reforms? Briefly discuss how each one aims to equalize spending across districts. Discuss the implication of each funding scheme for efficiency.

9. Both the Springfield public schools and the Shelbyville public schools are fully financed by local taxes of 1% on all property. In Shelbyville,

the average house is worth $150,000, while houses in Springfield are only worth $100,000 on average. Each town has 10,000 houses and can decide to spend its tax revenue on schooling (R) or on other community goods (X).

a. What is the total amount of tax revenue in each town? On the same graph, draw the budget constraint for both school districts.

b. The state government wants to equalize spending in the two districts. To do this, it provides a block grant to Springfield for the difference in the tax revenues between the two towns. Assuming there is no effect on property values, will this necessarily lead to the same amount of spending across districts? Explain.

c. Concerned that offering unrestricted grant aid to Springfield is not working to equalize spending, the state restricts the grant aid to be spent on education. Under what conditions will this lead to an increase in education spending in Springfield equal to the grant amount?

d. The government now offers a matching grant to Springfield, such that for every dollar spent by Springfield on education, the state will provide a grant of $1. What is the formula for the new budget constraint? Draw the budget constraint. Is this grant likely to increase, decrease, or keep constant the spending on education relative to all other community goods in Shelbyville?

10. The Simpsons are worried about the quality of the education Lisa is receiving in Springfield. Along with lawyer Lionel Hutz, they sue the state to alter the way in which schools are financed. The state sides with the Simpsons and now has to determine how to reform the school finance system. Assume that all town revenues go to the schools and that each town has 2,000 students.

a. The state proposes a foundation grant system that guarantees each district a foundation level of $8,000 at a tax rate of 1%. Assuming no effect on property values, calculate each town's foundation grant level and the effect on overall spending.

b. Realizing the expense of this plan, the state decides to redistribute funds across districts in a way that equalizes spending without costing any more money. What foundation grant level will equalize spending at current property values and tax rates? What effect do you think this funding scheme will have on property values and tax rates in Shelbyville? Will this lead to more, the same, or less overall spending on education?

c. Now the state proposes a power equalization program. What is the guaranteed property wealth base that would make Springfield's spending equal to Shelbyville's spending before the reform? If the state sets the guaranteed property wealth base at this amount, is it guaranteed to equalize spending across towns on schooling?

11. When a district increases local taxes by increasing the property tax or the local sales tax, will all of the additional revenue be available for school funding? How do state school finance equalization policies affect your answer?

Does Money Matter? The Relationship Between Education Inputs and Educational Outcomes

The Coleman Report

The landmark 1964 Civil Rights Act included a requirement that the government produce a report on equality of educational opportunities by race and ethnicity. The Department of Health and Human Services hired noted sociologist James Coleman to conduct such a study, and his 1966 report, entitled *Equality of Educational Opportunity* (commonly referred to as the Coleman report), was a watershed moment for education policy. Coleman conducted an enormous survey of 645,000 students in 4,000 public schools throughout the United States, with the goal of understanding the relationships between racial segregation, school resources, family backgrounds, and academic achievement.

> **Quick Hint:** While the 1954 Supreme Court Case *Brown v. Board of Education* made having separate schools for Black and White students unconstitutional, by the early 1960s many schools had yet to desegregate, especially in the South. Title IV of the 1964 Civil Rights Act was designed to further encourage desegregation and to give the U.S. attorney general expanded powers to file desegregation lawsuits against school districts.

While many observers at the time expected the Coleman report to provide strong evidence linking resource differences to differences in student outcomes by race and socioeconomic status, the results were much less definitive and, broadly, appeared to indicate that differences in observed school resources explained little of the observed variation in student performance. The authors summarize their findings best in the report: "It is known that socioeconomic factors bear a strong relation to academic achievement. When these factors are statistically controlled, however, it appears that differences between schools account for only a small fraction of differences in student achievement" (pp. 22–23).

3DDock/Shutterstock

Although they do find evidence of a stronger correlation between school resources and academic achievement among racial and ethnic minority students relative to White students, this effect is small in relation to the importance of family characteristics and socioeconomic status. Many of the methodological choices made in the Coleman report merit scrutiny, but the lasting impact was to open serious—and often contentious—investigation of the link between school resources and student outcomes among economists and other social scientists.

The Coleman report set the stage for how education researchers and policy makers have thought about education policy since the 1960s. One of the fundamental questions we ask in the economics of education and in education policy is whether we can boost student achievement by giving schools more money. This is such a fundamental question because of the wide disparity across states and school districts in the amount they spend per student. At one extreme, New Jersey spends over $16,000 per student on public education, while Utah spends about $6,300. Some of this difference is due to the different prices of inputs across states: It is more expensive to hire a qualified teacher in New Jersey than in Utah. Even after accounting for the input costs, there is wide variation in per-student spending across states.

Do these funding differences translate into achievement differences? Would reduction in funding disparities reduce inequality in educational outcomes? Is there evidence that certain inputs like small classes and high-quality teachers are important drivers of student achievement? Economists seek to determine what roles are played by policies that increase school resources more generally, or specific education inputs (such as teachers), to increase student academic performance. To echo the title of an influential book that addresses these questions, we want to know *Does Money Matter?* (Burtless, 1996).

This chapter focuses on the empirical research surrounding these questions. We first review the arguments and data on the research that has been brought to bear since the Coleman report. A number of people argue that the data continue to show at most a weak correlation between schooling resources and academic performance in the context of the current organizational structure of public schools. However, the interpretation of these data has been controversial. We discuss the arguments made by proponents of total resource policies who disagree that the data suggest a weak link between school resources and student achievement. The evidence is not straightforward, which leads to considerable uncertainty about the efficacy of total resource schooling policies.

Beyond the question of whether money in general matters for education outcomes, we are interested in whether the specific inputs money buys affect achievement. Teachers are one of the most important inputs into the education process, so we examine what the empirical research says on how the two education inputs most related to teachers—class sizes and teacher quality—affect measured student outcomes.[1] On the whole, the results from these studies point to large effects of both inputs on student achievement, which highlights their importance even when total resource policies appear ineffective. We conclude with a discussion of the policy implications of the findings from this research.

---

[1] The quality of one's peers, or peer effects, also is a potentially important input that has received considerable attention in economics. We do not discuss the K–12 peer effects research because it is very technical in terms of econometrics and because peer quality cannot be "purchased" by schools in the same way that class sizes or teachers can be. We discuss peer effects in higher education in Chapter 15. Sacerdote (2011) provides an excellent overview of peer effects research for interested students.

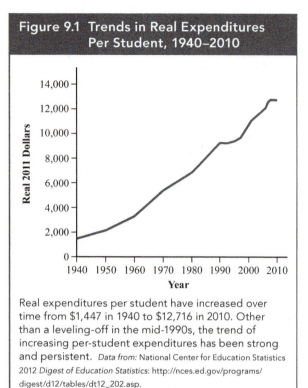

Figure 9.1 Trends in Real Expenditures Per Student, 1940–2010

Real expenditures per student have increased over time from $1,447 in 1940 to $12,716 in 2010. Other than a leveling-off in the mid-1990s, the trend of increasing per-student expenditures has been strong and persistent. *Data from:* National Center for Education Statistics 2012 *Digest of Education Statistics:* http://nces.ed.gov/programs/digest/d12/tables/dt12_202.asp.

Hanushek critique The argument that there is little correlation between the amount schools spend on students and measured academic outcomes in the context of the observed organizational structure of schools.

9.1 The Hanushek Critique

The Relationship Between Total Resource Policies and Outcomes

One of the most influential arguments since the Coleman report to cast doubt on the role of monetary resources for schools in driving educational outcomes is provided by economist Eric Hanushek. In a series of papers, Hanushek brings to bear two core pieces of evidence that we will call the **Hanushek critique**.

1. **Aggregate time-series evidence.** The large increases in per-student expenditures over time have not been met with gains in measured student achievement.
2. **Education production function evidence.** Research has not found consistent evidence of a positive link between total school resources and student outcomes or between key inputs such as teacher salaries or student–teacher ratios and student performance.

Taken together, the two points of the Hanushek critique suggest that both total resource policies and input-based policies foused on teacher pay and class size reduction may be ineffective.

Since the 1960s, per-student expenditures and many key education inputs have grown dramatically. Figure 9.1 shows the trends in real per-student expenditures: Between 1960 and 2010, per-student expenditures grew *in real terms* by almost 300%. That is, they almost quadrupled, from $3,246 to $12,716. Other than a leveling-off in the mid-1990s, the trend of increasing per-student expenditures has been strong and persistent. Figure 9.2 presents trends in two school inputs that have received much policy attention: teacher salaries and student–teacher ratios.

Figure 9.2 Trends in Teacher Salaries and Student–Teacher Ratios, 1960–2010

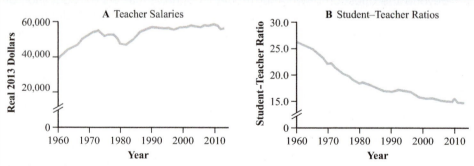

Teacher pay has increased by 43% between 1960 and 2013, with much of the increases occurring in the 1960s and 1980s. More teachers are being hired over time as well; the average student–teacher ratio in U.S. public schools dropped from 26.4 in 1960 to 14.8 in 2013, a 44% decline.

Data from: National Center for Education Statistics 2012 *Digest of Education Statistics:* http://nces.ed.gov/programs/digest/d12/tables/dt12_076.asp (student–teacher ratio) and http://nces.ed.gov/programs/digest/d13/tables/dt13_211.50.asp (teacher salary).

Teacher pay has increased by 43% over this period, with much of the increase occurring in the 1960s and 1980s. At the same time as teachers are becoming more expensive, more of them are being hired. The average student–teacher ratio in U.S. public schools dropped from 26.4 in 1960 to 14.8 in 2013, a 44% decline. Thus, at least some of the spending increases in Figure 9.1 have gone to support smaller classes, as measured by the student–teacher ratio.

A key point of Hanushek's argument is that measured education outcomes have not changed dramatically with these large increases in spending on education. One important way we measure trends in student knowledge is through the National Assessment of Education Progress (NAEP). The NAEP is administered by the National Center for Education Statistics, which has been testing a nationally representative set of students on a comprehensive set of subjects, including mathematics and reading, since the 1970s.[2] The tests are designed to be comparable over time, so these exams provide much insight into the knowledge and skills of U.S. students. We focus on the mathematics and reading exams, which have been administered to 9-, 13-, and 17-year-olds at intermittent periods since 1973.

Figure 9.3 presents trends in NAEP reading and math scores over time. In 2004, the exams were changed slightly. Both exams were given in that year, and we plot two scores for 2004 to aid in cross-time comparisons. As shown in the top panel, the changes in test scores are quite small. For 17-year-olds, reading scores have changed negligibly, while for 9- and 13-year-olds they have increased modestly. However, most of these increases have come since 2000, with relatively flat score trends between the early 1970s and 2000. This is an important point, because as Figures 9.1 and 9.2 show, school resources were growing steadily during this period. It seems odd to attribute the increases in 9- and 13-year-olds' test scores to increases in school resources in the 2000s, as similar increases prior to 2000 did not have such an effect.

The bottom panel of Figure 9.3 shows similar trends for NAEP mathematics scores. Again, we see that trends in mathematics scores for 17-year-olds are ostensibly flat, while they are increasing among younger children. The magnitude of the increases for smaller children is quite large, pointing to significant increases in the mathematics skills of 9- and 13-year-olds over time. That these gains are not reflected in the test scores of 17-year-olds is troubling. If gains among younger children fade out by the time they are 17, then we need to question how important those gains are. The difficulty in interpreting the differences across age patterns and whether the lack of a trend among 17-year-olds is indeed evidence that spending effects fade out remains a major source of controversy surrounding these time trends.

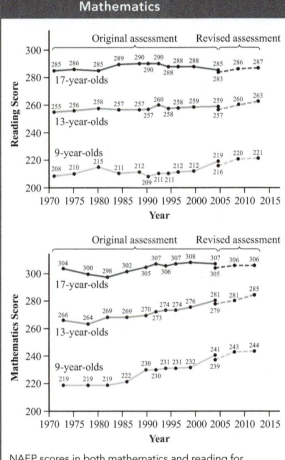

Figure 9.3 NAEP Scores: Reading and Mathematics

NAEP scores in both mathematics and reading for 17-year-olds have remained flat over time. NAEP scores for math among younger students have increased since the 1990s, while there have been more recent increases in test scores for reading. *Data from:* NAEP (2012) http://nces.ed.gov/nationsreportcard/subject/publications/main2012/pdf/2013456.pdf.

---

[2] See Appendix A for a more detailed overview of NAEP data.

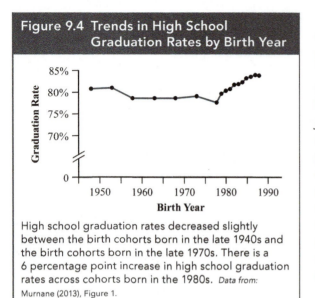

Figure 9.4 Trends in High School Graduation Rates by Birth Year

High school graduation rates decreased slightly between the birth cohorts born in the late 1940s and the birth cohorts born in the late 1970s. There is a 6 percentage point increase in high school graduation rates across cohorts born in the 1980s. *Data from:* Murnane (2013), Figure 1.

Changes in educational attainment are similar in many ways to the changes in NAEP scores. Trends in high school graduation rates by birth cohort are shown in Figure 9.4.[3] These trends suggest, at most, a modest increase in the high school completion rate since the late 1960s, when the 1948 birth cohort would have graduated. In fact, graduation rates *fell* modestly for the birth cohorts in the 1950s and then remained flat. While they increased by about 6 percentage points between the 1980 and 1990 birth cohorts, the lack of an increase in earlier periods when expenditures were growing rapidly casts doubt on whether the recent high school completion changes can be explained by school spending increases.[4] Indeed, high school completion rates among cohorts born at the beginning of the 1990s were only slightly higher than they were among cohorts born in the early 1950s.

Eric Hanushek (1986) sums up this evidence:

> Constantly rising costs and "quality" of the inputs of schools appear to be unmatched by improvement in the performance of students. It appears from the aggregate data that there is at best an ambiguous relationship and at worst a negative relationship between student performance and the inputs of schools. Such conclusions cannot, however, be made on the basis of aggregate data.

The last sentence of the quotation raises a very important point: While the lack of a strong correlation between aggregate trends in student performance and school expenditures is suggestive, it is not causal evidence. Such trends do not control for other school policies changing over the course of time, nor do they account for changes to the composition of students from immigration and other demographic shifts in the U.S. population.

The second part of the Hanushek critique consists of a review of studies examining the relationship between school resources and student achievement (Hanushek, 1986, 1997, 2003). Table 9.1 presents results taken from Table 3 of Hanushek's 2003 review of existing research. Overall, these studies have struggled to find a positive and statistically significant effect of various types of inputs on student performance. For example, of the 163 separate estimates of the effect of per-pupil expenditures, only 27% are positive and statistically significantly different from zero. What's more, 7% are negative and statistically significant, while the majority are not significantly different from zero. The same conclusion holds when looking at teacher salary and student–teacher ratios. For student–teacher ratios, the estimates are as likely to be positive and significant as they are to be negative and significant. The sum total of the evidence from the body of research examined by

---

[3] These data were taken directly from Murnane (2013).

[4] Recent research suggests that the enormous expansion in the 1980s and 1990s of Medicaid, the federal program that provides health insurance to low-income Americans, can explain about one-sixth of this increase (Cohodes, Sarah R., Daniel S. Grossman, Samuel A. Kleiner, and Michael F. Lovenheim. 2016. "The Effect of Child Health Insurance Access on Schooling: Evidence from Public Insurance Expansions." *Journal of Human Resources* 51(3): 727–759.

Table 9.1 An Overview of Study Findings for the Education Production Function				
		Percent		
Resource	Number of Estimates	Statistically Significant Positive	Statistically Significant Negative	Not Statistically Significant
Student–teacher ratio	276	14	14	72
Per-student expenditures	163	27	7	66
Teacher salary	118	20	7	73

Data from: Hanushek (2003).

Hanushek provides little support for the notion that higher school inputs raise academic achievement.

A caveat to this review is that estimating the causal effect of school spending on education outcomes is an extremely difficult undertaking. What we would like is to randomly assign schools different amounts of money and see what happens to student achievement. Such an experiment is infeasible, and in the absence of an experiment, researchers must use naturally occuring variation to try to tease out the causal effect of school spending on students.

One way to proceed is to compare outcomes across schools that spend different amounts per student. This approach is problematic because schools that spend more per student may have a more affluent student body or, in the other direction, they may serve students who receive substantial supplemental aid. Alternatively, we can relate changes in funding within a school to changes in student outcomes. This would allow us to control for fixed attributes of schools, such as the affluence of local residents. However, within-school changes over time could be due to a local community becoming wealthier, which would independently lead to test score increases. If school funding is compensatory, less wealthy schools will receive more state and federal aid, which could increase funding when other factors in the school are putting downward pressure on student achievement. The difficulties in conducting a causal analysis of this question have led economists to spend considerable time and energy trying to isolate "as good as random" variation in spending across schools.

DEEP DIVE: The Relationship Between State Spending and Student Test Scores

States vary considerably in their per-student expenditures, which provides an opportunity to examine whether these large funding differences translate into differences in student achievement. In the top panel of Figure 9.5, we show a plot of log NAEP scores at the state level between 1990 and 2012 on log state per-pupil expenditures. We have pooled math and reading NAEP exams, and the slope of the *linear regression line* gives the elasticity of NAEP test scores with respect to spending. This estimate is 0.055 (with a standard error of 0.015):

A 1% increase in expenditures is associated with only a 0.055% increase in test scores. Thus, the elasticity of NAEP scores with respect to state spending is positive, but it is quite small.

> **Quick Hint:** Taking the natural log of both variables is commonly done in economics because the resulting slope is the elasticity. Thus, the regression line that best fits the point in the figure is the elasticity of NAEP scores with respect to per-pupil expenditures (i.e., the percentage change in NAEP scores when expenditures change by 1%).

The correlation between the two variables shown in the top panel of the figure is problematic because there are lots of differences between states that affect student achievement beyond spending on schooling. One way states likely differ is in labor market conditions that affect the price of inputs to schooling, particularly teacher salaries. For example, districts must pay higher wages to hire teachers in California or New York than in Nebraska or Utah. In addition, there are large differences in family economic circumstances and parental education among districts that also affect measured achievement beyond school resources. That is, higher-spending districts that spend more also tend to have families with higher income and with more completed education. To account for many of these factors, we control for fixed differences across states, across years, across math and reading tests, and across grades 4 and 8 that may be correlated with state spending. This is accomplished by the use of state, year, subject, and grade fixed effects. Essentially, this model compares how *changes* in expenditures relate to *changes* in NAEP scores within states over time. In the bottom panel of Figure 9.5, we plot log NAEP scores against log per-student expenditures after accounting for these fixed differences. Now, there is no relationship between state per-student spending and NAEP exam scores. The estimated elasticity is 0.027 (standard error = 0.017), and it is not statistically significantly different from zero. This elasticity indicates that for every 1% increase in per-student spending (corresponding to about $111 in 2011), NAEP scores will only increase by 0.027%. While this evidence is unlikely to be causal due to concerns about why per-student spending varies within states over time, the relationship in Figure 9.5 is sufficiently weak that it raises serious concerns about whether education spending has any effect on measured academic achievement.

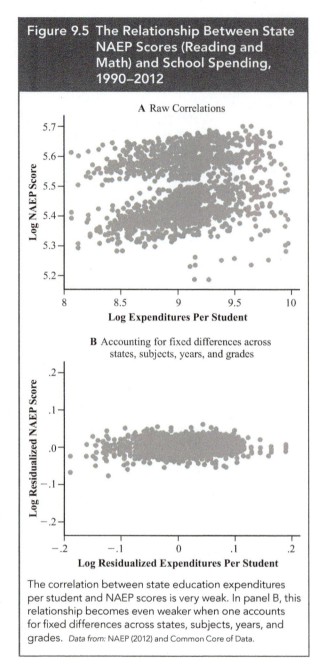

Figure 9.5 The Relationship Between State NAEP Scores (Reading and Math) and School Spending, 1990–2012

The correlation between state education expenditures per student and NAEP scores is very weak. In panel B, this relationship becomes even weaker when one accounts for fixed differences across states, subjects, years, and grades. *Data from:* NAEP (2012) and Common Core of Data.

> **Quick Hint:** Recall from Chapter 3 that fixed effects are a set of indicators that control for fixed characteristics. State fixed effects are a series of 49 dummy variables that control for unchanging characteristics of each state. Similarly, year fixed effects are composed of an indicator variable for each year and control for common factors across all states in each year. Conditional on these fixed effects, the remaining (or residual) test score variation is within state and over time.

Explanations for Small Total Resource Effects

In Chapter 7, we described the properties of the education production function and showed that efficiency in the use of resources means equating the marginal product per dollar of expenditure across all inputs. Contrary to what the data show, the education production function model suggests that increasing school budgets and allowing them to allocate these resources to employ more inputs should be the most efficient way to increase student achievement. How do we make sense, then, of the weak correlation between spending on education and student achievement? Economists have offered several explanations grounded in economic theory to explain the weak measured relationship between school resources and outcomes:

- Spending levels are sufficiently high to put spending on the flat of the curve. That is, spending is sufficiently high that the marginal returns to additional spending are low. This explanation stems directly from diminishing marginal returns to educational expenditures.
- There may be political considerations driven by parents' perceptions and preferences as well as by special interest groups; these considerations can distort the use of unrestricted school funds.
- Lack of competition in local schooling options means principals do not face competitive pressures to produce better outputs. This leads to inefficient use of resources.

The first explanation differs from the second two in terms of its implications for policy because it is consistent with efficient resource allocation. Inputs may be allocated efficiently, such that the marginal product per dollar is equated across all inputs, but increasing total resources has little effect because of diminishing marginal returns. Indeed, this explanation is consistent with the stronger positive link between total resources and student outcomes among older cohorts who attended school when school spending levels were lower (Betts, 1996). In this case, it will be difficult to raise student achievement without a technological change to the education production function that makes resources more productive at current levels.

The second two explanations suggest that total resource policies are ineffective because of inefficiencies in how resources are allocated within schools and/or school districts. The importance of political considerations in driving input allocation decisions has received much attention among policy makers and researchers, focused in large part on teachers unions. These unions may use negotiating power with districts to put resources toward inputs that do not have the highest marginal product per dollar. In other words, they may distort the allocation of resources in an inefficient manner, such that revenue increases are not spent on the most effective inputs.

Several scholars have argued as well that school resources have little effect on education production due to a lack of competition. In a Tiebout model, competition stems from families' ability to move across localities in response to differences in the provision of government services. In practice, parents likely face constraints in their ability to change schools within districts or between districts, and these constraints can dampen competition among schools. There also may be information barriers that keep parents from knowing which schools are the most productive (Hastings & Weinstein, 2008).

Without a need to compete for students, schools have little incentive to allocate resources efficiently. This could lead to small total resource effects.

Measurement Problems in Capturing Resource Effects

The previous section outlined theoretical reasons why we might expect per-student expenditures to be only weakly correlated with academic outcomes. Another class of explanations for this finding is that resource effects are indeed positive but are not captured by the ways researchers have measured either resources or student outcomes. Indeed, several arguments suggest that the correlations discussed in the first section miss important aspects of the story:

- Inequality in achievement has fallen along with spending inequality.
- There has been a compositional change in the types of students in U.S. schools over time that has made them more expensive to educate.
- Test scores provide an incomplete measure of academic achievement; once longer-run measures (such as earnings) are used, school resources appear to be very important.
- School resource increases lead to a reduction in the high school dropout rate, which affects the set of 17-year-old students taking the NAEP exam.

The first argument is based on the observation that inequality in academic achievement has fallen dramatically since the 1970s. Recall from Chapter 8 that a major target of the school finance reform movement was to equalize spending inequities across districts. If these spending equalizations led to better student performance, they should do so predominantly for students from lower-SES (socioeconomic status) backgrounds.

Figure 9.6 presents trends in White–Black and White–Hispanic differences in NAEP mathematics scores since the early 1970s. Among both groups and at all ages, the gaps have declined. For example, in 1971, the White–Black math test score difference was 40 points among 17-year-olds. By 2013 the gap had declined by 35%, to 26 points.

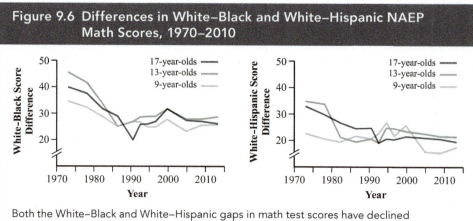

Figure 9.6 Differences in White–Black and White–Hispanic NAEP Math Scores, 1970–2010

Both the White–Black and White–Hispanic gaps in math test scores have declined substantially over time. These declines have occurred for all ages of students who take the NAEP. Among 17-year-olds, the gap declined by 35% for Black students and by 40% for Hispanic students. *Data from:* NAEP (2012) http://nces.ed.gov/nationsreportcard/subject/publications/main2012/pdf/2013456.pdf.

The White–Hispanic difference, while smaller, fell by 11 points (or 40%). Of course, examining aggregate trends cannot provide causal evidence of the effect of spending on student outcomes, but the narrowing of these test score gaps suggests that changes in school financing could have been a contributing factor.

The second critique of interpreting the weak link between resources and student achievement as an indicator of inefficiency is that analyses fail to take into consideration increased expenditures on students with special needs and other changes in demographics that made recent cohorts more likely to be "disadvantaged." Failing to account for the changes in the student population and the expansion in the range of services provided could be seen as a problem of omitted variables. Some argue that if researchers compared the delivery of educational services to populations with similar characteristics over time, the link between resources and achievement would increase. Large increases in the proportion of Hispanic immigrants, the numbers of students with disabilities, and the proportion of children from single-headed households over time are consistent with this story, as students from these backgrounds have lower test scores on average and often are more expensive to educate. However, parental education has increased markedly over time, which should increase test scores holding all else equal (Hanushek, 2003). While changes in the composition of U.S. students are a potential source of bias in aggregate trends, it is difficult to know in what direction any such bias goes.

The use of test scores as the measure of educational outcomes, while very common, has garnered much criticism as well. The argument often made is that test scores fail to capture the depth and breadth of skill acquisition in the educational context. In response to such criticism, a set of studies has focused on relating changes in education resources available to school-age children to long-run outcomes of those children. A series of path-breaking studies by economists David Card and Alan Krueger assessed how the variation in school resources available to students during the 1920s, 1930s, and 1940s affected their earnings observed in 1980.[5] They find substantial effects of changes in school inputs on the return to education.

Further research examines the rise of Rosenwald schools in the U.S. South between 1913 and 1931 on the long-run outcomes of Black youths exposed to these schools (Aaronson & Mazumder, 2011). This program, which was a collaboration between Booker T. Washington and Chicago philanthropist Julius Rosenwald, resulted in the building of 5,000 new schools for rural Black children in the South. These schools were of much higher quality and had more financial resources than the schools to which these students previously had access. The researchers collected detailed information on the timing of the opening of these schools in different areas and examined the long-run outcomes of the children who lived near a Rosenwald school. They find that these higher-resource schools had large effects on educational attainment of students, as well as on literacy and northern migration. Although they do not examine earnings, these outcomes all are tied so closely to earnings potential that it is likely earnings rose as well. Together, these papers indicate a substantial role for school resources in promoting long-run labor market outcomes of students, especially those from disadvantaged backgrounds.

---

[5] These studies are Card and Krueger (1992a, 1992b, 1996). Betts (1996) presents a comprehensive review of this research.

DEEP DIVE: The Effects of Education Resources on Long-Run Outcomes

One very important implication of the education production function is that students who are exposed to more resources (i.e., to higher school "quality") should receive more human capital from their education. In a series of influential papers, economists David Card and Alan Krueger (1992a, b) test whether this is the case by estimating how the returns to education vary with the quality of K–12 schools to which students were exposed as children. Their empirical approach has two stages. In the first stage, they estimate the return to education for individuals based on their state and year of birth. This produces a set of average returns to education for each state-of-birth and year-of-birth cohort in their data. They next examine how the returns to education experienced by different cohorts over time within states is related to state-level changes in measured K–12 resources. Ostensibly, this method examines whether the growth in school resources over time within a state is linked to the returns to education experienced by the students who were exposed to those increased resources.

The main difficulty faced by Card and Krueger in the use of this estimation approach is that a bias can result from cross-state differences in labor market earnings and rates of return. For example, the earnings of men born in Illinois may be very different from those born in Arkansas for many reasons that are unrelated to school resources. In addition, earnings can be deeply influenced by the state of *current* residence, not just the state of birth.

The authors overcome this problem by employing a fixed-effects strategy that holds constant fixed differences across people based both on their state of current residence and on their state of birth. In this way, they can estimate the return to a year of education for each state-of-birth and year-of-birth cohort without having to worry about biases driven by fixed differences across states in labor markets and in the composition of people born in each state. The conceptual experiment underlying this estimation approach is relatively straightforward. Imagine a set of workers in a specific labor market. Some of these individuals attended school in states with high-quality schools and some attended school in states with low-quality schools. As long as there are no unobserved differences between these workers, a comparison of the relative earnings of these individuals will yield an unbiased estimate of the effect of school quality on the return to education.

To estimate this model, Card and Krueger (1992a) use data from the public use sample of the 1980 U.S. census and restrict their sample to males born between 1920 and 1949. Thus, their estimates only pertain to men, since women born in these years had very low rates of labor force participation. They divide their sample into three 10-year birth cohorts and estimate the return to education separately for every 10-year cohort–state-of-birth combination. They then relate these estimated rates of return to the cohort–state averages of three school quality measures workers would have been exposed to as children: student–teacher ratio, teacher wages, and length of school year.

With the state fixed effects, this strategy compares changes over time within each state in the returns to education and relates them to changes over time within each state in these K–12 education resources. In effect, they estimate whether states that increase their resources more have students who receive a higher return to their education when they are adults. For this estimation approach to yield unbiased results, three assumptions must be met: (1) It must be the case that school quality affects earnings only through the return to education; (2) there can be no selective migration across states that contaminate the results; and (3) changes in unobserved school and community characteristics cannot be correlated with both changes in the return to education and school quality.

Card and Krueger find that rates of return to education are higher for those who attended schools with higher resources. Figure 9.7, replicated from the original paper (1992a), shows the final outcome of their two-step estimation procedure, using the student–teacher ratio as the measure of school quality. This figure plots the within-state change in return to education between individuals born 1920–1929 and individuals born 1940–1949 against the change in the average student–teacher ratio within each state. The figure indicates that the rate of return to education rose more in states that experienced a large decrease in the student–teacher ratio (i.e., smaller class sizes) and implies that the return to education is positively correlated with the student–teacher ratio.

Their regression results suggest a very similar story: A class size reduction of 10 students is associated with

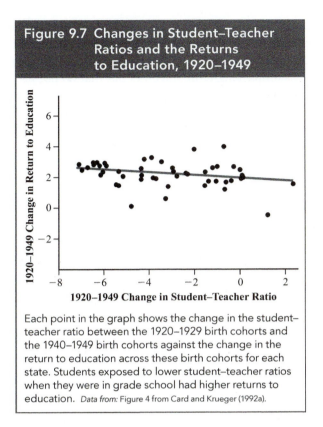

Figure 9.7 Changes in Student–Teacher Ratios and the Returns to Education, 1920–1949

Each point in the graph shows the change in the student–teacher ratio between the 1920–1929 birth cohorts and the 1940–1949 birth cohorts against the change in the return to education across these birth cohorts for each state. Students exposed to lower student–teacher ratios when they were in grade school had higher returns to education. *Data from: Figure 4 from Card and Krueger (1992a).*

an increase in the return to education of approximately 0.9 percentage points. Furthermore, a teacher salary increase of 30% is predicted to improve the rate of return to education by almost 0.3 percentage points. These results provide strong evidence for a relationship between school quality and the return to education, suggesting that policies targeted toward raising the quality of the school system can serve to improve the long-run economic prospects of students. Nevertheless, these variables explain very little of the overall variation in return to education even though they are statistically significant. This suggests that several other factors are important in explaining why the return to education varies so much across individuals.

Changes in school quality also can have important distributional consequences, especially if there is a narrowing of the gap between the resources at wealthy versus poor schools. Using a similar method to the one already discussed, Card and Krueger (1992b) investigate whether relative improvements in quality of schools serving Black students in the U.S. South post–World War II can account for the observed convergence between 1960 and 1980 in labor market earnings between Blacks and Whites. To perform this analysis, the authors utilize a two-step

procedure similar to the one discussed previously. They seek to relate variation in school inputs across segregated Black and White schools between 1915 and 1966 in the Southern states that practiced segregation to later-in-life earnings of individuals educated in those states.

Figure 9.8 (derived from the original paper) shows the result of this analysis for the student–teacher ratio as the measure of school quality. The figure plots the difference in the returns to education between Blacks and Whites against the difference in the student–teacher ratio between Blacks and Whites for men born between 1910 and 1939. The downward slope suggests that variation in the relative student–teacher ratio between Blacks and Whites can account for more than 60% of the interstate difference in the Black–White difference in the return to education. On the whole, the authors find that relative quality improvements of Black schools can explain 20% of the observed convergence in the Black–White earnings gap between 1960 and 1980. These results point to the importance of school quality in reducing long-run economic inequality.

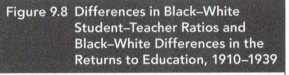

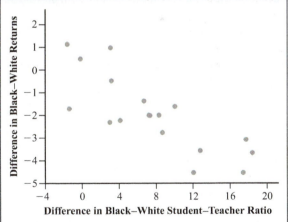

Figure 9.8 Differences in Black–White Student–Teacher Ratios and Black–White Differences in the Returns to Education, 1910–1939

Each point in the figure shows the difference in the student–teacher ratio between Blacks and Whites for men born between 1910 and 1939 versus the difference in the returns to education between Blacks and Whites among the same cohorts. Student–teacher ratio differences are negatively correlated with differences in returns; variation in the student–teacher ratio explains over 60% of the racial gap in the returns to education across states. *Data from: Figure V from Card and Krueger (1992b).*

So how do we reconcile the finding of substantial impacts of school resources on earnings with other evidence indicating little link between measured school resources and student achievement? One interpretation is that school administrators are making resource allocation choices that maximize long-term outcomes but that do not necessarily affect the short-term test score indicators.

Another explanation is the flat-of-the-curve argument discussed earlier: Initial increases in resources from low levels generated huge marginal gains in student achievement. This interpretation is consistent with the large gains in earnings from resource increases in the early part of the twentieth century as well as the lack of apparent effects from resource increases since the 1970s (Betts, 1996).

DEEP DIVE: The Effects of School Finance Reforms on Educational Outcomes

The landmark *Serrano v. Priest* school finance reform ruling triggered a reform movement that led almost every state to alter its school financing system to reduce inequality in funding across school districts. A natural question is whether these school finance equalization schemes, which generally succeeded in reducing funding disparities across school districts, also reduced gaps in student achievement. Economists have studied the effect of these reforms on short-run outcomes (test scores) as well as on long-run outcomes such as labor market earnings and educational attainment. Overall, these papers find mixed evidence on the effect of school finance reform on student achievement.

Card and Payne (2002) look at the effect of 1980s school finance reforms on school spending inequality and find that court-ordered school finance reforms led to an increase in relative funding to low-income school districts. After establishing this result, the authors use data on SAT scores of high school students for the same period to relate the degree of spending inequality in a state to the SAT score gap between children from families with different backgrounds (as measured by parental education). Their rationale is that families tend to sort into districts based on family income, so if school finance equalization reforms affect relative test scores, and if parental education can be used as a proxy for family income, such reforms should lead to a reduction in the achievement gap between children from different family backgrounds.

Their results suggest that reductions in interdistrict inequality in school spending had a small but significant effect on the SAT test score gap between the highest parental education group (father has some postgraduate education and mother has at least some college) and both the middle group (father has 13–15 years of education; mother has 12–15 years) and the lowest group.

This finding suggests that school finance equalization reforms have a very modest effect on narrowing the student achievement gap between children from different family backgrounds.

A different case is the Michigan school finance reform (Proposal A) that shifted financing away from local property taxes and resulted in districts with previously low spending levels receiving larger foundation grants from the state. The size of the foundation grant varies only because of prior spending levels and yearly growth in the amount of money the state has to spend on education. Thus, conditional on prior spending, the foundation grant variation should be uncorrelated with unobserved aspects of the school that are related to student academic performance. In a 2005 study, Papke finds that the increased spending from foundation grants had a positive, albeit small, effect on test pass rates. A 10% increase in spending is associated with an increase in the pass rate of 1 to 2 percentage points, and is approximately 1 percentage point larger for initially underperforming schools. Hyman (2015) extends this analysis to examine long-run outcomes. He finds students who received $1,000 in additional aid money due to Proposal A were 3.9 percentage points more likely to enroll in college and 2.5 percentage points more likely to earn a bachelor's degree. Hence, the long-run effects of Proposal A appear larger than the short-run effects on test pass rates.

Recall from Chapter 8 that Hoxby (2001) estimates how overall spending on education and spending inequality respond to the inverted tax price, the foundation tax rate, income and sales tax rates in support of school spending, and flat grants. Using the same estimation strategy but replacing the spending measures with student outcome measures, she finds little evidence of a relationship between these school finance reform mechanisms and dropout rates. There is a small negative effect of flat grants, which suggests that dropout rates decline in schools that were very low spending and that therefore increased spending due to the flat grant, but on the whole the spending changes induced by school finance reforms did not translate into higher educational attainment among high school students.

With nearly a half-century of school finance reforms since the *Serrano* decision, a recent study completed by Jackson, Johnson, and Persico (2016) examines the long-run outcomes of children who experienced increases in school funding because of school finance reforms. The researchers use detailed panel data that follow individuals from childhood into adulthood and that contains information on the primary and secondary schools that respondents attended. They examine how earnings and educational attainment differ among those who grew up in the same school district but who were differentially exposed to school finance reforms because of the timing of those reforms. They find that a 10% increase in school spending due to school finance reform leads students to complete 0.3 more years of schooling and to 7% higher earnings in adulthood. These results are even larger for students from low-income households, which is consistent with the fact that school finance reforms target aid to such families. The findings in this study, along with those in Hyman (2015), suggest there can be substantial positive effects of school finance reforms on long-run outcomes.

The final argument economists have levied against the Hanushek critique is that if total resource policies increase high school completion, the composition of 17-year-old students taking the NAEP exams will differ over time. Looking at Figure 9.3, NAEP scores have risen more for younger than for older students. Students need to be enrolled in school to take the exam. Thus, if total resource policies keep academically marginal students from dropping out of high school, overall test scores may not rise as the composition of students is getting weaker.

Overall, there is much disagreement over how to interpret the evidence on total resource policies. Much of the disagreement stems from the difficulty in understanding what the time-series evidence is showing. Furthermore, the education production function estimates Hanushek discusses rely on methods that are unlikely to solve the myriad selection problems discussed in Chapter 7. These disagreements have led economists to focus on estimating the effect of specific inputs to the education production function on short- and long-run student outcomes. We now turn to a discussion of the empirical research on the two most-studied inputs: class sizes and teacher quality.

9.2 The Effect of Class Size Reduction Policies

Beyond variation in total resources, a different approach considers the relationship between specific inputs, such as class size, and educational outcomes. Reducing class size or increasing the ratio of teachers to students may improve student achievement through a number of channels:

- Teachers may have more time per student to spend on individualized instruction.
- Teachers may need to spend a smaller share of class time on discipline and administration.
- Teachers may be able to tailor their lessons to the specific needs of the class.

Although there is a widespread belief among parents, teachers, and administrators that smaller classes are better for children, it is surprisingly difficult to know whether this is true.

A central concern in measuring how class size affects achievement is that districts, schools, or classrooms that have smaller classes also may differ in ways systematically related to student outcomes. As discussed in Chapter 7, the sign of this bias is ambiguous, and problems arise when one compares students in different class sizes both within and across schools. Within schools, smaller classrooms may be those that serve students with special needs, and as such, this resource is *compensatory*; it is targeted to students with particular disadvantages to narrow differences in outcomes. Alternatively, smaller classes could be found among gifted and talented students. This arrangement would make class sizes *complementary*, since they are allocated to the most academically advanced students. Thus, comparing outcomes between students who are exposed to different class sizes within a school can yield biased estimates of the effect of class sizes on their achievement.

Comparing class size differences across schools is similarly problematic. Schools or districts with greater resources per student (and lower class sizes) might include a high proportion of students with well-educated parents or parents who have a high demand for education. These confounding factors would make class size effects look more important than they actually are for achievement. It also is possible that schools serving low-income students have smaller classes in an attempt to compensate for the higher learning obstacles these students often face. This would make class sizes look less important for academic achievement than they are.

The economics research on the effect of class sizes on student achievement has sought to overcome these various concerns in several ways. Conducting an experiment in which students are randomly assigned to small and large classes is a clear approach to estimating the causal effect of class size reduction on student achievement. Because large-scale experiments are few and far between in education, we look as well at nonexperimental evidence in which researchers have used clever and varying methods based on specific policy rules to estimate the degree to which class size affects student outcomes. Table 9.2 provides an overview of the class size research.

Project STAR

One of the largest and most important social experiments ever conducted in the United States was a randomized controlled trial of the effect of smaller class sizes in Tennessee in the mid-1980s. In 1985, Governor Lamar Alexander and the Tennessee legislature introduced the **Project STAR**—or Student–Teacher Achievement Ratio—experiment. This four-year experiment focused on students in the early elementary grades, starting in kindergarten and then moving to third grade. The experiment included some 11,000 students in 80 elementary schools. To be included in the Project STAR study, each school needed at least 57 students in the entry grade, which allowed for at least a smaller class of 13–17 students, a regular class of 22–25 students, and a class of regular size that also would be assigned a teacher's aide. A key to the research design is that both students and teachers were randomly assigned to the three types of classrooms. Critically, the randomization was done within each school. This assured that, on average, the characteristics of students and teachers across the different classroom types *within each school* were the same. Thus, within-school comparisons of student test scores across different class sizes yields the causal effect of class sizes on student achievement.

In the most comprehensive study of the initial impacts of Project STAR on student test scores, Alan Krueger (1999) begins by examining the extent to which the random assignment was done properly. He shows that across all observed characteristics, those

Project STAR The largest randomized class size experiment in the United States, conducted in Tennessee in the mid-1980s among students in grades K–3.

Table 9.2 Summary of Class Size Research

Research Paper	Empirical Method	Data	Outcomes Examined	Main Findings
Krueger (1999)	Analysis of Tennessee STAR experiment	Administrative data on K–3 students in Tennessee	Percentile of Stanford Achievement Test	• Assignment to a small class increased test scores by 0.2 standard deviations. • Effects are largest in K–1 and in the first year students were treated. • Low-income and minority students had the largest test score increases. The effect eliminated two-thirds of the Black–White test score gap.
Krueger & Whitmore (2001)	Analysis of Tennessee STAR experiment	Administrative data on K–8 students in Tennessee; SAT/ACT scores	Comprehensive test of basic skills in fourth to eighth grades and SAT/ACT test outcomes	• Test score effects decline by half after the experiment ends in third grade. • A 3.7% increase in the proportion of students who take the SAT or ACT. • Black students assigned to small classes were 8.5% more likely to take the SAT or ACT.
Chetty et al. (2011)	Analysis of Tennessee STAR experiment	Administrative income tax records for those in the STAR experiment	College enrollment, earnings as an adult, and life outcomes such as homeownership, savings, and marriage	• Assignment to a small class in Project STAR increases college enrollment by 2%. • Smaller classes lead to increases in the quality of colleges students attend. • Treated students exhibit better life outcomes in terms of marriage, savings, homeownership, and neighborhood quality. • Little evidence of an effect of small classes on earnings.
Angrist & Lavy (1999)	Regression discontinuity using Maimonides' rule	Classroom-level data for Israeli elementary schools	Average third- to fifth-grade math and reading test scores	• Smaller classes led to increases in math and reading test scores for fourth- and fifth-graders. • No effect among third-graders.
Hoxby (2000)	Regression discontinuity using class size rules and population variation	School-level data from elementary schools in Connecticut	Statewide exams in fourth and sixth grades.	• No evidence of an effect of class size on test scores.
Jepsen & Rivkin (2009)	Examination of California's class size reduction policy	School-level data on student test scores and average class size	Stanford Achievement Test scores from second- to eleventh-grade students	• Class size reduction policy increased math and reading test scores by 0.05 and 0.09 standard deviations, respectively. • There were large reductions in teacher qualifications because of the need to hire many new teachers. • The teacher quality effect was larger in more disadvantaged schools.

assigned to a smaller versus a bigger classroom were identical on average within each participating school. The randomization had two components. First, all students were randomly assigned to one of the three class types upon initial enrollment in the school. The second component was that students randomly assigned to one of the large class groups were randomized again after kindergarten either to receive a teacher's aide or not. Most students entered in kindergarten, but many students also entered in each of first, second, and third grades. The experiment ended after the third grade.

The main findings of this experiment suggest that smaller classes lead to higher student achievement. Students who were assigned to the small classrooms did appreciably better during the K–3 grades than their peers assigned to large classrooms. A common metric for the differences in test scores between regular and small classes that can be generalized beyond the specific assessments given to students in Tennessee is the measure of the **effect size**. This measure captures the fraction of a standard deviation of difference in a group's performance that is due to the class size difference.

A summary of Project STAR findings in terms of effect sizes is reported in Table 9.3. Overall, the results of Project STAR showed that assignment to a small class was associated with an effect size of about 0.2. Interestingly, the estimates were largest in kindergarten and first grade, fading out somewhat in the higher two grades. This fade-out has led some researchers to question the conclusions drawn from this experiment, because if smaller classes raise student achievement, repeated exposure should produce higher and higher test scores. This does not appear to be the case in Project STAR.

Table 9.3 shows as well that minority students were particularly influenced by assignment to a smaller class, as were students from low-income backgrounds in second and third grades. In kindergarten, the effect is large enough to eliminate almost two-thirds of the Black–White test score gap. These sizable effects come from reductions in class size of about seven or eight students, or close to one-third of a normal-sized class.

effect size The impact of an intervention in standard deviation units of the outcome. For Project STAR, it is the effect of small classes in terms of the standard deviation of test scores.

Table 9.3 Summary of Project STAR Results in Standard Deviations

	(1)	(2)	(3)	(4)
Panel A: Overall	Kindergarten 0.187 (0.039)	Grade 1 0.189 (0.035)	Grade 2 0.141 (0.034)	Grade 3 0.152 (0.030)
Panel B: By race Black	Kindergarten 0.214 (0.074)	Grade 1 0.249 (0.063)	Grade 2 0.207 (0.054)	Grade 3 0.242 (0.060)
White	0.172 (0.042)	0.161 (0.040)	0.105 (0.042)	0.115 (0.034)
Panel C: By free lunch status Free lunch	Kindergarten 0.188 (0.046)	Grade 1 0.195 (0.042)	Grade 2 0.174 (0.041)	Grade 3 0.174 (0.039)
Not free lunch	0.177 (0.051)	0.194 (0.047)	0.126 (0.047)	0.118 (0.041)

Note: Standard errors in parentheses.
Data from: Schanzenbach (2006).

Social experiments are very difficult to run because it is hard to know how people will respond to being put in a randomized controlled trial. In the implementation of Project STAR, as with any social experiment, several threats to the randomization process can contaminate the results. Krueger (1999) provides a detailed discussion of these issues, most of which are based on the fact that while the experimenters could randomly assign students to class types, they could not compel parents to comply with this assignment. In particular, Krueger addresses the following threats to the experiment:

1. **Nonrandom reassignment.** Parents with children assigned to the larger classes complained to the principal and got their child reassigned. About 10% of students switched in this manner.

2. **Nonrandom attrition.** Those who were assigned to a larger class may have been more likely to leave the district for a private school or for another public school. There was about 50% attrition over the course of the study. The worry is that the highest-ability students in the control group left, thus biasing the estimates upward.

3. **Hawthorne effects.** Teachers assigned to smaller classes may have responded to the fact that they were involved in the experiment, thus biasing the estimates upward.

> **Quick Hint:** Hawthorne effects occur when participants know they are involved in an experiment; they often act in such a way as to make the experiment a success. In this context, teachers assigned to small classrooms might exert more effort because they were part of the experiment than they would if they were randomly given a small classroom outside of an experiment. Hawthorne effects make the results of experiments almost impossible to generalize to a broader policy context.

For the first concern, Krueger leverages the random nature of the initial assignment. While actual class size exposure might have been endogenous because of switching, initial assignment was not. Using the initial assignment rather than the actual class the student wound up in allows Krueger to estimate the effect of small classes among students whose class sizes differed because they complied with the experimental assignment.

> **Quick Hint:** Initial assignment serves as an instrumental variable for the realized class size. An instrumental variable (see Chapter 3) is correlated with the treatment—class size—but is uncorrelated with other determinants of the outcome—test scores. Because the initial assignment to a small or large class is random, it is uncorrelated with other determinants of test scores. The initial random assignment allows Krueger to isolate the random variation across students in class size.

Krueger handles nonrandom attrition in two ways. First, he assigns students who leave the sample their most recent test score. Effects using these imputed scores are virtually identical to the main results, suggesting attrition from the sample is not generating the main findings. However, this method only deals with students who show up at least once; scores for students induced by the experiment never to enroll in the school cannot be imputed. Krueger estimates that 2–4% more students in the control group relative to the treatment group withdrew from participating schools in this manner. He estimates that this is too small a percentage to affect the overall results.

To test for Hawthorne effects, Krueger examines the relationship between class sizes and test scores only among the control group. Variation in school size generated differences in the exact size of the large classes. He shows that this variation led to effects similar to the experimental estimates, which is inconsistent with the main effects being driven by teachers who might be influenced by their participation in an experiment.

Krueger's research shows that the effects of class size on contemporaneous test scores are large. However, in a 2003 article assessing the Tennessee STAR evidence, Hanushek raises the important point that the effects of class sizes in kindergarten do not increase appreciably with each additional year in a small class. That is, there appears to be a large initial effect of being in a small class, but with repeated exposure over time the effect does not grow. He argues that these results could be due to smaller classes having a socialization effect that helps students more quickly learn how to behave in the classroom. Socialization effects should lead to the largest increase in test scores in the first year of exposure to smaller classes, which is consistent with what the data show.

For evaluating educational interventions like class size reductions in lower grades, it also is critical to examine whether the gains in student achievement are permanent or transitory. Fortunately, a number of researchers have worked to collect data on the academic outcomes of Project STAR recipients for many years after the conclusion of the initial trial program. If the effects fade out over time, it suggests that the long-run returns are much smaller than the short-run returns. In such a case, it becomes necessary to think about extending the treatment to higher grades or to search for other interventions that have more persistent effects.

Using test scores beyond the end of third grade provides one type of longer-term assessment from Project STAR. Some research has analyzed effects on Tennessee standardized test scores up through eighth grade as well as on college entrance exam (i.e., ACT and SAT) testing rates (Krueger & Whitmore, 2001). There is evidence of positive long-run effects, but they are much smaller than the short-run test score gains that were apparent when the students were being treated with small classes. The effect of small classes on test scores drops immediately for all groups beginning in fourth grade. While some effects persist to eighth grade, they are less than half the size of the K–3 test score impacts. SAT/ACT test-taking rates also increase by 3.7 percentage points (or 9.3% relative to the mean test-taking rate among the control group). For Black students, the SAT/ACT test-taking effect was 8.5 percentage points, or 26.8% relative to the control mean. Small classes in K–3 thus reduced the Black–White SAT/ACT test-taking gap by 54%, which suggests that students who were exposed to smaller classes in early grades are more college-oriented when they reach high school. Thus, there are some long-run educational benefits of being in a small class in lower grades, but the long-run effects are clearly smaller than the short-run effects on test scores.

Beyond test scores, there is some evidence of modest long-term impacts of small classes in early grades on rates of college enrollment (Chetty et al., 2011). In addition, some studies indicate that initial assignment to a small class may reduce adverse teenage behavioral outcomes, such as pregnancy and juvenile delinquency (Schanzenbach, 2006). These results suggest that the effects of small classes in grades K–3 persist into adulthood and are economically meaningful in size.

DEEP DIVE: Long-Run Class Size Effects

"How Does Your Kindergarten Classroom Affect Your Earnings?" This question, which partially forms the title of a research paper by Chetty et al. (2011), is examined by linking individual student data from Project STAR to long-run labor market and education outcome data obtained from U.S. tax records. The authors manage to link 95% of the children who participated in the STAR project to their later-in-life tax records. This linkage allows them to analyze how class sizes, class characteristics, and teacher assignments in grades K–3 affect later-in-life education and labor market outcomes when the individuals are 27 years old. The importance of this analysis stems from the fade-out in test scores shown by Krueger and Whitmore (2001), which suggests it

is important to determine whether any effects persist into early adulthood.

The authors' empirical strategy consists of comparing the adult outcomes of individuals who were randomly assigned to different kindergarten classroom environments in Project STAR. Combined with their extraordinarily rich data, the fact that students and teachers were randomly assigned to each other enables them to look at whether class size, teacher quality, and peer quality in early grades affect later-in-life outcomes.

The children who were assigned to smaller classes were about 2 percentage points (or about 8%) more likely to attend college by the year 2000. They also exhibited better general life outcomes, such as homeownership, 401(k) savings, being married, and living in wealthier neighborhoods. Surprisingly, however, the results do not suggest that children assigned to smaller classes have higher labor market earnings than those assigned to larger classes.

One of the core contributions of this paper is to show that one's kindergarten class quality is extremely important and that class size is but a small part of such quality. For example, kindergarten students assigned to a teacher with more than 10 years of experience earn, on average, $1,093 more than those assigned to teachers with less experience.

And, the overall quality of the class as proxied by its average test score is strongly predictive of higher wages, more college attendance, attending a higher-quality college, and better overall life outcomes.

The overall takeaway from this paper is that early-grade classrooms differ markedly in quality in ways that translate to long-run differences in students' lives. The key for education policy is to understand what factors drive these quality differences to foster high-quality learning environments. Chetty et al. (2011) suggest that class size plays a small role, as does teacher experience, but neither is a dominant factor in determining classroom quality.

Nonexperimental Class Size Studies

While experimental evidence is certainly important for policy research, it is expensive—Project STAR cost $2.5 million per year for four years in 1985, which is just over $5.5 million in 2014 dollars—and politically difficult to implement. What is more, the time lag needed to observe many outcomes of interest, combined with concerns that predicted results may not apply to other demographic groups or grade levels, leaves researchers eager to find other techniques for measuring how class size affects student achievement. Nonexperimental studies therefore are critical to generating evidence of class size reduction effects across geographical areas and at different points in time.

Quick Hint: Recall from Chapter 3 that the ability to generalize findings to other groups not involved in the experiment or study sample is called *external validity*.

In Israel, class size is partially governed by the text of Maimonides, a twelfth-century rabbinic scholar (and budding social scientist) who declared that two teachers must be employed if there were 40 or more students in a grade level. The result is that in Israel there are relatively sharp discontinuities at increments of 40 students in the total number of students in each grade. So if one school has 40 first-graders and another school has 39, the first school will have two classes of 20 students, while the second will have one class with 39 students. Figure 9.9 shows this pattern for a hypothetical school and grade.

In general, researchers would be worried about drawing causal inferences from comparisons of achievement results by class size across very large schools (e.g., 150 kids at a grade level) and very small schools (e.g., 35 kids in a grade level). For example, one might be concerned that the large school would be in a major urban area, while the small school would

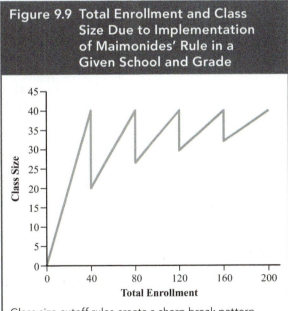

Figure 9.9 Total Enrollment and Class Size Due to Implementation of Maimonides' Rule in a Given School and Grade

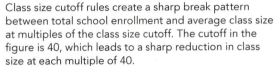

Class size cutoff rules create a sharp break pattern between total school enrollment and average class size at multiples of the class size cutoff. The cutoff in the figure is 40, which leads to a sharp reduction in class size at each multiple of 40.

be in a rural area, so it would be hard to ascertain whether any differences in student achievement were caused by class size policies or underlying demographic and family circumstances that also affect student achievement.

Joshua Angrist and Victor Lavy (1999) have a very clever solution to this problem. They note that schools just above and just below the break points generated by Maimonides' rule should be very similar. If this is the case, comparing student achievement when there are 39 students in one class to achievement when there are 41 students and class size is 20 or 21 will provide a good measure of how class size affects achievement. This method is an application of the regression discontinuity design discussed in Chapter 3. The researchers find large and significant effects of class size on student achievement for fourth- and fifth-graders but not for third-graders. Large declines in class sizes are associated with sizable increases in reading test scores. These estimates are highly consistent with those shown in Krueger (1999) from Project STAR.

Subsequent research has not found the same effect on students in other U.S. schools, however. In a 2000 study, Caroline Hoxby leverages class size variation due to population variation across 649 Connecticut elementary schools, combined with maximum and minimum class size rules that trigger large class size changes from small variations in school size. This is ostensibly the same method as that used by Angrist and Lavy, and yet she finds no evidence that smaller classes lead to higher test scores. These estimates cast doubt on whether class sizes truly influence test scores in a nonexperimental setting in the United States.

Evidence from Policy Variation

Why might there be differences between class size effects in an experimental versus a nonexperimental setting? Other than the Hawthorne effects discussed previously, a critical feature of the Tennessee STAR experiment was that each participating school had to be big enough to have one small and two larger classes. As a result, no new teachers had to be hired. Contrast this with the Hoxby (2000) design. There, schools likely need to hire new teachers, and as we will see in the next section, newer teachers, on average, demonstrate lower performance than more experienced teachers. This difference highlights the limitations of Tennessee STAR results for small-class policies, as any broad policy that requires schools to have small classes will require many new teachers to be hired in the short run. It is not possible to disentangle the effects of the change in the teacher workforce from the change in class sizes. The contrast further underscores the challenge of conducting policy analysis in a real-world setting.

A particularly salient example of this issue comes from California. Due in part to the evident successes of Project STAR in producing higher test scores, the California legislature created a strong incentive for schools to reduce class size by giving a financial reward to districts where every student was in a class of 20 or fewer students. Specifically, districts received $650 per student for meeting this condition, which was a bit more than 10% of the average per-pupil expenditure in California. It was, however, appreciably less than the full cost per student of class size reduction in most districts (Angrist, 2004).

The cost of achieving the class size targets within a grade varied appreciably across schools. For example, a school that originally had 50 second-graders divided between two classes of 25 faced a substantial cost of reaching the threshold of 20 students. To reach the threshold within the second grade, the school would need to hire an additional teacher, and class size would drop to 16 or 17. Similarly, if the school had 50 third-graders, another teacher would also need to be hired to meet the class size reduction objective.

School administrators in California quickly realized that the least expensive way to reduce class size in the example would be to add just one teacher and combine second and third grade into one class. Thus, the response to the policy would be to make two second-grade classes of size 20, two third-grade classes of size 20, and one combined class with 10 second-graders and 10 third-graders. There is strong empirical evidence that combining classes was indeed a very common practice in California in response to this policy, with nearly 15% of second- and third-graders assigned to combination classes (Sims, 2003). The startling result from the research that has been done on California's policy is that pooling classes on students' achievement has large adverse effects, and the negative effects on achievement for those who were assigned to the combination classes tend to cancel out the positive effects for students assigned to small classes.

Other researchers have shown that class size reduction may have had effects on the teacher labor market as well, in that experienced teachers from relatively disadvantaged districts were hired by relatively advantaged districts in response to the increased demand created by the class size reduction policy (Jepsen & Rivkin, 2009). As a result, relatively disadvantaged districts—home to many of the students with the greatest capacity to benefit from smaller classes—were forced to staff classrooms with a larger share of newly hired, inexperienced teachers, resulting in an unanticipated trade-off between class size and teacher quality in the education production function.

Writing in the *Oxford Review of Economic Policy*, Joshua Angrist (2004) provides a clear summary of the connection between research evidence and policy implementation related to class size reduction initiatives:

> Under relatively ideal circumstances (in particular, given long enough lead time and funding adequate to reduce class size without compromising other educational inputs), class size reductions can increase test scores. This is an important result and a performance standard that many and perhaps most programs, however well-intentioned, do not live up to.

DEEP DIVE: The California Class Size Reduction Policy

In 1996, California passed the most sweeping class size reduction law in the nation, reducing K–3 class sizes by about 10 students per class. The required class size reductions led to a large increase in demand for teachers: In the first two years, 25,000 new teachers had to be hired. Many of those teachers, particularly in low-income and high-poverty schools, were uncertified and had little or no prior work experience. This program provides a clear example of the trade-off between smaller classes and teacher quality.

What was the net effect on student achievement? A serious difficulty in studying this policy is that all schools and students in California were affected simultaneously, making it very difficult to identify an appropriate comparison group that can inform us about how student achievement would have changed in the absence of this policy. Such difficulties are common in the study of education policy, as state or federal laws often cover all students simultaneously.

Research by Jepsen and Rivkin (2009) approaches this problem using two methods. Although neither method is perfect, each one relies on different assumptions. To the extent that they yield similar results, together they can give us a clearer picture of the effect of the class size reduction policy. First, the researchers employ a difference-in-difference method, using the fact that some schools were late to adopt the class size reduction policy. This method links the timing of implementation to the timing of test score changes, but it requires one to believe the strong assumption that the timing of adoption of the class size reduction is unrelated to trends in student achievement.

The second method used by Jepsen and Rivkin is a fixed-effects strategy that relates changes in class sizes *in the same school grade over time* to changes in test scores and teacher composition. If the variation in class sizes within a school and grade is caused by the class size policy and not by unobserved factors that are correlated with the class size policy implementation, such as changes in student body composition, it will identify the causal effect of the program on test scores and teacher characteristics. One way to think about their approach is that school grades will be more heavily treated when they had larger classes prior to the reduction policy. The student-level panel data they use allow them to control both for fixed differences across school grades and school years, and so a central assumption they invoke is that school grades with different pretreatment class sizes would have had similar trends in outcomes absent the class size reduction policy.

The difference-in-difference estimates suggest that the class size reduction policy increased math and reading test scores by 0.05–0.09 of a standard deviation. These are sizable and statistically significant increases, although they are smaller than those found in the Tennessee STAR analysis. Importantly, when they implement their fixed-effects analysis and control for teacher characteristics, they find an almost identical effect of a 10-person class size reduction on student math and reading scores. The consistency of the findings from these two methods strongly supports their validity.

A further complication with this analysis is that holding teacher characteristics constant will tend to overestimate the effect of this policy; the California policy created thousands of new K–3 teaching jobs, and many of these were filled by inexperienced and nonqualified teachers. The reductions in teacher quality as a result of the class size reduction policy were likely to at least partially offset the class size effect on student performance. A very novel feature of the paper is that it explicitly estimates how the change in teacher quality induced by the class size policy affected student achievement. Their results suggest that having a teacher with no experience compared to having a teacher with two or more years of experience completely offsets the student achievement gain associated with the 10-student reduction in class size. They further find that having an uncertified teacher compared to a certified teacher has a smaller but similarly signed effect. This very important finding suggests that large-scale class size reduction policies may not yield substantial increases in student achievement unless there is a sizable number of qualified and experienced teachers who can step in to fill the new positions. This finding thus highlights a large complication in applying the results of experimental studies, such as Project STAR, to a real-world class size reduction policy. These studies ignore potential teacher quality effects associated with large-scale class size reduction policies and may overstate the effectiveness of such policies, at least in the short run.

The authors further found that the negative teacher quality effect was more pervasive among disadvantaged schools. While the affluent schools filled their new positions by recruiting experienced teachers from disadvantaged schools, disadvantaged schools had to rely more heavily on inexperienced and nonqualified teachers. Thus, class size policies could serve to increase inequality, which typically is counter to their aims. The central lesson learned from this analysis and from the California class size reduction policy more broadly is that policy makers need to account for the supply of teachers when constructing class size policies.

9.3 Teacher Quality

Teachers are perhaps the most important school-based input into the education process. They are with children on a day-to-day level, and they are responsible for actually teaching the information and skills that we believe constitute an important part of human capital. It therefore can be somewhat odd to ask questions like, Do teachers matter for education? The answer is almost certainly yes; almost every successful student can point to a teacher who changed the way he thought about a topic as well as one who was instrumental in stimulating his interest in learning. If teachers cannot influence student learning, then it is unlikely any school-based input into the education process will.

Thus, it is extremely important to understand the different ways in which teachers affect student academic achievement. In this section, we take a close look at what is known about teacher quality. How do economists measure teacher quality? How closely are our teacher quality measures linked to student academic outcomes? That is, how much of the variation in outcomes across students can be explained by the quality of the teachers they had? And finally, if teachers are very important for education, what are the characteristics that lead them to be effective? How can we identify such teachers and perhaps hire or develop more with such skills in our education system? These are some of the core questions that surround understanding the role of teacher quality in education production.

As we will see, teachers are immensely important for the education process. By far, teacher quality appears to be the most important school-based input that researchers have isolated in terms of the proportion of overall test score variation they explain (Goldhaber, 2002). At the same time, the observed characteristics of teachers seem only weakly correlated with their productivity in the classroom. Indeed, this is a core component of the Hanushek critique against input-based schooling policies: If the little we observe about teachers tells us how good they are at teaching, it is unlikely that policies that simply spend more money on teachers will be successful. The challenge for education policy, then, is how to develop hiring and firing policies as well as pay systems that appropriately reward teachers for their productivity. We discuss these issues in depth in Chapter 12 and concern ourselves here with the measurement and importance of teacher quality.

Value-Added and the Measurement of Teacher Quality

How Do Economists Think About Teacher Quality? We first start with the critical question, "What is teacher quality?" This is an important and often contentious question, and depending on whom you ask, you may get very different answers about what it means to be an effective teacher and who effective teachers are. This is especially the case since the outcomes of the education process are multifaceted. Here, we provide an overview of how economists think about and measure teacher quality, which is becoming an increasingly important component of education systems throughout the country in terms of teacher assessment, school accountability, and teacher pay.

The main way in which economists measure teacher quality is in terms of their ability to increase observed student outcomes. This has a rather intuitive appeal; after all, one of the main jobs of a teacher is to teach students the knowledge and skills that should show up in terms of their achievement. In practice, this typically means that teacher quality is measured by the ability of a teacher to raise student test scores. The effect of a teacher on her students' test score growth is called **value-added**, and the idea is to statistically isolate the contribution of each teacher to her students' test score gains. Teachers who produce higher test score gains, and thus have higher value-added, are considered higher-quality teachers under this measure.

This is admittedly a very data-driven approach to defining teacher quality, and it has associated strengths and weaknesses. The main strength of value-added analysis is that its data-driven nature allows us to actually produce measures of teacher quality.

value-added (of a teacher) His or her contribution to student test score gains.

There are deep measurement and estimation issues surrounding value-added analysis that we will discuss later, but the ability to generate objective measures of how much teachers are teaching to students is of high value. Its main weakness, however, is that value-added measures necessitate the focus on specific standardized tests. Thus, our measures of teacher quality will be specific to the skills being asked on a given exam, and this focus might cause us to miss important ways in which teachers are contributing to their students' human capital. For example, standardized tests may be quite poor at measuring creativity, social and emotional maturity, leadership skills, and civic engagement. These all are unquestionably important educational outcomes that many teachers may be quite adept at generating, and focusing only on test scores therefore may miss aspects of teacher quality.

Value-Added Analysis   Despite the drawbacks of value-added analysis, it is a powerful way to measure teachers' contributions to student learning. Consequently, a lot of work has been done to determine how good a job value-added models do in accurately estimating the causal effect of each teacher on his or her students' measured academic achievement. This research can get quite technical, and so, in this section, we provide a general overview of value-added modeling. In the subsequent sections, we discuss the evidence on how value-added translates into measured short- and long-run student outcomes as well as what observable features of teachers can predict their value-added.

Aside from rare circumstances, such as in Project STAR, students are not consistently randomly assigned to teachers. The nonrandom assignment of students to teachers raises an enormous problem for value-added analysis that is similar to the difficulties associated with estimating education production functions discussed in Chapter 7. To see the issues generated by such selection, imagine there are two teachers, Jamila and Zoe, who teach fourth grade in the same school. We want to identify each teacher's value-added. One simple but naïve comparison we can do is to compare the average test scores of Jamila's students to those of Zoe's students. If we see that Jamila's students score higher on the exams, does this mean she is a better teacher? Not necessarily—the students Jamila teaches may be systematically different from those Zoe teaches. What if the principal believes Jamila is better at teaching higher-ability students and Zoe is better at teaching students who are not as academically advanced? What if Jamila has been employed at a particular school for longer than Zoe and thus receives more requests than Zoe does from parents that their children be enrolled in her class? Both of these scenarios will lead to important differences in the composition of students across Jamila's and Zoe's classrooms that make average score comparisons very complicated to interpret.

Without random assignment, it would be wrong to ascribe the average test score differences across the students taught by Zoe and Jamila to their teaching ability. Comparing average test scores across teachers in a given year is an example of a cross-sectional estimator. Even if we controlled for observed characteristics of students, such as race, gender, family income, and parental education, it is unlikely we could overcome the biases associated with nonrandom sorting of students into classrooms with cross-sectional methods.

Instead of comparing test score levels, what if we looked at how the test scores of Zoe's and Jamila's students *changed* over time? That is, imagine we could collect information on their students' third-grade test scores, and instead of looking at the differences in test score levels across Zoe and Jamila, we examined how the average change between each student's third- and fourth-grade test score differed between Zoe and Jamila. This is an example of a first-difference estimator, and it will estimate how each teacher contributes to the growth in her student's test scores. Now the differences between them are less likely to be due to differences in the types of students they teach, as much of these differences will be encapsulated in the third-grade score. By estimating the change in scores, we can better isolate each teacher's contribution to her students' learning (as measured on the exam) in that year.

Instead of directly estimating the change in test scores, economists favor a model that controls for students' lagged test scores. This method is essentially the same as the first-difference approach, but it allows for a more flexible relationship between prior performance and current performance. The lagged test score model is highly prevalent, and it has become the standard model economists use to estimate value-added. Among its benefits is that it has a straightforward interpretation. Basically, the lagged test score acts as a control that accounts for selection of students to teachers based on test score levels. Prior test score levels reflect the history of educational inputs each student has received as well as differences in family circumstances and genetics. The argument behind this model is that controlling for lagged test scores allows one to account for these various difficult-to-observe factors that influence current test scores. Recalling Jamila and Zoe, Jamila is assigned higher-ability students than Zoe in our example. This will be reflected in their lagged test scores, however, and if the only difference between Jamila's and Zoe's students is that they differ in terms of prior performance levels, the lagged test score model will accurately estimate both teachers' value-added. The Toolbox provides a more technical overview of teacher value-added modeling and the relative benefits of different ways of estimating teacher value-added.

🧰 TOOLBOX: Estimating Teacher Value-Added

Imagine we have several years of student–teacher linked data for third- through fifth-grade students. In each year (y), we can identify the school (s), grade (g), and teacher (t) to whom each student (i) is assigned as well as the student's test scores. We could implement the first-difference estimator by first calculating, for each student and year, the change in the test score between grade g and grade $g - 1$. We call this change $\Delta Score_g$. We can estimate teacher value-added for each teacher with the following regression:

$$\Delta Score_{igsty} = \alpha + \theta_t + \delta_g + \rho_s + \tau_y + \beta X_{gsty} + \mu Z_{iy} + \varepsilon_{igsty}$$

This model amounts to a regression of the change in test score for student i in grade g, school s and year y assigned to teacher t on a set of teacher fixed effects (θ_t), grade fixed effects (δ_g), school fixed effects (ρ_s), and year fixed effects (τ_y). The term ε_{igsty} is the regression error. The regression therefore controls for fixed differences in test score changes across schools, grades, and years. X_{gsty} refers to observed characteristics of the classroom in the given year and grade, such as percentage Black, Asian, and Hispanic; the percentage who receive a free or reduced-price lunch; and perhaps even the average test score levels of students from the prior year. Typically, these means are calculated separately for each student in the classroom, using the values of all students other than the given student herself. The Z_{ty} term is a set of time-varying student characteristics, like free or reduced-price lunch status and parental income.

The coefficients of interest in this equation are the teacher fixed effects; they isolate each teacher's average test score gain in her classroom, controlling for these other factors. These θ_t estimates are the value-added measures. A teacher with a higher value of θ_t has higher test score growth in her class, conditional on the observed characteristics of the students in her class as well as the fixed characteristics of her school and grade and any fixed characteristics common to all teachers in that year.

The first-difference model embeds in it a strong assumption, namely that the effect of the prior year's test score does not decay. Put differently, this model assumes that the effect of last year's test score on a current test score is 1. This is a strong assumption and one that is easily relaxed by controlling for lagged test scores instead of using the first difference:

$$Score_{igsty} = \alpha + \theta_t + \delta_g + \rho_s + \tau_y + \beta X_{gsty} + \mu Z_{ty} + \pi_{i,g-1,sty} + \varepsilon_{igsty}$$

The first-difference model is akin to forcing $\pi = 1$, but a large body of research suggests that $\pi < 1$. This is called decay, as the impact of prior test scores on current test scores fades over time. Importantly, the lagged test score model is very easy to estimate, and the data requirements for this model versus the first-difference model are identical. One can even augment this model by controlling for more test score lags. This allows for researchers to control in a detailed manner for each student's prior achievement.

A final way that economists often estimate value-added models is to employ student fixed effects instead of (or in addition to) lagged test scores:

$$Score_{igsty} = \alpha + \theta_t + \delta_g + \rho_s + \tau_y + \sigma_i + \beta X_{gsty} + \mu Z_{ty} + \varepsilon_{igsty}$$

Here, the student fixed effects (σ_i) control for fixed differences across students in terms of their test scores. As with controlling directly for prior test scores, this model accounts for fixed family background factors as well as educational inputs that occurred prior to the start of the data. The fixed effects typically use more than two years of data, and so models like this control for student ability over a longer period of time.

Can Value-Added Models Be Trusted? Value-added models do a relatively good job of controlling for fixed differences across students, but they all face potential problems that can come from differences in trends or expected trajectories of student learning. Students may be matched to teachers based on expected trends in their measured achievement. For example, what if Jamila was given students who were expected to exhibit more test score growth than Zoe? This would bias any of the value-added estimators we've discussed. Furthermore, test score growth and test score levels can be correlated in complex ways. Higher-ability students could exhibit higher growth in each year as well as higher levels, or mean reversion could lead higher-performing students to grow less in the subsequent year (and vice versa for low-scoring students). Most tests also have score ceilings (such as 100%). Such ceilings will preclude students with very high ability from exhibiting much growth.

That these potential problems exist does not mean that value-added models necessarily give us the wrong answer; they just mean that there *could* be biases associated with these models. If this is the case, it is critically important to understand how well these models identify which teachers are producing the highest gains in measured student achievement before we base personnel and pay decisions on them.

The research, on the whole, suggests that value-added models that control for lagged student achievement do a good job at identifying teacher contributions to test score growth. One study of particular importance on this question was done by economists Thomas Kane and Douglas Staiger (2008). They conducted a randomized experiment in Los Angeles in which they first calculated value-added measures with preexperimental data (when the students were not randomly assigned to teachers), using models very similar to those just discussed. Then, using the random assignment of students to teachers from the experiment, they reanalyzed the models. They found that the value-added models that control for lagged test scores and average classroom characteristics in the prerandomization period did a good job of matching the experimental estimates. In short, their results indicate that the lagged test score model adequately controls for student sorting, such that the value-added estimates from such a model give you the same result as if there were random assignment of students to teachers.

DEEP DIVE: Nonexperimental and Simulation Evidence on the Validity of Value-Added Models

Statistical simulations provide a way to examine how different types of value-added models perform under different assumptions about how students are sorted to teachers. Guarino, Reckase, and Wooldridge (2014) use this strategy and show that while no value-added model is perfect, no matter the type of sorting, the lagged test score model exhibits the least bias in terms of misclassifying high-performing teachers as low-performing teachers. On the whole, their results suggest that lagged test score value-added models provide pretty accurate information about each teacher's contribution to his students' test score growth.

Research by economist Jesse Rothstein, however, casts doubt on the ability of value-added models to accurately estimate teacher quality. In a very influential and important 2010 paper, Rothstein employs a creative test of the validity of value-added models: fifth-grade teachers cannot affect fourth-grade value-added. He finds evidence that value-added models fail this test. The reason the data show a correlation between the fifth-grade teacher and fourth-grade value-added, he argues, is that students are sorted into fifth-grade classrooms based on trends in their test scores. This makes it appear as if fifth-grade teachers cause learning outcomes in fourth grade, which clearly cannot be the case. Although this is not direct evidence of bias in value-added estimates, the potential for sorting on trends to bias value-added estimates is worrying and points to potential problems with the prominent value-added models used by economists.

Recent research provides some reconciliation of the seemingly conflicting results from Rothstein and from Kane and Staiger. Using data from a large, unnamed school district in the United States from 1989 to 2009, comprising over 2.5 million students linked to U.S. tax data, the researchers first show that a detailed set of typically unobserved parent characteristics does not affect their value-added estimates when included in the model (Chetty, Friedman, & Rockoff, 2014a). Thus, the value-added model adequately controls for selection of students based on their unobserved background characteristics. The researchers also examine whether current teachers affect past performance, and they find no evidence this is so.

The research team then employs an innovative design to test the validity of value-added based on teacher mobility. They show that when a high-value-added teacher enters a school, the students in that grade perform better. When a high-value-added teacher leaves, the students in the school and grade perform worse. This is shown in Figure 9.10, which is reproduced from their research. While test scores exhibit no trend in the years prior to a high value-added teacher entering, when such a teacher enters, students in that grade perform better. This effect persists, and the jump is not evident in the grade just below in the same school. Figure 9.10 presents a strong case that value-added measures are picking up an important aspect of teachers' ability to increase student academic performance.

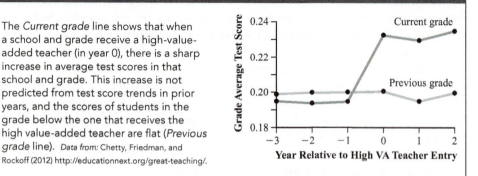

Figure 9.10 The Effect of High Value-Added Teachers

The *Current grade* line shows that when a school and grade receive a high-value-added teacher (in year 0), there is a sharp increase in average test scores in that school and grade. This increase is not predicted from test score trends in prior years, and the scores of students in the grade below the one that receives the high value-added teacher are flat (*Previous grade* line). *Data from:* Chetty, Friedman, and Rockoff (2012) http://educationnext.org/great-teaching/.

While it appears the Chetty, Friedman, and Rockoff study is at odds with Rothstein's work, both studies actually are based on similar findings. Both papers find evidence of sorting based on prior trends. However, Chetty, Friedman, and Rockoff can show that the sorting on prior trends does not affect value-added estimates. Their results are unchanged when they control for twice-lagged scores, and their analysis based on teacher mobility confirms that students exposed to higher-value-added teachers make larger gains. On the whole, the evidence to date points to value-added models providing informative data on teacher quality.

How Much Does Teacher Quality Matter?

Existing research supports the use of value-added as at least one measure of teacher productivity, but how important are teachers as inputs into the education production function? The answer should surprise few: Teacher quality as measured by teacher value-added is very important. In fact, it is the most important single school-based education input researchers have been able to measure to date, explaining 8–9% of the overall variation in student test scores (Goldhaber, 2002).

How successful are teacher value-added measures in predicting the learning gains of future cohorts of students? In other words, how does exposure to a teacher who is 1 standard deviation better in terms of value-added affect student test scores? In some of the earlier research on this question, Rockoff (2004) uses student–teacher linked data from K–sixth-graders in a single county in New Jersey. Estimating a student fixed-effects model, he finds that an increase of 1 standard deviation in teacher value-added is associated with an increase of 0.08–0.11 standard deviations in student test scores.

In one of the most influential papers on this topic, Rivkin, Hanushek, and Kain (2005) use detailed administrative data that contain test scores, schools attended, and grades attended for all students in Texas. They focus on third- through seventh-grade students in 1993–1995, leading to a dataset with over 200,000 students from over 3,000 public schools in the state. Although they cannot link students to teachers, they use the variation across school grade cohorts in teacher turnover that led to different cohorts being exposed to teachers of differing quality. Similar to Rockoff (2004), they find that an increase of 1 standard deviation in teacher quality increases student test scores by about 0.1 standard deviations in reading and math. According to their estimates, increasing teacher quality by 1 standard deviation is akin to reducing class size by 10 students. The range of teacher quality also is quite large: Some teachers achieve test score increases equal to 1.5 years of student learning, while others only achieve increases equal to 0.5 years.

In their study of a large urban school district, Chetty, Friedman, and Rockoff (2014b) estimate very similar-sized effects: an increase of 1 standard deviation in value-added raises student test scores by 0.08–0.09 standard deviations. Their teacher mobility analysis further supports this finding. When teacher mobility leads to an increase of 1 standard deviation in teacher value-added in the school and grade, student test scores increase by 0.08 standard deviations on average. The fact that evidence using different data from different periods tells a remarkably consistent story about how teacher value-added relates to student performance provides further support for the validity of these models.

An innovative aspect of Chetty, Friedman, and Rockoff's study is that they can link the students in their sample to long-run outcomes from U.S. tax data (similar to the data used in Chetty et al., 2011). There is concern from prior work that any effects of a specific teacher's value-added fade out, so that the long-run effects are much smaller than the short-run effects.[6] If teachers have only short-run effects on their students, it casts doubt on the importance of teacher quality in driving long-run educational outcomes. However, despite the fade-out of test score effects, this study shows large, long-run effects of teacher quality on a variety of student outcomes. An increase of 1 standard deviation in teacher value-added *in one grade* increases college enrollment by 0.49 percentage points by age 20 (1.3% of the baseline mean). It also leads to a significant increase in the quality of the colleges students attend.

In addition, student earnings increase at age 28 by over $180 per year (or 0.9% relative to mean earnings) for each standard deviation of increase in teacher value-added in one grade and year. Assuming this earnings increase persists for one's entire working life, the net present value of this earnings effect for a 12-year-old student is $4,600. If a single teacher teaches 25 students a year, exposing an entire class to a teacher who is 1 standard deviation higher in terms of value-added will produce a total net present value of earnings of $115,000. This is from one year's teaching. Making the strong assumption that these results can be extrapolated to one's entire schooling career, increasing the quality of teachers throughout the K–12 experience will produce extremely large earnings increases. These results underscore the importance of teacher quality in the education production function.

The Relationship Between Teacher Quality and Teacher Characteristics

Given the importance of teacher quality for student learning as measured by teacher value-added, a question of primary policy importance is how we can identify and hire more high-value-added teachers. Do teachers have observable characteristics that predict high value-added? Unfortunately, it turns out that the vast majority of what we can observe about teachers is uncorrelated with value-added. The one exception is experience: New teachers in particular tend to perform worse than more experienced teachers. For example, in their study of teacher value-added in Texas, Rivkin, Hanushek, and Kain show that teachers with a graduate degree do not have higher value-added,

---

[6] For more on teacher value-added fade-out, see Rothstein (2010) and Jacob, Lefgren, and Sims (2010).

but novice teachers perform 0.03–0.07 standard deviations worse than teachers with six or more years of experience. This experience effect is 30–70% of the effect of a standard deviation increase in value-added. Research on schools in New Jersey and in North Carolina show similar effects.[7] In fact, evidence from North Carolina suggests the experience effect for math is much larger than what was found in Texas and persists later into the teaching career (Wiswall, 2013).

Of course, experience is only one teacher attribute. From the perspective of a principal making hiring decisions, it is often difficult to only hire experienced workers. Indeed, not every school could do this if it so desired. Are there teacher characteristics that predict value-added and that principals could use to hire the most productive teachers? The research to date has not found strong links between teachers' value-added and their observable characteristics. One of the most prominent papers on this question uses matched student–teacher data from Chicago (Aaronson, Barrow, & Sander, 2007). First, they replicate the findings found in prior research, that 1 standard deviation increase in value-added increases student test scores by 0.13 standard deviations. However, they find that little about the teacher's background can explain this value-added variation. In particular, the researchers examine the type of certification teachers have, the quality of undergraduate schools teachers attended, their undergraduate major, and whether they have a master's degree. There is no evident relationship between these characteristics and value-added. This is a somewhat surprising result, as one would expect teachers' academic background and credentials to have some predictive power to determine their ability to generate test score gains. That this is not the case makes using value-added estimates for hiring decisions difficult. Although there is clear evidence that value-added measures an important component of teacher quality, we know very little about how to find high-value-added teachers using their observed characteristics. Thus, while teacher quality exists and is important, it is hard to identify ex ante.[8]

One important qualification to these findings is that while no one characteristic can predict value-added, the sum total of teacher characteristics might be more informative.[9] In fact, data from New York City show that changes in overall observed teacher characteristics in high-poverty schools can lead to sizable increases in student test scores (Boyd et al., 2008). Such findings highlight the critical need to understand how best to recruit and retain the highest-quality teachers.

9.4 Conclusion

Despite the enormous increases in school funding that have taken place over the past five decades, the evidence is at best inconclusive about any resulting effect on measured student achievement. The weak correlation between resources and student achievement

---

[7] Estimates from New Jersey come from Rockoff (2004). Clotfelter, Ladd, and Vigdor (2007, 2010) and Wiswall (2013) study North Carolina.

[8] The difficulty in identifying high-value-added teachers at the point of hire has led many to argue that teacher quality could be increased substantially if the lowest-value-added teachers were fired. This policy has been termed "teacher deselection," and many argue it can be used to overcome the problem that teacher value-added is hard to predict based on observable characteristics (Hanushek 2009; Gordon, Kane, & Staiger, 2006; Goldhaber & Hansen, 2010).

[9] These qualifications are made in research papers by Boyd et al. (2008) and Rockoff et al. (2011).

does not indicate that schools or teachers have little effect on student learning, however. Indeed, we show evidence from both experimental and nonexperimental methods that smaller class sizes and better teachers can have profound effects on students. Thus, the implication of the Hanushek critique is not that school inputs don't matter; it's that giving schools additional unrestricted resources does not seem to translate into the types of input changes that can influence student achievement.

Why might this be? As we discussed in Section 9.2, limits on the existing supply of teachers constitute a serious real-world barrier to enacting policies to reduce class size. Furthermore, while we know teacher quality is important, it still is unclear how to use this information to support hiring and retention practices that will maximize the quality of the teacher workforce.

Some of the problem as well is that education officials and policy makers may face strong political constraints in their use of funds and/or may not face strong enough incentives to use resources in a way that will maximize student achievement. The evidence discussed in Section 9.1 hence has been used as the foundation of arguments to inject strong market-based mechanisms into education in the form of more parental choice and higher school accountability. Such changes can increase the competitive pressures faced by educational institutions, which can lead to improved student learning. In the ensuing chapters, we will study the economics behind these market-based policies as well as the evidence on their effectiveness in generating growth in student achievement.

Highlights

- The data show a weak link between educational expenditures and student achievement. This is one part of the **Hanushek critique**, and it is based on the fact that expenditures on education have risen dramatically over the past several decades, without much increase in measured student performance.

- The second part of the Hanushek critique consists of reviews of the published research that tend to show little systematic evidence that increasing resources improves test scores.

- Evidence of closing racial/ethnic gaps in test scores, along with historical evidence that increases in school resources raised future earnings, indicates a potentially important role for school inputs, however.

- One explanation for the apparent large effects of resources for older cohorts and the lack of effects for more contemporaneous cohorts is that returns to additional school funding are approaching the flat of the curve.

- The prevalence of output-based schooling policies has been supported by the weak association between school spending and student achievement. If increasing funding does not affect student outcomes, policy makers must find ways to increase the incentives schools and teachers face to use resources more efficiently.

- The effect of class size on student achievement has received much attention among researchers. Many of these studies focus on the effects of **Project STAR**, a large randomized

controlled trial conducted by Tennessee in the mid-1980s. Generally, studies have found that reducing class sizes in early grades increases test scores. However, it also appears that the effects fade out over time, and there is only limited evidence of long-run effects on students as measured by earnings and collegiate attainment.

- The effect of class size reduction policies may differ from Project STAR results because in Project STAR no new teachers had to be hired. This is not the case when a state mandates smaller class sizes, as California did in 1996.

- Economists measure teacher quality using **value-added** models, which seek to isolate each teacher's contribution to his or her student's test score gains.

- Though value-added models have been controversial, the majority of the evidence points to them providing important information about teacher effectiveness in raising test scores and in driving long-run student outcomes, such as educational attainment and earnings.

- The evidence from the economics research points to teachers being one of the most important inputs to the education production process. However, there is only a weak relationship between observable characteristics of teachers and measured teacher quality. This makes it very difficult to use insights from value-added analyses to guide hiring practices, as little about the background characteristics of a teacher predicts whether he or she will be effective.

Problems

1. What is the Hanushek critique? What evidence does Hanushek use to support his critique?

2. Summarize the responses to the Hanushek critique. Why might we measure a weak link between resources and student achievement in recent work?

3. In 1985, then-governor Lamar Alexander and the Tennessee legislature implemented the Project STAR experiment.
   a. What was the goal of this experiment?
   b. Describe the experimental design.
   c. Describe the findings.
   d. Discuss the threats to the experiment and how Krueger (1999) proposed to address each threat.

4. Sometimes economists use similar research methods but find different results. For example, when studying the effects of class size, Hoxby (2000) found evidence conflicting the findings of Project STAR. What could lead to the difference in findings? How can we reconcile her findings with those from Project STAR? What is the implication of the difference between these studies for using the Project STAR results to support lower class size mandates?

5. How do economists define teacher quality? Discuss the strengths and weaknesses of this definition.

6. Prior to *Brown v. Board of Education,* many schools in the southern states maintained separate schools for Black and White students. Among states with segregated schools, differences in resources between the schools for Blacks and the schools for Whites varied, while by the middle of the twentieth century such differences had converged markedly. How might this variation provide evidence on the extent to which school resources affect outcomes?

7. Imagine that you are a principal of a school and want to use value-added information to hire teachers. Are there observable characteristics of teachers that predict high value-added? How might you use the results from value-added studies to hire the most effective teachers, or is it not possible to use them for this purpose? Can you think of any potential limitations to the use of value-added measures in schools?

CHAPTER 10

School Choice: A Market-Based Approach to Education Reform

This year, there are going to be millions of our children that we're going to needlessly lose, that we could—right now, we could save them all.... It is absolutely possible. Why haven't we fixed this? Those of us in education have held on to a business plan that we don't care how many millions of young people fail, we're going to continue to do the same thing that didn't work. —Geoffrey Canada, founder of Harlem Children's Zone

Parents want approaches that are vastly different from prevailing policies they believe hurt schools and students. They overwhelmingly choose strong neighborhood public schools over expanding choice, charters and vouchers.—Randi Weingarten, president of the American Federation of Teachers

The Founding of KIPP Schools

In 1994, recent Teach for America alumni Mike Feinberg and Dave Levin started an ambitious new program for fifth-grade students in the Houston public school system. The program, called the Knowledge Is Power Program (KIPP), was designed to give students from inner-city school districts the academic and behavioral skills needed for college. The following year, Feinberg opened the KIPP Academy Middle School in Houston, and Levin started the KIPP Academy in the South Bronx in New York. Today, there are over 140 KIPP charter schools in 20 states and Washington, D.C. They employ an approach to education that has come to be known as the *no-excuses model*. Both the school year and schools days are longer, children are held to very high academic and behavioral standards, and the academic focus of these programs typically is on mathematics and reading skills. The teachers in KIPP schools also tend to be younger and nonunionized, and they are expected to be on call for their students in the evenings and on weekends. Students (and their parents) actively *choose* to apply and to attend a KIPP charter school rather than their local public school.

There is some evidence that students who attend these schools demonstrate substantial achievement gains relative to students who wished to attend these schools but ultimately did not. As illustrated by the quotations at the start of this chapter, some view charter schools as an innovation with the power to transform

3DDock/Shutterstock

opportunities for inner-city youth, while others argue that these schools divert much-needed resources from the public schools without offering a viable model for all students. Our aim in this chapter is to put aside politics of school choice and focus on the key economic questions, including whether alternative schools of choice like KIPP improve student outcomes and how local public schools are affected by school choice policies.

School choice policies decouple the link between where students live and the schools to which they have access. School choice is not a single policy design but rather includes multiple policies that affect the supply of schooling options outside local public schools and the extent to which students can avail themselves of these options. While some forms of school choice have been in existence for decades, such as private and parochial schools, which tend to locate in urban areas, there has been a dramatic increase in the opportunities for school choice in recent decades. For example, all but seven states have laws allowing **charter schools**, which are schools that are independently managed and publicly funded, to operate.[1] As of 2013, the last year for which data are available, there were 6,079 charter schools in the United States. In 2001, there were fewer than 2,000.

Notably, policies expanding school choice have not been strictly partisan. For example, No Child Left Behind, the major education initiative of the George W. Bush administration, had provisions that expanded school choice for students in failing schools. President Obama's Race to the Top initiative, his signature education law, also contains strong incentives for states to expand access to charter schools and school choice programs for students in low-performing schools.

Given the rise in the prevalence of choice-based policies, a critical question is whether increasing the range of school options available to students and their families improves educational outcomes. In this chapter, we examine the two main questions surrounding school choice policies:

1. Are students who take advantage of school choice policies better off in terms of measured academic outcomes? This could occur either because nonpublic schools are more productively efficient than traditional public schools or because increased choice options allow parents to better select an educational environment that matches their preferences and their child's learning style.

2. Do the changes in the local market structure driven by school choice affect traditional public schools through increased competition?

In sum, we want to know whether separating the choices of where parents send their children to school and where they choose to live leads to greater efficiency in education markets. In this chapter, we focus on describing how the major school choice mechanisms used in the United States operate in practice and what the empirical evidence has to say about their effectiveness.

charter schools An independently managed and publicly funded school operated in accordance with a "charter" granted by the state or local government. Charter schools typically have some autonomy from local regulations while they maintain accountability for student performance.

10.1 Economic Theory of School Choice

Writing in the 1950s, Nobel laureate economist Milton Friedman identified a central challenge to the traditional provision of education by public schools. He argued that a system that separated public *funding* of education from public *provision* of education might better serve the needs of students and the public at large. Friedman's points were twofold: First, parents may be better able to assess the educational needs of their

---

[1] The seven states that do not allow charter schools are Kentucky, Montana, Nebraska, North Dakota, South Dakota, Vermont, and West Virginia.

children and identify when local schools are (or are not) meeting their needs than local bureaucrats. Second, competition among schools of all types in a local area uses the market mechanism to ensure relatively high quality and low cost in provision.

Friedman goes on to sketch a potential policy configuration:

> The arrangement that perhaps comes closest to being justified by these considerations—at least for primary and secondary education—is a mixed one under which governments would continue to administer some schools but parents who choose to send their children to other schools would be paid a sum equal to the estimated cost of educating a child in a government school, provided that at least this sum was spent on education in an approved school. This arrangement would meet the valid features of the "natural monopoly" argument, while at the same time it would permit competition to develop where it could. It would meet the just complaints of parents that if they send their children to private non-subsidized schools, they are required to pay twice for education— once in the form of general taxes and once directly—and in this way stimulate the development and improvement of such schools. The injection of competition would do much to promote a healthy variety of schools. It would do much, also, to introduce flexibility into school systems.—Friedman (1955, p. 130)

The configuration that Friedman proposes, which is similar to the voucher, open enrollment, and charter school policies discussed today, emphasizes the market features of **choice** and **competition**. We start with an examination of how families decide on the level of spending to devote to education under traditional public provision and under arrangements that explicitly encourage more choice. Then, we consider the supply side of the market and assess how the degree of competition may affect producer behavior.

Matching Student Demand and Local Public Schools

Under traditional public schooling, residents of a school district are assigned to a local public school through an **attendance zone**, which allocates each house to a specific school based on its location in the district. Having already paid local taxes, parents have free access to the local public school to which they are zoned. Without moving to another district, families have the choice of sending their children to the local public school or paying out of pocket to send their children to a private school. Families also could move to another attendance zone within the district.

A budget constraint provides a good starting point for representing the choices available to the family. If Y is family resources after taxes, they can spend money either on schooling (S) or on other consumption expenditures such as food, clothing, housing, or entertainment. We call all of these other goods the composite good X. This basic budget constraint is shown by the straight solid line in Figure 10.1. With a public schooling option, families can choose to send

choice (in education markets) The ability of students and families to select the school in which the student enrolls regardless of where the family lives.

competition (in education markets) Arises when students have a choice over which school to attend, leading schools to compete for enrollment.

attendance zone A geographic area in which all children are assigned to attend the same local school. The attendance zone thus determines which school in the district a student will attend at each level of schooling absent school choice.

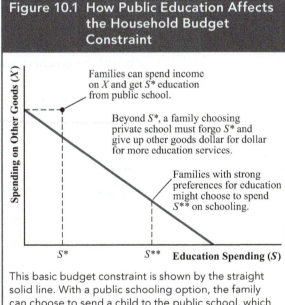

Figure 10.1 How Public Education Affects the Household Budget Constraint

Families can spend income on X and get S^* education from public school.

Beyond S^*, a family choosing private school must forgo S^* and give up other goods dollar for dollar for more education services.

Families with strong preferences for education might choose to spend S^{**} on schooling.

Spending on Other Goods (X) / *Education Spending (S)*

S^* S^{**}

This basic budget constraint is shown by the straight solid line. With a public schooling option, the family can choose to send a child to the public school, which provides education level S^*, or it can purchase private school services higher than S^* at additional cost. The budget constraint the family faces with public schooling is the dashed kinked line and the solid line to the right of S^*. By sending a child to public school, the family can spend all of its income on X.

their children to the public school, which provides education level S^*, or they can purchase private school services higher than S^* at additional cost. Since families already have paid taxes, they can receive S^* of educational services at no additional cost and then can spend the remainder of their income on the composite good. The budget constraint the family faces with public schooling is the dashed line in Figure 10.1. By sending their children to public school, they can consume more of X than if they purchased S^* level of education on the private market, but they are forced to consume only S^* of education.

Recall that in the Tiebout model discussed in Chapter 8, S^* will be set separately for each community based on the preferences of local residents. If sorting is efficient, then localities will set S^* to match the local preferences for education, and there will be no demand for additional education services. Under the assumptions of the model, therefore, Tiebout sorting will have worked to align parents' educational preferences with the offerings of local schools. However, the assumptions of the Tiebout model are very restrictive and are unlikely to be met in practice.

> **Quick Hint:** If S^* matches the demand for education among parents in the district, we sometimes say that parents are on their demand curve. This implies that at the given "price" of schooling, parents will want to invest no more and no less in schooling than they currently do.

The provision of local public schooling at resource level S^* ensures that every child will receive at least this level of education services. This is important because if the social marginal benefits to educational investments are larger than the private marginal benefits, some parents will underinvest in education when they have to pay out of pocket for schooling. Thus, completely relying on private funding to finance the education system is unlikely to generate an efficient level of investment in education, which supports at least some public role in education.

Many parents may want to consume more than S^* of education. Under the Tiebout model, parents have two options. First, they can move to a district that spends their desired amount on education. Many families face resource and mobility constraints, however, such that it is not possible for them to move to the district that provides their preferred level of education services (Nechyba, 2003). The second option is to opt out of the public schools altogether, thus forgoing the opportunity of "free" public education. Some parents will choose to spend some greater amount to send their child to private school. One example of such a choice is shown by S^{**} in Figure 10.1. In this case, parents are paying double for education: They are still paying local school taxes and in addition are paying private school tuition.

If one cannot opt out of paying for local schooling, as is the case throughout the United States, purchasing private education becomes extremely expensive. To see this point, let's consider an example. Suppose the Dunphys would choose to spend $10,000 per year of their $50,000 after-tax income on education for their son in the absence of a free public school option, leaving $40,000 for other expenses. Now, with a public school option that provides $7,500 per student in resources, they face a choice between allocating $50,000 to consumption (receiving $7,500 in public education) and spending $10,000 on private schooling (forgoing the $7,500 in public education) and only $40,000 on other expenditures. In effect, it would cost this family $10,000 in private expenditures to increase spending on their child's schooling by $2,500.

An important insight from Peltzman (1973) is that in-kind lump transfers such as for education can actually lower the utilization of these services. We first need to understand how much schooling parents would optimally choose in the absence of the public schooling option in Figure 10.1. Which point on the budget constraint a family will select were they to pay out-of-pocket depends on the strength of its preferences for schooling relative to other goods. Families with strong relative preferences for schooling will choose a point closer to S^{**}, while parents who value other goods more will choose a point closer to (and perhaps to the left of) S^{*}. The accompanying Toolbox provides an overview of consumer choice analysis in economics and introduces the concepts of utility functions, utility maximization, and indifference curves.

🧰 TOOLBOX: Utility Maximization and Optimal Consumption Decisions

How do individuals decide how much of each good to consume? This fundamental question in economics in many ways mirrors the question of how firms decide what goods to produce, which we discussed in Chapter 7. Decisions about how much of each good to consume are determined by two factors:

1. A budget constraint that details the trade-off between goods and the total amount that can be spent
2. Individuals' preferences for different goods

Take the case in which there are two goods a consumer can purchase, juice (J) and beer (B). Each individual has a total income, I, and the prices of juice and beer are given by P_J and P_B, respectively. The budget constraint is shown in Figure 10.2, where the position is determined by total income and the slope is given by the price ratio: $-\frac{P_J}{P_B}$. Thinking about how much juice and beer to purchase, certainly you would want to choose a mix that is on the budget constraint. If you choose a mix of goods interior to the budget constraint, you are not spending all of your money and thus can make yourself better off by consuming more of at least one of the goods. Consumption bundles outside of the budget constraint are infeasible because they cost more than I.

How does one decide which point on the budget constraint is best? It depends on one's preferences. Individual preferences reflect how much a person desires each good. In economics, we represent these preferences using a **utility function**. A utility function shows how each person's happiness or well-being is associated with consuming different combinations of goods and services. Different combinations of goods may lead to the same level of well-being. For example, having one container of juice and six cans of beer may lead to the same level of utility (or happiness) as having two containers of juice and three cans of beer. In such a case, the individual is willing to trade off three cans of beer for one container of juice. This trade-off reflects the fact that the individual values juice more than beer when juice is scarce relative to beer.

An **indifference curve** shows different combinations of goods that produce the same level of utility. Figure 10.2 shows an indifference curve for juice and beer. Movements along each indifference curve produce the same

utility function How each *Happiness from more or less of something* person's happiness or well-being is affected by the addition or subtraction of an additional good, holding all other goods constant.

indifference curves Different combinations of goods that produce the same level of utility (well-being).

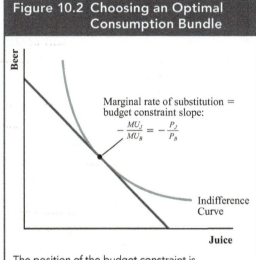

Figure 10.2 Choosing an Optimal Consumption Bundle

Marginal rate of substitution = budget constraint slope:

$$-\frac{MU_J}{MU_B} = -\frac{P_J}{P_B}$$

Indifference Curve

The position of the budget constraint is determined by total income, and the slope is given by the price ratio: $-\frac{P_J}{P_B}$. The optimal consumption bundle occurs at the tangency between the budget constraint and the indifference curve. This is the point at which the marginal rate of substitution equals the price ratio, and it is the utility-maximizing consumption bundle given the prices of the goods and the individual's income.

level of utility, while an outward shift of the indifference curve represents an increase in utility. The slope of the indifference curve in Figure 10.2 is given by the ratio of the marginal utilities:

$$\textit{Indifference curve slope} = -\frac{MU_J}{MU_B}.$$

> **Quick Hint:** Let the utility function be given by $U = U(J, B)$. In terms of calculus, the marginal utility of juice is $\frac{\partial U(J, B)}{\partial J}$ and the marginal utility of beer is $\frac{\partial U(J, B)}{\partial B}$. These are the partial derivatives of the utility function with respect to each good. In other words, they represent the change in utility associated with a small change in the consumption of a good, holding constant the consumption of other goods.

marginal rate of substitution The ratio of marginal utilities of two goods. It shows the utility trade-off between these goods.

The ratio of the marginal utilities is called the **marginal rate of substitution**, and it shows the utility trade-off between goods. Diminishing marginal utility of each good gives the indifference curve its shape. As we move leftward along the indifference curve, purchasing more beer and reducing juice consumption, the marginal utility of each can of beer declines and the marginal utility of each container of juice increases. Thus, the slope becomes steeper. As we move rightward along the indifference curve, the reverse situation occurs: The marginal utility of beer increases and the marginal utility of juice decreases. As a result, the slope flattens.

Graphically, the optimal consumption bundle occurs when the individual is on the highest indifference curve she can afford. As shown in Figure 10.2, the indifference curve is at its highest affordable level when it is just touching the budget constraint. Any higher indifference curve (and thus utility) would require more income, and a lower indifference curve does not maximize the individual's well-being. This tangency point therefore is the point at which an individual's income is being used efficiently; any change in the consumption bundle that is affordable will reduce utility. At this tangency point, the slope of the budget constraint equals the marginal rate of substitution (the slope of the indifference curve). That is, the marginal rate of substitution equals the price ratio of the goods. Rearranging this formula, we see that setting the ratio of the marginal utilities equal to the price ratio is the same as equalizing the marginal utility per dollar of each good:

$$-\frac{p_J}{p_B} = -\frac{MU_J}{MU_B} \Rightarrow \frac{MU_B}{p_B} = \frac{MU_J}{p_J}.$$

This is the condition that characterizes optimal consumption, and thus it shows which point on an individual's budget constraint—the combination of juice and beer—she will choose to maximize her utility. Note that the optimal allocation rule for individuals is very similar to the optimal allocation rule for firms discussed in Chapter 7. While the choice between beer and juice is rather trivial, the same theory applies to how a family divides its resources between spending on education (S) and spending on other goods and services (X).

In Figure 10.3 we show an example in which the introduction of a public schooling option reduces the amount of schooling purchased by the household. Indifference curve A shows a family's preferences over S and X, without a public schooling option. Recall that these indifference curves show combinations of S and X that leave the family equally well off. The optimal mix of S and X is the one that produces a tangency between the budget constraint and the indifference curve. This leads to S^A amount of schooling being chosen by the family.

When the public schooling option is introduced, a household can reach a higher level of utility by sending its child to a public school, which has schooling level $S^* < S^A$. This is shown by indifference curve A'. Thus, it is possible for public provision of education to reduce the amount of education services children receive. Figure 10.3 also shows that the kinked budget constraint that includes the public schooling option will cause many families to select S^*. This is because a family must have very strong preferences for schooling to make it worthwhile to pass up the "free" option of S^*. The result is that there will be bunching at the kink in the budget constraint, since those with a range of preferences for education will find it optimal to choose that point. This is indeed what we see in reality: Most students attend a local public school, with a small handful attending private schools that charge tuition.

Introducing School Choice Mechanisms

In reading through the example of the Dunphys, you might have seen a way to make some people better off without making anyone worse off. What if, rather than providing public education at the S^* level of resources, the district offered each family S^* per child, with the requirement that each family spend at least S^* on education? That requirement would prevent the potentially undesirable outcome of some parents choosing to spend no resources on their children's education. Offering S^* effectively changes the budget constraint to $Y + S^* = S + X$, where $S \geq S^*$. This is illustrated in Figure 10.4. In effect, S^* is an education voucher. All families for whom S^* is greater than the amount they would have spent on the education absent the voucher (shown by indifference curve A in Figure 10.4) now have education levels of at least S^*. For families that demand a level of schooling higher than S^* (shown by indifference curve B in Figure 10.4), the voucher acts as a pure income transfer, and they now consume more of all goods (including education). For no family will the amount of education consumed be lower when the voucher is introduced, and no family is made worse off by the vouchers. In fact, most will clearly be better off.

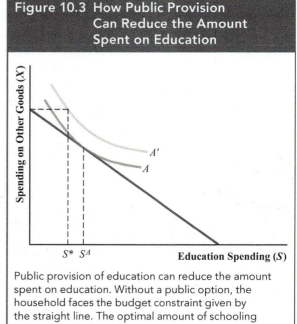

Figure 10.3 How Public Provision Can Reduce the Amount Spent on Education

Public provision of education can reduce the amount spent on education. Without a public option, the household faces the budget constraint given by the straight line. The optimal amount of schooling expenditure is shown by the tangency between the budget constraint and indifference curve A, which leads to S^A being spent on education. When the public option is available, as shown by indifference curve A', the household can achieve a higher level of utility, A', but spends less on schooling: $S^* < S^A$.

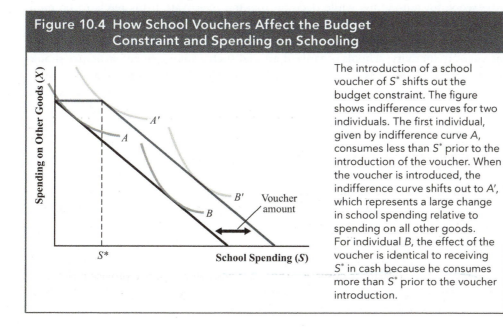

Figure 10.4 How School Vouchers Affect the Budget Constraint and Spending on Schooling

The introduction of a school voucher of S^* shifts out the budget constraint. The figure shows indifference curves for two individuals. The first individual, given by indifference curve A, consumes less than S^* prior to the introduction of the voucher. When the voucher is introduced, the indifference curve shifts out to A', which represents a large change in school spending relative to spending on all other goods. For individual B, the effect of the voucher is identical to receiving S^* in cash because he consumes more than S^* prior to the voucher introduction.

Thus far, we have discussed school choice only in terms of the level of resources expended. But it is natural to expand the discussion to think about parents choosing among schools that are equivalent in terms of costs but differ along other dimensions, such as student achievement or proximity, which parents may value.

Suppose that a private school or an alternative to the local public school could generate higher student achievement with the same level of resources. That is, the alternative school would be more efficient in production for the given level of resources. There are two explanations for schools with the same level of resources producing different levels of student achievement. One explanation is that there is a match-specific component to schools and students that make some schools a better fit for a particular type of student. For example, some students might learn better in a more structured environment, while others would fare better in schools that provide students more freedom to learn on their own. When there are gains from matching certain students to specific educational environments, introducing school choice could increase overall student achievement by producing better matches between students and schools. The second explanation is that one school is more productive for all students than the other school. If public schools are less efficient in production for all students than the alternatives, increasing school choice can raise overall student achievement by shifting students to more productive schools. In such a circumstance, all students could be made better off by switching to an alternative school!

Why might alternative schools be more productive? Theoretically, several arguments suggest that these types of schools may be more conducive to fostering learning. First, traditional public schools tend to lack strong incentives to maximize student achievement, as these schools cannot close and many parents face constraints that make them unable to move to a different school. Choice schools by definition need to compete for students, which likely generates stronger incentives to use resources in the most productive way to foster student achievement.

Second, critics of traditional public schools have argued that the structure of these schools is not conducive to the efficient allocation of resources. The argument is based on the idea that public bureaucracies (such as schools) tend to be centralized, with little scope for autonomy, while decision making in private firms tends to be more decentralized and customer focused. If the education production function is such that decentralizing the decision-making power to teachers and individual principals would increase productivity, schools organized around such a management structure should be more productive. It is an active empirical question in economics whether this is actually the case, but there are strong theoretical arguments that suggest we should expect choice-based schools to use resources more productively than traditional public schools.[2]

The Supply Side of the Market and School Choice

By introducing local schooling options that do not require families to move to take advantage of them, school choice policies can have large impacts on the supply side of education markets. If the public school system is the only educational option in a community, it is effectively a *monopoly*. A monopoly is simply a market containing one firm. School choice policies introduce competition with multiple providers of education

---

[2] These arguments are laid out in detail in Chubb and Moe (1990).

in the market, which can affect the functioning of local public schools and the achievement of students in these schools.[3]

As a benchmark, consider what would happen if there were free entry and exit of schools in a local market. A core tenet of economic theory is that a firm will enter a market only if it can at least cover its costs in the long run. For a school, revenues from students at the prevailing price must equal or exceed costs at the given scale. If revenues are less than costs, the school will be forced to close, and if revenues exceed costs, more schools will enter until economic profits are reduced to zero.

Barriers to Entry In practice, there are likely to be substantial barriers to entry for schools, which is different from the relatively free entry faced by many private firms (such as pizzerias). With such formidable barriers to entry, local public schools are likely to have substantial market power. These barriers to entry can be classified into three groups:

1. Regulatory barriers
2. Absence of public subsidies for alternatives to local public schools
3. Economies of scale

Regulatory barriers take the form of rules that govern how many of each type of nontraditional public school can open in a given place and year as well as standards that non-public schools must meet to remain open. For example, accreditation standards set rules and requirements for entry into the private schooling market that are designed to protect students and families from unscrupulous providers. Typically, there are explicit rules about the number of nontraditional public schools that can locate in a given area as well.

Public schools receive substantial subsidies from the government that allow them to overcome the fixed costs of operating a school (such as purchasing the land and building the school). Many private schools receive similar subsidies from religious organizations or private donors. Because subsidies reduce the need for revenues from sources, like tuition, for schools to be able to cover costs over the long term, for-profit and other entities that lack such resources will be deterred from entry.

A final limitation to entry in education markets is that public schools are able to take advantage of substantial economies of scale, in the sense that it costs less per student to educate 5,000 students than 50 students. This occurs because fixed administrative and facility costs as well as specialized services are divided over a larger number of students: *Average cost*, defined as fixed plus variable costs per student, declines with the number of students. As such, entry is very difficult for start-ups. Moreover, limits in the supply of talent—extraordinary principals and teachers—may make it difficult for a successful alternative school to expand to meet market demand.[4]

Economies of scale and the associated declining average cost curves lead to a situation in which marginal cost is below average cost over the range of enrollment

---

[3] Absent the school choice policies discussed in this chapter, school districts vary considerably in the extent to which they face competition due to the prevalence of private and parochial (largely Catholic) schools as well as due to historical accidents wherein some areas have many, but small, local school districts while some have a few, larger districts.

[4] Another potential constraint often noted in the literature is that in some markets, the supply of space suitable for schools may be particularly limited in commercial real estate markets.

that prevails in most districts. This is what economists call a *natural monopoly*: The local public school often is the sole or dominant provider of education services in a local area. Natural monopolies in school districts arise when average costs are lower for providing services like special education, busing, libraries, academic administration, and athletics to a relatively large number of students. Such cost structures create challenges for the entry of small, independent education providers. While natural monopolies may be productively efficient, they are not allocatively efficient. In the context of education, this means that they are unlikely to produce the right mix of education outputs.

School Choice and Competition   When schools enter the local market and compete with one another for students, a public school is no longer the only option or monopoly in the provision of local schooling. As long as students attend the school that maximizes their preferred mix of outcomes, the local public schools will face a choice: either lose large numbers of students or change the allocation of resources to produce those outcomes. Competition can provide incentives to teachers and administrators to use resources more efficiently to produce the set of academic outcomes that are valued by local residents.[5]

School choice policies are not guaranteed to increase competition, however. Several mechanisms can dampen competitive pressure from school choice:

- Parents must have information about each local school's productivity that allows them to make the choices that will generate competition between schools. Imperfect information effectively reduces choice, as parents do not have the requisite knowledge to assess the productivity of local options.
- If there is overcrowding in the public schools, school choice may be used as a release valve to reduce the pressure on the public schools to expand. In such a case, we would not expect school choice to generate competitive pressure on local public schools.
- "Cream skimming" occurs when the most academically capable students leave the traditional public schools. If having these students in a school has positive spillover effects, otherwise known as peer effects, on their fellow students, cream skimming could harm those left behind in the public schools.[6]

The introduction of school choice policies can affect public school financing through property taxes as well. Property taxes are used to at least partially fund local schools in most areas in the United States. By decoupling the link between where one lives and where one attends school, choice policies can affect the desirability of living in specific areas. For example, areas that are zoned to lower-quality public schools may become more desirable, and property values may rise. Furthermore, choice policies can bring some students back into the public school system from the private system, which would lead to changes in the overall cost of provision. Choice policies thus can affect local public school quality through changes in tax revenues and costs as well as through the mechanism of increased competition.

---

[5] What matters for competition to affect the outcomes at public schools is a legitimate threat of entry.

[6] Evidence on cream skimming and the effect of choice policies on how students sort across schools in the United States can be found in Figlio and Stone (2001), Lankford and Wyckoff (2001) and Altonji, Huang, and Taber (2010). Hsieh and Urquiola (2006) present evidence on this question in Chile.

10.2 School Choice Policies

While the majority of children continue to attend the public school to which they are assigned based on residential location, the past two decades have brought an increase in the share of families choosing other educational arrangements—including private and parochial schools, other public schools, or homeschooling. In 1993, about 20% of students were enrolled at a school other than the assigned public school, with this share increasing to 27% by 2007, the most recent year for which data are available. As shown in Figure 10.5, much of this increase in school choice has come from students attending alternative public schools, with this share rising from 11% to 16%. Attendance at private schools has held steady at about 10–12%.

School choice has a long history in the United States. As we discussed in Chapter 8, the choice of where to live is a basic element of school choice, with the capitalization of school quality in housing prices effectively capturing the valuation of differences in school quality. Moreover, private and parochial school options have a longstanding presence in the education market.[7] In many ways, the extent to which students and their families are exposed to choice in schooling depends on historical factors that determine the market structure in their locality.

In recent decades, the federal government, states, and localities have adopted a number of policies that make it easier for parents to choose schooling options for their children that are different from the assigned local public schools. While school choice policies come in many shapes and sizes that make succinct descriptions difficult, most policies can be grouped into one of five categories:

1. Charter schools
2. Open enrollment
3. Private and parochial school tuition vouchers
4. Magnet schools
5. Homeschooling

These policies change the supply of schooling options available to parents in different ways. In the rest of this section, we describe how each of the five school choice mechanisms works in practice. Implementation of these policies varies considerably across localities and states, so we describe the basic parameters and then offer some specific examples. Table 10.1 provides an overview of these school choice policies. After we have described the institutional framework, we turn to the important questions about how these policies affect student achievement.

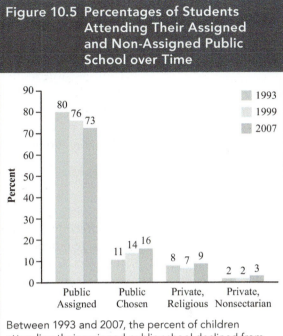

Figure 10.5 Percentages of Students Attending Their Assigned and Non-Assigned Public School over Time

Between 1993 and 2007, the percent of children attending their assigned public school declined from 80 to 73. Most of this decline was due to an increasing percentage of students attending alternative public schools through a school choice program. *Data from:* National Center for Education Statistics (2010).

---

[7] Some research has examined the effect of private and parochial school attendance on student outcomes. For example, see Altonji, Elder, and Taber (2005) for a seminal analysis of Catholic school effects. In this chapter, we focus on school choice policies that have increased schooling options for students rather than on choice options that arose for other reasons.

Table 10.1 School Choice Policies

Choice Policy	Characteristics
Charter schools	• Schools publicly funded, independently run. • Schools can be run by for-profit or not-for-profit organizations. • Schools cannot choose students; admission by lottery when oversubscribed. • A lot of variation in educational philosophy across schools, including no-excuses, learning by doing, and schools that closely resemble traditional public schools in their focus.
Open enrollment	• Students can attend any public school in the district or local area. • Schools cannot choose students; admission by lottery when oversubscribed.
Private and parochial school tuition vouchers	• Parents are given vouchers that they can spend on tuition for private and parochial schools. • Vouchers can be publicly or privately funded. • Programs operate on a relatively small scale and differ considerably in the generosity of the voucher.
Magnet schools	• Specialized public schools that typically focus on particular types of students or have targeted curricula. • Some do not practice selective admissions; admission is by lottery when oversubscribed. • Others, such as exam schools, are highly selective in admissions.
Homeschooling	• Children receive instruction at home rather than at a school. • Governed by state laws that vary considerably.

Charter Schools

Charter schools are relatively new in public education in the United States. They are privately run but publicly funded, and they enroll students regardless of the student's zoned school district.[8] Charter schools are public in the sense that they receive virtually all of their funding from state and local sources, and they get their name because they are authorized, or *chartered*, by these public authorities. Districts typically finance charter schools by assigning a dollar amount to each child in the district equal to the average cost per child of providing an education. Whichever school the child attends receives this money, whether it be her zoned public school or a charter school. Thus, charter schools and traditional public schools usually are in direct competition for public funds, which occurs through their competition for enrollment.

The main distinction between charter schools and regular public schools is that the charter schools are granted autonomy from many local regulations and direct administrative control. Most authorities date the development of charter schools to a 1988 speech by of Albert Shanker, then president of the American Federation of Teachers, who advocated for the creation of a new model of schools that would reduce

---

[8] In some states, charter schools give admissions preferences to students who live in the same district as the location of the school.

bureaucratic constraints and empower teachers. Minnesota passed the first legislation providing for charter schools in 1991, and a Minnesota legislative source offers the following description:

> The basic charter concept is simple: a group of teachers or other would-be educators apply for permission to open a school. The school operates under a charter, a contract with the local school board or state. Exempt from most state and local laws and regulations, the school must prove that students have gained the educational skills specified in that initial contract to renew the charter. The funding for charter schools parallels that of public schools.

The first charter school was in Minnesota, with the founding of the City Academy in St. Paul in 1992. Charter schools have expanded considerably since that time: The number of charter schools was 1,010 in 2000 and then 6,079 in 2013. The proportion of students attending a charter school increased over this period from 0.95% to 4.58%.[9] This dramatic growth in charter schools is illustrated in Figure 10.6. Charter schools have grown rapidly over a very short period, and the growth shows no signs of slowing down.

While charter schools represent a common type of policy, there is no single model of a charter school. Charter schools differ substantially in curriculum, philosophy about student learning, and educational practices, such as the length of the school day and teacher compensation. For example, in New York City, charter schools offer a broad range of curricula that include very progressive approaches, student development emphasizing learning by doing, and learning environments that promote strict academic standards.[10] The no-excuses model adopted by KIPP schools as well as others throughout the country employs long school days, strict discipline, considerable selectivity in teacher hiring, and student uniforms.

Charter schools can be for profit or not for profit, and they can be run by large national corporations or by a small group of local citizens. For example, the KIPP schools discussed at the beginning of the chapter are not-for-profit schools that are run by the nonprofit KIPP Foundation. National Heritage Academies, however, is a network of 80 charter schools in nine states that are run by a for-profit company. While KIPP schools adhere to the no-excuses model, National Heritage Academy schools more closely resemble traditional public schools in terms of curriculum and structure. Charter schools are so different in their focus and design that a very important area for researchers to investigate is what works to improve learning in such schools.

Although charter schools vary in terms of their organization, the students they serve, and their educational philosophy, they all share one important characteristic: They cannot directly select their students. As part of their

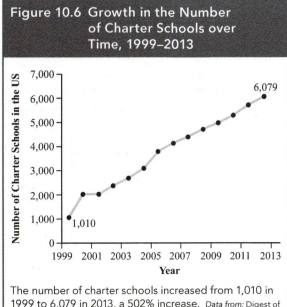

Figure 10.6 Growth in the Number of Charter Schools over Time, 1999–2013

The number of charter schools increased from 1,010 in 1999 to 6,079 in 2013, a 502% increase. *Data from:* Digest of Education Statistics, Table 216.20.

---

[9] These tabulations are from the *Digest of Education Statistics*, Table 216.20.

[10] Hoxby, Murarka, and Kang (2009) provide a comprehensive overview of charter schools in New York City.

charter, these schools typically are required to serve all students who are interested in attending. If the schools are oversubscribed, admission is done using randomized lotteries.[11] Many studies on charter schools' effectiveness use these lotteries for causal estimation, which makes them an important source of knowledge about how charter schools affect students. An implication of this feature of charter schools is that they are largely unable to focus on teaching specific types of students, because they cannot control the set of students who enroll. In this way, they are very similar to traditional public schools.

Many critics of charter schools contend that these schools select students indirectly through the quality of the programs they have and the way they treat students. For example, there is much worry that some charter schools discourage high-cost students from attending, such as those in special education and English language learner programs, by having low-quality services for these students. Similarly, there is concern that charter schools counsel out poorly performing or poorly behaved students, who are difficult to educate. Depending on who enrolls, these schools also could exacerbate income or racial segregation if children of parents with similar ethnic backgrounds or income tend to choose similar schools.[12]

Students who attend charter schools are likely to be systematically different from the students who stay in their assigned schools. When charter schools are located in more disadvantaged areas, charter school students are more likely to be Black or Hispanic, eligible for free or reduced-priced lunches, and to be residents of an inner-city area. Still, the direction of selection is indeterminate: students who attend charter schools may have had bad experiences in public schools or may have parents who are particularly active in trying to find the best educational opportunities for their children. Thus, particular attention to avoiding problems of self-selection is needed when estimating the effects of charter schools on student achievement.

Open Enrollment

open enrollment Policy allowing students to attend another school in the district or in the state regardless of where the student lives. The ability to enroll in another school depends on the school having space for additional students.

Open enrollment policies serve to decouple the link between where students live and the public schools they can attend by allowing students to attend any public school free of additional charges as long as there is space in the receiving school. Intradistrict open enrollment policies allow students to choose any school in the school district, while interdistrict policies allow students to choose schools anywhere in the state. One of the important factors in open enrollment policies, however, is that they usually do not provide for free transportation. Parents therefore are limited by distance, as it often is not feasible to transport a child to a school very far away.

As with charter schools, open enrollment rules do not allow receiving schools to select students. They must take all students for whom there is space, and if there is excess demand, spots are handed out randomly by lottery. These lotteries form the basis of much of our knowledge about how open enrollment affects students, as the lotteries generate random differences in schooling options among those who apply.

---

[11] The documentary *Waiting for Superman* focuses on several of these lotteries and shows how they operate, as well as their impacts on students and families.

[12] For example, Bifulco and Ladd (2007) show that North Carolina's charter school system has led to an increase in income and racial segregation. Hsieh and Urquiola (2006) find similar effects in Chile due to a widespread voucher program.

The first open enrollment law was passed by Minnesota in 1988, and 28 states have either inter- or intradistrict open enrollment policies. More than one in seven school districts in the United States have intradistrict open enrollment. Furthermore, more than one-third of large school districts, such as Chicago, Los Angeles, New York City, and Charlotte-Mecklenburg, have intradistrict open enrollment. In Los Angeles, fewer than 2% of students attend a noncharter public school other than their zoned school, largely because of space constraints in receiving schools. However, in Chicago, more than half of students opt out of their assigned public school. Thus, there is considerable variation in the extent to which open enrollment policies lead to higher levels of choice.

Private and Parochial School Tuition Vouchers

School vouchers are a straightforward manifestation of the idea of school choice. Under a voucher program, each family receives a lump sum per eligible child to apply toward private school tuition. As with any restricted grant, the family must spend at least the voucher amount but might choose to spend even more, depending on its tastes for education and on its income. As shown in Figure 10.4, school vouchers lead to an outward shift of the budget constraint. Under most voucher programs, the family can use the voucher at any recognized school, including sectarian or nonsectarian private schools. A key difference between vouchers and charter schools (as well as open enrollment) is that with vouchers families can spend more than the public allocation for schooling.

For families that would have sent their children to private schools without vouchers, the voucher simply acts as an income transfer from the government. They get more money to spend on other goods, as the amount they would have paid out of pocket in tuition is now lower. Families who would not have used a private school absent the voucher may increase their expenditures on education (depending on the generosity of the voucher) and may reduce consumption of other goods if the voucher does not fully cover tuition.

Voucher programs can be publicly funded through taxpayer assessments or funded from private sources. In recent policy experience, vouchers have been identified as a tool to help students from particularly low-income families and students in districts with low performance to afford private school attendance. In these circumstances, eligibility for the vouchers is often means-tested: Eligibility is restricted to families below a certain income cutoff.

To date, voucher programs in the United States operate on a relatively small scale and often are concentrated in metropolitan areas with public schools that have demonstrated weak performance in the academic achievement of students from traditionally disadvantaged backgrounds. Cities with voucher programs targeted to low-income students include Milwaukee, Cleveland, New York, and Washington, D.C. In contrast to the rise of charter schools, voucher programs have remained small and serve a modest fraction of students even in the cities in which they exist. This highlights the increasing primacy of charter schools over vouchers more generally in school choice policies in the United States.

Magnet Schools

Magnet schools are specialized public schools that typically focus on particular types of students or have targeted curricula. For example, most large urban districts have exam schools, such as the Bronx High School of Science in New York City and

school vouchers Money to students to apply toward tuition at a private school.

magnet schools Public schools that focus on teaching high-achieving students. They typically are high schools, and admission sometimes is determined using performance on standardized tests.

Boston Latin School in Boston, which admit only the highest-achieving students. Other magnet schools have curricula focused on certain themes, such as science, technology, engineering, and mathematics or fine and performing arts. Some magnet schools do not practice selective admissions and randomly allocate admissions spots when they are oversubscribed. Others are highly selective in their admissions. Magnet schools also can impact the composition of students enrolled in a district, since they may be an alternative to private schools for some families. As of 2011, there were over 3,200 magnet schools in the United States.

The existence of magnet schools can have important effects on students enrolling in traditional schools. Magnet schools allow more targeted instruction, and so the existence of these schools could allow traditional public schools to target instruction better to the remaining students as well. However, if there are positive peer effects from exposing students to those of different ability levels or with different interests, magnet schools could lead to worse educational outcomes among those remaining in traditional schools.

Homeschooling

homeschooling The practice of providing all education services at home rather than in a public or private school.

Homeschooling is the practice of providing education services at home rather than in a public or private school. The ability of parents to homeschool their children has grown in recent years, and currently about 3% of kids are homeschooled. This has grown from 1.7% in 1999. The reasons parents have for homeschooling vary, but in a survey conducted by the National Center for Education Statistics, 91% said they homeschool because of concern about the environment of local schools. While still small in scope, homeschooling is an option parents are increasingly turning to when they are displeased with their local schooling options.

States differ in their regulations concerning reporting requirements about student achievement among homeschooled children. The Home School Legal Defense Association has characterized state laws from those requiring no notice of homeschooling by parents (eight states as of 2016) to those with strict reporting requirements, including curriculum approval and notification of test score outcomes (five states).[13] All other states have laws that fall in between. Very little is known about how these differences in state regulatory environments surrounding homeschooling affect homeschooling decisions or student outcomes.

10.3 Effects of School Choice Policies on Student Outcomes

Do school choice policies improve student outcomes? The central challenge in answering this question is in estimating the unobserved counterfactual: What would have happened if a student had not attended a school other than the local public school? That is, we cannot observe the exact same student at the same time in different educational environments. Thus, we should consider whether students who opt out of their regular public schools are different from students who remain in their assigned public school in ways that may be systematically related to achievement.

---

[13] A map with the legal status of each state is available at http://www.hslda.org/laws/.

The Role of Selection in School Choice Studies

Think about why students who opt out of their local public schools may be different from students who persist at local schools. One reason is that the students who opt out are those who are struggling and possibly underachieving in their local public schools. A related issue is that because some types of schools of choice, like no-excuses charter schools, tend to locate near schools serving disadvantaged children, such children are much more likely to attend these schools. Simply comparing achievement levels of students in schools of choice with those in regular public schools will make it look like choice schools are performing worse (a downward bias). In reality, much of this difference is due to differences in the types of students served.

Alternatively, one might suspect that when a student or parent makes an extraordinary effort to attend a school other than the local public school, the family is very committed to education, and the student is likely to be highly motivated academically. In this type of case, comparing achievement of students in schools of choice to those in the regular public schools from whence they came likely will make choice schools look more effective than they actually are (an upward bias).

It is difficult to know a priori which effect will dominate, and the answer often lies in who the students attending the choice school are being compared to. Furthermore, the effects may differ across communities and are likely to be sensitive to the underlying quality of the public schools compared to the quality of the schools of choice. As a result, simple comparisons of outcomes between students in public schools and schools of choice are quite likely to get things wrong.

One of the most notable examples of a simple cross-tabulation that produced a very misleading estimate of the effect of school choice comes from a *New York Times* story on student achievement in charter schools and regular public schools.[14] Based on simple cross-tabulations using the National Assessment of Education Progress (NAEP), a front-page story reported that students at charter schools were appreciably less likely than students at regular public schools to score above standards of proficiency. Yet, the basic descriptive results failed to take into consideration the differences in student backgrounds—as the charter school students clearly came from much more disadvantaged circumstances. For example, 54% of the charter students were eligible for free and reduced-price lunch relative to only 46% of the public school students. When differences in circumstances are taken into consideration, the evidence from this article is far less clear-cut. The misleading nature of these tabulations highlights the need to develop strategies that overcome the biases from selection to estimate causal effects of choice programs on student achievement.

Empirical Evidence on the Effect of School Choice on Student Achievement

Researchers have approached the problem of estimating the causal effect of school choice policies on student outcomes in several ways. One set of studies uses randomization driven by lottery outcomes in charter schools and open enrollment schools or from explicit random assignment of vouchers to students. Thinking back to Chapter 3, in which we discussed methods for understanding how education policies affect student achievement, we presented a randomized controlled trial as an ideal way to overcome selection bias to determine whether an education policy improves student achievement.

---

[14] For further detail see Schemo (2004) and the associated critique (Howell and West 2005).

These studies approximate such randomized experiments and therefore provide a very clean and credible way to understand how choice policies affect outcomes.

Another set of studies, particularly for charter schools, examines how student outcomes *change* when students switch from a regular public school to a choice school. They compare these changes to those among students who remain in a public school. Rather than looking at differences in the level of student performance, looking at the change accounts for the observation that students start out at different levels of achievement. This research design is implemented through the use of student fixed effects, which control for fixed differences across students. These studies therefore can be thought of as difference-in-difference analyses that compare the changes in the treated group (those switching to charter schools) to changes in the control group (students remaining in public schools).

In the magnet school literature, researchers also have used regression discontinuity methods to estimate causal effects of exam schools on student outcomes. Because admission to these schools are exam-based, comparing outcomes of students just above and just below the test score admission threshold can yield insight into the causal effect of such schools. Below, we discuss findings from research examining each type of choice policy in turn.[15]

Charter School Studies   Table 10.2 provides an overview of the charter school studies discussed in this section that try to solve the selection problem in various ways. Ideally, to overcome the selection issues inherent in studying charter schools, one would want to run an experiment with random assignment of students to charter schools or traditional public schools. While it is often too expensive or logistically impossible to implement large-scale experiments in all cases, just this type of natural experiment can be found in a number of metropolitan areas. The natural experiment is generated by the rules that govern how charter schools are allowed to admit students when demand for spaces in the charter school exceeds supply.

Students interested in attending a charter school must first apply for enrollment. Because charter schools are typically prohibited from selecting students on attributes such as prior achievement or family characteristics (which may be used by private schools in choosing students), they must use a random process to select students from the list of applicants. So suppose that 100 students apply for 50 available positions in the sixth grade of a charter school. The charter school must use a lottery (which is, effectively, random assignment)[16] to offer 50 students the opportunity to enroll, while 50 students are placed on the waiting list. In effect, the 50 students on the wait list should be identical to the students who are offered the opportunity to attend the charter school. The subsequent evaluation is very straightforward: compare outcomes of students offered admission to a charter school to those of students placed on a waiting list.

As long as the lottery was done correctly, this method will uncover the causal effect of being offered admission to a charter school on student outcomes. These estimates thus compare those who are randomly offered a slot in the charter school to those who

---

[15] We do not discuss the homeschooling literature because too few studies examine this form of school choice.

[16] Typically, state laws require that the lotteries be done in a public setting by a disinterested party. The order of draw in the lottery then determines the student's position on the wait list, which is used to offer admission if students who were originally offered admission decline.

Table 10.2 A Summary of Charter School Studies

Study	Charter School Type	Method	Overview of Results
Abdulkadiroglu et al. (2011)	No-excuses (KIPP) schools in Boston	Lottery using randomized admission offerings	• Winning a middle school lottery increases English scores by 0.2 standard deviations and math scores by 0.4 standard deviations. • Winning a high school lottery increases English scores by 0.09 standard deviations and math scores by 0.19 standard deviations. • The effect of a year spent in a charter school is about 0.2 standard deviations for English and 0.4 standard deviations for math.
Hoxby, Murarka, & Kang (2009)	All charter schools in New York City, focused on early grades	Lottery using randomized admission offerings	• Winning a lottery increases math scores by 0.13 standard deviations and English scores by 0.13 standard deviations by third grade. • Continued accrual of test score gains over time, with gains actually rising in grades 4–8
Dobbie & Fryer (2011)	Three Promise Academy charter schools in New York City	Lottery using randomized admission offerings plus IV based on student address and cohort	• Winning an elementary school lottery increases math scores by 0.16 standard deviations and English scores by 0.10 standard deviations. • Winning a middle school lottery increases math scores by 0.3 standard deviations and English scores by 0.06 standard deviations. • IV estimates are similar but somewhat smaller. • The effects are driven by charter school attendance, not the associated community services.
Bifulco & Ladd (2006)	Charter schools in North Carolina	Individual fixed effects	• They examine how test scores change in North Carolina when students switch to a charter school relative to their counterparts who remain in nearby public schools. • Students who attend charter schools have slower test score growth, on the order of about −0.1 standard deviations for reading and −0.16 standard deviations for math, than students remaining in public schools.
Sass (2006)	Charter schools in Florida	Individual fixed effects	• Students who attend charter schools have slower test score growth than students remaining in public schools. • After several years of operation, there is no difference in math scores between charter and public school students.
Imberman (2011a)	Charter schools in a large, unnamed city in the Southwest	Individual fixed effects	• Test scores among students who switch to charter schools do not change relative to changes among students who remain in nearby public schools. • Charter schools increase attendance rates and reduce disciplinary infractions considerably.

are not offered admission. Comparing lottery winners and losers hence only captures the effect of being *offered a place* in a charter school. However, we would like to go further to have an estimate of the effect of *spending class time* at a charter school relative to a regular public school. Lottery offers translate directly to time spent at charter schools only when students offered a slot in a charter school enroll and persist in the school. This often does not hold true in practice—some students never accept their offer of enrollment; others leave quickly; and yet others originally denied enrollment will eventually be offered a place in the class. To measure effects adjusted for time spent in school, researchers adjust the simple comparison of outcomes for lottery winners and lottery losers based on how much time winners and losers spend in charter schools. The Toolbox provides details about how these causal parameters are related to one another and how they are calculated in practice.

Quick Hint: Those who lose a lottery still can spend time in a charter school because they might win another charter school lottery or be admitted off the wait list.

TOOLBOX: Calculating the Intent to Treat and the Treatment Effect on the Treated

intent-to-treat (ITT) The effect of being offered the opportunity to be treated on outcomes. In the context of charter schools, the ITT is the effect on outcomes of the student being offered admission to the charter school.

average treatment effect on the treated (ATT) The average effect of the treatment on those who participate in the treatment. In the context of charter schools, it is the effect on measured outcomes of enrolling in a charter school for a year.

Comparing outcomes among lottery winners and losers shows the causal effect of being offered a spot in the charter school. Economists call the resulting parameter in this comparison the **intent to treat (ITT)**, which is the effect of being offered the opportunity to be treated on outcomes. The ITT is relevant from a policy perspective because it is not possible to compel anyone who is offered admission to actually enroll in the charter school. Thus, the ITT shows the effect of offering charter school admission to students.

We also are interested in how charter schools affect the students who actually enroll in them. That is, we want to know how each year spent in a charter school affects students' outcomes. We call this parameter the **average treatment effect on the treated (ATT)** and it can be calculated in a straightforward way from the *ITT*:

$$ATT = \frac{Average\ score\ of\ winners - average\ score\ of\ losers}{Average\ charter\ years\ of\ winners - average\ charter\ years\ of\ losers}$$

$$= \frac{ITT}{Average\ charter\ years\ of\ winners - average\ charter\ years\ of\ losers}$$

Put differently, the *ATT* is the *ITT* effect divided by the effect of the lottery on time spent in a charter school. We often call the latter effect the first stage. For example, if the *ITT* is 0.2 and lottery winners spend 0.5 years more attending a charter school than those who lose a lottery, the effect of attending a charter school for a year on test scores would be $\frac{0.2}{0.5} = 0.4$. The idea here is that the change in test scores across lottery winners and losers is completely driven by the change in time spent in a charter school. Winning the lottery should not affect test scores if it does not alter the school in which the student enrolls. Under this assumption, this lottery setup can show us how much each charter school enrollment year affects test scores.

One of the most influential studies on charter schools comes from Massachusetts. Charter schools were first authorized in Massachusetts in 1993. Fifteen years later, when the study took place, there were 62 operating charter schools throughout the state, 16 of which were in Boston. State law limits the number of charter schools that can be opened in Boston; the limit is tied to both a total cap (120 in the state) and the share of charter school enrollment in a district. As a result, many charter schools in Massachusetts are oversubscribed (more students apply for admission than can be accommodated), leading to substantial waiting lists. Abdulkadiroglu et al. (2011) examine outcomes among students applying for admission to these charter schools, using the lottery draws to overcome the selection bias inherent in charter school studies.

They begin their inquiry by collecting historical lottery records from each of the currently operating charter schools at the middle school and high school level in Boston. In turn, this information on lottery applications was matched to individual data on test scores and demographic information for all students in the Boston public schools. As a first check of the lottery strategy, the authors compare differences in average characteristics among lottery winners and lottery losers for those who applied for charter school entry. In the main, the researchers find that these groups are not different, though lottery winners are a bit more likely to be female and have limited proficiency in English. One approach to measurement is to compare test score outcomes of the lottery winners and lottery losers (the ITT). Using this approach, they find that the lottery winners exhibit substantial achievement gains: for middle school students, about 0.2 standard deviations in English and language arts (ELA) and 0.36 standard deviations in math. For high school students, winning the lottery leads to an increase of 0.09 standard deviations in ELA and an increase of 0.19 standard deviations in math.

Since middle school lottery winners spend about one year more than lottery losers in charter schools, the ATT and ITT estimates are identical. Thus, spending a year in a charter middle school relative to a local public school predicts gains of 0.2 standard deviations in ELA and 0.36 standard deviations in math. The ATT estimates for high school students are similarly large. High school lottery winners spend only 0.55 years more in a charter high school than lottery losers, so we need to divide the ITT estimates by 0.55 to calculate the ATT effects. This calculation shows that spending a year in a charter high school increases ELA and math test scores by 0.16 and 0.35 standard deviations, respectively. As the authors of this research note, the results for both middle school and high school students are "extraordinarily large—equal to roughly half the [Black–White] achievement gap." These estimates also are as large as or larger than the 0.2 standard deviation effect from a seven-person class size reduction found in the Project STAR evaluation discussed in Chapter 9 (Krueger, 1999).

Large estimated effects associated with charter school attendance are by no means limited to Boston. Indeed, the Boston results parallel an earlier study in New York City by Hoxby, Murarka, and Kang (2009). They make a dramatic calculation by considering the substantial achievement gap observed in eighth grade between students attending school in a poor New York City neighborhood such as Harlem and a very affluent suburb like Scarsdale. They predicted that attendance at a New York City charter school would close about 86% of the achievement gap in math and nearly 66% of the achievement gap in English across these students. For advocates of charter schools in particular and for those who argue more generally that educational

DEEP DIVE: The Harlem Children's Zone

The Harlem Children's Zone (HCZ) is a nonprofit organization that operates a comprehensive set of programs in a 97-block area of Harlem in New York City. The organization provides to families living in the zone a multitude of free services designed to address the multiple facets of poverty and disadvantage these families face. The programs include parenting workshops (called the baby college), health clinics, and violence prevention programs.

One of the centerpieces of the HCZ is the three Promise Academy charter schools, which are very similar to the KIPP no-excuses charter schools studied by Abdulkadiroglu et al. (2011). Dobbie and Fryer (2011) study the effect of these schools on student achievement using randomized admission lotteries to overcome selection bias. As in the other lottery studies we have examined, they examine differences between lottery winners and lottery losers, which enables them to obtain estimates of the causal effect on student achievement of being offered admission to the Promise Academy.

To perform this analysis, the authors rely on Harlem Children's Zone lottery files for elementary and middle school children between 2004 and 2006. They merge this information with data from the New York City Department of Education to obtain student demographics and individual scores on standardized math and ELA tests administered to all children in grades 3–8 in New York State.

A problem that the authors encounter is that lottery files are unavailable for some of the years that they wish to investigate. To overcome this obstacle, the authors complement the lottery strategy with an innovative instrumental variable approach in which an interaction of the student's address and cohort year is used as an instrument for enrollment. This method builds on two fundamental aspects of the Promise Academy charter schools. First, although any child in New York City can apply, only children within the Harlem Children's Zone are actively recruited. Second, some cohorts of children are ineligible to apply either because of their age or because the school had not yet opened. Their empirical approach is to use the variation between cohorts across years to compare the between-cohort test scores of children in the zone as their eligibility for enrollment at the charter schools changes. As long as there are no systematic differences between children across cohorts, the ineligible students serve as a plausible control group for the eligible students. However, the authors acknowledge that there may be year-to-year variation in student performance induced by other school reforms or shocks. To prevent this issue from biasing the results, they use the difference in student performance between children from these cohorts who live in New York City but outside the zone to adjust for year-to-year fluctuations in student performance.

> **Quick Hint:** An instrumental variable is designed to isolate the variation in a given treatment that is essentially random. The goal is to use the variation in treatment driven by the variation in the instrument to mimic randomization of the treatment. See Chapter 3 for a detailed discussion of instrumental variables.

The results from the lottery strategy for middle school suggest that being offered admission (i.e., the ITT) is associated with an increase of 0.3 and 0.06 standard deviations in math and ELA, respectively. Dividing these figures by the average difference in time spent at the Promise Academy between lottery winners and lottery losers (1.2 years), the authors estimate the ATT: A year at Promise Academy leads to increases of 0.23 and 0.05 standard deviations in

math and ELA, respectively. These results point toward sizable effects of charter schools on student performance. The estimates from the instrumental variable method are smaller, especially for English: 0.206 and −0.053 standard deviations in math and English, respectively.

Lottery estimates for elementary school students also reveal substantial effects. The ITT parameters indicate that being offered admission is associated with 0.16 and 0.095 standard deviations of improvements in math and ELA, respectively. If children attend the Promise Academy from kindergarten through fifth grade, they will on average experience an increase of 1.146 and 0.570 standard deviations in math and ELA. The results from the instrumental variable method are even larger: 1.94 and 2.52 standard deviations.

Both estimation methods show that the effect of being offered admission to the Promise Academy on math performance is extremely large. However, the authors are worried that these results are biased by the host of other services that are accessible to children living in the HCZ. A novel feature of this paper is that the researchers are able to investigate whether their results are driven exclusively by the charter schools or by a combination of the charter schools and the community services.

They employ two methods to investigate this question. First, they exploit the fact that anyone in New York City can apply to the Promise Academy charter schools, but only children living in the zone are offered the additional community services. If the community services have an effect on student achievement, the effect of attending a Promise Academy charter school should be greater for children residing in the zone than for children living outside the zone. They therefore perform the lottery analysis separately for children in the zone and children outside the zone. The results suggest that there are no statistically significant differences in student achievement between lottery winners in the zone and outside the zone. The implication is that the community services provided in the zone have a small impact, at best, on student achievement.

Second, the authors note that siblings of Promise Academy enrollees are eligible to receive all the additional benefits that apply to Promise Academy students and their families, including but not limited to nutritious meals, parenting workshops, and travel allowances. If these services affect student performance, the siblings of Promise Academy students should benefit as well. However, they find having a sibling at a Promise Academy has little effect on test scores. Together, these results indicate that it is the charter schools themselves that are generating the large test score gains they estimate.

institutions can be a powerful agent for reducing differences in student outcomes associated with family economic circumstances, these are powerful results!

While the lottery-based estimates of the effectiveness of charter schools in New York City and Boston are unquestionably dramatic, we must be careful about the policy implications we draw from them, for several reasons. These issues all relate to the **external validity** of the results, or how much we can extrapolate these estimates to other students or environments. First, these lottery estimates are only possible because some charter schools are oversubscribed, which effectively means that demand among parents exceeds the supply of seats offered by these schools. Charter schools that do not have wait lists might not share the extraordinary characteristics of the schools where we observe lotteries. Indeed, research has shown that the large charter school effects in Boston are *only* due to charter schools that are oversubscribed. Those that do not tend to have excess demand for spots do not perform nearly as well.[17]

Second, large numbers of students do not apply to these charter schools and thus are uninterested in attending them. It is far from clear how they might be affected by charter school attendance. A third concern relates to the types of charter schools prevalent in New York City and Boston. Most charter schools in these cities follow the no-excuses model. (Many of them are KIPP schools.) This education model is particularly intense in terms of the amount of school time it requires and what is expected of students. Most charter schools in the United States do not follow this model and more closely resemble traditional public schools in terms of their approach to education.

The evidence on the effect of other charter schools on student achievement suggests these schools do not have positive effects on achievement. Some research even finds negative effects. These studies tend to employ student fixed effects; this is basically a difference-in-difference analysis that compares changes in outcomes among students who move to a charter school to those of students who remain in public schools. These studies, summarized in Table 10.2, find no effect or even negative effects of charter school enrollment on student test score growth, but there is some evidence that they increase attendance rates and reduce disciplinary infractions.[18]

Open Enrollment Studies As with charter school studies, analyses of the effects of open enrollment policies on student achievement have used lottery outcomes from oversubscribed schools to overcome selection problems. The open enrollment system in the Chicago public schools provides automatic access for all students to their zoned school, but students may apply for admission to any other school in the district as well. If the demand for spots exceeds supply, spaces are allocated using a lottery.

Economists Julie Cullen, Brian Jacob, and Steven Levitt (2006) link lottery data from 19 oversubscribed high schools in Chicago to individual student data. Their analysis is very similar to the charter school lottery studies in New York City and Boston, comparing outcome differences across kids who won versus lost a lottery. They first show that these lotteries were indeed random: Students who won and lost look observationally equivalent on average. Unlike the charter school analyses, this

external validity The extent to which a set of results from a particular experiment or setting can be applied more broadly to other settings.

---

[17] See Angrist, Pathak, and Walters (2013).

[18] These effects on noncognitive skills might be particularly important for driving long-run outcomes of these children, as research has shown a link between noncognitive skills and long-run life outcomes (Heckman, Stixrud, & Urzua, 2006).

research shows that lottery winners performed no better academically than lottery losers, and they may even have performed worse. Although those who won a place in the open enrollment school through winning the lottery attended schools with higher average test scores and of higher overall quality, those students themselves did not score higher.

Why might their performance decrease? One reason is that the chosen students are now in an environment with more academically advanced students. The authors show that lottery winners have a lower subsequent class rank than lottery losers. If they have trouble keeping up or if the instruction is targeted at too high a level, their academic performance might suffer.

Although students gaining access to their preferred public school did not score higher on tests and were less likely to graduate, results from survey questions indicate that they also were less likely to get in trouble at school and to get arrested. These effects were particularly large for students who won a lottery at a very high-achieving school (as measured by average test scores). This finding suggests that school quality increases brought about by more school choice can produce better noncognitive outcomes.

A more detailed look at how access to a high-quality school due to open enrollment policies affects crime comes from research by David Deming (2011) in Charlotte-Mecklenburg, North Carolina. He examines how intradistrict choice affects student involvement in the criminal justice system by linking student lottery data from oversubscribed schools to county and state criminal justice records. He finds a large, long-run effect on crime of winning a lottery for one's preferred school. Students who win an open enrollment lottery are about 50% less likely to engage in criminal activities, and most of this effect is in the long run after students leave school.

A related analysis using similar lottery data from Charlotte-Mecklenburg (Deming et al., 2014) shows that winning a lottery for one's first-choice school leads to higher postsecondary enrollment and attainment. These effects are particularly prevalent for girls, for whom attending a first-choice school after winning a lottery increases the likelihood of going to college by 17 percentage points and increases the likelihood of earning a four-year degree by 14 percentage points. These large impacts point to important long-run positive effects of increases in school quality that can be generated by open enrollment policies.

DEEP DIVE: Parental Information About School Quality and Open Enrollment Policies

Information is a central driver of the impacts of school choice programs on schools and students. Most choice programs assume parents have sufficient information about local schooling options and thus will make informed choices about which schools to select for their children. This also is a main assumption underlying the Tiebout model. However, if parents lack such information, it may lead to school choice policies being less effective.

It therefore is critical to ask whether parents have full information and, if not, how public policies might be designed to increase the amount of information they have.

Hastings and Weinstein (2008) implement two randomized experiments in the Charlotte-Mecklenburg school district (CMS) to estimate the effect of information on school choice behavior and on subsequent student academic achievement.

Intradistrict open enrollment was introduced in CMS in 2002. The program provides guaranteed admission for all students to an assigned school in their neighborhood but allows them to apply for admission to any other school in the district as well. If demand exceeds supply, spaces are allocated using a random lottery. To apply for admission to an alternative school, parents submit a school choice form in the spring, indicating the top three schools they wish their children to attend. To guide their choices, parents traditionally were referred to a 100-page book consisting of self-descriptions about the positive aspects of each school.

Because of No Child Left Behind (NCLB), in the spring of 2004 students in schools that were labeled failing under the law (see Chapter 11 for a detailed overview of NCLB) were given a three-page spreadsheet containing test score information on each school in the district. The spreadsheets and the information that a school was failing were distributed after the initial choices for the next fall were submitted, but parents of children in schools designated as failing were allowed to make another choice. The researchers thus can observe *changes* in choices parents make when they obtain the new information.

Their findings point to large parental reactions to this information, which indicates that parents were not operating under full information prior to receiving the score spreadsheet. Overall, there was a 5.1 percentage point increase in the number of parents choosing an alternative school. The results further reveal that, contingent on choosing an alternative school, the three-page spreadsheet led the average parent to choose a school whose average student-level test score was 0.485 standard deviation higher. This implies that parents do react to receiving direct information and that they do so by choosing higher-performing schools.

One of the drawbacks of this analysis is that being informed that the school was failing may have had an independent effect on school choice behavior. To increase the external validity of the results, the authors conducted a field experiment in the 2006–2007 school year. Through a randomized process, parents in low- and middle-income neighborhoods received one of three pieces of information attached to their school choice form: a one-page spreadsheet on the academic performance of each school, a one-page spreadsheet on the academic performance of each school and the odds of admission based on last year's acceptance rate, or no additional information. The authors' estimation method compares the school choice behavior of parents who received one of these documents with the behavior of those who received no additional information. The one-page document was simpler than the three-page spreadsheet and was targeted to children at both failing and nonfailing schools. Results from this experiment therefore should have greater external validity, as it targets all children in low- and middle-income neighborhoods.

The results suggest that parents with children at nonfailing schools respond positively to the information. Receiving the one-page test score document increased the number of parents choosing an alternative school by 7 percentage points. Furthermore, contingent on choosing an alternative school, these parents chose schools with 0.10 standard deviation higher student-level test scores.

The main takeaway from this study is that the information parents have about local schooling options matters a great deal. Their results suggest that parents do not typically have full information, and a central policy implication is that school choice policies can be rendered more effective if they are paired with clear information about local schooling options.

Private and Parochial School Tuition Voucher Studies A large body of research examines the performance of students at private schools relative to public schools. These studies usually show that students (or parents) who *choose* to attend private schools have higher educational attainment. In some circumstances, studies also point to improvements in achievement test scores and academic achievement due to private school enrollment, with these effects particularly large for students from the most economically disadvantaged circumstances.[19]

While such evidence may suggest the potential for larger-scale gains in student achievement if vouchers were to allow more disadvantaged students to attend

---

[19] See, for example, Neal (1997) and Altonji, Elder, and Taber (2005).

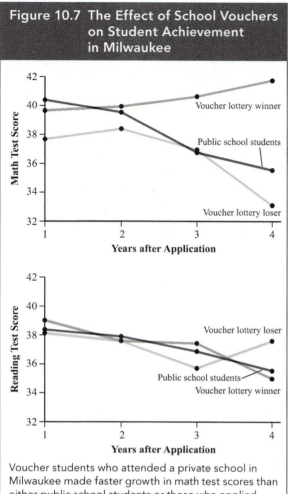

Figure 10.7 The Effect of School Vouchers on Student Achievement in Milwaukee

Voucher students who attended a private school in Milwaukee made faster growth in math test scores than either public school students or those who applied for but did not receive a voucher. In reading, however, test score changes do not differ systematically across groups. *Data from:* Rouse (1998), Figures I and II.

private school, it is difficult to extrapolate the results from these studies to a population of students who have not chosen to attend a private school. Although observed differences between students attending private schools and public schools, such as baseline test scores or parental education, can be incorporated into empirical models, systematic differences that are not observed by researchers, such as motivation and determination, may confound such nonexperimental estimates. It thus is difficult to use the findings from private school effectiveness studies to predict the effects of a tuition voucher program.

Fortunately, there have been several small-scale voucher programs in different cities in which private school vouchers were allocated randomly to a group of low-income students who signed up for the program. The randomization that was driven by oversubscription of the initial voucher programs provides a means to examine outcomes for students and families with the same desire to attend private schools, but only a random subset of whom actually receive vouchers.

One of the earliest and most prominent voucher programs was the Milwaukee Parent Choice program, introduced in 1990. Originally it was limited to enrollment of no more than 1% of Milwaukee public school children, and only those whose parents' income was under 1.75 times the national poverty line were eligible. The program limited participation to secular private schools (while the majority of private school enrollment was originally at religious schools).[20] The level of the voucher—$3,200 in 1994–1995—was sufficient to cover tuition at most of these schools.

Cecelia Rouse (1998)[21] uses the randomized voucher awards to compare outcomes among students who applied for and received vouchers to those who applied for but did not receive vouchers. These two groups of students, voucher and nonvoucher, are broadly similar in observed characteristics. This suggests that the randomization worked.

Her results show that students attending a private school because they received a voucher have higher math test scores, with effect sizes on the order of 0.08–0.12 standard deviations per year enrolled in the school. However, she finds few identifiable gains in reading scores. Figure 10.7 shows the results from Rouse's analysis

---

[20] In 1998, the voucher program was expanded to include religious private schools (Chakrabarti, 2008). Rouse (1998) notes that in the first year of the program there were seven voucher-eligible private schools, and this pool had expanded to 12 by 1995. Indeed, one can think of vouchers as providing incentives for entry and expansion on the supply side of the market as well.

[21] A number of other research teams have examined data on student choices and student achievement in Milwaukee related to the voucher program, such as Witte (1998) and Greene, Peterson, and Du (1999).

graphically. The figure indicates that math test scores of voucher students who attended a private (i.e., choice) school rose faster than for both public school students overall and those who applied for but did not receive a voucher.

Another major voucher program was initiated in 1997 in three cities (New York, Washington, D.C., and Dayton, Ohio) using private funds, with the goal of providing causal evidence of the effects of voucher receipt on student achievement. In an analysis of these three randomized controlled voucher experiments, Howell et al. (2002) find that Black students who switched to a private school from a public school because they randomly received the voucher made large test score gains relative to their counterparts who randomly did not receive the voucher. No effects are evident for other racial or ethnic groups, however.[22]

Magnet School Studies Similar to analyses of other school choice programs, the major hurdle to isolating the causal effect of magnet schools on student achievement is overcoming the selection problem built into the purpose of magnet schools. These schools are designed to focus on particular types of students, be it those who are high-achieving or interested in the performing arts. Thus, any comparison of the outcomes of magnet school students with other students in the district will struggle to overcome the fact that magnet school students are systematically different in terms of their interests and abilities than the traditional public school students. Simply put, there likely are few students in the other public schools who are equivalent to magnet school students.

Exam schools are one type of magnet school that admits only students with the highest academic achievement in the district. It is challenging to judge the effectiveness of exam schools because students who attend are *selected* for their achievement, making it hard to know how they would have done if they had attended a different school. One clever approach to this problem, which was pursued by Abdulkadiroglu, Angrist, and Pathak (2014) in the context of New York City and Boston, is to examine outcomes for students just above and just below the admissions cutoffs. These students should be very similar in achievement before secondary school enrollment. The researchers show this to be the case using the extensive amount of information they have about students: Students just above and just below the score cutoffs are the same in terms of their background characteristics and baseline academic achievement, on average.

Despite the fact that the exam schools have more resources and much higher-achieving peers, there is no difference across the admission threshold in subsequent standardized test scores or in the quality of colleges that students attend. In effect, this is a regression discontinuity estimate of the causal effect of these exam schools on student achievement and collegiate outcomes.[23] These regression discontinuity estimates provide effects of magnet school enrollment for students who are just academically eligible for admission. This is an interesting group, for sure, but this method does not tell us how magnet schools affect students who are not marginal to the cutoff. We therefore cannot

---

[22] Further analysis of these data by Krueger and Zhu (2004) found that these initial results are sensitive to the definition of racial groups. They also show evidence that the results are sensitive to the exclusion of students who did not take a baseline assessment.

[23] Dobbie and Fryer (2104) show virtually identical results for three magnet schools in New York City using the same regression discontinuity method as Abdulkadiroglu, Angrist and Pathak (2014).

know how these schools affect very elite students, whose scores place them well above the admissions cutoff.[24]

Little research has been done on other types of magnet schools. One exception is research by Cullen, Jacob, and Levitt (2005) that examines the effect of career academies on student outcomes in Chicago. Career academies focus on providing students with vocational skills as well as integrating direct work experience into the curriculum. The core concern the researchers face in attempting to estimate the causal effect of these schools is that students who select into these schools are systematically different from those in other schooling environments because they are more vocationally focused (and thus less academically focused). The researchers address this problem by using the fact that some students happen to live close to a career academy for reasons that appear unrelated to their academic or family background. Comparing outcomes among those who attend a career academy versus more traditional school types because of where they live, they find that attending a career academy leads to substantially higher high school graduation rates. While these results suggest career academies positively affect student outcomes, we emphasize that much work remains to be done to study how different types of magnet schools affect students.

10.4 Effects of School Choice Policies on Competition and Traditional Public Schools

Empirical Challenges

Recall that one of the rationales for school choice is to induce traditional public schools to change inefficient practices and resource allocations by means of increased competition for students. We thus want to assess empirically whether the presence of alternatives to public schools and the associated greater competition change outcomes in local public schools. In short, does increased school choice change the behavior of local public schools?

While this notion of competitive effects is a potentially powerful argument for increased school choice programs, it also is extremely difficult to evaluate. At base, there are two main challenges to estimating how choice-induced competition affects public schools:

1. Changes in the local choice environment are often related to underlying demand for education services and the quality of local schools that should exert independent influence on student achievement.
2. School choice induces a change in the composition of students in traditional public schools that can be difficult to disentangle from effects of choice on school productivity.

---

[24] Bui, Craig, and Imberman (2014) provide some evidence on this question using lotteries for admission to gifted-and-talented magnet middle schools in a large urban district in the Southwest. They find no evidence that being admitted to these schools affects measured outcomes, which suggests that even the highest-achieving students are not benefiting from such programs.

The first concern is that changes in the local choice environment reflect unobserved trends in the demand for education services and quality of the traditional public schools. For example, if charter schools are more likely to enter when public school quality is declining, then it will look like charter schools make traditional public schools worse. In reality, however, the declining public school outcomes and charter school entry will be driven by the same trend; this negative correlation does not tell us about the causal effect of charter schools on public school productivity. Conversely, if demand for education quality in an area is increasing, which leads to expanded school choice options, this could lead us to overstate the effect of choice on traditional public schools. The reason is that rising demand for education quality should exert an independent, positive influence on student outcomes. To overcome this problem, we need variation in school choice options that is unlikely to be related to these unobserved trends.

The second empirical challenge is that when choice expands, the composition of students in traditional public schools changes. Thus, if one has school-level data, these compositional changes will be very difficult to separate from effects of choice on student outcomes in the traditional public schools. This is why student-level data are highly preferred in this setting, but they are not always available.

Evidence on How School Choice Policies Affect Competition and Traditional Public Schools

These two empirical challenges motivate most of the research that has focused on the effects of school choice on traditional public school outcomes. Observing the same students over a number of years and their test scores at multiple points in time provides an opportunity to see how outcomes change with the introduction of charter schools in a community. Essentially, these studies examine how a change in school choice in a local area influences test scores among students who do not take advantage of the school choice program.

Table 10.3 provides an overview of the research on how traditional public schools are affected by school choice policies. Results that examine how student test scores change among public school students as a result of nearby charter school entry are mixed. Evidence from North Carolina suggests there is no effect, while in Florida, charter school entry is associated with small increases in public school student math scores but not reading scores. In Texas, increases in the prevalence of charter schools near to a public school leads to an increase in the public school's math and science test scores.[25]

A core concern with these studies is that they assume charter school entry is unrelated to trends in public school student performance. One novel approach to address this potential problem uses the fact that charter school entry is easier in areas where there is a higher supply of appropriate buildings—those with enough square footage for a school (Imberman, 2011b). As long as the building stock is uncorrelated with trends

---

[25] The North Carolina estimates are from Bifulco and Ladd (2006). The Florida results come from Sass (2006). The Texas results are from Booker et al. (2008). See as well Hoxby (2003) for similar evidence and results from Michigan and Arizona but using school-level data that has the associated empirical complications discussed previously.

Table 10.3 A Summary of Studies Estimating How School Choice Policies Affect Competition and Traditional Public Schools

Study	Choice Type & Location	Method	Overview of Results
Bifulco & Ladd (2006)	Charter schools in North Carolina	Nearby charter entry with student fixed effects	• No difference in the growth of math or reading test scores among students in traditional public schools when a charter school opens up nearby.
Sass (2006)	Charter schools in Florida	Nearby charter entry with student fixed effects	• Small increases in math test scores among students in traditional public schools when a charter school opens up nearby. • No change in reading test scores.
Booker et al. (2008)	Charter schools in Texas	Nearby charter entry with student fixed effects	• Small increases in math and reading test scores among students in traditional public schools when a charter school opens up nearby.
Hoxby (2003)	Charter schools in Michigan and Arizona	Charter school enrollment increases with school fixed effects	• In Michigan, schools that faced strong charter competition, defined as losing at least 6% of enrollment to charter schools, experience productivity increases (test score changes per dollar spent). • Estimates in Arizona are very similar.
Imberman (2011b)	Charter schools in a large, unnamed city in the Southwest	Appropriate building stock as an instrument for charter school supply	• Students in traditional public schools that face more charter school competition because there are more buildings appropriate for holding a charter school have lower test score growth. • Charter competition reduces disciplinary infractions.
Figlio & Hart (2010)	Private school vouchers in Florida	Compare effect of voucher program across areas with different private school supply	• Introduction of the voucher program had larger positive effects on math and reading test score changes in local public schools in areas in which the preexisting supply of private schools was larger (and thus where the program increased competition more).
Chakrabarti (2008)	Milwaukee voucher program	Expansion of program to include religious schools	• Traditional public schools in which a larger proportion of students were eligible for vouchers had test score increases when the program was expanded to include religious schools (and thus increased competition).
Hoxby (2000)	Interdistrict choice	Comparison of areas with different number of school districts due to natural boundaries	• Traditional public schools in metropolitan areas in which there are more school districts (and thus more competition for students) because of natural boundaries like rivers and streams exhibit higher productivity.

in student achievement, comparing achievement changes in areas with more versus fewer charter schools because of the number of appropriate buildings allows one to estimate the causal effect of charter schools on traditional public school students. The results using this method suggest that charter school entry is associated with *declines* in public school student performance in a large urban district in the southwest United States.[26] However, disciplinary infractions among high school students decline, suggesting there may be noncognitive benefits accruing to public schools due to competition from charter schools.

> Quick Hint: This is an example of an instrumental variables approach discussed in Chapter 3. The supply of appropriate buildings is used as an instrument for the supply of charter schools.

The majority of the work on the competitive effects of school choice focuses on charter schools, but a small number of studies examines the role of private school vouchers.[27] Prominent among them is a study of the Florida Tax Credit Scholarship Program, introduced in 2001, which is one of the largest voucher programs in the country. It offers private school vouchers that cover the cost of tuition at private schools to students who qualify for free or reduced-price lunches. Figlio and Hart (2010) study the effect of this program on local public schools, using the fact that some schools faced larger competitive pressures from the program because there were more private school options nearby. Thus, the introduction of the program should induce more competition in areas with more private schools. This is indeed what they find: The introduction of the voucher program increased math and reading test scores more among students in traditional public schools that are in areas with higher private school penetration.

Further studies, summarized in Table 10.3, have analyzed how traditional public schools have responded to choice-based competition in Milwaukee as well as how competition driven by having more school districts because natural boundaries affect local public school performance. These studies support the existence of a positive link between competition and public school productivity.[28] Overall, the evidence in Table 10.3 points to positive competitive effects of school choice policies on local public school performance. However, the estimates are not universally positive, and an important set of questions for research moving forward is to understand under what conditions school choice policies induce productivity-enhancing competition.

10.5 Conclusion

Innovations in school choice ultimately function on two important margins. First, they may introduce different ways of providing educational services to students. Whether these differences reflect educational standards or contracting arrangements for the hiring of

---

[26] Imberman is unable to name the district he studies under the confidentiality agreement that provided him access to his data.

[27] There also is literature that focuses on threat effects of vouchers that tend to be embedded in school accountability policies. We cover this research in Chapter 11.

[28] Bayer and McMillan (2005) provide similar evidence by estimating a school-specific measure of competition, an elasticity that shows how sensitive residents are to changes in school quality. They show that schools that face more competition because of this higher elasticity have higher measured outcomes in San Francisco.

teachers, alternative configurations of class size and school days, or new curricular and pedagogical methods, a central question that school choice innovations help to address is how to change the education production function to maximize student gains for any level of inputs.

Second, school choice holds the possibility of increasing competition among providers (between or within districts, as well as between private schools, charter schools, and local public schools). With sufficient opportunities for entry, parental demand for high-quality education services will reward the most efficient schools. This process can yield gains in efficiency throughout the education market as public schools improve in response to the potential loss of students. However, any such competitive effects are likely to be dependent on parents having sufficient information about the quality of the schools in their area.

There is growing evidence that certain types of charter schools can have large, positive effects on student achievement in some settings, as seen most notably in the recent cases of Boston and New York City. As well, there may be some capacity for open enrollment policies and vouchers to increase both test scores and long-run outcomes of students. Ultimately, the desirability of these policies rests on their ability to generate gains in learning through increasing both the productive and allocative efficiency of schools. Whether and under what conditions these policies are able to do so remains an open and important question in the economics of education.

Highlights

- School **choice** policies are those that allow students to attend a school other than the local public school in their **attendance zone**.

- There has been a significant trend over the past 20 years of an increasing prevalence of school choice policies. Economic arguments for school choice are that increased choice will allow for greater access to high-quality education for students at all levels of household income and that expanded choice will increase **competition** among local education providers, inducing improvements in traditional neighborhood public schools.

- In the United States, it is not an option to opt out of paying for local public schools (unless one fails to pay taxes and thus breaks the law). Hence, private schooling is very expensive because parents must pay for both private and public schooling services if they decide to send their child to a private school. School choice policies seek to increase educational choices by reducing the cost of attending a school other than the traditional public school to which the student is assigned.

- Alternative education providers face significant barriers to entry into the local public school market that can restrict competition: regulations, the lack of public subsidies, and economies of scale. Choice policies seek to reduce these barriers to entry to increase local competition among education providers.

- School choice policies include **charter schools**, private **school vouchers**, **open enrollment** policies, **magnet schools**, and **homeschooling**.

- Charter schools have risen in prevalence across the country. These schools are very different from each other, ranging from KIPP schools, which employ a no-excuses education model, to charter schools that are very similar to traditional public schools.

- Because charter schools cannot select students (admission is by lottery), there is a rich and growing literature using lottery-based studies to estimate the effect of charter schools on measured learning outcomes. The evidence suggests that no-excuses charter schools obtain dramatic increases in student achievement, while studies of other charter schools that typically employ difference-in-difference methods tend to find little effect. It is difficult to know whether these differences in results reflect differences in empirical methodology or differences across no-excuses versus other types of charter schools.

- Private school tuition vouchers are used in many areas of the country, although inconsistent funding tends to make these choice policies much less prevalent than charter school policies. Research on existing programs uses the randomized allocation of tuition vouchers to estimate the causal effect of these programs on student outcomes. The results are mixed, with some increases for certain demographic groups, and lingering questions over whether effects occur over the long run more than the short run.

- Open enrollment policies increased significantly with the implementation of No Child Left Behind. While proponents argue that these policies increase competition among district schools and thus can improve education and increase student achievement, the realities of space constraints within schools and transportation limitations (most districts do not bus students to schools outside their neighborhood even under open enrollment models) pose obstacles to the success of these programs.

- The research on open enrollment does not point to consistent effects of these programs on student outcomes. The evidence on these programs tends to come from lottery studies that use the random assignment of students to schools as a result of schools having too few spots to meet student demand. Results from Chicago point to little impact of open enrollment on student test scores and graduation rates, although evidence from North Carolina indicates an effect of these programs on crime and on long-run educational attainment for women.

- Magnet schools provide alternatives that focus on particular types of students, such as those who have high ability or are vocationally oriented. Despite the high success rate of exam school students, evidence from New York and Boston suggests that this success is not due to these schools per se but rather is driven by the high academic capability of the students who attend those schools. In contrast, career academies focused on vocational training in Chicago increase high school graduation rates.

Problems

1. Why did Milton Friedman argue that it would be best to separate public funding from the public provision of education?

2. Discuss how competition can lead to more efficient education outcomes and provide an argument against competition through school choice.

3. Traditionally, Hobbits have relied on private provision for their schooling. As the newly elected mayor of the Shire, Samwise Gamgee has decided to launch a public schooling option. The typical Hobbit family has the following budget constraint: $I = S + X$, where I is total family income, S is schooling expenditures, and X is expenditures on all other goods.

   a. Draw the Hobbit family's budget constraint prior to the opening of the public school.

   b. Hobbits are notoriously tax-averse, and as a result the level of services offered by the public school is small, at $1,000. Draw the new budget constraint the Hobbit family will face after the public school opens. Show an example in which the level of education services consumed by the Hobbit family declines because of the public school option.

   c. Samwise is concerned that the amount of schooling has declined. He therefore closes the public school and offers all students a $1,000 voucher that can be used only on education. Draw the new budget constraint. Will the voucher lead to any Hobbits receiving less education services than before the voucher program? In what case will the voucher lead Hobbits to spend exactly $1,000 more on education? In what circumstances will the voucher be treated just like a cash transfer?

4. Under what conditions would the complete privatization of schools generate an efficient level of education investment?

5. Describe the five types of school choice policies. For each one, explain what types of entities control the schooling option (i.e., public, private nonprofit, or private for-profit) as well as the way in which the schooling option is funded.

6. What is the no-excuses charter school model? How do no-excuses schools differ from other types of charter schools?

7. Without the five types of school choice policies, how can parents exercise choice over the schools in which their children enroll? What types of families are likely to face more constraints in exercising such choice, and how do these differences relate to the potential failures of the Tiebout model discussed in Chapter 8?

8. The archipelago nation of Tuvalu has enlisted you to study its school choice policies. Because the nation consists of a series of small islands, typically there was little school choice. However, the government recently implemented a charter school policy that led to a large increase in charter school prevalence.

Assume you have several years of student-level longitudinal data on math test scores, demographic characteristics, and what school each student enrolls in each year.

a. What would be the problem with simply comparing the math test scores of students attending a traditional public school with the outcomes of students who attend a charter school, even controlling for student demographic characteristics? Would this comparison yield the causal effect of attending a charter school on math test scores?

b. Explain how controlling for student fixed effects might overcome the problems you discussed in part a. In what way is this a difference-in-difference method? Under what assumptions will this method allow you to estimate the causal effect of charter school attendance?

c. Some charter schools are oversubscribed, and by law they are required to admit people by lottery. How would you use these lottery data to overcome the selection problems you discussed in part a? Would this method tell you how an average charter school in Tuvalu affects math test scores?

d. Using a variety of methods, you find that charter school enrollment leads to large increases in student math test scores. The government of Tuvalu uses this information to argue that it should expand charter school access to more students. Does this policy conclusion necessarily follow from your results? Explain.

9. You have a sample of individuals who applied for a private school voucher. Winners were awarded randomly among the applicants. You then estimate the following regression: $Y = \beta_0 + \beta_1 W + \varepsilon$, where W is a dummy variable indicating whether the student won the lottery ($W = 1$ if a student wins the lottery), Y is test scores in standardized units (so each one-unit change is a standard deviation) and ε is an error term. Conditional on winning, the probability of enrolling is 50%.

a. The estimated coefficient on β_1 is 0.35. Interpret this coefficient in words.

b. Calculate the causal effect of attending a private school on test scores.

c. Explain the difference between an intent-to-treat (ITT) estimator and a treatment-effect-on-the-treated (ATT) estimator. Which one is the estimator in part a and which one is the estimator in part b? Is one estimator more important for policy than the other?

10. No-excuses charter schools in New York City and Boston have been shown to have significant effects on student outcomes. Why can't this finding be generalized to all charter schools?

11. The price of office buildings differ between San Francisco and El Paso. How would this affect entry of new charter schools?

12. The North Pole School District provides public education to students and spends about $5000 per student on education. The families living in the district include reindeer, elves, and offspring of the Claus clan. There is a good bit of discontentment in the North Pole about public schooling, though the district is quite isolated leaving little opportunity for families to move to different districts. In particular, the reindeer think too much is spent on erudite learning and the Claus clan would like to see more resources spent on schooling.

a. Is the provision of public schooling in the North Pole *allocatively efficient*? Explain.

b. How would the introduction of a voucher system ($5000 could be used at a private school or would be paid to the public school) change the level and distribution of education in the North Pole? (Assume the voucher is non-refundable and must be spent on education.)

c. Instead of dismantling the public school system, the Santa Foundation (responding to research evidence from Milwaukee on vouchers) offers to provide vouchers of $5000 to one quarter of students in the North Pole. Discuss how this is likely to change student choices. Why might families decide to send their children to private schools even if the tuition (or funding per student) was just $5000?

Test-Based Accountability Programs

The Rise of Test-Based Accountability

Students likely have been complaining about having to take too many tests since the inception of formal schooling. In recent years, a notable increase in the number of standardized tests created by external authorities and mandated by schools has generated concerns that children actually are overtested. These concerns come from a broad array of groups, including teachers, parents, school administrators, and elected officials. A recent survey of parents found that 49% believe their children take too many standardized tests, and 2014 saw an historic rise in the number of parents who were voluntarily withdrawing their children from taking state standardized exams.[1] To be sure, U.S. schoolchildren take a lot of tests: a survey of 14 urban and suburban districts found that students take as many as 20 standardized exams per year and take 10 on average in third to eighth grade. These tests can be harmful insofar as they take time away from instruction and distort the curriculum. However, proponents of testing argue that these exams are critical components in assessing how much students know and how effective schools and teachers are at teaching them the curriculum.

Concurrent with the rise in the number of exams has been an increase in the consequences for schools, students, and teachers based on exam performance. Scores on state-designed exams not only affect a student's ability to advance in grade level but also determine a set of rewards or penalties the school will receive. The results of these exams often are used to produce school "report cards" that are released to the public, and exam outcomes in many states and school districts are used to make decisions about which teachers to fire and which teachers to promote. In short, standardized tests are being given with increasing frequency and are increasingly important in determining many facets of the educational environment.

The main reason for these substantial changes to the way the U.S. education system operates is the rise of **test-based accountability** policies, by which schools, teachers, and students are held accountable for their performance on standardized tests. It is important to emphasize that accountability policies can be focused on different education actors, such as schools, students, or teachers, and the specific set of incentives for meeting performance benchmarks under these systems can vary greatly. In this chapter, we focus most intensively on

---

[1] The statistics cited in this paragraph come from Lazarin (2014).

3DDock/Shutterstock

test-based accountability Policies that provide rewards or sanctions to teachers, schools, and students based on their performance on a set of measurable student outcomes, such as standardized tests.

school-based accountability policies, as these are the most prevalent in the United States. However, we also discuss student-based policies that provide explicit performance levels for students that they must reach to graduate. Chapter 12 covers teacher-based accountability, where we discuss teacher incentive pay.

The core argument in favor of accountability laws is that with limited information about student performance, there are insufficient incentives for students, teachers, and schools to address deficiencies in performance. Accountability laws can serve the following purposes:

1. Provide parents with information about the productivity levels of different schools and teachers to help them make informed educational choices.
2. Give local, state, and federal policy makers information about school and teacher productivity that they can use to allocate resources and target interventions.
3. Generate incentives for schools, teachers, and students to increase academic performance.

Test-based accountability policies can accomplish these goals by defining the objectives for student outcomes (expectations), monitoring student achievement (assessment), and providing rewards and sanctions based on student performance (incentives).

At the same time, accountability policies can have costs that are difficult to observe. For example, making students take lots of standardized tests may take time away from instruction in areas such as art or music, and it might make children feel less excited about being in school. Testing also entails administrative costs, and schools in which high-stakes accountability administrative requirements exist might be less enjoyable places to work.[2] As a result, accountability policies can lower teacher quality.

This chapter begins with an overview of the ways in which test-based accountability policies have been implemented in the United States, with particular attention paid to school-based accountability. We then discuss some of the theoretical and technical issues surrounding the measurement of student performance as it relates to accountability. Accountability programs will work only if they provide strong enough incentives for schools to focus on the "right" outcomes, and so understanding the challenges surrounding how to measure student performance is critical to correctly designing accountability policies. The final two sections of this chapter examine what research has shown regarding the efficacy of accountability policies in promoting student learning.

11.1 Accountability: Measurement, Rewards, and Punishment

What Is Test-Based Accountability?

Test-based accountability in education can take a variety of forms and can be focused on a number of different actors who might be held accountable:

- *School accountability* ties a system of rewards and punishments to measurable outcomes at the school level, such as average test scores, test score changes, or test pass rates.

---

[2] Existing evidence suggests that the administrative and test development costs of accountability are low. For example, payments to test makers are just 0.7% of the cost of elementary and secondary education, and the most any state spends on accountability policies is less than 0.5% of per-student expenditures (Hoxby, 2002).

- *Student accountability* provides explicit benchmarks that a student must meet on standardized exams to progress in the education system. Typically, these take the form of high-stakes high school graduation exams.
- *Teacher accountability* links teacher firing and promotion decisions as well as compensation levels to standardized exam or value-added scores.

Many actors might be affected by accountability policies even if they are not the target of those policies. For example, principals are likely affected by school accountability policies, as they are assessed on the overall performance of the school. Teachers also are impacted by school accountability rules, because they are responsible for teaching the material on the exams the students will take. Students are affected by all accountability laws, as it is their performance that forms the basis for the rating the school or teacher will receive or that the students themselves will receive.

Quick Hint: Recall from Chapter 9 that value-added is a teacher's contribution to student test score growth. It is a quantitative indicator of teacher quality.

Accountability policies come from several sources. The political process in a democratic society can exert strong accountability pressures on local education officials: Elected school board members and appointed school administrators all can lose their jobs if voters do not believe they are maximizing student achievement. Accountability also can come from human resource practices, with the fear of being fired (especially among novice teachers) generating implicit or explicit incentives to produce measured student learning outcomes. Tiebout sorting and school choice additionally can generate accountability pressures, as underperforming schools likely lose students whose parents decide to move to schools with higher perceived performance.

In this chapter, we will focus on accountability policies that tie aggregate test score performance in schools to explicit rewards and punishments. These policies seek to hold schools accountable for the performance of their students on certain test measures, often creating strong incentives for schools to raise test scores.

School Accountability in the United States

A History of School Accountability There is a long history in U.S. schools of using standardized tests to provide assessments of student progress and aptitude. These tests are typically designed by a third party other than the classroom teacher and administered to students across a number of schools. For example, the Iowa Test of Basic Skills, which gets its name because it was designed by faculty from the University of Iowa, originated in 1935 and has been widely administered to students in many states and used as a tool to track student progress in areas like reading comprehension, vocabulary, spelling, math, and social studies.

Historically, the administration of standardized tests at the school and district levels was done voluntarily and did not necessarily change the behavior of students, parents, teachers, or administrators. One main reason for the lack of influence of these tests was that their primary use was for diagnostic purposes, such as deciding how to place students in different academic tracks. As such, much of the early standardized testing in grades K–8 was low-stakes—there were few positive or negative consequences for students, teachers, or administrators for strong or weak performance.

The early push for more school accountability began in 1983 with the publication of *A Nation at Risk: The Imperative for Education Reform* (National Commission on Excellence in Education, 1983). This publication was a very influential report commissioned by the federal Department of Education and written by the National Commission on Excellence in Education that outlined the troubling state of education performance in the United States. It argued that the U.S. education system is systematically underperforming and sounded a warning bell for the long-run problems such performance would bring in terms of economic growth and prosperity. In a particularly notable passage, it states:

> If an unfriendly foreign power had attempted to impose on America the mediocre educational performance that exists today, we might well have viewed it as an act of war. As it stands, we have allowed this to happen to ourselves. We have even squandered the gains in student achievement made in the wake of the Sputnik challenge. Moreover, we have dismantled essential support systems that helped make those gains possible. We have, in effect, been committing an act of unthinking, unilateral educational disarmament.

The publication of *A Nation at Risk* helped spur increased attention by politicians to enact reforms that were intended to reduce inequality of outcomes in the education system and provide diagnostic information to policy makers on school productivity. In 1989, newly elected president George H. W. Bush convened an education summit that included all of the nation's state governors (including then-governor of Arkansas and future president Bill Clinton). The ensuing Charlottesville education summit led to an agreement on four principles: establishment of national education goals, more flexibility and accountability in the use of federal education spending to meet such goals, annual reporting on progress toward reaching these goals, and state-level restructuring of education systems.

As a result of these commitments to education reform, states in the late 1980s and early 1990s began to place greater emphasis on measured student and school performance and also sought methods to induce schools to raise those performance measures. These school accountability policies moved standardized test outcomes from a voluntary measure to a compulsory metric for the assessment of student and school performance. Of course, testing students in any grade presupposes a common set of curricular standards and expectations of learning in each grade; these benchmarks now had to be articulated in policies. Alignment of the curriculum with state assessments is a central tenet of standards-based reform initiatives. In effect, if passing the assessment requires a specific level of literacy or numeracy at the end of a grade level, then the curriculum should cover materials needed to meet these competencies. The idea behind school accountability policies is that well-defined expectations, standardized testing, and then some rewards (or sanctions) offered at the school level would encourage substantial gains in student achievement.

Texas was one of the early adopters of school test–based accountability, along with North Carolina, South Carolina, and Florida.[3] In 1990, Texas introduced the Texas Assessment of Academic Skills (TAAS) program. The initiative included the administration of

---

[3] School accountability policies were also adopted in a number of large metropolitan districts such as Chicago, where students had historically performed well below national norms. A central component of the Chicago plan was to end social promotion, or the advancement of students to the next grade even when the student is unable to demonstrate proficient performance at the current grade level. In March of 1996, the Chicago public schools introduced a policy linking testing in the third, sixth, and eighth grades to grade-level advancement. Students failing to achieve proficiency standards in the spring were assigned to summer school classes with an option to retest at the end of the summer period.

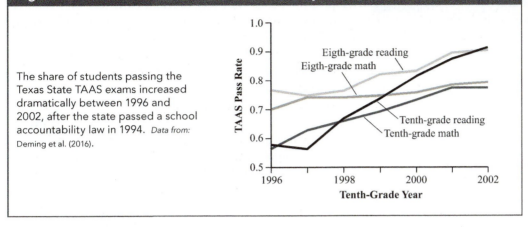

Figure 11.1 Trends in TAAS Exam Pass Rates by Grade and Cohort, 1996–2002

The share of students passing the Texas State TAAS exams increased dramatically between 1996 and 2002, after the state passed a school accountability law in 1994. *Data from:* Deming et al. (2016).

annual tests to students in grades three to eight, with the further requirement that students pass an additional examination (given in tenth grade) to graduate from high school. Beginning in 1994, the state introduced accountability requirements at the school level, requiring minimum pass rates if schools were to avoid sanctions from the state.

In subsequent years, scores on the TAAS exam increased dramatically. The changes in test pass rates are shown in Figure 11.1. These test score trends provided evidence to proponents of test-based accountability, including George W. Bush, that these programs work. At the same time, many have voiced skepticism that these gains truly reflect increased student learning from test-based accountability. For one, there is worry that the higher rates of test passage simply reflect easier exams and lowering of the scores required for passing. Indeed, Klein et al. (2000) show evidence that scores on the National Assessment of Education Progress (NAEP)[4] did not show the same increases, suggesting the rising pass rates do not reflect skill increases. Furthermore, there is evidence that districts systematically retained low-performing ninth-grade students as well as pushed them to drop out or reclassified them as special education (Haney, 2000). These issues highlight one of the central challenges to a successful school accountability policy: It is difficult to interpret state exam results when states and schools have incentives to make exam scores appear to be artificially high or to be artificially rising.

Following Texas and North Carolina, several other states moved to introduce accountability systems in the 1990s. While fewer than 5 states had any form of accountability system in place in 1993, five years later nearly 25 states had introduced statewide school accountability measures. By the start of the twenty-first century, more than 40 states had some accountability measures in place. This growth in state school accountability policies is shown in Figure 11.2.

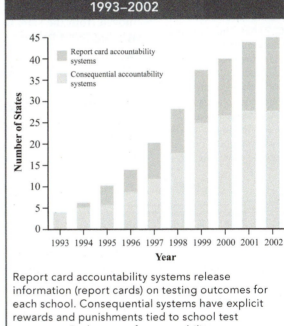

Figure 11.2 Expansion of School Accountability Systems, 1993–2002

Report card accountability systems release information (report cards) on testing outcomes for each school. Consequential systems have explicit rewards and punishments tied to school test outcomes. Both types of accountability programs increased in the 1990s and early 2000s, and more than 40 states had some accountability measures in place by 2002. *Data from:* Hanushek and Raymond (2005).

---

[4] See Appendix A for a detailed overview of the NAEP exam.

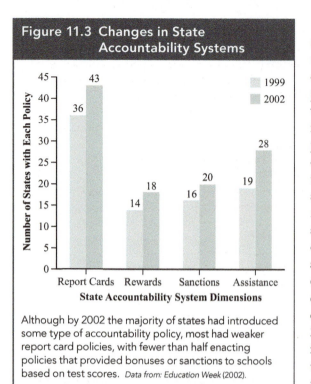

Figure 11.3 Changes in State Accountability Systems

Although by 2002 the majority of states had introduced some type of accountability policy, most had weaker report card policies, with fewer than half enacting policies that provided bonuses or sanctions to schools based on test scores. *Data from: Education Week (2002).*

Of course, not all state systems were the same, as states adopted provisions with very different curricular expectations, testing mechanisms, assessments of progress, and sanctions. One clear distinction is between states that simply mandated the full public disclosure of testing results ("report cards") and states that went further, not only to report results but to provide meaningful rewards or penalties to schools and districts based on test performance ("consequential systems"). School report cards, or disclosure, might be thought to affect outcomes to the extent that teachers or administrators in low-performing schools would adjust their effort, while parents would be able to use this information in making choices about schools. Yet, since report cards are simply informational, they might have much weaker effects on behavior than consequential systems. This is because consequential systems include bonuses to high-performing schools or sanctions for schools whose measured achievement is below expectations. Figure 11.3 shows the distributions of dimensions of accountability programs among states, and it is clear that, by 2002, the majority of states had introduced some accountability framework. However, the majority of states focused on the relatively weaker report card policies; less than half had policies that provided bonuses or sanctions to schools based on test scores.

No Child Left Behind (NCLB) Act The signature education initiative of the George W. Bush administration. A nationwide accountability system in which states would set goals for schools to meet. Those not meeting these goals would be subject to sanctions.

No Child Left Behind The governmental focus on the school accountability practices moved from the state level to the federal level with the passage of the **No Child Left Behind (NCLB) Act** in 2002. This was the signature education initiative of the George W. Bush administration, and it followed the structure of the Texas accountability law closely. In essence, all states were required to introduce standards of accountability and to assess student performance relative to these tests with annual assessments.

There was much concern, politically and among the public, that this law would be construed as an intrusion of the federal government on state and local control of education. As discussed in Chapter 2, the U.S. education system historically has been defined by local control of schools, with the federal government playing little role in setting education standards or regulations. Contrasting this education system with others from similarly

---

DEEP DIVE: The Politics of Common Core Standards

Since 1983, when the National Commission on Excellence in Education (NCEE) released its scathing report on the state of U.S. education entitled *A Nation at Risk: The Imperative for Education Reform*, policy makers and educators at the local, state, and federal level have scrambled to develop standards and teaching practices that would improve K–12 education in the United States. The NCEE report recommended a national set of common standards as part of the remedy to address deficiencies in the educational system, and efforts have been made repeatedly to develop and implement such a recommendation.

However, these efforts have been met with fierce opposition from state and local governments, who are reluctant to give up their local control over education policy.

The discussion over the Common Core State Standards (i.e., the Common Core) is the latest incarnation of the debate about the proper amount of local control in public schooling and is a clear illustration of the politics of federal education regulation. In 2009, governors and education commissioners from 48 states launched a program to develop a common set of education standards. Historically, states developed their own standards, leading to a large amount of variation across areas of the country in the academic curriculum and expectations for students. A task force created by Janet Napolitano, who was serving as chair of the National Governors Association, initiated the Common Core development as a recognition of the need for an internationally competitive system of education.

The Common Core represents a trade-off between local control and centralized control of the curriculum. To the extent that the Common Core outlines learning expectations that improve the organization of teaching and learning, it has the potential to increase productive efficiency and to help struggling districts improve outcomes. However, the Common Core also introduces constraints which—in some cases—may not be preferable to a course of instruction chosen at a district or state level that may be particularly well suited to the needs of local students. In such cases, the Common Core generates distortions that ultimately reduce allocative efficiency by weakening the extent to which students' needs are well matched with local schools.

While the intention of the Common Core was to create a national standard that continued to respect states' historic stronghold on education decisions, it brought a storm of controversy surrounding the standards that highlights the difficulty with increasing the federal government's role in regulating local schools. Proponents of Common Core emphasize that the development of the standards involved teachers and other education experts, that drafts of the standards were made public, and that criticism throughout the development process was welcomed and used to fine-tune the final set of expectations. The result, they assert, provides teachers and administrators with a clear, logical, and meaningful set of education standards by which they can gauge students' progress while leaving specific curriculum decisions to the discretion of local educators.

Prominent advocates include Michelle Rhee, founder of StudentsFirst and former superintendent of the Washington, D.C., public schools, who argues that Common Core addresses the inequity across schoolchildren of different backgrounds and from different districts.[5] Randi Weingarten, president of the American Federation of Teachers, states that "our members believe the Common Core Standards represent the best opportunity in a generation to put American students on a path to personal and professional success."[6] Support at the local, state, and national level can be found readily and on both sides of the political aisle as well, with supporters including the Republican former governor of Florida, Jeb Bush, and Democratic President Barack Obama.

Despite its bipartisan support, the very existence of a set of national standards remains problematic for a large population of Americans who believe the control of schooling content should be left to local communities. Representative of much of the backlash against any federal involvement in education, Senator Marco Rubio of Florida claimed that Common Core "is increasingly being used by the Obama Administration to turn the Department of Education into what is effectively a national school board. This effort to coerce states into adhering to national curriculum standards is not the best way to help our children attain the best education. Empowering parents, local communities and the individual states is the best approach."[7]

Indiana became the first state to adopt and then withdraw from the Common Core initiative, with then-governor Mike Pence stating, "I believe education is a state and local function,"[8] after signing legislation to make official the state's autonomy from the federal standard.

The fierce opposition to Common Core Standards among many proponents of local education control shows the complex relationships among federal, state, and local education policy makers. Some states have refused to adopt the Common Core, based on local control arguments. In states that have agreed to comply with the standards, many individual school districts disagree with the state's decision. Their arguments also surround the desire to keep the control of schools local. This argument over the "right" level of local versus state and federal control of education has been going on since the local public schooling system arose. The disagreement over the Common Core Standards is the most recent example, and it serves to illustrate the difficult tensions that arise between federal, state, and local officials in determining who should set education policy. It is important to recognize that any federal education policy will have to account for the political constraints imposed by many Americans' belief that education is and ought to remain the purview of local governments.

[5] Source: http://www.politico.com/magazine/story/2013/12/michelle-rhee-on-the-common-core-101041.html#.U5kAMPldWSo

[6] Source: http://www.corestandards.org/what-parents-should-know/

[7] Source: http://www.politifact.com/florida/statements/2013/oct/22/marco-rubio/common-core-obama-administration-national-school-b/

[8] Source: http://www.breitbart.com/big-government/2014/05/14/gov-mike-pence-federalist-not-when-it-comes-to-indiana-preserving-its-federal-education-waiver/

industrialized countries shows how unusual the U.S. system is. For example, there is a national curriculum in France that is set by the central government and that is required to be taught to all French children. The United Kingdom has national exams that are the same for all students and that determine whether a student can graduate from high school.

The U.S. federal government's role in education has traditionally been much smaller due to the strong desire among many Americans to retain local control of public schools. Historically, funding through **Title I** of the Elementary and Secondary Education Act, which provided federal funds to schools with high percentages of children from low-income families, was the main federal program affecting elementary and secondary education financing. It is left to the states to set the curriculum and the requirements for graduation, including the design and implementation of graduation exams, which is why the United States does not have a national curriculum or exit exams. This arrangement led to large differences across states in the curricula to which children were exposed and the requirements needed to obtain a high school degree.

The No Child Left Behind Act represented an historic and largely unprecedented expansion of federal influence in education. However, it stopped short of introducing national standards. Instead, the law ensures that the accountability systems and exams will be determined and administered by each state separately. The provisions of NCLB require that states test students in grades three through eight and at least once at the high school level. But each state can use its own exams with virtually no federal guidance or oversight into the content or difficulty of those exams. One key point of variation that has arisen among states is whether they measure performance in terms of *levels*, where the objective is for all students to achieve certain baseline competencies in achievement, or *growth*, where the objective is gains in performance independent of baseline levels of attainment.

The federal NCLB legislation also gives states considerable latitude in how passing standards, or proficiency, are defined. A given level of math or reading knowledge may allow students to be labeled proficient in one state but not in another. Similar to the concern over whether the changes in student performance in Texas actually reflect more student learning, a number of researchers have noted that NCLB creates incentives for states to lower the bar.[9] Peterson and Lastra-Anadon (2010) note: "States have strong incentives not to set world-class standards. If they do, more of their schools will be identified as failing under NCLB rules, and states will then be required to take corrective actions to bring students' performance up to the higher standard."

The original intent of NCLB was to ensure 100% proficiency in math and reading across the United States by 2014. As part of the law, each state had to set out a plan for each school regarding the change in proficiency rates expected each year to attain 100% by 2014. Again, states had virtually unlimited freedom to set the time pattern of changes expected, as long as the 100% proficiency goal was met by 2014. NCLB also requires that all teachers be "highly qualified," defined as being licensed by the state to teach. On the whole, NCLB gave states wide latitude to come up with exams and standards as well as a path to ensuring sufficient growth in performance to achieve full proficiency by 2014.

As 2014 approached, it became increasingly clear that states would not meet the goals of full proficiency. Beginning in 2011, the Federal Department of Education allowed states to apply for a flexibility waiver. The waiver would exempt them from most

---

Title I A federal grant program providing funding to schools that serve a large number of students from low-income families.

---

[9] Peterson and Lastra-Anadon (2010) cite the example of Tennessee, where over 90% of fourth-grade students are regarded as proficient in math based on state standards, while only 28% would be regarded as proficient using widely accepted national metrics.

DEEP DIVE: The Design of No Child Left Behind

The structure of NCLB is complex. Here, we provide an overview of how the law was structured. Our discussion highlights many of the incentives embedded in NCLB that have interested researchers. A core principle of NCLB was that schools should have to show progress overall and by relevant student subgroups. There are four subgroups:

1. Economically disadvantaged students
2. Special education students
3. Limited-English-proficient students
4. Students from major racial and ethnic groups (e.g., Black, Hispanic, Asian, and White)

Schools have annual targets for proficiency rates both overall and by subgroup. A school that meets each of these criteria is said to achieve **adequate yearly progress (AYP)**. Importantly, as long as a school has a sufficiently large number of students in each subgroup, failure of even one of the subgroups to meet AYP leads the entire school to be labeled as failing to meet the assessment target.

To see why this is relevant, consider a high-performing school with 20 students in a given subgroup. If those 20 students do not meet the AYP standard, the school is at risk of being sanctioned even though average scores are high. In this way, the law was focused on ensuring that no child, especially ones from disadvantaged backgrounds, fell through the cracks.

Contained within NCLB is an escalating set of sanctions targeted at schools that receive *Title I* funds. Title I is a federal grant program providing funding to schools that serve a large number of students from low-income families. As of the 2010–2011 school year, 66,646 schools—about 67% of public schools in the United States—receive these funds. Title I is the major source of federal funding for public schools, and it is the main mechanism through which NCLB sanctions are enforced.

The federal government enforced NCLB sanctions on schools that consistently did not meet AYP by threatening them with the withholding of Title I funds if they do not comply with the sanctions. For the first year a Title I–receiving school did not make AYP, there were no

sanctions. However, if such a school failed to make AYP for two consecutive years, it was labeled *in improvement* and faced the following sanctions:

- **Two consecutive years.** Year 1 of school improvement. The school must allow open enrollment among students to any other nonimprovement school in the district with room to admit the student. The school also must develop a school improvement plan.
- **Three consecutive years.** Year 2 of school improvement. Along with school choice, vouchers for supplemental education services are given to students from families that meet Title I income requirements. The vouchers can be used for both public and private providers of education services.
- **Four consecutive years.** Corrective action. In addition to school choice and supplemental education services, the school must take at least one of the following actions:
  - Replace the school staff that are relevant to the failure
  - Institute and implement a new curriculum
  - Significantly decrease management authority in the school
  - Appoint outside experts to advise the school
  - Extend the school year or school day
  - Restructure the internal organization of the school
- **Five consecutive years.** School restructuring (planning). In addition to all of the sanctions listed previously, the school must develop a plan to restructure. The restructuring must include at least one of the following:
  - Reopen school as a public charter school
  - Replace all or most of school staff, including the principal
  - Enter into a contract with an entity, such as a private management company, with a demonstrated record of effectiveness to operate the school
  - Any other major restructuring of the school's governance arrangement
- **Six consecutive years.** School restructuring (implementation). The school must implement the restructuring plan.

of the NCLB sanctions in exchange for the state setting up detailed and comprehensive plans to improve the academic performance of all students. Because of the impending increases in sanctions as a result of the largely unrealistic performance goals embedded in NCLB, most states applied for a waiver. By 2014, all but five states (including the District of Columbia) had been granted a waiver. Wyoming and Iowa had a waiver pending, while Nebraska, Montana, and North Dakota had not applied for a waiver.

adequate yearly progress (AYP) Defined by each state; refers to schools meeting certain benchmarks regarding the proportion of students passing state exams and graduating from high school.

In December of 2015, NCLB was replaced by the Every Student Succeeds Act, which greatly expanded state flexibility in setting and meeting performance standards. While students are still required to be tested in grades three through eight, the law made the states responsible for accountability rules related to those exams. This change basically ended federal sanctions related to NCLB.

11.2 School Accountability Measures

After several decades of school accountability policies at the state level and nearly a decade of operation of NCLB, policy makers and analysts have recognized that the theoretical benefits associated with a school accountability policy are countered by some practical limits in the measurement of student achievement:

1. Statistical noise in the test can generate imprecise measures of performance, especially for small schools and small classes.
2. Students far away from proficiency cutoffs will not contribute to accountability measures.
3. There are many schooling outcomes we care about, only some of which can be measured and included in accountability systems.

Policy makers and parents are interested in the level of knowledge and the change in knowledge over the course of a school year for a student or a group of students. Let's call this true level of knowledge for student i at the end of one year T_{1i}^*, with the baseline level T_{0i}^*. When we give students assessments, we will inevitably get a noisy or error-ridden measure of their true knowledge. In this sense, what we will observe is $T_{1i} = T_{1i}^* + \varepsilon_{1i}$ and $T_{0i} = T_{0i}^* + \varepsilon_{0i}$. The observed level of achievement at the level of a classroom or school is then the average over all N students:

$$\overline{T}_1 = \frac{1}{N}\sum_{i=1}^{n} T_{1i}.$$

If, on average, the error terms ε_{0i} and ε_{1i} are small or equal to zero, then such testing error will not matter. However, there are a number of reasons to suspect that these errors may be large and that they are unlikely to be equal to zero on average. One example of noise is a student experiencing a temporary illness or even a poor night of sleep that might have led to test performance that understates her true achievement. Similarly, a dog barking or construction outside a classroom might lead an entire class to record scores lower than their true capacity. These are examples of events that are random with respect to the given student, but they all reduce test scores. What is more, the impact of these measures of statistical noise may be relatively large if our accountability measures emphasize changes or growth rather than levels.

A number of analysts have noted that the impact of noise at the individual level will be greater when the number of students in a grade or a school is smaller. To see this, consider the average and note that because $\overline{T}_1 = \frac{1}{N}\sum_{i=1}^{n} T_{1i}$, adding or subtracting one student with high or low achievement will have a much larger impact on the average score level or pass rate when N is small compared to when N is large. In effect, the variance of the mean will be greater when the number of students is relatively small.[10]

This type of variation in pass rates and test scores turns out to have important implications in practice for some accountability mechanisms. Because small schools will naturally see more year-to-year fluctuation in test scores, it is these schools that will be more likely to be rewarded and punished for year-to-year changes in performance. Figure 11.4 provides the intuition for this result. The graph shows the distribution of test score means for a small school (say, 50 students) and a big school (say, 500 students) when students in these schools are expected to be similar. There is less dispersion in the average test results for the big school than the small school, and as a result, the likelihood of observing a value in the right tail or the left tail—representing very good or very poor performance—is much lower for the big school. Indeed, a North Carolina program that rewarded schools with test score improvements made more than one-quarter of its awards to schools in the bottom decile of school size (Kane & Staiger, 2002).

Many other well-intentioned proposals for school accountability metrics also are problematic in practice. For example, efforts to define school-level proficiency in terms of the performance of subgroups like minority students or low-income students in addition to the overall performance of students in a school may generate a much more difficult target with greater susceptibility to the effects of random variation. While the intent of such policies may be to ensure that schools do not ignore outcomes for minority children and other disadvantaged groups, such a mandate likely presents a more onerous accountability standard for schools with substantial minority populations. Kane, Staiger, and Geppert (2002) offer the following illustrative example:

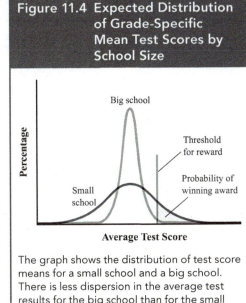

Figure 11.4 Expected Distribution of Grade-Specific Mean Test Scores by School Size

The graph shows the distribution of test score means for a small school and a big school. There is less dispersion in the average test results for the big school than for the small school. The probability of observing a value in the right tail or the left tail—representing very good or very poor performance—is much lower for the big school.

> Suppose that a school is solidly on the path to improvement, with a 70 percent chance of increasing the proficiency of any racial subgroup in a given year. A school with two racial subgroups in its student body would have less than a 50–50 chance for achieving an increase for both groups in a given year—because the year-to-year fluctuations are nearly independent for each racial group (therefore the probability is 0.7 times 0.7, or 0.49). The odds would be even longer for a school with three racial subgroups (0.7 times 0.7 times 0.7, or 0.34). (p. 58)

The implication is that students at schools with multiple racial subgroups are more likely to be subject to sanctions, which in turn generate some costs. These educational disruptions are a result of chance variation rather than a sustained and reliable measure of poor academic performance.

Careful consideration of these measurement issues associated with school accountability requirements has produced some clear recommendations as to how incentives can

---

[10] For example, suppose that individual test scores follow a normal distribution in the population such that $T_i \sim N(\mu, \sigma^2)$, where μ is the mean and σ^2 is the variance. It follows that a sample mean from this distribution will have the distribution $\overline{T} \sim N(\mu, \frac{\sigma^2}{N})$. Intuitively, as the number of students we observe gets larger, the observed mean test scores will be less susceptible to random variation or noise in individual test performance.

Figure 11.5 The Relationship Between API Rank and Value-Added Rank in Los Angeles

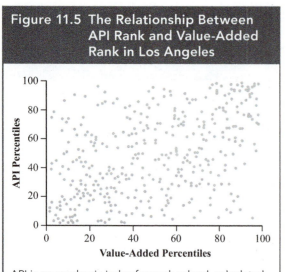

API is an academic index for each school, calculated largely from standardized test pass rates (proficiency rates). The school value-added is a measure of student learning. There is little relationship between the two measures of school performance. *Data from:* Imberman and Lovenheim (2016), Figure 4.

best be structured. First, the reliability of indicators of school performance will be improved by using several years of observation and avoiding too much emphasis on single-year changes in test scores. Second, incentives targeting the extremes of the distribution of student outcomes—either rewarding exceptionally strong performance or penalizing exceptionally low performance—will yield particularly weak incentives for large schools, where large moves in measured performance are very unlikely.

The strong focus on student proficiency measures under NCLB raises another measurement issue: Learning that occurs high and low in the test distribution is not detected. Changes in student proficiency can lend insight into how students around the test score cutoff for proficiency are faring. However, if a school has a high proportion of low-performing students, the proficiency measures will show that the school is performing poorly while in actuality it might be teaching the students quite a lot. Student learning at the bottom of the performance distribution is unlikely to show up in proficiency measures. Because sanctions under NCLB are targeted at schools with low proficiency rates, it may be targeted at the wrong place if the real goal is to sanction schools in which student learning is low.

To see that sanctions targeted at low-proficiency schools may produce outcomes different from those of sanctions targeted at low-growth schools, Figure 11.5 shows a scatter plot of *API rank* and *school value-added rank* in Los Angeles among elementary schools in 2010. *API* (Academic Performance Index) is an academic index for each school, calculated largely from standardized test pass rates (i.e., proficiency rates). The *school value-added* is a measure of student learning: the school's contribution to the *change* in test scores, controlling for student demographics and lagged test scores at the student level. Figure 11.5 shows that a school's *API rank* and *value-added rank* are very weakly correlated. There are many schools with low test pass rates that contribute highly to student learning (bottom right quadrant) as well as many schools with high proficiency rates and low value-added (top left quadrant). Targeting accountability measures at proficiency rates will lead to sanctions on schools that are producing considerable gains in student test scores.

The weak correlation between test pass rates and school value-added highlights the importance of the measurement instrument used in the accountability program. Depending on what types of exams and what types of outcomes are included in the measures, school accountability programs can have vastly different effects on student outcomes. The right policy question therefore is not, "Does school accountability work?" but instead, "How can we structure accountability programs to maximize their effectiveness?" In the next section, we turn to the evidence on whether school accountability affects student academic performance. We underscore that any lack of effects on student performance shows us that a particular program is ineffective, not that accountability policies are necessarily ineffective if structured differently.

Another central critique of school accountability policies surrounding measurement is that the outcomes from schooling that parents and policy makers value extend beyond outcomes on standardized tests. It often is argued that the emphasis of school accountability policies on subject areas that are easily tested on standardized exams crowds out time devoted to other subject areas, such as art, music, and even social studies and science. Moreover, critics note that within subject areas, school accountability policies may lead to an emphasis on rote learning at the expense of higher-order critical thinking and problem-solving skills. Suppose we think about policy makers as caring about easily observed testable knowledge (T) and unobserved abstract skills (A). If school accountability policies lead to rewards for increasing T while A remains unobserved, it follows that teachers will respond by shifting their effort away from producing A toward producing T.

The consequences of this shift in effort toward producing the outcome that is easily observed depend critically on whether T and A are substitutes or complements in the education production function (Holmstrom & Milgrom, 1991). At one extreme, classroom drills on vocabulary might completely crowd out the time that a language arts teacher had to devote to critical analysis of plot in literature. At the other extreme, adding to students' vocabulary might help them better interpret literature and facilitate discussion of plot and narrative. Thus, there is a potential for crowding out difficult-to-measure dimensions of student learning by school accountability initiatives, but we should also understand that such consequences are neither inevitable nor mechanical.

Even if accountability policies cause teachers to teach to the test in ways that lead to the production of only certain types of knowledge, there are situations in which students still may learn more under an accountability regime (Lazear, 2006). Basically, if learning is costly, broad-based exams may induce students to give up and learn nothing. However, they still may invest in learning the more limited set of skills tested on a narrow exam. An illustrative analogy is speeding: If a small number of police locate randomly to enforce speed limits, then people may decide to speed more because the likelihood of being caught is low. However, if the police announce where they will be, then people will at least obey the speed limit in those areas. Announcing the location of speed traps therefore may reduce overall speeding. Similarly, targeted testing may increase overall learning if learning costs are high.

11.3 Do School Accountability Policies Change Student Performance?

The Effect of School Accountability Policies on Student Achievement

What would student achievement have been without NCLB? This is not easy to answer. By 2002, many states already had accountability systems in place; hence, the alternative to NCLB was not a landscape lacking in school accountability. The experience and outcomes in states that were early adopters of accountability provide one source of evidence to inform the understanding of how standards-based accountability practices affect student achievement.

Evaluation of the impact of accountability policies on student achievement requires an assessment instrument or standardized test used across many states. The National Assessment of Educational Progress (NAEP) turns out to be a particularly good metric for assessing the effects of state and federal accountability on broad constructs of student learning because it is not tied to a specific course of instruction. Since results for districts, schools, and individuals are not reported, there are few incentives to cheat, prep, or otherwise game performance on this exam. In short, the NAEP results are thought to have considerable validity as a measure of student achievement. Students in the fourth and eighth grades are tested every four years—in 1992, 1996, and so forth for math and in 1994, 1998, and so forth for reading. To assess the impact of school accountability practices in general and the NCLB provisions in particular, researchers have used changes in NAEP scores in two types of analyses that examine changes in student performance between states with different accountability provisions in place.

When NCLB was implemented in 2002, the best way to predict its effects was to compare the change in student performance in states that had adopted accountability standards to the change in states without meaningful accountability standards. However, to examine such a question only using variation across states in a given year is quite problematic. For example, comparing Massachusetts to Missouri will capture differences in accountability policies as well as differences in other demographic characteristics and policies (such as spending per student) that can affect student achievement. Rather than looking at differences between states at a single point in time, which will reflect a multitude of factors beyond accountability, a clear strategy for assessment is to compare the *change* in outcomes over time in states that implement an accountability system to changes in states that do not change their accountability policies in the same year. This is a straightforward example of a difference-in-difference strategy. The states that do not alter their accountability system act as the control group; ostensibly, their change in outcomes tells us what would have happened in the states that do implement an accountability policy had they not instituted this new policy.

Research studies that use this approach find substantial impacts on fourth- and eighth-grade test scores on achievement of passing consequential school accountability policies in the 1990s.[11] States passing such reforms produced faster test score growth over this period than other states. For example, states adopting consequential accountability policies had about 3.2 points more growth in math and reading NAEP scores than states that did not pass these laws (Hanushek & Raymond, 2005). While consequential accountability seems to benefit overall performance, there is less evidence to suggest that these policies narrowed racial gaps in student achievement. In fact, estimates for Black and Hispanic students indicate that accountability policies are associated with increasing achievement gaps.

More recent evidence on school accountability using NAEP performance focuses on the period surrounding the introduction of NCLB. Suppose that NCLB had little impact on states that already had a consequential accountability system in place in 2002 (such as Texas). Then, the effect of the introduction of NCLB can be estimated by comparing changes in NAEP scores in states without a preexisting consequential accountability system to changes in states with a preexisting system. In essence, states with accountability policies in place prior to 2002 serve as a control group. Dee and Jacob (2011) follow this research design and find substantial effects of NCLB on student performance.[12] NCLB is associated with an increase in fourth-grade math achievement of about 8.2 points (0.26 standard deviation) and an effect on eighth grade math of 5.3 points (0.14 standard deviation). However, the estimates for reading are smaller and generally are not statistically significantly different from zero.

A different type of question researchers have posed about school accountability policies is whether the provision of school or district ratings, which typically are accompanied by penalties or rewards, affects student achievement. Many states and large school districts issue grades of A to F to schools, and they tie financial rewards to receiving

---

[11] Studies that have used this approach are Hanushek and Raymond (2005) and Carnoy and Loeb (2002).

[12] For a comprehensive literature review on school accountability effects, see Figlio and Loeb (2011).

high grades (usually A or B) as well as sanctions for schools receiving failing grades (usually D or F). As you may recognize from your own academic experience, a grade such as an A or B is a discrete measure for ranges of performance, and it is frustrating to be the highest-scoring B+ and a bit of a relief to find out that you just squeaked out an A. Of course, how close you were to the cutoff will never be known by your employer or others who look at your transcript! When examining the performance of schools, however, researchers typically observe the underlying test scores on which these grades are based. In turn, they can implement a regression discontinuity strategy in which they compare outcomes among schools that barely passed to schools that barely failed.

The authors of these studies argue that receiving a failing grade leads to increased pressure to improve, and thus we should see improvement among schools that receive failing grades relative to their counterparts who barely received passing grades. This is exactly what the data show. Studies from New York City and Florida that use this method point to sizable gains in math test scores and, often, in reading scores among students in schools

DEEP DIVE: The Effect of the Florida Accountability System on Student Achievement

In 1999, Florida enacted a statewide school accountability system in an attempt to raise the quality of low-performing schools. Through this system, the state provides each school with a grade from A to F based on the school's average performance on the Florida Comprehensive Assessment Test (FCAT), which consists of standardized tests in math, reading, and writing in certain high-stakes grades. If fewer than 60% of a school's students pass the math test, fewer than 60% pass the reading test, and fewer than 50% pass the writing test, the school receives an F and is labeled a failing school. If a school obtains a grade of F in at least two of the four most recent years, its students are provided with school vouchers (opportunity scholarships) that can be used to transfer to higher-performing schools in their district.

This program has two components that can influence public school behavior. First, the pressure from the grading system, and in particular the fear of being labeled a failing school, might spur schools to increase their performance on these test measures. Second, the desire to not lose students through the voucher program could induce schools to increase test scores. Thus, we want to know the total effect on student performance as well as to portion the total effect into the part due to accountability and the part due to vouchers. Economists David Figlio and Cecelia Rouse (2006) provide an in-depth analysis of how this accountability system affected the performance of failing schools. A serious difficulty in analyzing this policy is that it affected all schools in Florida simultaneously. Thus, it is incredibly difficult to identify a control group

that can inform us about how school performance would have changed in the absence of this policy.

Figlio and Rouse solve this problem by employing a difference-in-difference method that links the change in a school's average test score between 1999 and 2000 to the grade received by the school in 1999. By comparing the changes in average test scores of schools that received an F to those that received passing grades, this method enables the authors to estimate the test score response to receiving an F. The main assumption of this estimation approach is that schools receiving an F would have had the same student test score trends as schools that did not receive an F absent the policy.

The results suggest that the test score response to receiving an F is approximately 0.09 standard deviation in reading and 0.23 standard deviation in math on the FCAT. Given the low cost associated with enacting this system, these are economically significant effects.

The authors do a lot of work to attempt to control for all potential threats to the validity of their estimation approach. First, they acknowledge that the results could be biased because the grading system may have affected student and parent school choice, and thus the composition of students at the various schools could have changed. To overcome this obstacle, the authors control for prior test scores to ensure that the test score response is not driven by changes in student characteristics. Controlling for previous student knowledge leads to a sizable reduction in the estimated test score response in reading but leaves the math estimate unchanged. Thus, while student composition appears to change when the school receives an F grade, the main results remain when prior test scores are used to control for these changes.

Second, Figlio and Rouse worry that teachers may be teaching to the test. If this is the case, then the estimated test score response to receiving an F does not necessarily represent an increase in student learning. To explore this possibility, the authors repeat their analysis using student performance on the low-stakes Stanford-9 Achievement Test rather than on the FCAT test. If teaching to the test is present, one would expect this adjustment to reduce the estimated test score responses to receiving an F, since the state did not use the low-stakes tests to grade the schools. The results from this alternative specification suggest that this indeed was the case: The test score response in math is reduced by almost 50%, and the test score response in reading ceases to be significantly different from zero.

Third, the authors acknowledge that some schools may have been on an upward or downward trajectory when the system was enacted in 1999. This would bias the authors' results, because their estimation method would accidentally attribute test score changes reflective of pre-existing trends to the implementation of the accountability system. To address this concern, they repeat their analysis for the longer time horizon from 1995 to 2000, which allows them to control for any school-specific trends prior to 1999. As a consequence of this modification, the test score response in reading becomes statistically indistinguishable from zero, while the test score response in math continues to have a modest effect.

An innovative feature of this paper is that the authors provide some evidence on whether the estimated effects are due to the opportunity scholarships or to accountability-induced stigma (the shame of being labeled as a failing school). They do this by exploiting the fact that Florida experimented with an earlier version of this system between 1996 and 1998. Under this system, schools with low average student test scores were put on a critically low-performing schools list, but they were not subject to sanctions. If the voucher aspect of the 1999 plan was the main driving force underlying the test score response, then the test score response should be greater under the 1999 system than under the earlier system. However, the results indicate that the effects of these two systems are indistinguishable from each other. This suggests that it is stigma, and not the voucher aspect of the system, that drives the test score response to receiving an F.

Overall, this paper suggests that there are large effects of accountability pressure and accountability-driven stigma from receiving a failing grade on public school performance. The effects seem particularly large on the incentivized exams, although there are some spill-over effects to other, low-stakes exams. Putting these effect sizes in context, the 0.06 standard deviation effect on low-stakes math exam scores (in high-stakes grades) is substantially smaller than the effects from Project STAR, for example. However, this policy also is much cheaper. The main takeaway from this research is that this type of school accountability system may be a cost-effective method for raising student achievement in certain subjects in underperforming schools.

under pressure from receiving failing accountability grades.[13] One of the core components of school accountability policies is not only to generate information on school-level student performance but also to share it with the public. These findings suggest that putting public pressure on schools to improve does indeed lead to increases in student test scores.

As with studies of the effect of teacher quality and class sizes on student test scores, there is a strong concern that any short-run test score gains may be temporary. If the test score effects fade out over time, the long-run benefits of these programs might be smaller than the short-run returns. Emerging research, however, suggests there are substantial long-run positive effects on students who are in schools that face accountability pressure because those schools are at risk of being labeled low-performing (Deming et al., 2016). Using data from Texas that link K–12 education records to both college outcomes and labor market earnings later in life, this research shows that increased accountability pressure on high schools leads to higher tenth-grade test scores as well as higher postsecondary attainment and earnings. That is, students in schools that face the threat of being low-performing have higher test scores, are more likely to go to college and to complete a four-year degree, and earn considerably more in the labor market in their early- to mid-20s

---

[13] Rockoff and Turner (2010) study New York City, while Rouse et al. (2013) conduct their analysis using data from Florida.

than students whose schools do not face accountability pressure from being labeled low performing. However, low-performing students perform worse in schools that are most likely to receive the highest academic rating under the accountability system. Thus, while there are potentially large positive long-run effects of low-performance accountability threats on student outcomes, lower-achieving students in high-performing schools may be hurt by the accountability system.

Effects on the Distribution of Student Achievement

The research discussed thus far focuses on average student test score gains. However, because of the focus of accountability systems on pass rates, the effects may not be the same for all students. As discussed in Section 11.2, students at the margin of passing are likely to be most affected by accountability pressures, as raising their scores is the easiest way for a school to increase test passage rates. Thus, students near the passing margin are the beneficiaries of educational triage in this setting.

The earliest evidence on this question examines the experience of Texas, which had a system nearly identical to NCLB in the 1990s (Reback, 2008). Using student-level data on all students in Texas to calculate whether increasing each student's test score changes the likelihood that a school receives a higher accountability rating, one can isolate students whose performance has a large impact on the rating the school receives. The incentives schools face under the accountability program predict that students whose test score changes will have the largest effects on the school's accountability rating should experience the largest test score increases. This is what the data show. Low-achieving students also tend to have higher scores when more of their classmates' math scores are important for the school's rating. These results are consistent with the idea that school accountability leads to uneven performance increases across students, depending on the importance of the student to the school's rating.

While the administration of the Illinois Achievement Test (ISAT) was considered a low-stakes exam before the introduction of NCLB, the test immediately became the exam used for NCLB assessment in 2002. Thus, comparison of the performance of students in Chicago public schools on the ISAT before and after the introduction of the NCLB provides a clear demonstration of how accountability incentives differentially affect student performance.

Research by Neal and Schanzenbach (2010) examines how performance changed across the distribution of students—looking at gains in the bottom, middle, and top of the baseline test score distribution. Figure 11.6 illustrates their results. The decile of the initial (i.e., before 2002) test score distribution is shown along the horizontal axis, so students in the lowest 10% are at the far left and students in the top 10% are on the far right. The

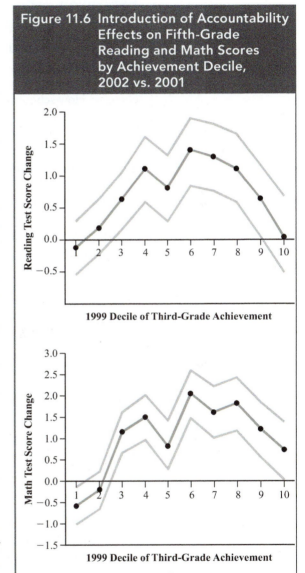

Figure 11.6 Introduction of Accountability Effects on Fifth-Grade Reading and Math Scores by Achievement Decile, 2002 vs. 2001

1999 Decile of Third-Grade Achievement

1999 Decile of Third-Grade Achievement

The decile of the initial (i.e., before 2002) test score distribution is shown along the horizontal axis, so students in the lowest 10% are at the far left and students in the top 10% are on the far right. The vertical axis measures the gains in test performance between the low-stakes (2001) and the high-stakes (2002) year of assessment. Students in the middle of the distribution gain much more than students who started out at either the bottom or the top. *Data from:* Neal and Schanzenbach (2010).

measures along the vertical axis show the gains in test performance between the low-stakes (2001) and the high-stakes (2002) year of assessment. What is unambiguously clear is that students in the middle of the distribution gain much more than students who started out at either the bottom or the top. This evidence suggests that schools are following the incentives of the program to raise passing rates, which paradoxically can hurt or at least fail to impact many of the low-scoring students that the NCLB Act was designed to help.

Explaining Achievement Effects: School Responses to Accountability Pressure

The evidence discussed thus far suggests that accountability systems increase average student test scores and that schools facing accountability pressure from receiving low grades increase the performance of their students. How do schools accomplish these changes? How schools react to accountability pressures provides some insight into the education production function by showing us how input changes affect educational outputs.

There are many ways in which schools can respond to accountability pressures. They can change their mix of inputs, they can alter instructional practices, or they can engage in (often shady) accounting practices by shifting students to special education or retaining them to alter the composition of test takers. A major hurdle in understanding what schools are doing when they face pressure from an accountability system is data. As suggested by evidence in the case of Texas, states may be making tests easier to help ensure that they meet accountability standards. It also is extremely hard to know what schools are doing on a day-to-day level in response to accountability pressures.

One innovative study attempts to overcome some of these data problems by linking administrative student-level test score data in Florida to detailed surveys on specific educational practices and resource allocation fielded over the course of several years surrounding the implementation of Florida's accountability system (Rouse et al., 2013). Using a variety of methods to isolate the causal effects of accountability pressure, including a regression discontinuity design surrounding the threshold for receiving a D versus an F rating, this study shows that schools facing threats from a low rating alter their behavior along several dimensions. In particular, they lengthen instruction time, restructure the curriculum to focus more on tested subjects (e.g., reading and math), put more attention toward low-achieving students, and increase teachers' resources and autonomy. Furthermore, they present evidence that the test score effects of the Florida accountability policy can be explained by these school responses.

Unintended Effects: Evidence of Gaming and Cheating

Accountability policies create strong incentives for schools to raise academic achievement as measured by test scores. Indeed, this is the main purpose of these policies. However, like any set of incentives, these policies may lead to unintended consequences as schools attempt to raise their test scores through means other than increasing their students' knowledge and abilities. They also may affect teacher mobility or school resource allocation more broadly in unintended ways. A full evaluation of the effects of the introduction of school accountability policies cannot simply focus on the *intended* dimension of changes in achievement on standardized tests but also should explore the magnitude of the changes in behavior on other margins.

DEEP DIVE: How Schools and Teachers Respond to Accountability Pressure

An important study that examines how schools and teachers respond to accountability pressure on a national scale in the NCLB period was conducted by Reback, Rockoff, and Schwartz (2014). They use a very inventive research strategy, which recognizes that states differ dramatically in the standards necessary for proficiency on exams. As a result, a school might be labeled as meeting AYP in one state but an identical school in another state would not. They compare differences in outcomes between schools in each state that are close versus far from an AYP passing threshold to the differences among observationally equivalent schools in another state that are not close to any threshold. The difference in their location relative to an AYP threshold is due to state-specific rules and is what allows them to isolate the effect of accountability threats on teacher and student behavior.

As in many of the other studies we have discussed, they find that accountability pressure from NCLB raises student test scores. Importantly, they study low-stakes exams that are not used in calculating AYP. That students do better on these tests suggests that accountability threats do not just induce teachers to teach to the test but lead to performance increases on exams that are not linked to incentives. Schools that face accountability pressure also report changes in structure and curriculum that could be important drivers of the test score effects. Those close to an AYP threshold report a shift from general instruction to more specific reading and math instruction. This shift largely comes at the expense of science and social studies. Teachers also say they have less job security, suggesting that human resource practices have changed to place more emphasis on observed student outcomes.

One way in which teachers and administrators can raise test scores is to change the pool of students who are present on testing days. In short, school- and classroom-level results will be improved if the high-scoring kids are present and the low-scoring kids are not. Figlio (2006) shows that one way schools alter the pool of tested students is to change disciplinary practices around test dates. He finds that schools in his sample reduced suspension penalties for higher achievers in high-stakes grades during the testing window, while suspensions for lower achievers increased in those grades.[14]

In other work, Figlio and Getzler (2006) examine whether the state accountability policies in Florida led schools to reclassify students as disabled and therefore ineligible to contribute to school average test scores.[15] If students likely to be reclassified would have scored poorly on the assessment, then such behavior would increase observed test scores without meaningful changes in student achievement. The researchers find that schools did tend to reclassify low-performing students as disabled, with this type of action most concentrated among the schools with a high fraction of low-income students and those at risk for failing to meet the state's proficiency standards. Figlio and Getzler provide a nuanced interpretation of these results:

> One interpretation of reclassification results is that schools are behaving in an insidious manner, reclassifying potentially low-performing students into test-excluded categories to make average test scores look better. But it is also unclear whether this behavior is desirable or undesirable, given that one could

---

[14] Figlio studies Florida's accountability program prior to NCLB. A core component of NCLB was the requirement that virtually all students be tested to avoid schools systematically excluding certain students from testing.

[15] In most pre-NCLB accountability programs, including Florida's studied here, students with learning disabilities were excluded. NCLB ended this exclusion and made students with learning disabilities one of the groups that needed to meet AYP each year.

legitimately make the argument that rather than "gaming the system" this pattern reflects an increased attention to assessment and students who may have slipped through the cracks are now appropriately classified.

Similar effects on student reclassification as well as on student retention have been found in Chicago (Jacob, 2005) and in Texas (Cullen & Reback, 2006), which suggests these practices are pervasive among schools facing accountability pressures.

In a creative paper, Figlio and Winicki (2005) show that schools facing accountability pressure increase the caloric content of school lunches on test days. Because students tend to perform better when they have more energy, the argument is that feeding them more before they take the exam will boost scores. This is indeed what they find, which highlights that the short-run test score gains might be very different from long-run gains; long-run gains should not be affected by caloric intake on the test day.

In addition to schools changing the base of students who are tested, placing incentives to raise test scores on teachers may encourage outright cheating. In a very innovative paper, Brian Jacob and Steven Levitt (2003) use data from the Chicago public schools to attempt to identify the prevalence of cheating on assessments. Their evidence suggests that cheating occurred in 3–5% of the elementary classrooms in the sample. Indicators of cheating at the classroom level include unusually large test score gains followed by unusually small gains or even declines in the following year. In addition, they found that answers in classrooms where cheating was likely to have occurred often display unusual patterns; an identical block of answers among many students in the class suggests that a teacher or administrator systematically adjusted answers for a group of students.

To test their method of identifying classrooms in which cheating took place, Jacob and Levitt implemented retesting in suspect classrooms and in a control group. While the control classrooms largely replicated their original scores, the suspect classrooms showed substantial declines in the second round of testing. They then examined whether there was an increase in the prevalence of cheating in 1996, when Chicago implemented a school accountability system based on these tests, dramatically increasing their importance. They find that by their measure, cheating rose substantially after this policy change, particularly in classrooms that were low-achieving and that faced the largest likelihood of sanctions under the accountability policy.

Cheating increases, while large, are still small enough that they are unlikely to be the sole driver of aggregate test score gains from accountability. That we see growth in low-stakes NAEP test scores as well as in long-run student outcomes from school accountability policies also is evidence that the gains we are measuring are not solely from cheating. Nonetheless, it is important to understand all of the distortions caused by a given policy. This is true especially for cheating behavior, as an increase in the incidence of cheating is not an inevitable consequence of the introduction of accountability. It is possible to counteract this incentive by improving the mechanisms for detecting cheating (increasing the probability of catching those who cheat) or by increasing the penalties for cheating.

Finally, accountability policies may have unintended effects on the inputs available to schools. As argued in Chapter 9, teachers are one of the most important inputs to schooling. Clotfelter et al. (2004) examine how the introduction of the school accountability system in North Carolina in 1996 affected teacher turnover and the composition of teachers in low-performing schools. Using administrative data on all children, teachers, and schools in North Carolina,[16] they find evidence of increases in teacher turnover in lower-performing schools when the accountability system was implemented. It is less clear whether the composition of teachers shifted in such a way that would lead to worse student outcomes, but the disruption of high turnover rates themselves are likely to lower student performance. The consequences of accountability for the teacher workforce thus may be an important aspect of how these policies affect student academic achievement.

11.4 Do Student Accountability Policies Change Student Performance?

A sizable component of the accountability movement has focused on holding students accountable for their own test scores in making grade promotion or graduation decisions. The underlying theory behind these policies is to create incentives for students to work harder to meet promotion benchmarks and to ensure that those who obtain a degree have a minimum set of skills. Indeed, one tagline often associated with these policies is the need to end social promotion, which allows students to move forward in grade levels even when they have not mastered core competencies.

The effects of imposing test score cutoffs for grade-level advancement can be seen by comparing graduation outcomes of students just below to those just above the cutoff. That is, researchers estimate regression discontinuity models that compare outcomes among those who barely pass the cutoff with those who barely miss the cutoff. Because human capital likely moves continuously through these thresholds, these analyses show how imposing cutoffs for graduation or promotion affect students right around these cutoffs.

The two research papers that have used this strategy find evidence that these cutoffs tend to reduce high school graduation rates for students just below the cutoff. One of these studies examines tenth-grade exit exams in Massachusetts (Papay, Murnane, & Willett, 2010). The findings indicate that overall, failing one of these exams has little impact on graduating, since students can retake the exams. However, failing a math test reduces the likelihood that low-income students will graduate. The second study examines how being on either side of a score cutoff to be promoted to the next grade in Chicago for sixth- and eighth-grade students affects high school enrollment and graduation (Jacob & Lefgren, 2009).[17] While there are no effects of failing the sixth-grade exam, retaining eighth-grade students significantly reduces the likelihood that they will graduate from high school. They argue that the difference in findings is due to the fact that the retained sixth-grade students are able to catch up to their peers over time, whereas the eighth-grade students are not.

Overall, this research suggests that imposing graduation or grade promotion cutoffs reduces the likelihood of graduating for those right below the cutoffs. A concern with interpreting this evidence as it relates to accountability is that the existence of any cutoff for promotion or graduation might increase effort among all students due to

---

[16] See Appendix A for a description of the administrative North Carolina education data.

[17] Often, grade retention rules require or allow students to attend summer school to try to avoid being retained. Jacob and Lefgren (2004) show that the net effect of summer school and grade retention on future academic achievement is positive, with the summer school portion of these policies driving much of this effect.

the threat of failing a high-stakes test. No study has examined such a question, as the regression discontinuity results cannot tell us whether introducing student accountability policies increases overall student performance.

The evidence suggests, however, that these cutoffs do not alter the return to a high school degree: There is no difference in earnings among those who barely pass versus barely fail high school completion exams in Texas (Clark & Martorell, 2014). Similar to the research discussed earlier, failing these exams reduces the likelihood of receiving a high school degree. But, there is no effect on earnings after high school. There is little evidence that imposing graduation cutoffs increases the signaling value of a high school degree, but it does discourage many students from receiving such a degree.

11.5 Conclusion

Accountability policies are now well established at the state and national level after more than a decade of NCLB and even longer periods of accountability in many individual states. Despite the difficult measurement issues associated with constructing meaningful accountability policies, the evidence to date suggests they have led to higher student achievement both in the short and long run. However, there is considerable variation across different types of students in how they are affected by accountability policies. As well, the incentives schools face under accountability policies can lead to unintended effects as teachers and schools game the system or even outright cheat. These are important factors to consider when designing such policies.

This chapter has focused on both school and student accountability policies, but many accountability policies directly affect teachers by determining their retention or tenure as well as their pay. We examine teacher accountability in more detail in Chapter 12, when we discuss teacher incentive pay policies.

Highlights

- School accountability policies contain expectations, assessments, and incentives (in the form of rewards and/or sanctions) that are tied to measured student academic outcomes.
- The 1983 publication of *A Nation at Risk*, followed by the 1989 Charlottesville education summit, spurred education reform that mandated a set of national education goals, more flexibility and accountability for the use of federal education spending, annual progress reports, and state-level restructuring of education systems. This marked a significant shift in U.S. education policy and was the beginning of a dramatic increase in measuring student academic performance to hold schools, teachers, and students accountable.
- The first state to adopt strong **test-based accountability** measures was Texas. Many states followed suit and instituted similar accountability policies, some of which contained strong measures similar to those in Texas and some of which contained much weaker measures.

- In 2002, the **No Child Left Behind Act** was passed under the leadership of President George W. Bush. While this policy marked the first federal education accountability policy, the act left the responsibility of developing standards and assessments to each individual state. Common across all states were the NCLB provisions setting up a system of punishments for schools receiving **Title I** funds that did not meet **adequate yearly progress** for multiple years in a row.
- A central concern with school accountability policies is what measures to use to specify achievement benchmarks. Statewide policies that provide incentives for test score improvement often have larger impacts on smaller schools, whose test score changes have higher variance associated with them than larger schools. The provisions in NCLB that require all racial and socioeconomic subgroups to meet adequate yearly progress also place more of a burden on schools with more diversity.
- Accountability policies also have proved to be controversial because many believe they favor the development of

certain types of knowledge and skills, such as the ability to do well on a state math test, over other potentially important skills, like teamwork and creativity.

- Empirical evidence suggests that strong accountability policies generate increases in test scores on average. Part of this effect comes about because of the pressure for schools to increase test scores that comes from making accountability results public. There also is evidence that accountability raises long-run student outcomes, such as educational attainment and earnings.

- While test scores increase on average, they do not appear to do so for all students. NCLB provided incentives to raise achievement among students close to the passing threshold. The research indicates that it is these students who experience increases in achievement, while very high- and low-performing students are less affected by the policy.

- Many concerns have been raised about the unintended consequences of accountability policies. Chief among these concerns is that school accountability policies provide incentives to lower the bar by writing more lenient state assessments, to shift students to different classifications, to change who is present on test day, and/or to alter test results by cheating. There also is evidence that accountability policies can increase teacher turnover in low-performing schools.

Problems

1. Briefly explain what school accountability policies are and provide the economic arguments that support these policies.

2. Describe the No Child Left Behind Act. What was its original intent, how does it mandate that states assess adequate progress, and what are the sanctions that schools face if they do not meet these goals?

3. Why are schools with multiple racial and economic subgroups more likely to experience sanctions?

4. What are the main critiques of school accountability policies?

5. Suppose "proficiency" is determined when a student scores above a threshold of 80, and exam scores vary between 1 and 100. A teacher faces a class that, without further instruction, would have scores distributed uniformly over this range. If the teacher's objective is to maximize the pass rate of her students, should she devote the same amount of time to each student? Discuss.

6. Imagine you are a principal who wants to implement a school accountability system. You can either base this system on average test scores or on the percentage of students exceeding a specific score (the proficiency rate). How might the response of teachers to the accountability system vary based on which measure is used? How might student outcomes be affected?

7. How does school finance reform affect the ability of schools to respond to accountability pressures? Do these two types of reforms potentially interact, especially given the evidence on how schools respond to accountability pressure?

8. How might schools affect test score performance by altering the composition of students taking exams? How might policymakers design accountability guidelines to guard against such gaming?

9. Suppose one city (let's call it Grinchville) has an elementary school with 100 students in the third grade, while another city (let's call it Maxtown) has an elementary school with 500 students in the third grade. The students and families in Grinchville and Maxtown are, on average, alike. School resources are the same in Grinchville and Maxtown. For any third grader (like our friend Cindy Lou) from either Grinchville and Maxtown, we can expect a score on the accountability exam of x_i, where $x_i \sim N(\mu, \sigma^2)$.

   a. Is the variance of the mean test scores the same in each town?

   b. Would both towns be equally likely to win a state bonus for year-to-year test score gains of 10%? Why or why not?

3DDock/Shutterstock

Teacher Labor Markets

Classrooms Without Teachers: The Teacher "Shortage" Problem

Nearly every August, there are stories in national and local newspapers about teacher shortages. A *New York Times* headline is indicative of such articles, with a title that proclaimed "Teacher Shortages Spur a Nationwide Hiring Scramble (Credentials Optional)."[1] At the start of the 2015 school year, Las Vegas was short about 3,000 new teachers for its schools. As a result, 600 classrooms were staffed by long-term substitutes who were not full-time certified teachers at the start of the school year. Nearby, California is experiencing its own shortfall in the number of teachers available to staff classes. A week before the start of the 2015 school year, there were 21,000 teacher vacancies to fill across the state.

Concerns about teacher "shortages" are by no means unique to California and Nevada; this is an issue that affects nearly every state in the United States. Claims that teachers are in short supply are most common among schools in rural areas, those that serve disadvantaged populations, and those that face budgetary problems. Within school districts, it is often the case that those who teach special education, mathematics, and science are in short supply. Teacher shortages reflect *excess demand* for teachers, which occurs when the supply of teachers is lower than the demand for teachers at the existing wage rate. Why do these shortages persist in the teacher labor market? In most labor markets, a situation of excess demand is met with an increase in wages and the entry of additional workers. For example, during the housing boom of the early 2000s there was a large increase in the demand for construction workers driven by the quick rise in the demand for new homes. In the short run, there was excess demand for these workers in many areas. This caused an increase in construction workers' wages, which drove many people to enter that line of work until the supply of construction workers again equaled the demand for those workers. Wages therefore adjust to equilibrate supply and demand in labor markets, much as price does in commodity markets. The persistence of teacher shortages suggests that this process of adjustment is far from seamless in the labor market for teachers.

In this chapter, we discuss some of the determinants of the supply of teachers and the labor market demand for teachers, along with some of the reasons why market adjustments to changes in the supply and demand for teachers may be limited. On the demand side of the market, we consider how school policies,

---

[1] The article was written by Motoko Rich and published on August 9, 2015.

funding, and demographics determine the number of teachers that schools want to hire. On the supply side of the market, we examine how individuals make choices to enter the teaching profession and where they choose to work. Teaching is an occupational choice, and we model how wages and working conditions in teaching and other professions affect the supply of teachers. The model we present provides a useful framework for interpreting the data regarding who becomes a teacher, how selection into teaching over time has changed, and how changes in labor markets that are external to teaching (such as expanding opportunities for women) have changed the teacher labor force.

In the second part of this chapter, we examine teachers unions. We begin by providing an historical overview of the unionization movement in an attempt to better understand how we arrived at the current policy environment, after which we discuss what union contracts look like and how they have shaped the compensation system for teachers. We conclude this section by discussing the evidence on how teachers unions affect school district resources and student academic achievement.

A major argument among opponents of teachers unions is that the protections given to teachers by union contracts do not provide proper incentives for them to put forth effort. One policy that has gained increasing traction in recent years is teacher incentive pay. These policies give teachers monetary incentives to raise students' test scores and academic achievement. The increasing prominence of these policies makes them an ever more common feature of teacher labor markets. We first examine the economic justification for these policies using a *principal–agent* model. We then examine what research has shown about the effectiveness of teacher incentive pay. The chapter concludes with a discussion of *certification* regulations, which govern who can teach; alternative certification policies; and programs such as Teach for America that take highly academically successful recent graduates and place them in classrooms serving disadvantaged students.

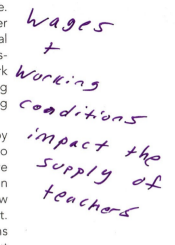

[handwritten margin note: wages + working conditions impact the supply of teachers]

12.1 Supply and Demand in Teacher Labor Markets

Teacher Supply, Demand, and Wage Schedules

As in any labor market, the teacher labor market can be described in terms of supply and demand. Figure 12.1 shows an example of a labor supply and a demand curve for a teacher labor market. The intersection of supply and demand determines both market *wages* (W^*) and *employment* (E^*). Labor supply is upward sloping because workers typically want to supply more labor when wages are higher.[2] The downward-sloping demand curve is driven by the fact that the **marginal product of labor** is diminishing in the number of teachers hired. The marginal product of labor is the worker's contribution to overall output.

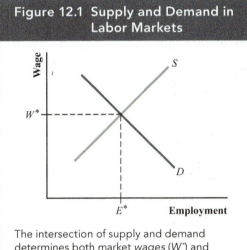

Figure 12.1 Supply and Demand in Labor Markets

The intersection of supply and demand determines both market *wages* (W^*) and *employment* (E^*). Labor supply is upward sloping because workers typically want to supply more labor when wages are higher. The demand for teachers is downward sloping because of the diminishing marginal product of labor.

marginal product of labor A worker's contribution to overall firm profits or output.

---

[2] For individuals, decisions about the amount of labor to supply involve trading off labor and leisure. As wages increase, the income effect induces workers to work more hours, but the substitution effect puts negative pressure on hours of work because the worker is wealthier and leisure is a normal good. At lower levels of labor supply, the income effect outweighs the substitution effect and the labor supply curve is upward-sloping. At high hours of work the substitution effect can dominate, causing the labor supply curve to bend backward.

In Chapter 7, we discussed how inputs to the education production function exhibit diminishing marginal productivity. As an input to education, teachers are no different: Holding all other inputs constant, the added gain in student achievement from hiring another teacher will be greater when class size is large than when class size is small. A core feature of any competitive labor market is that workers will be paid the value of their marginal product. This means that teachers will be hired until their wage is equal to the value of the education outcomes they produce in the school. The demand for teachers is downward sloping because as more teachers are hired, their marginal product will be lower, which lowers the wage that the school is willing to offer.

Several factors shift the demand for teachers:

1. **The number of students in a district.** If there is population growth with lots of young children, more teachers will be needed.
2. **The level of available resources and the incomes of families in the district.** When districts face budget cutbacks, demand for teachers typically falls.
3. **The education production function and the state of knowledge about how teachers affect students.** If there is an innovation that makes teachers more effective, resources should be shifted from other inputs such as administrators to hiring more teachers.

What factors shift the supply of teachers? Perhaps the most important factor affecting the supply of teachers is the outside option available to potential teachers. Wages and working conditions in other occupations affect whether young people choose to enter the teaching profession. The size of the cohort of recent college graduates also affects the supply of teachers.

In a competitive labor market in which workers are paid the value of their marginal product, a more productive worker will command a higher wage, while a less productive worker will be paid a lower wage. Teachers, however, tend to face a salary schedule that does not vary with individual productivity. Most school districts have a fixed salary schedule that varies only with respect to two characteristics: years of experience and level of education. As an example, Figure 12.2 shows the salary schedule for a New York City public school teacher by whether she has a bachelor's degree (BA) or a

Figure 12.2 Salary Program for New York City Teachers Who Begin with No Prior Teaching Experience

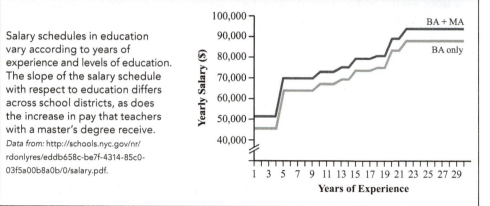

Salary schedules in education vary according to years of experience and levels of education. The slope of the salary schedule with respect to education differs across school districts, as does the increase in pay that teachers with a master's degree receive.

Data from: http://schools.nyc.gov/nr/rdonlyres/eddb658c-be7f-4314-85c0-03f5a00b8a0b/0/salary.pdf.

master's degree (MA) and by years of experience. The salary increases both with years of teaching experience and with the educational attainment of the teacher. Teachers move along each experience profile as they gain experience, and teachers with only a BA can jump up to the higher salary schedule by obtaining the more advanced degree.

Although teacher salary schedules are nearly universal in terms of having a return to experience and a return to a master's degree, the shape of the return to experience and the size of the wage increase from earning an advanced degree can vary considerably across districts. For example, some districts may have higher starting salaries but lower experience-based increases, while others may backload teacher pay toward the end of a career.

That teacher wages vary only with experience and education level means that schools typically are unable to pay teachers differently depending on what they teach. This feature of teacher labor markets contributes to teacher shortages (and in some cases surpluses). When teachers differ in their specific skills and in turn their potential employment options outside of teaching, we predict that their wages should differ as well. This variation in teacher wages does not occur with the type of single-scale salary structure shown in Figure 12.2.

Consider the cases of someone prepared to teach math in high school and someone prepared to teach in the elementary grades. These two teachers would face very different labor market options if they chose not to teach: the math teacher might have options as an accountant or a banker, which are relatively high-paying professions, while the elementary teacher might have options as a social worker or an editor, which typically pay less than teaching. Figure 12.3 illustrates such circumstances. The left panel shows supply and demand curves for math teachers. While the wage that equilibrates supply and demand is W^M, the district must pay the single salary wage. At this wage, the supply of math teachers (E^S) is less than the demand for math teachers (E^D). The exact opposite situation occurs for elementary school teachers. Because in this example they have a set of skills that are less in demand in the labor market, they are paid above their market wage. The result is a

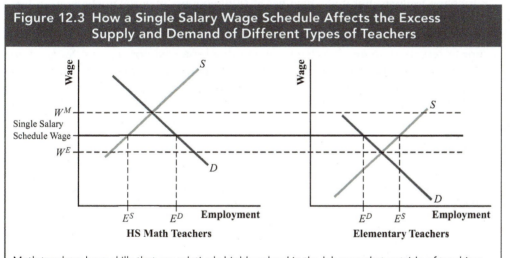

Figure 12.3 How a Single Salary Wage Schedule Affects the Excess Supply and Demand of Different Types of Teachers

Math teachers have skills that are relatively highly valued in the labor market outside of teaching. With a single salary offered for all teachers, math teachers are paid less than their market wage (W^M), while elementary school teachers are paid more than their market wage (W^E). As a result, there is an excess supply of elementary teachers and an excess demand for math teachers.

shortage of math teachers and an excess supply of elementary school teachers at the single wage offered by the district.

The fact that teacher wage schedules are not tied to performance or demand for particular subjects is a feature of teacher labor markets that make them differ substantially from competitive labor markets in the commercial sector. With a single-scale salary structure, poorly performing teachers earn the same as very productive teachers with the same experience and education level in the same district. However, on average, teacher contracts such as the one shown in Figure 12.2 *could* more generously reward more productive teachers. If there are positive effects of MA degree receipt and experience on teacher productivity, workers with these attributes should be paid more. Prior work on these questions has found a strong link between early career teacher experience and both value-added and future earnings of students.[3] We therefore would expect wages to increase with teacher experience, but it remains an open question whether the exact shape of the earnings–experience profile in school districts matches the productivity–experience relationship of teachers. In contrast, there is no evidence that teachers with advanced degrees are of higher productivity (Rivkin, Hanushek, & Kain, 2005).

Compensating Differentials

compensating differential
The wage increase necessary to compensate a worker for taking a job with an attribute he does not like.

Workers care about more than just wages when they select a job. There are pecuniary benefits, such as health insurance and pensions, as well as nonpecuniary factors, such as how pleasant or unpleasant it is to work in a given job. For teachers, there are a lot of nonpecuniary benefits, including how well-behaved the students are, how easy the students are to teach, class size, instructional time, the quality of the school administration, school facilities, and the community in which teachers live. The extent to which teachers value each of these amenities is called a **compensating differential**. A compensating differential is the wage increase necessary to compensate a worker for taking a job with an attribute he does not like. Note that the value placed on particular job characterstics will likely vary across individuals. For example, a teacher may not want to work in an old school with crumbling facilities. But if you paid her $5,000 more per year, she might agree to teach there. In this case, her compensating differential for teaching in this school is $5,000.

That teacher salaries tend not to differ across schools in a district is a core contributor to teacher shortages in schools serving disadvantaged populations. Such schools tend to be more difficult to work in, and students in these schools face many disadvantages that make them more challenging to teach. Without paying teachers more to work in these schools, it is hard to find a sufficient number of teachers. Effectively, compensating differentials shift the teacher labor supply curve, changing the amount of labor teachers are willing to supply at a given wage.

12.2 Who Becomes a Teacher, and Does It Matter?

The Roy Model and Occupational Choice

Now that we have gone over the basics of supply and demand in teacher labor markets, we can consider who decides to become a teacher. This is a question of fundamental

---

[3] See Rivkin, Hanushek, and Kain (2005), Rockoff (2004), Clotfelter, Ladd, and Vigdor (2007, 2010), Wiswall (2013), and Chetty, Friedman, and Rockoff (2014).

importance, because as shown in Chapter 9, teacher quality is a major input into education production. Without modeling how people make the decision to go into the teaching profession, it is almost impossible to design policies that will effectively attract the most capable teachers. People differ in their abilities for different professions and in their preferences over occupations, and they face wage rates that vary across labor markets. There also are costs to entering certain occupations: Some careers require many years of specialized training, including graduate education, while other jobs have fewer barriers to entry. These factors all interact to drive individuals' occupational decisions.

To see this point, consider two workers, Angela and Renee. They both are interested in teaching as a profession but differ in terms of their skill. Angela has a large amount of skill that is valued in the labor market, such as critical thinking and analytical and mathematical ability. Renee has fewer such skills. Both Angela and Renee need to decide whether to choose teaching or an alternative profession, such as law or medicine. Because teacher salaries do not vary with their marginal product of labor, there is a very low return to skill among teachers: The teaching profession does not reward Angela's skills with a higher salary. The same is not true in these other professions, where those with the highest skill levels make considerably more than less-skilled workers.

The result of this difference across professions is that Renee will become a teacher and Angela will go into another high-skilled profession. Although both workers have similar preferences, the labor market they face leads them to make different choices. Consider what this means for the average skill level of teachers. Because the return to skill is so high outside of teaching, the most-skilled workers will choose other professions, and the less-skilled workers will become teachers. Thus, the return to skill across professions can have large impacts on the quality of the teacher labor market.

The idea that workers select occupations based on their individual skills and the characteristics of the labor market was originally formulated by Roy (1951).[4] The *Roy model*, as it has come to be called, remains the primary way economists think about and model occupational choices (as well as education and immigration decisions). Recall that a foundation of economic models is that people make decisions to maximize their utility. The Roy model is no different: workers differ in their skills, jobs differ in their returns to skills, and workers choose the job in which their relative rewards will be the greatest. The insights that come from this model guide our thinking about who decides to become a teacher.

The main intuition of the Roy model can be gleaned by considering a worker's choice between two professions, teaching and banking. Ignoring for a moment the fact that individuals may have different preferences over the different professions, as some people may feel a particular calling, or aversion, to teaching (or banking), the decision over which profession to join will be based on the relative wages the worker expects to earn. The Roy model predicts that each individual's decision about whether to be a teacher or a banker is based on three factors:

1. Average wages of bankers versus teachers
2. The return to skill in both professions
3. The **complementarity of skills** in the two professions

complementarity of skills (across occupations) The extent to which occupation-specific skill or ability in one occupation is positively correlated with occupation-specific skill or ability in another occupation.

---

[4] See Borjas (1987) for a mathematical formulation of the Roy model.

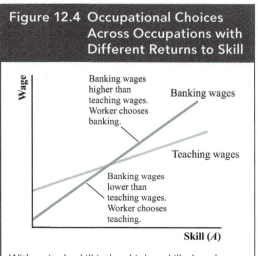

Figure 12.4 Occupational Choices Across Occupations with Different Returns to Skill

With a single skill index, higher-skilled workers will earn more in banking than in teaching, while lower-skilled workers will earn more as teachers than as bankers. This results from the fact that teaching and banking have the same average wage, but the return to skill is much higher in banking than in teaching.

The first condition is perhaps the most straightforward. If bankers make a lot more on average than teachers, workers will be much more likely to select into banking. It is not just the average wage that matters. In a labor market in which workers have different abilities that make them more or less productive, the return to skill in each profession also drives behavior. This was illustrated by the example of Angela and Renee: The banking profession provided a higher return to Angela's skill than did teaching, which led her to not become a teacher. For Renee, the return to teaching was higher than the return to banking, which drove her to become a teacher. This selection pattern can hold true even if the average wages in the two professions are identical.

Figure 12.4 illustrates occupational decisions by worker ability when teaching and banking have the same average wage but banking has a higher return to skill. As the figure demonstrates, such a wage structure will lead lower-ability workers to select into teaching and higher-ability workers to select into banking. This is completely driven by the fact that the benefit to a high-ability worker of becoming a banker is very high, as wages increase strongly with ability. In the teaching profession, wages vary much less with ability. This makes teaching a more lucrative career choice for lower-ability workers and banking the better option for high-ability workers. The critical implication of this model is that the wage premium for skill in different professions will have important consequences for the skill distribution of workers who join each profession.

At this point, you may have noticed that we are treating all worker skill (A) as the same. It could be the case that the skills that make one a good teacher are not skills that make one good at banking. Teaching is very different from banking, after all, and there may be workers who are high-ability teachers and low-ability bankers and vice versa. The extent to which skills are equally important in each occupation is called the complementarity of skills across occupations. In this example, teaching skill and banking skill are perfect complements. Thus, we could consider only one measure of worker ability. Now, we can allow for a teacher-specific skill level (A_t) and a banking-specific skill level (A_b).

Figure 12.5 shows occupational choices among workers as a function of A_t and A_b when average wages and the return to occupation-specific skills are identical for teaching and banking. The decision rule in this example is simple: workers will select into teaching if $A_t > A_b$ (above the 45-degree line) and will select into banking if $A_b > A_t$ (below the 45-degree line). The figure shows two cases that differ in terms of how A_b and A_t covary among workers. In panel A, A_b and A_t are negatively correlated, so that those with high teaching aptitude have low banking aptitude. In panel B, teaching and banking skills are positively correlated. At low overall skill levels, $A_t > A_b$ and workers select into teaching. At higher overall skill levels, this relationship switches and workers select into banking. Here, more highly skilled workers have more of both skill levels, but A_b grows faster than A_t, which leads to the highest-skilled workers becoming bankers.

In reality, all three factors in the Roy model are relevant simultaneously. Professions differ in terms of average wages and in the return to skill, and workers differ in their occupation-specific skill levels. Workers also can differ dramatically in their preferences (which may be correlated with their skill levels). Some people really want to be teachers, and some are driven to own their own business or to brew beer for a living. Such preferences unquestionably play a role in occupation choices, but we tend not to focus on them because they are very hard to influence with public policy.

What are the implications of this model for selection into the teaching profession? The pay structure for teachers is very compressed because it often is determined by a fixed scale. That is, there is less difference between the highest- and lowest-paid teachers than there is between the highest- and lowest-paid workers in other high-skilled professions. This feature is illustrated in Table 12.1. The table shows the mean and standard deviation of earnings for K–12 teachers as well as several other high-skilled professions: consultant, computer programmer, engineer, accountant, lawyer, and doctor. Aside from engineers and accountants, the standard deviation of teacher wages is substantially below that in all of these other professions. This is true particularly for lawyers and doctors, the two most prevalent high-skilled occupations in the data aside from teaching.

As Figure 12.4 shows, when one profession has a compressed wage schedule and a low return to skill, this will serve to induce lower-skilled workers to select into that profession at higher rates. Table 12.1 demonstrates that teaching has a relatively compressed wage distribution, which suggests that less-skilled workers might be more attracted to teaching than to other professions that require at least a college degree. Data from a variety of sources and time periods suggest that this is the case. Using data from the Survey of Recent College Graduates, a nationally representative survey conducted by the National Science Foundation, Hoxby and Leigh (2004) classify teachers by the average SAT score of the college from which they graduate. Their data show that:

- 36% of teachers come from the bottom quartile of colleges in the SAT distribution.
- 5% come from the top 15 percentiles of colleges in the SAT distribution.
- 1% of teachers come from the top 5 percentiles of colleges in the SAT distribution.

Consistent with these results, among those who report having considered entering teaching, those with higher college entrance exam scores and who attend more selective colleges are less likely to actually join the teaching profession (Goldhaber & Liu, 2003). What's more, college selectivity and college entrance exams are not correlated with wages for teachers, while they are strongly positively correlated with wages in other occupations. Together with the results from Hoxby and Leigh, these estimates suggest that there is a lower return to skill in the teaching profession and that those

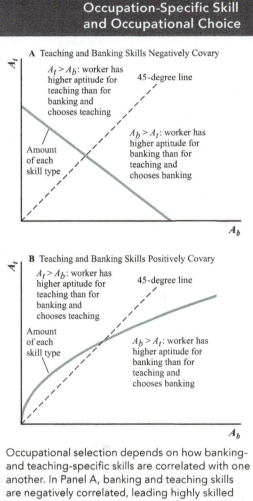

Figure 12.5 The Relationship Between Occupation-Specific Skill and Occupational Choice

A Teaching and Banking Skills Negatively Covary

$A_t > A_b$: worker has higher aptitude for teaching than for banking and chooses teaching

45-degree line

Amount of each skill type

$A_b > A_t$: worker has higher aptitude for banking than for teaching and chooses banking

A_b

B Teaching and Banking Skills Positively Covary

$A_t > A_b$: worker has higher aptitude for teaching than for banking and chooses teaching

45-degree line

Amount of each skill type

$A_b > A_t$: worker has higher aptitude for banking than for teaching and chooses banking

A_b

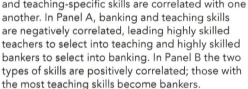

Occupational selection depends on how banking- and teaching-specific skills are correlated with one another. In Panel A, banking and teaching skills are negatively correlated, leading highly skilled teachers to select into teaching and highly skilled bankers to select into banking. In Panel B the two types of skills are positively correlated; those with the most teaching skills become bankers.

Table 12.1 Mean and Standard Deviation of Hourly Wages for Various High-Skilled Professions (2011–2012, real 2012 dollars)		
Occupation	Mean	Standard Deviation
K–12 teacher	32.28	14.88
Consultant	35.11	15.47
Computer programmer	38.33	15.20
Engineer	34.25	14.36
Accountant	30.27	14.31
Lawyer	41.62	16.80
Doctor	40.37	21.43

Data from: 2011 and 2012 Current Population Survey.

being drawn into teaching are drawn disproportionately from less selective and less elite schools.[5] These findings are consistent with the predictions of the Roy model.

To the extent that teachers who graduate from less selective schools and who have lower measured academic ability have lower teaching aptitude, it suggests that the workers who would be the most productive teachers are not selecting into the teaching profession. This is not guaranteed to be true, because many of the most selective postsecondary schools do not have teaching programs, and less selective schools overall may have high-quality teacher training programs. As well, if teacher-specific skill is sufficiently different from the skills needed to do other professions that highly educated workers do (like banking, medicine, law, and engineering), then the lower quality of colleges from which teachers tend to graduate may be less of a concern for the productivity of the teacher workforce. This would be the case especially if those with higher teaching aptitude *chose* these less selective schools because of their teaching programs. Indeed, researchers have not found a relationship between measures of college quality and calculated teacher value-added.[6] The data are clear that teachers are much less likely to come from elite colleges and universities, but to date there is little evidence that this one characteristic of selection into teaching is meaningfully related to measured teacher productivity.

Changes in the Composition of Teachers over Time

The composition of the teacher labor force has changed markedly over the past 40 years. There is much evidence from several data sources to support this contention. In one of the most influential research papers to examine the changes in the composition of teachers over time, Corcoran, Evans, and Schwab (2004) painstakingly combine five longitudinal datasets that follow five cohorts of high school graduates from 1957 to

---

[5] More research using the NLS72 (Manski, 1987), HS&B (Hanushek & Pace, 1995), and high school graduates in Missouri (Podgursky, Monroe, & Watson, 2004) shows consistently that college students with higher measured academic aptitude are far less likely to go into the teaching profession. See Appendix A for a description of the NLS72 and HS&B datasets.

[6] Research papers that examine the relationship between teacher value-added and the quality of the college a teacher attended are Aaronson, Barrow, and Sander (2007) and Rockoff et al. (2011).

1992. Each longitudinal survey includes aptitude tests that were administered in high school, and the respondents were followed as they transitioned to college and then into the workforce. This makes it possible to examine what types of individuals are selecting into the teaching profession and how this has changed over time.

There are three important findings from this study:

1. Those who go into teaching have lower high school test scores than college graduates overall, scoring about 0.1–0.2 standard deviations lower.
2. Measured academic aptitude among teachers has dropped considerably over time: There was a 23% decline in the high school test scores of teachers across the cohorts examined in this study.
3. Much of the decline is due to reductions in women in the top test score decile who go on to become teachers.

Several studies have corroborated these findings. For one, the quality of schools from which entering teachers graduate has declined considerably over time (Hoxby & Leigh, 2004). In 1963, 17% of teachers came from colleges in the top 15 percentiles of the SAT distribution, and 16% came from the bottom 25% of SAT score schools. As discussed previously, by 2000 the proportion coming from the top schools had dropped to 5% and the proportion coming from the bottom schools had increased to 36%. Second, teachers in the 1960s were as likely to have high IQ scores as lower IQ scores. By the 1980s, those with lower IQ scores were far more likely to enter teaching than their high-IQ counterparts (Murnane et al., 1991).

In short, there is ample evidence that the academic aptitude of teachers has fallen since the 1960s. What is less clear is how these changes might translate into the ability of teachers to increase students' knowledge and skills. The evidence is mixed as to whether teacher test scores translate into higher teacher performance.[7] It therefore is still an open question as to whether the decline in the test scores of people entering teaching is evidence of reductions in teacher quality.

What has caused this shift? We focus on two very important trends in labor markets that have occurred over this period:[8]

1. The labor market opportunities for women have changed.
2. The return to skill in most professions that require at least a college degree has grown, while teaching has exhibited increasing pay compression.

In the 1960s, job opportunities for women were extremely limited, with a majority of highly educated women going into either teaching or nursing. Since that time, reductions in discrimination in labor markets and educational institutions have led to an enormous expansion in the types of fields and occupations women select. Figure 12.6 shows the share of men in several high-skilled occupations from 1979 to 2012 among workers aged 25–34. Except for computer programmers,

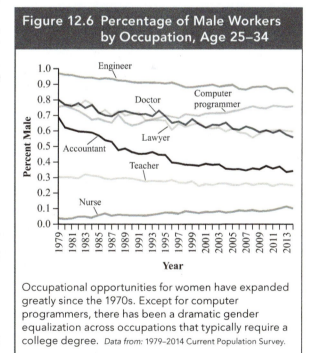

Figure 12.6 Percentage of Male Workers by Occupation, Age 25–34

Occupational opportunities for women have expanded greatly since the 1970s. Except for computer programmers, there has been a dramatic gender equalization across occupations that typically require a college degree. *Data from:* 1979–2014 Current Population Survey.

---

[7] Rockoff et al. (2011) find no effect, while Ehrenberg and Brewer (1995) and Ferguson and Ladd (1996) show a positive relationship between teacher test scores and student performance.
[8] A detailed discussion of these trends and their causes can be found in Eide, Goldhaber, and Brewer (2004).

Figure 12.7 Ratio of High-Skilled Professions' Median Wages to Teachers' Median Wages, Age 25–34

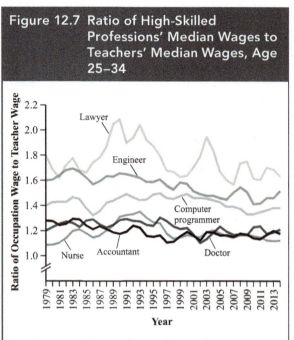

A ratio greater than 1 indicates that median wages are higher in the given profession than median wages in teaching. This is the case for all of the occupations shown. For all but accountants, median wages have been constant over time relative to median teacher wages. *Data from: 1979–2014 Current Population Survey.*

"I don't want an apple, Danny—do you have any money?"

Michael Maslin The New Yorker Collection/The Cartoon Bank

there has been dramatic gender equalization across occupations that typically require a college degree. For example, among both doctors and lawyers, the percent male dropped from 80% to virtual gender parity over this period. Although engineering remains male-dominated, there has been a trend of increasing gender parity over time in this field as well. This figure highlights the fact that the occupational opportunities for women have expanded greatly since the 1970s.

Changes in the return to skill and the compression of teacher wages also are important labor market trends that affect the changing composition of teachers. High-skilled women are increasingly selecting into professions with high pay and high returns to skill. Figure 12.7 shows the trends in the ratio of median wages in the professions shown in Figure 12.6 relative to median teacher wages. A ratio greater than 1 indicates that median wages are higher in this profession than in teaching; this is the case for all of the skilled occupations considered. Furthermore, for all but engineers, median wages have been relatively constant over time relative to median teacher wages.

A focus on median wages might miss important changes at the top of the wage distribution, which should have more influence on the decisions of high-skilled workers. As Table 12.1 shows, the wage variance in these occupations is, for the most part, higher than in teaching, which likely reflects the higher return to skill. In Figure 12.8, we show trends in the ratio of the 75th percentile of the wage distribution for each occupation to the 75th percentile of the teacher wage distribution. The patterns in Figure 12.8 are even starker than in Figure 12.7: top wages are much higher for all professions listed than among teachers, and particularly for lawyers relative wages have increased substantially over time. The Roy model predicts that increases in labor market opportunities of high-skilled women in occupations with high returns to skill should lead to reductions in the highest-skilled women selecting into teaching. This is exactly what the data show is happening.

Hoxby and Leigh (2004) provide a direct assessment of these two forces on the change in the composition of the teacher workforce. They use changes in public sector union laws, which we discuss in detail in Section 12.3, as a natural experiment that generates variation in pay compression in the education sector. The idea behind this approach is that as teachers unions have grown, they have compressed the wage distribution for teachers, and they have done so in an era when the returns to skill were growing in other occupations.

Hoxby and Leigh find evidence that workers are highly sensitive to relative pay both within teaching and across teaching and other occupations. Consistent with the Roy model, their evidence suggests that compression of pay in teaching

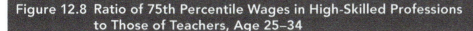

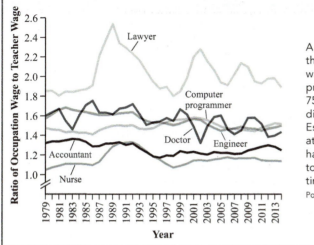

Figure 12.8 Ratio of 75th Percentile Wages in High-Skilled Professions to Those of Teachers, Age 25–34

A ratio greater than 1 indicates that the 75th percentile of the wage distribution in the given profession is higher than the 75th percentile of the wage distribution in teaching. Especially for lawyers, earnings at the top of the distribution have gone up with respect to top-earning teachers over time. *Data from:* 1979–2014 Current Population Survey.

has led to a rise in the share of workers going into teaching from less selective colleges and a decline in those from the highest-quality schools becoming teachers. They also show that the reduction in the male–female wage gaps in other occupations, due in large part to reductions in discriminatory labor practices over time, leads the most academically elite women to go into nonteaching professions. While both factors are important in explaining changes in teacher composition, they find the former is empirically larger because of the large amount of pay compression in teaching from the 1960s to 2000. On the whole, the Roy model appears to do a very good job of predicting how and why the composition of teachers has changed over time.

DEEP DIVE: The Link Between Teacher Compensation and Student Outcomes

There is considerable empirical evidence to support the predictions of the Roy model that changes in the wages of teachers relative to other high-skilled professions influence the types of workers who go into teaching. It is natural to ask whether students in districts that pay teachers particularly well relative to other professions requiring a college degree also have higher levels of achievement.

A natural approach to measure the effect of teacher wages on student performance is to examine how differences in teacher wages across school districts relate to cross-district differences in student academic performance. As long as there are no unobservable differences between districts that are correlated with both teacher wages and student performance, a comparison of student achievement in high- and low-wage districts will yield a measure of the wage effect. This estimation approach has been used extensively in the past, and the results suggest a weak link, at best, between teachers' wages and students' outcomes. This is surprising, as one would expect higher wages to attract higher-quality teachers and thus to improve student outcomes.

But there are likely many differences between districts beyond wages: nonpecuniary job characteristics and alternative job opportunities also differ across districts. That is, some districts provide more pleasant working environments, and some are located in areas that have more alternative job opportunities for teachers than do others. These factors both influence the relative attractiveness of going into teaching, and they are likely to be correlated with teacher wages. This correlation comes from the fact that in areas with better nonteaching job opportunities, teachers' wages will have to be higher. Furthermore, districts that offer better nonpecuniary compensation (such as more class prep time and smaller classes) likely can offer lower wages because of compensating differentials. Failure to account for these factors will lead to a downward bias of the estimated wage effect.

To overcome these problems, Susanna Loeb and Marianne Page (2000) proposed an empirical method that incorporates nonpecuniary job characteristics and alternative job opportunities into the estimation approach. Rather than relying on cross-district variation in teacher wages, their method estimates the effect of teacher wages on student achievement by relating *changes* in relative salaries in an area (measured as the ratio of the average teacher wages to the average nonteacher wages among college graduates) to changes in student academic outcomes in the same areas. They accomplish this by employing state fixed effects, which also hold constant fixed differences across states in nonpecuniary job benefits. In this way, they can isolate variation in the relative attractiveness of teaching, as measured by relative wages of college graduates in a state, without having to worry about biases driven by differences in cross-state labor market composition or nonpecuniary job factors for teachers.

The authors rely on state-level panel data drawn from the 1960 to 1990 Public Use Microdata Samples from the U.S. Census. They restrict their sample to individuals between the ages of 20 and 64, and they exclude all individuals who worked less than 26 weeks during the year. Unfortunately, reliable and consistent information on test score performance is not available for this period, so they use information on high school dropout and college enrollment rates to measure student outcomes.

Loeb and Page first illustrate that there is no evidence of a relationship between teacher wages and student outcomes if one relies solely on cross-state variation in teacher salaries. Thus, they can replicate the findings of the previous literature, an important first step in their analysis. They then employ their preferred model, which controls for nonwage attributes and alternative job opportunities through the use of state fixed effects. The results from this approach suggest a clear link between teacher salaries and student outcomes: a 10% increase in teacher wages is associated with a 3–4 percentage point reduction in the high school dropout rate and a 2 percentage point increase in college enrollment. The findings of this paper suggest strongly that student academic performance is tied to teachers' wages, which highlights the importance of understanding the labor market for teachers and what policies can be used to attract the most productive teachers into the teaching profession.

Teacher Mobility over the Career Cycle

How teachers sort across school districts can have profound effects on educational disparities across schools. To underscore this point, consider what would happen if wealthy school districts paid their teachers more than poor districts. Most teachers would want to work in the higher-paying district. Thus, the wealthy school district would get its choice of teachers, and high-quality teachers in poorer districts would be very likely to transfer to wealthier districts over the course of their career.

In fact, this story is highly consistent with the data. In their seminal analysis of teacher sorting patterns over their careers, Lankford, Loeb, and Wyckoff (2002) examine the career trajectories of the universe of teachers in New York State from 1984 through 2000. First, they show that there is massive inequity in the characteristics of teachers across schools in the state. Some schools have highly qualified teachers, as measured by their experience levels, whether they have an advanced degree, whether they failed the state certification exam, and whether they graduated from a top-ranked college. Second, they show that most of this variation is occurring across both school districts and schools *within* each of the six broad regions of New York State. This finding suggests that these inequities are not due to differences in the characteristics of teachers across regions in New York but rather reflect teacher sorting within region. Their data demonstrate that these differences across schools in the qualifications of teachers are highly related to the wealth and urbanicity of the school district. In virtually every region of New York State, urban schools, compared with suburban schools, have a higher percentage of inexperienced teachers, a higher proportion who have failed a certification test, and a lower proportion who graduated from a very competitive college. What's more, these same differences occur across student characteristics, with poor and nonwhite students being much more likely to be in schools with less qualified teachers.

The mobility of teachers over their career exacerbates these inequalities. Loeb and Wyckoff (2002) follow the 1993 cohort of entering teachers over a five-year period and are able to see who moves across schools and districts. Teacher mobility is high: 18% of teachers entering in 1993 switch schools within a district over the first five years of their career and another 11% switch districts. They find as well that the urban and poorer schools have much higher turnover than suburban schools, and the teachers who move districts and schools tend to have better qualifications than those who stay. Together, this evidence points to the more highly qualified teachers leaving poor urban districts to go to wealthier suburban districts over time. Indeed, this interpretation is consistent with the findings in Jepsen and Rivkin (2009) discussed in Chapter 9. In response to a small-class-size requirement in California, they show that poor schools were more likely to hire novice teachers with worse qualifications. The implication is that the large demand increase for teachers led many of the most qualified teachers in urban schools to move to suburban areas. The evidence in Lankford, Loeb, and Wyckoff suggests that such mobility occurs broadly and systematically among teachers over the course of their working life.

A similar analysis was conducted in Texas (Hanushek, Kain, & Rivkin, 2004). Using administrative data on teachers and students, researchers can track teachers over time and link them to the characteristics of the students in the schools in which they work.[9] The findings from this study show that teachers are much more likely to leave urban districts for suburban ones, and those teachers tend to go from schools that are higher in minority populations and lower in income to ones that are wealthier and have a higher proportion of White students. While there is a modest role for teacher salaries, student demographic characteristics and academic achievement have the most explanatory power in predicting teacher mobility.

Further evidence consistent with the difficulty of urban and low-income schools to attract and keep highly qualified teachers comes from the comparison of teacher value-added across poor and nonpoor schools (Sass et al., 2012). Using detailed student-level data from North Carolina and Florida, this research shows that teacher value-added in schools that serve a high proportion of poor students is lower on average and is more variable than teacher value-added in other schools. These differences are in large part due to the higher prevalence of teachers with very low value-added in high-poverty schools. There also is a lower return to teacher experience in high-poverty schools. This result is consistent with the most productive teachers moving out of these schools over the course of their career, such that the experienced teachers remaining in high-poverty schools are of lower productivity on average. However, it also could be the case that experience gained in very difficult educational environments may be of lower value.

In addition to relatively high rates of moving across schools or districts, the teaching profession exhibits high rates of exit. Many teachers, especially early in their career, leave teaching for other professions. For example, in New York over 30% of new teachers entering in 1993 were no longer teaching in New York State by 1998 (Lankford,

---

[9] The Texas School Project data are described in more detail in Appendix A of this book.

Loeb, and Wyckoff, 2002). In their study of public school teachers in Texas, Hanushek, Kain, and Rivkin (2004) find lower but still substantial exit rates, on the order of 9% for teachers with five years of experience or less. As with mobility across schools, teachers are more likely to exit when they begin their career in urban schools and when they are in a school with a higher minority share or with students who perform lower on standardized tests.

The high turnover rate among teachers may be harmful or beneficial for overall quality, depending on which teachers exit. In New York State, teachers who exit teaching are more likely to have graduated from a competitive college and are slightly less likely to have failed a teacher certification exam than teachers who remain in their school. In North Carolina, those who leave the teaching profession tend to have higher certification exam scores than those who remain, as well (Murnane et al., 1991). This is suggestive evidence that teachers with better qualifications are more likely to exit.

The weak link between teacher observable characteristics (such as test scores and college quality) and student achievement makes it important to directly assess the relationship between measured teacher productivity (i.e., value-added) and attrition from teaching. Two studies that have addressed this question using data from Washington State and from North Carolina both show that, on the whole, teacher value-added is negatively correlated with attrition:[10] the highest value-added teachers are the most likely to stay in teaching. Their results suggest that despite the propensity for teachers with better observed qualifications to exit teaching, these are not, on average, the highest value-added teachers.

12.3 Teachers Unions

What Are Teachers Unions?

collective bargaining The process by which a union negotiates a labor contract with an employer. For teachers, their union collectively negotiates their contract with the school district in which they work.

Unions are one of the most prominent features of teacher labor markets in the United States. The main function of teachers unions is to engage in **collective bargaining** with the school district to decide on teacher compensation (wages, health care, pension plans) as well as workplace practices and grievance rules. Collective bargaining refers to the negotiation process that takes place between employee union representatives and their employers to determine a mutually agreed upon employment contract. About 60% of teachers in the United States are covered by a collectively bargained contract with the district (Frandsen, 2016). As teachers are public employees, their right to collectively bargain is determined by state law. All but seven states have laws that either allow teachers to collectively bargain or that require a district to bargain with teachers if they are unionized. Of the remaining seven states, four outlaw teacher collective bargaining altogether, and the remainder have no regulations regarding teacher bargaining.[11]

Teachers differ from unionized workers in other sectors, such as manufacturing and service. The main difference is that teachers tend to work in the public sector,

---

[10] Krieg (2006) studies Washington State, while Goldhaber, Gross, and Player (2011) examine North Carolina.

[11] The seven states that do not allow for collective bargaining among teachers are Alabama, Georgia, North Carolina, and Virginia (collective bargaining prohibited) and Mississippi, Missouri, and Wyoming (no public sector collective bargaining law).

and their labor therefore provides a public service. Other public sector unions include firefighters, police officers, and in some cases, nurses. These workers are very different from a worker in a car plant or a hotel, who works for a private company, because the public sector workers are needed on a day-to-day basis for our society to function. If police officers or firefighters strike even for a day, it would create a large threat to public safety. The same is not true for workers in a car manufacturing plant, who typically are members of a private sector union. While long-run strikes can have negative consequences for the company they work for and for the car industry, the harm to public safety is much lower.

Another key difference between private and public sector unions is that private industries can shut down or move their operations. Public schools, police stations, and fire stations do not have this option: by design they serve a local area, and they cannot shut down in the same way a private firm can. Some argue that this feature of the public sector makes unionization inappropriate for public sector workers, since public sector employers have no option but to operate in the local labor market in which they find themselves. However, public sector unions remain quite strong in the United States. In the past several decades, there has been a precipitous decline in private sector unionization. As a result, unionization and collective bargaining in the United States is increasingly a public sector phenomenon. Because they are the largest group of public sector workers, teachers also are the single largest set of workers engaged in collective bargaining.

A Brief History of the Teacher Unionization and Collective Bargaining Movement

Today, teachers unions and collective bargaining are synonymous in all but the few states that do not allow teacher collective bargaining. This was not always the case. Until the 1960s and 1970s, collective bargaining was almost nonexistent among teachers. While a few unions in large districts, such as New York City, Chicago, and Detroit, attempted collective bargaining, district administrators and school boards had little reason to take the negotiations seriously. This led to a process that was described by many teachers as "collective begging," rather than collective bargaining, and as a result very few districts had a negotiated contract as of 1960 (Murphy, 1990). Although widespread collective bargaining is a fairly recent phenomenon in U.S. education, the existence of professional teachers unions is not. Loose organizations of teachers have been around since the late nineteenth century. Today, all local teachers unions are affiliated with one of two national organizations: the National Education Association (NEA) and the American Federation of Teachers (AFT). The NEA was established in 1857, four years before the Civil War, while the AFT began in 1916 in Chicago. In the beginning, teachers unions were simply professional organizations that advocated for better working conditions for teachers, higher pay, and more government funding, especially from the federal government in a time when the federal government had only a minor role in financing K–12 education. These advocacy activities did little to generate contracts between teachers and school districts that established the terms of compensation, the conditions under which a teacher could be fired, and the job expectations for teachers.

After World War II ended in 1945, the coalescing of several forces led to a persistent increase in the desire of teachers to unionize and to engage in collective bargaining. Ultimately these forces, listed below, led to the high levels of unionization we see today.

- A growing desire for academic freedom for teachers in the wake of anti-Communist firings in the 1940s and 1950s
- The low wage growth for teachers relative to other professions, driven by the lack of resources for public schooling to handle the large number of children born during the baby boom
- The reluctance of the federal government to provide funding for education
- The persistence of work practices that many workers found onerous, including strong restrictions on female teachers' lives outside of school and arbitrary human resource practices

Teachers' displeasure with compensation levels and perceived unfair work practices was likely the dominant driver of the unionization movement. The post–World War II baby boom caught the education system off guard, and it struggled to find the resources necessary to educate the resulting influx of children. Efforts by teachers unions to advocate for more federal funds for K–12 education were largely unsuccessful, and in the ensuing budget crunch teacher pay suffered significantly. In contrast, the postwar boom led to significant increases in wages in other industries, which made teaching less and less attractive to highly skilled workers. The stagnation in teacher pay was a major impetus for teachers to collectively bargain.

As shown in Figure 12.6, teaching has historically been a female-dominated profession. However, school administration was male-dominated, and the work conditions faced by the largely female teaching staff often reflected the power dynamics associated with this gender difference. Prior to the 1960s, the principal had virtually complete control over the administration of a given school (Becker, 1953). Therefore, he was allowed to hire and fire teachers at will; he could set long work hours and mandate that teachers work on the weekend; and he could set restrictive rules for conduct outside the classroom.

Restrictive work rules, particularly for women, were an historical staple of K–12 education. For example, in the early twentieth century Chicago contracts stipulated that teachers must wear skirts of a certain length, could not receive "gentleman callers" more than three times a week, and must teach at least one Sunday school class. Teachers also were fired for attempting to organize or for joining a labor union (American Federation of Teachers, 2014). As of 1938, 60% of cities had a policy against hiring and keeping married women, and into the 1940s teachers were routinely fired for being married or for having a child (Murphy, 1990). Furthermore, teachers who were married found that their employers had considerable market power, as most women would not move far from their husband's job.

> **Quick Hint:** Failure of perfect competition because there is only one or a few employers in the market is called a monopsony.

The treatment of female teachers was part of a broader set of unfavorable work policies that were very unpopular with teachers. Elementary school teachers often were expected to teach without a break for the full school day; there was little preparatory time built into the day; and teachers were expected to participate in extra duties, such as being lunchroom monitors (Murphy, 1990). Teachers also disliked the fact that school start and end times were left up to the arbitrary decision of the principal and that administrators had unfettered access to their classrooms. In short, a strong desire arose among teachers to detail the expectations and duties in a contract, which is one of the primary goals of collective bargaining.

Despite the rise in the desire to engage in collective bargaining and the increasing membership in the NEA and AFT from the 1920s through the 1950s, collective bargaining was rare. The main factor holding it back was that aside from strikes, teachers had little leverage with which to force administrators to bargain in good faith. Beginning in the 1960s, however, states began passing public sector bargaining laws that drastically changed the landscape for teachers. These laws arose from a combination of increasingly pro-union views held by many Americans and strong political lobbying for bargaining rights by teachers and public sector workers more generally.

Public sector bargaining laws were typically of two types. The first was *meet and confer*, which allowed districts and teachers to collectively bargain if they so chose. The second type of law was a **duty-to-bargain law**. Duty-to-bargain laws legally require administrators to bargain with an elected teachers union if the teachers organize such a union. These laws were seen as highly pro-union insofar as they made it illegal for districts to refuse to bargain with teachers unions.

duty-to-bargain law
Employers' legal duty to engage in collective bargaining in good faith with their employees' elected union of choice.

Figure 12.9 shows the time pattern of types of union law adoption in the United States from 1955 to 1996. (Collective bargaining laws have been relatively stable since 1996.) In 1955, three states had meet-and-confer statutes that covered teachers, but the vast majority of states had no public sector collective bargaining laws that applied to teachers. In 1960, Wisconsin passed the first public sector duty-to-bargain law for teachers in the United States. Many states quickly followed suit, such that by 1970, 15 states had duty-to-bargain laws, and by 1980, 30 states had such laws. Since the 1980s, only four states explicitly outlaw teacher collective bargaining: Alabama, Georgia, North Carolina, and Virginia. Teachers in these states can (and do) join unions, but they are not allowed to collectively bargain with the school district. As a result of these legal changes, between 1960 and 1980 throughout the country there was a massive increase in teacher unionization for the purposes of collective bargaining. This increase led to the large proportion of K–12 teachers who today are covered by a collectively bargained contract.

The Structure of Union Contracts

What do teachers and districts bargain over? The specific details of the contracts vary, depending on the preferences of local teachers and administrators as well as on individual district budgets. Several researchers have done detailed work on this topic, collecting and characterizing some of the common components of teachers' contracts. In general, teachers unions bargain over several factors:[12]

- Wages
- Health insurance and retirement benefits

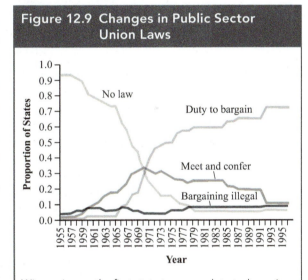

Figure 12.9 Changes in Public Sector Union Laws

Wisconsin was the first state to pass a duty-to-bargain law, in 1960, and by the early 1990s 33 states had passed such laws. Currently, four states explicitly outlaw teacher collective bargaining: Alabama, Georgia, North Carolina, and Virginia. The rest either have no law or allow but do not require that districts collectively bargain with teachers unions. *Data from:* NBER Public Sector Collective Bargaining Law Data Set. These data come from Freeman and Valletta (1988) and were updated by Kim Reuben to 1996. The data can be accessed at http://www.nber.org/publaw/.

---

[12] Much of this research can be found in Freeman (1986), Moe (2009), Strunk (2011), and West (2015).

- Hiring and firing policies
- Promotion policies
- Work rules detailing the hours they are required to be at work and to teach
- Class assignments
- Class sizes
- Nonteaching duties (such as cafeteria monitoring and extracurricular activities)

One of the most prominent issues over which teachers and districts negotiate is compensation and, in particular, salaries. In Section 12.1 we presented an example of a typical salary schedule that varies only with teacher experience and education. To what degree are unions responsible for this type of salary schedule? While we see clear evidence from observing union-negotiated contracts that these salary schedules are part of the negotiated compensation system, teachers in nonunion districts and in states in which collective bargaining is outlawed have similar salary schedules. In fact, most districts in the country had a single salary wage schedule prior to the introduction of collective bargaining in education (Murphy, 1990), which suggests that the exact structure of teachers' wages are not driven by collective bargaining. Unions may affect wage levels as well as how wages change with both experience and education level, but the fact that teachers' wages vary only with education and experience appears to be more of an historical artifact than an outcome of unionization.

Quick Hint: Total compensation includes salaries, but it also includes other benefits such as health insurance and pension payments.

Teachers unions also are focused on negotiating over human resource policies, delineating the steps necessary to fire a teacher, the requirements for teachers to receive tenure, rules regarding mandatory break times, the distribution of teacher's aides, and student–teacher ratios. Teacher *tenure* refers to a common component of many education systems: teachers who have a certain number of years of experience and have demonstrated sufficient ability are awarded a contract that protects them from losing their job without due process and sufficient evidence of poor performance or misconduct. In the K–12 education system, it usually takes teachers between 3 and 5 years to receive tenure, but since very few teachers are dismissed due to low productivity, virtually all teachers who remain employed in a district for that period of time will receive tenure. The strong job protections provided by union rules and tenure about teacher dismissal and the relative ease of receiving tenure are major sources of controversy over unions, as they make it very difficult for a principal to fire a low-performing teacher (Chubb & Moe, 1988). The view that these contract provisions harm student learning is summed up by Terry Moe, who writes in his book *Special Interest: Teachers Unions and America's Public Schools*:

But when it comes to bad teachers alone, the [New York City School] district is wasting millions of dollars because the rules it is required to follow in operating the schools—rules that are embedded in the local collective bargaining contract and state law—prevent it from quickly, easily and inexpensively removing these teachers from the classroom. Getting bad teachers out of the classroom is essential if kids are to be educated effectively. Yet the formal rules prevent it.—Moe, 2011, p. 3.

While unions make it harder to fire teachers, the job protections they provide their members could have important impacts on the overall characteristics of the teacher workforce. Unionized teaching jobs have relatively high levels of compensation as well as job security, which makes them desirable, and thus these job protections could lead more productive workers to decide to go into teaching. Unfortunately, there is scant evidence to support either position. In careful descriptive work, West (2015) conducted a survey of unionized and nonunionized school districts regarding human resource practices. She finds no difference in teacher dismissal rates across unionized and non-unionized districts, which is inconsistent with unions systematically protecting bad teachers who would be fired in nonunionized settings.

Evidence on the Effect of Unions on School Districts and Students

Given that unions influence teacher compensation as well as work practices and job protection, it is necessary to ask two questions:

1. What effect do unions have on school district finances?
2. How do unions affect student achievement?

Theoretically, there is much ambiguity about the effects we might expect unions to have on these outcomes. There is a strong theoretical argument that unions can distort the inputs to education production in such a way as to lower student outcomes. Recall from Chapter 7 that the optimal allocation of inputs requires that the marginal product per dollar of each input be equalized across all inputs. Consider a simplified model in which there are two inputs to education production, teachers and computers. The optimal allocation across teachers and computers is:

$$\frac{MP_T}{P_T} = \frac{MP_C}{P_C}$$

where MP represents the marginal product and P represents the price of each input. A central goal of a teachers union is to advocate for higher pay for its members. If unions are successful in raising their members' pay, they will increase the price of teachers, P_T, without changing the marginal product of teachers (as the increased pay is not linked to performance). This will distort the inputs into the education production function and will lower output, as the same number of teachers and computers cannot be used without an increase in the budget. This often is called the *rent-seeking* model of teachers unions, because the teachers are extracting economic rents from the district without seeking to increase student performance. Opponents of teachers unions frequently use this model of union behavior to support their position.

A counterargument is that changes in the inputs favored by teachers may be beneficial to students. Unions are focused on improving working conditions as well as pay. Historically, teachers had very little power to influence their working conditions, and as a result schools often provided unappealing work environments with little job protection. The increase in job satisfaction from unionization is called the *union voice effect*, and such an effect can make teachers more productive as well as support the hiring of more effective teachers overall.

Teachers unions also can be beneficial for students by providing more accurate information on how to use education inputs. As we discussed in Chapter 7, there is considerable uncertainty over the form of the education production function. Because they are actually in the classroom and work directly with students, teachers may have a better sense of how to allocate educational resources than principals or administrators. Empowering teachers therefore may lead to a more efficient use of resources.

The theoretical ambiguities surrounding the role of unions in education production make it important to examine the empirical research on this question to see which model is more consistent with the data. Both theories have a similar prediction that unionization should lead to an increase in teacher pay and compensation. However, only the rent-seeking model predicts that student outcomes will decline with unionization.

What does the data show? Like many questions in the economics of education, the results from published empirical research do not tell a consistent story about how unions affect school district finances and student academic performance. Researchers have faced two main difficulties in estimating union impacts. The first is that it is very hard to identify which districts actually have a union that is recognized for the purposes of collective bargaining. This information is kept by public employment relations boards at the state level, and so it is necessary to go state by state to collect such data. In addition, historical records often are unavailable or incomplete, making it difficult to know when a district first unionized.

The second major difficulty is establishing causation: differences across school districts in whether they are unionized, especially within a state, likely are related to other characteristics that also are correlated with the outcomes of interest. For example, unionization is more prevalent in urban and low-income areas. Differences in unionization status across districts within a state are likely to reflect these differences in the types of schools unions operate in, making causal estimation challenging.

Early evidence on this question tended to find that unions increase teachers' wages but found either no effect or a small positive impact on education productivity.[13] Only a couple of studies of teachers union impacts attempt to overcome the issues associated with cross-sectional estimates by using changes in union status over time. A major challenge to undertaking such a study is the difficulty of observing district-level union status at different points in time.

In one of the most influential papers to date on this question, Caroline Hoxby (1996) uses data from the Census of Governments (COG) on teacher pay, district expenditures, and unionization status. The COG is a census of all government units, including school districts, that is conducted every five years. Between 1972 and 1987, the survey included a set of questions about collective bargaining. Hoxby considers a district as unionized if at least 50% of teachers are union members, the form of labor negotiations the school reports is collective bargaining, and the district has at least one contract or memorandum of understanding with *any* employee organization in effect as of October of the survey year.

This operational definition of union allows her to observe changes in district-level unionization status over time. Thus, she can examine how district-level outcomes change when unionization status changes, compared to changes in the

---

[13] Such studies include Eberts and Stone (1986), Baugh and Stone (1982), Moore and Raisian (1987), and Kleiner and Petree (1988). Freeman (1986) provides an overview of this literature as well as a detailed discussion of unionization in the public sector.

same time period among districts whose unionization status is not changing. This is an example of the difference-in-difference approach discussed in Chapter 3. Of course, there still is the concern about why district unionization status is changing. If teachers unionize because of increasing dissatisfaction with working conditions or with pay or if they unionize because of changes in student academic performance, the resulting estimates will be biased. Therefore, Hoxby also uses changes in state collective bargaining laws (Figure 12.9) as natural experiments, which provide variation in unionization status that likely is unrelated to teacher satisfaction in any one school district. This is an example of the instrumental variables approach discussed in Chapter 3.

The results from her paper are consistent with the rent-seeking model of unionization. Her findings suggest unionization increases teacher pay by about 5% and increases overall per-pupil spending by about 3%. While student–teacher ratios also decline significantly when a district unionizes, she finds evidence that unions both raise high school dropout rates and reduce the educational return to lowering student–teacher ratios and raising teacher salaries. That is, they make these inputs less productive, which is what the rent-seeking model predicts. Her results indicate that unionization leads to increased spending on education, particularly on teachers, but that student outcomes worsen because the unions are simply altering the inputs to education in a way that benefits teachers but not students.

Accurately measuring unionization status within districts over time is a central challenge in teachers union studies. While Hoxby (1996) was a major step forward, there is concern that her union measure is not ideal. Because it is based in part on there being *any* collectively bargained contract between the district and a union, this measure is potentially sensitive to contracts between districts and the cafeteria workers or bus drivers. In addition, the requirement that at least 50% of teachers be union members can be problematic because districts (which are responding to the survey) likely do not know exactly how many teachers are union members; many teachers also are covered by contracts even if they are not union members.

Quick Hint: Many states have agency shop rules that require workers to pay union dues even if they are not members of the union. These rules make actual union membership rates very hard to measure.

A follow-up study provides direct evidence on the problems associated with measuring union status: it collected the timing of the initial unionization decision in Iowa, Indiana, and Minnesota from public employment relations boards (PERBs) in those states (Lovenheim, 2009). When workers in a district decide to unionize, they hold a *representation election* to elect a union for the purpose of collective bargaining. These union votes often are on file with local PERBs, and Lovenheim uses an estimation strategy similar to Hoxby's with this particular unionization measure. In contrast to the prior results, Lovenheim finds no evidence that unions affect teacher salaries, district educational expenditures, student–teacher ratios, or high school dropout rates when this alternative unionization measure is used. Differences in the union measures used across the two studies can account for most of the differences in the results.

Another way to address the union measurement problem is to use changes in state collective bargaining laws as natural experiments that increase teacher unionization and collective bargaining rates in a state.[14] This method allows one to examine how teacher pay and district expenditures change when a state passes a more pro-union public sector bargaining law. Results from this approach suggest that unions have little effect on wages, hours worked, or per-student district expenditures (Frandsen, 2016).

While the evidence on the effects of teacher unions disagrees somewhat across studies, it points to a 5% effect at most on teacher wages. This is a relatively small effect, especially given the rancor associated with teachers unions and their stated purpose in raising teachers' wages. Indeed, talking to teachers and union representatives reveals their strongly held belief that unions significantly raise their wages. This is somewhat in contrast to what the data show.

Why might they be ineffective at raising teacher salaries? There are several potential explanations for these results:

- Unions could face restrictive district budget constraints that make it very hard to alter current compensation. They may focus on long-run compensation in the form of more generous pension packages instead.
- They may be influencing other aspects of the compensation package that are hard to observe, like health insurance.
- Union aggressiveness in negotiations may be limited by a fear of taxpayer backlash at the local level. If taxpayers become angry over union abuses, they could vote in less union-friendly school board members or reduce the funding to schools from local property taxes. Unions may react to this possibility by reducing the degree to which they attempt to influence educational inputs.
- They may focus much of their attention on bettering working conditions as well as giving teachers a voice in setting work rules and practices.

There is little evidence on these potential union impacts because of constraints on data availability, but this remains an important area for future work.[15]

12.4 Teacher Incentive Pay

incentive pay (merit pay) A contract under which a worker's compensation is tied to the amount of output he or she produces. For teachers, merit pay usually refers to the practice of paying teachers for their students' test score levels or gains.

Because teacher contracts tend to vary only with experience and educational level of the worker, there is considerable concern that teachers do not face adequate incentives to raise student achievement. Of course, the vast majority of teachers care deeply about their students and work hard, but the lack of monetary incentives to generate specific achievement outcomes may cause teachers to put forth too little effort, to focus their efforts in areas that are not preferred by school administrators or by parents, or to use methods that are not the most effective at increasing student achievement.

These concerns have led to a dramatic rise in teacher **incentive pay** or **merit pay** programs in the United States. As of 1993, over 12% of teachers were covered by a merit pay system (Ballou, 2001). This percentage has increased substantially in recent

---

[14] Hoxby (1996) does this as well with the use of these law changes as instruments for teacher unionization.

[15] Several studies also have examined the role of union contract restrictiveness on student outcomes: Do more restrictive union contracts affect students more than less restrictive contracts? These studies come to differing conclusions on this question (Moe, 2009; Strunk, 2011; Lott and Kenny, 2013). However, this research faces the problem that contract restrictiveness is likely to be correlated with unobserved characteristics of the districts that independently influence student outcomes. This omitted-variables bias problem makes it difficult to interpret the findings as representing a causal relationship.

years as large school districts, such as Denver, Colorado; Houston, Texas; Minneapolis, Minnesota; and Washington, D.C., as well as the states of Florida, North Carolina, and Tennessee, have implemented such systems. Incentives for teacher performance also play a large role in the Obama administration's largest education policy program, the Race to the Top initiative, suggesting that such programs are likely to be an important aspect of education policy in the near future.

The motivation for these programs is to provide monetary incentives for teachers to increase effort and to try new strategies that lead to higher student achievement. Much like the school accountability policies discussed in Chapter 11, the goal of teacher incentive pay is to provide explicit incentives for raising measured student performance. The main difference between teacher incentive pay and school accountability is that the former focuses on teacher-specific outcomes, while the latter is based on schoolwide outcomes. However, many teacher incentive programs have been at the school level, which makes them very similar to school accountability systems. In this section, we examine the theoretical foundation for teacher incentive pay, and then we review some of the emerging evidence about how these policies affect student achievement.

The Principal–Agent Model

We first examine the economic theory that motivates teacher incentive pay policies. Under what conditions does economic theory suggest that linking teacher pay to student performance will improve student academic achievement? Our model starts with the recognition that the parents and policy makers who ultimately manage schools have only a limited capacity to monitor what teachers do in classrooms. In many ways this problem is very similar to a more general class of problems in economics known as **principal–agent models**. These models are designed to capture the phenomenon that the goals of an employee (or agent) are not always perfectly aligned with the goals of the employer (or principal).

principal–agent models
Models of worker and employer behavior when the goals of the employee (the agent) are not perfectly aligned with those of the employer (the principal).

> **Quick Hint:** The language we use comes from the traditional economics literature. In these models, the principal typically is the manager and the agents are employees. With respect to schooling, it is a fortunate coincidence that the principal often is the actual school principal or administrator.

To take an example, suppose an employer (principal) pays a worker (agent) by the hour to sell souvenirs. The employer benefits if the worker is entrepreneurial, efficient, and responsive to customers, because this will lead to more sales. If the employee is only paid by the hour, he will get the same wages even if he does not work very hard and is not outgoing. He therefore may choose to exert only minimal effort. The principal–agent problem is that the employer's goal of getting the worker to make every effort to sell souvenirs is inconsistent with the employee's desire to make the most money with the least exertion of effort. If the principal can devise a way to align his incentives with those of the agent, it will fix this problem. One such fix would be for the employer to pay the worker a commission for each souvenir sold rather than by the hour. The incentives of the employee to work hard then would be better aligned with the principal's desire to maximize profits. Selling as many souvenirs as possible would be in the interests of both the employer and employee! This model explains why many salespeople are paid on commission rather than by the hour.

Paying teachers on the basis of student test score performance is broadly similar to this example. Teachers who are most successful at increasing measured student performance will receive monetary rewards, while those who are less successful will not. It thus is expected that linking incentives to compensation will improve student performance. The actual magnitude of these changes is a question for empirical analysis—if the rewards are small or if teachers have a relatively modest effect on student achievement, we would expect the change in student performance to be relatively modest.

> **Quick Hint:** Theoretically, those who perform poorly could receive sanctions (such as being fired) under a teacher incentive pay system. In practice, there rarely, if ever, are sanctions associated with bad performance in teacher merit pay systems. However, sanctions often are part of teacher evaluation systems that use value-added measures.

A central challenge to pay-for-performance incentive structures in education is that such compensation mechanisms create incentives to shift effort in ways that improve measures of objective performance but may hinder the overall mission of the organization (Holmstrom & Milgrom, 1991; Neal & Schanzenbach, 2010). One common example from outside education is CEO compensation. Compensation for CEOs often is tied exclusively to short-term changes in stock prices, which can lead to trade-offs between short-term gains and long-term productivity that ultimately are not in the best interests of shareholders. One parallel in education is the concern that teaching to the test will limit students' long-term retention of basic content and impede the acquisition of abstract and critical thinking skills. Moreover, emphasis on classroom performance may generate harmful competition among teachers, erode teamwork within schools, and increase incentives for outright cheating on exams. These potential problems with teacher merit pay make it very important to ensure that these policies are leading to increases in the outcomes schools care about most and to fully examine whether there are unintended consequences of merit pay systems on teacher behavior that can undermine the effectiveness of these policies.

Different Forms of Teacher Merit Pay

Teacher incentive pay can take many forms; it is critical to ascertain which program features (if any) are most effective at boosting student achievement. One important point of distinction across incentive pay programs is the unit that is given the incentive. Individual incentive pay plans link each teacher's individual performance to a merit award. Group-based incentive pay plans, however, tie the average output of a given group to monetary rewards. Group sizes can vary significantly across programs; a plan may use all teachers in a school, teachers in a school and grade, or teachers in a school, grade, and subject. Some merit pay policies use all teachers in a subject and school as a group as well. If the group wins the award, everyone in the group receives the merit bonus.

Group-based awards are much more popular in the United States because they are seen as a way to foster cooperation among teachers and reduce within-school competitiveness that can have negative consequences for teacher behavior. Teachers tend not to like feeling competitive with their colleagues, which makes group-based awards more popular with teachers as well. The drawback of group awards is what is called the $1/n$ problem, or the **free rider problem** (Kandel and Lazear, 1992). This issue stems from the

free rider problem This problem as it relates to teacher incentive pay stems from the fact that as the size of the group on which the award is based increases, each individual's effort is less important to whether the group wins the award. As a result, as group size increases, each individual teacher will provide too little effort, effectively free riding on the effort of others.

fact that as the group size increases, the fixed award gets split among a larger and larger number of teachers. Thus, the size of the monetary incentive for any one teacher declines with group size. In addition, as the group size grows, the impact of any one teacher on the eventual outcome declines, and this reduces the effort incentives for all teachers. To take a concrete example, consider a group with 2 teachers and a group with 100 teachers. In the small group, the effort of both teachers clearly is important in driving the average group outcome. But in the 100-teacher group, the behavior of any one teacher has a small impact on the average output, which makes the per-teacher incentives much weaker. Therefore, larger groups produce less powerful incentives for teachers.

Another important difference across incentive pay programs is the form of the incentive itself. We can separate these policies into *piece rates* and *tournaments*. *Piece rate* incentives pay workers per unit of output. This is akin to paying a teacher a set amount per unit of test score level or value-added. *Tournaments* are designed such that workers are competing either against a fixed threshold or with each other. The most popular tournament form for teacher incentive pay is the *rank order tournament*: teachers are ranked based on an outcome measure, and some prespecified proportion of teachers receives a bonus. For example, in the Houston, Texas, incentive pay system, the top 50% of teachers as measured by their value-added receive a bonus and the top 25% receive double the amount. Alternatively, one could structure a tournament to be against a fixed standard, so that everyone who achieves a value-added score above a certain level, for example, would receive merit pay.

The differences in these components of merit pay may play a large role in determining how responsive teachers will be to an incentive pay program. From a policy standpoint, the question is not necessarily "Does incentive pay work?" but, rather, "What type of incentive structure will produce the largest gains in student achievement per dollar spent?" The latter question is quite difficult to answer, particularly because such programs are relatively new to the education landscape. There has not yet been enough variation in the types of teacher incentive pay programs to generate adequate data that can inform consistent and effective design of merit pay systems in education. We now turn to a discussion of what research does exist on teacher incentive pay, focusing on specific program features and the role they might have in driving the results from various studies.

Does Teacher Incentive Pay Affect Student Achievement?

Some of the most straightforward evidence on teacher incentive pay comes from Israel, where economist Victor Lavy (2009) was able to make use of an unusual policy design. In 2001, the Israeli government began an incentive pay program in 49 high schools based on their high school matriculation exams in English and mathematics. The program was a rank order individual incentive pay system. Tenth- to twelfth-grade teachers were ranked based on the difference between their students' actual scores and their predicted performance based on their grade, school, education level, and socioeconomic characteristics. Thus, the ranking was based on how much teachers "outperformed" their expected score given the composition of their students. The awards ranged from $1,750 to $7,500 per teacher, a significant portion of their mean salary of $30,000.

Only schools with matriculation rates of 45% or lower in 1999 were eligible to participate. However, the data used to assign treatment was flawed, meaning some schools that should have been eligible were not and some that had lower matriculation rates were ruled ineligible. Among schools that had similar actual matriculation rates, the error produced essentially random assignment of the incentive pay regime. The comparison of schools with similar matriculation rates but that differ with respect to whether they had access to the merit pay system shows positive effects of incentive pay on student test-taking rates, on student-pass rates, and on average test scores.

In addition to the inventive study design, one of the main contributions of Lavy's paper is to examine how teaching methods and teacher effort changed as a result of the merit pay incentives. He conducts a survey of teachers that asks detailed questions about teaching practices, and by comparing such practices across treated and untreated teachers he can explore some of the mechanisms that drive the test effects. Pairing a strong program evaluation with detailed surveys on behavior is an extremely promising research strategy that can teach us a lot about *why* certain education interventions influence student achievement. Lavy finds that teachers who were exposed to the incentive pay program more frequently used small-group instruction and increased instruction time before the exam. It is likely these changes played a large role in driving the test score and test passage effects of the program.

While the results from Israel are very important, it is unclear how generalizable they are to the United States, as the specifics of the Israeli and U.S. education systems can be quite different. Indeed, the results from the United States are far more mixed and tend to suggest little effect of incentive pay on student performance. Why incentive pay programs have such a large impact in Israel but not in the United States is an open question, but the differences likely are related to differences in the structure of the education systems in each country as well as differences in the design of the incentive pay programs themselves.

Much of the U.S. evidence comes from two randomized controlled experiments done in Nashville, Tennessee, and in New York City. The Nashville experiment was an individual teacher incentive pay system that was implemented in middle schools between 2006–2007 and 2008–2009. The focus of the experiment was on mathematics teachers, and all math teachers in the district were eligible. The teachers who signed up were randomly assigned to treatment and control groups. The treatment group was eligible for a bonus of up to $15,000 per year on the basis of test score gains on the Tennessee state mathematics exam. Despite the large bonus amounts for which treated teachers were eligible, no difference was found between the performance of students who had teachers randomized into the incentive pay system and those who had teachers randomized into the control group (Springer et al., 2010). This result indicates that incentive pay did not lead to a rise in math test scores.

The other randomized controlled trial on teacher incentive pay is at the school level in New York City (Fryer, 2013). Over 200 schools participated, and they were ranked according to a combination of school environment measures (e.g., attendance), performance (e.g., percent proficient on state exams), and progress (e.g., changes in proficiency and graduation rates). The system was based on school-specific score targets, so it was not a rank order tournament. All schools that met their target could earn the award. Schools earning the merit bonus then decided how to split it up among the teachers, with the proviso that it could not be based on teacher seniority. Similar to the Tennessee experiment, the treated schools did not experience increases in outcomes relative to the control schools. In fact, achievement may have declined. The findings from this study provide little evidence for the contention that school-based teacher incentive pay systems can increase student test scores.

Although the design of the New York City experiment is compelling, several important caveats pertain to the interpretation of the results:

1. The design of the incentive system was particularly odd, as schools got to decide how much of the money went to each teacher. It was unclear how much teachers expected to make if their school won, and there likely was a lot of variation across schools in the way the money was split among the teachers and in the expectations of the teachers.
2. The incentives were schoolwide, and many of these schools are quite large. The average school had almost 60 teachers, and thus each teacher had a very limited impact on the overall likelihood of award receipt.

A reanalysis of the data from this experiment was done to examine whether schools of different sizes reacted differently to the incentive pay system (Goodman & Turner, 2013). The idea here is that in smaller schools, the free rider problem should be smaller and teachers should be more responsive to the incentives. This is indeed what is found. The estimates suggest a small positive effect of the incentives on reading in small schools but no effect on math. In large schools, the effect of the program on math and reading test scores is negative. Thus, it is likely that the design of the program—in particular the school-based nature of the incentives—is at least partially responsible for the lack of test score effects in this experiment.

Further evidence that the size of the group has important implications for how teachers respond to merit pay incentives was found in a study on schools in Houston, Texas (Imberman & Lovenheim, 2015). The Houston Independent School District (HISD) implemented an incentive pay system called ASPIRE, a rank order value-added tournament that began in 2007. In high schools, it is a group-based system at the *department* level. Departments are defined as a school–subject–grade combination, so all ninth grade math teachers in a school are in one department, while all tenth grade math teachers in the same school are in a different department. Each department competes in a value-added rank order tournament with all of the same grade and subject departments across HISD in a given year. Departments over the 50th percentile win a base award, and the top 25% of departments earn double. The award amounts are substantial, with a maximum of $7,700 per teacher in the 2009–2010 school year (the last year of the study).

Using administrative data on all high school students in HISD from 2003–2010, Imberman and Lovenheim examine how the group size affects a teacher's response to the program. They measure group size by the share of students in a group a teacher is responsible for teaching, which they term the *teacher share*. The hypothesis is that a teacher who teaches, say, 30% of the students in the group will be more responsive to the incentives than a teacher who teaches 5% of the group.

This study estimates how the relationship between teacher share and student test scores changes when the incentive pay system comes into place. The empirical approach is another example of a difference-in-difference method that is discussed in Chapter 3. The results show that test scores change significantly as a function of teacher share when the program is implemented: post-2007, teachers who teach a higher share of students have higher test score growth in math, English, and social studies (but not science). What's more, this effect is large at low shares but fades out between shares of 0.2 to 0.3. This means that teachers in very large groups, such as those in the New York City experiment, are not very responsive to merit pay incentives. As the group becomes smaller, responsiveness increases until there are about three to five teachers in the group. At this point, the return to reducing group size disappears. These results suggest that small groups may be optimal for incentive pay, as they balance the free rider problem associated with large groups with the desire of many teachers to maintain a noncompetitive and collaborative environment with their colleagues. This research also highlights the fact that the design of incentive pay systems is very important.

12.5 Teacher Certification

teacher certification policies Rules about the amount and type of education and apprenticeship experience a teacher must have to work in public schools in the state.

Teacher certification rules set out the steps individuals must take to be licensed to teach in a given state. They are intended to ensure that all teachers are trained and qualified to teach. The standards for teaching qualification are set by states and thus differ markedly across areas of the country. All states require teachers to have at least a bachelor's degree and to complete a teacher preparation program. Many states also require teachers to pass a certification exam, and others have strict requirements about the acceptable undergraduate majors and programs that count toward certification. There also tend to be provisions that require prospective teachers to spend a certain number of hours as a student teacher as well as continuing education and training requirements throughout one's career.

The intended benefit of these requirements is to ensure that all teachers are well trained both in their subject matter and in modern pedagogical practices. They thus are designed to guarantee a minimum level of teacher quality for all students. However, these regulations also have costs that can undermine their intent. They significantly raise the cost of becoming a teacher, particularly in terms of the time and effort needed to take the required courses for certification. These costs are largest for those who are not sure they want to have a career in teaching and for those who have a high opportunity cost of time because they are paid high wages in other occupations. It thus can be very challenging for a midcareer professional or for an early-career worker who did not plan on being a teacher while in college to transition into teaching. Teacher certification policies could significantly restrict the supply of high-quality teachers, which is counter to the intent of these rules.

To take a particular example, Michigan has certain undergraduate majors that count toward certification. The certification requirements in that state mean that any student who did not major in one of these areas has to complete another undergraduate degree to teach in the state. This is potentially important for high school teachers who are responsible for more specialized teaching (like a chemistry teacher), but for K–6 teachers this can be a serious barrier to entry that can reduce the supply of high-quality teachers.

alternatively certified teachers Teachers working in public schools who have not yet met all the requirements for certification. Typically, these teachers are working toward traditional certification while they are teaching.

There is a trade-off with teacher certification laws between the restriction of teacher supply and helping ensure the teacher workforce is properly trained. As discussed in the introduction to this chapter, many areas of the country face chronic teacher shortages that make it very difficult for them to hire the desired number of certified teachers. As a result of such shortages, there has been a growth of uncertified and **alternatively certified teachers** working in many schools. Alternatively certified teachers typically have not met all of the requirements for full teacher certification but have either met an alternative and less stringent set of requirements and/or are teaching while completing their traditional teacher certification. A question of central concern is whether these alternatively certified teachers perform better or worse than traditionally certified teachers. If they do not perform worse, then it suggests current teacher certification rules restrict supply without generating benefits in terms of higher quality.

One of the earlier and most influential studies to empirically examine this question was done using the NELS:88 longitudinal dataset to relate student math and science test scores in twelfth grade to the certification status of their teachers (Goldhaber & Brewer, 2000).[16] Controlling for a rich set of observed characteristics to help account for the fact that teachers are not randomly assigned to students, this study finds a negative correlation between having an uncertified teacher and students' math scores. The effect is sizable, about 0.1 standard deviations. However, there is less evidence of an effect for science. Students with alternatively certified teachers perform similarly to students with traditionally certified teachers. While these results must be interpreted cautiously because the study likely is unable to fully account for the fact that students from more disadvantaged backgrounds are more likely to have an uncertified teacher, the estimates are suggestive of a modest effect of certification on student performance. The type of certification a teacher has does not appear to matter very much, however.

Subsequent work on this question has been able to improve on these methods, using a panel of teachers and students over a six-year period in New York City. Access to panel data allows the researchers to control for lagged test scores, which likely go a long way to account for the nonrandom sorting of teachers with varying certification levels to students of different academic backgrounds. This approach leads to a measure of teacher value-added, which then is related to certification status. The findings indicate little relationship between teacher certification status and student test score growth. They also indicate that failure to account for lagged test scores makes teacher certification status look more important than it actually is because of the way teachers with different certifications sort with respect to students (Kane, Rockoff, & Staiger, 2008).

A series of studies using a similar estimation strategy with all students in North Carolina, however, finds a positive and sizable relationship between teachers being traditionally certified and licensed and student test score growth (Clotfelter, Ladd, & Vigdor, 2007, 2010). One reason for the differences between these studies is that in New York City, a large proportion of uncertified teachers are from Teach for America or the NYC Teaching Fellows program, which is not the case in North Carolina. Teachers in these programs come from elite colleges and universities but do not have much formal teacher training. It could be that certification is less important for such teachers.

The mixed evidence on the effect of teacher certification rules suggests that sometimes these laws are beneficial and sometimes they are harmful for student achievement. Given the potential for these regulations to restrict the supply of teachers, it is important for education policy to understand under what conditions these rules provide schools with maximum flexibility in hiring a highly skilled teacher workforce.

---

[16] See Appendix A of this book for an overview of the NELS:88 dataset.

DEEP DIVE: The Effect of Teach for America Teachers on Student Achievement

Teach for America (TFA) is a nonprofit organization that aspires to reduce educational inequality in the United States by enlisting high-achieving college seniors from top-rated U.S. colleges and universities to teach in low-income communities for two to three years. Wendy Kopp started the TFA program in 1990, based on her undergraduate senior honors thesis at Princeton University, and it now operates in 49 cities in 26 states. The idea behind TFA is to use highly motivated students from the most selective schools to fill teacher shortages in lower-income schools and districts. The majority of TFA teachers thus work at schools that qualify for Title I funding and that struggle to hire a sufficient number of teachers to meet demand. In 2012, the organization placed approximately 5,800 applicants at schools across the nation, making TFA one of the largest suppliers of teachers in the United States.

The majority of TFA recruits do not have any teaching experience and lack a formal teaching certificate. Instead, the recruits receive alternative certification through coursework taken at a five-week intensive training program held in the summer. In addition to this training, the TFA recruits participate in weekly professional development workshops throughout the school year and often are enrolled in alternative certification programs while they teach. This alternative certification program is substantially cheaper than the formal certification process and is considerably less demanding in terms of time. Once a TFA recruit has been placed at a school, he earns a normal school district salary, receives all the teacher benefits, and is provided with a modest education voucher.

How do students of TFA teachers fare relative to students with regularly certified teachers? Researchers Margaret Raymond and Stephen Fletcher (2002) conduct an in-depth analysis of the academic performance of TFA teachers' students. Their empirical strategy consists of comparing changes in test scores of students with TFA teachers to those of students with non-TFA teachers. This empirical approach hinges on the assumption that the test score performance of students with TFA teachers would have been the same as that of students with non-TFA teachers absent the TFA program.

To perform this analysis, the authors link student- and teacher-level data from Houston between 1996 and 2000. They focus their analysis on students in third through fifth grade. Student outcomes are measured by test score performance on state standardized math and reading tests. Their approach compares the test score gains among students of TFA teachers versus those of non-TFA teachers. They use value-added models that include controls for student demographic characteristics, lagged student test scores, school characteristics, and classmate characteristics (i.e., peer composition) to isolate the causal effect on academic performance of having a TFA teacher. In essence, the researchers seek to estimate how the teacher value-added among TFA teachers compares to the value-added of other teachers in the district.

Results from their analysis are reproduced in Figure 12.10. For reading, the results suggest that the performance of students with TFA teachers is similar

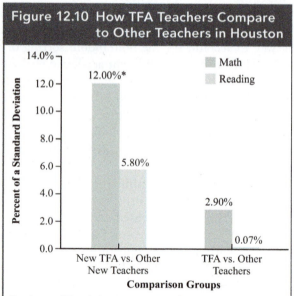

Figure 12.10 How TFA Teachers Compare to Other Teachers in Houston

Students of Teach for America Teachers experienced additional test score gains of 12% of a standard deviation in math and 6% of a standard deviation in reading relative to new teachers in Houston. Compared to all teachers, TFA teachers had test score gains for their students 3% higher in math and 0.7% higher in reading, but these differences were not statistically distinguishable from zero. *Data from:* Figure 2, Raymond and Fletcher (2002) and authors' calculations.

*Denotes statistical significance at $p < 0.05$.

to the performance of students with non-TFA teachers. However, students of TFA teachers gain almost 6% of a standard deviation more than students of other *new* teachers in the district. The results also imply that more than 60% of the TFA teachers perform better than the median performance of new teachers in the district, and there are fewer very low- and high-performing TFA teachers. That is, TFA teachers are more consistent in generating reading gains.

The results for math performance are very similar: the performance of students with TFA teachers is identical to the performance of students with non-TFA teachers. But when compared to other students who had newly hired teachers, the TFA-taught students gained 0.12 standard deviations more. As with the reading results, over 60% of TFA teachers obtain higher gains than the median new non-TFA teachers, and the gains are more consistent.

Overall, these results suggest that if a district is choosing between two candidates for a teaching position and knows nothing about them except that one is a TFA teacher and one is not, then the district should hire the TFA teacher. Although these teachers do not remain in the district for as long, they are better at increasing student test scores than other newly hired teachers. To the extent that the higher turnover does not exert a large negative effect on these schools, the findings from this research suggest that the TFA program provides high-quality teachers to low-income schools, which leads to larger test score increases.

12.6 Conclusion

The notion that teachers are one of the most important drivers of student learning is not likely to be controversial among most people, and the data strongly support this contention. Developing an understanding of teacher labor markets therefore is essential to designing sound teacher recruitment and retention policies to ensure that we have as highly qualified and high-performing a teacher workforce as possible. In this chapter, we examined several key features and patterns related to teacher labor markets. First, we discussed what types of workers decide to go into teaching and how this has changed over time. Although changes in the returns to skill in professions that require a college degree combined with increasing labor market opportunities for women have led to shifts in the composition of teachers, the implications for student achievement are not fully known.

This chapter also examines teachers unions, which are one of the most prominent teacher labor market institutions. Teachers unions, through the collective bargaining process, have potentially large impacts on the level and structure of compensation as well as on workplace practices and human resource decisions. Despite the unions' large role in setting these policies, there is conflicting evidence about how they affect student achievement, teacher pay, and school district resources. Even studies that find a role for unions in influencing these outcomes suggest their impact is not large, which is surprising given how prevalent unions are and the controversy that surrounds them.

Teacher incentive pay is a policy model that is growing in importance in the United States. Arguably, incentive pay systems have arisen in response to the decoupling of teacher pay and student achievement that is a feature of union contracts. Although merit pay systems are becoming an ever more prominent feature of U.S. K–12 education, the evidence does not strongly support the contention that these policies as they currently exist increase achievement in the United States. However, it is likely that a large reason for these findings is the poor design of many of the incentive pay systems that have been studied, and thus an important question for further research is how to design these programs to maximize their effect on student achievement. The chapter concludes with a discussion of teacher certification policies.

Highlights

- Teacher wages are set as a function of experience and education level, which means that teachers tend not to be paid their **marginal product of labor**. This can generate shortages of specialty teachers whose skills are highly valued by the labor market. Wages also do not vary across schools within a district. The lack of **compensating differentials** generates shortages in schools that are less desirable places in which to teach.

- The Roy model provides an important framework for understanding teacher labor markets. According to this model, workers will choose the profession that will maximize their utility, both in terms of earnings and preferences for different jobs.

- Teaching offers a very compressed wage structure and little to no link between pay and student performance. This means that the return to skill is low in teaching relative to other professions that contain large proportions of college-educated workers. According to the Roy model, these two factors should induce lower-skilled workers to join the teacher profession and dissuade higher-skilled workers from entering the teaching workforce. This is not necessarily the case if there are multiple dimensions of skill and the **complementarity of skills** is such that teaching skill is negatively correlated with other skills valued by the labor market.

- The data are consistent with the predictions of the Roy model: teachers are less likely to come from more selective schools, and they have lower test scores and academic aptitude measures than those in other high-skilled professions. This gap has gotten larger over time as the return to skill in non-teaching professions has increased. However, it is not clear that these teacher characteristics affect student learning.

- The data show that over the course of their career, teachers are likely to move out of urban, lower-performing schools to suburban, higher-performing schools. This pattern leads to a teacher quality gap across schools serving more- versus less-advantaged students.

- Teachers unions have a long history in the United States but only gained **collective bargaining** power at a significant level beginning in the 1960s with the passage of state **duty-to-bargain laws**. Unions and districts bargain over salary and compensation as well as over human resource policies.

- Proponents of teachers unions argue that the resulting improved working conditions and compensation lead to more satisfied and effective teachers. Opponents argue that unions cultivate *rent-seeking* behavior, causing districts to overspend on teacher salaries and compensatory benefits at the expense of student achievement. The research on how unions affect school district resources and student achievement comes to mixed conclusions.

- The **principal–agent model** provides a useful framework in which to consider the limited capacity of parents and policy makers to monitor teachers and to provide incentives for effort. **Teacher incentive pay** or **merit pay** programs were born out of concern that there are insufficient incentives for teachers to exert more effort to increase student academic achievement because pay is usually not related to performance measures.

- Incentive pay policies can differ in the unit that receives the reward (an individual teacher versus a group) and in the form of incentive (piece rates or rank order tournaments). While teachers and policy makers tend to prefer group-based incentive systems, the **free rider problem** can render these policies ineffective if the group is too large.

- The research on teacher incentive pay does not find consistent evidence that these policies increase measured student achievement. Particularly in the United States, most studies find no effect of the provision of financial incentives for teachers to increase test scores on the test scores of their students. It does appear that the size of the group involved in the incentive pay system matters, however, which points to the importance of the design of incentive pay programs in generating test score changes.

- **Teacher certification policies** are designed to ensure that all teachers are well-trained. They can significantly restrict the supply of teachers by raising the cost of becoming a teacher, especially for midcareer professionals and students who are not sure they want to become a teacher. Growing teacher shortages have led to a rise in the use of **alternatively certified teachers**. Existing evidence suggests such teachers perform just as well as or better than traditionally certified teachers, especially when these teachers come from Teach for America.

Problems

1. Describe the structure of most teacher salary schedules. What factors affect wages? How do these contracts differ from typical labor market contracts? (Hint: In a perfectly competitive labor market, how are wages set?)

2. If teachers generally prefer to teach at schools in low-crime neighborhoods, how would this affect the supply of teachers across schools? How might this factor affect the distribution of teachers with different skill levels?

3. How does the use of a single-scale for teacher salaries within districts affect the quality of teachers at schools in which students are disproportionately low-income?

4. Consider two professions that a college-educated worker might choose: teaching and investment banking. Investment banking and teaching both value a single measure of skill, which we will call X. (You can think of X as entrepreneurial spirit). Increases in X receive greater rewards in investment banking than teaching. Discuss how each of the following scenarios will affect the selection of those with different levels of X into teaching.

   a. A nonunionized charter school opens that pays all teachers a base salary of twice what public school teachers make.

   b. The state passes a duty-to-bargain law that facilitates collective bargaining among teachers.

   c. A teacher incentive pay system is implemented that provides high-performing teachers with large monetary bonuses.

   d. The stock market crashes.

   e. Teach for America is launched.

5. What implication does the reduction in labor market discrimination against women have for the quality of the teacher workforce?

6. Explain why local labor market conditions can affect the quality of teachers. How does this answer depend on whether those who select into teaching have strong preferences for being teachers?

7. In an effort to ensure that all students have access to high-quality teachers, the governor of New York, Andrew Cuomo, decides to mandate that all elementary teachers have an undergraduate degree with a major in education. Under what conditions will this positively impact student performance and under what circumstances will it negatively impact students?

8. What is a duty-to-bargain law? How do these laws facilitate collective bargaining among teachers?

9. What is the goal of teacher incentive pay contracts? Explain why the design of typical teacher pay schedules might make it desirable to provide merit pay.

10. What are the different forms of teacher incentive pay? How might the characteristics of these programs influence how they affect teacher behavior and thus student academic performance?

11. In a group incentive pay system, why would you expect a group of 3 to react differently to the monetary incentive than a group of 50? Is there empirical evidence to support this prediction for teachers?

12. Do the findings that teacher incentive pay in the United States does not lead to positive effects on student achievement necessarily mean that incentive pay for teachers "doesn't work?" What is an alternative explanation for these findings?

13. In recent years, there has been much discussion of whether teachers entering the labor force through alternative pathways like Teach for America (TFA) are more or less effective than traditionally certified teachers. Suppose students in classrooms led by TFA teachers score lower than students in classrooms led by traditionally certified teachers. Would this type of evidence prove that TFA teachers are less effective? Discuss in the context of the research evidence on how teacher certification affects student outcomes.

Market Dimensions of Higher Education in the United States

The Higher Education Market in Chicago

In the Chicago metropolitan area, there are 210 distinct postsecondary institutions. These institutions vary immensely in academic focus; in the degree to which they are controlled by public, private, or for-profit entities; and in the amount of resources they can devote to their students. Two highly selective universities that draw students from across the nation, as well as from all over the world, are Northwestern University and the University of Chicago. These schools are extremely selective in terms of admissions, with acceptance rates of 10.7% and 7.6%, and they have very high per-student instructional expenditures, at $25,921 and $57,199, respectively.

These are but two of the 83 private four-year schools in the Chicago area. A quite different type of private four-year institution in Chicago is Roosevelt University, which has a more open-access mission in terms of admissions: It currently accepts about three-fourths of all students who apply. It spends much less than its more selective counterparts as well, with per-student instructional expenditures of $5,854. Chicago also is home to 100 private schools that offer two-year degrees or vocational training. The vast majority of these schools are focused on providing students with vocational training in areas such as health care, criminal justice, and various service industries. For example, the Worsham College of Mortuary Science, the Rosel School of Cosmetology, and the Star Truck Driving School all prepare students for careers in specific occupations. These schools typically are nonselective in the sense that all students who meet basic requirements can enroll. They also tend to be very small, with average enrollments of 427 students.

Still, the majority of college students in Chicago are enrolled in public four-year and two-year colleges and universities. There are five public four-year universities in the city, including Northern Illinois University and the University of Illinois Chicago. Although there are only five such schools, their undergraduate enrollments are large, at almost 12,000 students on average. As a result, these schools are responsible for the majority of the four-year enrollment in the city. The 22 public two-year schools, also called *community colleges*, enroll a large number of the students in Chicago as well. Many of these schools are part of the City Colleges of Chicago system, which operates seven branch campuses throughout the city. As public colleges, they have little financial endowment and have large average enrollments of over 18,700 students per campus. The per-student instructional expenditures at these schools tend to be low, however, at about $1,900.

Unlike the market for elementary and secondary education, where geography limits choice, students from Chicago are not limited to institutions in Chicago or even in Illinois when they are selecting a college. Not only will students from Illinois consider attending colleges out of state, but students from all over the world will come to Chicago to study at institutions like Northwestern University, the University of Chicago, and the University of Illinois at Chicago.

Across the United States, there were 7,151 postsecondary education institutions in 2014, including 4,627 degree-granting colleges and universities. As in the microcosm of Chicago postsecondary institutions, they are differentiated by their academic focus, in the types of degrees offered, in the resources they have available, and in the extent to which they compete for students in local, regional, national, and global markets. Overall, more than 20.7 million students enrolled in United States colleges and universities in 2014. While many of these students are recent high school graduates pursuing BA degrees, the reach of higher education is much broader and includes more than 2.9 million graduate students and nearly 5 million students over the age of 25.

Colleges and universities in the United States constitute the domestic market for postsecondary education. In this chapter, we analyze the institutions and structure of higher education markets. Market structure is important to understand because to explain (or change) the level of collegiate attainment in a country or state, we need to understand the organization, the institutional objectives of different colleges and universities, and the funding of higher education institutions. What do these institutions produce, and how do they compete? How do they produce research and educational outcomes? And, importantly, who is able to enroll and complete study at different colleges and universities?

We highlight many of the core features of the United States higher education market that are essential to analyzing student education investment decisions, their resulting educational and labor market outcomes, and how institutions make resource allocation decisions that affect students as well as society more broadly. One of the unique aspects of the United States postsecondary market is that it is decentralized: Institutions are largely autonomous, and they often compete directly for students. Unlike many Asian and European countries, in which admissions at both undergraduate and graduate levels are determined centrally and by exam scores, colleges and universities in the United States compete for students on the basis of both price and academic achievement. In turn, students compare collegiate options and choose where to apply and where to attend, with the aim of finding the best match with their aptitude, financial resources, and aspirations. The result is a competitive marketplace: Institutions compete with each other for students, faculty and—in the particularly unusual American twist—dominance on the athletic field. Although competition among postsecondary institutions is widespread in the sense that all institutions compete with one another, it is also incomplete in the sense that the competitors of any one institution will vary by geography and by type of school.

Heterogeneity and **stratification** are defining characteristics of the market for higher education in the United States. Colleges and universities differ markedly in the types of degrees and training they provide and whether they have a substantial research function: They are heterogeneous in terms of the educational services they offer. Some institutions focus on certificates or degrees in vocational and technical fields; others award the vast majority of their degrees at the undergraduate level; while many universities award professional degrees like the JD and MD as well as

heterogeneity Across higher education institutions; refers to the fact that there are many types of postsecondary institutions in this country. They differ along many dimensions, including their academic focus, selectivity, resources available, and whether they are publicly or privately controlled.

Stratification In higher education; describes the hierarchical distribution of resources in which some institutions have markedly higher resource levels than others.

doctorates or PhDs. In addition to heterogeneity, there is stratification in resources. As the microcosm of Chicago illustrates, resources are concentrated in a small number of postsecondary institutions, leading to much inequality in spending per student across different schools even in the same geographic area.

We begin with an examination of what it is that universities do, in particular considering in what ways traditional economic *theory of the firm* models apply and in what ways the higher education market is unique. We then provide a brief history of higher education in the United States, including the evolution of government funding for higher education. The second part of this chapter takes a close look at costs and revenues; understanding the budget constraint in higher education and the differences in funding across institutions is key to understanding the market and the effects of public policies. In this section, we also address tuition pricing in higher education and the determinants of increases in tuition charges over time. In the final section, we consider heterogeneity and stratification in the market and discuss arguments for why stratification has increased in recent decades.

13.1 **What Do Universities Do?**

The University as a Firm

An accurate—if broad—description of the main business of colleges and universities is that they are engaged in the creation *and* diffusion of knowledge (Goldin & Katz, 1999). In effect, teaching students (diffusion of knowledge) and research (creation of knowledge) are the main activities of colleges and universities, though there are vast differences across institutions in what is taught, how it is taught, to whom it is taught, and the extent to which research is a central function. What makes studying the postsecondary sector interesting yet complicated?

1. Universities have many outputs, some of which are hard to measure.
2. Asymmetric and incomplete information affects students' choices, and it may be very difficult to know which educational environment will lead to the highest returns.
3. The production of student knowledge is a **customer input technology**: student effort is both an input to and output of the production process.
4. The market for higher education in the United States is a **mixed market**, where there is overlap among public, private **non-profit**, and private for-profit institutions.

In addition, the substantial public sector role in the production and financing of higher education highlights the potential public benefits to the production of research and postsecondary attainment.

The Varied Outputs of Postsecondary Institutions Teaching and research are the functions through which higher education institutions produce and diffuse knowledge. What differ across institutions, however, are the balance between teaching and research, the way in which knowledge is produced, and the particular areas of specialization.

One measurable output of higher education is the number of degrees awarded, which vary in level (for example, an associate's degree versus a bachelor's degree) and subject matter concentration (for example, majoring in mathematics or English). In 2014, colleges and universities awarded more than 175,000 doctoral degrees, 755,000 master's degrees, 1.9 million BA degrees (typically requiring 4 years of study) and more than a

---

customer input technology A production technology in which those who purchase the outputs are also inputs. In terms of education, student effort is an important input into the production of the knowledge and skills that form the output of the education process. This is in contrast to the production of a typical commodity, where the quality of the final product is unrelated to which consumers purchase it.

mixed market A market in which institutions controlled publicly and privately are in competition with each other.

nonprofit Enterprise in which there are no residual shareholders; all differences between revenue and expenses are retained to fulfill the organization's mission; no individual can take that profit for personal use. Non-profit and public universities in the United States benefit from tax-favored status. The difference between revenues and expenditure is exempt from taxation, and these institutions can receive tax-deductible charitable donations.

million associate degrees (typically requiring 2 years of study). In addition, postsecondary institutions awarded nearly 1 million certificates, often in vocational and technical fields.

> Quick Hint: Doctoral degrees are not to be confused with a medical degree (MD). The PhD ("doctor of philosophy") is the most common doctorate, and completing a PhD generally requires at least 4 years of specialized study as well as original research (a dissertation). Generally, doctorate degrees are needed to hold faculty positions at universities.

Beyond the courses of study in which students enroll, the second major product of higher education institutions is research, or the creation of new knowledge. While research is not limited to universities, its production tends to be highly concentrated at a fairly small set of institutions. Indicators of research production include patents and publications. Universities often concentrate in *basic research*, which has very general application and produces innovations that can be widely shared or that advance knowledge in areas with no commercial application (and, as a result, would not be produced by for-profit firms). Still, universities often generate innovations with commercial applications, such as seatbelts (Cornell University), the Google search engine (Stanford University), GPS (MIT), Gatorade (University of Florida), the polygraph (University of California—Berkeley), rocket fuel (Clark University), the polio vaccine (University of Michigan), and pacemakers (University of Minnesota).

To be sure, the outputs of universities are not limited to teaching and research. As many universities also include medical schools, these universities typically operate hospitals and produce medical care as well. In addition, the presence of programs of study in the visual and performing arts on college campuses contributes to culture of the community in the form of theater, art museums, concerts, and so forth. Finally, we would be remiss if we did not note the substantial role of colleges and universities in producing athletic entertainment.

Complexity of operations and existence of multiple outputs does not distinguish higher education from other sectors in the economy. For example, enormous multinational firms like General Electric and Microsoft produce a range of products that are delivered to a wide variety of consumers. One distinction for colleges and universities is that some of their products—in terms of both teaching and research—would not be produced by a for-profit firm. For-profits underproduce basic research because benefits are often widely diffuse, and for-profits are not likely to train students in areas that have high fixed costs (big lab science) or that may have limited labor market returns (Sanskrit, classics, etc).

What is more, only some of the outputs, such as degrees awarded and labor market success of their students, are easy to measure. Similar to schooling in the K–12 context, which we covered in earlier chapters, many outputs in higher education are very difficult to measure. Universities often claim that they want to endow their students with a sense of honesty, integrity, and civic engagement to prepare them for a life and career benefiting society at large. It is very hard for one to measure systematically whether a university is indeed successful at generating such outcomes.

Asymmetric Information and Uncertainty Unlike tangible capital purchases like a car, it may be very difficult for students to assess the quality of a particular degree program at the time of enrollment. Producers—colleges and universities—may have much more information about resources and quality in a particular program than do potential students. Compare the information structure in higher education to the one in the new car market. Most people do not have the technical knowledge to fully evaluate a car. However, it is relatively easy to find out the relevant aspects of a new car and to compare prices, mileage per gallon, space, and engine power. You also can test-drive a car before you buy it, but you cannot enroll in a school for a while before paying tuition. In addition, many of the benefits of a college education are experienced long after college ends, such as the impact on one's career options and earnings. These effects are difficult to evaluate at the time the enrollment decision is made. Students and their families must make large financial commitments under much uncertainty about the quality of the educational environment they will face and the returns to a given enrollment decision, which makes this market quite different from a normal commodity market.

When students choose a particular college and course of study, they face uncertainty along several dimensions. First, they may have incomplete information about their own skills and aptitudes and thus may not be able to accurately predict success. It is hard to know beforehand whether the teaching style of the professors will match the learning style of the particular student, how easy it will be to get the number and distribution of credits needed to complete a degree in a timely manner, and the overall level of resources to which one will be exposed when one is enrolled. While students can obtain information to reduce these uncertainties somewhat, a policy concern is that those from the most disadvantaged families have the most limited access to such information. In turn, students may face considerable uncertainty about the labor market opportunities after the degree is earned. For example, people who enrolled in college in 2005 certainly did not predict that the unemployment rate would spike to nearly 10% by the time they graduated from college.

Customer Input Technology The characteristics and behavior of students affect learning outcomes, in addition to purchased inputs like faculty labor. College is not a passive experience; the more effort a student puts in, the more he or she will learn while enrolled. That student effort is itself an input into the production of student knowledge in college (and in education more generally) and makes the production function different from the production of a physical commodity. To see this difference, compare the purchase of a new car to the purchase of a college education. A car will work the same and have the same value for all consumers who buy the same make and model. For a college education, the same students at a given school can get much different value out their investment, depending on how much effort they put in while enrolled.

Student learning in the postsecondary sector is not generated just by the faculty and academic classes. One's peers can play an important role in learning as well. Such *peer effects* can operate through many channels, including direct learning from one's college peers as well as learning good or bad study habits and/or health behaviors from those peers. Peer effects therefore are more likely to be important at institutions in which a large proportion of students live on or close to campus, rather than commuter campuses at which students commute to school each day from an area that is not proximate to the school. As a result of peer effects, which we discuss in more detail in Chapter 15, the quality of the education one receives is made better by having more academically capable students at the university. Again, this makes the production of student knowledge very different from the production of typical physical commodities, where the quality of one input does not affect the quality of the other inputs.

Mixed Market Competition: Public, Nonprofit, and For-Profit Higher Education
Most of the institutional participants in the higher education market are either public entities or private nonprofit organizations. In the United States in 2014, 71% of the

20.7 million postsecondary students were enrolled in public colleges or universities, meaning the land they are on is publicly owned and state or local governments are responsible for their operation and governance. Another 19% were enrolled in schools that were private and nonprofit, and only 8% of students were enrolled in private for-profit organizations (see Table 13.1). Among students enrolled in public institutions, about 56% were enrolled in institutions that grant four-year degrees, while nearly all students at nonprofit colleges were in the four-year sector.

Even as the majority of students are enrolled in public colleges and universities, there are slightly fewer public institutions (1,621) than nonprofit institutions (1,666), while the number of for-profit institutions is 1,327 (see Table 13.2). Comparing enrollment and institution counts, it follows that the public institutions are much larger

Table 13.1 Postsecondary Enrollment by Type of Institution (Fall 2014)

	Total Enrollment	Public	Private Nonprofit	Private For-Profit
Total	20.7 million	14.7 million	4 million	1.6 million
Four-year institutions	13.5 million	8.3 million	4 million	1.3 million
Two-year institutions	6.8 million	6.4 million	30,365	286,355
Less than 2 years, nondegree	325,036	50,891	9,579	264,566

Data from: *Digest of Education Statistics, 2015*, Table 301.10 from United States Department of Education, National Center for Education Statistics, Integrated Postsecondary Education Data System (IPEDS), spring 2014.

Table 13.2 Number of Institutions by Type and Average Enrollment, Fall 2014

	Public		Private Nonprofit		Private For-Profit	
	N =	Average Enrollment	N =	Average Enrollment	N =	Average Enrollment
Total	1,621	9,041	1,666	2,399	1,327	1,173
Doctoral, highest research output	73	32,859	34	16,611		
Doctoral, high research output	73	20,576	24	12,728		
Doctoral, lowest research output	29	14,484	48	6,723	11	10,187
Master's	274	9,791	363	4,371	38	8,912
Baccalaureate	207	5,636	520	1,562	126	993
Special-focus institutions	45	1,940	591	633	547	1,269
Two-year	920	6,954	86	353	605	473

Data from: *Digest of Education Statistics, 2015*, Table 317.40. Doctoral, Master's, and Baccalaureate institutions refer to the highest degree awarded.

than the nonprofits, with the for-profits having the smallest average scale. However, the for-profit institutions have the largest variance in enrollment, as some of the smallest institutions and some of the largest institutions, like the University of Phoenix (with an enrollment of 216,000), are in this category. Table 13.2 shows the number of institutions and average enrollment by highest degree and research intensity. It is notable that all research (doctoral) universities are either public or nonprofit institutions. Still, among the schools that do not award doctorate degrees, there is considerable for-profit, public, and nonprofit provision.

Given the prevalence, what are the economic arguments for nonprofit and public provision in higher education? A central argument is that nonprofit and public higher education institutions are able to produce specific types of education and research that would be underprovided by for-profit firms. In turn, nonprofit and public institutions often receive substantial subsidies from private philanthropy or from public (governmental) appropriations. The result is that the price that students at these institutions pay for instruction is often far less than the cost of production.[1]

The public and nonprofit control of many colleges and universities also affects entry and exit. In the for-profit sector, firms enter when there is an opportunity to generate economic profit and close when they are unable to cover costs. Public institutions, in contrast, face barriers to entry in that they generally require legislative approval. Thus, nonprofit and public institutions may persist beyond the point where they are economically viable.

The Government's Role in Higher Education

The government's role in the higher education market affects what types of education are offered to students, the level of support for research and innovation on topics with great public return but insufficient private return, and the extent to which students are able to finance investments in human capital development. The role of the government in higher education is substantial, comes from multiple layers of government (federal, state, and local), and takes several forms that include the direct control of universities, the provision of resources to institutions for both general support and to pursue particular lines of inquiry, and support to students in the form of financial aid.

Governments are directly involved in the production of higher education when they charter or operate institutions of higher education. The vast majority of public institutions are under state control. Typically, states have a stratified and differentiated set of public institutions, which includes some institutions with a research focus and graduate professional degrees, along with colleges that are open access and target students within commuting distance. Aside from the four military academies, the federal government does not run any schools in the United States. In the next section, we discuss the evolution of public institutions of higher education in the United States.

---

[1] Writing in 2003, Gordon Winston notes: "The price the student-customer pays for his or her education is strikingly less than the cost of its production. It cost $12,400 a year to educate a student at the average United States college in 1995–96. But he or she paid a price of $4,000. So each student got a subsidy of $8,400 a year on average. It's as if the Taurus that cost your Ford dealer $20,000 to put on the showroom floor were sold for less than $7,000—regularly and routinely. If you were poor or an exceptionally good driver, you might pay even less. Clearly, no ordinary Ford dealer would survive." http://www.nebhe.org/info/journal/articles/2003-Winter_Winston.pdf

Public colleges and universities are governed by state and local governments through the appointment of governance boards (sometimes called a board of trustees or a board of regents). Because public universities receive substantial subsidies from state governments, they are constrained in matters such as tuition setting and admissions—either implicitly or explicitly—as policy moves in opposition to the majority of legislators would likely lead to reductions in public support. In exchange for these subsidies, in-state students at public colleges and universities pay markedly lower tuition and fee levels than their counterparts who are not state residents. To illustrate, the differences in tuition for in-state versus out-of-state students at two public institutions in the 2014–2015 academic year were $13,208 (in state) versus $42,394 (out of state) at the University of Virginia and $13,486 (in state) versus $41,906 (out of state) at the University of Michigan. The out-of-state tuition charges at these institutions approach those of similarly selective private universities.

Governments also play a substantial role in funding higher education, as discussed in greater detail in Section 13.3. Three important and identifiable channels of support include:

- *Appropriations* (generally from states) to public colleges and universities to support operating expenses, which implicitly provide a subsidy to students.
- *Financial aid*, which is sent directly to students, is funded by both states and the federal government. In the 2012–2013 school year, the federal government spent over $148 billion on grants and loans to students for financial aid. State financial aid grants were another $9.7 billion.
- *Research support* is provided by governments to support particular lines of research inquiry at universities, including those in both the private and public sectors. Funding is provided by entities like the National Science Foundation, the National Institutes of Health, the Institute of Education Sciences, the Department of Defense, and the Department of Agriculture.

A final way in which the public provides support for postsecondary schools is through tax breaks, particularly on land and endowment income. The land on which public and nonprofit institutions are located is not subject to property taxation. This amounts to a large subsidy for most of these schools: Consider the value of the land on which New York University, Harvard University, and Stanford University sit. These schools are located in the middle of some of the highest-value real estate markets in the world. Of course, one reason property in these areas is so expensive might be because of the universities themselves, but the value of their land is immense. Local and state governments provide a large subsidy to these institutions by making them exempt from property tax levies.

Furthermore, these schools do not pay taxes on the income derived from their often substantial endowments. In 2012, five schools (Harvard, Yale, Princeton, Stanford, and MIT) had endowments of over $10 billion. Many more have endowments of over $1 billion. The tax-free status of the income derived from these endowments is a large government subsidy to higher education institutions. Additionally, when individuals make philanthropic contributions to colleges and universities, they are able to deduct these contributions from their taxable income.

What economic reasons could there be for the large public sector role in the provision and financing of higher education? Put differently, why do we need government intervention in these markets at all? The motivation for government provision of higher education is distinct from the argument for government funding or subsidies for higher

economies of scale When average costs are declining with additional students; in this sense, it will cost less per student to operate one relatively large school than multiple small schools. Large fixed costs of operation can generate economies of scale.

credit constraint Arises when an individual cannot borrow money or cannot borrow money at a sufficiently low interest rate to finance a desired educational investment that has a positive rate of return.

education, which could occur at public or private institutions. The rationale for government provision follows from the complementarity of higher education with other public functions, **economies of scale** in provision, and market failures that would lead to underinvestment in education.

There are two broad arguments for government subsidy or financing of higher education:

1. Positive externalities, or spillovers, from college and university research and teaching
2. Financial barriers, or **credit constraints**, that limit college enrollment and college choice

Do the positive externalities from collegiate attainment generate a convincing rationale for substantial subsidies for higher education? As discussed in prior chapters, there is a strong link between the size of the college-educated workforce and economic growth (Delong, Goldin, & Katz 2003; Vandenbussche, Aghion, & Meghir 2006; Aghion et al., 2005; Moretti, 2004). This comes about because highly skilled workers are more likely to provide innovations and the type of labor that is demanded in our advanced and skill-based economy. Yet, there also are substantial private benefits to higher education: on average the earnings gains over a lifetime from obtaining a college degree exceed the prices students pay.

Academic research often has positive spillovers as well. For example, the polio vaccine was invented by a medical researcher, Jonas Salk, at the University of Michigan in 1957. This vaccine eradicated one of the largest public health concerns in the world at the time, which had clear positive benefits to society at large. Virtually every study mentioned in this book was conducted at a postsecondary institution as well (as was this book itself). To the extent that this research helps guide education policy to better our education system, it has positive benefits that accrue to the entire country.

As we identified in early chapters of this book, the very nature of educational investments and the embodiment of human capital produce incomplete markets that limit individual capacity to finance and insure investments in education as well as insure against bad educational outcomes. The result is that without public financial aid in the form of grants and loans, students are likely to underinvest in collegiate attainment. Moreover, the consequences of these limited markets are likely to disproportionately impact students from low-income families, contributing to inequality and an absence of a pathway to upward mobility.

Financial aid and the reduced tuition at public institutions also serve to relax credit constraints. Credit constraints arise in the human capital model when a student has a positive return to the education investment but lacks the funds to finance the investment. We will examine the evidence on credit constraints in higher education as well as the effect of financial aid on student behavior in Chapter 14. But if lower tuition and financial aid reduce credit constraints by allowing low-income students to invest in a college education, the efficiency of the higher education system can be increased.

Risk and uncertainty also may limit collegiate investments that are efficient in aggregate. Because individuals may not have full information about their own likelihood for success in college, they may underinvest in college. Further, individuals may be unable to predict either future aggregate economic conditions or circumstances that would affect individual benefits from college. Individuals cannot insure fully against such circumstances because individual effort also affects outcomes. Financial aid, which lowers the cost of college, effectively limits individual losses in the event of adverse outcomes.

In the absence of full information about the characteristics of colleges and universities and because poorly informed decisions lead to considerable social costs, the government may have an additional regulatory and consumer protection role in the higher education market. Some information about expected outcomes at colleges and universities, such as employment rates and earnings of graduates, may be difficult for potential students to observe, yet they are highly relevant in assessing collegiate options. There is an important role for public provision of this information as a result. Additionally, when there exists a profit motive in higher education and students have dificulty in observing long-term outcomes, regulations may limit predatory behavior by colleges. Such behavior stems from students incurring large costs without receiving returns.[2]

The Optimization Problem for Colleges and Universities

Even though most colleges and universities do not maximize a profit function, we still expect them to make optimizing decisions in deciding what to produce and how to produce. These decisions reflect both the goals of the institution and the production function for different outcomes. We want to know the mix of postsecondary outcomes, such as research and student learning each university wants to produce, and how it goes about producing those outcomes. One thus might legitimately ask: What do universities maximize? The answer is surely: It depends.

Institutional Goals: The Objective Function For colleges and universities that are for-profit in control, there is a straightforward institutional goal. We expect a for-profit college to choose what programs to offer and what combination of faculty and other resources to employ to maximize the difference between total revenue and total costs given the tuition students are willing to pay. That is, they maximize profit, as would any firm producing a physical commodity. While some colleges and universities are organized as for-profit firms and choose what courses to offer, a method of instruction, and tuition levels to maximize profits, many colleges and universities in the United States maximize something other than economic profits. What do these nonprofit and public universities maximize?

Certainly, little guidance is provided by college and university mottos: *Terras irradient* (let them illuminate the lands, Amherst College), *Vox clamantis in deserto* (the voice crying in the wilderness, Dartmouth College), *Artes, Scientia, Veritas* (arts, science, truth, University of Michigan), and *Die Luft der Freiheit Weht* (the wind of freedom blows, Stanford University). In his inaugural address to the first class of Cornell students in 1868, Ezra Cornell laid out the goals of his new university as follows:

> I desire that this shall prove to be the beginning of an institution which shall furnish better means for the culture of all men of every calling, of every aim; which shall make men more truthful, more honest, more virtuous, more noble, more manly; which shall give them higher purposes and more lofty aims, qualifying them to serve their fellow men better, preparing them to serve

---

[2] The federal government requires that any school receiving federal funds be accredited by a licensed accrediting body. Accreditation provides information to students about whether a school has met a minimum quality standard. Regulations that preclude schools in which a large percentage of students default on their federal student loans also help to crack down on low-quality providers and give information to prospective students about institutional quality.

society better, training them to be more useful in their relations to the state, and to better comprehend their higher and holier relations to their families and their God (Bishop, 1962, p. 88).

Such lofty and wide-ranging language characterizes a large variety of university mission statements. In this statement, Cornell articulates many different objectives of his university, many of which are difficult to measure. What colleges and universities maximize (along with the nature of student demand) is important if we are to understand the nature of competition in the marketplace.

Production Function How do colleges and universities combine inputs to produce outputs? In essence, the organization of faculty with different types of expertise, students, and other material resources like computers, libraries, and laboratories to produce student learning and new knowledge represents the university production function. With considerable heterogeneity in higher education outputs and stratification in the market, it should be clear that there is no single production function in higher education. Rather, production functions are differentiated by institutional mission. Still, some features that distinguish production functions in higher education include economies of scale generated by high fixed costs and **economies of scope**.

economies of scope
Occur when there are complementarities across the production of various outputs of a firm or institution. These complementarities make it less expensive to produce these outputs jointly rather than separately in different institutions.

There are substantial economies of scale in higher education, which are driven by high fixed costs of production and which generate barriers to entry. Examples of such costs include buildings for classrooms and dormitories, expensive laboratory equipment, and access to a large library. These are important requirements for both teaching and research that make it far less expensive on a per-student basis to teach many students at one school than to teach few students each at several schools. When universities produce multiple outcomes, such as undergraduate education, graduate education, and research, there also can be substantial economies of scope. Economies of scope occur where the cost of producing the outcomes together is less than it would be if separate institutions were devoted to each activity.

A longstanding question related to economies of scope in higher education production concerns the complementarity between teaching and research in the allocation of faculty time. On the one hand, time spent teaching is time that cannot be spent in a laboratory or doing original research. Yet the activities and discovery of research may improve the quality of teaching, while questions that arise in teaching may well challenge research. One university leader quipped: "Research is to teaching as sin is to confession. If you don't participate in the former you have very little to say in the latter."[3] The quote highlights the basic point that engaging in research may improve the content of what faculty teach; still, it is the case that increasing time spent teaching will likely come at a cost of less time spent doing research.

To be sure, the market for higher education is characterized by a wide array of institutions, and it is only a small fraction of colleges and universities that actively produce research. Overall, colleges and universities in the United States produce a range of outputs differentiated by subject matter, varying from applied fields like medical technology and accounting to abstract fields like philosophy or physics, as well as the mix of research and ancillary services. In turn, what institutions produce is integrally related to how they produce these educational outcomes.

---

[3] Frank Rhodes (1998) quote of John Slaughter of Occidental College.

13.2 The History and Structure of Higher Education in the United States

How did the peculiar market of higher education in the United States arise? After all, it is not obvious that student education and academic research should be produced by the same institutions, nor is it clear that a market dominated by the public sector and characterized by many different types of schools with different foci and resources is the best way to organize a higher education market.

Eighteenth- and Nineteenth-Century Higher Education

Universities have been around for a long time and are anything but an American invention. The University of Bologna (1088), Oxford (around 1096), and Cambridge (1209) were in existence for several hundred years before Christopher Columbus first sailed to America. On this side of the Atlantic, Harvard traces its roots to 1636, more than a century before the Revolutionary War. But at their founding, these old universities looked nothing like the institutions we see today. They were small, unspecialized, and focused much more on teaching and the diffusion of knowledge than on its production

---

DEEP DIVE: The Founding of Cornell University

Although it would have been hard to predict at the time, July 2, 1862, was a watershed day for the U.S. system of higher education. President Abraham Lincoln signed the Morrill Act, which donated federal lands to several states to establish colleges of agriculture or "mechanical arts." A significant number of today's large public universities, the so-called land grant schools, are a direct result of this act. The law gave to each state 30,000 acres for each congressional senator and representative. States were required to sell this land and to use the proceeds from the sale plus the interest from investing this money to fund higher education institutions.

New York was the largest beneficiary of this land grant, receiving almost a million acres of land. At the low land prices during the U.S. Civil War, this translated into about $400,000 (about $7.5 million today).[4] The decision of how to allocate the money was deeply contentious, with the 20 existing colleges in the state all vying for control of the funds. State Senator Ezra Cornell took the opportunity to propose a bold plan: He would donate $500,000 of his personal telegraph-based wealth toward a new university to be located in his home town of Ithaca, New York, as long as the state would put all

proceeds from Morrill Act land sales into the university as well. Cornell, along with fellow State Senator Andrew D. White, got the New York state legislature to agree to this plan. Cornell University was founded in 1865, with White as its first president.

When Cornell first opened for instruction in the fall of 1868, it bore little resemblance to what we might recognize as an elite higher education institution today. There were fewer than 500 students and only one completed building on campus. While the faculty was considered to be of high quality for its time, the individual faculty members were broadly educated and knowledgeable rather than disciplinary specialists, and there was almost no focus on or interest in research.

Almost 150 years later, Cornell has a total enrollment of over 20,000 students that includes undergraduates, professional master's students, and highly specialized PhD students. In addition to the liberal arts school, there are schools of agriculture, law, medicine, hospitality, labor relations, veterinary medicine, engineering, and human ecology. The faculty are specialists in a given field and/or discipline, with a primary focus on research and the production of new knowledge.

---

[4] Much of the history of Cornell discussed here is taken from Morris Bishop's excellent and detailed history of Cornell University (Bishop, 1962).

through research. They likely resembled the small liberal arts schools of today (such as Amherst and Swarthmore) more than the major research-oriented institutions that can be found across the current postsecondary landscape.

Like Harvard, the first postsecondary schools in the United States were private, typically religiously affiliated schools, and taught a very small number of students. In 1776, right before the start of the American Revolutionary War, there were 18 private colleges in the 13 colonies, with a combined enrollment of 750 students (Bowen, Kurzweil, & Tobin 2005). College enrollment in this time period was exceedingly rare: Only 0.1% of the population had enrolled in college. Today, almost 60% of Americans over 25 years old have enrolled in college at some point in their lives.

Schools in the late eighteenth to the mid-nineteenth century were almost universally connected to religious organizations, most of which were one of the various Protestant denominations in the United States at the time. Unlike most European universities, however, many different Christian denominations were represented, making the United States system far more open and accessible than its European counterparts. While these colleges differed in terms of their focus on religious studies and to the extent to which they would allow those of other (Christian) faiths to enroll, religion played a much larger part in higher education institutions than it does today. In addition, colleges in the early to mid-nineteenth century were mostly private: The first public university charter was for the University of Georgia in 1785, and by 1860 publicly controlled institutions were only 24% of the total postsecondary schools in the United States (Goldin & Katz, 2008). Typically these schools served students from wealthy backgrounds as well, since these were the students who both could afford to pay tuition and received enough secondary schooling to enroll in college. Thus, around the middle of the nineteenth century, the small number of higher education institutions that did exist were mostly religious in nature, small, and teaching-oriented.

While the majority of institutions founded in the nineteenth century were private, seeds were planted for the subsequent growth of postsecondary education with the opening of public universities funded through the Morrill Acts of 1862 and 1890. The 1862 Morrill Act granted resources to states to endow universities and colleges that specialized in agriculture and the mechanical fields. The resources came in the form of a grant of federal land (hence the term *land grant university*), which had to be sold or developed in support of higher education.[5] A second iteration of the Morrill Act in 1890 established many of what we now call historically Black colleges and universities (HBCUs).

Origins of U.S. Research Universities

If you were to visit a public or private university in the second half of the nineteenth century, you would have found it looked very different from what we see today. The range of graduate and professional programs in areas like law and medicine would have been absent, and very few institutions awarded a doctorate degree. In a very careful historical analysis of U.S. higher education, researchers Claudia Goldin and Lawrence Katz (1999) argue that the research universities of today can trace their roots to massive

---

[5] The purpose of these institutions, as stated in the authorizing legislation was "to teach such branches of learning as are related to agriculture and the mechanic arts, in such manner as the legislatures of the States may respectively prescribe, in order to promote the liberal and practical education of the industrial classes in the several pursuits and professions in life." While "other scientific and classical studies" were not to be excluded, the focus of these institutions was intended to be in the applied, vocational, and technical areas.

changes in the way knowledge was structured, produced, and valued at the turn of the twentieth century. These changes were brought about by several factors:

- In the late nineteenth century, there was a growth in demand for workers with knowledge of the sciences, specifically chemistry and physics, which were important in the manufacturing and production sectors.
- The demand for scientists spurred a growth in science departments and fields in existing universities. Course offerings expanded and academic departments became increasingly specialized to meet the demands of industry.
- A general growth in the demand for specific disciplinary knowledge in the sciences, social sciences, and agriculture led to more specialized faculty and academic departments.
- Proliferation of the scientific method across disciplines increased the production of knowledge.

What happened between 1890 and 1910 is that existing schools expanded both their scale in terms of increased enrollment and their scope in terms of the breadth of disciplines covered, leading to the formation of the modern research university. As the structure of science changed significantly, broad subjects were divided, which led to the establishment of new fields and departments within the university structure. Fields splintered, and respected universities no longer had general science faculties but departments of biology, chemistry, and physics, with individuals working in subfields within these disciplines. One manifestation of this greater division in areas of study is the expansion of separate learned societies in the late nineteenth and early twentieth centuries, illustrated by the founding of societies for economists (1885), psychologists (1892), anthropologists (1902), political scientists (1903), and sociologists (1905; Goldin & Katz, 1999).

With greater division of labor within broad areas of study, the optimal scale of a university necessarily increased. To illustrate, in 1897, the average private college had 256 students and the average public university had 415 students. By 1924, these numbers had increased to 755 and 2,156, respectively (Goldin & Katz, 1999). Thus, the scale of all institutions increased while enrollment shifted to public institutions that grew considerably in size. Although in the early and mid-nineteenth century enrollment in private colleges was about as likely as enrollment in a public university, this began to shift such that by the early twentieth century higher education became mostly public.

The *modern university* encompassed an expanded scope of institutions of higher education with a deeper and greater emphasis on research. As described by Goldin and Katz (1999), the universities that emerged in the United States took a unique institutional form:

> A "university," then, would appear to be a department store of higher education, combining the specialized disciplines with the broader ones of the past and adding the various professional subjects like law, medicine, dentistry, pharmacy, theology, and even business. But the modern university is far more than a collection of higher education services brought together under one roof. It is a production center in which the research of one part enhances the teaching and research of other parts. The "university" form was an organizational innovation enabling the exploitation of technical complementarities among its various components (p. 46).

The institutions that most closely resembled the university structure in the late nineteenth and early twentieth centuries were mostly—but not exclusively—public. Because much of the science pursued by researchers in this period was complementary to local industry, public universities were able to attract much state support for their research. This was followed by a growth in specialized fields of study that could specifically benefit local labor markets, such as hybrid corn at Iowa State, dairy products at the University of Wisconsin, and petroleum engineering at the University of Texas. The state support for research deepened over the early and mid-twentieth century. For example, in World War II and the following decades, substantial government investments related to basic science and military technology were placed directly in the hands of universities. As Rhodes (1988) notes, "The ascendancy of science, both as a professional study and as a dominating influence, has notably changed the culture of the university. Unlike most other countries, the United States concentrates much of its basic research in universities rather than in government laboratories and institutes" (p. 7).

The ways in which these public universities grew allowed them to take advantage of both economies of scale and economies of scope, which increased their competitive advantage over their private counterparts. Public institutions absorbed the majority of the increased demand for collegiate training, which led to increased economies of scale in the public sector of higher education. Private universities also expanded but by less than their public counterparts.

Public universities took advantage of economics of scope driven by complementarities between the production of undergraduate education, graduate education, and research. Because of such complementarities, producing these outcomes together under one roof can be done at a lower cost than if institutions pursued any one of these activities separately. Since public universities were expanding their ability to teach all levels of students as well as their research capacity simultaneously in the late nineteenth century, they were able to reap the benefits from these economies of scope. Economies of both scope and scale remain very important features of the way universities operate today.

While the growth of the modern research university was one structural change in the U.S. higher education system, by the 1930s higher education still was reserved for a relatively small minority of the population. Figure 13.1 shows college enrollment from 1870 to 1940 relative to the size of the 20- to 24-year-old population. In 1870, the rate of college attendance was only 1.4%. By 1940, it had risen to 12.9%, but the proportion of Americans who went to college still was extremely low.

"Mass" Higher Education

While college enrollment was on a clear upward trajectory, a transformation occurred in the post–World War II era that greatly expanded investment in higher education. On January 11, 1944, President Roosevelt made a speech in which he pronounced that every American should have a "right to a good education"—since high school completion was already widespread, postsecondary attainment was the

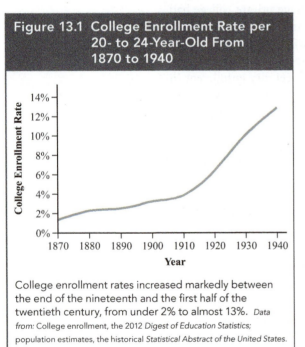

Figure 13.1 College Enrollment Rate per 20- to 24-Year-Old From 1870 to 1940

College enrollment rates increased markedly between the end of the nineteenth and the first half of the twentieth century, from under 2% to almost 13%. *Data from:* College enrollment, the 2012 *Digest of Education Statistics;* population estimates, the historical *Statistical Abstract of the United States.*

new frontier. An accelerant to the process was the Serviceman's Readjustment Act of 1944, what is now called the *GI Bill*, which provided very generous educational benefits to the many men returning home from military service. Such benefits were equal to tuition and a living stipend for each year of military service.

The upward trend exhibited in Figure 13.1 continued and accelerated after World War II, such that today the majority of students attend some form of postsecondary schooling. This extraordinary increase in postsecondary attainment in the modern period is sometimes called the era of "mass higher education." What led to these increases? Both demand-side and supply-side factors contributed to this change.

The high school movement (discussed in Chapter 2) made the United States one of the leaders throughout the world in high school completion rates by the mid-twentieth century. As a result, more and more students were academically qualified to pursue postsecondary education. At the same time, the returns to obtaining such an education were growing with the advent of new technologies and manufacturing procedures that made more educated workers more productive. These two factors led the demand for a college education to grow precipitously in the postwar period.

At the federal level, President Truman created the President's Commission on Higher Education (known as the Truman Commission) in 1946; it produced a set of reports under the heading *Higher Education for American Democracy*. These reports not only identified the role of universities in technological advance and national security but also underscored the importance of opportunities in higher education for low- and moderate-income youth. The report noted, "One of the gravest charges to which American society is subject is that of failing to provide a reasonable equality of educational opportunity for its youth."[6] Analysis afforded by tests of ability of servicemen in World War II further demonstrated that there was a large segment of the population well prepared to complete both two-year and four-year postsecondary programs but who were not attending college. One of the recommendations of the commission was a substantial expansion of community colleges, with the aim of providing two years of either general or vocational training at a very low cost. Another recommendation was to increase subsidies and opportunities in the four-year collegiate sector (Bowen et al., p. 35).

With the assistance of substantial federal funding, many states dramatically expanded their postsecondary systems. The advent of standardized testing and the increased scale also afforded the stratification of institutions within states, with at least one research university available to very strong students, multiple regional four-year institutions with BA-level programs, and many local community colleges providing access to nearly all students in proximity to their home. Perhaps the most formally defined and best-known state system of higher education came out of the California Master Plan of 1960. The master plan defined the specific roles (and admission requirements) for different tiers: the University of California institutions (UC), comprised of the most selective BA-granting universities; the California State University (CSU) system, comprised of minimally selective four-year colleges; and the California Community Colleges (CCC) system, comprised of open-access two-year colleges.[7] California and other states added institutions to meet the growing postsecondary demand.

---

[6] As cited from Bowen, Kurzweil, & Tobin (2005, p. 33)

[7] Initially, the top one-eighth (12.5%) of graduating high school seniors would be guaranteed a place at a campus of the University of California, the top one-third (33.3%) would be able to enter the California State University system, and the community colleges would accept any student with the ability to benefit. Today, test scores and high school grades are used as the determinants of admissions.

The rising demand for postsecondary schooling led as well to the establishment of a large community college system in most states. These colleges have become an increasingly important part of the U.S. higher education system, with over half of current higher education students enrolled in one of these schools. Community colleges originally were designed to mimic the programs found at four-year schools, with the idea that students would obtain a two-year associate's degree and then transfer. Over time, they have expanded to focus on vocational degrees and certificates, continuing adult education programs, and workforce and community development programs (Kane & Rouse, 1999). As their name suggests, these schools are designed to be "open access" for the local community, meaning that typically only a high school diploma and local residency are required for attendance (as well as the payment of tuition). Unlike their four-year counterparts, two-year colleges have little research mission; the main goal is the diffusion of knowledge through teaching students.

The rise of community colleges occurred in several stages. The first occurred after World War II in response to the GI Bill. The four-year system lacked the capacity to handle all of these students, and many were not academically ready for a four-year degree. As a result, a large number of students enrolled in their open-access local two-year school. A second wave of community college expansion occurred in the 1960s due to the massive increase in demand for college among the baby boom generation (i.e., the children of the World War II veterans). Over the course of the decade, the number of community colleges doubled, and enrollment in them quadrupled (Witt et al., 1994).

Beyond changes in the supply side of the market, another major contributor to the rise of mass higher education was the increased participation of women in the postsecondary system. Figure 13.2, reproduced from Goldin, Katz, and Kuziemko's (2006) analysis of rising female college participation rates, shows college graduation rates by birth cohort for men and women from 1870 to 1980. Prior to 1920, male and female college graduation rates were very low and were not very different from each other. In the first half of the twentieth century, college completion rates among men and women increased, but they did so at a much faster rate for men. However, around the 1960 birth cohort, these rates converged, and then female college completion rates grew much faster than those of men. As a result, currently there are far more women who complete college than men. This elimination and then reversal of the gender gap in postsecondary attainment is a major contributor to the overall growth in collegiate attainment rates in the postwar period.

One of the most important historical changes that helped create the current higher education market is the increased geographic integration that occurred post World War II. Prior to World War II, the system of higher education was highly localized. There was little national market for colleges but instead a "collection of local autarkies" (Hoxby, 2009). Both technological changes and institutional developments led to a significant change in this system to the more integrated system we have today. Among

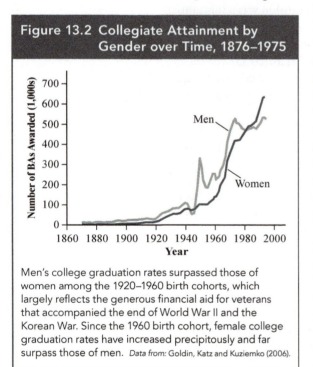

Figure 13.2 Collegiate Attainment by Gender over Time, 1876–1975

Men's college graduation rates surpassed those of women among the 1920–1960 birth cohorts, which largely reflects the generous financial aid for veterans that accompanied the end of World War II and the Korean War. Since the 1960 birth cohort, female college graduation rates have increased precipitously and far surpass those of men. *Data from:* Goldin, Katz and Kuziemko (2006).

the innovations identified by Hoxby are institutional policies facilitating the evaluation of student characteristics, including (1) the advent of standardized admissions testing (approximately 1943–1948)[8] and (2) the introduction of a standardized needs analysis system for financial aid (1956). Moreover, technological changes lowered transportation costs (the cost per mile of airline travel) and communication (the widespread availability of long-distance service), making it much easier for students to leave home to attend colleges out of state. A more detailed discussion of the resulting increased stratification in the market for higher education follows in Section 13.4.

The post–World War II era not only defines the period of a massive increase in access to U.S. higher education in terms of increased enrollment rates, but it also captures a rise to preeminence in graduate education and research innovation. Before World War II, it was common for United States scholars to obtain much of their early career training in Europe (Goldin & Katz, p. 258).[9] Innovations during World War II, such as radar and the atomic bomb, led to the creation of the National Science Foundation, which represented a commitment to extend federal support of scientific research beyond the military. Total federal funding for research at colleges and universities increased by more than a factor of 5 between 1955 and 1970. Investment in scientific research also was spurred by the Soviet Union's launch of the Sputnik I satellite in October 1957. The U.S. public's panicked reaction to an alleged educational crisis guaranteed that there would be federal intervention in higher education. The result was the rapid passage of the National Defense Education Act (NDEA) in September 1958, which provided loans for college students (with partial forgiveness for those entering elementary and secondary school teaching), graduate fellowships, and aid for programs supporting science, mathematics, modern foreign languages, and area studies. Research funding increases were not limited to engineering or to military sciences, as federal investments extended to medicine and the social sciences.

With a heavy emphasis on competition and peer review, the allocation of federal research dollars went disproportionately to a small number of research universities. By one estimate, 20 universities received 79% of research funds in 1963, with this group dubbed the "federal grant universities" by Clark Kerr (Graham & Diamond, 1997, p. 42). Doctorate education also was concentrated at a modest number of universities. In 1952, the National Science Foundation established the Graduate Research Fellowship program, which provided generous multiyear support for those pursuing doctorate study in the sciences and engineering. In addition, the NDEA fellowships for graduate study were passed by Congress in 1958 as part of a broader package of legislation intended to improve funding of education in the sciences and other areas of national need (including foreign languages), partly in response to the launching of Sputnik.

---

[8] Although standardized admissions tests have come to be used as "objective" means by which to screen college applicants, they have a somewhat nefarious beginning rooted in ideas about genetic intelligence differences across different racial and ethnic groups. See Lemann (1999) for a detailed history of admissions testing in the United States.
[9] An excellent illustration of this is the statistics presented by Goldin and Katz (2008): "Among United States Nobel Prize winners in the fields of chemistry, physics or medicine who received PhDs before 1936 and were born in the United States, 44% did some part of their formal education in Europe. Among PhDs before 1936, the United States accounted for just 18% of Nobel Prizes in science and medicine; among those with PhDs after 1955, 48% of the science Nobel Prize winners hailed from America."

Twenty-First-Century Supply-Side Changes

The growth in enrollment at for-profit colleges and the rise of online higher education providers are two developments of the early twenty-first century that have changed the structure of the postsecondary market. While there is overlap among for-profit and online offerings, it is neither the case that all for-profits are online nor the case that all online offerings are for profit. A substantial share of for-profit education is provided by "brick and mortar" colleges, while a number of public and nonprofit institutions have entered the online space.

As of 2013, over 8% of total enrollment in higher education was in private for-profit schools. In contrast, 1.5% of enrollment in 1990 and 2.9% of enrollment in 2000 was in such institutions; 42% of higher education growth between 2002 and 2012 was due to the for-profit sector. By any measure, these types of schools have become much more important in the higher education over the past 20 years. For-profit providers are diverse in terms of the programs of study offered and the extent to which they offer two-year or four-year degrees. A large percentage of these schools have a vocational focus and offer only sub-baccalaureate training. For-profit schools are more directly affected by market forces, such as demand for different course offerings and degree programs, so they have the potential to respond quickly to demand changes for various education services. However, some—though by no means all—for-profit colleges have low completion rates and high student loan default rates. This has led to much concern from policy makers over the quality of such schools and whether they are helpful or harmful for students.

Concurrent with the rise of for-profit schools has been a growing importance of online coursework and degrees in the U.S. postsecondary sector. Online higher education takes three basic forms:

1. Students at traditional brick and mortar schools who take some classes online
2. Students whose entire degree program is online
3. Massive open online courses (MOOCs)

Many traditional postsecondary schools are turning to online courses as a way to meet student demand and to allow students more flexibility in the timing of when they can take the course. These courses are taught by faculty members at the university, but all lectures are online and interactions among students and faculty are through online chat boards rather than in person. Online degree programs have a similar structure, with the distinction being that all courses are online for the entire degree program. These programs sever the link between where students live and where the instructors are located. Online degree programs typically are operated by for-profit firms and have grown dramatically over time: As of 2012, 6.5% of all higher education students in the United States were enrolled in an online degree program.

MOOCs are of a very different character from the other type of online programs. As the name suggests, these courses enroll large numbers of students, they are free and completely online, but they do not lead to a degree. Often, students receive certificates from finishing the course, but rates of completion are usually very low. MOOCs typically are offered by more elite postsecondary institutions, such as Harvard, Stanford, and MIT, as a way to provide education services to a broader population. These schools currently offer such course content for free. As Hoxby (2014) describes, this business model is unsustainable in the long run, and it is unclear whether elite post-secondary institutions have a comparative or absolute advantage in offering mass post-secondary education. Online programs are relatively new in higher education, and so it remains to be seen how this part of the market develops and how more traditional universities are affected.

13.3 The Financing of Higher Education

Each college and university in the market has a budget constraint that is determined by costs and revenues. Understanding the sources and uses of funds on both sides of this equation is fundamental to understanding the stratified market for higher education, the role of public funding, and the determinants of changes in tuition.

Revenues and Expenses

A college or university—just like any other institution—must balance its budget to remain financially viable, which means that revenue streams must match expenses. For colleges and universities, the primary sources of revenue include:[10]

- Tuition payments by students
- Appropriations from government
- Gifts and endowment returns from private philanthropy
- Grants and contracts

There are substantial differences between institutions (as well as over time) in the sources of revenue. Typically, public colleges and universities receive a large share of revenues from state appropriations. Grants and contracts tend to be concentrated at research universities. Gifts and income from endowments tend to be concentrated at selective private nonprofit colleges and universities, although public universities do receive some funding from private gifts.

Table 13.3 shows the sources of revenue for educational activities for different types of institutions, distinguishing between public and private institutions as well as between other degree-granting four-year and two-year colleges. The table shows revenues per full-time equivalent student from the key sources for academic year 2012–2013: net tuition, state appropriations, federal grants and contracts, and private support. The sum of these categories constitutes the revenue available to support the educational enterprise. Tuition revenue shown in the first column of the table is net of institutional grants for financial aid. Another category, *auxiliary enterprises*, includes revenues from sources unrelated to instruction, such as hospitals, vending contracts, and so forth.

A first point to note is the differences in sources of funds between public and private institutions. For public institutions, between $5,700 (community college) and $7,388 (research university) in revenue comes from state appropriations, while less than $1,000 per student in state appropriations flows to private institutions. Net tuition revenues are much higher at private institutions than public institutions, and across

---

[10] For this purpose of this discussion, we exclude what are often called auxiliary enterprises, which include revenues from hospitals.

Table 13.3 Sources of Revenue and Educational Expenditures, by Type and Control of Institution, 2012

	Net Tuition	State and Local Appropriations	Gifts & Endowment Income	Federal Appropriations & Grants	Non-auxiliary Revenue	Auxiliary Enterprises	Total Revenue	Educational Expenditures
Public Colleges and Universities								
Public Research	$9,844	$7,388	$1,607	$8,093	$26,792	$11,966	$38,758	$28,921
Public Master's	7,143	5,470	326	1,884	14,751	3,715	18,466	15,476
Public Bachelor's	6,402	6,538	544	2,335	15,486	4,072	19,558	16,262
Public Associate's	3,702	5,765	146	1,692	11,186	1,296	12,482	12,016
Private Colleges and Universities								
Private Research	$21,809	$755	$13,859	$11,628	$47,207	$25,124	$72,331	$52,856
Private Master's	16,210	323	1,803	765	18,765	4,472	23,237	18,835
Private Bachelor's	14,949	363	5,282	1,289	21,419	6,992	28,411	23,445

Data from: Delta Cost Project, Trends in College Spending: 2013.

the public and private sectors research universities are able to draw in greater revenues from tuition. There also are stark differences in the extent of funding from private gifts and endowments across school types: private research universities average about $13,859 per student, while even public research universities draw no more than $1,600 per student from this source. From the perspective of students, the levels of appropriations and private support are critical because they define the extent of subsidy for higher education.

On the other side of the ledger, colleges and universities face expenses that include faculty salaries, academic support services, the costs of plant and equipment, and student financial aid. The cost of faculty is perhaps the largest single item for a university, accounting for about two-thirds of expenditures. As shown in Table 13.3, expenditures per student differ markedly by type of institution. Research universities spend far more than the other types of institutions. The difference is particularly noteworthy among the private research universities, which spend about $52,856 per student on average.

Higher Education Costs and Prices

"Why does college cost so much?" This is a frequent refrain from parents and public policy makers, especially as tuition levels have increased over time. It is important to distinguish higher education *costs* from higher education *prices*, which mean something quite different in the market for higher education. We define the cost of higher education as the value of the inputs required to produce a unit of output. In other words, what does it cost in terms of expenditures on faculty and facilities to produce an undergraduate degree? Price refers to the amount that a student (or his family) pays for a unit of higher education. We distinguish between *sticker price*, which is the listed tuition level, and *net price*, which is the difference between tuition and all financial aid. Net price is what an individual actually pays to attend a given college or university. Net tuition revenue is what a college receives in tuition revenue; it is the total tuition and fee bill (if all students paid full price) less financial aid provided by the institution. Focusing on the part of the budget supporting instruction, the budget constraint for a given college thus sets costs (expenditures) equal to revenues:

$$\text{Costs} = \text{net tuition revenue} + \text{subsidy}$$

Quick Hint: Net price paid by families is the sticker price minus all grant aid, which may come from the federal government, the state, the institution or other sources. Net tuition revenue is the sticker price less grant aid provided by the institution. Chapter 14 discusses all sources of aid in more detail.

where the subsidy is the sum of state appropriations, endowment income, and private gifts. Subsidies in higher education thus are defined as revenues not coming from tuition, since these alternative revenue streams subsidize expenditures on students.

All of the pieces of this equation have changed over time, differing in magnitude across different types of institutions. Because institutions cannot spend more than they take in, this relationship is fundamentally an identity: If costs increase, either net tuition or subsidies must rise or expenditures per student must fall, with the latter implying a potential decline in the quality of education. Thus, tuition can rise either because of a decline in other sources of revenues (holding costs constant) or because of an increase in costs (holding other sources of revenue constant).

Increasing Costs Higher education is a very labor-intensive industry, and the majority of people holding instructional positions have advanced degrees. Thus, as wages of college-educated workers in the economy rise, there has been upward pressure on the salaries of faculty. The cost of faculty members is a core reason for the increase in university costs. This is true particularly in the four-year private sector, where the average real faculty salary increased from $67,735 in 1970 to $83,695 in 2011 (*Digest of Education Statistics*, 2012). This average increase hides the large rise in salaries for faculty members in technical and professional fields, such as engineering, economics, medicine, law, and computer science. For example, the starting salary for a newly minted economics PhD faculty member at research-oriented universities typically is over $100,000. For law and medical professors as well as for business school faculty, salaries are even higher. As the demand for students trained in these areas has risen, a lot of the growth in academic departments has been in these areas. Hiring more faculty in high-cost areas has resulted in an increase in faculty-based costs.

Absent changes in how teaching is organized—the production technology—colleges and universities will find their costs rising faster than those of industries in which it is possible to substitute labor-saving technology or capital for increasingly expensive labor inputs. In the 1960s, economists William Bowen and William

Baumol wrote about the economics of the performing arts. They argued that in sectors like university education and the performing arts there is less opportunity to increase productivity by substituting capital or other inputs for expensive labor. Because it is the overall labor market that determines the wages for comparably qualified individuals, the higher education sector would have no choice but to pay higher wages for its very educated labor pool, resulting in unit labor costs rising faster than in the overall economy. This phenomenon, known as **Baumol's law** or **Baumol's cost disease** (Baumol & Bowen, 1966), states that due to an economy-wide general increase in labor productivity, labor costs will rise in labor-intensive sectors that have not necessarily experienced productivity increases.[11] Robert Frank (2012) provides an intuitive example:

> While productivity gains have made it possible to assemble cars with only a tiny fraction of the labor that was once required, it still takes four musicians 9 minutes to perform Beethoven's String Quartet in C minor, just as it did in the nineteenth century.[12]

Baumol's law (Baumol's cost disease) Faculty salaries in higher education will increase in response to increases in high-skilled labor productivity in other sectors of the economy. This forces costs up in higher education if there are no labor-saving productivity changes to compensate.

The argument is that the education and research outputs of universities are very labor-intensive—it is very difficult to allow machines to do research, to teach a class, or to advise students. An increase in labor productivity in sectors other than education will raise wages in those sectors, which will draw faculty out of higher education and into these other sectors if universities do not offer them a higher salary as well. Thus, even though worker productivity in the higher education sector may not have increased, the fact that the value of faculty skills has grown outside of education generates an increase in their salaries as universities compete with other sectors for the best workers.

To take an example, consider the career choices faced by a student who has recently graduated from a top law school. The student can practice law or she can become a faculty member at a university. Even if she is predisposed to want to become a professor, if the salary of practicing lawyers rises enough relative to the professor's salary, she will choose to practice rather than to teach law. Thus, an increase in the salary of practicing lawyers will put upward pressure on faculty salaries of academic lawyers, as universities and private firms are competing for the same workers. Indeed, it is exactly in the fields in which labor productivity is rising that we have seen the largest growth in faculty salaries. That these fields of study are more and more popular among students due to the high associated wages exacerbates this phenomenon.

Research costs also have risen over time, due largely to the cost of space for labs and the cost of labor inputs to producing research. Increases in graduate student tuition as well as wages for undergraduate and graduate students make research more expensive. This increases overall university costs, particularly in research-centered schools.

---

[11] Bowen, a former president of Princeton University, documented what then seemed like an "inexorable tendency" for instructional cost per student to increase in *The Economics of Major Private Universities* (1968). Bowen (2012) revisits the question in the recent essay "The 'Cost Disease' in Higher Education: Is Technology the Answer?" He argues that the claim of limited productivity growth in higher education may be misplaced. He notes, "It seems evident that information technology has been extremely consequential in higher education over the last 25 years, but principally in 'output enhancing' ways that do not show up in the usual measures of either productivity or cost per student." http://www.ithaka.org/sites/default/files/files/ITHAKA-TheCostDiseaseinHigherEducation.pdf

[12] Robert H. Frank, "The Prestige Chase Is Raising College Costs," *New York Times*, March 10, 2012.

In addition to Baumol's Law, there are several other explanations for cost increases:

- *Growth in administrative spending.* Administrative costs have risen substantially over time, driven in part by expansions in the number of administrators. Of central concern is whether administrative expansions enhance productivity or whether they indicate managerial rent-seeking that does not increase productivity.[13] Bowen and McPherson (2016) argue the former is more likely. They note that the rise in administrative positions accompanied an overall increase in enrollment and that there is some evidence of a shift from nonprofessional staff to professional staff. This shift is consistent with the replacement of low-skilled jobs, like filing and typing, with positions that require greater skill, such as computer support.

- *Expansion of expenditures on consumption amenities.* Many colleges and universities spend considerable amounts on amenities that seem to have little to do with their core educational mission. These amenities include recreational facilities, plush dormitories, and high-quality dining halls. If students (and parents) value such features, competition over these dimensions of quality could lead to higher costs. In the provocatively titled paper "College as Country Club: Do Colleges Cater to Students' Preferences for Consumption?" Jacob, McCall, and Stange (forthcoming) consider whether these types of amenities affect enrollment decisions. They find that, particularly among private institutions outside the most academically competitive, students respond to amenity spending in their college-going decisions. Competition over consumption amenities therefore could be an explanation for cost increases among these types of institutions.

- *Increased expenditures on financial aid.* Many universities use financial aid to provide opportunities for lower-income students and to recruit high-achieving students ("merit aid"). They are effectively giving up tuition revenue to attract students who help them satisfy institutional goals. Such financial aid is an expense, and it has increased considerably over time as universities seek to attract more students from lower-income families and to increase the academic aptitude of incoming classes.

Such changes in costs necessarily require either an increase in revenues from tuition or fees or an increase in subsidies to maintain the budget balance condition.

Subsidies in Higher Education When the price that a student pays for higher education is less than the cost of producing that education, the student receives a subsidy. Some subsidies reduce prices for all students attending an institution; other subsidies are specific to particular students. Suppose either a private donor or the state government fully funded a new library at a college; all students would have the opportunity to benefit. Subsidies that take the form of financial aid are student-specific and are based on characteristics like capacity to pay, academic achievement, or athletic ability. We discuss these subsidies in relation to net price later in the chapter and in Chapter 14.

As previously noted, state appropriations and private philanthropy are the two main sources of general student subsidies. The relative importance of these subsidies differs markedly by type of institution, with public institutions disproportionately receiving

---

[13] See Paul F. Campos, "The Real Reason College Tuition Costs So Much," *New York Times*, April 4, 2015, for a further description of this argument.

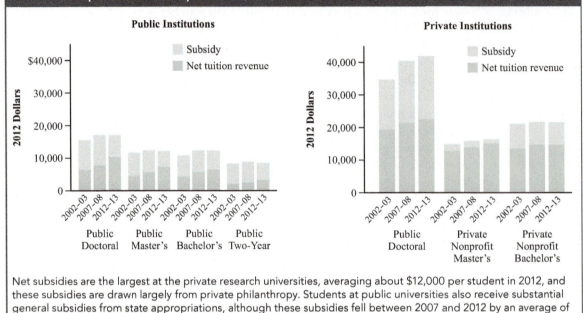

Figure 13.3 Net Tuition Revenues, Subsidies, and Education and Related Expenditures per Full-Time Equivalent (FTE) Student in 2012 Dollars

Net subsidies are the largest at the private research universities, averaging about $12,000 per student in 2012, and these subsidies are drawn largely from private philanthropy. Students at public universities also receive substantial general subsidies from state appropriations, although these subsidies fell between 2007 and 2012 by an average of about $1,600 at public research universities and by about $1,400 at public community colleges. Over this period, the balance between state appropriations and tuition revenues shifted toward a greater reliance on tuition revenues.

From: The College Board, *Trends in College Pricing 2015,* Figure 19A & 19B.

subsidies in the form of state appropriations and private universities receiving the bulk of subsidies from private philanthropy. The magnitude of subsidies differs considerably by institutional selectivity. Figure 13.3 shows the overall level of subsidy and share of educational services spending by type of institution. Net subsidies are the largest at the private research universities, averaging about $12,000 per student in 2012, and these subsidies are drawn largely from private philanthropy. Students at public universities also receive substantial general subsidies from state appropriations, although these subsidies fell between 2007 and 2012 by an average of about $1,600 at public research universities and by about $1,400 at public community colleges. Over this period, the balance between state appropriations and tuition revenues shifted toward a greater reliance on tuition revenues.

These declines in subsidies per student mirror the aggregate decline in state appropriations over this period, from $92.3 billion to $75 billion (2014 constant dollars).[14] Why has public support for higher education fallen so dramatically in recent years? A first explanation is that the recession beginning in 2008 put downward pressure on state budgets. However, as shown in Figure 13.4, which depicts state appropriations per full-time equivalent (FTE) student at public colleges and universities, the decline began in the 1990s. The figure shows a dramatic reduction in per-student state appropriations, from about $12,000 per FTE in the mid-1980s to less than $7,000 per FTE in the most recent year. Generally, there is a strong negative trend in appropriations

---

[14] *Trends in College Pricing,* Figure 16B.

per-student, with clear downward cycles following recessions in 1990, 2001, and 2008. One explanation for this pattern is that states' capacity to fund higher education, particularly during cyclical economic downturns, has been constrained by increasing commitments for states to match federal spending on other programs such as Medicaid and K–12 education. As well, tax revenues in the last two decades have been increasingly volatile, which reduces the ability of states to make longer-run financial commitments to higher education institutions (Kane, Orszag, & Apostolov, 2005).

The other source of major subsidy, private gifts and endowment, is concentrated at private colleges and universities and at very selective public universities. Overall endowment values and the flow of new private gifts have increased in recent decades, albeit with variability that mirrors the stock market. Figure 13.5 presents endowment asset deciles per FTE across different institution types. The left panel shows the distribution of endowment per student at private nonprofit institutions by decile rank, and the right panel presents the same figure for public institutions. The scales differ dramatically between public and private institutions; while the top decile of private institutions has $1.1 million in endowment per student, the top decile of public institutions has about $110,000 in endowment per student. For both types of institutions, endowment support deciles rapidly to near zero below the top couple deciles.

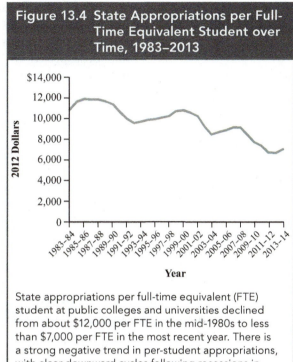

Figure 13.4 State Appropriations per Full-Time Equivalent Student over Time, 1983–2013

State appropriations per full-time equivalent (FTE) student at public colleges and universities declined from about $12,000 per FTE in the mid-1980s to less than $7,000 per FTE in the most recent year. There is a strong negative trend in per-student appropriations, with clear downward cycles following recessions in 1990, 2001, and 2008. *Data from: Trends in College Pricing and Digest of Education Statistics, various years. All figures are deflated by the Higher Education Price Index (HEPI).*

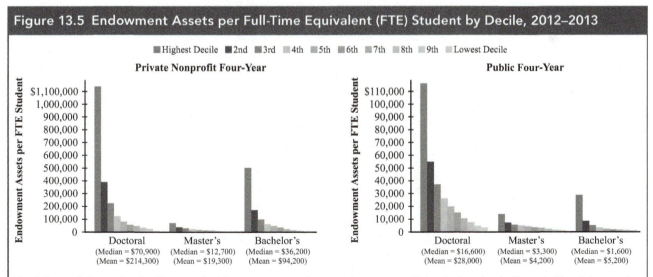

Figure 13.5 Endowment Assets per Full-Time Equivalent (FTE) Student by Decile, 2012–2013

The left panel shows the distribution of endowment per student at private nonprofit institutions by decile rank. The right panel presents the same figure for public institutions. While the top decile of private institutions has $1.1 million in endowment per student, the top decile of public institutions has about $110,000 in endowment per student. For both types of institutions, endowment support declines rapidly to near zero below the top decile. *From: The College Board, Trends in College Pricing 2015, Figure 20.*

How should you think of $1 million in endowment affecting spending? A reasonable rule of thumb is to multiply the endowment value by 0.05, if 5% is the expected annual real rate of return for an asset in *perpetuity*. So, an endowment of $1 million could be expected to produce $50,000 in annual operating expenditures, while $100,000 would be expected to produce $5,000 in such expenditures per student.

> **Quick Hint:** A perpetuity is an asset that provides an infinite series of payments. The value of a perpetuity (E) is the payment (Y) divided by the rate of return (r): $E = Y/r$.

To link the different sources of support—endowment from private gifts and state appropriations—it is sobering to consider the needed additions to endowment if state funding were to decline permanently. Suppose an institution like the University of Michigan, which received about $300 million in state support in 2016, were to face a 10%, or $30 million, cut in appropriations. It would take nearly $600 million in increased endowment ($E = $30 million/0.05) to replace these revenues on a permanent basis!

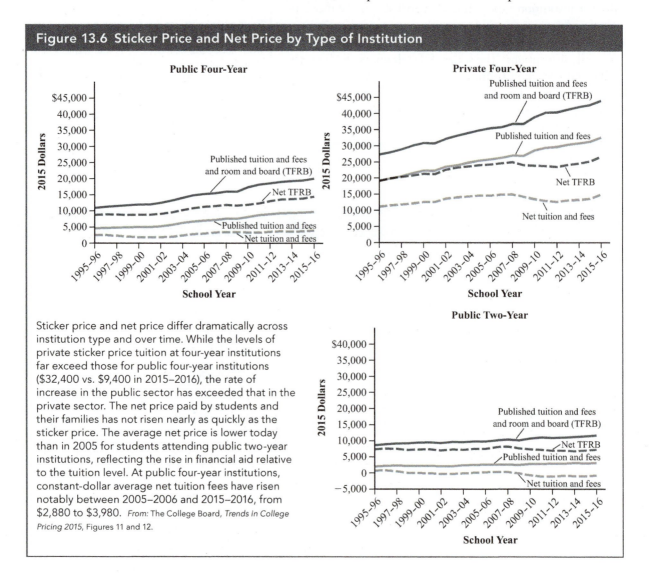

Figure 13.6 Sticker Price and Net Price by Type of Institution

Sticker price and net price differ dramatically across institution type and over time. While the levels of private sticker price tuition at four-year institutions far exceed those for public four-year institutions ($32,400 vs. $9,400 in 2015–2016), the rate of increase in the public sector has exceeded that in the private sector. The net price paid by students and their families has not risen nearly as quickly as the sticker price. The average net price is lower today than in 2005 for students attending public two-year institutions, reflecting the rise in financial aid relative to the tuition level. At public four-year institutions, constant-dollar average net tuition fees have risen notably between 2005–2006 and 2015–2016, from $2,880 to $3,980. *From: The College Board, Trends in College Pricing 2015, Figures 11 and 12.*

Changes in Sticker Price and Net Price Rarely a year has gone by in recent memory in which there has not been a series of media stories about the rise in the price of college. This outcry is not without merit: Tuition levels have increased at rates far above standard cost indices like the consumer price index (CPI). As we noted previously, one reason is that the underlying input cost of producing a college education of a given quality has increased. Yet, increases in tuition have not been uniform across sectors, as shown in Figure 13.6. While the levels of private tuition charged at four-year institutions far exceed those for public four-year institutions ($32,400 vs. $9,400 in 2015–2016), the rate of increase in the public sector has exceeded that in the private sector since 2000: Constant-dollar tuition at public four-year institutions increased by 94% between 2000 and 2015 and increased by 46% at private institutions over this period.

The dramatic increases in tuition charges at public universities are clearly related to changes in the level of state appropriations, as shown in Figure 13.7. Institutions face a difficult choice when state support falls: either reduce educational services (offer fewer classes or increase class size) or increase tuition charges. Beyond changing subsidies, rising tuition levels may reflect decisions to spend more per student, either because costs of inputs increase or because the institution chooses to increase inputs per student (with an eye to competing on quality). These explanations account for much of the increase in the level of tuition at private universities.

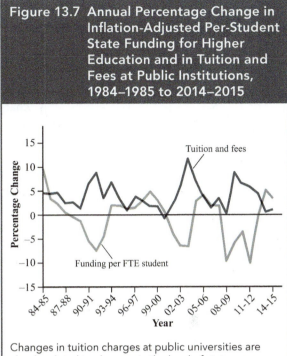

Figure 13.7 Annual Percentage Change in Inflation-Adjusted Per-Student State Funding for Higher Education and in Tuition and Fees at Public Institutions, 1984–1985 to 2014–2015

Changes in tuition charges at public universities are clearly related to changes in the level of state appropriations. When state support falls, public institutions increase tuition to make up for at least part of the lost revenue. *From: The College Board,* Trends in College Pricing 2015, *Figure 16A.*

The sticker price may differ considerably from the net price. The net price paid by students and their families has not risen nearly as quickly as the sticker price. As Figure 13.6 shows, the average net price is actually lower today than in 2005 for students attending public two-year institutions, reflecting the rise in financial aid relative to the tuition level. At public four-year institutions, constant-dollar average net tuition has risen notably between 2005–2006 and 2015–2016, from $2,880 to $3,980. Accounting for room and board charges leads to even larger increases in costs to students.

The distinction between net price and sticker price is important in understanding changes over time in net tuition revenues. For institutions that promise to meet student need by financial aid, increasing tuition by a dollar will not increase net tuition revenue by a dollar. Every student receiving financial aid will have a dollar more of need, while additional students may also become aid eligible.

Increasing the sticker price can generate revenue if it allows for **price discrimination**. Price discrimination occurs when a firm charges different prices to different consumers, irrespective of the cost of providing the good to the consumer. To understand how price discrimination works through tuition discounting in higher education, start with a downward-sloping demand schedule as in Figure 13.8. The demand curve illustrates the number of students willing to attend a college at any given price. Suppose we observe the enrollment quantity E_1 and tuition price T_1. The capacity of the institution is E_C, leaving $E_C - E_1$ empty seats. What should an institution do to fill seats and increase net revenue? If the marginal cost of enrolling students is less than T_1, the institution could offer students financial aid—a scholarship of $F = T_1 - T_C$, where T_C is the resulting tuition

price discrimination
Occurs when a firm charges different customers different prices for reasons that are not related to the cost of providing the good or service.

Figure 13.8 Price Discrimination in Higher Education

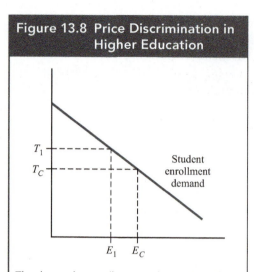

The demand curve illustrates the number of students willing to attend a college at any given price. At tuition level T_1, enrollment is E_1, but the capacity of the institution is E_c, leaving $E_c - E_1$ empty seats. If the marginal cost of enrolling students is less than T_1, the institution can offer students a scholarship of $T_1 - T_c$. The college generates additional revenue of $T_c \times (E_c - E_1)$, and the sum of the revenue from the scholarship students and those paying the full fare would be greater than what the institution would have received if E_c students paid T_c.

Bennett hypothesis
Increases in financial aid will lead to increases in tuition as schools attempt to capture some of the financial aid funds for themselves.

amount. Given the demand schedule, the college would generate an additional revenue of $T_C \times (E_C - E_1)$, and the sum of the revenue from the scholarship students and those paying the full fare would be greater than what the institution would have received if E_1 students paid T_1.

Colleges that do not face excess demand and therefore that need to attract more students may find implicit price discrimination—charging a higher sticker price but awarding many students aid or discounts—an effective way to increase revenue. In contrast, for selective institutions with excess demand, providing institutional aid is appropriately considered as an expenditure or cost because it does not add to net revenue.[15] Institutional aid in this case is an expenditure that is used to satisfy institutional goals.

Some colleges and universities use a significant portion of their tuition revenue to provide institutional grants in the form of tuition discounts to students. The average discount rate among private non-profit colleges was 46.4% in 2014, which rose from 37.2% in 2000 (Rivard, 2014). What this means is that for a college to raise $1 of tuition revenue, it needs to increase tuition by $1.87. This number is found using the following formula: $\frac{1}{1 - 0.464}$. In essence, these schools are engaging in price discrimination, charging wealthier students more to attend so that they can charge students from lower-income backgrounds less. The result is a steep rise in the posted tuition of colleges and universities, with an ever-declining fraction of the student bodies who attend these schools paying the full price.

Changes in financial aid from public sources—primarily state and federal government—provide another channel through which financial aid policies might affect college tuition charges. In a 1987 *New York Times* Op-Ed piece titled "Our Greedy Colleges," then–Secretary of Education William Bennett charged, "If anything, increases in financial aid in recent years have enabled colleges and universities blithely to raise their tuitions, confident that Federal loan subsidies would help cushion the increase." His hypothesis, now known as the **Bennett hypothesis**, predicted that colleges will raise tuition when federal and state financial aid increases to capture these funds. To take a simplified example, suppose the federal government increased financial aid to all college students by $1,000. What would stop all colleges from raising tuition by $1,000 (or reducing institutional grant aid by this amount), so they can take all of the increased aid as added revenue and make students no worse off? If the college market were not very competitive, such behavior might occur. More generally, as with any subsidy the incidence depends on the relative elasticities of supply and demand. There are a number of reasons to think that the Bennett hypothesis would not apply across the board to institutions of higher education. Many who objected to Bennett's claim noted that at many public and private nonprofit institutions like Yale and Stanford, which were explicit objects of Bennett's scorn, only a minority of students were affected by changes in the generosity of aid. So it would make little sense to respond to federal changes by raising tuition for all students at these schools.

---

[15] For a more detailed discussion, see Bowen and Breneman, "Student Aid: Price Discount or Educational Investment?" *College Board Review,* 167 pp. 2–6, 35–36, spring 1993.

Ultimately, the question of whether the Bennett hypothesis is valid is an empirical one. The challenge is one of establishing causality: It is difficult to find a source of financial aid variation that is uncorrelated with the composition of students and with other institutional and state or federal education policies. Moreover, the impact of changes in financial aid is likely to vary across the sectors of higher education. It therefore is not surprising that the available empirical evidence is quite mixed.

One clever test of the Bennett hypothesis examined tuition differences among for-profit institutions in vocational–technical fields. Postsecondary training in some occupations, like cosmetology, is provided by institutions that are eligible for federal financial aid, while others are not eligible. An empirical analysis by Goldin and Cellini (2014) shows that the institutions eligible for federal aid charge tuition that is about 78% higher than that charged by comparable institutions whose students are not eligible for federal aid. In turn, the dollar value of the premium parallels the amount of grant aid and loan subsidy received by students in eligible institutions, which is consistent with the Bennett hypothesis.

A study examining a wider set of institutions by Lesley Turner (2014) examines how need-based federal aid affects the amount of institutional aid a student is offered. Turner's findings indicate that for every $1 increase in federal grant aid, institutional aid declines by 20 cents. This result suggests that federal aid does reduce the price for students, just not by as much as was intended by federal policy makers. That the Bennett hypothesis has some truth to it highlights the role financial aid can play in increasing college tuition levels.

13.4 Heterogeneity and Stratification in the Market for Higher Education

Heterogeneity in Higher Education

A central point that we have highlighted throughout this chapter is that colleges and universities comprise a very heterogeneous set of institutions. There is certainly competition in the market, but institutions are by no means perfect substitutes! It is not the case that "a college is a college," with the implication that a student will get nearly the same education at any institution. Three important dimensions distinguish postsecondary institutions:

1. Public, nonprofit, or for-profit control of the school
2. Levels of degree offered (two-year, four-year, graduate, undergraduate)
3. The academic quality and resources of the institution

What is more, some institutions specialize in particular types of educational experiences. Caltech and Swarthmore are both highly selective private nonprofit institutions with very low student–faculty ratios. Yet they produce a very different distribution of degrees by level and subject matter: Caltech produces many degrees in engineering and the natural sciences, while Swarthmore does not have an engineering program and awards a large percentage of degrees in the arts and humanities. It is difficult to find another market where the institutions that constitute the market are so varied in their scope, quality, control, and focus. The closest is probably the health care market: doctors and hospitals have specialties in different areas, there are public and private hospitals, and hospital and doctor quality can vary immensely. However, the health care market is far less geographically integrated than the higher education market; few travel across the country for any medical care, much less emergency treatments. Many students travel quite far to go to college or graduate school, however.

One of the defining characteristics of the higher education market is the degree to which it is stratified by expenditures per student and the academic characteristics of students. There are many ways to categorize schools into different groups, and as discussed in Chapter 6, measuring college quality is very difficult. Nevertheless, we split the higher education sector into six mutually exclusive groups that broadly define the different types of institutions in the higher education system:

1. Public four-year flagship universities
2. Public four-year nonflagship colleges and universities
3. Highly selective private colleges and universities
4. Less selective private colleges and universities
5. Public community colleges
6. Private two-year schools

flagship universities The most selective and highest-resource four-year public universities in each state. Most states explicitly designate one or two schools as their flagship institution.

Public four-year **flagship universities** are the most selective and highest-resource public universities. Every state has at least one university designated at the flagship, which means it serves the academically highest-performing students and tends to have far higher resource levels. Thus, categories 1 and 2 are public four-year schools that differ in resources and degree offerings.

We also split private four-year schools according to quality. For the highly selective private schools, we take the 65 top-ranked private universities according to *U.S. News and World Report* as well as the 50 top-ranked liberal arts schools. These schools all have very competitive admissions and admit a small proportion of students who apply. While the *U.S. News* ranking can seem quite arbitrary, they do a good job of separating schools into broad groups on the whole. We note that none of the conclusions we draw from the data are sensitive to the specific method we use to categorize schools. Finally, we combine all public two-year schools together and all private ones together.[16]

Table 13.4 shows the degree of stratification across these higher education sectors in terms of financial resources, graduation rates, student–faculty ratios, and the academic achievement level of incoming students as measured by SAT and ACT scores. The differences across the school types are immense and show a strong positive correlation between per-student resources and student academic achievement levels. At one end of the spectrum, the highly selective private schools spend $78,373 per student and have a graduation rate of 86%. Public flagship universities also have very high per-student expenditures and graduation rates, although not as high as the highly selective private sector. Furthermore, students in these two sectors are very high-achieving as measured by SAT and ACT scores. Both the less selective privates and the nonflagship publics have much lower expenditures per student and graduation rates than their higher-quality counterparts. In fact, the characteristics of the less selective privates and nonflagship publics are very similar to each other on all of these dimensions except for tuition. Tuition at the less selective four-year private schools is over twice the in-state tuition at the nonflagship public schools.

---

[16] Stange (2012) shows that quality measures of community colleges do not translate into differences in student outcomes. Furthermore, most students attend their local community college rather than searching for the best two-year school. Thus, it is not very informative to split the community colleges into groups according to quality measures.

Table 13.4 Average Characteristics of Schools across Sectors in 2012

School Characteristic	Public Flagship	Public Non-flagship	Highly Selective Private	Less Selective Private	Public two-year	Private two-year
Resources						
Per-student expenditures	$43,897	$28,047	$78,373	$20,545	$6,225	$8,769
Per-student instructional expenditures	$13,873	$7,978	$23,894	$5,982	$3,690	$3,532
Student–faculty ratio	15.1	22.3	9.3	18.7	29.0	27.8
25th percentile math SAT score	549.8	462.0	625.0	462.4		
75th percentile math SAT score	663.7	569.3	720.7	575.1		
25th percentile ACT score	23.6	19.3	27.7	19.8		
75th percentile ACT score	28.7	24.1	31.6	25.1		
Graduation rate	0.71	0.43	0.86	0.45		
Tuition and Fees						
In state	$9,083	$7,205	$41,043	$19,278	$3,595	$13,461
Out of state	$23,712	$16,020	$41,130	$19,291	$7,055	$13,480
Revenues per Student						
Tuition	$8,957	$4,700	$21,350	$10,634	$1,629	$7,267
Federal	$5,523	$180	$12	$269	$83	$861
State	$6,436	$5,899	$140	$70	$1,787	$42

Data from: 2012 IPEDS. ACT scores are composite, while SAT scores are for mathematics only. In-state and out-of-state tuition and fees are for full-time undergraduate students and show the amount owed if a student pays full price without financial aid. All per-student measures are relative to all enrolled students, graduate and undergraduate. SAT and ACT data are not reported for two-year schools because very few students who attend these schools take these college admissions exams. Instructional expenditures include categories that support research as well as teaching, which is why the difference between overall educational expenditures and instructional expenditures is particularly large at selective universities.

The differences across the two-year and four-year sectors are even larger than the differences across the different types of four-year schools. On the whole, community colleges are characterized by very low resources, high student–faculty ratios, and low graduation rates. Although SAT scores are not available for community college students because these schools do not require entrance exams, two-year college students tend to be much lower performing academically (Bound, Lovenheim, & Turner 2010; Lovenheim & Reynolds, 2011). Thus, two-year students have fewer financial resources, faculty resources, and peer resources than four-year students.

Stratification in Public Higher Education

The inequality in resources across higher education institutions is unambiguous, as shown in Table 13.4. Among public colleges and universities, much of the stratification in resources occurs within states, with appropriations or government subsidy per student historically greater at the more selective and research-intensive universities. Is this stratification simply historical accident, or can it be explained with an economic model? How would a social planner—a decision maker who attempted to generate the best result for all potential students—choose the assignment of students to colleges with different levels of resources? This allocation problem depends on both the production function and the effect of resources on achievement for students with different aptitudes for college.

One useful way to approach this problem is through an economic model first presented by Sallee, Resch, and Courant (2008). They begin with the assumption that we are concerned only with maximizing the skills (A) that students acquire in college and that these skills are the only thing that colleges produce. The resulting production function with student aptitude (S) and instructional expenditures (E) can be shown as $A = f(S,E)$. This setup disregards peer effects in production and the other outputs of a university, such as research. One assumption that the authors make is that there is a *complementarity* between student aptitude and instructional expenditures: A dollar of instructional expenditures is more productive when spent on higher-aptitude students. For this reason, it is efficient to match higher-aptitude students with more resource-intensive collegiate experiences. At the extreme, one might think of matching students and universities such that each student receives a customized resource allocation. Such a matching algorithm is shown graphically by the upward-sloping line $r(S)$ in Figure 13.9. Because there are economies of scale in the production of collegiate education, colleges will need to be of a minimum scale. A perfect sorting of students by aptitude leads to different institutions that aggregate students into ability groups. Figure 13.9 shows the case with two institutions. An optimal allocation is reached when total learning could not be improved by altering the number of institutions. An implication of this model is that a policy of selective admissions is necessary because all students would likely prefer access to the most resource-intensive institutions.

This sorting system that leads higher-ability students to be allocated to institutions with higher resource levels broadly resembles the public postsecondary systems in many states. California is a clear example of such a system, with a group of elite public schools that receive considerable state subsidies, a group of less selective colleges that also spend less per student, and a large assortment of open-access community colleges. In this system, the students with the greatest aptitude receive the largest subsidies in public support. But just how many tiers a public university system should optimally have is far from certain, though it is logical that this should depend on the population size, the distribution of student characteristics, and the

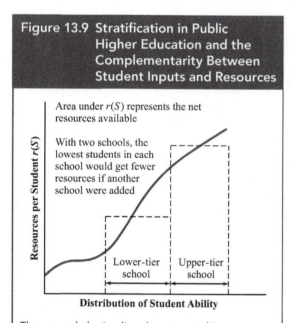

Figure 13.9 Stratification in Public Higher Education and the Complementarity Between Student Inputs and Resources

Area under $r(S)$ represents the net resources available

With two schools, the lowest students in each school would get fewer resources if another school were added

Resources per Student $r(S)$

Lower-tier school | Upper-tier school

Distribution of Student Ability

The upward-sloping line shows a matching algorithm in which each student receives a customized resource allocation. Because there are economies of scale in the production of collegiate education, colleges will need to be of a minimum scale. A perfect sorting of students by aptitude leads to two different institutions that aggregate students into ability groups.

production technology. It follows that states with larger populations are likely to have more tiers and stratification will be greater, with the greater selectivity in the top tier institution. This is indeed what Sallee, Resch, and Courant (2008) find. Even as there is a strong theoretical rationale for some stratification in higher education, it is not at all clear whether there is too much or too little in the current allocation of resources.

Stratification in Private Higher Education

Among private nonprofit colleges and universities, the stratification we observe in resources per student follows from differences across institutions in subsidies generated from private donations, largely in the form of endowment. When a university's relative wealth or endowment increases, it is either because the returns on these invested funds increased or because the university received additional gifts.

Many of the private and nonprofit institutions with very high levels of endowment per student were founded more than a century ago. To this end, the wealth and, effectively, per-student subsidy can grow in a dynastic fashion if an institution's graduates are both financially successful and inclined to give back by adding to the endowment. One way to think of the situation of the elite private research universities and liberal arts colleges suggested by Caroline Hoxby (2015) is that they behave like intellectual venture capitalists. With a mission to invest in advanced human capital in people and new knowledge, the university aims to select students and research projects (along with faculty researchers) to further this goal. The endowment funds provide the seed money and subsidy for these objectives, which would be difficult to fund in traditional capital markets given the expertise needed to identify talent and the risk associated with such investments. For students, Hoxby models the university as a venture capitalist investing expertise and resources. The investment is represented by the tuition subsidy, which is the difference between the cost of a student's education and what he or she actually pays. Just as a venture capitalist is compensated when an investment proves successful, the university would like to hold an equity stake in the future earnings of its graduates. While an explicit contract on future labor is not feasible given prohibitions on indentured servitude, the university nevertheless seeks to create an obligation for students to repay to finance investments in future generations. Colleges and universities thus aim to create a sense of commitment and loyalty among alumni with the aim of promoting philanthropy to the institution. When successful, the result is a virtuous cycle of funding for universities, yielding substantial subsidies for students.

Competition and Stratification over Time in the Higher Education Market

When there are many colleges and universities competing to attract students, the market for higher education is seen as competitive. Because of the customer input nature of higher education, colleges and universities compete for students with high aptitude, not just customers with the capacity to pay.

Market Integration If a market is local or regional, it will be less competitive than a market that is national with many participants. Over time, higher education has become a more nationally **integrated market**, particularly among the most resource-intensive

integrated market
Combines markets that are separated geographically, thus increasing the effective market size for a given consumer. When markets are more integrated, there are increased opportunities to differentiate products, resulting in better matching of consumer (student) preferences to choices over products (colleges).

universities. While it would have been rare for a student to travel out of state to college before World War II, today it is fairly common for students to explore college choices far away from home. What changed to make the market more nationally integrated?

An insightful analysis by Caroline Hoxby (2009) identifies some of the innovations that reduced the cost of applying to and attending colleges far from home, thus increasing the national integration of the higher education market. Changes that spurred the integration of the higher education market include the widespread adoption of standardized admissions assessments such as the SAT and ACT exams, along with the introduction of a standardized needs analysis system. In addition, technological changes such as the introduction of large-scale air travel, the more general reduction of travel costs, and the rise of widespread long-distance phone service surely made it easier to attend college out of state. Table 13.5 provides some supporting evidence on reductions in some of the costs associated with geographic integration. Since the mid-1950s, there has been a large reduction in the cost of cross-country calls as well as the cost of air travel. These changes make it easier for students to attend school far from home. There also has been a dramatic rise in the number of colleges requiring the SAT or ACT—from 143 in 1955 to 1208 in 1975. The adoption of standardized exams increases the ability of students across the country to signal their academic aptitude to all schools.

Concurrent with these changes, the percentage of in-state students at private colleges and universities fell from 80% in 1949 to about 55% in 1994 (Hoxby, 2009). While the proportion of in-state students also fell at public universities in aggregate, it is only at the modest number of public universities that are close substitutes with nationally recognized private universities that the number of out-of-state students increased markedly.

The increase in the capacity of students to apply to colleges and universities across the country suggests that higher education institutions have become more selective. While it is unambiguously the case that the elite colleges and universities have become much more selective, increased selectivity does not apply across the board. As Hoxby (1999) shows, the supply of college seats open to moderately qualified students has actually increased over time.

Table 13.5 Institutional and Price Changes Affecting College Market Integration

High School Graduating Cohort	Cost of 10-Minute Cross-Country Call (2007 Dollars)	Cost per Air Passenger Mile	Colleges Requiring SAT	SAT Test-Takers per Freshman
1955	52.73	41.38	143	0.23
1965	42.45	39.88	783	0.75
1975	17.34	29.63	1208	0.6
1985	9.31	23.74	1787	0.65
1995	3.67	18.36	1831	0.75
2005	2.61	13.05	1429	0.87

Data from: Hoxby (2009).

Increased Stratification Over the course of the last quarter-century, resources per student among the most selective institutions have increased markedly. There has been a fanning out of expenditures per student at the most elite universities. Figure 13.10 shows trends in real per-student expenditures by school type from 1980 to 2012. The magnitude of the changes in resources is simply striking, with enormous increases among selective four-year private schools and flagship universities and much more modest increases across the other institution types. For example, in 1980 the selective private-sector schools spent 5.5 times the amount per student as public two-year schools. By 2012, this difference almost doubled, so that now the selective private schools spend 9.2 times per student what community colleges spend. Between 1980 and 2012, per-student spending in the two-year and less selective four-year sectors increased by 600–800%. Expenditures per student in the flagship sector increased by over 1,100%, and in the selective four-year schools spending increased by over 1,300%.

Taking a focused look at institutions in the top part of the distribution of selectivity, Hoxby (2009) examines how resources per student have changed over time differentially according to 1962 selectivity. Her results are similarly dramatic: Per-student resources among the top 1% selectivity colleges in 1962 grew enormously, from less than $20,000 to over $90,000 in 2006 (when her study ends). The 96th to 98th percentile schools also grew, from about $10,000 per student to about $40,000 per student, as did the 91st to the 95th percentile universities. However, schools below the 90th percentile of 1962 selectivity saw at most a small increase in per-student expenditures. Hoxby (2009) thus indicates that the most selective schools became higher resource and more elite over time, while the vast majority of less selective schools experienced a very small increase in resources per student. Clearly, resource stratification has increased substantially over this time period.

Table 13.6 shows that the source of these expenditure increases differs across sectors. The table presents per-student expenditures, net tuition revenues, and subsidies for a set of elite public and private institutions in 2012 dollars. Among the private universities, tuition revenues have either held constant or declined slightly while expenditures rose substantially. Thus, subsidies have grown among the highly selective private universities, mostly driven by endowment growth and private donations. For the elite public schools, tuition revenues have grown markedly while subsidies have mostly remained constant. Constant subsidies reflect declining state appropriations and growth in endowment income and charitable donations.

The large increases in per-student resources in highly selective institutions comes at a time when demand for postsecondary education is growing. However, the most resource-intensive institutions have not responded to increased demand with growth in capacity, as evidenced by vastly increased selectivity and very low admission rates. Highly selective institutions tend not to increase the number of students they admit when there is a demand increase. An explanation for limited enrollment growth at many of these institutions is that they are providing substantial subsidies to each student, which allow

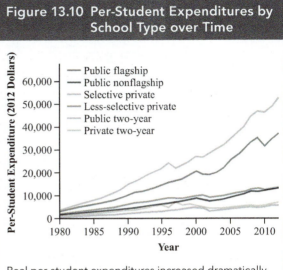

Figure 13.10 Per-Student Expenditures by School Type over Time

- Public flagship
- Public nonflagship
- Selective private
- Less-selective private
- Public two-year
- Private two-year

Real per-student expenditures increased dramatically in the selective private and flagship public sectors between 1980 and 2012. Increases in the other postsecondary sectors were more modest, leading to increased resource stratification across higher education institutions. *Data from: 1980–2012 IPEDS.*

Table 13.6 Education Expenses, Net Tuition Revenues, and Subsidies per FTE (2012 Dollars)						
	2007–2008			2012–2013		
School	Education Expenses (1)	Net Tuition (2)	Subsidy per FTE (2) − (1)	Education Expenses (3)	Net Tuition (4)	Subsidy per FTE (4) − (3)
Private Sector						
Columbia University	$75,900	$30,436	$45,464	$96,070	$34,297	$61,773
Harvard University	86,424	22,211	64,213	84,207	21,978	62,229
Massachusetts Institute of Technology	76,287	23,115	53,172	70,975	25,835	45,140
Princeton University	67,893	15,344	52,549	80,253	10,433	69,820
Stanford University	88,170	18,075	70,095	95,412	15,552	79,860
University of Chicago	85,536	26,516	59,020	92,420	26,617	65,803
Yale University	144,989	14,789	130,200	157,636	10,877	146,759
Public Flagship Sector						
University of California-Berkeley	$26,060	$9,173	$16,887	$27,452	$15,483	$11,969
University of California-Los Angeles	40,610	9,137	31,473	50,979	15,090	35,889
University of Michigan-Ann Arbor	28,535	16,636	11,899	31,253	19,252	12,001
University of North Carolina at Chapel Hill	37,654	9,715	27,939	33,856	13,001	20,855
University of Virginia	21,220	12,817	8,403	24,461	16,340	8,121

Data from: Delta Cost Project.

for competition for the highest achieving students. To admit more students would necessitate a decline in resources per student and loss of positional rank in terms of selectivity.

Where will the increased number of students demanding a higher education go? They will sort into the large set of less selective and nonselective four-year schools and community colleges. As Bound and Turner (2007) demonstrate, it is these schools that absorb the larger number of students from a demand increase. They show that when there is a demand shock driven by a large birth cohort size, more selective schools do not let in more students, while less selective schools let in many more. The result is that less selective public and private schools have fewer resources along two dimensions: (1) The academic ability of their student body declines and (2) the per-student resources at these institutions decline because tuition pays for only a portion of the cost of educating a student. As with geographic integration, increased demand therefore will tend to exacerbate the cross-sector stratification of resources.

A very important question raised by the high and rising stratification in the higher education market is whether it matters for student collegiate outcomes. That is, do the higher financial and peer resources at the more selective schools translate into better student academic performance? We discuss the evidence on this question in Chapter 15.

13.5 Conclusion

Higher education markets are characterized by two features: heterogeneity and stratification. In this chapter, we presented an overview of the varied market for higher education, focusing on the many different types of schools that exist, the dimensions along which they differ, and the increasing concentration of resources in a small number of highly selective public and private institutions. We also examined the history of higher education expansion in the United States to understand how this market evolved, explored the arguments for the large government role in higher education, and discussed the sources of funding for the current higher education system.

A main takeaway message from this overview of the U.S. higher education system is that postsecondary institutions are incredibly varied. Thus, college enrollment means very different things to different students, depending on where they enroll. The varied nature of the higher education market also necessitates an understanding of how students sort into institutions and how different schools make admission decisions. Of particular concern is whether low-income students are receiving the same opportunities to enroll in the most selective and highest-resource schools as students from wealthier backgrounds. The high degree of stratification in the U.S. higher education system, combined with the evidence that institutional resources affect college outcomes, makes it important to understand not only income differences in college attendance but also whether and how students from different backgrounds sort into the various higher education sectors.

Much of the remainder of this book is motivated by these questions. In the next chapter, we focus on the financial aid system, providing details on the design of the system and the evidence on how it impacts students' postsecondary education choices and outcomes. Chapter 15 provides an in-depth analysis of college admissions and differences in student application and enrollment decisions across the socioeconomic distribution. On the whole, we will present evidence that low-income students invest very differently in higher education than do higher-income students. In the next two chapters, we will examine the reasons behind these differences and the evidence on whether educational interventions can be effective at reducing this inequality.

Highlights

- The higher education market in the United States is characterized by both **heterogeneity** and **stratification.** Heterogeneity refers to the fact that postsecondary institutions differ dramatically in terms of their academic focus, whether they are public or private, for-profit or not-for-profit, and the amount of resources they have. Stratification comes about because resources are increasingly concentrated in a small proportion of the colleges and universities in this country.

- In many ways, we can think of universities as firms. However, universities differ from typical profit-maximizing firms in a number of ways: They have many objectives as well as outputs that differ across schools and are hard to measure; there is asymmetric information on the part of students; production of knowledge is a **customer input technology**; and there is a **mixed market** that is dominated by public and **non-profit** firms.

- The government has two main roles in higher education: direct provision of education services and financing of schools through research, student aid, and tax breaks. The large government role in postsecondary markets is supported by two potential market failures in higher education: positive externalities from having an educated citizenry and **credit constraints** that bring about unequal access to higher education across the income distribution.

- Universities make optimizing decisions in deciding what to produce and how to produce it. Institutions vary considerably in their goals: for-profit schools seek to maximize profits, while nonprofit and public colleges and universities typically have broader and less well-defined objectives. Institutions also differ considerably in their method of production. There is no single production function in higher education, and production functions likely differ according to institutional goals.

- Before the mid-nineteenth century, there were few institutions of higher education in the United States, and they were mostly private, religiously affiliated, small, and focused on liberal arts education. These schools generally were teaching colleges at which little or no research was done.

- The growth of the modern research university began around the late nineteenth century, spurred by several factors: a growth in the demand for highly skilled workers trained in the sciences, an increasing specialization of academic departments, and proliferation of the scientific method across disciplines. These changes led to increases in the size and scope of higher education institutions, as schools took advantage of both economies of scale and economies of scope. Public universities were most able to take advantage of **economies of scale** and **economies of scope** and had the funding to expand, which led to a large increase in the proportion of students in public universities.

- The era of "mass higher education" began after World War II and was driven by the GI Bill as well as the increasing demand for skilled workers. Public support for postsecondary education increased, with states building community colleges and structuring their higher education systems hierarchically to help accommodate the growing demand for a higher education. This change was accompanied by higher education markets becoming more geographically **integrated**: the link between where students live and the colleges in which they enroll was significantly weakened. Additionally, enrollment of women in postsecondary institutions grew considerably.

- The first part of the twenty-first century has witnessed considerable growth in online higher education and for-profit education providers that have the potential to significantly change higher education markets. Online higher education takes three forms: students at traditional institutions taking online classes, fully online degree programs, and massive open online courses (MOOCs).

- Heterogeneity among higher education institutions occurs along three dimensions: public or private control, the level of degree offered, and the academic quality and resources of the institution. The evidence suggests this market is becoming more stratified over time in terms of resources being increasingly isolated in a small set of highly selective private institutions and public **flagship universities**.

Problems

1. Claudia Goldin and Larry Katz (1999) write: "Universities had long existed in Europe, where they took several forms: the classical studies of British universities, the scientific training of French grand ecoles, and the graduate research institutes of Germany. The modern university of the New World, however, was a different creature than its European counterpart, for it served a far broader clientele of students and the state …." During what period—and why—did the U.S. university take shape in its current form? Did this development favor public or private institutions?

2. Think about a flagship university, such as the University of Michigan or the University of Nebraska. In what ways are these institutions similar to profit-maximizing firms and in what ways are they different?

3. What is meant when economists describe a market as *perfectly competitive*? Discuss the violations of perfect competition in higher education. Do colleges and universities compete? Give two examples of the ways in which they compete.

4. Describe what a customer input technology is. Is the production of normal commodity goods, such as pencils, a customer input technology? Why or why not?

5. Suppose a university could educate undergraduates (U) at one campus at a cost of $C(U) = 40,000U$ and graduate students (G) at a different campus at a cost of $C(G) = 20,000,000 + 20,000G$. Alternatively, the university could educate undergraduates and graduates at the same campus at a cost of $C(U,G) = 20,000,000 + 20,000G + 20,000U$.

a. Under what circumstances should the university offer graduate and undergraduate education on the same campus?

b. Does this cost structure exhibit economies of scale? Does this cost structure exhibit economies of scope? Explain.

c. In addition to producing undergraduate and graduate education, describe two other outputs of a public university. Are these activities complementary with either graduate or undergraduate education?

6. Before the 2008 recession, Tiger State University's (TSU) endowment was valued at $5.1 billion. Several years later, the endowment was valued at $3.8 billion.

a. Assuming an expected rate of return of 5%, how much did the annual level of spending in perpetuity that Tiger State's endowment can support decrease?

b. Assume there are 20,000 students at TSU, paying an average of $15,300 per year in tuition. How much does tuition have to increase to offset the decrease in the endowment if spending is held constant?

c. The state also cut state funding to TSU by $23 million. How much does tuition have to increase to offset this decrease if spending is held constant? How much will tuition have to increase to offset the losses from the endowment decline and from state funding?

7. Count von Count wants to open a counting school, and he can do so at three locations: Sesame Street, Main Street, and ElectricCo Street. The marginal cost of a school on Sesame Street is $MC^S = 40$, and the marginal cost of a school on Main Street or ElectricCo Street is $MC^M = 30$. On Sesame Street the Count can perfectly price-discriminate because he knows everyone's willingness to pay, while on Main Street and ElectricCo Street he charges one price to all. Main Street is a competitive market (there are lots of other counting schools), and on ElectricCo Street the Count would have a monopoly. At all locations he faces the same demand curve, $P = 100 - 5Q$. (Assume the markets are geographically separate and students do not travel between markets.)

a. For Sesame Street, Main Street, and ElectricCo Street identify the profit for Count von Count and the quantity of enrollment.

b. Discuss the distinction between the price discrimination exercised by Count von Count on Sesame Street and financial aid awards at a nonprofit college with excess demand in admission.

8. Consider the price elasticity of demand for college. Is the elasticity of demand greater or smaller (i.e., is demand more or less elastic) if we consider the demand for one college versus any college? Is the elasticity of demand greater or smaller when measured over a five-year horizon versus a one-month horizon? Explain.

Paying for College: Student Financial Aid Policies and Collegiate Enrollment

3DDock/Shutterstock

Financing a College Investment

For recent high school graduates, a college education is typically the largest investment they have ever made. The total amount of money required in terms of direct tuition expenses and forgone earnings is easily in six figures. How do students (and their families) finance such a large investment? It is expected that as an investment, current costs for college will yield future returns. Yet few recent high school graduates have savings sufficient to pay the full cost of college. How do they do it? Who pays? As the *sticker price* of a college education has increased markedly in recent decades, the question of how students finance a college education has become more pressing.

The capacity to pay for college has a substantial impact on the overall demand for college and the extent to which individuals are able to make privately optimal investments in human capital. Individuals' college choice is also a central concern for public policy makers who aim to provide liquidity and insurance for worthwhile collegiate investments, with the aim of responding to increases in earnings inequality by assisting students of low and moderate income to gain human capital. Colleges and universities have the potential to serve as "engines of opportunity" by providing access to human capital for well-qualified students independent of family circumstances. Yet, if access to higher education is limited by capacity to pay, colleges and universities risk becoming "bastions of privilege,"[1] exacerbating existing inequality in economic circumstances and limiting intergenerational mobility.

The differences in collegiate attainment by family income are quite marked, reflecting both differences in *whether* students enroll in college and *where* they enroll; low- and moderate-income students are underrepresented at some of the most resource-intensive institutions. These gaps raise fundamental questions of both equity and efficiency, particularly when we examine the extraordinary levels of public and private subsidy at the nation's most elite colleges.

---

[1] This phrase is from Bowen, Kurzweil, and Tobin, *Equity and Excellence in American Higher Education* (2005).

The demand for higher education reflects the relationship between price and desired attendance. Student financial aid alters the price of college for potential students; thus, it potentially affects whether and where students choose to attend college. Our aim in this chapter is to examine the demand for higher education and the role of financial aid. We focus on understanding the financial aid system in the United States as well as the evidence on how different types of aid affect students' higher education investment decisions.

Financial aid for college comes in the form of grant aid, which does not have to be repaid, and loans, which have to be repaid at some interest rate. Grants and loans come from several sources:

- Federal government (loans and grants)
- State government (grants)
- Postsecondary institutions (grants)
- Private market (loans)

The first part of this chapter examines the economic argument for government-provided financial aid. While private loan markets dominate for other large expenditure items like automobiles and homes, the federal government is the major source of financial aid for college. Why might it be desirable to have a significant government role in providing student financial aid? We address the question of why private markets may underprovide financing for human capital investments. Additionally, we consider why many institutions provide so much funding for financial aid for their students. What institutional goals might this aid achieve?

We next turn to a detailed examination of the structure of financial aid in the United States. In particular, we focus on how student aid is calculated, the different types and sources of student aid, and trends in student financial aid receipt. In the third section of the chapter, we explore the empirical research on how the financial aid system affects students' enrollment decisions and postsecondary outcomes. We consider how government and institutions determine eligibility for need-based financial aid and whether the complexity of the process may disadvantage some students. In the final section, we discuss the economics of student loans in greater depth and examine arguments for changing the structure of student loans and student loan repayment in the United States.

14.1 Inequality and Inefficiency in Collegiate Enrollment and Attainment

Over the course of the past three decades, the increase in the college wage premium has been met with an anemic response in college completion.[2] The fact that rising returns to collegiate investment have not been met with large increases in collegiate attainment is a central puzzle in the economics of higher education: A core tenet of economics is that when the financial returns to a given activity increase, more people should engage in that activity. The level of collegiate attainment is fundamentally a function of supply and demand. We cover the supply-side explanations for sluggish increases in college completion in Chapter 15. Here, we focus on the demand-side factors related to students' capacity to pay for college.

---

[2] It is worth noting that BA degree attainment rose between 2007 and 2014, from 30% to 34%, perhaps reflecting increased collegiate attainment during the period of slack labor demand following the financial crisis. Bowen and McPherson (2016) provide a full discussion of these trends.

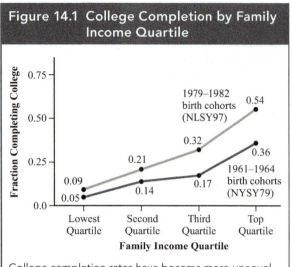

Figure 14.1 College Completion by Family Income Quartile

College completion rates have become more unequal across the income distribution over time. While the difference between the top and bottom quartile in college completion rates was 29 percentage points among NLSY79 respondents, it was 45 percentage points among NLSY97 respondents. *Data from:* Bailey and Dynarski (2011); tabulations from the NLSY79 (1961–1964 birth cohorts) and the NLSY97 (1979–1982 birth cohorts).

Differences in College Investment by Income

While the idea of mass postsecondary education gained much traction after World War II, the realization of this ideal has been far more limited. Figure 14.1 shows the fraction of young adults attending and completing college by family income for those born between 1961 and 1964 and those born between 1979 and 1982. There are two important trends illustrated by the figure. First, among both birth cohorts there is a steep family income gradient in college completion: Students in low-income families are much less likely to complete college than their counterparts from high-income families. Second, the income gap in college completion has increased over this nearly two-decade interval. While the college completion rate for students in the bottom income quartile increased from a mere 5% to 9%, the fraction in the top quartile completing college jumped by 18 percentage points, from 36% to 54%. As well, the near-poor students in the second quartile gained only modestly, from 14% to 21%. Figure 14.1 understates the income gaps in collegiate investment because it ignores quality differences in the types of colleges students attend. The connection between family income and college quality contributes to potential inequality in outcomes through two channels: First, the fraction of those enrolling who complete is greater at more resource-intensive institutions, and second, the earnings gain or returns to a college degree may be greater at a high-quality institution.

These gaps in college investment across the income distribution raise questions of equity and efficiency that have important implications for economic productivity and the level of income in the United States. The correlation between family circumstances and collegiate attainment *may* be an indication of an **allocative inefficiency:** There are likely to be many low-income students whose labor market productivity would be increased markedly by obtaining a college degree but who do not graduate from college. Conversely, there may be students from wealthier backgrounds whose productivity changes little from the college investment. These students might go to college because it is a consumption good rather than an investment in their future productivity. Allocative inefficiencies brought about by the income gap in college investment provide scope for government intervention.

allocative inefficiency Requires that no reorganization of production or consumption could make everyone better off. In the case of higher education, allocative efficiency occurs when it is not possible to reallocate students across institutions in a way that will increase aggregate output.

Short-Run Versus Long-Run Credit Constraints

Although differences in collegiate attainment by parental income may support government intervention, it is critical to understand why these gaps exist to develop appropriate policy responses. Thus, we aim to understand why there is such a strong positive correlation between family income and collegiate attainment. The first answer most students would give to such a question is that college is expensive: Low-income families have trouble financing the sizable cost of college attendance for their children. This is an example of a **short-run credit constraint.** A short-run credit constraint arises when a student has a positive rate of return to a given educational investment but he or she cannot obtain the money to finance the investment. It is a short-run constraint because the lack of access

short-run credit constraint Occurs when a student has a positive return on an education investment but is unable to borrow at a sufficiently low interest rate to finance the investment.

to financial capital is a problem that is specific to the small time period around which the student is trying to make the educational investment. Recall from Chapter 4 that a central reason for an inability of students to borrow enough to pay for a human capital investment is the fact that one cannot collateralize human capital; selling your human capital to an employer would be indentured servitude or slavery, which is illegal in almost all countries today. While the prohibition against slavery is undoubtedly good, it creates a problem for loan markets. How can we expect private companies to provide loans at low rates to people with no collateral? We cannot, which is a main reason why the government role in the financial aid system is so large.

Capacity to pay for college is not necessarily the only reason why students from richer versus poorer families differ in their postsecondary investments. Family income also is correlated with the academic achievement levels of students by the time they reach the end of high school. Students who are less academically prepared for college likely have diminished capacity to benefit from a given postsecondary investment. An underlying reason for these differences in achievement by family income are disparities in the resources families have to spend on education throughout the lives of their children. Children from lower-income families are often exposed to fewer educational inputs and lower educational quality, which reduces human capital accumulation. Such disparities are unlikely to reflect parental preferences: It is surely the case that many low-income families would like to move to a district with higher-quality schools or spend money for cocurricular activities to improve achievement. However, capacity to pay often limits families' ability to make these choices.

Financing limitations generate what economists Pedro Carneiro and James Heckman (2002) term **long-run credit constraints**. Long-run credit constraints arise when resources are lacking throughout a child's life that can be used to invest optimally in her education. While low-income parents might wish to borrow to increase the ongoing amount they can spend on their children's education, no such loan market exists. Parents who face a long-run credit constraint will be forced to invest less in their child from a young age. This lower investment will translate to lower academic achievement by the time the child is of college age, but it also can compound itself by reducing the efficacy of further investments. That is, lower investments when young can reduce the returns to investing in education when students are older.[3]

Disentangling the relative importance of short-run versus long-run credit constraints is critical to understanding how large public expenditures for financial aid should be. On the one hand, if the gap in collegiate attainment by family income is due to long-run credit constraints, expanding financial aid will have little impact on the attainment gap—spending money on financial aid would be an inefficient use of public funds. On the other hand, financial aid will help boost enrollment among lower-income students in the presence of short-term credit constraints. Indeed, there are many low-income students who are well-prepared to enroll in and complete college. Thus, spending on financial aid will lead to a high return on public investments when there are short-run credit constraints.

To see the different implications these types of credit constraints have for policy, consider each one in terms of the human capital model. Take two individuals, Taryn and David, each with the same level of academic ability. However, David is from a lower-income

long-run credit constraints Occur when the lack of access to financial resources throughout a child's life leads to persistent underinvestment in human capital. The result is the student will be less academically prepared for college by the end of high school than if his or her family had access to resources that would have allowed them to make human capital investments at their desired levels throughout the student's life.

---

[3] This has been termed dynamic complementarity. For a detailed treatment of dynamic complementarities, see Cuhna and Heckman (2007).

Figure 14.2 Education Investment With Short-Run Credit Constraints

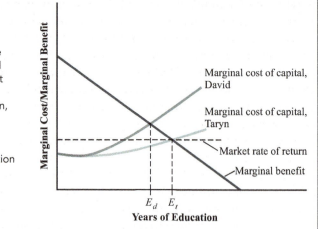

David and Taryn have the same academic ability level (marginal benefit curve) but face different costs of capital. David faces a higher cost of capital than Taryn, which causes him to invest in less education: $E_d < E_t$. David is subject to a short-run credit constraint that limits his education investment.

family and thus faces a higher marginal cost of capital. That is, it is much more expensive for David to obtain money for a given educational investment than it is for Taryn. One reason this would occur is if Taryn's family could pay the full tuition price and David only could borrow money at very high rates of interest to finance his college degree.

Figure 14.2 shows this situation. David has a higher cost of capital than Taryn, and the gap increases for more years of education. This increasing gap represents the fact that David likely will find it increasingly expensive to raise the money to finance more education. The same is true for Taryn, but she has access to much less expensive financing, which likely stems from having parents with financial assets they can use to help her pay for her education. In the figure, David obtains less education than Taryn ($E_d < E_t$), and this occurs *despite* the fact that they have the same academic preparation for college and face the same marginal benefit curve for education. For Taryn, the intersection of her cost of capital and the marginal benefit is also the intersection with the market rate of return. Recall from Chapter 4 that the optimal educational investment level is achieved when the marginal benefit equals the market rate of return (i.e., what one could do with the money if it is not invested in education). Taryn therefore obtains the optimal level of education, because her marginal benefit and cost curves intersect at the market rate of return. David, however, obtains too little education, as the cost of obtaining sufficient funds to obtain the same level of education as Taryn is too expensive for him. He faces a short-run credit constraint, and therefore he obtains less education than Taryn.

How does this situation differ from long-run credit constraints? In a long-run credit constraint situation, families are constrained from investing as much as they want in education throughout a child's life. This difference in educational investment is crystalized into academic achievement levels among college-age students. Were this the case as shown in Figure 14.3, by the time David and Taryn reach the end of high school, Taryn will be better academically prepared for college than

Figure 14.3 Education Investment With Long-Run Credit Constraints

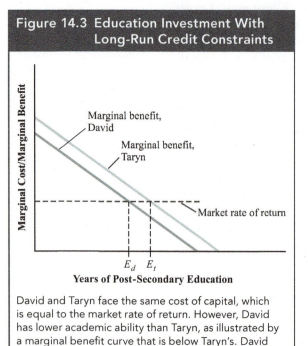

David and Taryn face the same cost of capital, which is equal to the market rate of return. However, David has lower academic ability than Taryn, as illustrated by a marginal benefit curve that is below Taryn's. David faces a long-run credit constraint that causes him to invest less in education: $E_d < E_t$.

David because of the differences in education resources they have received throughout their lives. David's lower level of academic achievement shifts his marginal benefit curve inward, as shown in Figure 14.2. Each person still invests in education up until the point that the marginal benefit equals the marginal cost, which here is the market rate of return for both Taryn and David. A comparison of Figures 14.2 and 14.3 thus shows that long-run credit constraints produce the exact same effect as short-run credit constraints: $E_d < E_r$.

Now, let's consider what happens if we introduce financial aid targeted toward low-income students in each situation. In the short-run credit constraint scenario, this just would involve providing David access to a loan to lower his marginal cost of capital. Graphically, providing credit to allow low-income students to borrow for college flattens the marginal cost of capital curve, which leads to an increase in the amount of education David obtains.

How does the story change in the presence of long-run credit constraints? Long-run constraints lead to differences in marginal benefits, as shown in Figure 14.3, such that even when David and Taryn face the same cost of capital, David will choose to invest in less education. The problem that David faces is that he lacks the academic preparation due to insufficient prior educational investments, rather than a facing a challenge in financing college. Thus, providing him with financial aid for college enrollment would not allow him to receive the same rewards from college that Taryn receives.

The importance of this difference for education policy cannot be overstated. We see evidence that students from low-income backgrounds invest less in college. If short-run credit constraints are to blame, then financial aid policies to help alleviate such constraints are very sensible. However, students whose parents have low income when they are of college age likely also had low incomes throughout their childhood. If the resulting long-run credit constraints are responsible for the education differences across the income distribution, providing financial aid for less wealthy students will not solve the problem. What is needed in this case are interventions to increase the ability of low-income parents to invest in their children's education when they are young. Indeed, this is a central goal of the K–12 policy interventions we discussed in Chapters 9–12.

Empirical Evidence on Short-Run Credit Constraints

Of course, both long-run and short-run credit constraints might be at work in producing disparities in educational attainment across the income distribution. To determine the extent to which financial aid can be used to support the college investment of low-income students, we would like to be able to discern how many and which students face short-run credit constraints. The way economists have approached this question is by attempting to estimate the causal effect of family resources on college enrollment patterns of students. Family resources primarily enter the education decision by shifting the marginal cost of capital. If resource constraints increase the marginal cost of capital above the marginal benefit to the education investment, the investment will not be undertaken. Thus, if we see evidence that family income differences among college-age students with similar academic preparation for college lead to differences in college investment, it is an indication of short-run credit constraints.

Students from families with different income levels differ along a number of dimensions, such as information about college, noncognitive skills, and preferences for education. So the patterns in Figure 14.1 are likely a function of a set of factors beyond financial resources at the time of college going. The economics literature has attempted to deal with this difficulty in two ways. The most prominent set of studies uses the rich set of student observable characteristics in national longitudinal datasets, such as the NLSY and the NELS:88,[4] to control directly for differences in parental characteristics and high school cognitive test scores across students. The assumption underlying this research is that these characteristics and test scores account for all the reasons why college enrollment varies across students from families with different income levels, except for the causal effect of the income itself.

Focusing on the individuals born in the early 1960s and attending college in the late 1970s and early 1980s from the NLSY79 dataset, Carneiro and Heckman (2002) conduct such an analysis.[5] While there are sizable gaps between high- and low-income students in their college investment patterns, once they control for student demographic characteristics and Armed Forces Qualification Test (AFQT) scores, much of the income gaps in college enrollment disappear. They conclude from this analysis that the impact of academic ability on college enrollment is much more important than the effect of short-run family income variation. Their calculations using these results suggest that at most, 8% of the college-age population in the United States faces short-run credit constraints.

Since this early period, there have been substantial changes in the cost to families of attending college, potentially increasing the importance of family income. Belley and Lochner (2007) update the Carneiro and Heckman (2002) study to include the NLSY97 cohorts. The results from their BA completion analysis are shown in Figure 14.4,[6] which depicts the difference between college completion rates for students in each family income quartile relative to students in the bottom family income quartile (income quartile 1) after controlling for student test scores and background characteristics. In the NLSY79, those in income quartiles 2 and 3 are slightly less likely to obtain a BA than those in quartile 1 after student background factors and precollegiate academic achievement levels are accounted for. There is a positive difference between the top and bottom quartiles, but it still is not large, at 5 percentage points. However, among the NLSY97 cohorts that were making college enrollment decisions nearly two decades later, the importance of family income is larger. There now is a 3 percentage point gap between the college completion rates of the third versus the first family income quartile, and students in the top income quartile have BA attainment rates 10 percentage points higher than their low-income counterparts. This evidence points strongly to the conclusion that family resources have become more closely tied to college completion over time. Families with incomes below the median likely face increasing difficulties in financing college.

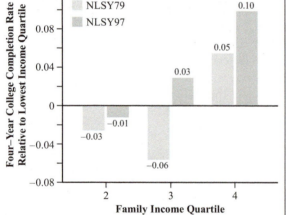

Figure 14.4 The Relationship Between Family Income and BA Completion, Controlling for High School Test Scores and Student Demographic Characteristics

Differences in college completion rates across family income quartiles relative to the lowest income quartile, controlling for student and family background characteristics as well as precollegiate cognitive test scores. About 5% of those in the bottom income quartile in the NSLY79 completed college, while 9% in the NLSY97 did so. The difference in completion between the top and bottom quartile doubled between the NLSY79 and the NLSY97 cohorts. *Data from:* Authors' tabulations from Belley and Lochner (2007).

---

[4] These datasets are described in Appendix A of this book.

[5] The data that these authors use is from the NLSY79. See also the similar analysis using NELS:88 data in Ellwood and Kane (2000).

[6] Belley and Lochner (2007) also examine enrollment rate differences by family income. The results from their enrollment analysis closely mirror those of the completion rate analysis in showing that gaps between low- and high-income families have grown over time.

DEEP DIVE: Credit Constraints and Housing Markets

To examine the extent of short-run credit constraints, we would like to find a source of quasi-experimental variation in family resources that is unrelated to variation in student ability. It would be ideal to run an experiment in which we randomly assign some families to receive more income right around the time their children are making college decisions. Clearly, such an experiment is unlikely to happen, but we can look for events that mimic this experimental setup.

During the period from the late 1990s to 2007, there were considerable differences across cities in housing price changes, resulting in substantial variation in household wealth held in housing that was not related to students' academic ability. Housing wealth is an extremely important component of total household wealth: Particularly for middle-class households, the majority of Americans have little savings outside of their home. The housing boom brought about two important changes in housing markets. First, the value of homes increased dramatically over this period. Between 1990 and 2005, real home prices increased by 55%. Second, it became much easier to use one's housing wealth to make purchases without having to sell the house, through the use of home equity loans, home equity lines of credit, and cash-out refinances. Lovenheim (2011) uses this variation to estimate the effect of wealth on college enrollment.

The main thought experiment on which this study is based is to imagine two observationally similar students who live in different cities. For example, take one student who lives in Rochester, New York, and another student who lives in New York City. Between 1993 and 2003, home prices in New York City rose by 90%, while in Rochester they rose only by 20%. Thus, a high school senior in 2003 in New York City would

have experienced a large recent home price increase relative to the family in Rochester. Furthermore, the timing of the housing boom differed across areas. For example, home prices in San Francisco rose by more in the late 1990s, while in New York City and Miami they rose by more in the early 2000s. Thus, comparing the college enrollment of students who experienced different recent house price changes due to fluctuations in the housing market when they were in high school allows Lovenheim to isolate the causal role of family housing wealth in college enrollment decisions of students.

These findings point to housing wealth variation affecting college enrollment decisions of students. For each $10,000 increase in housing wealth, college enrollment increases by 0.7 of a percentage point. This might not sound like a lot, but between 2000 and 2005 average housing wealth in the United States increased by over $57,000. This means that the housing boom generated an increase in college enrollment of 4 percentage points. Furthermore, these effects are largest among relatively low-income families. For families with earnings below $70,000 per year, a $10,000 home equity increase leads to a 5 percentage point increase in college enrollment. In a follow-up analysis, Lovenheim and Reynolds (2013) show that housing wealth affects the types of schools students enroll in as well. Those who experience housing wealth increases while in high school are more likely to enroll in a public flagship university and are less likely to enroll in a community college. Together, these estimates point to the sensitivity of college enrollment and college choice to short-run housing wealth fluctuations, which is consistent with the prevalence of short-run credit constraints among a sizable subset of the U.S. population.

It is tempting to focus exclusively on the market failure generated by credit constraints, but it is worth emphasizing that it is not simply the undersupply of credit for college that limits enrollment with high potential return. After all, if the problem were only credit constraints, addressing the market for student loans would be the sole focus of federal student aid policy. Two other market imperfections likely place college attainment from purely private financing well below the social optimum. First, if there are positive externalities, or spillover effects, from increasing collegiate attainment, there is a potential role for public subsidy. Second, the inability to collateralize human capital, discussed in Chapter 4, implies that individuals will be limited in their capacity to diversify risks associated with poor collegiate outcomes. This yields underinvestment in education when individuals are risk averse; even if students face a high average return, the risk associated with a postsecondary investment might dissuade many of them from undertaking the investment.

> **Quick Hint:** The riskiness of an investment from an individual perspective refers to the variance of returns associated with an investment, as distinct from the mean return. Individual risk in higher education investment comes from the differences across students in the return to a given education investment, even among students who attend the same college or university. The variance in returns is driven by such factors as unexpected family challenges as well as unforeseen academic difficulties that deter completion. The riskiness or variance in the return to collegiate investments may well vary across colleges, fields of study, and individuals with different levels of preparation.

Other Barriers to Enrollment

While analysis of inefficiency and inequality in students' collegiate decisions tends to focus on financial barriers to attending college, there are other challenges that affect students' choices. Beyond short-run credit constraints, students may face information constraints that make it difficult for them to make optimal postsecondary investment decisions. These information constraints can take several forms:

- Lack of information about what college will actually cost due to the inability to observe the net price of college (including financial aid) at the time one applies
- Lack of information about how to access the financial aid system and how to get all of the aid for which one is eligible
- Lack of information about the returns to higher education in general and the returns to investing in higher-quality schools in particular

When students do not have full information about what a college investment will cost them or what the returns are to making such an investment, they will underinvest in postsecondary education or make college-going decisions that do not maximize their own well-being. These constraints are likely to be larger for students from lower-income families and for those who do not have parents or close relatives who have completed college. As we highlight later in this chapter and in Chapter 15, the complexity of the financial aid system and the substantial strategic and informational requirements to choose among colleges may lead to inefficient levels of collegiate investment and, in turn, may exacerbate inequalities in postsecondary enrollment across the income distribution. To this end, policies addressing these information constraints can have a higher return in some circumstances than simply increasing the generosity of financial aid.

14.2 The Structure of Financial Aid in the United States

The Different Types of Aid Policies

How can policy makers and higher education leaders use the toolkit of financial aid to improve investments in higher education? There are two broad types of tools available to policy makers: (1) Provide grants that reduce the net price students must pay to invest in college and (2) provide loans that increase access to capital and can reduce the short-run credit constraints.[7]

---

[7] Work–study is another form of aid that generally involves access to capital (funding in exchange for working) along with a subsidy, to the extent that the compensation exceeds the market wage.

A grant is a transfer of money for college attendance and is a subsidy for college going. The basic economics of a grant (G) is to reduce the net price students must pay from the base (sticker price) tuition level of T to $T - G$. Grants thus shift out student demand for college, as shown in Figure 14.5. The impact of the grant will depend on the elasticity of demand relative to the supply elasticity. When demand is inelastic—a situation in which a student's decision to attend college (or a specific college) is not very responsive to the price charged—an increase in grant aid will not generate much of a change in enrollment behavior. This situation is depicted by the more steeply sloped demand curves in Figure 14.5. Conversely, when demand is elastic, students' decisions are more sensitive to changes in price. The flatter demand curves in Figure 14.5 show such a case. The figure demonstrates that the enrollment response to grant aid will be larger when demand is more elastic (for a fixed supply elasticity).

Quick Hint: Recall that in Chapter 13 we discussed how more inelastic supply provided an opportunity for colleges and universities to capture increases in aid through higher tuition. That institutions might raise prices in response to financial aid is termed the Bennett hypothesis.

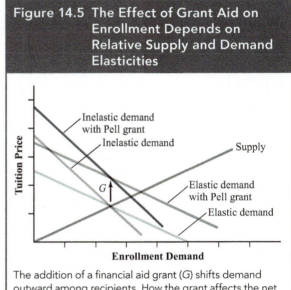

Figure 14.5 The Effect of Grant Aid on Enrollment Depends on Relative Supply and Demand Elasticities

The addition of a financial aid grant (G) shifts demand outward among recipients. How the grant affects the net price paid by students and the ultimate enrollment level depends on the relative elasticities of supply and demand at the point of the initial equilibrium.

Grants differ not only in their financial generosity but also in the extent to which they are portable across institutions rather than being specific to enrollment at a given college or university. Many grants also entail categorical restrictions that depend on factors like financial circumstances, place of residence, and academic achievement.

A central policy concern with grants is the extent to which they induce higher enrollment or simply subsidize students who would have enrolled in college absent the grant. Suppose the government decided to give a grant of $5,000 for college attendance to all 18-year-olds. Some young people who were not otherwise planning to attend college might enroll (marginal students). Many students who were already planning to attend (inframarginal students) would receive a price reduction, thus enabling the consumption of more of other goods and services. The funding of many inframarginal students with public dollars raises the question of whether it is possible to generate a higher return on use of these resources in terms of either other public programs or a reduced tax burden.

The second financial aid policy tool addresses the limited private market for student loans through government participation in credit markets. A loan is by definition a commitment that requires repayment in the future. As Figure 14.2 demonstrates, loans can overcome short-run credit constraints by reducing the cost of capital. If a family faces a cost of capital too high to justify a given investment that would be optimal at the market rate of return, or if an absence of loan markets makes borrowing impossible for some families, government intervention in the loan market could increase college going. In addition to offering loans, policy makers can adjust the exact terms of a loan along several dimensions: the length of the repayment period, the interest rate, and the rate of repayment.

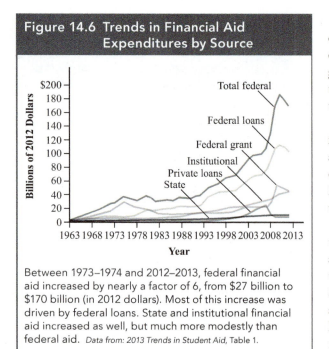

Figure 14.6 Trends in Financial Aid Expenditures by Source

Between 1973–1974 and 2012–2013, federal financial aid increased by nearly a factor of 6, from $27 billion to $170 billion (in 2012 dollars). Most of this increase was driven by federal loans. State and institutional financial aid increased as well, but much more modestly than federal aid. *Data from: 2013 Trends in Student Aid, Table 1.*

Although grants and loans form the core financial aid tools available to policy makers, these tools can be deployed by the federal government, state governments, and individual postsecondary institutions. Figure 14.6 presents trends in grants, loans, and total federal aid for these different groups. Between 1974–1975 and 2014–2015, federal commitments to financial aid in constant dollars increased by nearly a factor of 6, from $27 billion to $161 billion. Most of this increase was driven by federal loans. A driving factor behind the dramatic increases in aid over this period is an increase in college enrollment, from 10.2 million to 20.2 million students. State and institutional financial aid increased much more modestly, and as a result the federal government currently is the dominant provider of financial aid in the United States. We now provide an overview of the history and structure of financial aid policies, with a particular focus on the federal programs that constitute the majority of aid disbursements.

Federal Financial Aid

The History of Federal Aid The beginning of the modern federal financial aid system dates to the GI Bill (Servicemen's Readjustment Act, Public Law 346) at the end of World War II. Prior to the passage of the GI Bill, there was very limited federal support for students seeking to finance a higher education investment. The GI Bill was passed to reward veterans for their military service in World War II, and for the first time generous grant support was provided to all veterans. This was a watershed event in the provision of financial aid in the United States; many historical accounts cite the GI Bill as having "democratized" higher education by making college a viable option for men from a range of sociodemographic backgrounds, including minorities, first-generation Americans, and those from low-income households.

Benefits under the GI Bill included up to $500 in tuition and educational expenses per academic year, which was sufficient to cover the charges even of expensive private colleges at the time. Beneficiaries also received a monthly cash allowance of $65 for single veterans and $90 per month for married veterans to help cover living expenses. By providing grants directly to individuals, the program ensured that benefits were portable across institutions. The number of years of benefits varied 1 to 1 with years of active-duty service for up to 4 years. Notably, these awards were contingent on neither financial background nor academic ability, and about 50% of returning servicemen born between 1923 and 1928 took advantage of them.

While the GI Bill continued with some modification for those participating in later conflicts such as the Korean War, there would not be another major federal financial aid initiative until the National Defense Education Act (NDEA) of 1958 (PL85-864). The NDEA legislation was spurred by the Soviet launch of Sputnik and the more general concern that the United States was falling behind in science and technology. While many of the elements of the law focused on education tied to science and national security, Title II provided for the establishment of campus-based student loans that would be funded directly by the government. This program, originally known as the National Defense Student Loan program, is the precursor to today's Perkins Loan program. An addition to the loan program was the authorization of the College Work Study program through the 1964 Economic Opportunity Act, which gave institutions funds to provide needy students with part-time employment. Today, approximately 3,400 institutions participate, and funds are distributed to schools that then disperse them to students through employing them in specific jobs. While many students participate in work–study, the actual level of expenditures is small relative to other student aid programs.

The Higher Education Act of 1965 (PL89-329) laid the groundwork for much of the current structure of federal grant and loan aid for postsecondary enrollment. This law, which has been amended a number of times in the past 50 years, is the basis for the current law authorizing federal student financial aid. Student financial aid programs fall under Title IV of this act. The major grant component of this law is the Educational Opportunity Grant Program, which aimed to provide grants for the most financially needy students. This program was later renamed the Supplemental Educational Opportunity Grant (SEOG) program and still exists today.

The Higher Education Act of 1965 also introduced the Guaranteed Student Loan (GSL) Program. The existing loan system consisted of all direct loans from the federal government. In contrast, the GSL program allowed for education loans that were guaranteed by the federal government but were issued by private banks. This reduced the cost of the loans to the federal government but also reduced the risk of education loans to banks, thereby ensuring banks would actually offer these loans.[8] In 1988, the GSL program was renamed the Stafford Loan program after Vermont Senator Robert Stafford. Stafford loans currently are the dominant source of loans offered by the federal government.

The last significant addition to the federal financial aid portfolio was the 1972 reauthorization of the Higher Education Act,[9] which produced the Basic Educational Opportunity Grant (BEOG). These grants were later renamed in honor of the late Rhode Island Senator Claiborne Pell and are now known as Pell grants. The Pell grant program is intended to provide grants that are fully portable across institutions to the neediest students. Eligibility is based on a standardized needs formula that relates the cost of attendance to a family's capacity to pay.

Today, federal financial aid is a patchwork of grant and loan programs:

- Pell grants
- Grants to military veterans
- Supplemental Educational Opportunity grants (SEOG)
- Stafford loans
- PLUS loans
- Perkins loans
- Tax credits

---

[8] In recent years, the funding mechanism has shifted back from guaranteed loans in which financial institutions originated loans with federal guarantees to a system in which the federal government originates "direct" loans to students.

[9] The 1972 reauthorization also produced a number of other notable changes, including allowing students attending for-profit or proprietary schools eligibility for aid while also explicitly providing eligibility for aid to students who were no longer dependent on parents' capacity to pay.

By far, the two largest programs are Pell grants and Stafford loans. Together, they make up the vast majority of all aid disbursements by the federal government. In the subsequent sections, we provide a more detailed description of these programs, trends in aid generosity, and the way in which the federal government determines eligibility for financial aid.

Federal Grant Aid The central way through which the federal government provides grant aid to financially needy undergraduate students is the Pell grant. Students from the lowest-income backgrounds receive the maximum Pell grant amount. The amount students are eligible for differs according to their family's financial situation and the cost of college enrollment they face. Pell grants are targeted toward the lowest-income students, and as a result recipients come from disadvantaged backgrounds: in the 2013–2014 school year, 75% of dependent students who received a Pell grant came from families with yearly income under $40,000, and 94% came from families with yearly income under $60,000.

Figure 14.7 shows trends in the value of the maximum Pell grant. In the 1974–1975 school year, an eligible student would receive a maximum of $1,400 ($7,529 in 2014 dollars), which could be used for tuition, fees, and living expenses. The nominal value of the Pell grant changes only with Congressional authorization, and it has risen steadily over time. However, there is considerable variation in the real value of the Pell grant due to inflation, with a number of periods of decline. While the maximum Pell grant award level for the 2014–2015 school year was $5,730, the minimum was $582. Thus, depending on college costs and family resources, the specific amount of Pell grant aid can vary considerably among recipients.

Federal Student Loans Most federal financial aid loans are made through the Stafford Loan Program. There are two types of Stafford loans: subsidized and unsubsidized. Both types of loans carry the same interest rate, but subsidized loans do not start accumulating interest until a student graduates or leaves college. In contrast, interest begins accumulating on unsubsidized loans directly after they

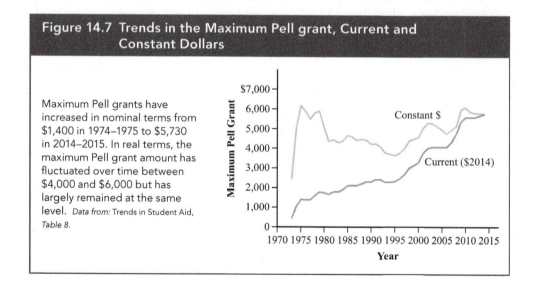

Figure 14.7 Trends in the Maximum Pell grant, Current and Constant Dollars

Maximum Pell grants have increased in nominal terms from $1,400 in 1974–1975 to $5,730 in 2014–2015. In real terms, the maximum Pell grant amount has fluctuated over time between $4,000 and $6,000 but has largely remained at the same level. *Data from:* Trends in Student Aid, Table 8.

are issued. Interest rates for these loans are fixed over the course of the loan: in the 2016–2017 school year, the interest rate was 3.76% for undergraduate students and 5.31% for graduate students. Interest rates on Stafford loans are set by Congress and are well below interest rates charged on other uncollateralized debt, such as credit cards.

There are two important characteristics of Stafford loans that make them quite different from noneducation loans. Unlike a car loan or mortgage, in which the banker will take into consideration one's credit score and likely capacity to repay, these loans are not differentiated in terms of a student's credit risk or educational prospects. A further feature of student loans is that they are not dischargeable in bankruptcy, so one cannot declare bankruptcy and erase government educational debt the way one can with credit card debt and auto loans.

Currently, Stafford loans are capped at $5,500 in the first year of college, $6,500 in the second year, and $7,500 in the third year and beyond. These include unsubsidized loans, which cannot exceed $3,500 in the first year, $4,500 in the second year, and $5,500 in the third year. Thus, the total amount of Stafford loans available to all students is the same, but students differ in the amount of unsubsidized versus subsidized loans they can take out depending on their family's economic circumstances. There is a loan limit of $31,000 under this program, with no more than $23,000 allowed to come from unsubsidized loans.

Total spending on Stafford loans in the 2014–2015 academic year was $76.4 billion, of which 32% was subsidized and the remainder unsubsidized. The true cost of this program is much lower. This is because, as with all loans, the government charges students interest on the loans, and the loan amounts plus interest need to be paid back. However, there is a cost to the government because it charges interest rates below market value, and some students default on their loans before they are repaid. Recent estimates suggest the federal government winds up recouping about 80 cents per dollar loaned.[10] Thus, one should divide the total expenditure on these loans by 5 to determine the cost to the federal government of this loan program.

PLUS loans constitute the other major federal loan program. These loans are designed to meet student financial needs that are not met by Pell grants and Stafford loans. Unlike Stafford loans, PLUS loans are dependent on parents' credit ratings. Parents with adverse credit histories often cannot secure these loans as a result. The interest rates on these loans also are higher, currently at 6.31%, and they are fixed for the life of the loan.

The volume of student loans is very cyclical, increasing when unemployment (and enrollment) rises and decreasing when unemployment falls. In constant dollars, Stafford loan spending rose from $64 billion in 2007–2008 to a peak of $95 billion in 2010–2011, before falling somewhat to the current levels.

Tax Credits and Tax Deductions A final arm of federal financial aid comes in the form of *tax credits* and *tax deductions*, which essentially shift the provision

---

[10] This estimate is from the Congressional Budget Office, average by loan volume over the different loan types: http://www.cbo.gov/sites/default/files/cbofiles/attachments/44509_StudentLoanSubsidyRatesUnder May2013Baseline.pdf.

DEEP DIVE: The Price of Borrowing

The interest charged on a loan is a way of quantifying the cost of capital or the cost of borrowing funds from the government or a private source to repay in a future year.[11] In general, bankers determine the rate of interest based on the likelihood the loan will be repaid, whether there is an asset or collateral to take in the event of nonpayment, and how long it will take to repay the loan.

Students first will borrow from the lowest cost of capital source, which is why students generally first make use of subsidized Stafford loans (if eligible) and unsubsidized Stafford loans before turning to private capital markets. As of the 2016–2017 school year, Stafford interest rates were 3.76% for undergraduate students and 5.31% for graduate students. The interest rates on PLUS loans to parents were higher, at 6.31%.[12]

How high are these interest rates? Compared to a securitized loan, such as for a car or a house, they are somewhat high. The average 30-year fixed interest rate on a home loan was about 3.7% in June of 2016. For a five-year auto loan, the average interest rate is around 3%. However, these are somewhat unfair comparisons: If you default on a home or auto loan, the bank can seize the property and resell it to recoup much of its losses. This significantly reduces the amount of risk banks face when making these loans, and lower risk leads to lower interest rates. Education loans are unsecured, since the bank or federal government cannot seize your human capital if you default. The most common unsecured loans given in the United States are through credit cards, and these interest rates are much higher than education loan rates. Credit card interest rates typically range from 15–20%, but they can get much higher in some circumstances if consumers have poor credit histories. Thus, compared to credit cards, which are the likely alternative source of credit for most Americans, Stafford and PLUS loans are given at very favorable interest rates.

Another source of credit on which many families rely is *home equity*, the difference between the value of the home and the amount remaining on the mortgage. Home equity can be used to finance investments like college because families can take out loans on this equity through cash-out refinances, home equity loans, and home equity lines of credit. Because home equity-based loans are collateralized, they typically are a less expensive way to finance college than PLUS loans.

of federal student aid from the expenditure side of the budget to the revenue side through reductions in tax revenues. The Taxpayer Relief Act of 1997[13] created two tax benefits for higher education, the Hope Scholarship credit and Lifetime Learning credits; these provisions were restructured under the American Recovery and Reinvestment Act (ARRA) of 2009 and renamed the American Opportunity Tax Credit (AOTC). The Hope credit allowed a taxpayer (including the parents of a dependent student) to claim a tax credit for 100% of the first $1,200 and 50% of the next $1,200 in qualified tuition and related expenses (including books and materials) for the first 2 years of at least half-time enrollment in college. The AOTC supplanted the Hope credit and allowed a taxpayer to claim 100% of the first $2,000 and 25% of the next $2,000 in qualified tuition and related expenses (for a maximum credit of $2,500) for the first 4 years of college enrollment. The AOTC is partially refundable (up to maximum credit of $1,000), while income phase-outs eliminate eligibility for high-income taxpayers. The Lifetime Learning credit provided for a nonrefundable credit of 20% of up to $10,000 in qualified tuition and related expenses per taxpayer per year.

---

[11] A further cost of borrowing is the origination fee, which is a fee charged to cover the processing of the loan. Stafford loans have an origination fee of 1% of the loan amount, while to take out a PLUS loan costs 4.3% of the loan amount.

[12] Federal information on interest rates can be found at: https://studentaid.ed.gov/sa/types/loans/interest-rates.

[13] The Taxpayer Relief Act of 1997 also made the interest on student loans tax deductible.

> **Quick Hint:** A tax credit reduces dollar for dollar an individual's tax liability by reducing the level of taxable income. If the original tax liability is $t \times Y$, a credit of C reduces liability to $t \times (Y - C)$. Tax credits vary by whether they are refundable or nonrefundable. A refundable tax credit can be claimed when there is zero tax liability, generating a refund from the government. A nonrefundable tax credit can be claimed only up to the point where tax liability becomes zero. Nonrefundable credits therefore affect higher-income taxpayers more because these taxpayers tend to have higher tax liability.

Other Sources of Financial Aid

State Aid One might think of the large state appropriations discussed in Chapter 13 that lead to lower tuition charges for in-state students as an implicit source of financial aid. These appropriations are larger than the entire federal aid budget, at $81 billion in 2014–2015. However, these subsidies are not typically recorded in the financial aid ledger. Aside from these subsidies, states provide financial aid to students in two forms:

1. Grants and need-based scholarships
2. Merit scholarships

Eligibility for grants and need-based scholarships usually depends on whether a student is a resident of the state and on the economic circumstances of his or her family. These awards are mostly restricted to residents attending a public college or university in state. For example, New York State has the Tuition Assistance Program (TAP), which provides college aid to students from low-income families who attend in-state public universities. The majority of states have such a financial assistance program, and many states have programs that focus on different populations to try to assist students going into high-need professions (such as nursing and teaching) and to subsidize students who want to help underserved communities.

The second type of state aid is state merit scholarships. Unlike need-based aid, merit scholarships are given to high-achieving students in the state, regardless of parental income, as long as the student attends an in-state public university.[14] The goals of such programs are to help keep high-achieving students in the state and to provide financial incentives for students to work hard while in high school. The first state merit aid program was started by Arkansas in 1991, but the program that has received the most research attention is the Georgia HOPE Scholarship, which was started in 1993. Students who graduate from a Georgia high school after 1993 are eligible as long as they have a high school GPA of at least 3.0. While at first there was an income cap, it was eliminated after a couple years, and currently all Georgia residents who meet the GPA requirement are eligible for the scholarship. The scholarship pays for a large portion of tuition at any public school in Georgia.

The apparent success of Georgia's program (see Section 14.3) led to a rapid increase in the number of states with such programs. Table 14.1 contains a list of these states and the year that each program was enacted. Currently, 18 states have a substantial merit aid program for which at least 15% of students are eligible. Another 13 states have smaller programs. As Table 14.1 shows, there are large differences across states in the generosity of this aid. In some states, full tuition is provided, while in others the awards are capped at relatively small amounts. Program rules differ in terms of obtaining and keeping eligibility. Virtually all states restrict merit aid to high-achieving students, but the measures used to determine whether students are high

---

[14] Some states, including Georgia, extend portable grant aid to private universities within the state. In addition, some states adjust the generosity of merit-based scholarships according to family circumstances.

Table 14.1 Merit Aid Program Details in States With Broad Merit Aid Plans

State	Name	Start Year	Max Amount	Renewal Eligibility
Alaska	Alaska Performance Scholarship	2011	$4,755	2.0 GPA first year 2.5 GPA after
Arkansas	Academic Challenge Scholarship	1991	$4,500 (4 years) $2,200 (2 years)	2.5 GPA
Florida	Florida Bright Futures	1997	$43–$101 per credit hour	2.75–3.0 GPA
Georgia	Georgia HOPE Scholarship	1993	$71–$242 per credit hour	3.0 GPA
Kentucky	Kentucky Educational Excellence Scholarship	1999	$1,000	2.5 GPA first year 2.5–3.0 GPA after
Louisiana	Taylor Opportunity Program for Students	1998	Public tuition + some fees	2.3 GPA first year 2.5 GPA after
Maryland	HOPE Scholarship	2002	$3,000 (4 years) $1,000 (2 years)	3.0 GPA
Massachusetts	Adams Scholarship	2005	Public tuition	3.0 GPA
Michigan	Merit Award	2000	$4,000 over 4 years	2.5 GPA
Mississippi	Mississippi Tuition Assistance Grant	1996	$500 first 2 years $1,000 second 2 years	2.5 GPA
North Dakota	North Dakota Academic Scholarship	2010	$1,500	2.75 GPA
Nevada	Millennium Scholarship	2000	$1,980 (4 years) $920 (2 years)	2.6 GPA first year 2.75 GPA after
New Mexico	Legislative Lottery Scholarship	1997	Public tuition + fees	2.5 GPA
South Carolina	LIFE Scholarship	1998	$5,000 + $2,500 for math/science majors	3.0 GPA
South Dakota	Opportunity Scholarship	2004	$1,000 first 3 years $2,000 fourth year	3.0 GPA
Tennessee	Tennessee HOPE	2003	$4,000 (4 years) $2,000 (2 years)	2.75 GPA first year 3.0 GPA after
West Virginia	West Virginia PROMISE	2002	Public tuition + fees	2.75 GPA first year 3.0 GPA after
Wyoming	Hathaway Scholarship	2006	$3,200	2.5 GPA

Data from: Fitzpatrick and Jones (2012). This table shows all states with a broad merit scholarship program, defined as covering at least 15% of all students statewide. Alabama, California, Hawaii, Indiana, Illinois, Minnesota, Missouri, New Jersey, New York, North Carolina, Oklahoma, Texas, and Washington all have smaller merit aid programs as well.

achieving differ across states, with some using test scores and some using high school GPAs. Furthermore, these programs require students to maintain some minimum GPA to retain eligibility once enrolled in college. For example, Georgia requires students to maintain at least a 3.0 GPA in each year, while in West Virginia students are expected to have at least a 2.75 GPA in their first year and a 3.0 GPA in subsequent years.

Merit aid not only is likely to have different behavioral effects than need-based aid due to the GPA requirements, but the beneficiaries are likely to be different. Need-based

DEEP DIVE: Place-Based "Promise" Programs

In recent years, there has been a growth of "promise" scholarships, which provide grants to students who graduate from a high school in a certain area. The first and best-known such program is the Kalamazoo Promise, which was begun in Kalamazoo, Michigan, by a group of anonymous donors. All students who attend a high school in Kalamazoo for all 4 years and who graduate receive a grant to pay for their tuition and fees at an in-state college or university. In an initial analysis of this program, Andrews, DesJardins, and Ranchhod (2010) show that this scholarship increased the likelihood a Kalamazoo student attended college in the state of Michigan.

Since the Kalamazoo Promise scholarship began in 2005, similar programs have been launched in 40 communities across the United States.[15] However, not all of them are as generous as the Kalamazoo Promise program. Unlike federal financial aid programs, promise scholarship programs are place-based rather than income- or resource-based. They exist only in districts that serve predominantly low-income and underrepresented minority communities, but all students who attend these schools can receive this aid. The idea behind a place-based scholarship is that it can be used to spur economic development in an area in addition to helping low-income students invest in college. However, this can come at some cost in terms of targeting benefits at the most needy students, since some students who receive a scholarship may not be of high financial need.

aid targets lower-income students, while the academic achievement requirements for merit aid generally favor higher-income students because of the positive correlation between high school achievement and family financial circumstances.

Institutional Aid In Chapter 13, we noted the importance of institutional funds for financial aid in college and university expenditures. By construction, this source of support is not portable but rather is tied to specific college choices. Not all colleges and universities have sufficient resources or tuition structures to permit sizable institutional aid. Aid given by colleges and universities is disproportionately concentrated at private universities and selective public universities.

The modern era in institutional need-based aid began with the founding of the College Scholarship Service (CSS) in 1954, which was an effort by about 95 private colleges to develop a standardized system of assessment of financial need and a family's capacity to pay based on analysis of tax data and other holdings. The CSS methodology is the precursor to the approach currently used by the federal government to assess financial need. A number of private universities developed policies of need-based financial aid (and associated need-blind admissions) as a signal that a lack of financial resources would not limit the enrollment of students from modest circumstances. In addition, universities sought common policies to limit financial aid to students with demonstrated financial need to avoid bidding wars that would be a drain on scarce institutional resources (Bowen, Kurzweil & Tobin, 2005).

Beyond recruiting very able students from modest economic circumstances, colleges and universities use institutional aid for other competitive purposes. First, institutions may award aid on the basis of student merit to change the composition of a class. There are surely many dimensions of merit an institution may think important to its mission, including recruiting students with high academic scores or students with exceptional talent in athletic areas. In an era in which institutional rankings (such as those that appear in *U.S. News and World Report*) depend on the test scores of matriculating students, it may well make sense to offer aid targeted to those who raise the institution's academic profile. In turn, a college's competitiveness in sports like football

---

[15] See Andrews (2014) for a comprehensive overview of promise programs in the United States.

and basketball may directly affect revenues, while alumni contributions and reputation more generally may depend on the capacity to field competitive teams in a range of sports. Finally, as discussed in Chapter 13, institutions may award financial aid as a price discount aimed at increasing net revenue.

Private Loans Another notable source of financing for college is the private loan sector. Since this source of financial aid first started being tracked in 1995, private loans have risen from $1.67 billion to $7.20 billion (Figure 14.6). However, this comparison obscures a large rise in the prevalence of private loans between 2002 and 2008. Private loan payments peaked in 2006 at $23.21 billion, which represents a 1,290% increase from 1995! The large recession and the collapse of many areas of the financial sector reduced the prevalence of these loans after 2008, but private loan levels have again begun to increase. If students are increasingly constrained by federal student loan limits, it is likely such loans will be an increasingly important part of the financial aid system.

How Is Need-Based Aid Determined?

Economic Principles of Needs Assessment The principle of need-based financial aid is straightforward: Policy makers and college administrators want to allocate financial aid in a way that eliminates short-run credit constraints and reduces differences in the burden of paying for college by family circumstances.[16] Several types of economic tensions plague efforts to design a method of needs assessment that is both equitable and efficient. First, a persistent challenge is the trade-off between simplicity and targeting. Whether it be the analysis of eligibility for social welfare programs like food stamps or financial aid, an objective is to make application sufficiently accessible and low-cost that those most in need of aid will not be deterred from applying. However, needs analysis must be sufficiently detailed so as to capture meaningful differences in economic circumstances. An aid analysis system that is too simple may be inefficient because it reduces the ability to target aid to the most needy. An aid system that is overly complex also would reduce efficiency if intended beneficiaries were deterred from applying.[17]

vertical equity Effort to pay or burden among agents from different circumstances is the same in the distribution of subsidies or the assessment of taxes. In the context of financial aid, it requires that all families put forth the same effort in paying for college relative to their financial resources.

Recognizing that potential college students come from very different financial backgrounds, an objective of need-based aid is to achieve **vertical equity,** which is defined by equality of effort in paying for college across families with different resources. Vertical equity means that those with greater financial resources will pay more than those who are less well off. Financial aid is the means through which vertical equity can be realized, which requires aid to be targeted to lower-resource families.

horizontal equity Agents from the same circumstances face the same burden or receive the same benefit in a tax or transfer system.

In addition to vertical equity, optimal needs assessment should generate **horizontal equity**. Horizontal equity occurs when economic agents with the same characteristics are treated the same by a tax or transfer system. In the context of financial aid, this would lead families with the same earnings capacity to be eligible for the same amount of aid. In practice, needs assessment focuses on current income and wealth, not earnings capacity (which is much harder to measure). The use of current financial resources leads to horizontal inequity because it treats families with the same lifetime earnings but different savings behavior differently.

---

[16] For a very good summary of the details of needs assessment, students are encouraged to view the short film *Form and Formula: How the Federal Government Distributes Aid to Students.* http://www.ihep.org/video/form-and-formula-how-federal-government-distributes-aid-students.

[17] See https://www.luminafoundation.org/files/resources/form-and-formula-viewing-guide.pdf for a history of needs analysis in the context of financial aid.

Consider two otherwise identical families: the Griffins and the Simpsons. They have identical lifetime earnings, but the Griffins take lots of family vacations and spend their money. In contrast, the Simpsons save their money. Although they have the same lifetime resources, the financial aid system treats them differently: The Griffins will be eligible for more aid because they have lower wealth and thus appear poorer. This feature of the financial aid system not only introduces horizontal inequities but can lead to substantial distortions in savings because families are essentially penalized for saving. To the extent families are reducing savings or changing the timing of income, there is a potentially large efficiency loss associated with using current resources to determine financial aid eligibility. The accumulation of wealth or assets is particularly challenging for the consideration of the optimal design of needs analysis.

How Need-Based Aid Is Determined With the reauthorization of the Higher Education Act in 1972, which created what we now know as the Pell grant, Congress had to grapple with how it would define need and eligibility. In 1986, Congress aimed to generate some independence in the allocation of federal aid from the approach used by colleges and created the *Congressional Methodology*. Congress also introduced a single form for federal aid known as the Application for Federal Financial Aid, later known as the **Free Application for Federal Student Aid (FAFSA).**[18] The 1992 Higher Education Act reauthorization brought substantial changes in the formula and relabeled it the *Federal Methodology*. These changes included the removal of home equity from needs assessment. Subsequent changes have introduced an online form and adjusted the formula to provide a streamlined analysis for very low-income students.

All federal financial aid and most of the financial aid awarded by states and public institutions use the Federal Methodology to determine student need and family ability to pay. However, about 350 postsecondary institutions use an additional formula called the *Institutional Methodology*. This formula provides a way for institutions to measure household assets more carefully. The largest difference between the federal and institutional methodologies is that the latter includes housing wealth in family financial assets and includes more categories of investment income and net worth. Most schools that use this methodology are private, although some of the more selective public universities also use this method. It is designed to more fully capture family assets to better target aid toward those students with financial need. Colleges and universities with high sticker prices find that financial need extends up the income distribution to include middle-income families. As needs analysis for these institutions includes a broader set of financial circumstances, increases in complexity and more information are needed to assess capacity to pay and eligibility for financial aid.

The primary components of the federal assessment formula are the determination of **expected family contribution (EFC)**, which is the amount a student and his family could be expected to pay for college, and the cost of attendance, which includes tuition and fees as well as an allowance for expected living costs. The total amount of aid a student is eligible for is calculated as:

$$\text{Cost of attendance} - \text{EFC} = \text{demonstrated need}$$

Demonstrated need refers to the maximum amount of aid a student could expect to receive, though simply because an individual has calculated need does not mean that

Free Application for Federal Student Aid (FAFSA) The application all students must fill out to receive federal financial aid.

expected family contribution (EFC) The government's assessment of how much each family can afford to contribute toward paying for college costs.

demonstrated need The maximum amount of financial aid a student can receive under the Federal Methodology.

---

[18] This legislation also created an explicit distinction between dependent and independent students. Students under the age of 24 are considered dependent for the purpose of determining capacity to pay for college, and parents' financial circumstances are required to determine need. Independent students are either over the age of 24 or meet an alternative criterion such as veteran, married, or with children.

available income (AI) The amount of parental income net of allowances for financial aid determination.

discretionary net worth The difference between total assets (excluding housing) and the asset protection level that applies to the given household.

adjusted available income (AAI) The sum of 12% of discretionary net worth and available income.

colleges or the federal government will provide sufficient aid to meet this need. Those institutions that are able to meet full need may provide financial aid through an aid package that can include loans as well as grants.

How is the EFC calculated? The actual formula is rather complex (and varies between the Federal Methodology and the Institutional Methodology), but the broad goal is to determine a family's ability to pay (i.e., the expected family contribution) and provide financial aid for costs in excess of this amount. There are several important components to financial aid determination:

- Parental income
- Parental assets
- Student income and assets
- Allowances for taxes paid and for income protection

These components are combined and run through a formula that shows how much financial aid each family is eligible for.

If a family has an EFC of $10,000 and a student is planning on attending a community college with costs of $6,000 per year, the demonstrated need would be –$4,000. As a result, the family would qualify for no federal financial aid. Yet if the same student were planning on attending a private four-year school with yearly costs of $30,000, demonstrated need would be $20,000. This student would be eligible to receive $20,000 in aid from federal, state, and institutional sources. However, this does not guarantee that he or she will receive this amount of financial aid.

Importantly, the EFC is increasing in a family's income and assets. Figure 14.8 contains expected family contributions for a family of four at different income levels. We have done these calculations two ways. First, we assume the family has $20,000 in assets at each income level. Second, we assume that assets grow with income and that at each income level families have twice their income in assets. Thus, a family with income of $100,000 per year would have $200,000 in assets.

The figure shows how the EFC rises steeply with income and assets. Under both asset assumptions, families with incomes below $30,000 per year are not expected to contribute anything to paying for their child's college attendance. Between $30,000 and $70,000, for every dollar more in income the low-asset family is expected to contribute 15 to 20 cents more. The high-asset family is expected to contribute between 17 and 28 cents more toward their child's education for each additional dollar between $30,000 and $60,000. Above these income thresholds, the low-asset family's EFC grows by 30 cents per dollar and the high-asset family's contribution grows by about 40 cents per additional dollar of earnings. Thus, the rate at which family income translates into EFC is increasing with income until family income is about $70,000. After that point, another dollar of earnings has the same effect on the EFC. The accompanying Deep Dive provides further details on how financial aid eligibility is calculated.

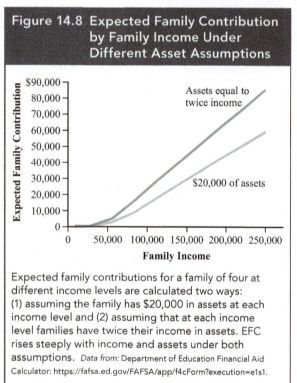

Figure 14.8 Expected Family Contribution by Family Income Under Different Asset Assumptions

Expected family contributions for a family of four at different income levels are calculated two ways: (1) assuming the family has $20,000 in assets at each income level and (2) assuming that at each income level families have twice their income in assets. EFC rises steeply with income and assets under both assumptions. *Data from:* Department of Education Financial Aid Calculator: https://fafsa.ed.gov/FAFSA/app/f4cForm?execution=e1s1.

DEEP DIVE: Calculating Financial Aid Eligibility

The first step of the process is to sum up parents' income. Both taxable income and untaxed income and benefits (such as child support payments, tax-exempt interest, and payments to tax-deferred pension and savings plans) are included in the determination of parental income. Several allowances then are subtracted from parental income, such as federal income taxes, state and local tax allowances, Social Security taxes, and employment expenses. There also is an income protection allowance, which is determined by the number of household members and the number of college students in the household. In 2013, a family of two with one college student had an income protection allowance of $17,100. For each additional household member, the allowance increases by $4,000–$5,000, while the allowance declines by about $2,900 for each additional college student. The total allowances are then subtracted from total income to generate **available income (AI)**.

The next step is to calculate parental assets. These assets include money in checking and savings accounts, stock market and other investments, and the value of a business or farm. Note that housing wealth on a family's primary residence is not included in this calculation. A result of this exemption is that a family can have an expensive home and still qualify for financial aid if the value of its other assets as well as its income are low enough. In practice this situation is rare, but the exemption of housing wealth creates such opportunities. The values of the various assets included in the federal aid formula are summed and an asset protection allowance is subtracted that varies by parent age and by the number of parents (but not by the household size or the number of children in college). Older parents are given more asset protection, ostensibly because of the desire to protect their savings for retirement. The difference between total assets and the asset protection level is called **discretionary net worth**, and the federal formula includes 12% of this net worth towards the EFC.

The total parental contribution is calculated by summing contributions from assets and income (AI) to form **adjusted available income (AAI)**. Thus, AAI is the sum of 12% of discretionary net worth and available income. AAI is then run through a payment schedule that determines how much parents are expected to contribute toward college costs. Figure 14.9 shows this schedule as of the 2013–2014 school year. The schedule has several bend points, where the percentage of AAI parents are expected to contribute increases. The contribution rates range from zero to 47% on AAI over $30,900.

Student income and assets also play an important role in financial aid calculations. Student income is included from the same sources as parental income, which for students typically consists of labor market earnings. Tax allowances are then applied, as is an income protection allowance that equaled $6,100 in 2013. Any income over this amount (net of taxes) is considered available to help pay for college. Fifty percent of students' available income is expected to be contributed toward college costs. That is, for every additional dollar of earnings over the protection threshold, EFC increases by 50 cents. The value of student assets is calculated in a similar manner to parents', except that 20% of student assets contribute toward the EFC. The total student contribution is equal to 50% of income above the protection amount and 20% of assets.

Expected family contribution is the sum of the parental contribution and the student contribution:

$$EFC = parental\ contribution + student\ contribution$$

These calculations were done for a dependent student. Such students typically attend college directly after high school. Older students (generally older than 24) often are independent, and their financial aid is calculated differently. We focus on dependent students here because they constitute the majority of undergraduate students in the United States.

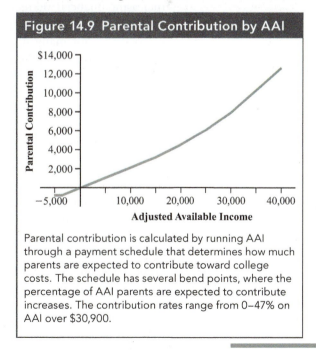

Figure 14.9 Parental Contribution by AAI

Parental contribution is calculated by running AAI through a payment schedule that determines how much parents are expected to contribute toward college costs. The schedule has several bend points, where the percentage of AAI parents are expected to contribute increases. The contribution rates range from 0–47% on AAI over $30,900.

14.3 The Effect of Net Price and Financial Aid on Behavior

One of the most basic predictions from economics is that lowering the price of a good or service will yield an increase in the quantity demanded; in effect, demand schedules slope down. The extent to which the rate of going to college changes relative to a change in price is the price elasticity of demand. In turn, we might expect students to be indifferent between a decline in $1,000 in tuition and an increase of $1,000 in financial aid—after all, the net effect on the student would be the same. Critically, this hypothesis depends on the assumption that students are fully informed about their eligibility for financial aid.

How do we determine the effect of changing tuition or financial aid on college choices? Ideally, our assessment would cover not just whether individuals enroll in college but also the type of college they choose, degree outcomes, and long-run outcomes like employment and earnings. Answering these questions is complicated because it is rare that changes in financial aid and tuition are independent of other factors that affect college going. Changes in tuition levels generally occur in relation to market conditions that also influence college investment decisions. For example, tuition increases at public colleges often follow from declines in state appropriations in economic downturns, and such adverse labor market conditions may well have an independent effect on college going. Similarly, need-based aid and merit-based aid are—by construction—not randomly assigned, and it is likely that students receiving such aid differ systematically from the broader pool of potential college students.

This section focuses on empirical approaches researchers have used to test whether and how enrollment and attainment respond to the availability of financial aid.

Empirical Framework and Estimation Challenges

Increasing financial aid reduces the cost of investing in college. For some students, the addition of aid doesn't change their decisions, as they would have attended without aid. Alternatively, for many students the availability of aid is insufficient to make college a good investment. The students for whom financial aid affects behavior are those for whom the net benefits switch from negative to positive. The empirical challenge is to figure out just how large this group is.

A good starting point for understanding this problem is to consider the following simple regression:

$$Y_i = \beta_0 + \beta_1 aid_i + \varepsilon_i$$

where Y is an indicator variable representing college enrollment of student i and aid is the amount of financial aid he or she is eligible for. If the aid was randomly assigned ($[\varepsilon_i | aid] = 0$), the estimated coefficient β_1 would be the causal effect of financial aid eligibility on enrollment. In such a case, this coefficient would be equal to the difference in the enrollment rates for those eligible for different levels of aid. In Section 14.2, we detailed the factors affecting different types of financial aid distribution, including family background. These factors are undoubtedly related to other, unobserved student attributes that also are correlated with the likelihood of college enrollment. For example, students from higher-income backgrounds are likely to have parents who went to college and are likely to be more academically prepared for college. These factors are independently correlated with college enrollment, which creates a bias in the regression.

What we would like is an experiment that randomly assigns financial aid to some students but not to others. While such an experiment would be very informative, it is extremely unlikely that someone will allocate aid to students in such a way. Thus, we are left with trying to find sources of financial aid variation that are uncorrelated with student characteristics and academic ability. Researchers have approached this problem in several ways:

- Use the implementation of federal financial aid programs, such as the Pell grant, to examine how student enrollment and educational outcomes change when the program is implemented.
- Examine changes in federal financial aid programs that affect only certain students, such as veterans or students eligible for federal survivorship benefits from having a deceased parent. This allows one to conduct a difference-in-difference analysis, since only some students are affected by the rule changes.
- Use the implementation of state merit aid laws, comparing changes among students in the affected state to those in other states that did not implement a merit aid program in a difference-in-difference analysis.

Virtually all financial aid studies done by economists conform to one of these three methods. We will now discuss these studies in more detail, starting with federal aid programs and then focusing on what is known about state merit aid.

Federal Aid

The Introduction of the Pell Grant One of the central ways in which researchers have estimated the effect of federal financial aid on collegiate outcomes is to examine how these outcomes changed surrounding the implementation of the Pell grant in 1973. In one of the earliest and most influential examples of this approach, Kane (1994) uses Current Population Survey (CPS)[19] data from 1970–1978, which is a period that surrounds the introduction of the Pell grant program. He estimates whether low-income students who would have been Pell-eligible experienced a change in their college enrollment rates after 1973. Both for Black and White students, he finds little evidence to suggest that the introduction of the Pell grant altered the enrollment behavior of low-income students. Simple trends in enrollment among low- and higher-income Blacks and Whites further support this conclusion: While enrollment among low-income Blacks and Whites increased post 1973, so did enrollment among higher-income students of both ethnic groups (Hansen, 1983; Kane, 1994). Hansen's review of the evidence highlights that the implementation of the Pell grant program, which greatly expanded the scope and targeting of federal grant aid, did little to alter the postsecondary outcomes of young adults from disadvantaged backgrounds.

Unlike the early evidence for low-income youth, the effects on college participation for nontraditional students have been sizable. Research by Seftor and Turner (2002) finds that the introduction of the Pell program, as well as expansions in program eligibility, have a positive and significant effect on the college enrollment decisions of older students. Pell grant introduction increased male enrollment by about 1.7 percentage points and female enrollment by 1.4 percentage points. While these percentages may appear modest, they are large relative to the underlying college enrollment rate of each

---

[19] See Appendix A for a description of CPS data.

group. For men, only 9.1% of 22–35-year-olds were enrolled prior to 1973, and so the 1.7 percentage point increase represents an 18.7% change in the college enrollment rate. For women, the mean enrollment rate was only 3.3%, so the introduction of the Pell grant increased female enrollment by 42.2%. Many of the most significant changes in benefit determination associated with the Pell program have affected nontraditional students.

> **Quick Hint:** To translate percentage points into percent effects relative to baseline, you divide the percentage effect by the pretreatment mean. In this case, (1.7/9.1) × 100 = 18.7%.

The Social Security Student Benefit Program From 1965 to 1982, the Social Security Administration provided the children of deceased, disabled, or retired Social Security beneficiaries monthly payments while they were enrolled full time in college. On average, the annual payment for college expenses in 1980 was $9,217 in 2015 dollars. Obtaining the Social Security student benefits was uncomplicated, and it was easy for students to know their eligibility because the Social Security Administration sent form letters to child beneficiaries nearing age 18. If recipients responded that they would be continuing their education, they would receive a monthly benefit check until they left school or turned 22. In 1981, the federal government ended the provision of these benefits for college enrollment. While some potential recipients were eligible for other forms of financial aid, there is no question that students with a deceased parent experienced a large negative shock to their ability to pay college expenses in 1981.

The elimination of the Social Security student benefits presents an opportunity to assess how such a change in aid affects students' college going and attainment. Sue Dynarski (2003) compares how college enrollment changed among students with a deceased father when the SSI program was eliminated to enrollment of students without a deceased father, using data from the NLSY79.[20] This is a difference-in-difference approach that assumes there would have been no change in the difference between enrollment patterns of the two groups in the absence of the policy change. That is, the difference-in-difference method is predicated on the idea that enrollment and attainment rates of youths with deceased fathers would have changed similarly to changes in these rates among youths without a deceased father if the benefit had not been repealed. Of course, students with a deceased father are going to be different from students with a live father, but any constant differences across these groups is accounted for.

The top part of Table 14.2 presents comparisons of observed characteristics, such as family income and parental education, by fathers' mortality status. Young people with a deceased father tend to come from families with both lower income and lower parental education, but critically, these characteristics change little with the policy change. Dynarski's results, shown in the bottom part of the table, are striking: Before the SSI benefit repeal, students with a deceased father were much *more* likely to enroll in college and had more educational attainment. After the SSI program was eliminated, enrollment and attainment among students with a deceased father fell significantly below those of other students. Taking the difference-in-difference in the final column, there is an 18 percentage point decline in college enrollment due to the

---

[20] See Appendix A for an overview of the NLSY79 dataset.

Table 14.2 The Effect of Eliminating the College SSI Benefit Program on College Enrollment

| | High School Seniors 1979–1981 | | High School Seniors 1982–1983 | | |
	Father Not Deceased	Father Deceased	Father Not Deceased	Father Deceased	Difference-in-Differences
Student Characteristics					
Household Income ($2,000)	54,357 (537)	32,875 (1,837)	50,842 (788)	32,298 (2,958)	2,938 (4,816)
AFQT Percentile	61 (0.51)	58 (2.36)	53 (0.91)	45 (3.92)	6 (5.33)
Black	0.135 (0.007)	0.235 (0.036)	0.151 (0.011)	0.297 (0.063)	0.046 (0.068)
Hispanic	0.051 (0.004)	0.055 (0.020)	0.062 (0.007)	0.059 (0.032)	0.007 (0.026)
Father Attended College	0.331 (0.009)	0.184 (0.033)	0.299 (0.014)	0.158 (0.050)	0.006 (0.079)
Outcomes					
Attended College by Age 23	0.502 (0.010)	0.560 (0.043)	0.476 (0.015)	0.352 (0.066)	0.182 (0.096)
Complete Any College by Age 23	0.487 (0.010)	0.560 (0.043)	0.459 (0.015)	0.361 (0.066)	0.171 (0.097)
Years of School at Age 23	13.410 (0.030)	13.440 (0.130)	13.250 (0.050)	12.900 (0.200)	0.380 (0.296)
Number of Observations	2,745	137	1,050	54	3,986

Data from: Dynarski (2003), Table 1. Standard errors are in parentheses.

program change.[21] There also is evidence of a large decrease in the likelihood of completing college, which is consistent with the lower enrollment rates of these students. These results suggest that providing money for students to enroll in college can have large impacts on their enrollment and completion behavior. Dynarski calculates that each $1,000 of aid increased college enrollment by 3.6 percentage points.

The GI Bill The GI Bill was the first large-scale portable federal financial aid program. Studying the effects of this program is difficult, since service in World War II was nearly universal. Simply comparing veterans to nonveterans in a given birth cohort is likely to give misleading answers because those who did not serve were a very unique group. Veterans and nonveterans are likely to differ in ways that might also be related to collegiate attainment, as physical and mental disabilities were primary reasons for

---

[21] Regression-based estimates controlling for student characteristics that change slightly over this interval lead to an even larger (and statistically significant) estimated effect of 22 percentage points.

not participating in the military for cohorts born between 1923 and 1928. Bound and Turner (2002) solve this problem using the fact that military service *across* birth cohorts differed. They then compare the differences in years of education and college completion rates across cohorts to the differences across the same cohorts in the proportion of World War II veterans. As the authors note, this method will show the effect of the GI Bill plus military service on educational attainment: No one was eligible for GI Bill funds without having served in the military. They find the combined effects of the GI Bill and military service were substantial, increasing college completion among veterans by 50%. These results suggest that providing grants that cover the full cost of a college education to students will greatly increase college completion rates.[22]

The GI Bill and the Social Security student benefit results are particularly meaningful because they demonstrate effects on attainment, not just enrollment. The public and private return to programs that generate enrollment increases without attainment increases are much less likely to be positive.

So how do we reconcile the evidence on small enrollment responses to the Pell grant with larger estimates of the effect of grant aid from the GI Bill and the Social Security benefit elimination? One explanation is that transparency and communication may make a big difference: Pell eligibility may not be evident at the time an individual would apply to college because of the complexity and difficulty of federal aid programs that work through the FAFSA application process. In contrast, programs like the Social Security survivor benefits and the GI Bill provided clear notification of benefit eligibility and easy access to funds. These programs were very transparent and allowed students to easily determine eligibility; they provided support over a fixed duration that encouraged college completion; and they were sufficiently generous to cover a substantial share of college costs. These differences in program structure are likely a main reason why they differ in their effects on collegiate investment, which provides some guidance on how best to structure financial aid programs.

DEEP DIVE: The Role of Complexity and Student Knowledge

Taken together, the evidence discussed in the prior two sections suggests that in many circumstances providing students financial assistance for college can have large impacts on college going and on college completion. It therefore is curious that much of the work focusing on federal financial aid programs as they operate through the FAFSA application process, most notably the Pell grant, has little impact on traditional college students. This is an unexpected result: What could cause students to be responsive to financial aid more generally but not to the Pell grant specifically? One compelling argument that researchers have put forth is that the complexity of the financial aid system prohibits students from using it effectively.

Quick Hint: Traditional college students are those who attend college directly (or within a couple years) of high school graduation. Nontraditional students refer to those first attending college in their mid-20s or later.

Dynarski and Scott-Clayton (2006) highlight two particularly important aspects of the financial aid process that might make it less effective:

1. Timing
2. The length and complexity of the FAFSA

Traditional students typically apply to college in the fall or winter of their senior year. Yet financial aid determinations are not made until the spring. Dynarski and Scott-Clayton

---

[22] Barr (2015) examines the post-9/11 GI Bill, which greatly expanded veterans' education benefits. He finds large effects of these expansions on college investments among veterans.

highlight the difficulties this timing imposes, since students do not know the price of the school when they apply. Imagine shopping for a car in this manner. First, you would look around at different cars, each of which has a price attached to it that is far above what you will likely pay. Then, you have to decide which cars you are interested in, and only after you have made this decision are you told what each car costs. And, if you do not like the final price, you cannot go out and search for more cars. This makes shopping based on prices very difficult, and few people would argue this is an optimal way to operate a market for a consumer good. Yet this is exactly how the timing of financial aid works: You must first decide which schools you are going to apply to, and only after the admissions decision are you told the price you will have to pay. That many students do not know what different schools will cost when they apply undoubtedly reduces the effectiveness of the federal financial aid system.

The second issue highlighted by Dynarski and Scott-Clayton is the complexity of the FAFSA itself. The FAFSA is a five-page document with 127 questions about details of parental and student earnings and assets. To put this in context, this form is longer than any of the U.S. income tax forms, such as the 1040, that taxpayers routinely complain about. The complexity of this form produces considerable compliance costs that fall more heavily on low-income families, who may be less familiar with the specifics of the financial questions being asked. Furthermore, high school students are likely to exhibit what behavioral economists call "time inconsistency," which means that even though they may plan to fill out the lengthy FAFSA, when it comes time to do so they procrastinate and avoid applying for aid. Time inconsistency can lead small up-front costs to preclude individuals from engaging in behaviors that have large long-run benefits (such as college enrollment), and FAFSA costs are a prime example of this type of problem.

While the complexity of the FAFSA form is meant to ensure that aid is targeted correctly to low-income families, Dynarski and Scott-Clayton (2006) argue that such targeting could be accomplished with far fewer questions. Basically, because wealth and income are so highly correlated, most low-income parents also are low in wealth, which means you only need to know about the former to infer total household resources. They conduct detailed simulations that show the distribution of aid across families would be extremely similar if the government only asked eight questions about parent and child income as well as family structure. Using only parental income information that the government has through the income tax system would also produce largely the same distribution of aid as well. Thus, the complexity of the FAFSA

creates compliance costs with little benefit in terms of targeting aid to the most needy families.

While the argument that the FAFSA compliance costs could lead to students underutilizing the financial aid system is quite compelling, it is not evidence that complexity can explain the apparent weak response of students to federal financial aid programs. In a very important study, Bettinger et al. (2012) provide such evidence from an experiment in which they randomly fill out FAFSA forms for a set of low-income families. In conjunction with the tax preparation firm H&R Block, the researchers designed an experiment whereby low-income families who had members aged 15–30 without a bachelor's degree were randomly assigned to being offered help to fill out a FAFSA right after they completed their tax forms. Since the information on one's taxes and on the FAFSA overlap to a large degree, it was relatively straightforward for tax preparers to fill out these forms. Another set of families was randomly assigned to receive information about financial aid and likely eligibility, while the control group only received brochures about college and general information about costs and financial aid.

The randomization allows one to compare differences in college attendance and completion outcomes across treatment and control groups to isolate the effect of FAFSA simplification and assistance on these outcomes. The intervention had a large effect on student college investment. Dependent students whose families received assistance in filling out the FAFSA were 8.1 percentage points more likely to enroll in college, which is a 24% increase relative to the baseline college enrollment rate. These dependent students are mostly traditional college students who attend college directly after high school. Older, independent students with no prior college experience also increased enrollment by 1.5 percentage points (16%) due to being offered FAFSA assistance. Importantly, those who only received financial aid information had identical outcomes to the control group, suggesting that for the intervention to work families needed direct assistance in completing the financial aid application. Furthermore, retention and collegiate attainment increased substantially: Students treated with FAFSA assistance were significantly more likely to be enrolled in college for two consecutive years and completed more years of college than the control group.

These are very important results for education policy. In short, this research points to the large compliance costs faced by many low-income students, negatively affecting their likelihood of applying for aid and going to college. That these compliance costs are largely unnecessary to produce the targeting of aid for which they are intended makes them even more difficult to justify. In fact,

Dynarski and Scott-Clayton (2007) have proposed sending families information on federal financial aid availability on a postcard using data already collected by the income tax system. This policy would dramatically reduce the complexity in the financial aid system and would alleviate many of the timing issues surrounding financial aid awards. The analysis in Bettinger et al. (2012) suggests it would support college going and college completion among children from low-income families as a result.

Another important implication of the results in Bettinger et al. (2012) is that posted tuition might matter. If students have incomplete knowledge about the financial aid system, then they may mistake the college's posted tuition for the amount they actually have to spend. In such a case, colleges face a substantial challenge of communicating to students expected net price, which will be much lower than posted tuition with the inclusion of financial aid.

Further evidence supporting this argument comes from Kane (1994). He shows that students are much more responsive to posted tuition than they are to Pell grants, which economic theory would not predict if students had full information about the financial aid system. Hoxby and Avery (2013) also show that the majority of low-income, high-achieving students do not apply to any selective college or university. This is despite the fact that financial aid policies likely make such schools less expensive for them than the less selective alternatives they typically attend. Their behavior is consistent with these students having insufficient information about the financial aid system and college pricing policies to understand this point. In fact, a recent intervention aimed at alleviating these information deficiencies, which we discuss in more detail in Chapter 15, suggests that these students can be induced to apply to and attend more selective schools if given the proper information.

A main takeaway message from this research is that information matters. While much policy attention has been given to whether financial aid is generous enough, very little has been given to designing programs in such a way that they can be of most use to low-income students. The evidence from the SSI and state merit aid programs suggests that financial aid is very effective when it is easy to access and when knowledge about it is widespread among the target populations. Federal financial aid as it operates through the current FAFSA application does not, by and large, have these properties. Understanding how to reform this system to make it more accessible to the students it aims to help is an important policy problem that remains to be solved.

State Merit Aid

The political popularity of state merit aid programs is demonstrated by the adoption of such programs in 18 states over the past three decades, as shown in Table 14.2. State merit aid programs provide the *potential* of benefits to everyone, which makes these programs enormously popular with voters. At first glance, these systems share many of the same characteristics as the most successful federal initiatives—eligibility is straightforward and the level of benefits is clear. The nature of these programs, which generally have an academic threshold for eligibility and maintenance of benefits as well as the requirement for in-state enrollment, suggests they could affect many different outcomes. Such outcomes include high school achievement, college enrollment, collegiate attainment, and long-term labor market outcomes.

The Georgia HOPE Scholarship was one of the first programs to be enacted and has been the subject of a number of research inquiries. Dynarski (2000) provided an early analysis of this program by comparing changes in the college attendance rates of students in Georgia to those in nearby states. This difference-in-difference approach assumes that students in states near to Georgia would have experienced similar college enrollment patterns to Georgia students absent the merit aid program. Whether other students in the southeastern United States are a valid control group for Georgia students has been a debated question since this paper was published.

Dynarski (2000) finds that college enrollment among 18- and 19-year-olds in Georgia increased by between 7 and 8 percentage points when the HOPE Scholarship was introduced in 1993. Relative to the 30% enrollment rate in Georgia in the pretreatment period, these effect sizes translate to between 23% and 26% enrollment increases due to the merit aid program. Importantly, she also shows that students who were too old to be affected by the program experienced no change in their college enrollment rates. This falsification test provides considerable support for her conclusions, as it demonstrates that only those students who should have been influenced by this program actually changed their enrollment behavior.

Beyond evidence on whether college enrollment and attainment increases in response to state merit aid, a related question concerns how state merit aid affects *where* students enroll. State merit aid programs do not change the price of all colleges (like the Pell grant) but rather affect the relative prices of in-state public institutions in relation to out-of-state and private options. We thus would predict that merit aid will make it more likely that high-achieving students will attend college in state. This is exactly what Cornwell, Mustard, and Sridhar (2006) find in Georgia. They show that among first-time 4-year college entrants who enter college directly after high school, two-thirds of the enrollment increase is due to Georgia students shifting their enrollment from out-of-state to in-state schools.

The consequences of inducing high-achieving students to shift their attendance to in-state public schools depends on whether such shifts increase or decrease the quality of colleges student attend. There is a strong link between measures of college quality/college resources and student collegiate academic outcomes. If merit aid programs induce students to attend lower-resource in-state schools, their postsecondary attainment could be negatively affected. In a novel analysis of such unintended consequences of merit aid programs, Cohodes and Goodman (2014) show this to be the case with the Adams Scholarship in Massachusetts.

The John and Abigail Adams Scholarship Program provides tuition waivers to high-achieving students who attend public colleges and universities in state. The Massachusetts scholarship is based on tenth-grade state exam (MCAS) scores. If students score "advanced" on at least one portion of the exam, score at least "proficient" on the other portion, and are in the top 25% of scores in the school district, they are eligible for the tuition waiver. Cohodes and Goodman (2014) use these rules, which create strict cutoffs in eligibility based on exam scores, to examine college choice and attainment in a regression discontinuity framework. Essentially, this method compares outcomes among students who barely received the scholarship to outcomes of those who barely missed being eligible.

Their findings show that students who barely qualify for the Adams Scholarship attend colleges that have fewer resources and lower peer quality than those who barely miss the scholarship cutoff. The reason for this school quality effect is that the program induces students to go to in-state schools, which have fewer resources than the alternatives they otherwise would have attended. Furthermore, they find that the Adams Scholarship program leads to lower graduation rates among recipients, which they argue is due to the lower resource levels to which these students are exposed. These results highlight the potential unintended consequences of inducing students to sacrifice attending higher-resource schools to save money.

A general takeaway is that state-level merit aid systems are likely to have very different impacts on students, depending on the resource levels at public colleges and universities relative to the out-of-state and private alternatives. In states with high-resource public universities, such as Michigan, Texas, and California, the effect of merit aid programs that induce high-ability students to remain in state is likely to differ from the effect in states without more elite public universities.

In addition to giving students tuition assistance for attending college in state, most merit aid programs include performance incentives for students while enrolled in college. These achievement incentives may have positive effects on collegiate attainment. The West Virginia PROMISE scholarship is a prominent example of a program with built-in achievement incentives. Students who qualify for a scholarship by the end of high school must maintain a 3.0 GPA while enrolled in college (2.75 after the first year) and complete 30 credits per year. Scott-Clayton (2011) analyzes this program using two complementary methods that together provide strong support for her conclusions. The first approach is a regression discontinuity design, comparing college outcomes of students just above and just below the ACT(SAT) eligibility threshold of 21(1000). The second method she uses is to compare observationally similar students across cohorts when the PROMISE program was implemented. She finds that first-year GPA and credits accumulated increase due to scholarship eligibility. In addition, the program increases the likelihood a student obtains a BA after 4 years by between 6.7 and 9.4 percentage points. Receipt of a PROMISE scholarship significantly increases the likelihood a student has at least a 3.0 GPA as well. By providing incentives to college students for high academic performance to keep their scholarship, Scott-Clayton's research shows merit pay can have large impacts on college performance and academic attainment.

14.4 Student Debt

Levels and Trends of Student Debt

Eye-popping numbers, such as the presence of $1.2 trillion in student debt, which now exceeds consumer credit borrowing, have led to considerable public attention about whether there is a student borrowing crisis. Students and families are more reliant than ever on student loan financing: Between academic year 2002–2003 and 2014–2015, the share of undergraduate students borrowing from the federal student loan program increased from 24% to 36% (*Trends in Student Aid 2015*). Rising college costs, erosion of state support for public colleges and universities, and stagnant family incomes are all factors at play in the rise in student debt.

Importantly, the average loan amount per borrower in real terms has changed only moderately; there are simply more borrowers. For public university graduates, debt per borrower increased from $20,800 in 1999 to $25,000 in 2011, while for private university graduates with student loans, debt increased from $23,800 to $29,900.

Figure 14.10 contains the distribution of loan debt among the entering class of 2003–2004 as of 2009, broken down by degree type. Among BA recipients, only 23% have over $30,000 of debt, and only 8% have over $50,000. As expected, debt levels are lower for students earning associate's degrees, with only 12.4% having debt levels over $30,000 and fewer than 2% having debt over $50,000. Those who do not complete a degree also tend not to accumulate large amounts of debt: Only 5% have debt over $30,000 and fewer than 1% have debt over $50,000. With many stories in the popular press about students racking up hundreds of thousands of dollars to finance an undergraduate education, Figure 14.10 emphasizes that this is the exception, not the norm.[23]

---

[23] The rise of graduate student lending has added significantly to total student debt levels, because graduate student loans are over double undergraduate loans on average ($17,000 versus $7,000). Students typically do not have to pay back undergraduate loans while enrolled in graduate school, but interest on those original loans accumulates while they are working toward a graduate degree. This adds to the total amount of debt faced by students with a bachelor's degree.

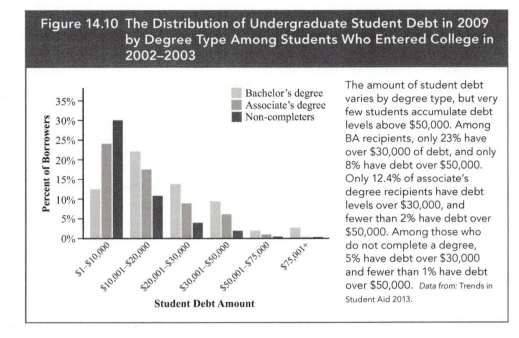

Figure 14.10 The Distribution of Undergraduate Student Debt in 2009 by Degree Type Among Students Who Entered College in 2002–2003

The amount of student debt varies by degree type, but very few students accumulate debt levels above $50,000. Among BA recipients, only 23% have over $30,000 of debt, and only 8% have debt over $50,000. Only 12.4% of associate's degree recipients have debt levels over $30,000, and fewer than 2% have debt over $50,000. Among those who do not complete a degree, 5% have debt over $30,000 and fewer than 1% have debt over $50,000. *Data from:* Trends in Student Aid 2013.

How do the debt levels faced by the average borrower translate into monthly payments after college? To do this calculation, we need to compute the payment of a fixed-interest loan occurring over a 10-year period (which is the length of most education loans). This is the same formula one would use to calculate home or car payments, except they typically would be over a different period of time. The loan payment formula is as follows:

$$P = \frac{r \times loan}{1 - (1 + r)^{-120}}$$

where we assume there are monthly payments over 10 years (120 months) at a fixed monthly interest rate of r and an original loan amount equal to *loan*. The monthly interest rate is found by dividing the yearly interest rate by 12. If the average student only took out Stafford loans, the yearly interest rate on the loan would be 3.76%. At this interest rate, a student with $25,000 of debt (the average among public graduates) would pay $250 per month, and a student with $29,900 in loans (the average among private graduates) would pay $299 per month.

Are these debt levels large or small? There is no right answer to this question, but we can put them into perspective. One way to do this is to consider how they relate to the college earnings premium. Student debt reflects the costs of obtaining a college degree, so to justify the expenditure there needs to be a sizable earnings return to college. Estimates from the Economic Policy Institute (EPI) suggest that yearly earnings among those with a college degree are $30,112 higher than those with only a high school degree, assuming workers work 2,000 hours per year. This difference translates into about $2,509 more in earnings per month for college-trained workers relative to workers with only a high school degree. The college earnings premium has risen since the late 1990s, when it was $26,878 per year, or $2,240 per month. Thus, over this period, the college earnings premium increased by $269 per month.

College debt has increased such that students graduating today can expect to pay about $44–$63 more per month for 10 years, while earnings of college- versus high school–trained workers have changed such that college workers can expect to earn $269 more per month *over their entire working life*. These calculations suggest that, although they undoubtedly feel burdensome to many students, student debt for undergraduates is low relative to the college–high school earnings gap and has grown at a slower rate than the earnings gap. In other words, the benefits have been growing faster than the debt burden.

Another way to think about the magnitude of the debt increases over the past 15 years is the **payment-to-income ratio.** The payment-to-income ratio is the ratio of monthly student loan payments to monthly income. This is not a perfect measure of the debt burden of students, as income is earned over the course of one's working life, while debt payments are made only over the life of the loan. But it is an informative measure of how the debt burden of students has changed relative to their incomes. Akers and Chingos (2014) calculate the payment-to-income ratio among workers aged 20–40 with any education debt between 1992 and 2010. They focus on "high" levels of debt, defined as the proportion of students with a ratio of 10%, 15%, and 20%. The proportion of students at each payment-to-income ratio has fallen over time, suggesting debt burdens relative to income have declined over their period of study. For example, in 1992, 25% of workers had a payment-to-income ratio of 10%, while by 2010 this proportion of workers had decreased to about 16%. The percent of workers with a payment-to-income ratio of 20% also has declined, from 10% to about 5%. These trends are consistent with trends in the college earnings premium and suggest that wages are rising faster than undergraduate student debt levels.

payment-to-income ratio The ratio of student debt payments to income.

cohort default rate (CDR) The proportion of a graduating class who enter default on their student loans over a given period. We typically focus on the two-year CDR, which shows the default rate over a two-year period.

Default and Repayment of Student Debt

How successful are students at repaying their student loans? Repayment rates typically are measured by the **cohort default rate (CDR),** which is the proportion of a graduating class who enter default over the following two-year period. Recall from Section 14.2 that students cannot be absolved of federal loan debt through bankruptcy. Thus, when a student goes into default, interest continues to accumulate until it can be repaid. Trends in two-year cohort default rates are shown in Figure 14.11. After rising to a high of 22% in the early 1990s, CDRs fell to below 5% between 2003 and 2005. Since that time, they have risen to about 10%. Thus, as of 2011, about 10% of students entering repayment defaulted on their loans over the course of the following two-years. Furthermore, CDRs vary considerably across schools types. Among public two-year schools, the CDR in 2011 was 15%, while it was 6.8% among public four-year students. Private for-profit two-year students have a default rate of 14.1%, and the four-year private nonprofit CDR is 5.1%.

What is the source of the post-2005 CDR increases shown in Figure 14.11? It is critical to understand the source of this increase to develop policies to reduce loan default rates. In careful descriptive work, Looney and Yannelis (2015) combine administrative data on tax records, student loans, and enrollment outcomes that provide an incredibly detailed look

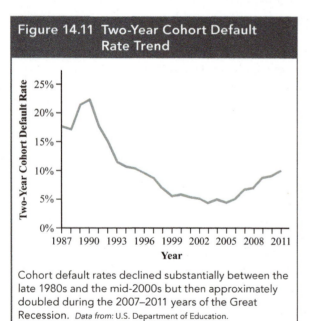

Figure 14.11 Two-Year Cohort Default Rate Trend

Cohort default rates declined substantially between the late 1980s and the mid-2000s but then approximately doubled during the 2007–2011 years of the Great Recession. *Data from:* U.S. Department of Education.

at which types of students were defaulting and what factors led to the CDR increases. They document a number of important facts:

- Most of the increases in student debt and loan defaults come from nontraditional borrowers, whom they define as students attending for-profit, two-year, and nonselective institutions. These students tend to come from lower-resource backgrounds and have worse labor market outcomes.
- By 2011, borrowers at for-profit and two-year institutions represented almost half of student loan borrowers leaving school and starting to repay loans; they accounted for 70% of student loan defaults.
- Median loan balances of for-profit borrowers jumped almost 40%, from $7,500 to $10,500, and increased by about 35%, from $7,100 to $9,600, among two-year borrowers.

So, why did student debt and default rates increase by so much? To answer this question, Looney and Yannelis (2015) conduct a decomposition analysis, which amounts to asking how much of the observed change can be explained by borrowers' characteristics as distinct from changes in the likelihood of default for a borrower with a given set of characteristics. They focus on changes due to the demographic characteristics of borrowers and the types of schools borrowers attend, as well as changes in labor market outcomes among borrowers. Their analysis shows that these factors can explain between half and two-thirds of the total increase in default rates over time; changes in the types of schools students attend can explain between a quarter and half of the increase. These findings highlight that the worse debt outcomes reflect a change in who borrows and the types of schools they attend rather than a worsening of outcomes among students attending four-year institutions soon after high school graduation.

Interestingly, nontraditional borrowers tend to borrow much less than traditional borrowers, even though they default at higher rates. How could this be? A core explanation is that those who borrow more, on average, are more likely to complete a degree and have stronger labor market prospects after graduation. Thus, despite their lower debt levels, students at two-year and for-profit institutions default at much higher rates than their four-year counterparts. Part of this is likely due to the fact that the returns to these degrees are lower (see Chapter 6) and that there is a lower likelihood that students who go to these schools will obtain a degree. In short, many of these schools may not represent a good investment for students, which leads to high default rates.

Repayment Alternatives

There are high social returns to facilitating investments in college by addressing private market failures in student lending. Yet high default rates come with not only a toll on the public purse but also adverse effects on individuals. For example, default can lead to long-term harm to an individual's capacity to borrow in other markets, such as consumer credit and home borrowing. Might there be a way to restructure student loan repayment in a way that helps both individuals and the public purse?

Several dimensions of student lending point to a mismatch between the traditional 10-year fixed repayment structure of student loans and the nature of collegiate investments:

- *Structure of payments and productive life of asset.* With most physical assets, it is common to tie the length of payments to the useful life of the asset. Because cars depreciate much more rapidly than houses, it is not surprising that car loans tend to be 3–5 years while home loans are often spread over 30 years. With a college education, we would expect the returns to accrue throughout the working life, so a 10-year horizon surely understates the expected working life of the asset.

- *Structure of returns to college.* The expected profile of earnings increases rapidly in the early career years, and then the rate of increase in earnings typically decreases later in an individual's career, yet payments are constant in these early career years. This leads to a proportionately greater burden of repaying student loans in the early career years.

- *Private risk.* College is a risky investment because future returns are uncertain and subject to a number of factors beyond an individual's control, including unpredictable personal circumstances and labor market fluctuations. For a large group of individuals with a positive expected return to college, such risk is diversified. However, an individual would like to be able to insure against such risks. Because collegiate outcomes are also a function of individual effort, such insurance is generally not available in the market.

Quick Hint: The reason insurance is underprovided is that there is a *moral hazard* problem: Individuals who know they are fully insured against poor academic or labor market outcomes might exert less effort in college and in the labor force.

Policy makers have considered ways to address these issues with alternative repayment structures. The first type of approach is to allow borrowers to adjust the shape or duration of repayment. In effect, borrowers pay somewhat more in interest over the loan in exchange for postponement of at least some repayments to later years. These policies address the challenge of the timing of payments and earnings, but they do not address problems related to the nondiversifiable risk of collegiate investments.

Economists dating back to Nobel Laureates Simon Kuznets and Milton Friedman in the 1940s have considered ways to take innovations from the financing of corporations to inform the optimal design of student lending policies. The policy prescription advanced by these scholars is to allow students to repay loans through a fixed proportional assessment of their income for a specified number of years; these instruments are known as *income-contingent loans*.[24] Income-contingent loans are defined by a small set of parameters: (1) length of repayment period, (2) rate at which income is taxed and the associated exclusion of income for basic living expenses, (3) share of the loan that can be forgiven, and (4) minimum and maximum payments.

Given the concern about rising defaults beginning in 2005 (Figure 14.11) and the hardship that some borrowers faced in the Great Recession of the mid-2000s, policy

---

[24] Income-contingent loans require people to pay a fixed percentage of income for a fixed period of time, with payments not to exceed the principal plus accrued interest. A variant on the income-contingent loan framework is a structure known as a graduate tax, which requires a fixed percentage of income for a fixed period with the possibility that students may pay more (high earner) or less (low earner) than the principal plus accrued interest. At one point in the early 1970s, Yale University implemented such a program, in which participants were expected to pay 0.4% of earnings per $1,000 borrowed, with group retirement of debt at a horizon of 35 years (or when the principal and interest were repaid in full). There was also a buyout provision at 1.5 times current debt. While Yale graduates have been extraordinarily successful, this program was not: Yale terminated the program in 2001, absorbing a loss of about $5 million.

makers and some economists have advocated the adoption of an income-based repayment plan for students with outstanding federal student loans. In the United States, income-based repayment programs were initially available only to those with some demonstrable financial hardship. In the past decade, the terms have evolved to include a broader range of borrowers, to reduce the duration of repayment, and to lower the income share required on an annual basis.

Are income-based repayments unambiguously an improvement over conventional loans in terms of improving the allocation of scarce financial aid subsidies and improving students' educational investments? There is no clear answer to this question. Consider some of the unintended consequences of income-based repayment, which are classic problems in markets in which there is incomplete information. The first type of problem is moral hazard: The contingency of repayment levels on performance may change individual effort. That is, the insurance component may reduce the student's effort while in college, and the presence of a tax on income may reduce effort in the labor force. The second type of problem is adverse selection: Students who expect to have high balances forgiven are the most likely to participate, while students who will likely repay in full are the least likely to participate, particularly if there are other sources of financing. There is some anecdotal evidence that this second issue has led to changes in behavior by students and colleges. As an example, even in a well-regarded program like Georgetown Law School, administrators counseled students on ways to allocate income so that they would reduce loan payments and increase the amount of debt likely to be forgiven.[25]

There also are important distributional impacts of income-based repayment plans to consider. The borrowers who necessarily benefit the most from these programs are those with the largest balances. These students are, disproportionately, students with graduate school debt and those who have attended very expensive institutions. The large number of students struggling with relatively small debt levels are not the biggest beneficiaries, even as this pool may include some of the most disadvantaged borrowers who enrolled at community colleges. As federal policy makers have promoted income-contingent repayment, there has been a notable increase in the use of income-based repayment, rising from 11% of borrowers in 2013 to 20% of borrowers in 2015. The percent of loan dollars in income-based repayment has risen more over this interval, from 23% to 37% (*Trends in Student Aid 2015*), which suggests that students with higher debt levels are increasingly likely to use this repayment method.

Thinking about the problem of student loan default, the incentives tied to income-based repayment raise a fundamental question. To the extent that student loan default rates are too high, is the primary cause the postcollegiate structure of repayment or the college choice decisions made by students? It is quite possible that improved decisions about college choice might have a substantial impact by reducing default rates, which highlights the potential role for more information among college-bound high school students to positively impact loan outcomes. We turn to the role of information problems in the higher education market in Chapter 15.

---

[25] This example, along with a number of others, is available in the reports such as "Beware Savvy Borrowers Using Income-Based Repayment" http://www.edcentral.org/beware-savvy-borrowers-using-income-based-repayment/.

14.5 Conclusion

When students can finance high-return postsecondary educational investments, individuals and society more broadly benefit. Achieving this objective is more difficult in practice than in theory. At a fundamental level, the objective of government spending on student aid is to address challenges of credit constraints and underinvestment in education using market-based tools.

The practical design and funding of aid mechanisms poses substantial challenges. First, determining who is credit constrained and who would benefit from additional loans and grants is difficult. The combination of unique individual financial circumstances and the potential to adjust behavior in distortionary ways suggests fairly complex needs analysis designs, yet complexity itself may harm the intended beneficiaries by increasing the cost of application for the most economically disadvantaged students.

A second challenge concerns the optimal design of financial aid delivery. Of course, individual students prefer grants to loans, but grants are appreciably more costly than loans, such that for a fixed budget, a much smaller number of students would have access to financing assistance without considerable loan utilization. As an empirical point, federal and state student aid programs reach a much broader group of students than they did four decades ago, with increased support for students older than recent high school graduates, students from moderate and upper income families, and graduate students.

How we evaluate the efficiency of aid allocation depends on the empirical questions of how aid impacts behavior. Does aid simply provide a subsidy for students without affecting college choice, or does aid allow students to make better choices about whether and where to enroll? We highlight that analyses of how aid affects outcomes should not stop at the point of college enrollment but also should focus on longer-term outcomes, such as degree completion and later-life outcomes like earnings.

Now that we have examined the supply side of the higher education market and the financial aid system in detail, in Chapter 15 we turn to a set of topics that describe the economics of college admissions and the collegiate experiences of students. We also examine factors that influence how students select colleges as well as how different institutional features of the schools in which they enroll affect their paths through the higher education system.

Highlights

- Financial aid comes from four sources: the federal government, state governments, postsecondary institutions, and private loan companies.
- Financial aid is one tool that can be used to address the fact that college investment by students from lower-income families is much lower than investment by students from higher-income families. This can produce **allocative inefficiency** from underinvestment in higher education by students from low-income backgrounds, leading to lower aggregate productivity in the economy.

- **Short-run credit constraints** arise when a student has a positive rate of return to a given educational investment but he or she cannot obtain the money to finance the investment. This type of credit constraint can be addressed using financial aid. **Long-run credit constraints** come about because families lack the resources throughout a child's life to invest sufficiently in their education. As a result the student will not be as academically qualified to attend college. Financial aid will do little to address this type of credit constraint. Empirical evidence suggests that long-run credit constraints are more important for collegiate attainment than short-run constraints, but studies from recent years suggest short-run credit constraints are increasingly prevalent.

- Financial aid policies include both grants and loans. A grant is a transfer of money for college attendance that reduces the net price students must pay to enroll. The effect of grants on college enrollment depends on the relative size of supply and demand elasticities. Loans are a financial commitment that require repayment in the future at some interest rate. Loans can relax short-run credit constraints by reducing the cost of capital.

- The current financial aid system is a patchwork of federal, state, and institutional programs, with the vast majority of aid coming from the federal government.

- Federal financial aid programs began with the post–World War II GI Bill but expanded into their modern form in the 1960s and 1970s with Title IV of the Higher Education Act of 1965 and its reauthorization in 1972. Federal financial aid comes in the form of Pell grants, Stafford loans, and PLUS loans. Stafford loans can be either subsidized or unsubsidized. The interest rates are the same across these two loan types, but with subsidized loans interest does not begin to accumulate until after college. Pell grants and Stafford loans are targeted toward lower-resource families, while all families can take out PLUS loans up to their demonstrated need. There also is a set of federal tax credits and tax deductions that allow families to deduct set amounts of higher education expenses from their taxable income.

- State aid comes in the form of grants and need-based scholarships as well as state merit aid fellowships. Institutional aid is almost entirely made up of grants and tends to be restricted to highly selective private and public universities.

- There are many difficulties in designing a method of financial aid needs assessment that is both equitable and efficient. There is a trade-off between simplicity and targeting: More accurately targeting financial aid to those who are indeed most needy necessarily requires a more complex system that dissuades students from taking up financial aid. Need-based aid seeks to achieve **vertical equity**, which requires that families with different resources expend the same effort in paying for college. Optimal needs assessment also entails **horizontal equity**, whereby families with the same earnings capacity are eligible for the same amount of aid. The use of current financial resources in needs assessment leads to horizontal inequity because it treats families with the same lifetime earnings but different savings behavior differently, and it also creates a disincentive for families to save.

- Need-based financial aid is largely determined through the **Free Application for Federal Student Aid (FAFSA).**

The primary component of federal aid determination is the **expected family contribution (EFC)**, calculated using information on student and parent income (**adjusted available income [AAI]** and **available income [AI]**) and assets (**discretionary net worth**). Families are eligible for financial aid amounts equal to their **demonstrated need**, which is the difference between the cost of college attendance at a given school and the EFC. The system is structured such that families with fewer resources have lower EFCs and thus are eligible for more aid.

- Economists have used several methods to attempt to estimate the causal effect of financial aid on student behavior. One prominent method is to compare changes in college enrollment among low-income students when financial aid policies change. Evidence from the introduction of the Pell grant in 1973 suggests little effect of this type of aid on enrollment behavior.

- Studies that examine changes in financial aid from the elimination of Social Security student benefits for college students as well as from the World War II GI Bill indicate that financial aid has large positive effects on college going. Dynarski (2003) estimates that each $1,000 of aid increases college enrollment by 3.6 percentage points.

- State merit aid programs have garnered much study among economists. Typically, these studies use a difference-in-difference framework comparing changes in enrollment in states that implement a program to changes in states that do not. There is evidence that merit aid programs increase college enrollment, but much of the effect of these programs appears to be to induce students to enroll in in-state rather than out-of-state universities. In some cases, this can reduce the quality of the college students attend and can worsen postsecondary outcomes. However, by providing incentives to students to obtain good grades, these programs also can lead to better student performance.

- The complexity of the aid system is a challenge for education policy and may be one explanation for the research that shows little effect of federal aid programs on student postsecondary enrollment. Evidence indicates that the lengthy set of family finance questions on the FAFSA are not needed to achieve better targeting of aid to needy students. In a randomized study of the effects of simplifying the financial aid process, researchers found that the complexity of the aid system reduces college enrollment among individuals from low-income families.

- Student debt has increased substantially in the past 15 years, but most of this increase is driven by the number of borrowers rather than debt per borrower. Very few college students take on large amounts of debt, as measured both by debt levels and by the **payment-to-income ratio**. The rise in student debt has been more than offset by increases in the college wage premium.

- Loan default rates, as measured by the **cohort default rate (CDR)**, are high and have grown markedly over the past decade. Much of this increase is due to a change in the types of students who borrow, with increased borrowing among students attending for-profit and two-year schools who are from more disadvantaged backgrounds and who tend to have worse labor market outcomes.

- Growing cohort default rates have led some economists to propose income-based repayment plans in which payment is a fixed proportion of one's postcollege income for a given set of years. This repayment scheme will reduce the likelihood of default but can lead to problems associated with lower effort while in college and in the labor market (moral hazard) and adverse selection of students who expect to have the highest balances choosing income-based repayment plans.

Problems

1. Both the federal government and individual colleges typically use needs analysis, which considers available income and assets, to determine eligibility for financial aid. Consider a simplified version of needs analysis in which grant aid is awarded in the following manner:

   - Line A: Total adjusted gross income as reported on income tax form
   - Line B: Supplement from assets, equal to $0.2 \times$ assets per year
   - Expected Family Contribution (EFC): $0.35 \times$ [Line A + Line B]
   - Aid Rule: Grant = max(0,$15,000 − EFC)

   a. What are the maximum levels of income (assuming zero assets) and assets (assuming zero income) at which an individual could be expected to receive financial aid?

   b. Under what circumstances does this aid formula create a disincentive for parents to save?

   c. Is this aid policy horizontally equitable? How about vertically equitable? What are the potential efficiency consequences of this policy?

2. Suppose some students are able to borrow for college at a rate of 5%, which also is the market rate of return. For other students, the only source of funds to borrow for college is Louie the Loanshark, who charges an interest rate of 20%. What are the consequences for the educational attainment of these different students? Is there a potential role for government intervention in the education market?

3. Explain the difference between a short-run and a long-run credit constraint. Give an example of

   a policy that could overcome each type of constraint. Why is it important for financial aid policy to distinguish between short- and long-run credit constraints?

4. In 1973, the Basic Education Opportunity Grant (later renamed the Pell grant) was established to provide grant aid to low-income students—not just recent high school graduates ("traditional students") but also older students who might be returning to school ("nontraditional students"). The program was intended to increase college enrollment among the students most likely to face difficulties financing a college education.

   a. How is the effect of the Pell grant on college enrollment different for a student who is in his mid-20s than for a recent high school graduate?

   b. In addition to federal financial aid (Pell grants, Stafford loans, and PLUS loans), what other forms of state and federal assistance may affect the decision of older students to return to college?

5. When a bank holds private student loans or when the federal government issues student loans, the promise to repay can be thought of as an asset. What factors would you consider if you were asked to value a portfolio of student loans? What factors in the overall economy would you expect to affect the valuation of such a portfolio?

6. Using sources like the College Board or the Department of Education, describe the trend in student loan defaults over the last two decades. What factors explain the increasing default rate between 2010 and 2015?

7. Beginning in October 2016 for the 2017–2018 academic year, the Free Application for Federal Student Aid (FAFSA) will be available earlier—in October, rather than January—and the FAFSA will now use tax information from two years ago ("prior-prior" year)—as opposed to last year.
   a. What economic problem does this policy change address in the allocation of student aid?
   b. Who benefits from this policy change?
   c. What are the costs of this policy change? Are there any losers?
   d. How would you propose to evaluate this policy change?

8. In a paper appearing in the *National Tax Journal*, titled "The cost of complexity in federal student aid: Lessons from optimal tax theory and behavioral economics," Sue Dynarski and Judith Scott-Clayton examine the current federal methodology for determining eligibility for financial aid. At the time they wrote, it was true that "The FAFSA, at five pages and 128 questions, is lengthier than Form 1040EZ and Form 1040A. It is comparable to Form 1040 (two pages, with 118 questions)." Why might the complexity of the FAFSA reduce efficiency in the distribution of financial aid?

The Economics of College Life: Admissions, Peer Effects, and Graduation

3DDock/Shutterstock

College Choices as Economic Choices

When you make decisions about how many schools to apply to, where to apply, and where to attend college, you are solving an optimization problem. Similarly, when you make a decision about whether to major in economics or English, you are implicitly weighing the benefits and costs of the alternative choices. As you decide how to divide your time among working for pay, doing homework, and enjoying some leisure, you are making a choice subject to a constraint. In short, college choices are economic choices. On the other side of the market, colleges and universities make choices about how many students to admit and, among applicants, which students to admit. They face constraints, such as the number of dorm rooms and the size of the faculty, which limit the number of students they can enroll. Subject to such constraints, colleges and universities set policies about admissions, financial aid, and the curriculum that are intended to improve student outcomes; but do they? The only way to find out is to evaluate.

This chapter examines several topics in the economics of higher education: the economics of college application and admission, the matching of students to colleges, peer effects and student effort, how students make choices about courses of study once enrolled in college, and some of the major factors driving college completion rates. Through an economic lens, we explore how students and institutions make some of the core decisions that affect how people progress through the postsecondary system.

We begin with an analysis of how students make decisions about where to apply as well as how the college admission process operates. We then discuss differences in application behavior across the income distribution and the role of information in driving differences in the way students from low- versus high-income households apply to college. The section concludes by examining race-based affirmative action policies. We next turn to how students' time allocation affects their postsecondary outcomes as well as the extent to which they are influenced by their peers (*peer effects*). Collegiate outcomes include not only degree receipt but also choice of major and other learning outcomes. We therefore assess what factors influence how students decide on a course of study as a way to understand some of the gender differences in major selection. The chapter ends with an analysis of college completion, with a focus on some of the reasons for changes in college completion rates over time.

15.1 The Economics of College Choice

College Application and Admissions

Economists are interested in college application behavior and college admission policies because they involve the way in which schools and students allocate scarce resources—spaces in entering classes and the supply of academically qualified students—to meet individual and institutional objectives. Students (and their parents) are trying to find a college that provides the highest return given their preparation and ability to pay. Colleges and universities want to choose students who will make the most of available resources while also ensuring sufficient tuition dollars to pay for expenses. The application and admission problems for both sides of the market are complicated by uncertainty: Students do not know which institutions will admit them, how much financial aid they will receive, or which college will maximize their outcomes, though they may form expectations about these factors. In turn, colleges and universities are uncertain about which students will accept offers of admission.

Although there are many dimensions to consider when assessing the match quality between students and colleges (extracurricular activities, social life, athletics, academics), researchers tend to focus on the alignment between student achievement levels and the average achievement level of students at a given college. For example, we might compare a student's SAT score to the average SAT score at a university. While we sometimes use such comparisons for simplicity, an optimal matching algorithm likely takes into account a much broader set of characteristics and individual preferences, such as geography, particular courses of study, demographic background, and extracurricular options.

The process of matching with a college occurs in steps: (1) students apply, (2) colleges make admissions offers (along with financial aid offers), (3) students choose among the schools that have offered them admission. For students applying to multiple selective institutions, the timeline for this process is extended, creating a long period of uncertainty. Applications usually are submitted in December. Students and their families submit additional information about finances (the FAFSA) early in the following calendar year. Colleges and universities deliver decisions about admission and financial aid in early April, and matriculation decisions are typically due before the start of June.

College matching is in many ways similar to how people search in other markets, such as jobs or housing. The complexity of the timing of the application and decision processes leads to the concern that some groups of students, for example first-generation college students or students from low-income families, may find it particularly difficult to navigate the matching process. To the extent that the complexity of this system generates suboptimal matches, education policies have the potential to increase the quality of the student–college matching process.

Applying to College: Students Choosing College Each student's objective in applying to college is fairly straightforward: A student wants to maximize his or her return on the education investment, subject to the constraint that he or she will have to be admitted to a school and be able to afford to attend. Note that the returns to education for a student can be monetary or nonmonetary: If a university will increase a student's utility by giving her access to a specific occupation or by exposing her to a mode of thought that increases her happiness, such factors should be included in the decision of where to enroll.

Deciding how many applications to submit and where to apply is fundamentally an optimization problem, albeit a fairly complicated one. One of the reasons that the college application decision is a difficult problem is that students (and their families) face considerable uncertainty in predicting whether they will be admitted to any particular school as well as the financial aid offered by different schools. It is also difficult for a student to evaluate the expected return associated with attendance at any particular institution, the probability of graduating at each of these institutions, or the cost of application.

Evaluating benefits and costs of applying to every institution in the United States would take an immense amount of time! What is more, there are a huge number of potential application combinations for a student to consider—at the extreme, with more than 3,000 four-year colleges and universities in the United States, there are 2^{3000} potential combinations of application. Even if a student were to limit potential applications to those in her state and nationally ranked institutions outside of her state, the potential choice set and informational requirements are onerous. Of course, some simple logic helps to rule out many of these options. For example, if a student knows he will be admitted to college A with 100% certainty, there is no reason to apply to any college that is not preferable to college A.

Because applications are often due at about the same time,[1] it is generally impossible to wait for a decision from one school before considering another. Economists describe this matching process as *nonsequential*. The long time horizon between application, admissions, and financial aid makes investing in a college decidedly different from other major purchases, like buying a house or a car. When buying a house, you do not have to wait several months between deciding to purchase it and knowing whether your offer is accepted. You also know the approximate price of the house at the time a purchase offer is made. In contrast, the long lag between application and receiving information on financial aid offers makes actual prices very hard to observe at the point of application for most students.

What factors do we expect to influence a student's decision to apply to a particular school? There are several:

- Labor market return to the school
- Net price (tuition, fees, room and board less financial aid)
- Alignment of academic interests with the strengths of the school
- Existence and strength of nonacademic programs, such as athletics and performing arts
- Community and social environment of the school—whether it is urban or rural, big or small
- The likelihood of admission, as there is no point in spending time and energy on an application that will be rejected with certainty

---

[1] Early application options, wherein students submit applications earlier to obtain an earlier (and often binding) decision, are notable counterexamples to this generalization.

One difficulty faced by many students is that the data required to assess these factors, even for a small number of colleges, are immense and not always easily available in the public domain. Remember that for each of these benefits and costs, what matters is the outcome for you—or a person just like you—not the outcome for someone much stronger (or weaker) in academic preparation or someone much richer (or poorer) in family circumstances. Such outcomes are extremely hard to assess when students are making application decisions.

Even if students can form good estimates of these factors in advance, the question of to how many and to which institutions to apply is challenging.[2] What a student needs to do is to craft an optimal portfolio of applications, with the actual number depending on the degree of risk in each college application (the likelihood of admission) and the extent to which expected admissions offers are correlated. For example, if it is likely that a student will either be admitted to Harvard and Yale or denied admission to both schools, he need only apply to his preferred option. Alternatively, if the likelihoods of admission are only weakly correlated, it may make sense to apply to both. As an empirical matter—which you may have observed first-hand—it is not the case that admissions outcomes are perfectly correlated across similarly selective institutions.

Because admission cannot be known with certainty at many selective schools, even for students with excellent credentials, the optimal strategy is for students to apply to a portfolio of schools. In effect, this is the same strategy of diversification as when financial investors build a portfolio that includes both high-risk and low-risk investments. It turns out the standard rules of thumb encouraging students to apply to a group of schools that include "reach," "match," and "safety" options is close to the optimal strategy (Hoxby & Turner, 2013; Hoxby & Avery, 2013). In short, the application set is critical, because if you don't apply, you can't enroll!

> **Quick Hint:** In finance, a portfolio is a range of investments such as stocks and bonds held by an individual, where the risk and expected return of the portfolio depend on the variance in the return of individual securities and the extent to which returns are correlated. A portfolio of college applications has some of the same characteristics: Some applications may yield a 100% probability of admission, while admission probabilities for others are much lower.

Admissions: Colleges Choosing and Recruiting Students Colleges have two potential levers with which to craft a class of students. First, colleges can alter their price by offering financial aid on the basis of student characteristics to affect who enrolls. Second, colleges and universities can use admissions policies to select students with particular characteristics. It is important to highlight that not all colleges and universities in the United States employ selective admissions strategies. Institutions of higher education in the United States differ quite dramatically in their goals as well as in the degree to which they are selective in the admissions process (see Chapter 13). Indeed, some colleges may have excess capacity and actively recruit students to cover costs, while nonselective schools tend to expand and contract with student demand.

---

[2] For a demonstration of the theoretical complexity of this problem, see Chade, Lewis, and Smith (2014) and Chade and Smith (2006).

There are a large number of open-access (or nonselective) schools in the United States that offer both two-year and four-year degrees. Community colleges and other two-year schools have open-access missions that preclude them from turning away students who live in the area, have a high school diploma, and can finance their enrollment. Many four-year institutions also have an open-access mission. For these schools, there is little uncertainty in the admissions process. Most community colleges and many local public institutions have standards for acceptance that include minimum high school grades or placement exam scores,[3] but they do not require application essays or multiple letters of recommendation. For these schools, admissions often occur on a rolling basis—students are informed shortly after application about whether they will be accepted for attendance.

At the other end of the selectivity spectrum is a set of institutions that are incredibly selective in terms of who gets in. For example, Harvard University has a 6.1% acceptance rate, followed by Stanford, Columbia, Yale, and Princeton, with acceptance rates below 8%. Many of the highest-ranked small liberal arts schools are similarly selective: Amherst College and Pomona College have acceptance rates of 13%, while Williams, Swarthmore, Bowdoin, Middlebury, and Claremont-McKenna have rates under 18%.[4] A large share of colleges and universities fall in the spectrum between these extremely selective colleges and universities and the nonselective two- and four-year institutions.

Whenever there are more students who wish to attend an institution than there are slots available, there is excess demand.[5] As we discussed in Chapter 13, the presence of nonprofit and public colleges and universities introduces the capacity for institutions to maximize outcomes other than profits, like knowledge production and study in fields where costs of education are very high. Because tuition covers only a small proportion of the costs of education, especially at resource-intensive institutions, expansion of capacity at such colleges and universities only reduces resources per student. Moreover, students may not be just customers or investors but also inputs in the production of higher education: Higher-achieving students can generate *peer effects* that increase learning among other students at an institution.

Examining the college admissions process in the United States can help us answer one of the main economic puzzles of university admissions: Why is the complex admissions apparatus necessary at all? Typically in economics, scarcity will be accounted for

---

[3] Students who fail these placement exams often are placed in remedial courses that are designed to prepare them for college-level classes. Empirical evidence on college remediation is mixed, with some studies finding assignment to remedial classes increases persistence (Bettinger & Long, 2009; Calcagno & Long, 2008) but has little effect on college completion (Martorell & McFarlin, 2011; Scott-Clayton & Rodriguez, 2012; Calcagno & Long, 2008).

[4] These admissions rates are taken from the 2014 *U.S. News and World Report* college rankings.

[5] In their classic paper, Rothschild and White (1995) present a model in which students ("customers") are inputs to the education production process and universities charge differentiated prices based on the impact of peer inputs in education production. A key result of the Rothschild and White analysis is that a frictionless decentralized market in which colleges charge zero-profit prices produces an efficient allocation of students to schools, and students are allocated to schools through the price mechanism. What distinguished the U.S. higher education market from the Rothschild–White model is that students in the United States receive large institutional subsidies and access is rationed through selective admissions. Sallee, Resch, and Courant (2008) model the optimal allocation of resources across students. When they assume complementarity between student ability and college resources, either because better prepared and better motivated students are in a better position to make the most of generous resources or because more capable students benefit disproportionately from having like-minded peers, efficient allocation will match well-prepared students with highly resourced schools.

by prices: When a good is increasingly scarce, the price of that good will rise to clear the market, such that supply equals demand. One could make a similar argument for higher education. The low admission rates at selective schools such as Harvard University and Pomona College suggest that the supply of spaces in these schools is scarce. Why, then, would we not expect prices to adjust such that the admission rates are equalized across all institutions?

> **Quick Hint:** The U.S. market for higher education is distinguished from those in many European and Asian countries, where admission to college is a deterministic function of scores on a national exam. Such systems often match students to majors or courses of study upon entry and offer much less flexibility for students to transfer across schools or switch majors.

Consider for a moment what might happen in this case. If capacity to pay determined access to higher education, the most resource-intensive schools would be filled with the most affluent students. This would occur despite the fact that there are higher-achieving students from more modest economic circumstances who stand to gain more from attending these institutions than many of their higher-income counterparts. The most selective schools, then, would be filled with students who have the financial ability and desire to pay the exorbitant cost of attendance, not those who have the highest returns. Such an outcome is strongly at odds with institutional goals of selective colleges. It also is at odds with colleges' and universities' best interests, which include graduating students who will in turn make productive use of their educations to give back in philanthropy.

Thus, admissions decisions at selective colleges and universities are based on more than a student's willingness to pay. But this still does not tell us why U.S. colleges and universities collect a broad array of information beyond academic performance on standardized tests, including extracurricular activities, letters from teachers, and even essay questions. One explanation for the collection of substantial multidimensional information in college applications is that this information helps administrators to better identify who will succeed while also crafting a class that will yield productive learning dynamics. A second explanation is that colleges and universities may wish to impose some nonmonetary costs on applicants to identify those applicants who are likely to matriculate if offered admission.

DEEP DIVE: College Admissions Essays

To obtain admission to one of the more selective postsecondary institutions in the United States, a college admissions essay usually is required. These essays typically are straightforward and ask why a student is interested in studying at the given institution. Two examples from Cornell Univserity and the University of Chicago are illustrative of these types of essay questions:

- *Cornell University:* Describe your intellectual interests, their evolution, and what makes them exciting to you. Tell us how you will utilize the academic programs in the College of Arts and Sciences to further explore your interests, intended major, or field of study.

- *University of Chicago:* How does the University of Chicago, as you know it now, satisfy your desire for a particular kind of learning, community, and future? Please address with some specificity your own wishes and how they relate to UChicago.

Some colleges and universities have much less straightforward essay questions that underscore the varied nature of the college admissions processes across institutions in the United States:

University of North Carolina—Chapel Hill: What do you hope to find over the rainbow?

University of Chicago: Winston Churchill believed "a joke is a very serious thing." From Off-Off Campus's improvisations to the *Shady Dealer* humor magazine to the renowned Latke-Hamantash debate, we take humor very seriously here at the University of Chicago (and we have since 1959, when our alums helped found the renowned comedy theater the Second City). Tell us your favorite joke and try to explain the joke without ruining it.

Brandeis University: If you could choose to be raised by robots, dinosaurs, or aliens, who would you pick? Why?

University of Virginia: To tweet or not to tweet?

Amherst College: Sartre said, "Hell is other people," but Streisand sang, "People who need people/Are the luckiest people in the world." With whom do you agree and why?

University of Chicago: So where is Waldo, really?

University of Pennsylvania: You have just finished your 300-page autobiography. Please submit page 217.

Tufts University: Kermit the Frog famously lamented, "It's not easy being green." Do you agree?

University of Chicago: Alice falls down the rabbit hole. Milo drives through the tollbooth. Dorothy is swept up in the tornado. Neo takes the red pill. Don't tell us about another world you've imagined, heard about, or created. Rather, tell us about its portal. Sure, some people think of the University of Chicago as a portal to their future, but please choose another portal to write about.

While many of these questions are light-hearted and whimsical, we suspect that answering the questions occupies hours of time for students and evaluating responses requires much effort among admissions officers. It is worth pondering what skills are under assessment and what information colleges and universities gain from these essays.

How do institutions make admissions decisions, then? Colleges and universities solve a constrained optimization problem in making decisions to admit students: They are generating admissions policies to meet some set of institutional goals, subject to capacity constraints. Within this broad framework, there are likely to be a number of student characteristics that the college considers in making admission decisions. Some of these:

- Whether a student has the academic preparation to make the best use of the college's faculty and curricular resources
- How a student's academic interests align with specific programs or majors, like literature or engineering
- Whether a student has a particular extracurricular skill, such as the capacity to play tuba in the band or cornerback on the football team, that is in short supply
- How a student may bring diversity in background, ethnicity, or political perspective to the campus environment
- Whether a student is from in state, which may be particularly important at public universities where providing opportunities for local students is an explicit part of their mission
- Whether a student is a legacy, or child, of alums
- Whether a student is likely to enroll if he or she is admitted
- Whether a student and her family require substantial institutional financial aid; only a small group of high-resource schools are need-blind and do not pay attention to capacity to pay when making admissions decisions

Admissions selectivity is a form of market power. As the number of applicants relative to spaces increases, a school's ability to craft a specific class of its choice increases. As admissions selectivity declines, a school has less and less ability to decide which students to admit and which students to reject. This is likely to differ across the public and private sectors as well. Public colleges and universities have an explicit mission to serve the students in their state. As a result, more in-state students are admitted to public institutions (and more apply because of the lower cost of attendance). In effect, we can think of public schools as having two admissions regimes, one for in-state students and one for out-of-state students.

As college selectivity increases, the importance of nonacademic qualifications of students increases, in addition to the expectation of exceedingly strong academic achievement. While the most selective schools tend to admit only the most academically elite students, factors aside from the academic qualifications of students may be important to meet institutional goals. For example, schools want to have students represented across a range of academic programs and want to ensure that there are top-tier participants in key extracurricular activities ranging from band to athletic teams. Some colleges emphasize "spiky" applicants, who demonstrate extraordinary excellence in some area, such as receiving a Westinghouse prize in science, demonstrating athletic prowess, or being a concert violinist. Other schools seek out "well-rounded" applicants, who have strong skills in a number of domains.[6] Colleges and universities also have an interest in presenting a class that is both socioeconomically diverse and racially/ethnically diverse. In the admission process, colleges often face a trade-off between admitting students with particular nonacademic characteristics and admitting students with somewhat higher measured achievement.

Finally, colleges and universities are heavily invested in admissions because outcomes of this process—what percentage of students are admitted and the test scores of those who choose to enroll—are inputs to college rankings, such as the widely cited *U.S. News and World Report* metrics. In effect, how high an institution is ranked this year likely will affect the number and characteristics of students choosing to apply to the institution in subsequent years.

In making admissions decisions, each institution also has to be mindful of the likelihood that a given admitted student will enroll (often called the *yield*). Admitting a student who does not decide to enroll has costs in terms of the time it took to develop financial aid for the student, the time it took to recruit the student, and the uncertainty it can cause over the final size of the incoming class. Selective schools have complex algorithms that help them predict what types of students will come, and these algorithms can determine admissions. If a university believes a student is very unlikely to matriculate—because it is likely she gets into a higher-ranked school, because she has interests that are not well aligned with the school's strengths, or because she is from a region in which few students tend to enroll—the likelihood the student will be admitted declines. That admission officers account for student behavior in their admissions decisions illustrates that they understand the matching process is two-sided.

Deciding Where to Attend College: Matriculation The optimal strategy for students is to pick the institution among those offering admission that best matches their interests and preferences and for which the expected net returns are the highest. The labor market return to enrolling in a given school is going to depend, in part, on the level of school resources, the quality of the instruction, the ease of getting the classes required for graduation, the likelihood of graduation, and a student's own effort and ability.

---

[6] Shulman and Bowen (2002) provide a more complete discussion of such college admissions practices.

In theory, the best collegiate choice for a student should not depend on the availability of financial aid, so long as the net present value of enrolling in the school is the greatest. In practice, a student may be limited in his or her ability to make the best choice if sufficient financial aid is not available. In Chapter 14, we discussed how credit constraints may limit enrollment choices among students from lower-income backgrounds.

A number of features of the college choice process, from application to matriculation, present challenges for students and their families. A key point is that limited information about opportunities and expected outcomes, as well as how to navigate the process, can limit students' capacity to optimize.

College Enrollment Choices by Student Circumstances When students go to high schools where attendance at selective colleges is a norm or when parents or other trusted adults have completed college, they are likely to have much more information about the college application and admissions process. Those without such peer, school, and family resources may have very limited information about the differences among colleges in quality, the availability of financial aid, and how to navigate the complex admissions process discussed previously. This may be a particular problem for lower-income students, for whom college costs are a much larger consideration and for whom the information environment is likely to be much worse than among wealthy students.

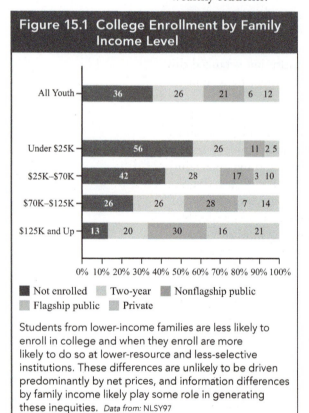

Figure 15.1 College Enrollment by Family Income Level

Students from lower-income families are less likely to enroll in college and when they enroll are more likely to do so at lower-resource and less-selective institutions. These differences are unlikely to be driven predominantly by net prices, and information differences by family income likely play some role in generating these inequities. *Data from: NLSY97*

Consistent with these arguments, there are large differences across the income distribution in the types of colleges and universities in which students enroll. Figure 15.1 shows college enrollment patterns for recent high school graduates for students from the NLSY97.[7] These patterns are shown for the entire sample and by parental income group. As discussed in Chapter 14, students from lower-income families are much less likely to enroll. When students from low-income backgrounds do enroll in college, they are much more likely to attend a lower-resource school in the form of a community college or a nonflagship public four-year school. Figure 15.1 shows that students from families with more than $125,000 in yearly income are eight times more likely to enroll in a public flagship university than are students from families that earn less than $25,000 per year.

Some of the gaps shown in Figure 15.1 undoubtedly reflect differences in academic preparation for college. However, they are unlikely to be driven predominantly by net prices students actually have to pay. An unusual feature of the U.S. higher education market is that the most selective and resource-intensive colleges and universities often offer the lowest net prices for low-income students. Hoxby and Turner (2013) provide some striking calculations: In 2009–2010, the most competitive colleges in terms of admissions had an average sticker price of $45,540, but for students at

---

[7] See Appendix A for a detailed description of the NLSY97 data set.

the 20th percentile of family income net price would average $6,754. In contrast, schools that have competitive admissions had an average sticker price of $24,166 but a net price of $19,400 for such lower-income students. At public two-year schools, sticker price was $10,543 on average, whereas average net price for a 20th income percentile student was $7,573. Thus, for a low-income student, tuition at an elite postsecondary institution was lower than at a community college.

As these calculations highlight, highly selective schools tend to be less expensive for low-income students to attend than less selective schools once financial aid offers are taken into consideration. However, if low-income students do not know that their net price at such institutions will be low, high sticker prices may dissuade them from applying. That is, there may be an information constraint that reduces the effectiveness of generous financial aid policies at selective colleges and universities. One test of the role information plays in driving the differences shown in Figure 15.1 is the degree to which low-income, high-ability students apply to and enroll in different schools than their high-income, high-ability counterparts. Bowen, Chingos, and McPherson (2009) provide such a test by linking secondary school academic records with collegiate outcomes for the state of North Carolina. They find that 40% of the students with SAT scores and high school grades in the range needed to enroll at a very selective university failed to do so. This enrollment effect is appreciably more pronounced among students in the bottom quartile of family income than among students from the top quartile.

Relatively high-income students apply to more colleges and include somewhat higher-quality institutions in their choice sets than do their low-income counterparts. To the extent that more applications generate more choices after admission decisions, differences in college application behavior by family circumstances are a significant determinant of the income gap in collegiate outcomes among students with similar high school achievement levels.

In a careful empirical analysis of the supply of low-income, high-achieving students, Hoxby and Avery (2013) argue that there is a large supply of such students but that they are "hidden." This comes about because they are geographically dispersed and thus are difficult for any given university to find. Hoxby and Avery focus on a particularly important group of students: those in the top 10% of SAT or ACT scores but in the bottom quartile of the income distribution (under $41,472). The starting point for their analysis is the idea that college counselors have very specific advice for students, which is to apply to a couple of reach schools, a group of peer institutions in which the likelihood of admission is high, and one or two safety schools in which one is almost assured admission. What they find is that among high-achieving students, only those from higher-income families seem to follow this advice.

Figure 15.2, reproduced from their paper, shows the distribution of the first and second most selective schools to which high- and low-income high achievers apply. The scores have been adjusted so that they show the difference between the median score of the school and the student's score. A score of zero thus means the student has the same ACT or SAT score as the median student at the institution. Focusing on the top row, the differences are striking: Almost 40% of high-achieving, low-income students apply to *only* nonselective schools, while none of the high-income students apply to these schools. Among high-income students who apply to a selective school, the applications are centered around zero (where there is no difference between

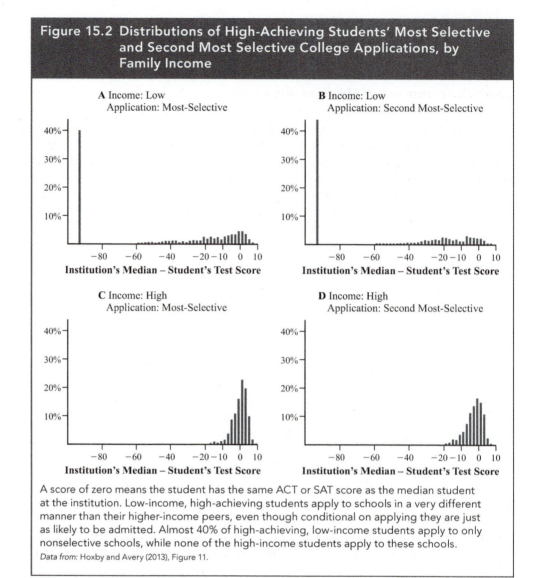

Figure 15.2 Distributions of High-Achieving Students' Most Selective and Second Most Selective College Applications, by Family Income

A score of zero means the student has the same ACT or SAT score as the median student at the institution. Low-income, high-achieving students apply to schools in a very different manner than their higher-income peers, even though conditional on applying they are just as likely to be admitted. Almost 40% of high-achieving, low-income students apply to only nonselective schools, while none of the high-income students apply to these schools.
Data from: Hoxby and Avery (2013), Figure 11.

the student's test score and the median student at the institution). This suggests that most students are applying to reach schools or peer institutions, as a college counselor would instruct. A small percentage of low-income students do this as well, but they apply in much higher numbers to safety schools that are well below those to which high-income students apply. On the whole, low-income, high-achieving students apply to schools in a very different manner than their higher-income peers, even though conditional on applying they are just as likely to be admitted. As a result, low-income, high-achieving students enroll in lower proportions in more selective schools.

One important question that arises from this work is what determines whether a low-income student will apply to college in a way that aligns with the suggestions of admissions experts (and more closely matches what higher-income students do). Low-income students who do not send applications to peer or reach schools are more likely to come from small districts without high-performing public high schools, are not in areas with a large number of high achievers, and are unlikely to have had a teacher who attended a selective college. In contrast, low-income students who do apply to selective schools tend to come from large cities with elite magnet high schools that have highly trained college application counselors.

Evidence that a large number of well-qualified low-income students are not applying to and attending very selective institutions demonstrates that the correlation between family income and college preparation does not explain in full the proportional underrepresentation of low-income students at very selective institutions. One explanation for the observed underrepresentation is that low-income students may lack the information and guidance needed to navigate successfully the process of applying to selective colleges and universities; an alternative hypothesis, also consistent with the data, is that students differ systematically across the income distribution in their preferences for different types of collegiate experiences.

What policy levers might affect the application behavior of high-achieving, low-income high school students? The answer to this question depends on the source of these information constraints such students face:

- *Net price:* Students may overestimate net price if they assume it is correlated with sticker price, often assuming that high-resource institutions are financially infeasible.
- *Application guidance:* Low-income students may be missing guidance on the needed application steps and the recommendation to apply to a portfolio of schools.
- *Application fees:* Low-income students may be unaware of eligibility for fee waivers and overestimate the cost of applications.

A large-scale experiment conducted by Hoxby and Turner (2013) provides a test of whether college application decisions and enrollment choices respond to improved information along these dimensions. The information experiment focused on low-income, high-achieving high school students. Among this group, students were randomly assigned to receive application information and guidance or were assigned to a control group that did not receive the information. Those randomly assigned to treatment were mailed binders that included:

- A personalized letter of introduction, so that the student knew the information was coming from a third party and was not a recruiting tool of a given school
- A guide to application strategies that included the advice to apply to safety schools, reach schools, and peer schools as well as reminders about application deadlines and the financial aid process and deadlines
- Information on graduation rates of the nearest colleges, the state flagship, other in-state selective schools, and some randomly selected out-of-state selective colleges
- Information on net costs of college attendance for low- and middle-income students at the state flagship, another in-state public school, nearby colleges, and in-state and out-of-state private universities and liberal arts colleges
- Eight application fee waivers that were personalized with the student's name

Results suggest that this information had dramatic effects on the application and enrollment behavior of these students. Those who received the materials applied to 19% more schools, were 22% more likely to apply to a peer institution with a median SAT–ACT score close to their own, and were 31% more likely to apply to a school that had a median test score 5 or more percentiles above their own (i.e., a reach school). However, these estimates understate the effect of receiving the information, because many students simply ignored or threw away the materials without reading them. By surveying treated students, the researchers estimate that 40% of students who were mailed the information could recall having seen it. To calculate the effect of actually seeing the information, they need to divide all of their estimates by 0.4. This is the treatment-on-the-treated effect discussed in Chapter 10. When they do this calculation, Hoxby and Turner find that receiving the college information increased the number of applications submitted by 47.6% (over two applications), increased the likelihood of applying to a peer school by 55.8%, and increased the probability of applying to a reach school by 78%.

One important question to consider is whether the change in application behavior led to changes in enrollment. After all, if the intervention simply increases applications, it is less important than if it changes actual student behavior. The researchers show that the effect of the intervention on enrollment behavior was similar to the effect on applications: There was an increase of over 46% in the proportion of students attending a peer school, and the likelihood a low-income, high-achieving student enrolled in a reach school increased by over 150%. These are enormous changes in enrollment patterns for such a small intervention. The authors explain that the intervention cost only $6 per student. That such large enrollment changes can be accomplished for so little money suggests information is indeed a key barrier to enrolling in highly selective schools for low-income, high-achieving students and that reducing these barriers can be done effectively and cheaply.

Further evidence that fairly small, low-cost changes can greatly influence student application behavior comes from Pallais (2015). She studies a change in the number of free ACT scores a student can send to colleges and universities. In 1997, the ACT increased this number from three to four. Pallais examines how this change affects the set of schools to which low-income students apply and enroll. She uses two estimation strategies:

1. Compare changes in applications and enrollment among ACT test takers when the change occurs, controlling for time trends and student characteristics
2. Use SAT takers (for whom there was no change) as a control group in a difference-in-difference setting, comparing changes among ACT takers to changes among SAT takers

She finds that low-income students increased the number of scores they sent and the likelihood of applying to a more selective school, and the quality of colleges and universities in which they enrolled increased significantly after the change. No such effect occurred for high-income students. This small change in the cost to a student of sending a test score to a school—an additional score only cost $6 to send—has large impacts on application and enrollment behavior of low-income students. This is consistent with the existence of information barriers about the application process and about the value of applying to many schools that disproportionately affect students from less wealthy backgrounds. The evidence discussed in Chapter 6 on the returns to higher education quality suggests such changes can have profound impacts on the long-run outcomes of these students.

15.2 Policies to Improve Matching Students and Colleges

Early Decision and Early Action

One prominent component of higher education admissions in the United States is the prevalence of *early decision* and *early action* policies. Early decision and early action refer to admission rules that allow students to apply for admission earlier in the year, typically in October or November, to receive an admissions decision earlier as well. Early decision policies preclude students from applying to other schools at the same time, and the admission decision is binding. If the student gets admitted, she must attend the school (unless there is a financial reason to decline the offer). Early action policies have a similar timing, but the admission decision is not binding, and students therefore can apply to several schools under early action.

Early admissions are a common staple of higher education admissions among the most selective private universities and colleges. Almost 70% of the 281 private schools in *U.S. News and World Report*'s rankings of private universities and liberal arts colleges have an early action or early decision admission policy (Avery, Fairbanks, & Zeckhauser, 2003). In addition, public colleges and universities in 18 states have early action programs; very few public schools have binding early decision admissions.

Avery, Fairbanks, and Zeckhauser (2003) provide an in-depth analysis of early admissions policies from an economic standpoint. They highlight the following five facts about early admissions:

1. Almost all highly selective private colleges have early admissions programs.
2. Rules and deadlines differ across schools, which increases confusion.
3. Higher-income students are more likely to apply early.
4. Some early admissions programs have grown so large that few spots remain for normal applicants. However, most schools admit a minority of their students through early admissions.
5. Acceptance rates are higher among early applicants relative to on-time applicants.

Avery, Fairbanks, and Zeckhauser conduct statistical analyses of the early admissions advantage using five years of admissions data from 14 private schools in the United States, spanning the period 1991–1992 through 1996–1997. They also use data from a survey of 3,000 students from 400 prestigious high schools throughout the country who are most likely to be able to take advantage of early admissions policies. They estimate that applying early confers a significant advantage on students in terms of the likelihood of admission, equal in magnitude to a 100-point increase in SAT score.

Why do these admissions regimes exist? At first glance, they seem quite odd, and they create more work for admissions committees who need to go through two rounds of admissions instead of one. It therefore is important to consider the economic rationale for early admissions and why they have proven to be so popular with students. From an institutional perspective, an early admissions policy is attractive for several reasons:

1. It allows colleges to appear more selective, as the percentage of students accepted in the regular pool will decline, thus improving one of the metrics commonly recorded in rankings like those of *U.S. News and World Report*.
2. It creates a competitive edge over their closest rivals to the extent that students have an incentive to choose to apply to a school that offers an early decision program over close competitors that do not.

3. It gives them more certainty over the size of the incoming class, because students admitted under early decision must make a decision early (typically in January).
4. It helps to identify those students who are likely to enroll, as applying early provides a signal to a college about the student's preferences.
5. It may minimize financial aid awards, because students will be more limited in their capacity to shop around other institutions for improved financial aid.

From the student's perspective, the decision to apply early almost certainly is based on the perceived idea that doing so increases one's likelihood of being admitted. Avery, Fairbanks, and Zeckhauser (2003) show this to be true for elite private schools, and thus students are correct to make application decisions under this assumption. In addition, students might like to get their admissions process over with early.

Early admissions policies have costs as well as benefits. One of the main costs is that students who are induced to apply under early admissions often are making college choices with much less information than those who apply normally. They have had less time to acquire information, and financial aid awards have not made. This is true particularly for early decision admissions, where the decision is binding. Early admissions policies therefore may exacerbate the information barriers already inherent in the higher education market. What is more, early decision policies may lead to distortions in students' preferences over college options if the advantage to applying early to a second-best school is sufficiently large that a student prefers this option to taking the risk of not being admitted to a preferred school.

Race-Based Affirmative Action Policies

Race-based affirmative action policies give preference in admissions to students from underrepresented minority groups, which in the United States typically means Black and Hispanic students. These policies elicit strong opinions from politicians, voters, and stakeholders in higher education. While economics cannot answer the normative question of whether affirmative action is "good" or "bad," the models and empirical tools from economics provide a framework to assess the costs and benefits of these institutional-level policies.

Quick Hint: There are no federal affirmative action policies in higher education. Decisions about whether and how to consider race as a factor in admissions are made predominantly at the institutional level. For many public universities, such decisions also are guided by state law.

The history of affirmative action in U.S. higher education dates to the period of the 1960s, immediately following a set of court rulings that made racial discrimination and segregation illegal in higher education. While the University of Alabama and the University of Mississippi remained segregated until the early 1960s,[8] there were few minorities at selective northern institutions as well. For example, Blacks made up about 1% of the enrollment at selective New England schools in 1965

[8] The University of Mississippi was desegregated with the enrollment of James Meredith in 1962, while the desegregation of the University of Alabama followed President Kennedy's dispatch of the National Guard in 1963.

(Bowen & Bok, 1998). At this time, the difference in collegiate attainment between Blacks and Whites also was large: In 1970, 17.4% of Whites aged 25–29 held a college degree, relative to about 6% of Blacks. This gap has declined appreciably since the start of the twentieth century, which underscores the large disadvantages Blacks faced in higher education historically.

For colleges and universities, affirmative action in admissions is a voluntary institutional action in which a student's race is considered "affirmatively" as a factor in admissions. As discussed previously, other nonacademic factors, such as whether a student's parents are alums (legacy status) or whether the student is an exceptional athlete, also are considered by college and university admissions. Thus, race-based affirmative action can be thought of as part of a university's larger goal of crafting a class that meets its institutional objectives.

The concept of affirmative action is often linked to Lyndon Johnson's commencement speech in 1965 at Howard University in which he outlined the need for nondiscriminatory hiring practices: "You do not take a person who, for years, has been hobbled by chains and liberate him, bring him up to the starting line of a race and then say, 'You are free to compete with all the others,' and still justly believe that you have been completely fair." President Johnson went on to include affirmative action in federal policy via Executive Order 11246, which mandated nondiscriminatory practices in hiring for federal contractors and required contractors to "take affirmative action to ensure that applicants are employed, and that employees are treated during employment, without regard to their race, color, religion, sex or national origin." Despite these federal rules, the consideration of race in the admissions policies of colleges and universities is a matter of institutional policy: It is imperative to keep in mind that there is no such thing as a uniform affirmative action policy. Because colleges and universities choose students to achieve institutional goals such as academic excellence and producing knowledge, it follows that institutions that choose to engage in affirmative action in admissions see some educational benefits to these policies.

What Is Race-Based Affirmative Action? Race-based affirmative action in higher education means that race is considered as one factor along with measures of academic achievement and extracurricular activities in college admissions decisions. The result is that the probability of admission is likely to be higher for a minority student than for a nonminority student, conditional on pre-collegiate academic achievement. A seemingly obvious point that is often missed is that a school must practice selective admissions to engage in affirmative action; a nonselective school cannot practice affirmative action.

Because colleges and universities tend not to make their admissions rules public, it is difficult to know exactly how extensively affirmative action is practiced. It is tempting to interpret the difference in incoming academic credentials between Blacks and Whites or Hispanics and Whites as a measure of affirmative action. Indeed, affirmative action can lead to widened racial gaps in SAT–ACT scores or high school GPAs within an institution. However, racial gaps in these measures are not necessarily evidence of affirmative action policies, because average test scores are lower for underrepresented minorities than for Whites even as there are many underrepresented minority students who score as well as their White peers. When there is an overall difference by race in the distribution of test scores in the applicant pool to a college, average test scores among admitted students will differ across races unless the college discriminates against the lower-scoring group.

Figure 15.3 Average Test Score Differences Emerge Across Groups With Different Underlying Score Distributions From a Uniform Score Admission Rule

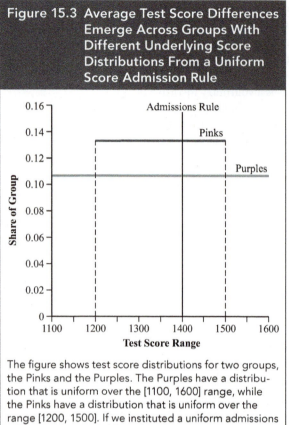

The figure shows test score distributions for two groups, the Pinks and the Purples. The Purples have a distribution that is uniform over the [1100, 1600] range, while the Pinks have a distribution that is uniform over the range [1200, 1500]. If we instituted a uniform admissions rule at 1400, we would need to discriminate against the Pinks to have equal means among admitted students.

Figure 15.3 shows an illustrative example of this principle. The figure shows test score distributions for two groups, the Pinks and the Purples. The Purples have a distribution that is uniform over the [1100, 1600] range, and the Pinks have a distribution that is uniform over the range [1200, 1500]. Suppose we instituted a uniform admissions rule at 1400: Those above are admitted, and those below are rejected. While such a rule is blind, or neutral, to group membership, the means of the admitted students would differ by group membership. Indeed, one would need to discriminate against the Pinks to have equal means among admitted students. Because between-group average test score differences among students attending a given college capture both the potentially different distributions of applicant characteristics and the extent to which race is considered in the admission process, it is very difficult to know how extensive race-based admission preferences are in the United States. As well, affirmative action differs substantially across institutions depending on institutional admissions policies and on the selectivity of admissions.

The Legal Status of Affirmative Action in College Admissions Over the past 35 years, there have been a number of legal and legislative challenges to affirmative action. The 1978 case *Bakke v. California Board of Regents* considered admissions to the medical school at the University of California, Davis, in the context of the 1964 Civil Rights Act. The Supreme Court was sharply divided over whether the university's admission policy, which set aside 16 of 100 seats for minority applicants, violated the Equal Protection Clause of the Fourteenth Amendment. The deciding opinion, from Justice Lewis Powell, "concluded that it was permissible to take race into account, as one among many factors, in seeking to secure educational benefits of diversity" (Bowen, Kurzweil, & Tobin, 2005). The court struck down the use of quotas and also required a rationale that extended beyond past discrimination to focus on expected benefits of racial diversity. Thus, institutions can practice affirmative action only if it satisfies an institutional goal. In two landmark cases involving the University of Michigan in 2003, *Gratz v. Bollinger* and *Grutter v. Bollinger*, the court ruled it illegal to have an explicit quota system or a separate admissions matrix by race. Still, the 5–4 Supreme Court decision in *Grutter v. Bollinger* ruled that affirmative action was not unconstitutional because schools have a "compelling interest" in maintaining diversity.

As a result of these rulings, the legal arguments for affirmative action tend to focus on whether affirmative action in admissions furthers educational quality, essentially benefiting all students through the creation of a diverse learning environment. Courts and legislators have also asked whether affirmative action policies are sufficiently "narrowly tailored"—in essence, could the same diversity be achieved without considering race per se?

Benefits and Costs of Affirmative Action There are likely to be both costs and benefits to affirmative action, and the challenge for researchers is to assess the empirical magnitude of each. This is very difficult in practice, which contributes to controversies surrounding affirmative action. It also is important to emphasize that just because a policy such as affirmative action has particular costs or benefits does not by itself tell us whether the policy is desirable. What matters is the sum total of the costs and benefits, each of which is weighted by its importance to social welfare. While we cannot provide a full cost-benefit analysis of affirmative action here, it is useful to consider what some of these benefits and costs are, starting with the benefits:

1. *Educational benefits of diversity for all students:* Students from all racial and ethnic groups may benefit from knowing and working with students from different racial and ethnic backgrounds. Affirmative action helps institutions to achieve student diversity to enrich the learning environment.

2. *Educational benefits for minority students:* Race-sensitive policies may help students from minority backgrounds obtain access to high-quality postsecondary schools that they otherwise would not be able to attend. These benefits may accrue in terms of higher graduation rates or greater future earnings associated with attending selective colleges and universities.

3. *External benefits to race-sensitive admissions:* Race-sensitive admissions policies may have increased substantially the number of minority students who have gone on to assume positions of leadership in the professions, academia, military, and the government (Bowen, Kurzweil, & Tobin, 2005). Such benefits of diverse leadership may be distributed broadly, as suggested by testimony from military and corporate leaders in the *Gratz* and *Grutter* cases.

Now consider the potential costs:

1. *Mismatch or "fit":* Affirmative action may hurt minority student educational outcomes by allowing students who are less prepared for college into more selective schools. Note that this hypothesis is counter to the potential benefit of improving opportunities for minorities mentioned earlier.

2. *Stigma:* Minorities who would have been admitted in the absence of race-sensitive admissions may face some costs to the extent that other students or employers infer that their admission is based on race-based preferences. That is, employers may infer a different signal from a minority having attended an elite school than a nonminority, which would translate into differences in wages in a signaling model (see Chapter 5).

3. *Forgone admissions for nonminorities:* There is no question that the opportunity cost of admitting any particular student is that another strong applicant is not chosen. Thus, any preference given to one group involves a potential cost to another. Bowen, Kurzweil, and Tobin (2005) note that these costs are likely overstated in many cases, as the elimination of race-sensitive policies at one set of very selective institutions would have only increased admission rates for White students from 25% to 26.5%. Still, the *perception* of a substantial change in admission likelihood created by race-sensitive policies is nevertheless a cost.[9]

---

[9] Kane (1998) notes that the assessment of the costs of racial preferences is likely complicated because most students and their families cannot accurately assess how racial preferences change their own likelihood of admissions. He notes that handicapped parking provides a useful example. "Suppose that one parking space in front of a popular restaurant is reserved for disabled drivers. Many of the nondisabled drivers who pass by the space while circling the parking lot in search of a place to park may be tempted to think that they would have had an easier time finding a space if the space had not been reserved. Although eliminating the space would have only a minuscule effect on the average parking search for nondisabled drivers, the cumulative cost perceived by each passing driver is likely to exceed the true cost simply because people have a difficult time thinking about small probability events."

It could be the case that the costs and benefits are oppositional, to the extent that race-sensitive policies may benefit minorities by providing access to high-quality colleges or may harm the intended beneficiaries by encouraging enrollment in institutions that are poorly matched with individual aptitude. This is what Arcidiacono and Lovenheim (2016) term the "quality–fit trade-off." While there is fairly voluminous empirical literature on this question, the empirical evidence does not produce a strong conclusion for several reasons:

- Given that there is no single affirmative action policy, the effect of race-sensitive admissions on student outcomes likely varies across settings.
- Most empirical analyses rely on variation in policy regimes (whether race-sensitive policies are permitted), yet it is likely that other institutional factors, such as the availability of support services and racial climate on campus, may change with such policies.
- Very few policy changes can be used to study the effect of affirmative action, and because of selection problems, simply comparing outcomes of minority students who attend schools of varying selectivity or contrasting the outcomes of Whites versus minorities at similarly selective schools is unlikely to lead to causal estimates.

Are There Race-Neutral Alternatives to Affirmative Action? Is it possible to achieve racial diversity without considering race per se in college admissions? Put differently, is it possible to achieve the benefits of racial diversity without the costs of an affirmative action policy? This is the very practical question considered by college administrators responding to the affirmative action bans in states like California and Texas. If a college can identify a characteristic correlated with race, it is possible to target students with this characteristic in the admissions process. Two research papers on this question cast serious doubt on the validity of such an approach.[10] Their analyses show that when schools are precluded from using race as a factor in admissions, they shift the importance given in the admission decision to factors correlated with race rather than correlated with the likelihood of academic success. The result is a lower-performing class that also has lower representation among underrepresented minorities.

In practice, several states that have banned race-based affirmative action in higher education, such as Texas, California, and Florida, have adopted *percent plans* as a potential replacement. Percent plans give automatic admissions to all students above some rank threshold in each high school. The most prominent of the percent plans is the Texas Top Ten Percent Plan. Passed in 1997, this rule gives automatic admission to *any* public postsecondary school in Texas to students in the top 10% of their class. In California, any students in the top 9% of their class or in the top 9% of students in the state are guaranteed admission to *some* University of California school. Florida's percent plan, called the Talented 20, gives automatic admission to at least one of the public universities in Florida to the top 20% of students in each high school class who complete a college preparatory curriculum.

These policies come with high costs in other dimensions. First, because race and income are only weakly correlated, particularly among high-achieving students, it requires a much larger admissions pool of both White and minority students to generate the same number of minorities as admitted under affirmative action policies. Second, it is possible that students admitted under a percent plan from weak high schools

---

[10] These papers are Fryer, Loury, and Yuret (2007) and Long (2015).

may not be well positioned to succeed at top flagship universities. Furthermore, Long (2004) argues these policies will have little impact on minority enrollment because most minority students in the top decile of their class who apply to a flagship get in. While these policies are designed to be an alternative to race-based admissions, in practice they tend to lead to lower enrollment among Hispanic and Black students at flagship universities when they replace an affirmative action policy (Arcidiacono & Lovenheim, 2016).

In his preface to the empirical study *The Shape of the River* (Bowen & Bok, 1998), economist Glenn Loury notes the importance of "the backdrop of our unlovely racial history" as a motivation for serious consideration of the role of race per se in the academic environment. While evidence can help in making "prudential judgments," it will not resolve "principled disputes" about race-conscious policies. Loury writes, "It is essential that we confront our fears and speculations about controversial public undertakings with the facts, as best they can be discerned." The takeaway, then, is that there is an important positive role for employing the tools of economics to assess the impact of affirmative action, as well as other policies potentially affecting racial inequality in higher education.

15.3 Peer and Student Inputs in Knowledge Production

Colleges choosing students and students choosing colleges determines the institutional resources and peers available during the college years. Once students arrive on campus, how does this community of students affect the skills they build and how they learn? In turn, how do students' own choices about how they spend time affect their college outcomes? After all, college is not a spectator sport; rather, as we've noted throughout the book, learning is a customer input technology.

Peer Effects

Peers are an input to the college education production function just like other factors, such as the quality of faculty. Students may gain knowledge and perspective from their peers, while peers may also affect behaviors—both positive and negative. Indeed, the very idea that students learn from their peers is fundamental to the case for college and university investment in carefully crafting a class through undergraduate admissions, along with attention to the representation of a diverse group of students in an undergraduate class.

That one's learning outcomes can be affected by one's peers is referred to as *peer effects*. Research-based evidence on peer effects is of first-order policy significance, as it may inform how colleges select students in the admissions process and how they arrange students in housing and course experiences. To examine the empirical relevance of peer effects, we need to isolate the causal role of one's peers in driving college outcomes. Simply looking at the association between a students' peers or friends and outcomes will be a flawed measure of peer effects, however. There typically are two problems associated with estimating the causal effect of peers on each other (Manski, 1993):

1. *Selection:* Students do not select their peer groups randomly. Who you decide to spend your time with is likely related to the unobserved characteristics that also influence your academic outcomes.
2. *Reflection:* If peer effects are in operation, you affect your peers, and they affect you.

What would greatly help in overcoming these problems is to randomly assign peers to each other. In effect, many colleges and universities do just this when they assign students to residential housing and roommates. Take the case of Dartmouth College: First-year students are given a questionnaire in which they are asked several questions about smoking, studying practices, and whether one is messy or not. They then are grouped according to their answers on these questions, and within each group students are randomly assigned to each other. This administrative random assignment overcomes the selection problem that would likely exist if students selected their own roommates. Observation of precollegiate high school performance measures, such as SAT scores and GPA, helps to address the reflection problem, since these outcomes are determined prior to a student meeting her roommate. These precollegiate measures cannot be influenced by a college roommate one has not met yet. Characterizing roommate academic quality using precollegiate measures therefore minimizes bias from the reflection problem.

Bruce Sacerdote (2001), an economics professor at Dartmouth, makes use of the data from this assignment to assess how the academic ability of one's roommate affects first-year college GPA. His paper asks, "Would having a smart (or not-so-smart) roommate improve (or erode) your academic performance?" It turns out that roommate academic achievement has modest but statistically significant effects on first-year GPA. Having a roommate in the top 25% of the precollegiate achievement distribution increases one's first-year college GPA by between 0.04 and 0.06 points. Average first-year GPA is 3.2, with a standard deviation of 0.43, so these effects are not large even though they are statistically significant.

In a parallel analysis, David Zimmerman (2003) examines how roommate assignment affects academic outcomes at Williams College. In his 2003 study, Zimmerman finds assignment to a roommate with a 100 point higher SAT verbal score (but not SAT math score) increases one's first-year and cumulative GPA by about 0.03. These effects are largest for the middle-scoring SAT students (those in the middle 70% of the Williams College SAT distribution), suggesting that the students most influenced by their peers are neither the most nor least academically advanced students.

While these studies demonstrate that student academic performance is affected by one's first-year roommate, they suggest the effects are not large. Why might this be so? Stinebrickner and Stinebrickner (2006) outline three potential explanations for these small effects:

1. It could be that first-year roommates are not relevant peers. If people do not study with their roommate or spend much time with him or her, it is unlikely that first-year roommates will have a large impact on academic performance while in college.
2. It may be the case that the very high-achieving pool of students from Williams and Dartmouth obscures the measurement of peer effects, given the absence of substantial variation in academic achievement at these colleges;[11] less academically elite students may be more susceptible to peer influence.
3. A main pathway through which peer effects may operate is through modeling of good time use and study habits as well as negative behaviors such as excess drinking. The peer quality measures used by prior researchers may not be those that correlate most strongly with these outcomes.

---

[11] In the Dartmouth data used by Sacerdote (2001), the mean (and standard deviation) of SAT scores is 691 (67) and 632 (70) for math and verbal, respectively, which is an appreciably narrower variance than in the overall population of college students. At Dartmouth, there is also minimal variation in high school GPA, with a mean of 3.56 and a standard deviation of 0.51.

Stinebrickner and Stinebrickner (2006) examine these three explanations using detailed survey data combined with roommate randomization at Berea College. Berea College is a small, private liberal arts school in Kentucky that enrolls only students from low-income backgrounds. Students do not pay tuition, but all students must work while enrolled. In short, this is a very different population from those attending Williams and Dartmouth.

Critical to their analysis as well as to the randomized roommate studies discussed previously, they first show that first-year roommates are indeed relevant peers. They report that, on average, students spend 21.7 hours per week with their roommate. Almost 50% of students spend more time with their roommate than with anyone else. However, only 37% report that the roommate is one of their four best friends, which suggests much of this time is out of necessity. Nonetheless, roommates are indeed relevant and important peers for first-year college students.

The authors then use detailed information on how students spend their time to show that ACT score is uncorrelated with time spent studying. However, high school GPA and parental income are strongly positively correlated with study time. If modeling good study habits is a main mechanisms through which peer effects operate, studies using test scores as the peer measure (e.g., Zimmerman, 2003) should find little in the way of peer effects. Using the randomization of roommates, they estimate the effects of roommate ACT score, family income, and high school GPA on first semester grades. Consistent with the time use explanation, they find that roommate high school GPA and family income have the largest effects on grades, with these effects most pronounced for women.

But grades are not the only outcome of the college years, as a range of other behaviors and outcomes reflect peer interaction in college. Indeed, alcohol abuse is often cited as a major problem in college life, with deleterious consequences including damage to health and increased sexual violence. Combining survey data with roommate assignment, researchers Michael Kremer and Dan Levy (2008) show how high school alcohol use translates to adverse collegiate outcomes, which clearly spill over to roommate peers. For men (but not women), assignment to a roommate who frequently drank alcohol comes with a cost of nearly 0.28 in college GPA (on a 4.0 scale). These effects are nearly as large for those with roommates who drank only occasionally. Eisenberg, Golberstein, and Whitlock (2014) find similar results: Random assignment to a roommate who drinks more increases drinking behavior of the student. These results suggest peers may have at least as much effect on the social aspects of college as the academic aspects of college.

While roommates are important peers, they are not the only important peers with whom students interact. What would be the impact of altering the academic quality of an entire peer group in college? Such a question may seem impossible to answer, but an innovative paper by Carrell, Fullerton, and West (2009) found a situation that allows for randomization of entire peer groups. These researchers study peer effects at the U.S. Air Force Academy. Air Force students are randomly assigned to a peer group that lives together, takes classes together, and studies together. There is limited ability to interact with those outside of one's assigned peer group, which makes this an ideal setting in which to estimate the effect of whole peer group effects.

They find much larger effects of peers than the roommate studies discussed previously. For every 100-point increase in group average SAT verbal scores, first-year GPAs increase by 0.4 (on a scale of 4.0). These effects are most prevalent for math and science courses as opposed to physical education and foreign languages, where students have less possibility for interaction. Thus, the effects are localized to subjects in which students tend to study together. In addition, the Air Force Academy randomizes roommates within peer groups. They therefore can compare the group peer effects to the roommate peer effects, and indeed the roommate effects are much smaller and in line with the prior literature. Taken together with the other roommate studies, this research demonstrates that one's college peers as a whole matter quite a lot for one's academic performance.[12] It also is important to keep in mind that these studies all focus on very specific populations, typically students at residential colleges and universities where students spend a great deal of time on campus. How peer effects work in other types of colleges where students typically commute remains an open question.

Working and Studying

How much students get out of their college education can be strongly influenced by their time allocation decisions while enrolled. Some students may spend their time partying and socializing, while others may be forced to work a lot to help pay college expenses. Many students also take part in extracurricular activities, such as athletics and performing arts that require significant time commitments. All of these activities can reduce the amount of time students spend studying and going to class, which can alter the amount students learn during their time in college. In turn, time use affects the length of time it takes a student to finish a degree. There is some evidence that how students spend their time has changed markedly over the past half century. Babcock and Marks (2011) combine five time-use surveys that span 1961 to 2004 and show that the time spent studying and in class has dropped dramatically over this period. In the 1961 data, 67% of students reported spending 20 hours a week or more studying. By 1988, this had dropped to 19%, and in 2004 it was 13%. Student class time also fell, but by less than study time.

> Quick Hint: Time use surveys are of growing interest in economics research, and they typically ask participants to record their activities in small intervals (usually 15–30 minutes) from the day before. Such data provide a rich picture of how people spend their time, but they can be complex to work with because individuals engage in a variety of activities that are difficult to code in a way that makes the data usable. There also is a concern about whether people can accurately recall the details of their time use from the day before; try to do this for your own time use yesterday and you will see how difficult it can be.

What are students doing if not studying? Almost certainly, time spent on extracurricular and social activities has grown. But Babcock and Marks also show a large increase in student labor supply. In 1961, only 7% of students worked more than 20 hours per week. By 2004, 17% did so. A full work week typically is about 35–40 hours, so this is a substantial amount of working hours for full-time students.

Reducing study time can have impacts on two margins. First, on the intensive margin, reduced time studying may negatively affect academic outcomes such as grades or learning outcomes from college courses. Second, on the extensive margin, if students

---

[12] Carrell, Sacerdote, and West (2013) provide a cautionary tale about the difficulty of using these peer effect results to maximize student learning. They use the results of Carrell, Fullerton, and West (2009) to design what appear to be outcome-maximizing peer groups. However, they find students assigned to these peer groups did worse because they formed more homogeneous smaller groups within their assigned group. This study illustrates the difficulty of using peer effect results to inform policy design.

substitute paid employment or extracurricular activities for coursework, time to degree may be extended. A typical BA degree requires the accumulation of 120 credits, or 30 credits per year; suppose a student reduces course taking even by one course per term (12 credits per term, or 24 credits per year), it would take that student an extra year to complete a degree!

The growth in student labor supply has been documented in other sources as well, most notably using Current Population Survey (CPS) data in Scott-Clayton (2012).[13] Figure 15.4 is reproduced from her paper and shows the trend in employment and in weekly hours among full-time students from 1970–2009. The probability a student works grew from about 35% in 1970, peaked during the early 2000s above 50%, and then fell to about 40% during the recent recession. As the bottom panel shows, hours worked conditional on working also have grown significantly. At the end of Scott-Clayton's sample, the average full-time student who works does so for about 20 hours per week. It is important to emphasize that this is for full-time students: Labor supply among part-time students is much higher.

Why has labor supply among full-time students increased so much over time? Scott-Clayton analyzes this question and shows that increases in different periods can be attributed to different factors. Between 1970 and 1982, her data show the rollout of the Federal Work Study (FWS) Program was important in increasing student labor supply. The FWS system is part of federal financial aid, and participating institutions can use FWS funds as part of financial aid packages (see Chapter 14). For eligible students, the federal government pays up to 75% of the student's wage (as long as it is over the minimum wage). Although the program was initiated in 1964, its roles grew considerably during the 1970s, which Scott-Clayton argued was a major contributor to student labor supply increases over this period.

FWS participation leveled off in the early 1980s, but there was a change in the types of students who were enrolling in college as well as overall economic improvements that drove student work increases between 1982 and 1994. After 1994, Scott-Clayton argues, student labor supply increased because of credit constraints: As college became more and more expensive, students began working more and more to be able to finance their enrollment. That these cost increases are continuing suggests labor supply among students will continue to rise as well, despite the reduction in working behavior that occurred during the most recent recession.

Beyond trying to understand *why* students are working more and more hours, it is critical to assess whether it matters. That is, are students trading off time spent working with time they otherwise would have been studying or going to class?

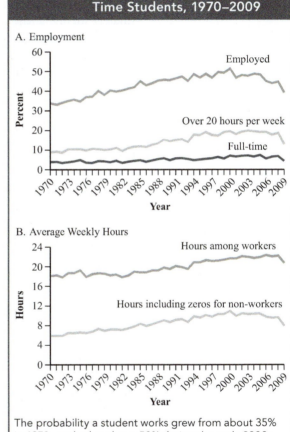

Figure 15.4 Employment and Weekly Hours Worked Among Full-Time Students, 1970–2009

The probability a student works grew from about 35% in 1970, peaked at above 50% during the early 2000s, and then fell to about 40% during the recent recession. As the bottom panel shows, hours worked conditional on working also have grown significantly: The average full-time student who works does so for about 20 hours per week by the end of the sample period. *Data from:* Scott-Clayton (2012), Figure 2.

---

[13] See Appendix A for an overview of the Current Population Survey.

A classical economic model of time allocation suggests this should be the case as long as study and work time are considered to be substitutes by students. As there is a clear daily time constraint of 24 hours (or less if the student wishes to sleep), time spent in one activity will come at the expense of all other substitute activities. If students do trade off study and work time, the rise in work time could be causing the reduced study time, which then may have negative consequences for student academic attainment.

Estimating whether more working hours lead to worse academic outcomes among college students is made difficult because, for the most part, students are not randomly assigned to working hours. Students who decide to work a lot while enrolled may be from lower-income backgrounds, or they may value studying less than students who work less. These background characteristics and preferences are likely to independently influence educational outcomes, making causal analyses very difficult.

Evidence on the effect of work time on student academic performance that best overcomes these empirical difficulties comes from Berea College (Stinebrickner and Stinebrickner, 2003). All students at Berea College are required to work. Fortunately for the authors, students are assigned randomly to jobs upon entering the college, and some jobs require students to work more hours than others. The random allocation of students to jobs creates variation in hours worked that is unrelated to student preferences or backgrounds. Although Berea College students are a select sample, the opportunity this study affords one to estimate causal effects of working on student performance is of extremely high value and is unique in the higher education literature.

Stinebrickner and Stinebrickner find strong evidence of a negative effect of work hours on academic performance: Working one extra hour per week reduces the semester GPA by 0.162 (on a 4.0 scale). This finding suggests that the work increases shown in Figure 15.4 could have profound impacts on academic performance of students. However, it is important to note that their results suggest a stronger negative relationship between hours worked and student academic performance than much of the rest of the literature that examines this question. These differences could be due to the types of students who attend Berea College, but they also could be driven by the fact that students are randomly assigned to jobs instead of choosing them. It further is plausible that studies without randomization are biased toward zero, which could explain the differences in results.

Focusing on national data, there is evidence that broad increases in working time have contributed to increases in the amount of time undergraduates are taking to complete degrees in the United States (Bound, Lovenheim, & Turner, 2012). Between the high school classes of 1972 (NLS72) and 1992 (NELS:88),[14] the average number of years it took to obtain a BA increased from 4.5 to 4.8, and the median student went from taking 4 to 5 years. At non–top 50 ranked public universities and community colleges, increases were even larger (Bound, Lovenheim, & Turner, 2012).

Using these data, Bound, Lovenheim, and Turner calculate that for each hour increase in time spent working, students study 0.3 hours less. This is direct evidence that working time crowds out time spent on coursework among college students. With this measure, they then calculate that increases in working hours across these two cohorts of students can explain 47% of the increases in the time to degree. Thus, the rise in student labor supply is lengthening the amount of time it takes students to graduate, which has costs in terms of delaying the labor market returns to higher education.

---

[14] See Appendix A for a description of these data sets.

15.4 Choosing a Major

Beyond choosing a college, choosing a major or an area of academic specialization identifies the types of skills and knowledge a student is expected to carry forward to the labor market. Even within institutions, college majors differ markedly in the different requirements they impose upon students in terms of the amount of mathematics preparation needed, the amount of reading and writing necessary, and the difficulty of the courses. Two students at the same school who major in vastly different subjects, say, physics and history, will graduate with a very different set of skills and opportunities for postbaccalaureate study. College major and occupation are closely coupled, though the mapping is far from 1 to 1. College major also may indicate preparation for different types of postbaccalaureate study, including professional programs in law and medicine or advanced graduate degrees in particular subjects. While it is relatively well established that there is a substantial correlation between choice of major and future earnings,[15] there is a clear selection challenge, as students who choose to major in, say, math may have very different preparation and interests than those who choose to major in English or French literature.

It is instructive to get a sense of which majors are the most prevalent in U.S. higher education. Table 15.1 shows the number and distribution of degrees awarded

Table 15.1 The Number and Distribution of Majors Among Degree Recipients, 2012

Major	Number	Percent	Major	Number	Percent
Engineering	141,684	3.2	Religion and theology	32,179	0.7
Physical sciences	3,349	0.1	Arts and music	152,372	3.4
Geosciences	8,831	0.2	Interdisciplinary	28,794	0.6
Math and computer sciences	163,495	3.7	Education	384,013	8.6
Life sciences	571,128	12.9	Business and management	784,273	17.6
Psychology	144,919	3.3	Communication and librarianship	108,340	2.4
Social sciences	252,743	5.7	Law	57,767	1.3
Science and engineering technologies	508,493	11.4	Social service professions	48,362	1.1
Architecture and environmental design	19,961	0.4	Vocational studies/ home economics	222,966	5.0
Humanities	136,990	3.1	Other	672,972	15.1

Data from: 2012 IPEDS Earned Degrees Conferred Survey.

---

[15] For example, using data on recent graduates in Texas that are linked to labor market earnings, Andrews, Li, and Lovenheim (2012) show that business majors earn 51% more than those who major in liberal arts. Engineering majors earn 70% more than liberal arts majors as well. A study by Carnevale and Cheah (2013) comparing earnings of workers who had different majors comes to similar conclusions: Median earnings of recent graduates ranged from $54,000 per year in engineering to around $30,000 for recreation and arts degree holders. Altonji, Blom, and Meghir (2012) show as well that the earnings difference across graduates of different majors is at least as large as the average earnings gap between high school and college graduates.

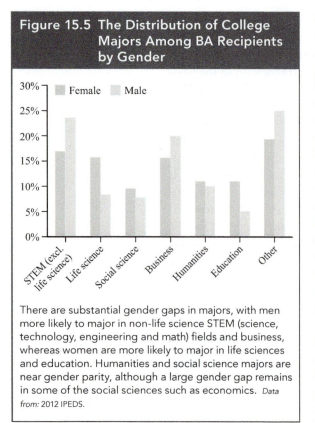

Figure 15.5 The Distribution of College Majors Among BA Recipients by Gender

There are substantial gender gaps in majors, with men more likely to major in non-life science STEM (science, technology, engineering and math) fields and business, whereas women are more likely to major in life sciences and education. Humanities and social science majors are near gender parity, although a large gender gap remains in some of the social sciences such as economics. *Data from:* 2012 IPEDS.

in the United States in 2012 by broad major category. The single most popular major is business and management, at almost 18% of all degrees awarded. Education also is very popular, at about 9%. There is much interest in this country in promoting STEM majors, which are science, technology, engineering, and mathematics. Summing across all of these categories in the table, STEM majors make up 18.6% of all majors excluding life sciences and 31.4% including life sciences. Social science majors also are rather popular among students, at 9% of all majors (including psychology), while humanities majors constitute only 7% of all degrees awarded (including religion and art and music). The distribution of degrees awarded also differs markedly by type of institution, with degrees in broad-based liberal arts subjects more concentrated at selective colleges and universities, while professional degrees in areas like business, communications, and education dominate at many public colleges and universities.

Large differences exist as well between men and women in their major choices. Figure 15.5 shows the proportion of degrees awarded to men and women by broad major group in 2012. Men are much more likely to major in fields like physics, computer science, math, and engineering, as well as in business. Women are more likely to select education or life sciences as their major, while the social sciences aggregate and humanities have roughly equal gender distributions (although women are substantially underrepresented in economics).

Large increases in the labor force participation of women, combined with substantial gains in the overall educational attainment of women in the past half century,[16] have not brought about a closing in the gender gap in choice of major. Three explanations merit consideration:

- *Preparation:* Do men and women enter college with different preparation and skills in subjects that are prerequisites for success in particular fields? Of particular concern is whether women are less well prepared in mathematics, which is prerequisite in a number of quantitative sciences, than their male peers.
- *Study and career preferences:* Do men and women, on average, differ in the types of subjects they enjoy? Do they have different preferences for the types of occupations and employment patterns?
- *Institutional barriers and discrimination:* Are women with similar preparation treated differently by faculty (or students) in male-dominated fields in college? In turn, do women shy away from particular fields because they expect to find discrimination in the labor market?

Distinguishing among these expectations is critical for providing opportunities and achieving the best matching of students with particular courses of study, both to

---

[16] Women now graduate from college at rates far greater than men, while women also graduate from high school with far greater academic achievement.

maximize individual outcomes and to ensure the best allocation of talent for innovation and economic growth. The first explanation places the cause of differences earlier in the educational pipeline, potentially limiting the role of colleges and universities in narrowing the gap. The second explanation, based on preferences, need not suggest a policy problem or market failure in education, as it is quite possible that the distributions of preferences of men and women differ.[17] The third explanation does suggest a policy challenge for the postsecondary system—while academic institutions are broadly committed to equality of opportunity and labor market discrimination is illegal, it is nevertheless possible that differential treatment of men and women in the academic environment and the labor market contributes to the observed differences.

While there are some observed differences in preparation in quantitative fields between men and women, these differences are insufficient to explain the observed gaps in choice of major. The historic (but declining) gender gap in math achievement in high school therefore could contribute to male–female differences in college majors. Using SAT test scores for students at 12 elite private schools in the United States in 1989, Turner and Bowen (1999) show that less than half of the male–female difference in math and physical science majors can be explained by differences in math SAT scores. For engineering, precollegiate math scores can explain about one-third of the major gap. These results suggest the skills students come to college with have substantial influences on the types of major they select, though differences in pre-collegiate skills do not account for the full gender gap. Since this paper was written, male–female math test score gaps have declined significantly, but as Figure 15.5 shows, important gender gaps in STEM and business majors still remain. Thus, there must be other important factors that impact major choice and that differ across men and women. Understanding what these factors are is a ripe area for research.[18]

There is some evidence as well that students make major choices in part based on their perceived returns to these majors. This is what both the human capital and signaling models would predict: Students will select the majors in which their returns are the highest. Wiswall and Zafar (2011) conduct an information experiment on undergraduate students at New York University in which they give a randomly selected set of students information about earnings among workers in the United States with economics, engineering, natural sciences, and humanities degrees. They find that this information differs greatly from what students believed their returns to a given major would be. Furthermore, a sizable fraction of students report an increase in the likelihood they will major in one of the subjects with high earnings, suggesting perceived returns is an important component of student major choice.

---

[17] This is not a statement that all women prefer, say, biology to computer science but rather that more women than men prefer biology to computer science. Some women will likely prefer computer science, while some men will prefer biology.

[18] One such factor is how men and women respond to competitive environments. Lab experiments conducted by Gneezy, Niederle, and Rustichini (2003) show in an experimental setting that women are less productive in environments in which they have to compete against others. This is particularly the case when they have to compete against men. Additionally, experiments by Niederle and Vesterlund (2007) show that women tend to avoid competitive environments. STEM majors in particular are quite difficult, competitive, and male-dominated. While these results suggest such factors could contribute to the gender gap in STEM, no study to date has directly shown this to be the case.

15.5 College Completion

Nearly twice as many young people start college as finish college. Yet the economic returns accrue disproportionately to those with degrees, primarily BA degrees but also AA degrees. The median lifetime earnings measured in 2009 for someone with some college but no degree was $1.54 million, only slightly above the $1.3 million a high school graduate is expected to earn (Carnevale, Rose, & Cheah, 2014). Median expected lifetime earnings for a BA degree recipient totaled $2.27 million, and those who continued on to receive professional degrees could expect median lifetime earnings of more than $3.6 million. The last decade has brought an uptick in college degree receipt, with the percentage of young people (ages 25–29) with a BA degree rising from 30% to 34%. Yet these shares are far below the nearly 65% of this age group who have enrolled in college.

The optimal rate of college completion is likely to be appreciably less than 100%. Some students may try college, only to find that they are unlikely to benefit or that their true interests lie in other domains. In this sense, enrolling in college provides an *option value*; that is, college attendance gives one the option of continuing on and obtaining a college degree. Thus, students can incorporate new information about personal ability as they make sequential decisions about whether to persist.[19] While some attrition may be efficient, it is unlikely that all of the degree noncompletion in U.S. higher education follows such a model; credit constraints and other impediments to academic progress may contribute to some of the observed college dropout behavior.

College completion rates are difficult to measure using aggregate data. Figure 15.6 shows trends in the ratio of workers aged 30–40 with a BA versus some college. Since most people who obtain a BA do so by age 30, this can be interpreted as the relative size of the BA completer to college dropout population over time. The figure shows trends in this proportion overall and separately by gender. There is a clear pattern: the number of BA recipients relative to non-completers fell precipitously until the mid to late 1990s. Since that time, it has recovered somewhat. For women, the proportion of college goers who obtain a four-year degree is higher now than in the early 1980s, which is consistent with the long-run trends in increasing female educational attainment (Goldin, Katz, & Kuziemko, 2006). Among men, though, this ratio continues to be lower than it was in the 1980s. Looking at the scale in Figure 15.6 reveals an important fact: Just over half of college attendees complete a BA. That college completion rates are so low makes it very important to understand the factors that influence how students progress through the higher education system toward a degree.

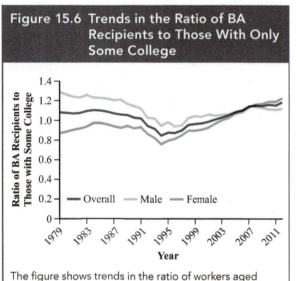

Figure 15.6 Trends in the Ratio of BA Recipients to Those With Only Some College

The figure shows trends in the ratio of workers aged 30–40 with a BA versus some college, overall and separately by gender. The proportion of college attendees who complete a BA degree fell precipitously until the mid to late 1990s and then recovered somewhat. For women, the proportion of college goers who obtain a four-year degree is higher now than in the early 1980s, consistent with the long-run trends in increasing female educational attainment. *Data from: 1979–2012 CPS.*

Quick Hint: In this section, unless otherwise specified, completion rates refer to the rate of completion of four-year (BA) degrees.

---

[19] Manski (1989) is the first to lay out the argument for the option value of schooling. See Stange (2012) for an empirical examination of the role of option value in driving student investment decisions.

The current upward trajectory of college completion rates follows an interval in which completion rates fell from a peak in the early 1970s. For students from the high school graduating class of 1972 who enrolled in college, 50.5% received a BA degree, while two decades later only 45.9% of the high school graduates of the class of 1992 attending college received a BA degree. What is particularly striking about this result is that it occurred during a time when the return to a college degree was increasing. What hypotheses might explain this trend?

- *Student preparation:* Students entering in the later cohort may have been less prepared academically for college.
- *College and university quality:* Students in the later cohort may have entered different types of institutions, in particular open-access and lower-resource institutions.
- *Collegiate resources:* Within college and university sectors, resources may have declined.

Using longitudinal data from the NLS72 and NELS:88 studies, Bound, Lovenheim, and Turner (2010) examine how completion rates have changed over time differently for students beginning in one of five sectors of higher education: top 50 public schools, non–top 50 public schools, less selective privates, more selective privates, and community colleges.[20] Table 15.2 shows the completion rate changes in their data, both overall and separately by gender. They define completion rates as the proportion of students who enter college and obtain a BA within eight years after high school graduation. Consistent with Figure 15.6, it is among men that completion rates declined most dramatically, and in particular it is among men who first enter the postsecondary system in a non–top 50 ranked public school or at a community college. The decline at less-elite public schools is the most dramatic, at almost 10 percentage points. Among the high school class of 1992 (the NELS:88 sample), barely 50% of those who attended a non–top 50 ranked public college or university had obtained a BA degree after eight years.

Table 15.2 Changes in College Completion Rates Between the NLS72 and NELS:88 High School Cohorts

Panel A: Full Sample			
	NLS72	NELS:88	Difference
Full sample	50.5	45.9	−4.6
Initial School type			
Non–top 50 public	61.8	56.9	−4.9
Top 50 public	73.5	82.5	9.0
Less selective private	58.2	70.5	12.3
Highly selective private	80.1	90.3	10.3
Community college	20.2	17.6	−2.5

(continued)

[20] See Appendix A for a description of these data sets.

Table 15.2 *(continued)*

Panel B: Men			
	NLS72	**NELS:88**	**Difference**
Full sample	51.7	43.2	−8.5
Initial School type			
Non–top 50 public	61.2	51.6	−9.6
Top 50 public	73.8	77.5	3.8
Less selective private	59.9	67.7	8.0
Highly selective private	82.7	89.2	6.5
Community college	21.6	17.7	−3.9
Panel C: Women			
	NLS72	**NELS:88**	**Difference**
Full Sample	49.2	48.5	−0.8
Initial School type			
Non–top 50 public	62.4	61.8	−0.6
Top 50 public	73.1	87.7	14.6
Less selective private	56.5	72.6	15.9
Highly selective private	75.6	91.4	15.8
Community college	18.6	17.5	−1.1

Data from: Bound, Lovenheim, and Turner (2010), Table 2. The data used in this table are from the NLS72 and NELS:88 data sets (see Appendix A) and show college completion rates for the high school classes of 1972 (NLS72) and 1992 (NELS:88), respectively.

When more students apply to four-year schools, more selective schools will not expand the size of their class much; more students will attend less selective and open-access four-year schools and community colleges where supply of admission spots is more elastic. This interaction of a demand increase with differentially elastic supply across the sectors of higher education leads to the following predictions:

- The increased demand for college enrollment will lead more students who are less academically prepared for college to enroll.
- These less prepared students will sort into the least selective schools, which also have the fewest resources.
- Per-student resources will decline in the less selective schools because state and federal funding are very slow to respond to demand increases, and student tuition covers only a small part of the cost of education provision.
- The more selective schools will become even more competitive, and the academic ability of the students attending these schools will increase.

In short, the authors argue, a demand increase for college will lead to higher completion rates among the more selective schools and declining completion rates at less selective schools. The result will be increased stratification of completion rates across higher education sectors. This is exactly what the pattern in Table 15.2 shows.

Why have completion rates declined among students attending less selective schools? Bound, Lovenheim, and Turner (2010) examine the importance of demand-side factors and supply-side factors. The main demand-side factor is that there has been an increase in less academically prepared students attending college. Since less prepared students are much less likely to complete college, even conditional on enrolling, this could lead to reductions in completion rates at the schools these students attend. The supply-side factors are twofold:

1. Students are increasingly attending schools in the lower-resource sectors, such as non–top 50 ranked public schools and community colleges.
2. Per-student resources at these schools have declined over time with the influx of students and tightening state budgets that have reduced state support for higher education (see Chapter 13).

They conduct an analysis in which they decompose the change in completion rates into the parts driven by each of these explanations. Overall, their results indicate that declines in student academic preparation for college (as measured by high school math test scores) can explain about one-third of the decline in the completion rate. Declines in institutional resources can explain about one-fourth of the change, and three-fourths of the decline is due to changes in the types of schools in which students enroll. Together, these explanations predict a larger decline than is observed in the data, which means some other force is making the completion rate decline smaller than it otherwise would be. The authors argue this is likely to be the increasing collegiate attainment of parents over time. Overall, this paper highlights the importance of the supply side of college education, particularly in understanding the implications of a demand increase.

While Bound, Lovenheim, and Turner (2010) focus on institutional resources in driving completion rates, it also could be the case that individual family resources impact the likelihood a student who enrolls in college obtains a degree. One very important set of programs to consider is financial aid. In Chapter 14, we reviewed the financial aid literature with a focus on college attendance. But if financial aid is successful at getting students to enroll in college but not to finish, it may not be as successful as the enrollment analyses suggest in boosting collegiate attainment among low-income students.

Surprisingly, there is not much research on the effect of financial aid on college persistence and graduation, and the research that does exist tends to come to somewhat mixed conclusions about the importance of financial aid programs. Much of the evidence on how financial aid affects persistence comes from analyses of older programs, such as the GI Bill and the introduction of the Pell grant, which bear little relationship to current federal financial aid programs. These studies are discussed in Chapter 14. Evidence on how the current federal financial aid system impacts college completion is extremely sparse.

One of the few studies that exists starts with the observation that at some income levels a small change in income introduces a discontinuous change in Pell eligibility. Bettinger (2004) combines detailed administrative data from the Ohio Board of Regents and employs a regression discontinuity approach, comparing students just below the threshold to those just over the threshold for Pell grant eligibility. He finds suggestive evidence that Pell grants increase student persistence, but his results are not terribly conclusive. Small changes to the model yield different results, which is not ideal from a research perspective.

Short-run credit constraints also may play an important role in driving college completion rates. If completion is responsive to variation in family resources, it implies that at least some families may have trouble obtaining sufficient funds to adequately support their children while enrolled in college. The clearest evidence on the importance of resource constraints for college completion comes from Berea College. Stinebrickner and Stinebrickner (2008) conduct a detailed survey of students in which they ask them about their financial background, their desired expenses, and whether they would like to be able to take out more money in loans (at fair market rates). They classify students as constrained if they report they would like to take out more money in loans.

Despite the fact that completion rates at Berea College are around 50%, only 20% of students answer they would like to take out more loans. For those who answer affirmatively to this question, the average amount they would like to borrow is only $889 for the academic year. Students who report being constrained do drop out at higher rates than unconstrained students; however, the low proportion of constrained students combined with the difference in dropout rates suggests that resource constraints cannot explain the vast majority of student dropout behavior.

While this discussion focused on BA completion at four-year schools, low completion rates are arguably an even larger problem at community colleges. The proportion of students who complete any degree, including associate's degrees or certificates, is typically around 20% but varies considerably across colleges. Community college students tend to come from more disadvantaged backgrounds than four-year college students, and they thus face considerable disadvantages that include lack of academic preparation for college, few financial resources, and lack of access to information about the postsecondary system.

A series of interventions by the research institute MDRC has begun to examine how more holistic interventions that address this set of disadvantages affect community college completion.[21] The Accelerated Study in Associate Programs (ASAP) was launched in the community colleges in New York City in 2007. The programs encourage students to attend full-time; provide tutoring, career services, and advising; and provide tuition waivers to help students cover college costs. Their main findings across several studies are that these interventions dramatically increase retention rates and graduation rates among disadvantaged students and among students who require remedial coursework. These studies highlight the potential importance of interventions that address the multiple disadvantages faced by many community college students.

15.6 Conclusion

College choices are economic choices. Where to apply, where to attend, whether to work while in school, and what major to choose can be modeled with the tools of economics. In turn, universities' behavior in admitting students also reflects a constrained optimization problem. A persistent question in modeling these outcomes is whether agents (students and colleges) are fully informed and whether credit constraints may limit choices and outcomes. We also highlighted the role of salient and customized information in helping students to make better college-going decisions. To the extent

---

[21] See their Web site, http://www.mdrc.org/publications, for the specifics of the research design and results.

that low-income students face greater barriers than their more affluent peers in navigating the college application process, policy innovations to reduce these barriers may increase efficiency.

How students interact in colleges and how students spend their time also affect outcomes. Even as self-selection limits what we can learn from the association between student outcomes and peer characteristics, there are clear cases, such as roommate and class assignments, where peers are randomly assigned. The academic impact of peers is small but nonzero, and peers impact other behaviors, including alcohol consumption. As you may know well, time is one of the biggest constraints for students (not to mention faculty). Over the past several decades, there has been a shift in the allocation of student time away from studying, with clear evidence of increased time spent working.

Whether students receive degrees and the specialization of those degrees (major) also reflects the productivity of higher education and predicts the future earnings of students. One point of emphasis is that group differences in outcomes—whether they be by gender or by race—merit consideration of the underlying explanatory factors. Finally, our examination of student completion rates brought together the supply and demand sides of the market for higher education that we have studied separately in prior chapters. We discussed research showing that the increase in student demand for a higher education has had large and differential impacts on the various sectors of higher education. This in turn has led to increased stratification of college outcomes. From a policy perspective, this research points to the important role of institutional resources in reducing this stratification by increasing the low completion rates at less selective colleges and universities.

With ever-tightening budgets, it might not be politically feasible for states to meaningfully increase their financial support for higher education. How to increase completion rates in an era of growing student demand and declining state support while keeping college tuition at affordable levels for students is a preeminent policy challenge that we will be faced with for quite some time. Our goal in this book was to provide you with the economic tools and knowledge of the literature to understand fully the importance and scope of this policy problem.

Highlights

- Economists are interested in college application behavior and college admissions policies because they involve the way in which schools and students allocate scarce resources to meet personal and institutional objectives. Students (and their parents) are trying to find a college that provides the highest return given their preparation and ability to pay. Colleges and universities want to choose students who will make the most of available resources while also ensuring sufficient tuition dollars to pay for expenses.

- Deciding how many applications to submit and where to apply is fundamentally an optimization problem. Complicating these decisions is that students (and their families) face considerable uncertainty in predicting whether they will be admitted to any particular school, the financial aid offered by different schools, and the likely educational and labor market returns to choosing a given school.

- A college's goal is to admit students who will help attain institutional goals; however, many institutions do not practice selective admissions and therefore have little control over the types of students who enroll. Colleges can alter their price by offering financial aid on the basis of student characteristics to affect who enrolls, and they can use admissions policies to select students with particular characteristics.

- Institutions have preferences for a socioeconomically diverse class, which precludes them from setting prices that would equilibrate supply and demand. As a result, selective institutions in particular consider a wide range of factors when admitting students that allow them to craft a class that meets their institutional goals. This leads to a rather complex admissions process, especially for highly selective schools.

- There are large gaps across the income distribution in the types of schools to which students apply and in which they enroll. Students from lower-income backgrounds tend to enroll in lower-quality schools, even conditional on their academic preparation for college. A growing body of evidence suggests differences in the information environment across the income distribution are important contributors to these gaps.

- Early decision and early action policies, wherein students apply and are admitted (or denied) early, are a staple of most selective universities. Colleges like these policies because they provide more control over the class and they allow students to signal their interest. But there is concern that they have adverse effects on low-income students by exacerbating information barriers.

- Affirmative action policies give preference in admissions to students from underrepresented minority groups. While economics cannot answer the question of whether affirmative action is "right," what it brings to the question are the models and empirical tools to inform and measure the costs and benefits of these institutional-level policies.

- The potential benefits of affirmative action include the educational benefits of diversity to all students, benefits to minority students of attending a higher-quality school, and benefits to society at large. The potential costs include worse outcomes among minority students due to mismatch, stigma effects, and forgone admissions opportunities for nonminority students.

- Peer effects are likely to be an important aspect of how institutional quality affects student outcomes. Still, it is very hard to isolate the causal role of peers due to the selection and reflection problems. Evidence from random assignment of college roommates suggests an important role for one's peers in driving collegiate academic success, but peers also affect other outcomes, such as alcohol consumption.

- Student time allocation has changed markedly over the past several decades, with students studying less and working more. The reasons for the increase in student labor supply differ across time periods, but the available evidence suggests the growth in the amount students work while enrolled has negative effects on collegiate outcomes.

- Various factors drive student decisions about which major to choose, including perceived labor market returns, academic preparation (in particular in math), and individual preferences for different subjects. These factors make it very difficult to estimate the labor market returns to college major choices, but the large differences in earnings across majors and the persistent gender gap in many majors underscore the importance of understanding how college major choices affect long-run outcomes.

- The rising demand for college over the past several decades has led to increased stratification in student outcomes across the different sectors of higher education. Less academically prepared students are attending college, and they are sorting increasingly into lower-resource schools. As a result, completion rates have fallen in less selective public schools and have risen in selective schools, which are becoming increasingly selective as demand for enrollment increases.

Problems

1. Low-income, high achieving students are underrepresented at the most selective colleges and universities. Does this underrepresentation stem from differences in application behavior, differences in the likelihood of admission for students with similar preparation, or differences in matriculation decisions? What are some of the economic explanations for this underrepresentation?

2. Suppose a college employs a simple admissions rule: Students with SAT scores greater than 1300 will be admitted, while students with lower SAT scores will be denied admission. There are two different types of students applying to the institution: Red people and Blue people. The distribution of scores among Red people is uniform over the range 1000 to 1600; the distribution of scores among Blue people is uniform over the range 1200 to 1500. Assume matriculation rates are identical and do not depend on color or test scores.
   a. What are the admission rates for Red people and Blue people?
   b. What are the mean SAT scores in the population of Red people and Blue people?
   c. What are the mean SAT scores among admitted students for Red people and Blue people?
   d. Are either Blue people or Red people favored in admission? Do differences in test scores conditional on admission provide any evidence of differential treatment in admission?

3. Mary Winters, the president of a major research university, recently received a letter arguing that the lower performance of female BA degree recipients

relative to male BA degree recipients on a mathematics test given at college graduation is indicative of discrimination in teaching, grading, and mentoring among senior faculty, some of whom were appointed before coeducation. Rather than making off-the-cuff comments outside her own area of research, President Winters has appointed a committee to study the question.

a. Discuss the potential explanations for this gender difference in mathematics performance that you would expect a social science committee to explore.

b. One researcher on the committee notes that men and women differ in SAT math scores on average at the time of university enrollment. In fact, men have average math scores of 700 and women entering the university have average math scores of 650. The researcher notes that for men and women, there is a linear relationship (indicated here) between SAT scores and the mathematics test at graduation on average:

$$GradTest_m = 20 + 0.1SAT_{Math}$$
$$GradTest_f = 15 + 0.1SAT_{Math}$$

What is the difference between men and women in the expected graduation test scores? Using the Oaxaca decomposition, calculate how much of this differential is due to differences in entering (SAT) test scores.

4. Many large public universities have recently seen dramatic increases in the number of undergraduate students from abroad, and as a result, it is natural to ask how these students impact domestic students.

a. Discuss the costs *and* benefits of the flow of foreign students on the education received by domestic, particularly in-state, students.

b. Discuss potential peer effects of the change in demographic composition of a college's cohort generated by foreign students. What is an empirical strategy you could use to measure such effects?

5. Assume that the following table represents the number of high school seniors in the state of Virolina disaggregated by race (minority versus White) and by income status (low income versus middle class and above).

		Low Income	Middle Class or Above
Overall	White	50,000	100,000
	Minority	25,000	25,000

a. If the students at the flagship University of Virolina were representative of the population of the state, what would be the fraction of low-income students and minority students at the university?

b. The observed representation of low-income students at Virolina is 10%; discuss two potential explanations.

c. The observed representation of minority students at the University of Virolina is 5%. Discuss whether preferences based on economic circumstances can increase racial diversity in this case. Include the associated trade-offs in your discussion.

Description of Data Sets Commonly Used in the Economics of Education

3DDock/Shutterstock

The data used for education research come in many forms. One important distinction across data sets is whether they are cross-sectional or longitudinal. Cross-sectional data provide a snapshot of individuals or institutions in any one time period. For example, the set of test scores in each school in California in 2009 is an example of a cross-sectional data set. Longitudinal data allow one to follow individual units over time. A data set with a cross-sectional and longitudinal component, such that it follows the same units over time, is called a panel data set. Data on test scores of all schools in California from 2000–2012 is an example of panel data. Another example of panel data is a nationally representative survey that follows the individuals surveyed over time. The use of panel data is extensive in economics of education; indeed, most data sets used by researchers in this area use panel data of one form or another.

Another important distinction across data sets is whether the data are collected by surveys of individuals or through administrative records. Survey data have the benefit of including detailed information about people, including their beliefs, preferences, and aspirations. Administrative data, however, typically include only outcomes that are measured through a specific government program, such as standardized tests or income from tax returns. Administrative data sets tend to be large, as they include all individuals in a state or in the country, but they include only a limited set of background characteristics about those who are in the data. These data also have the benefit over survey data of being less prone to measurement error from incorrect individual responses or nonresponses to questions.

The purpose of this appendix is to provide an overview of the main data sets used in the economics of education and in the studies discussed throughout this book. The appendix is organized into several sections that characterize the type of data. These sections as well as the data sets described in each are listed here:

1. Large, nationally representative government surveys
   a. Current Population Survey (CPS)
   b. U.S. Census and American Community Surveys
2. Longitudinal individual-level data sets
   a. National Longitudinal Study of 1972 (NLS72)
   b. High School and Beyond (HS&B)

   c. National Education Longitudinal Study of 1988 (NELS:88)
   d. Educational Longitudinal Study of 2002 (ELS:2002)
   e. Early Childhood Longitudinal Study, Kindergarten Class of 1998–99 (ECLS-K)
   f. National Longitudinal Survey of Youth 1979 and 1997 (NLSY79, NLSY97)
   g. Panel Study of Income Dynamics (PSID)
3. State administrative data sets
   a. Texas
   b. North Carolina
   c. Florida
4. Institutional-level data from the Department of Education
   a. Integrated Postsecondary Education Data System (IPEDS)
   b. Common Core of Data (CCD)
5. National Assessment of Education Progress (NAEP)

A.1 Large, Nationally Representative Government Surveys

Current Population Survey (CPS)

Overview: The Current Population Survey (CPS) is conducted by the U.S. Census Bureau and the U.S. Bureau of Labor Statistics. It is a monthly nationally representative household survey designed to measure labor force statistics in the United States. The CPS also collects information on earnings and education that make it an important source of knowledge about how earnings and labor force participation vary over time for individuals with different education levels. Each month is a nationally representative sample, but households are surveyed for four months, are out of the sample for eight months, then are surveyed again for four months. Each month, respondents are given topical modules that ask more detailed questions about specific aspects of their lives. The most commonly used among education researchers are the October module, which asks detailed education questions, and the March module, which asks about earnings. Also commonly used is the *outgoing rotation group*, which is comprised of the set of households that are rotating out of the sample in each month.

Years: The CPS has been conducted since 1948 and continues to the present.

Frequency: Monthly.

Sample: All individuals 16 and older who are not institutionalized are eligible to be in the sample. Institutionalized individuals are those who are in prison, a long-term care hospital, or a nursing home.

Sample size: About 60,000 households are sampled each month.

Geographic information: The data contain state of residence as well as city of residence for those living in large metropolitan statistical areas (MSAs).

Major variables of interest: The most commonly used variables in the CPS among education economists are the variables asking about demographics (race, sex, household composition, age), educational attainment, labor force participation, hours worked, and earnings. The earnings questions are asked only for non–self-employed workers, which is a limitation. Prior to 1992, the CPS asked respondents about the highest grade completed. In 1992 it switched the question to ask about highest degree completed. This can make comparisons of educational attainment over time in the CPS difficult. Jaeger (1997, 2003) and Jaeger and Page (1996) have detailed discussions of the implications of the change in the way education is measured in the CPS and suggestions for researchers on how to use these data appropriately.

Data access: The data can be downloaded from the Census Bureau Web site: http://www.census.gov/cps/data/. The NBER data archive contains monthly CPS data from 1976 onward, at http://www.nber.org/data/cps_basic.html, as well as consistently coded and formatted outgoing rotation group data back to 1975: http://www.nber.org/morg/annual/.

U.S. Decennial Census and American Community Survey (ACS)

Overview: The U.S. Decennial Census is conducted every 10 years in the year ending in zero and is designed to obtain information on every resident of the United States. In 2000 and before, the Census had both a short form and a long form. The short form asked basic demographic questions, such as name, sex, age, race, and household composition. The long form asked more detailed questions about educational attainment, labor supply, income, and housing. About one-sixth of households received the long form. In 2010, the long form was discontinued. Since 2005, the detailed socioeconomic, labor supply, education, and housing data previously collected on the long form have been collected through the American Community Survey (ACS). The ACS also is run by the Census Bureau, and its goal is to replace the long form Census with more frequent data: The survey collects data about all communities each year rather than once every decade. Only a small proportion of the population receives it in any one time during a 10-year span, with no household receiving the ACS more than once every 5 years.

Years: The decennial census has been collected every decade in the year ending in zero since 1790. The ACS began in 2005 and continues yearly to the present.

Frequency: Decennially or yearly, depending on the time period.

Sample: All households (and thus individuals) in the United States are required to fill out the Census and, if asked, the ACS.

Sample size: The entire population of the United States. Public-use census data are available as a 1% or 5% sample of people or housing units.

Geographic information: The data contain many types of geographic identifiers. Both current state of residence and state of birth are recorded. In addition, the U.S. Census Bureau breaks all areas into census tracts, made up of a series of census block groups, which themselves are constituted by census blocks. The Census also contains county and metropolitan statistical area (MSA) codes. In the individual micro data, only the large counties, MSAs, and census tracts are identified. Aggregated data at each geographic level are available, however. In the ACS, the aggregated data at smaller levels of geography are either 3-year or 5-year averages from all individuals sampled over that timeframe.

Major variables of interest: The most commonly used variables in the Census and ACS among education economists are the variables asking about demographics (race, sex, household composition, age), educational attainment, labor force participation, hours worked, and income. Prior to 1990, the Census asked respondents about the highest grade completed. In 1990 and after, it switched the question to ask about highest degree completed. (This is identical to the CPS questions about educational attainment.) The different measures can make comparisons of educational attainment over time in the Census difficult. Economists also use the geographic information in the Census and ACS as well as the information about state of birth and mobility over the last 1 or 5 years.

Data access: Decennial census data can be downloaded from the Census Bureau Web site: http://www.census.gov/main/www/cen2000.html. ACS data also are available from the Census Bureau Web site: https://www.census.gov/programs-surveys/acs/data.html. Additionally, both datasets can be downloaded through IPUMS: https://usa.ipums.org/usa/

A.2 Longitudinal Individual-Level Data Sets

Beginning in the early 1970s, the National Center for Education Statistics (NCES), a division of the U.S. Department of Education, began conducting longitudinal studies of nationally representative sets of students. These studies are designed to follow students as they progress through secondary education and into young adulthood, going either to college or directly into the workforce. The NCES has now conducted four of these studies that focus on the transition to young adulthood (NLS72, HS&B, NELS:88, and ELS:2002) and one that focuses on early childhood (ECLS-K). These studies all have similar sampling frames, include cognitive test scores developed and conducted by the NCES, and for the studies examining older children, provide linkages to college transcripts and high school records. Three other longitudinal studies, NLSY79, NLSY97, and PSID, have a similar structure but differ along several important dimensions including the lack of college transcripts and, for the PSID, the lack of cognitive test scores. Together, these data sets are used in a large proportion of economics of education research studies.

National Longitudinal Study of 1972 (NLS72)

Overview: The NLS72 is the first of a series of nationally representative longitudinal data sets conducted by the National Center for Education Statistics, which is designed to follow students as they transition into young adulthood. This data set is a stratified random sample of all high school seniors in the United States in the spring of 1972. Follow-ups were conducted repeatedly until 1986, allowing one to follow students as they made postsecondary decisions and moved into the labor force. The data at every follow-up contain an extensive set of questions about family background, life goals, learning environments, and activities in which the respondent is engaging.

In addition, the data contain test scores from cognitive ability exams given to high school seniors in the baseline survey. High school records were included in 1984. The data are further linked to postsecondary transcript files for the majority of students who attended college. Those transcripts detail the institution attended, courses taken, grades received, and the dates of enrollment. The transcript data allow one to measure in detail where and when respondents enrolled in college.

Years and Frequency: The baseline survey was conducted in 1972, with follow-ups in 1973, 1974, 1976, 1979, and 1986 (for a subsample only).

Sample: A nationally representative sample of high school seniors was drawn from a stratified random sample of the population of U.S. high school seniors. The sampling strategy was stratified by school, surveying 1,200 schools with 18 seniors per school.

Sample size: The baseline sample was 19,001 students, but there was considerable attrition across survey waves.

Geographic information: The data contain high school identifiers, college identifiers, and information on the state of residence in each survey wave.

Major variables of interest: The most commonly used variables among education economists are those that detail how much education a student received, the timing of educational attainment, high school test scores, and the postsecondary transcript files that show where students attended college. The detailed student background information, including parental income and education, also is used extensively.

Data access: The data can be ordered on a CD from the National Center for Education Statistics at http://nces.ed.gov/surveys/nls72/index.asp or can be downloaded from ICPSR at the University of Michigan at http://www.icpsr.umich.edu.

High School and Beyond (HS&B)

Overview: The HS&B is the second installment of the National Center for Education Statistics' series of longitudinal studies to examine the progression of students through secondary school and into young adulthood. This survey followed two cohorts, the 1980 sophomore and senior classes. The data set is a stratified random sample of all high school seniors and sophomores in the United States in 1980. Follow-ups were conducted every other year until 1986; a 1992 follow-up for the sophomore class of 1980 also was conducted. The data contain a set of questions similar to those of the NLS72 survey, including at every follow-up an extensive set of questions about family background, life goals, learning environments, and activities in which the respondent is engaging. The data also contain test scores from cognitive ability exams given to students in the first year of the survey. This survey includes information on twins as well: If a student reported being a twin, his or her twin also was surveyed. Additionally, information on friend networks and teacher questionnaires was included in the baseline survey. The data are further linked to high school transcripts and, for the majority of students who attended college, to postsecondary transcript files that detail the institution attended, courses taken, grades received, and the dates of enrollment. The transcript data allow one to observe in detail where and when students enrolled in college.

Years and Frequency: The baseline survey was conducted in 1980, with follow-ups in 1982, 1984, and 1986. The sophomore sample was followed up in 1992.

Sample: A nationally representative sample of high school seniors and sophomores was drawn from a stratified random sample of the population of U.S. high schools. The sampling strategy was stratified by school, surveying 1,122 schools with 36 seniors and sophomores per school.

Sample size: The baseline sample was 58,270 students, but there was considerable attrition across survey waves.

Geographic information: The data contain high school identifiers, college identifiers, and information on the state of residence at each survey wave.

Major variables of interest: The most commonly used variables among economists looking at education-related questions are those that detail how much education a student received, the timing of educational attainment, the high school test scores, and the postsecondary transcript files that report where students attended college. The detailed student background information, including parental income and education, also is used extensively.

Data access: The data can be ordered on a CD from the National Center for Education Statistics at http://nces.ed.gov/surveys/hsb/ or can be downloaded from ICPSR at the University of Michigan at http://www.icpsr.umich.edu.

National Education Longitudinal Study of 1988 (NELS:88)

Overview: The NELS:88 is the third installment of the National Center for Education Statistics' series of longitudinal studies to examine the progression of students through secondary school and into young adulthood. This survey followed the eighth-grade cohort of 1988. The data set is a stratified random sample of all eighth-grade students in the United States in 1988. Five follow-ups were conducted through 2000. The data contain a similar set of questions to the NLS72 and HS&B surveys, including at every follow-up an extensive set of questions about family background, life goals, learning environments, and activities in which the respondent is engaging. The data also contain test scores from cognitive ability exams given to students in the first year of the survey. Information on high school achievement is included in the survey, but high school transcript files are not included. For the majority of students who attend college, however, the data are linked to postsecondary transcript files that detail the institution attended, courses taken, grades received, and the dates of enrollment. The transcript data allow one to observe in detail where and when students enrolled in college. Students' teachers, parents, and school administrators also were surveyed, and a separate survey focuses on high school dropouts. Beginning with the NELS:88, access to transcript files and many of the achievement test outcomes are restricted to researchers who obtain clearance from the Department of Education to use the data.

Years and Frequency: The baseline survey was conducted in 1988, with follow-ups in 1990, 1984, 1986, and 2000.

Sample: A nationally representative sample of eighth-graders was drawn from a stratified, random sample of the population of eighth-graders. The sampling strategy was stratified by school, surveying 1,052 schools with about 25 individuals per school. Refresher samples were included in the first two follow-ups to account for attrition.

Sample size: The baseline sample was 25,000 students. There was considerable attrition across survey waves, but the refresher samples kept overall sample numbers relatively constant across waves.

Geographic information: The data contain high school identifiers, college identifiers, and information on the state of residence at each survey wave. All geographic identifiers are contained in the restricted-access data.

Major variables of interest: The most commonly used variables among education economists are those that detail how much education a student received; the timing of educational attainment; the test scores from eighth, tenth, and twelfth grades; and the postsecondary transcript files that report where a student attended college. The detailed student background information, including parental income and education, also is used extensively.

Data access: The data can be ordered on a CD from the National Center for Education Statistics at http://nces.ed.gov/surveys/nels88/ or can be downloaded from ICPSR at the University of Michigan at http://www.icpsr.umich.edu. A restricted-data license application can be found at http://nces.ed.gov/pubsearch/licenses.asp.

Educational Longitudinal Study of 2002 (ELS:2002)

Overview: The ELS:2002 is the fourth installment of the National Center for Education Statistics' series of longitudinal studies to examine the progression of students through secondary school and into young adulthood. This survey followed the tenth-grade cohort of 2002 and the twelfth-grade cohort of 2004. The data set is a stratified random sample of all tenth-grade students in the United States in 2002 and all twelfth-grade students in 2004. Three follow-ups have been conducted to date through 2012. The data contain a similar set of questions to the NLS72, HS&B, and NELS:88 surveys, including at every follow-up an extensive set of questions about family background, life goals, learning environments, and activities in which the respondent is engaging. The data also contain test scores from cognitive ability exams given to students in the first year of the survey. As of 2005, high school transcript files are available, and as of 2013, postsecondary transcripts also have been collected. The postsecondary transcript data allow one to observe in detail where and when students enrolled in college. Students' math and English teachers, parents, and school administrators also were surveyed. As with the NELS:88 data, access to transcript files and many of the achievement test outcomes are restricted to researchers who obtain clearance from the Department of Education to use the data.

Years and Frequency: The baseline survey was conducted in 2002, with follow-ups in 2004, 2006, and 2012.

Sample: A nationally representative stratified random sample of U.S. tenth-graders and twelfth-graders was drawn. The sampling strategy was stratified by school, surveying 752 schools with about 26 individuals per school. Refresher samples were included in the first two follow-ups to account for attrition.

Sample size: The baseline sample was 15,352 students. There was considerable attrition across survey waves.

Geographic information: The data contain high school identifiers, college identifiers, and information on the state of residence at each survey wave. All geographic identifiers are contained in the restricted-access data.

Major variables of interest: The most commonly used variables among education economists are those that detail how much education a student received, the timing of educational attainment, the test scores from tenth- and twelfth-grade assessments, and the secondary and postsecondary transcript files that measure high school achievement levels and where a student attended college. The detailed student background information, including parental income and education, also is used extensively.

Data access: The data can be ordered on a CD from the National Center for Education Statistics at http://nces.ed.gov/surveys/els2002/avail_data.asp or can be downloaded from ICPSR at the University of Michigan at http://www.icpsr.umich.edu. A restricted-data license application can be found at http://nces.ed.gov/pubsearch/licenses.asp.

Early Childhood Longitudinal Study, Kindergarten Class of 1998–99 (ECLS-K)

Overview: The ECLS-K is part of the National Center for Education Statistics' series of longitudinal studies, but unlike the studies previously discussed, this one focuses on early childhood. The data follow students in the kindergarten class of 1998–1999 as they progress through elementary school and into middle school, ending when most students are in eighth grade. The students in the study came from both private and public kindergarten programs, and in addition to extensive student-level information, parent and teacher surveys are included. NCES-designed tests are given to students to measure cognitive development, and detailed survey data from parents and schools are used to measure emotional, social, and physical development; the characteristics of the home environment; and the quality of the schooling environment. The child data were collected from trained evaluators who observed students while in school.

Years and Frequency: The baseline survey was conducted in 1999, with follow-ups in 1999–2000, 2002, 2004, and 2007.

Sample: A nationally representative sample of kindergartners was drawn from a stratified random sample of the population of kindergarten-age children. The sampling strategy was stratified by school, surveying 1,000 schools with about 22 individuals per school.

Sample size: The baseline sample was 22,000 children.

Geographic information: The data contain school identifiers, which are contained in the restricted-access data.

Major variables of interest: The most commonly used variables among education economists are those that measure cognitive outcomes and psychological outcomes. The data on school and home environments also have been valuable for examining early childhood environments. The detailed student background information, including parental income and education, is used extensively as well.

Data access: The data can be ordered on a CD from the National Center for Education Statistics at http://nces.ed.gov/ecls/kindergarten.asp or can be downloaded from ICPSR at the University of Michigan at http://www.icpsr.umich.edu. A restricted-data license application can be found at http://nces.ed.gov/pubsearch/licenses.asp.

National Longitudinal Survey of Youth (NLSY), 1979 and 1997

Overview: The National Longitudinal Survey of Youth, run by the Bureau of Labor Statistics, has been conducted twice. The first study began in 1979 with a nationally representative group of youths aged 14–22. They were surveyed annually between 1979 and 1980 and on a biennial basis since 1994. The second study began in 1997 with a set of nationally representative youths aged 12–16. Follow-ups are conducted every year. The data include extensive questions on educational enrollments, employment, earnings, demographics, household composition, marriage, and fertility. Respondents also are asked about a set of health outcomes and about involvement with the criminal justice system. Extensive data on student background characteristics include household income, parental education, the number of siblings, and mother's age at respondent's birth. Children of female NLSY79 respondents also have been followed since 1986 in a separate survey. A set of restricted-access data contains information on the specific postsecondary schools in which respondents enroll as well as the MSA in which they live. Finally, respondents in the NLSY79 were given the Armed Forces Qualifying Test (AFQT) in the base year, while the NLSY97 respondents took the Armed Services Vocational Aptitude Battery (ASVAB). Both exams are developed by the military and are considered to accurately measure one's cognitive ability.

Years: The NLSY79 baseline survey was conducted in 1979 and the NLSY97 baseline survey was conducted in 1997. Both surveys include follow-ups that are every year or every other year up to the present.

Frequency: Follow-ups to the baseline surveys are conducted yearly or biannually.

Sample: The NLSY79 is a nationally representative sample of youths aged 14–22. The NLSY97 is a nationally representative sample of youths aged 12–16.

Sample size: NLSY79 has a sample of 12,686 and the NLSY97 has a sample of 9,000.

Geographic information: The data contain state of residence and the data in the restricted-access version contain MSA of residence.

Major variables of interest: The most commonly used variables among education economists are those that describe educational attainment, the detailed set of student and household background characteristics, and the AFQT and ASVAB cognitive test scores. Many economists also use the geographic and postsecondary enrollment data that are included in the restricted-access version of the data. The labor force measures in the NLSY79 have been used extensively by economists examining the relationship between schooling and earnings, especially because the long nature of the panel allows one to examine earnings throughout much of the life course. The information on marriage and fertility and the data on students' noncognitive skills also have been used widely by economists.

Data access: The data can be accessed at the Bureau of Labor Statistics Web site at http://www.bls.gov/nls/. A restricted data license application can be found at http://www.bls.gov/nls/geocodeapp.htm.

Panel Study of Income Dynamics (PSID)

Overview: The Panel Study of Income Dynamics (PSID) is the longest-running longitudinal study in the United States. The panel began in 1968 with a nationally representative sample of 18,000 families. Every year since 1968 (every other year since 1997), these families and their lineal descendants have been surveyed. The PSID works like a household-level survey, except that when one member (usually a child) leaves the household, he or she is split off into his or her own household and is followed. Thus, it is possible to trace all PSID members descended from an original member back to the original member. The focus of the survey is on obtaining labor force and household demographic information, although limited information on educational attainment exists. The PSID also contains a child development supplement, which was conducted in 1997, 2002, and 2007 for children aged 0–12 in 1997 and their families. Detailed information on educational outcomes, test scores, psychological measures, and time use diaries are included in the child development supplement. One also can link these respondents to the main PSID data.

Years: The PSID began in 1968 and has been updated continually until today.

Frequency: Yearly until 1997, biannually after 1997.

Sample: The original sampling frame consisted of a random sample of U.S. households (the SRC sample) and an oversample of low-income families (the Survey of Economic Opportunity sample). Refresher samples have been added over time to help rebalance the demographic composition to reflect the U.S. population. In particular, in 1990 a set of 2,043 Hispanic households was added to help account for the post-1968 immigration of people from Mexico, Cuba, and Puerto Rico. In 1997, another immigrant sample was added.

Sample size: The current sample size is over 70,000 and can span as much as four decades of an individual's life.

Geographic information: The data contain MSA, county, census tract, and census block group of residence. These geographic codes are available only in the restricted-access version of the data.

Major variables of interest: The most commonly used variables among education economists are those that describe labor market outcomes, such as labor force participation, earnings, and hours worked. The PSID contains data only on years of education completed, not on degrees completed. In addition there is not information on the postsecondary schools students attend. The detailed set of student and household background characteristics as well the time use and child development measures in the child development supplements also are widely used. The child development supplement contains cognitive test scores, but the main sample was not given exams. The PSID also has widely used detailed information on marriage, fertility, and household composition changes over time.

Data access: The data can be accessed at the PSID Web site: http://simba.isr.umich.edu/data/data.aspx. A restricted-data license application can be found at http://simba.isr.umich.edu/restricted/RestrictedUse.aspx.

A.3 State Administrative Data Sets

Recent years have witnessed a rise in the use by education researchers of administrative state data sets on K–12 and postsecondary student outcomes. In some cases, these data sets also have links to earnings records reported through state unemployment insurance records. These data sets have the benefits of being administrative, so there is little measurement error in the variables that can come with individually reported outcomes, and the samples are large. Typically, the data include every student in the state. In this section, we describe the administrative data sets from the three states that have the best-established and most widely used data: Texas, North Carolina, and Florida.

Texas

Overview: The Texas administrative data come from three sources. This first, from the Texas Education Agency (TEA), is data on all K–12 students in public schools in Texas. The data include information on standardized test scores for all state standardized tests, grade and school, and yearly enrollment information. The data also contain information on a limited set of students' demographic characteristics, such as whether the student qualified for free and reduced-price lunch, race/ethnicity, sex, whether the student is limited in English proficiency or is gifted and talented, and whether the student qualifies for special education services. Which teachers are teaching in which schools and grades is contained in the data as well, but one cannot link students to specific teachers in the Texas data.

The second source of data is the Texas Higher Education Coordinating Board (THECB). It provides administrative data on all higher education students attending public colleges or universities (including community colleges) in Texas. The THECB data do not contain full transcripts, but they do contain semester-by-semester enrollment information, grade credits attempted and earned (from which one can calculate GPA), major, and degrees earned. For students applying to a four-year school, the data contain parental income and education from the college application as well. Beginning in 2000, financial aid data are included in the data. Students in the THECB data can be linked to students in the TEA data with a unique ID, which allows one to follow a Texas student from kindergarten through the completion of college if he or she remains in Texas.

The third source of data is quarterly earnings data for all workers in Texas from the Texas Workforce Commission (TWC). Most workers in Texas pay unemployment insurance, and as part of this payment their quarterly earnings are reported to the TWC. These data can be linked to the TEA and THECB data, so that one can link the education outcomes to earnings outcomes. A main limitation of these data is that those who leave the state or do not work are not in the earnings data. Thus, it is not possible to know whether a Texas student left Texas or is simply not working. It also is not possible to determine industry or occupation or to measure hours of work with these data.

Years: The TEA and THECB data are available from 1992 to the present. The TWC earnings data are available from 1990 to the present.

Sample size: The sample sizes of the various data sets vary, but there are over 1.4 billion observations in total.

Geographic information: Full information on the high school and all colleges attended are in the data. No information on place of residence is recorded in these data sets, however.

Data access: Access to these data is highly restricted and is approved by an appointed board on a project-by-project basis. A synthetic version of the data that contains the correct structure and variable names with fake information is available at http://www.utdallas.edu/research/tsp-erc/data-holdings.html. Information on applying for a data license can be found at http://www.utdallas.edu/research/tsp-erc/access.html.

North Carolina

Overview: The North Carolina administrative data share many features with the Texas data. These data are stored at the North Carolina Education Research Data Center (NCERDC), and they contain administrative data on all North Carolina public school students and teachers. The student data contain a detailed battery of state test scores, behavioral and disciplinary outcomes, demographic information on race/ethnicity and sex, free and reduced-price lunch status, parental education, special education status, and limited English proficiency. Like the Texas data, the North Carolina data contain unique student IDs that allow one to follow students over time, even as they switch public schools. The school in which each student enrolls in each year is known, as are the grade and specific classroom of each student. High school transcripts are available from 2005 onward, and SAT scores are available beginning in 2009. Unlike the Texas data, the North Carolina data do not contain links to higher education and earnings outcomes. But they do allow one to link students to specific teachers. Furthermore, the data contain information on teachers' characteristics, such as experience, absences, licensure, teacher certification exam scores, the college from which the teacher graduated, and whether the teacher has a master's degree.

Years: The NCERDC data are available from 1995 to the present, but not all information is available in every year.

Sample size: All K–12 students attending public schools (including charter schools) in North Carolina are in the data.

Geographic information: The address of each student's house, as well as the location of the school he or she attends, is in the data.

Data access: Access to these data is highly restricted and is granted by NCERDC on a project-by-project basis. Information on applying for a data license can be found at http://childandfamilypolicy.duke.edu/wp-content/uploads/2013/08/Procedures-for-Obtaining-Data.pdf.

Florida

Overview: The Florida PK-20 data set contains administrative data from pre-kindergarten through college completion for all students enrolling in public schools in Florida. In this way, it is very similar to the Texas data, and researchers also have been successful in combining these data with unemployment insurance data from Florida. The data contain detailed information on courses taken, student demographics, and any student disabilities. Thus, one can construct GPAs for students, and as in the other state data sets, a complete set of state standardized test results is included. The data also link students to the specific instructors who teach their courses, much as in the North Carolina data. As with all of these data sets, one can follow students longitudinally using unique identification numbers combined with information about what school, grade, and classroom each student is in in each year. The PK-20 data set also has extensive information about teachers, including compensation, demographics, whether the teacher has a master's degree, experience, and licensure. The higher education data contain SAT scores, institutions attended, the timing of all enrollment spells in a given school, financial aid amounts from different sources, student employment, courses taken, and any educational awards received.

Years: The PK-20 data are available from 1995 to the present, but not all information is available in every year.

Sample size: All PK–12 and higher education students attending public schools (including charter schools) in Florida are in the data.

Geographic information: The school each student attends is in the data, which makes it straightforward to link each student to a geographic area.

Data access: Access to these data is highly restricted and is granted by the Florida Department of Education on a project-by-project basis. Information on applying for a data license can be found at http://www.fldoe.org/accountability/data-sys/edw/.

A.4 Institutional-Level Data from the U.S. Department of Education

The U.S. Department of Education collects administrative data on all institutions of higher education and K–12 schools operating in the United States. These data are essential to measuring the number of schools in each area, the types of schools in each area, the distribution of student enrollments across different school types, and school district and institutional finances. Because these data include a census of every school in the country, they are used extensively among education researchers.

Integrated Postsecondary Education Data System (IPEDS)

Overview: IPEDS is the main source for information on postsecondary institutions in the United States. The data come from a series of nine surveys conducted by NCES, and completing a survey is mandatory for any postsecondary institution that participates in federal financial assistance programs. This covers virtually every school in the United States. The data cover an extensive range of institutional characteristics and outcomes. There is detailed information on institutional characteristics, such as the institution's level (less than two-year, two-year, four-year), control (public or private), location, types of programs, and admissions requirements. Information on institutional prices, including room and board, tuition, and fees for undergraduate and graduate students (separately for in-state and out-of-state students), are collected as well. IPEDS includes detailed financial data: revenues by source (e.g., federal, state, local, tuition, and endowment), expenditures by category (e.g., instructional, student services, research), and financial aid expenditures. As well, the data contain detailed yearly enrollment numbers by the level of the student, race, sex, full- or part-time status, prior postsecondary experience, age, and residence. Information on the faculty and staff of each college and university, including faculty salaries, the numbers of each level of faculty member (e.g., lecturer, assistant, associate or full professor), and faculty race/ethnicity and sex, are collected by IPEDS. As well, in recent years institutional outcomes have been collected, such as retention rates and 150% graduation rates (i.e., the proportion of an entering class who graduate in three years from a two-year school or in six years from a four-year school). Finally, IPEDS contains information on the number and types of degrees conferred, including the number of degrees of each type given in each major in each year.

Years: The data collections began in 1980, and in 1984 they began to be collected on a yearly basis. Many of the institutional outcomes data for the early years are not available. Prior to IPEDS, the U.S. Department of Education conducted the Higher Education General Information Survey (HEGIS). Beginning in 1965, this survey collected information similar to, although less extensive than, IPEDS.

Sample size: All postsecondary institutions in the United States participating in Title IV financial aid programs are included in the data. This is about 7,500 institutions per year.

Geographic information: Each school's address is included in the data, allowing one to map the specific location of each college and university.

Data access: These data are publicly available. IPEDS data can be downloaded at the IPEDS Datacenter: http://nces.ed.gov/ipeds/datacenter/. HEGIS data are available at ICPSR at the University of Michigan: http://www.icpsr.umich.edu.

Common Core of Data (CCD)

Overview: The Common Core of Data data set contains the characteristics and location of every school in the United States that teaches pre-K through twelfth grade. The data contain information aggregated to the district level and for each school; private, public, and charter schools are all included. The main focus of the data is on providing the characteristics of schools and school districts. The data include the location of each school, the control (public, charter), the grades covered, whether the school received Title I funding, and the proportion of students on free or reduced-price lunch. Overall enrollment, enrollment by grade, race/ethnicity, and sex, and the number of teachers also are included in the data. At the school district level, the CCD contains detailed information on finances, such as revenues by source and expenditures on broad areas (e.g., faculty salaries, support services, administration). Finally, the CCD data report the number of high school degrees granted in each year. These degree numbers often are used to calculate high school graduation rates. However, several researchers have documented problems with using these data to calculate high school graduation rates (Heckman and LaFontaine, 2010; Mishel and Roy, 2006); it is important to be aware of these limitations when using these data for this purpose.

Years: The CCD data collections began in the 1986–1987 school year and have been done annually since then.

Sample size: All public PK–12 schools and school districts in the United States are included in the data. This is about 103,000 schools per year and about 18,500 districts (local education agencies). However, exact numbers vary from year to year because of school openings and closings and school district mergers. Private schools are not included in the CCD.

Geographic information: Each school's address as well as the latitude and longitude is included in the data, allowing one to map the specific location of each school.

Data access: These data are publicly available and can be downloaded at http://nces.ed.gov/ccd/.

National Assessment of Education Progress (NAEP)

Overview: The National Assessment of Education Progress is a nationwide exam that is written and administered by the National Center for Education Statistics and is designed to measure what U.S. elementary and secondary students know. The exam is conducted among a stratified random sample of students in every state. It tests students in mathematics, reading, science, writing, arts, civics, economics, geography, and U.S. history. However, the mathematics and reading assessments are done with the most regularity, so these are the exam scores most used by economists and other researchers. The tests are changed only minimally over time, which allows one to use trends in NAEP scores as a benchmark with which to measure changes in the knowledge of U.S. students over time. National exam scores as well as scores for most states and by race/ethnicity and sex are available.

There are two versions of the NAEP. The main NAEP is administered to fourth-, eighth-, and twelfth-grade students across the country in a broad set of subjects. Results by subject for the United States and by state are publicly available. These data are mostly used to compare students' knowledge across states using a common baseline.

The long-term trend NAEP is given to 9-, 13-, and 17-year-old students in math and reading every four years. This version of the NAEP is specifically designed to track students' knowledge and skills in math and reading over time. Results from the long-term trend NAEP are available only at the national level and by race/ethnicity and sex.

Scoring is done either by computer for multiple-choice questions or by trained evaluators using detailed scoring guidelines for open-ended questions. Scorers are independent, and thus they are not teachers or employees of the schools in which the students are enrolled. The NAEP is administered as a stratified random sample across schools, much as sampling is done for the NCES longitudinal data sets. First, a nationally representative and state representative set of schools is selected, and then students at each school are randomly selected to take the NAEP exam. Each year, a new set of schools is selected, although because the selection of schools is random (conditional on a set of characteristics), some schools participate more often than others. Both scaled scores that provide a measure of knowledge in each subject and the proportion of students hitting "basic," "proficient," and "advanced" benchmarks are reported.

Years: The main NAEP has been conducted every two to four years since 1990. The long-term NAEP has been conducted every four to five years since 1971.

Sample size: The number of students who take the NAEP varies. For the main NAEP, about 3,000 students across 100 schools are selected in each state. For the long-term trend NAEP, the sample sizes vary from about 6,000 to 20,000 students. Individual student scores are not available, however, and so the sample sizes in each year are limited to either one number for the nation (separately by race/ethnicity and sex) or to a score for each of the 50 states.

Geographic information: State identifiers are available. In some cases, school district identifiers can be obtained through a restricted data license from the National Center for Education Statistics.

Data access: These data are publicly available and can be downloaded at http://www.nationsreportcard.gov/. A restricted-data license application can be found at http://nces.ed.gov/pubsearch/licenses.asp.

Glossary

ability bias The bias that occurs when differences in underlying labor market productivity or ability lead people to obtain different levels of education. In such a case, comparing earnings across workers with different education levels will provide a biased estimate of the returns to education, as these workers also differ in terms of their underlying productivity.

academic tracking Separating students by academic ability groups.

adequate yearly progress (AYP) Defined by each state and refers to schools meeting certain benchmarks regarding the proportion of students passing state exams and graduating from high school.

adjusted available income (AAI) The sum of 12% of discretionary net worth and available income.

allocative efficiency When there is no reorganization of resources across schools or students that could improve outcomes for at least some students without making any worse off.

allocative inefficiency Requires that no reorganization of production or consumption could make everyone better off. In the case of higher education, allocative efficiency occurs when it is not possible to reallocate students across institutions in a way that will increase.

alternatively certified teachers Teachers working in public schools but who have not yet met all the requirements for certification. Typically, these teachers are working towards traditional certification while they are teaching.

asymmetric information Arises when one individual or group in a market transaction has more information about the product or good being sold than another individual or group in the transaction.

attendance zone A geographic area in which all children are assigned to attend the same local school. The attendance zone thus determines which school in the district a student will attend at each level of schooling absent school choice.

available income (AI) The amount of parental income net of allowances for financial aid determination.

average treatment effect on the treated (ATT) The average effect of the treatment on those who participate in the treatment. In the context of charter schools, it is the effect on measured outcomes of enrolling in a charter school for a year.

Baumol's law (Baumol's cost disease) Faculty salaries in higher education will increase in response to increases in high-skilled labor productivity in other sectors of the economy. This forces costs up in higher education if there are no labor-saving productivity changes to compensate.

Bennett hypothesis Increases in financial aid will lead to increases in tuition as schools attempt to capture some of the financial aid funds for themselves.

biased estimator A method of estimating causal effects is biased if, on average, the resulting estimate differs from the true causal effect.

budget constraint The trade-off between inputs given input prices. The slope of the budget constraint is given by the relative prices of inputs, and the location of the constraint is determined by the overall amount of money the school has to spend.

capitalization (of school quality into home prices) The extent to which quality differences across schools are reflected in price differences across houses in different school attendance zones.

categorical aid Revenue that is directed to students who fit into a defined category, such as being from a low-income family or having a learning disability.

causal link (between two variables) altering one variable leads directly to a change in the other variable. That is, a change in one variable results in a change in another.

charter schools An independently managed and publicly funded school operated in accordance with a "charter" granted by the state or local government. Charter schools typically have some autonomy from local regulations while they maintain accountability for student performance.

choice (in education markets) The ability of students and families to select the school in which the student enrolls regardless of where the family lives.

cohort default rate (CDR) The proportion of a graduating class who enter default on their student loans over a given period. We typically focus on the two-year CDR, which shows the default rate over a two-year period.

collateralized loan A loan in which there is a physical asset (such as a house or car) that the lender can seize if the loan is not paid back. The existence of a physical asset significantly reduces the financial risk to the lender, as the asset can be sold to recoup at least some of the lender's money if the borrower defaults.

collective bargaining The process by which a union negotiates a labor contract with an employer. For teachers, their union collectively negotiates their contract with the school district in which they work.

compensating differential The wage increase necessary to compensate a worker for taking a job with an attribute he does not like.

compensatory resource allocation Provides more resources to students from disadvantaged backgrounds whose families have fewer nonschool resources.

competition (in education markets) Arises when students have a choice over which school to attend, leading schools to compete for enrollment.

complementarity of skills (across occupations) The extent to which occupation-specific skill or ability in one occupation is positively correlated with occupation-specific skill or ability in another occupation.

complementary resource allocation Provides more resources to students who have access to higher levels of resources outside of the schooling environment.

constant returns to scale Doubling all inputs exactly doubles output.

correlation The extent to which variables move together in the data.

cost minimization The objective of a firm that is analogous to profit maximization. The firm's goal is to produce a given output at the minimum possible cost. This will lead to the same allocation as trying to maximize profits.

counterfactual What would have happened to an individual in the absence of the treatment.

credit constraint Limitation that arises when an individual cannot borrow money or cannot borrow money at a sufficiently low interest rate to finance an educational investment that would have a positive rate of return if the individual could borrow at the market rate.

customer input technology A production technology in which those who purchase the outputs are also inputs. In terms of education, student effort is an important input into the production of the knowledge and skills that form the output of the education process. This is in contrast to the production of a typical commodity, in which the quality of the final product is unrelated to which consumers purchase it.

decreasing returns to scale Doubling all inputs less than doubles output.

demonstrated need The maximum amount of financial aid a student can receive under the Federal Methodology.

dependent variable In a regression, the variable we are seeking to explain with the independent or explanatory variables. It is the outcome of interest in a regression.

diminishing marginal product The marginal product of a given input declines as additional units of the input are added, holding all other inputs fixed. Adding additional units of an input, holding other inputs fixed, eventually will make each of those units less and less important for production.

diminishing marginal returns Productivity of a given input declines as additional units of the input are added, holding all other inputs fixed. Adding additional units of an input, holding other inputs fixed, will eventually make each of those units less important for production.

discretionary net worth The difference between total assets (excluding housing) and the asset protection level that applies to the given household.

dummy variable A binary variable that takes on a value of 1 if a condition is met and zero if not. For example, the variable *Georgia* takes on a value of 1 if the observation is for Georgia and a value of zero if the observation is for any other state.

duty-to-bargain law Employers' legal duty to engage in collective bargaining in good faith with their employees' elected union of choice.

econometrics The use of statistical techniques to measure relationships among variables in data.

economics The study of how limited resources are allocated to help satisfy unlimited human wants.

economies of scale Refers to a situation in which the average costs of operation decline with the scale of the operation. In terms of schooling, this means the average operating cost of a school or district is declining with the number of kids enrolled. Economies of scale occur in firms in which there are large fixed costs of operation: As scale increases, fixed costs are spread over a larger number of outputs, which leads to declining average costs.

economies of scope Occur when there are complementarities across the production of various outputs of a firm or institution. These complementarities make it less expensive to produce these outputs jointly rather than separately in different institutions.

education production function The process by which the outcomes of education, such as cognitive ability and knowledge, are produced from the "raw" inputs.

effect size The impact of an intervention in standard deviation units of the outcome. For Project STAR, it is the effect of small classes in terms of the standard deviation of test scores.

efficient in production Refers to the case of when there is no way to combine the school's resources to produce a higher level of outputs.

equalization aid Revenue that is distributed based on the socioeconomic or financial characteristics of the school district, with the intent of equalizing per-pupil expenditures across districts.

equity–efficiency trade-off To make allocations more equal, distortionary taxes are needed that make production less efficient.

expected family contribution (EFC) The government's assessment of how much each family can afford to contribute towards paying for college costs.

external validity The extent to which we can generalize results from an empirical study to other settings.

fixed effects estimator Fixed effects control for fixed differences across units of observation and across different units of time with a series of indicator variables for each unit of analysis and each unit of time. For example, a fixed effects estimator with observations of students in each year would include an indicator variable for each student and an indicator variable for each year.

flagship universities The most selective and highest-resource four-year public universities in each state. Most states explicitly designate one or two schools as their flagship institution.

foregone earnings The earnings one would have received in the labor market during the period of enrollment in school if he or she had not been in school.

Free Application for Federal Student Aid (FAFSA) The application all students must fill out to receive federal financial aid.

free rider problem A situation that occurs when people can benefit from goods and services without paying for them, often resulting in underprovision of collective and public goods. Because each person's contribution is a small part of the total and as all members of the community receive these goods and services, individuals will find it in their best interest to spend little and free-ride on the donations of others. This leads to underprovision of the good or service.

fuzzy regression discontinuity design A regression discontinuity design in which the likelihood of treatment changes by less than 1 at the threshold.

Hanushek critique The argument that there is little correlation between the amount schools spend on students and measured academic outcomes in the context of the observed organizational structure of the schools.

Hawthorne effects What happens when people know they are part of an experiment and behave in a way that is more likely to make the hypothesis being tested seem true.

heterogeneity Across higher education institutions; refers to the fact that there are many different types of postsecondary institutions in this country. They differ along many dimensions, including their academic focus, selectivity, resources available, and whether they are publicly or privately controlled.

heterogeneous treatment effects When the treatment has different effects on those with different background characteristics. For example, financial aid policies likely have heterogeneous effects on low- versus high-income students.

homeschooling The practice of providing all education services at home rather than in a public or private school.

horizontal equity Agents from the same circumstances face the same burden or receive the same benefit in a tax or transfer system.

human capital The skills, knowledge, and attributes of a worker that have value in the labor market.

human capital earnings function An equation that relates how earnings change with respect to years of schooling and work experience.

human capital model This model, pioneered by Gary Becker, explains the decision to invest in human capital (such as education) that is rewarded with higher future earnings.

incentive compatibility constraints A set of conditions that ensure workers will only behave in such a way that maximizes their net benefit. In terms of the signaling model, this means they will not invest in a signal unless the benefit of the investment outweighs the cost.

incentive pay (merit pay) A contract under which a worker's compensation is tied to the amount of output he or she produces. For teachers, merit pay usually refers to the practice of paying teachers for their students' test score levels or gains.

increasing returns to scale Doubling all inputs more than doubles output.

independent variable (explanatory variable) The variable in a regression used to describe the dependent variable or outcome of interest.

index A worker characteristic that cannot be changed, such as race/ethnicity or gender. An index is distinguished from a signal by the fact that workers can obtain a given signal by investing in it, while an index cannot be changed.

indifference curves Different combinations of goods that produce the same level of utility (well-being).

inputs Factors used in the process of production. With respect to education, any factors or resources that contribute to building an individual's cognitive ability or knowledge.

inputs into education Any factors or resources that contribute to building an individual's cognitive ability or knowledge.

instrument (instrumental variable) A variable that isolates variation in the treatment that is uncorrelated with underlying characteristics of those who are treated or untreated.

integrated market Combines markets that are separated geographically, thus increasing the effective market size for a given consumer. When markets are more integrated, there are increased opportunities to differentiate products, resulting in better matching of consumer (student) preferences to choices over products (colleges).

intent-to-treat (ITT) The effect of being offered the opportunity to be treated on outcomes. In the context of charter schools, the ITT is the effect on outcomes of the student being offered admission to the charter school.

internal validity The extent to which the estimated causal effect of the treatment is unbiased.

isoquant Shows combinations of inputs that can be combined to produce the same amount of an output.

local average treatment effect (LATE) The treatment effect among those individuals who are induced to change their behavior because of an intervention or natural experiment. In an instrumental variables setting, the LATE refers to the group whose behavior is impacted by the instrument. The effect estimated is therefore local to this group.

long-run credit constraints Occur when the lack of access to financial resources throughout a child's life leads to persistent underinvestment in human capital. The result is the student will be less academically prepared for college by the end of high school than if his or her family had access to resources that would have allowed them to make human capital investment at their desired levels throughout the student's life.

magnet schools Public schools that focus on teaching high-achieving students. They typically are high schools, and admission sometimes is determined using performance on standardized tests.

marginal product (MP) The change in output generated by employing one more unit of a particular input, holding all other inputs fixed.

marginal product of labor A worker's contribution to overall firm profits or output.

marginal rate of return The percentage gain in earnings, net of costs, from purchasing an additional unit of the investment. With respect to schooling, it is the percentage change in earnings, net of costs, to obtaining an extra year of education.

marginal rate of substitution The ratio of marginal utilities of two goods. It shows the utility trade-off between these goods.

marginal social rate of return (MSRR) The rate of return to an individual's education investment that accrues to society at large. The *MSRR* depends on both the private and social returns to education.

market for education or **education market** The mechanism through which education services are exchanged.

market rate of return The financial return an individual can expect from investing money in typical financial vehicles, like stocks or bonds.

mixed market A market in which institutions controlled publicly and privately are in competition with each other.

natural experiments (quasi-experimental designs) Use of variation in treatment exposure determined by nature or changes in policy that are outside the control of the researcher but nevertheless approximate random assignment.

net present value The value today of a stream of current and future inflows and outflows of cash. In education, the net present value of a schooling investment is the value today of the change in wages that will be earned sometime in the future because of the increase in education net of the cost of investing in an education today.

No Child Left Behind (NCLB) Act The signature education initiative of the George W. Bush Administration. A nationwide accountability system in which states would set goals for schools to meet. Those not meeting these goals would be subject to sanctions.

nondistribution constraint Because there are no residual shareholders in a nonprofit, those who exercise control over the organization cannot receive residual earnings. In theory, this should reduce incentives to take advantage of consumers and ensure that donations are used for their intended purposes.

nonprofit Enterprise in which there are no residual shareholders; all differences between revenue and expenses are retained to fulfill the organization's missions; no individual can take that profit for personal use. Non-profit and public universities in the United States benefit from tax-favored status. The difference between revenues and expenditures is exempt from taxation, and these institutions can receive tax-deductible donations.

normal good A good whose consumption increases when income increases. That is, when people have more money, they purchase more of a normal good.

omitted variables In a regression, any variables that are correlated with both the treatment and the outcome that are not included in the estimation.

omitted variables bias The bias that occurs when a variable is correlated with both the treatment and the outcome but is not included in the regression. This creates a bias in the estimate of the causal effect of the treatment, the sign of which depends on how the omitted variable is correlated with the treatment and with the outcome.

on-the-job training Employer-provided training that occurs while workers are employed and that increases worker skills.

open enrollment Policy allowing students to attend another school in the district or in the state regardless of where the student lives. The ability to enroll in another school depends on the school having space for additional students.

opportunity cost The value of the other goods or activities you have to give up to engage in an activity or purchase a given good. For example, the opportunity cost of studying for this class is the value to you of studying for other classes, or of sleeping, working, or spending time with your friends.

outcome of education Any knowledge, skill, or attribute that is a result of participation in the education process.

payment-to-income ratio The ratio of student debt payments to income.

perfectly competitive market (perfect competition) A market in which it is easy to enter and exit and all firms are price takers in the sense that the quantity they sell does not affect the market price.

pooling equilibrium A signaling equilibrium in which all workers invest identically in the signal and therefore are paid identical wages.

preference revelation How localities can learn the true preferences of residents to be able to tax them in accordance with their desired level of the public good or service.

present value The value today of inflows of cash (e.g., wages) that will be earned sometime in the future.

price discrimination Occurs when a firm charges different customers different prices for reasons that are not related to the cost of providing the good or service.

principal-agent models Models of worker and employer behavior when the goals of the employee (the agent) are not perfectly aligned with those of the employer (the principal).

private return to education The return on an education investment that accrues only to the individual.

production function Specifies the way in which a set of inputs are combined to produce a final product.

production possibilities frontier (PPF) The combinations of outcomes that are feasible when all available resources are employed efficiently.

productive efficiency (efficiency in production) When a school is distributing inputs in such a way as to maximize total output.

Project STAR The largest randomized class size experiment in the United States, conducted in Tennessee in the mid-1980s among students in grades K–3.

publicly funded education Education that is paid for by government revenues. Education that is publicly financed does not need to be publicly provided.

publicly provided education Education that is operated and controlled by a public entity.

randomized controlled trial (RCT) An experiment in which people are randomly assigned to the treatment and control groups. On average, this makes the two groups identical but for receiving the treatment.

return to scale The rate of increase in output in relation to an increase in the inputs.

running variable (forcing variable) The variable that describes how close an individual is to a treatment threshold in a regression discontinuity design.

scarcity Having too few resources to satisfy individuals' unlimited desire to consume goods and services.

school finance The revenue sources that fund schooling. We are interested in the source of these funds, the level of funds, and the distribution of funds across schools.

school finance reform The set of legal and legislative changes designed to decouple the link between property values

and education spending and to increase equity in per-pupil spending across schools within a state, as well as the adequacy of education services.

school vouchers Money to students to apply toward tuition at a private school.

selection bias The bias that occurs because individuals choose whether they are part of the treatment or control group based on characteristics or preferences related to an outcome. This can lead to the characteristics of those in the treatment group being systematically different from those in the control group.

separating equilibrium A signaling equilibrium in which workers of different productivity levels obtain different schooling amounts and thus get paid different wages.

sheepskin effect The phenomenon that the return to a year of education is higher when that year includes the awarding of a degree or education credential.

short-run credit constraint When a student has a positive return on an education investment but is unable to borrow at a sufficiently low interest rate to finance the investment.

signal A malleable characteristic of a worker that can provide information to employers about the worker's underlying productivity.

signaling equilibrium When employers' beliefs about the relationship between worker productivity and a signal are true. In turn, wages reflect the expected value of productivity among workers who invest in the signal. A signaling equilibrium exists when the productivity of workers who invest in a given signal matches the initial beliefs of the employer about the productivity of these employees.

skill-biased technological change (SBTC) Growth or changes in the economy that favor higher-skilled workers over lower-skilled workers. An example of SBTC is the introduction of computers, which made higher-skilled workers who knew how to use computers more productive and replaced many low-skilled jobs.

social returns to education The returns on an individual's education investment that go to society at large rather than to the individual herself.

spillovers (externalities) Occur when an individual's market transaction affects other members of the economy.

stratification In higher education; describes the hierarchical distribution of resources in which some institutions have markedly higher resource levels than others.

teacher certification policies Rules about the amount and type of education and apprenticeship experience a teacher must have to work in public schools in the state.

test-based accountability Policies that provide rewards and/or sanctions to teachers, schools, and students based on their performance on a set of measurable student outcomes, such as standardized tests.

Tiebout sorting The process by which families will sort across localities to find the locality that has the right mix of taxes and public services to match their preferences.

Title I A federal grant program providing funding to schools that serve a large number of students from low-income families

treatment effect The causal effect of the treatment on a specific outcome.

utility function How each person's happiness or well-being is affected by the addition or subtraction of an additional good, holding all other goods constant.

value-added (of a teacher) His or her contribution to student test score gains.

vertical equity Effort to pay or burden among agents from different circumstances is the same in the distribution of subsidies or the assessment of taxes. In the context of financial aid, it requires that all families put forth the same effort in paying for college relative to their financial resources.

References

Chapter 1

Gruber, Jonathan. *Public Finance and Public Policy*, 5th ed. New York: Worth Publishers, 2016.

Hanushek, Eric A., and Ludger Woessmann. "The Role of Cognitive Skills in Economic Development." *Journal of Economic Literature* 46, no. 3 (2008): 607–68.

Hanushek, Eric A., Paul E. Peterson, and Ludger Woessmann. *Endangering Prosperity*. Washington, DC: Brookings Institution Press, 2016.

Neal, Derek, and Diane W. Schanzenbach. "Left Behind by Design: Proficiency Counts and Test-Based Accountability." *Review of Economics and Statistics* 92, no. 2 (2010): 263–83.

Chapter 2

Autor, David H. 2014. "Skills, Education, and the Rise of Earnings Inequality Among the 'Other 99 Percent'." *Science* 344(6186): 843–51.

Autor, David H., Lawrence F. Katz, and Melissa S. Kearney. "Trends in U.S. Wage Inequality: Revising the Revisionists." *Review of Economics and Statistics* 90, no. 2 (2008): 300–23.

Bayer, Patrick, Fernando Ferreira, and Robert McMillan. "A Unified Framework for Measuring Preferences for Schools and Neighborhoods." *Journal of Political Economy* 115, no. 4 (2007): 588–638.

Black, Sandra. "Do Better Schools Matter? Parental Valuation of Elementary Education." *Quarterly Journal of Economics* 114, no. 2 (1999): 577–99.

Currie, Janet, and Duncan Thomas. "Does Head Start Make a Difference?" *American Economic Review* 85, no. 3 (1995): 341–64.

DeLong, Bradford J., Claudia Goldin, and Lawrence F. Katz. "Sustaining U.S. Economic Growth." In *Agenda for the Nation*, edited by H. J. Aaron, J. M. Lindsay, and P. S. Nivola. Washington, DC: The Brookings Institution, 2003.

Deming, David, and Susan Dynarski. "The Lengthening of Childhood." *Journal of Economic Perspectives* 22, no. 3 (2008): 71–92.

Elder, Todd E., and Darren H. Lubotsky. "Kindergarten Entrance Age and Children's Achievement: Impacts of State Policies, Family Background, and Peers." *Journal of Human Resources* 44, no. 3 (2009): 641–83.

Fitzpatrick, Maria D. "Starting School at Four: The Effect of Universal Pre-Kindergarten on Children's Academic Achievement." *The B. E. Journal of Economic Analysis & Policy* 8, no. 1 (2008): 46.

Friedman, Milton. *The Role of Government in Education*. New Brunswick, NJ: Rutgers University Press, 1955.

Freeman, Richard. *The Overeducated American*. New York: Academic Press, 1976.

Garces, Eliana, Duncan Thomas, and Janet Currie. "Longer-Term Effects of Head Start." *American Economic Review* 92, no. 4 (2002): 999–1012.

Goldin, Claudia. "America's Graduation from High School: The Evolution and Spread of Secondary Schooling in the Twentieth Century." *Journal of Economic History* 58, no. 2 (1998): 345–74.

Goldin, Claudia. "A Brief History of Education in the United States." In *Historical Statistics of the United States*. New York: Cambridge University Press, 2005.

Goldin, Claudia, and Lawrence F. Katz. *The Race Between Education and Technology*. Cambridge, MA: Harvard University Press, 2008.

Goldin, Claudia, Lawrence F. Katz, and Ilyana Kuziemko. "The Homecoming of American College Women." *Journal of Economic Perspectives* 20, no. 4 (2006): 133–56.

Hansmann, Henry. "The Rationale for Exempting Nonprofit Organizations from Corporate Income Taxation." *Yale Law Journal* 91(November 1980): 54–100.

Heckman, James J., and Paul A. LaFontaine. "The American High School Graduation Rate: Trends and Levels." *Review of Economics and Statistics* 92, no. 2 (2010): 244–62.

Imberman, Scott, and Michael F. Lovenheim. "Does the Market Value Value-Added? Evidence from Housing Prices after Public Release of Teacher Value-Added." *Journal of Urban Economics* 91 (2016): 104–121.

Ludwig, Jens, and Douglas Miller. "Does Head Start Improve Children's Life Chances? Evidence from a Regression Discontinuity Design." *Quarterly Journal of Economics* 122, no. 1 (2007): 159–208.

Murphy, Kevin, and Finis Welch. "Wage Premiums for College Graduates: Recent Growth and Possible Explanations." *Educational Researcher* 18, no. 4 (1989): 17–26.

Winston, Gordon C. "Subsidies, Hierarchy and Peers: The Awkward Economics of Higher Education." *Journal of Economic Perspectives* 13, no. 1 (1999): 13–36.

Chapter 3

Angrist, Joshua D., and Alan B. Krueger. "Does Compulsory School Attendance Affect Schooling and Earnings?" *Quarterly Journal of Economics* 106, no. 4 (1991): 979–1014.

Angrist, Joshua D., and Jörn-Steffen Pischke. *Mostly Harmless Econometrics*. Princeton: Princeton University Press, 2009.

Angrist, Joshua, D. "American Education Research Changes Tack. *Oxford Review of Economic Policy* 20, no. 2 (2004): 198–212.

Bailey, Martha J., and Susan M. Dynarski. "Inequality in Postsecondary Education." In *Whither Opportunity? Rising Inequality, Schools, and Children's Life Chances*, edited by G. J. Duncan and R. J. Murnane. New York: Russell Sage, 2011.

Bonomi, Amy E., Julianna M. Nemeth, Lauren E. Altenburger, Melissa L. Anderson, Anastasia Snyder, and Irma Dotto. "Fiction or Not? *Fifty Shades* Is Associated with Health Risks in Adolescent and Young Adult Females." *Journal of Women's Health* 23, no. 9 (2014): 1–9.

Bui, Sa A., Steven G. Craig, and Scott A. Imberman. "Is Gifted Education a Bright Idea? Assessing the Impact of Gifted and Talented Programs on Students." *American Economic Journal: Economic Policy* 6, no. 3 (2014): 30–62.

Cornwell, Christopher, David B. Mustard, and Deepa J. Sridhar. "The Enrollment Effects of Merit-Based Financial Aid: Evidence from Georgia's HOPE Program." *Journal of Labor Economics* 24, no. 4 (2006): 761–86.

Dynarski, Susan. "Hope for Whom? Financial Aid for the Middle Class and Its Impact on College Attendance." *National Tax Journal* 53, no. 3 (2000): 629–61.

Goswami, Nina. "The Greater Your Weight, the Lower Your IQ, Say Scientists." *The Telegraph*, October 15, 2006. Accessed August 29, 2014. http://www.telegraph.co.uk/news/uknews/1531487/The-greater-your-weight-the-lower-your-IQ-say-scientists.html/.

Hahn, Jinyong, Petra Todd, and Wilbert Van der Klaauw. "Identification and Estimation of Treatment Effects with a Regression-Discontinuity Design." *Econometrica* 69, no. 1 (2001): 201–09.

Heckman, James J., and Jeffrey A. Smith. "Assessing the Case for Social Experiments." *Journal of Economic Perspectives* 9, no. 2 (1995): 85–110.

Kaplan, Karen. "Study: To boost Your Odds of a Successful Marriage, Have a Big Wedding." *Los Angeles Times*, August 20, 2014. Accessed August 29, 2014. http://www.latimes.com/science/sciencenow/la-sci-sn-high-quality-marriage-study-20140819-story.html#page=1.

Lovenheim, Michael F., and Emily G. Owens. "Does Federal Financial Aid Affect College Enrollment? Evidence from Drug Offenders and the Higher Education Act of 1998." *Journal of Urban Economics* 81 (2014): 1–13.

Murnane, Richard J., and John B. Willett. *Methods Matter: Improving Causal Inference in Educational and Social Science Research*. Oxford: Oxford University Press, 2011.

Smith, Philip H., Gregory G. Hornish, R. Lorraine Collins, Gary A. Giovino, Helene R. White, and Kenneth E. Leonard. "Couples' Marijuana Use Is Inversely Related to Their Intimate Partner Violence Over the First 9 Years of Marriage." *Psychology of Addictive Behaviors* 28, no. 3 (2014): 734–42.

Wang, Xiaoping, Roxana Odouli, and De-Kun Li. "Maternal Caffeine Consumption During Pregnancy and the Risk of Miscarriage: A Prospective Cohort Study." *American Journal of Obstetrics and Gynecology* 198, no. 3 (2008): 279.e1–279.e8.

Wooldridge, Jeffrey M. *Introductory Econometrics: A Modern Approach*. Boston: South-Western, Cengage Learning, 2009.

Chapter 4

Autor, David H., Lawrence F. Katz, and Melissa S. Kearney. "Trends in U.S. Wage Inequality: Revising the Revisionists." *Review of Economics and Statistics* 90, no. 2 (2008): 300–23.

Autor, David H., Frank Levy, and Richard J. Murnane. "The Skill Content of Recent Technological Change: An Empirical Exploration." *Quarterly Journal of Economics* 118, no. 4 (2003): 1279–333.

Becker, Gary S. "Investment in Human Capital: A Theoretical Analysis." *Journal of Political Economy* 70, no. 5 (1962): Part 2: Investment in Human Beings: 9–49.

Becker, Gary S. *Human Capital: A Theoretical and Empirical Analysis, With Special Reference to Education*. Chicago: University of Chicago Press, 1964.

Becker, Gary. *The Age of Human Capital*. 2002. Accessed June 19, 2014. http://media.hoover.org/sites/default/files/documents/0817928928_3.pdf.

Cascio, Elizabeth U., and Ayushi Narayan. "Who Needs a Fracking Education? The Educational Response to Low-Skill Biased Technological Change." Dartmouth College Working Paper, 2005.

Goldin, Claudia D., and Lawrence F. Katz. *The Race Between Education and Technology*. Cambridge: Harvard University Press, 2009.

Griliches, Zvi. "Estimating the Returns to Schooling: Some Econometric Problems." *Econometrica* 45, no. 1 (1977): 1–22.

Heckman, James J., and Bo E. Honore. "The Empirical Content of the Roy Model." *Journal of Political Economy* 58, no. 5 (1990): 1121–149.

Kane, Thomas J. *The Price of Admission: Rethinking How Americans Pay for College*. Washington, DC: Brookings Institution Press, 2010.

Katz, Lawrence F., and Kevin J. Murphy. "Changes in Relative Wages, 1963–1987: Supply and Demand Factors." *Quarterly Journal of Economics* 107, no. 1 (1992): 35–78.

Mincer, Jacob A. *Schooling, Experience, and Earnings: Human Behavior & Social Institutions No. 2*. New York: Columbia University Press for National Bureau of Economic Research, 1974.

Murphy, Kevin, and Finis Welch. "Wage Premiums for College Graduates: Recent Growth and Possible Explanations." *Education Researcher* 18, no. 4 (1989): 17–26.

Smith, Adam. *An Inquiry into the Nature and Causes of the Wealth of Nations*. London: W. Strahan and T. Cadell, 1776.

Story, Louise. "Schools That Train Real Estate Agents Are Booming, Too." *New York Times*, July 2, 2005.

Willis, Robert J., and Sherwin Rosen. "Education and Self-Selection." *Journal of Political Economy* 87, no. 5 (1979): 7–36.

Chapter 5

Cameron, Stephen V., and James J. Heckman. "The Nonequivalence of High School Equivalents." *Journal of Labor Economics* 11, no. 1 (1993): 1–47.

Clark, Damon, and Paco Martorell. "The Signaling Value of a High School Diploma." *Journal of Political Economy* 122, no. 2 (2014): 282–318.

Heckman, James J., and Paul A. LaFontaine. "Bias-Corrected Estimates of GED Returns." *Journal of Labor Economics* 24, no. 3 (2006): 661–700.

Hungerford, Thomas, and Gary Solon. "Sheepskin Effects in the Returns to Education." *Review of Economics and Statistics* 69, no. 1 (1987): 175–77.

Jaeger, David A., and Marianne E. Page. "Degrees Matter: New Evidence on Sheepskin Effects in the Returns to Education." *Review of Economics and Statistics* 78, no. 4 (1996): 733–40.

Spence, Michael A. "Job Market Signaling." *Quarterly Journal of Economics* 87, no. 3 (1975): 355–74.

Stiglitz, Joseph E. "The Theory of 'Screening,' Education, and the Distribution of Income." *American Economic Review* 65, no. 3 (1975): 283–300.

Tyler, John H., Richard J. Murnane, and John B. Willett. "Estimating the Labor Market Signaling Value of the GED." *Quarterly Journal of Economics* 115, no. 2 (2000): 431–86.

Chapter 6

Acemoglu, Daron, and Joshua D. Angrist. "How Large Are Human-Capital Externalities? Evidence from Compulsory-Schooling Laws." In *NBER Macroeconomics Annual* 15. Boston: MIT Press, 2001.

Andrews, RodneyJ., Jing Li and Michael F. Lovenheim. "Quantile Treatment Effects of College Quality on Earnings." *Journal of Human Resources*, 51, no. 1 (2016): 417.

Angrist, Joshua D., and Alan B. Krueger. "Does Compulsory School Attendance Affect Schooling and Earnings?" *Quarterly Journal of Economics* 106, no. 4 (1991): 979–1014.

Ashenfelter, Orley, and Alan B. Krueger. "Estimates of the Economic Return to Schooling from a New Sample of Twins." *American Economic Review* 84, no. 5 (1994): 1157–1173.

Ashenfelter, Orley, and Cecilia Rouse. "Income, Schooling, and Ability: Evidence from a New Sample of Identical Twins." *Quarterly Journal of Economics* 113, no. 1 (1998): 253–84.

Ashenfelter, Orley, and David J. Zimmerman. "Estimates of the Returns to Schooling from Sibling Data: Fathers, Sons, and Brothers." *Review of Economics and Statistics* 79, no. 1 (1997): 1–9.

Becker, Gary S. *Human Capital: A Theoretical and Empirical Analysis, With Special Reference to Education.* Chicago: University of Chicago Press, 1964.

Ben-Porath, Yoram. "The Production of Human Capital and the Life Cycle of Earnings." *Journal of Political Economy* 75, no. 4 (1967), Part 1: 352–65.

Behrmen, Jere R., and Mark R. Rosenzweig. "'Ability' Biases in Schooling Returns and Twins: A Test and New Estimates." *Economics of Education Review* 18, no. 2 (1999): 159–67.

Behrmen, Jere R., Mark R. Rosenzweig, and Paul Taubman. "Endowments and the Allocation of Schooling in the Family and in the Marriage Market: The Twins Experiment." *Journal of Political Economy* 102, no. 6 (1994): 1131–174.

Belzil, Christian. "The Return to Schooling in Structural Dynamic Models: A Survey." *European Economic Review* 51, no. 5 (2007): 1059–105.

Belzil, Christian, and Jorgen Hansen. "Unobserved Ability and the Return to Schooling." *Econometrica* 70, no. 5 (2002): 2075–091.

Bennett, William J., and David Wilezol. *Is College Worth It?: A Former United States Secretary of Education and a Liberal Arts Graduate Expose the Broken Promise of Higher Education.* Nashville, TN: Thomas Nelson, 2013.

Black, Dan A., and Jeffrey A. Smith. "How Robust Is the Evidence on the Effects of College Quality? Evidence from Matching." *Journal of Econometrics* 121, no. 1–2 (2004): 99–124.

Black, Dan A., and Jeffrey A. Smith. "Estimating the Returns to College Quality with Multiple Proxies for Quality." *Journal of Labor Economics* 24, no. 3 (2006): 701–28.

Bound, John, and David A. Jaeger. "Do Compulsory School Attendance Laws Alone Explain the Association Between Quarter of Birth and Earnings?" *Research in Labor Economics* 19 (2000): 83–108.

Bound, John, and Gary Solon. "Double Trouble: On the Value of Twins-Based Estimation of the Return to Schooling." *Economics of Education Review* 18, no. 2 (1999): 169–82.

Bound, John, Michael F. Lovenheim, and Sarah E. Turner. "Why Have College Completion Rates Declined? An Analysis of Changing Student Preparation and Collegiate Resources." *American Economic Journal: Applied Economics* 2, no. 3 (2010): 129–57.

Brewer, Dominic J., Eric R. Eide, and Ronald G. Ehrenberg. "Does It Pay to Attend an Elite Private College? Cross-Cohort Evidence on the Effects of College

Type on Earnings." *Journal of Human Resources* 34 , no. 1 (1999): 104–23.

Brock, William A., and Steven B. Durlauf. "What Have We Learned from a Decade of Empirical Research on Growth? Growth Empirics and Reality." *World Bank Economic Review* 15, no. 2 (2001): 229–72.

Buckles, Kasey S., and Daniel M. Hungerman. "Season of Birth and Later Outcomes: Old Questions, New Answers." *Review of Economics and Statistics* 95, no. 3 (2013): 711–24.

Card, David. "Using Geographic Variation in College Proximity to Estimate the Return to Schooling." In *Aspects of Labor Market Behaviour: Essays in Honour of John Vanderkamp*, edited by L. N. Christofides, E. K. Grant, and R. Swidinsky. Toronto: University of Toronto Press 1995.

Card, David. "The Causal Effect of Education on Earnings." In *Handbook of Labor Economics*, edited by Orley Ashenfelter and David Card, vol. 3A (1999). Amsterdam: Elsevier.

Card, David. "Estimating the Return to Schooling: Progress on Some Persistent Econometric Problems." *Econometrica* 69, no. 5 (2001): 1127–160.

Carneiro, Pedro, James J. Heckman, and Edward J. Vytlacil. "Estimating Marginal Returns to Education." *American Economic Review* 101, no. 6 (2011): 2754–781.

Carrell, Scott E., Richard L. Fullerton, and James E. West. "Does Your Cohort Matter? Measuring Peer Effects in College Achievement." *Journal of Labor Economics* 27, no. 3 (2009): 349–64.

Cascio, Elizabeth U., and Ethan G. Lewis. "Schooling and the Armed Forces Qualifying Test: Evidence from School-Entry Laws." *Journal of Human Resources* 41, no. 2 (2006): 294–318.

Dale, Stacey Berg, and Alan B. Krueger. "Estimating the Payoff to Attending a More Selective College: An Application of Selection on Observables and Unobservables." *Quarterly Journal of Economics* 117, no. 4 (2002): 1491–527.

Dale, Stacey B., and Alan B. Krueger. "Estimating the Effects of College Characteristics over the Career Using Administrative Earnings Data." *Journal of Human Resources* 49, no. 2 (2014): 323–58.

Dee, Thomas. "Are There Civic Returns to Education?" *Journal of Public Economics* 88, no. 9–10 (2004): 1697–720.

DeLong, J. Bradford, Claudia Goldin, and Laurence Katz. "Sustaining U.S. Economic Growth." In *Agenda for the Nation*, edited by H. Aaron, J. Lindsay, and P. Nivola, 17–60. Washington: Brookings Institution, 2003.

The Economist. "Is College Worth It?" April 5, 2014. http://www.economist.com/news/united-states/ 21600131-too-many-degrees-are-waste-money-return-higher-education-would-be-much-better.

Figlio, David N., Jonathan Guryan, Krzysztof Karbownik, and Jeffrey Roth. "The Effects of Poor Neonatal Health on Children's Cognitive Development." *American Economic Review* 104, no. 12 (2014): 3921–955.

Grilliches, Zvi. "Estimating the Returns to Schooling: Some Econometric Problems." *Econometrica* 45, no. 1 (1977): 1–22.

Hanushek, Eric A., and Ludger Woessmann. "The Role of Cognitive Skills in Economic Development." *Journal of Economic Literature* 46, no. 3 (2008): 607–68.

Heckman, James J., and Sergio Urzúa. "Comparing IV with Structural Models: What Simple IV Can and Cannot Identify." *Journal of Econometrics* 156, no. 1 (2010): 27–7.

Heckman, James J., Lance J. Lochner, and Petra E. Todd. "Earnings Functions, Rates of Return and Treatment Effects: The Mincer Equation and Beyond." *Handbook of the Economics of Education*, 1 (2006): 307–458.

Hoekstra, Mark. "The Effect of Attending the Flagship State University on Earnings: A Discontinuity-Based Approach." *Review of Economics and Statistics* 91, no. 4 (2009): 717–24.

Hoxby, Caroline M. "The Changing Selectivity of American Colleges." *Journal of Economic Perspectives* 23, no. 4 (2009): 95–118.

Kane, Thomas J., and Cecilia E. Rouse. "Labor Market Returns to Two- and Four-Year Colleges: Is a Credit a Credit and Do Degrees Matter?" NBER Working Paper No. 4268, 1993.

Kane, Thomas J., and Cecilia E. Rouse. "Labor-Market Returns to Two- and Four-Year College." *American Economic Review* 85, no. 3 (1995): 600–14.

Keane, Michael P., and Kenneth I. Wolpin. "The Career Decisions of Young Men." *Journal of Political Economy* 105, no. 3 (1997): 473–522.

Leigh, D.E., and A.M. Gill. "Do Community Colleges Really Divert Students from Earning Bachelor's Degrees?" *Economics of Education Review* 22, no. 1 (2003): 23–30.

Lemieux, Thomas. "The Mincer Equation Thirty Years after Schooling, Experience and Earnings." In *Jacob Mincer, A Pioneer of Modern Labor Economics*, edited by S. Grossbard Schechtman. New York: Springer Verlag, 2006.

Lochner, Lance, and Enrico Moretti. "The Effect of Education on Crime: Evidence from Prison Inmates, Arrests, and Self-Reports." *American Economic Review* 94, no. 1 (2004): 155–89.

Long, Bridget Terry, and Michal Kurlaender. "Do Community Colleges Provide a Viable Pathway to a Baccalaureate Degree?" *Education Evaluation and Policy Analysis* 31, no. 1 (2009): 30–53.

Long, Mark. "Changes in the Returns to Education and College Quality." *Economics of Education Review* 29, no. 3 (2010): 338–47.

Mincer, Jacob. "Investment in Human Capital and Personal Income Distribution." *Journal of Political Economy* 66, no. 4 (1958): 281–302.

Mincer, Jacob. *Schooling, Experience, and Earnings. Human Behavior & Social Institutions No. 2.* New York: Columbia University Press for National Bureau of Economic Research, 1974.

Moretti, Enrico. "Estimating the Social Return to Higher Education: Evidence From Longitudinal and Repeated Cross-Sectional Data." *Journal of Econometrics* 121, no. 1–2 (2004): 175–212.

Oreopoulos, Philip. "Estimating Average and Local Average Treatment Effects of Education When Compulsory Schooling Laws Really Matter." *American Economic Review* 96, no. 1 (2006): 152–75.

Reynolds, C. Lockwood. "Where to Attend? Estimating the Effects of Beginning College at a Two-Year Institution." *Economics of Education Review* 31, no. 4 (2012): 345–62.

Rouse, Cecilia E. "Democratization or Diversion? The Effect of Community Colleges on Educational Attainment." *Journal of Business and Economic Statistics* 13, no. 2 (1995): 217–24.

Rouse, Cecilia E. "Further Estimates of the Economic Return to Schooling from a New Sample of Twins." *Economics of Education Review* 18, no. 2 (1999): 149–57.

Roy, Andrew D. "Some Thoughts on the Distribution of Earnings." *Oxford Economic Papers* 3, no. 2 (1951): 135–46.

Sacerdote, Bruce. "Peer Effects with Random Assignment: Results for Dartmouth Roommates." *Quarterly Journal of Economics* 116, no. 2 (2001): 681–704.

Sandy, Jonathan, Aruto Gonzalez, and Michael J. Hilmer. "Alternative Paths to College Completion: Effect of Attending a 2-Year School on the Probability of Completing a 4-Year Degree." *Economics of Education Review* 25, no. 5 (2006): 463–71.

Stinebrickner, Ralph, and Todd R. Stinebrickner. "What Can be Learned about Peer Effects Using College Roommates? Evidence from New Survey Data and Students from Disadvantaged Backgrounds." *Journal of Public Economics* 90, no. 8–9 (2006): 1435–454.

Willis, Robert J., and Sherwin Rosen. "Education and Self-Selection." *Journal of Political Economy* 87, no. 5 (1979): 7–36.

Zimmerman, David J. "Peer Effects in Academic Outcomes: Evidence from a Natural Experiment." *Review of Economics and Statistics* 85, no. 1 (2003): 9–23.

Zimmerman, Seth. "The Returns to Four-Year College for Academically Marginal Students." *Journal of Labor Economics* 32, no. 4 (2014): 711–54.

Chapter 7

Angrist, Joshua, and Victor Lavy. "New Evidence on Classroom Computers and Pupil Learning." *The Economic Journal* 112, no. 482 (2002): 735–65.

Cunha, Flavio, and James Heckman. "The Technology of Skill Formation." *American Economic Review* 97, no. 2 (2007): 31–47.

Holmstrom, Bengt, and Paul Milgrom. "Multitask Principal-Agent Analyses: Incentive Contracts, Asset Ownership, and Job Design." *Journal of Law, Economics, & Organization* 7 (1991): 24–52.

Malamud, Ofer, and Cristian Pop-Eleches. "Home Computer Use and the Development of Human Capital." *Quarterly Journal of Economics* 126, no. 2 (2011): 987–1027.

Chapter 8

Bayer, Patrick, Fernando Ferreira, and Robert McMillan. "A Unified Framework for Measuring Preferences for Schools and Neighborhoods." *Journal of Political Economy* 115, no. 4 (2007): 588–638.

Black, Sandra. "Do Better Schools Matter? Parental Valuation of Elementary Education." *Quarterly Journal of Economics* 114, no. 2 (1999): 577–99.

Black, Sandra, and Stephen Machin. "Housing Valuations of School Performance." *Handbook of the Economics of Education* 3 (2011): 485–519.

Card, David, and A. Abigail Payne. "School Finance Reform, the Distribution of School Spending, and the Distribution of Student Test Scores." *Journal of Public Economics* 83, no. 1 (2002): 49–82.

Figlio, David N., and Maurice E. Lucas. "What's in a Grade? School Report Cards and the Housing Market." *American Economic Review* 94, no. 3 (2004): 591–604.

Fischel, William A. *Making the Grade: The Economic Evolution of American School Districts*. Chicago: University of Chicago Press, 2009.

Gruber, Jonathan. *Public Finance and Public Policy.* New York: Worth Publishers, 2012, 183–206.

Hanushek, Eric A., and Alfred A. Lindseth. *Schoolhouses, Courthouses, and Statehouses: Solving the Funding-Achievement Puzzle in America's Public Schools*. Princeton, NJ: Princeton University Press, 2009.

Hoxby, Caroline M. "Are Efficiency and Equity in School Finance Substitutes or Complements?" *Journal of Economic Perspectives* 10, no. 4 (1996): 51–72.

Hoxby, Caroline M. "Does Competition among Public Schools Benefit Students and Taxpayers?" *American Economic Review* 90, no. 5 (2000): 1209–38.

Hoxby, Caroline M. "All School Finance Equalizations Are Not Created Equal." *Quarterly Journal of Economics* 116, no. 4 (2001): 1189–1231.

Hoxby, Caroline M. "Does Competition among Public Schools Benefit Students and Taxpayers? Reply." *American Economic Review* 97, no. 5 (2007): 2038–55.

Hoxby, Caroline, and Ilyana Kuziemko. "Robin Hood and His Not-So-Merry Plan: Capitalization and the Self-Destruction of Texas' School Finance Equalization Plan." NBER Working Paper No. 10722, 2004.

Jackson, C. Kirabo, Rucker C. Johnson, and Claudia Persico. "The Effect of School Finance Reforms on the Distribution of Spending, Academic Achievement, and Adult Outcomes." NBER Working Paper No. 20118, 2014.

Murray, Sheila E., William N. Evans, and Robert M. Schwab. "Court-Mandated School Finance Reform and the Distribution of Resources." *American Economic Review* 88, no. 4 (1998): 789–812.

Rothstein, Jesse. "Does Competition among Public Schools Benefit Students and Taxpayers? Comment." *American Economic Review* 97, no. 5 (2007): 2026–37.

Silva, Fabio, and Jon Sonstelie. "Did *Serrano* Cause a Decline in School Spending?" *National Tax Journal* 48, no. 2 (1995): 199–215.

Tiebout, Charles. "A Pure Theory of Local Expenditures." *Journal of Political Economy* 64, no. 5 (1956): 416–24.

Chapter 9

Aaronson, Daniel, and Bhashkar Mazumder. "The Impact of Rosenwald Schools on Black Achievement." *Journal of Political Economy* 119, no. 5 (2011): 821–88.

Aaronson, Daniel, Lisa Barrow, and William Sander. "Teachers and Student Achievement in the Chicago Public High Schools." *Journal of Labor Economics* 25, no. 1 (2007): 95–135.

Angrist, Joshua D. "American Education Research Changes Tack." *Oxford Review of Economic Policy* 20, no. 2 (2004): 198–212.

Angrist, Joshua D., and Victor Lavy. "Using Maimonides' Rule to Estimate the Effect of Class Size on Children's Academic Achievement." *Quarterly Journal of Economics* 114, no. 2 (1999): 533–75.

Betts, Julian R. "Is There a Link between School Inputs and Earnings? Fresh Scrutiny of an Old Literature." In *Does Money Matter? The Effect of School Resources on Student Achievement and Adult Success*, edited by Gary Burtless. Washington, DC: The Brookings Institution, 1996.

Boyd, Donald, Hamilton Lankford, Susanna Loeb, Jonah Rockoff, and James Wyckoff. "The Narrowing Gap in New York City Teacher Qualifications and Its Implications for Student Achievement in High-Poverty Schools." *Journal of Policy Analysis and Management* 27, no. 4 (2008): 793–818.

Card, David, and Alan B. Krueger. "Does School Quality Matter? Returns to Education and the Characteristics of Public Schools in the United States." *Journal of Political Economy* 100, no. 1 (1992): 1–40.

Card, David, and Alan B. Krueger. "School Quality and Black-White Relative Earnings: A Direct Assessment." *Quarterly Journal of Economics* 107, no. 1 (1992): 151–200.

Card, David, and Alan B. Krueger. "Labor Market Effects of School Quality: Theory and Evidence." In *Does Money Matter? The Effect of School Resources on Student Achievement and Adult Success*, edited by Gary Burtless. Washington, DC: Brookings Institution, 1996.

Card, David, and A. Abigail Payne. "School Finance Reform, the Distribution of School Spending, and the Distribution of Student Test Scores." *Journal of Public Economics* 83, no. 1 (2002): 49–82.

Chetty, Raj, John N. Friedman and Jonah E. Rockoff. "Great Teaching: Measuring Its Effects on Students' Future Earnings. *Education Next* 12, no. 3 (2012): 58–68.

Chetty, Raj, John N. Friedman, Nathaniel Hilger, Emmanuel Saez, Diane Whitmore Schanzenbach, and Danny Yagan. "How Does Your Kindergarten Classroom Affect Your Earnings? Evidence from Project Star." *Quarterly Journal of Economics* 126, no. 4 (2011): 1593–660.

Chetty, Raj, John N. Friedman, and Jonah E. Rockoff. "Measuring the Impacts of Teachers I: Evaluating Bias in Teacher Value-Added Estimates." *American Economic Review* 104, no. 9 (2014): 2593–632.

Chetty, Raj, John N. Friedman, and Jonah E. Rockoff. "Measuring the Impacts of Teachers II: Teacher Value-Added and Student Outcomes in Adulthood." *American Economic Review* 104, no. 9 (2014): 2633–679.

Clotfelter, Charles T., Helen F. Ladd, and Jacob L. Vigdor. "Teacher Credentials and Student Achievement: Longitudinal Analysis with Student Fixed Effects." *Economics of Education Review* 26, no. 6 (2007): 673–82.

Clotfelter, Charles T., Helen F. Ladd, and Jacob L. Vigdor. "Teacher Credentials and Student Achievement in High School: A Cross-Subject Analysis with Student Fixed Effects." *Journal of Human Resources* 45, no. 6 (2010): 655–81.

Cohodes, Sarah, Daniel Grossman, Samuel Kleiner, and Michael Lovenheim. "The Effect of Child Health Insurance Access on Schooling: Evidence from Public Insurance Expansions." *Journal of Human Resources* 51, no. 3 (2016): 727–759.

Coleman, James. "Equality of Educational Opportunity." ICPSR06389-3. Ann Arbor, MI: Inter-university Consortium for Political and Social Research, 2007-04-07. http://doi.org/10.3886/ICPSR06389.v3

Goldhaber, Dan. "The Mystery of Good Teaching." *Education Next* 2, no. 1 (2002): 50–5.

Goldhaber, Dan, and Michael Hansen. "Using Performance on the Job to Inform Teacher Tenure Decisions." *American Economic Review* 100, no. 2 (2010): 250–55.

Gordon, Robert, Thomas J. Kane, and Douglas O. Staiger. "Identifying Effective Teachers Using Performance on the Job." Hamilton Project White Paper 2006-01.

Guarino, Cassandra, Mark Reckase, and Jeffrey Wooldridge. "Can Value-Added Measures of Teacher Performance Be Trusted?" *Education Finance and Policy* 10, no. 1 (2014): 117–56.

Hanushek, Eric A. "The Economics of Schooling: Production and Efficiency in Public Schools." *Journal of Economic Literature* 24, no. 3 (1986): 1141–177.

Hanushek, Eric A. "Assessing the Effects of School Resources on Student Performance: An Update." *Education Evaluation and Policy Analysis* 19, no. 2 (1997): 141–64.

Hanushek, Eric A. "The Failure of Input-Based Schooling Policies." *The Economic Journal* 113, no. 485 (1997): F64–F98.

Hanushek, Eric A. "Teacher Deselection." In *Creating a New Teaching Profession*, edited by Dan Goldhaber and Jane Hannaway. Washington, DC: Urban Institute, 2009.

Hastings, Justine S., and Jeffrey M. Weinstein. "Information, School Choice, and Academic Achievement: Evidence from Two Experiments." *Quarterly Journal of Economics* 123, no. 4 (2008): 1373–414.

Hoxby, Caroline M. "The Effects of Class Size on Student Achievement: New Evidence from Population Variation." *Quarterly Journal of Economics* 115, no. 4 (2000): 1239–285.

Hoxby, Caroline M. "All School Finance Equalizations Are Not Created Equal." *Quarterly Journal of Economics* 116, no. 4 (2001): 1189–231.

Hyman, Joshua. "Does Money Matter in the Long Run? Effects of School Spending on Educational Attainment." Working Paper (2015): http://www-personal.umich.edu/~jmhyman/Hyman_Does_Money_Matter.pdf.

Jackson, C. Kirabo, Rucker C. Johnson, and Claudia Persico. "The Effects of School Spending on Education and Economic Outcomes: Evidence from School Finance Reforms." *Quarterly Journal of Economics* (2016): 157–218.

Jacob, Brian A., Lars Lefgren, and David P. Sims. "The Persistence of Teacher-Induced Learning." *Journal of Human Resources* 45, no. 4 (2010): 915–43.

Jepsen, Christopher, and Steven Rivkin. "Class Size Reduction and Student Achievement: The Potential Tradeoff between Teacher Quality and Class Size." *Journal of Human Resources* 44, no. 1 (2009): 223–50.

Kane, Thomas J., and Douglas O. Staiger. "Estimating Teacher Impacts on Student Achievement: An Experimental Evaluation." NBER Working Paper No. 14607, 2008.

Krueger, Alan B. "Experimental Estimates of Education Production Functions." *Quarterly Journal of Economics* 114, no. 2 (1999): 497–532.

Krueger, Alan B., and Diane Whitmore. "The Effect of Attending a Small Class in the Early Grades on College-Test Taking and Middle School Test Results: Evidence from Project Star." *The Economic Journal* 111, no. 486 (2001): 1–28.

Murnane, Richard. "U.S. High School Graduation Rates: Patterns and Explanations." *Journal of Economic Literature* 51, no. 2 (2013): 370–422.

NAEP. *Trends in Academic Progress.* National Center for Education Statistics: Washington, DC, 2012: http://nces.ed.gov/nationsreportcard/subject/publications/main2012/pdf/2013456.pdf.

Papke, Leslie E. "The Effects of Spending on Test Pass Rates: Evidence from Michigan." *Journal of Public Economics* 89, no. 5–6 (2005): 821–39.

Rivkin, Steven G., Eric A. Hanushek, and John F. Kain. "Teachers, Schools, and Academic Achievement." *Econometrica* 73, no. 2 (2005): 417–58.

Rockoff, Jonah E. "The Impact of Individual Teachers on Student Achievement: Evidence from Panel Data." *American Economic Review* 94, no. 2 (2004): 247–52.

Rockoff, Jonah E., Brian A. Jacob, Thomas J. Kane, and Douglas O. Staiger. "Can You Recognize an Effective Teacher When You Recruit One?" *Education Finance and Policy* 6, no. 1 (2011): 43–74.

Rothstein, Jesse. "Teacher Quality in Educational Production: Tracking, Decay, and Student Achievement." *Quarterly Journal of Economics* 125, no. 1 (2010): 175–214.

Sacerdote, Bruce. "Peer Effects in Education: How Might They Work, How Big Are They and How Much Do We Know Thus Far?" In *Handbook of the Economics of Education, Vol. 3*, edited by Eric A. Hanushek, Stephen Machin, and Ludger Woessman. Holland: Elsevier, 2011.

Schanzenbach, Diane Whitmore. "What Have Researchers Learned from Project STAR?" *Brookings Papers on Education Policy* 9 (2006): 205–28.

Sims, David. "How Flexible Is Education Production? Combination Classes and Class Size Reduction in California." MIT Department of Economics, 2003.

Wiswall, Matthew. "The Dynamics of Teacher Quality." *Journal of Public Economics* 100 (2013): 61–78.

Chapter 10

Abdulkadiroglu, Atila, Joshua D. Angrist, Susan M. Dynarski, Thomas J. Kane, and Parag A. Pathak. "Accountability and Flexibility in Public Schools: Evidence from Boston's Charters and Pilots." *Quarterly Journal of Economics* 126, no. 2 (2011): 699–748.

Abdulkadiroglu, Atila, Joshua D. Angrist, and Parag A. Pathak. "The Elite Illusion: Achievement Effects at Boston and New York Exam Schools." *Econometrica* 82, no. 1 (2014): 137–96.

Altonji, Joseph G., Todd E. Elder, and Christopher R. Taber. "Selection on Observed and Unobserved Variables: Assessing the Effectiveness of Catholic Schools." *Journal of Political Economy* 113, no. 1 (2005): 151–84.

Altonji, Joseph G., Ching-I Huang, and Christopher R. Taber. "Estimating the Cream Skimming Effect of School Choice." NBER Working Paper No. 16579, 2010.

Angrist, Joshua D., Parag A. Pathak, and Christopher R. Walters. "Explaining Charter School Effectiveness." *American Economic Journal: Applied Economics* 5, no. 4 (2013): 1–27.

Bayer, Patrick, and Robert McMillan. "Choice and Competition in Local Education Markets." NBER Working Paper No. 11802, 2005.

Bifulco, Robert, and Helen F. Ladd. "The Impacts of Charter Schools on Student Achievement: Evidence from North Carolina." *Education Finance and Policy* 1, no. 1 (2006): 50–90.

Bifulco, Robert, and Helen F. Ladd. "School Choice, Racial Segregation, and Test-Score Gaps: Evidence from North

Carolina's Charter School Program." *Journal of Policy Analysis and Management* 26, no. 1 (2007): 31–56.

Booker, Kevin, Scott M. Gilpatric, Timothy Gronberg, and Dennis Jansen. "The Effect of Charter Schools on Traditional Public School Students in Texas: Are Children Who Stay Behind Left Behind?" *Journal of Urban Economics* 64, no. 1 (2008): 123–45.

Bui, Sa A., Steven G. Craig, and Scott A. Imberman. "Is Gifted Education a Bright Idea? Assessing the Impact of Gifted and Talented Programs on Students." *American Economic Journal: Economic Policy* 6, no. 3 (2014): 30–62.

Chakrabarti, Rajashri. "Can Increasing Private School Participation and Monetary Loss in a Voucher Program Affect Public School Performance? Evidence from Milwaukee." *Journal of Public Economics* 92, no. 5–6 (2008): 1371–393.

Chubb, John E., and Terry M. Moe. *Politics, Markets, and America's Schools.* Washington, DC: The Brookings Institution, 1990

Cullen, Julie Berry, Brian A. Jacob, and Steven Levitt. "The Impact of School Choice on Student Outcomes: An Analysis of the Chicago Public Schools." *Journal of Public Economics* 89 (2005): 729–60.

Cullen, Julie Berry, Brian A. Jacob, and Steven Levitt. "The Effect of School Choice on Participants: Evidence from Randomized Lotteries." *Econometrica* 74, no. 5 (2006): 1191–230.

Deming, David J. "Better Schools, Less Crime?" *Quarterly Journal of Economics* 126, no. 4 (2011): 2063–115.

Deming, David J., Justine S. Hastings, Thomas J. Kane, and Douglas O. Staiger. "School Choice, School Quality, and Postsecondary Attainment." *American Economic Review* 104, no. 3 (2014): 991–1013.

Dobbie, Will, and Roland G. Fryer, Jr. "Are High-Quality Schools Enough to Increase Achievement Among the Poor? Evidence from the Harlem Children's Zone." *American Economic Journal: Applied Economics* 3, no. 3 (2011): 158–87.

Dobbie, Will, and Roland G. Fryer, Jr. "The Impact of Attending a School with High-Achieving Peers: Evidence from the New York City Exam Schools." *American Economic Journal: Applied Economics* 6, no. 3 (2014): 58–75.

Figlio, David N., and Cassandra M.D. Hart. "Competitive Effects of Means-Tested School Vouchers." NBER Working Paper No. 16056, 2010.

Figlio, David N., and Joe A. Stone. "Can Public Policy Affect Private School Cream Skimming?" *Journal of Urban Economics* 49, no. 2 (2001): 240–66.

Friedman, Milton. "The Role of Government in Education." In *Economics and the Public Interest*, Robert A. Solo (Ed.), Rutgers University Press: New Brunswick, 1955.

Greene, Jay P., Paul E. Peterson, and Jiangtao Du. "Effectiveness of School Choice: The Milwaukee Experiment." *Education and Urban Society* 31, no. 2 (1999): 190–213.

Hastings, Justine S., and Jeffrey M. Weinstein. "Information, School Choice, and Academic Achievement: Evidence from Two Experiments." *Quarterly Journal of Economics* 123, no. 4 (2008): 1373–414.

Heckman, James J., Jora Stixrud, and Sergio Urzua. "The Effects of Cognitive and Noncognitive Abilities on Labor Market Outcomes and Social Behavior." *Journal of Labor Economics* 24, no. 3 (2006): 411–82.

Howell, William G., and Martin R. West. "Gray Lady Wheezing: The AFT Hoodwinks the *Times*." *Education Next*, Winter 2005: 74–7.

Howell, William G., Patrick J. Wolf, David E. Campbell, and Paul E. Peterson. "School Vouchers and Academic Performance: Results from Three Randomized Field Trials." *Journal of Policy Analysis and Management* 21, no. 2 (2002): 191–217.

Hoxby, Caroline M. "Does Competition among Public Schools Benefit Students and Taxpayers?" *American Economic Review*, 90, no. 5 (2000): 1209–238.

Hoxby, Caroline M. "School Choice and School Productivity: Could School Choice Be a Tide that Lifts All Boats?" In *The Economics of School Choice*, Caroline M. Hoxby (Ed.). Chicago: University of Chicago Press, 2003.

Hoxby, Caroline, Sonali Muraka, and Jenny Kang. "How New York City's Charter Schools Affect Achievement, August 2009 Report," Second in series. Cambridge, MA: New York City Charter Schools Evaluation Project, 2009.

Hsieh, Chang-Tai, and Miguel Urquiola. "The Effects of Generalized School Choice on Achievement and Stratification: Evidence from Chile's Voucher Program." *Journal of Public Economics* 90, no. 8–9 (2006). 1477–503.

Imberman, Scott A. "Achievement and Behavior in Charter Schools: Drawing a More Complete Picture." *Review of Economics and Statistics* 93, no. 2 (2011): 416–35.

Imberman, Scott A. "The Effect of Charter Schools on Achievement and Behavior of Public School Students." *Journal of Public Economics* 95, no. 7–8 (2011): 850–63.

Krueger, Alan B. "Experimental Estimates of Education Production Function." *Quarterly Journal of Economics* 114, no. 2 (1999): 497–532.

Krueger, Alan B., and Pei Zhu. "Another Look at the New York City Voucher Experiment." *American Behavioral Scientist* 47, no. 5 (2004): 658–98.

Lankford, Hamilton, and James Wyckoff. "Who Would Be Left Behind by Enhanced Private School Choice?" *Journal of Urban Economics* 50, no. 2 (2001): 288–312.

National Center for Education Statistics. *Trends in the Use of School Choice: 1993 to 2007.* National Center for Education Statistics Paper No. 2010-004. Washington, DC.

Neal, Derek. "The Effects of Catholic Secondary Schooling on Educational Achievement." *Journal of Labor Economics* XV (1997): 98–123.

Nechyba, Thomas J. "Centralization, Fiscal Federalism, and Private School Attendance." *International Economic Review* 44, no. 1 (2003): 179–204.

Peltzman, Sam. "The Effect of Government Subsidies-in-Kind on Private Expenditures: The Case of Higher Education." *Journal of Political Economy* 81, no. 1 (1973): 1–27.

Rouse, Cecilia E. "Private School Vouchers and Student Achievement: An Evaluation of the Milwaukee Parental Choice Program." *Quarterly Journal of Economics* 113, no. 2 (1998): 553–602.

Sass, Tim R. "Charter Schools and Student Achievement in Florida." *Education Finance and Policy* 1, no. 1 (2006): 91–122.

Schemo, Diane J. "Nation's Charter Schools Lagging Behind, U.S. Test Scores Reveal." *New York Times*, August 17, 2004.

Shanker, Albert. National Press Club Speech. 1988. http://reuther.wayne.edu/files/64.43.pdf.

Witte, John F. "The Milwaukee Voucher Experiment." *Education Evaluation and Policy Analysis* 20, no. 4 (1998): 229–51.

Chapter 11

Carnoy, Martin, and Susanna Loeb. "Does External Accountability Affect Student Outcomes? A Cross-State Analysis," *Educational Evaluation and Policy Analysis* 24, no. 4 (2002): 305–31.

Clark, Damon, and Paco Martorell. "The Signaling Value of a High School Diploma." *Journal of Political Economy* 122, no. 2 (2014): 282–318.

Clotfelter, Charles T., Helen F. Ladd, Jacob Vigdor, and Roger Aliaga Diaz. "Do School Accountability Systems Make It More Difficult for Low-Performing Schools to Attract and Retain High-Quality Teachers?" *Journal of Policy Analysis and Management* 23, no. 2 (2004): 251–71.

Cullen, Julie B., and Randall Reback. "Tinkering Toward Accolades: School Gaming under a Performance Accountability System." *Advances in Applied Microeconomics* 14 (2006): 1–34.

Dee, Thomas S., and Brian Jacob. "The Impact of No Child Left Behind on Student Achievement." *Journal of Policy Analysis and Management* 30, no. 3 (2011): 418–46.

Deming, David J., Sarah Cohodes, Jennifer Jennings, and Christopher Jencks. "School Accountability, Postsecondary Attainment, and Earnings." *Review of Economics and Statistics* 98, no. 2 (2016): 848–862.

Figlio, David N. "Testing, Crime and Punishment." *Journal of Public Economics* 90, no. 4–5 (2006): 837–51.

Figlio, David N., and Joshua Winicki. "Food for Thought: The Effects of School Accountability Plans on School Nutrition." *Journal of Public Economics* 89, no. 2–3 (2005): 381–94.

Figlio, David N., and Lawrence S. Getzler. "Accountability, Ability and Disability: Gaming the System?" *Advances in Applied Microeconomics* 14 (2006): 35–49.

Figlio, David N., and Cecelia E. Rouse. "Do Accountability and Voucher Threats Improve Low-Performing Schools?" *Journal of Public Economics* 90, no. 1–2 (2006): 239–55.

Figlio, David, and Susanna Loeb. "School Accountability." In E. Hanushek, S. Machin, and L. Woessman (Eds.), *Handbooks in Economics*, Vol. 3 (pp. 383–421). The Netherlands: North-Holland, 2011.

Haney, Walt. "The Myth of the Texas Miracle in Education." *Education Policy Analysis Archives* 41, no. 8 (2000).

Hanushek, Eric A., and Margaret E. Raymond. "Does School Accountability Lead to Improved Student Performance?" *Journal of Policy Analysis and Management* 24, no. 2 (2005): 297–327.

Holmstrom, Bengt, and Paul Milgrom. "Multitask Principal–Agent Analyses: Incentive Contracts, Asset Ownership, and Job Design." *Journal of Law, Economics, & Organization* 7 (1991): 24–52.

Hoxby, Caroline M. "The Cost of Accountability." NBER Working Paper No. 8855 (2002).

Imberman, Scott A. and Michael F. Lovenheim. "Does the Market Value Value-Added? Evidence from Housing Prices After a Public Release of School and Teacher Value-Added." *Journal of Urban Economics* 91 (2016): 104–21.

Jacob, Brian A. "Accountability, Incentives and Behavior: Evidence from School Reform in Chicago." *Journal of Public Economics* 89, no. 5–6 (2005): 761–96.

Jacob, Brian, and Lars Lefgren. "Remedial Education and Student Achievement: A Regression–Discontinuity Analysis." *Review of Economics and Statistics* 86, no. 1 (2004): 226–44.

Jacob, Brian, and Lars Lefgren. The Effect of Grade Retention on High School Completion." *American Economic Journal: Applied Economics* 1, no. 3 (2009): 33–58.

Jacob, Brian, and Steven Levitt. "Rotten Apples: An Investigation of the Prevalence and Predictors of Teacher Cheating." *Quarterly Journal of Economics* 118, no. 3 (2003): 843–877.

Kane, Thomas, and Douglas Staiger. "The Promise and Pitfalls of Using Imprecise School Accountability Measures." *Journal of Economic Perspectives* 16, no. 4 (2002): 91–114.

Kane, Thomas J., Douglas O. Staiger, and Jeffrey Geppert. "Randomly Accountable." *Education Next* 2, no. 1 (2002): 56–61.

Klein, Stephen P., Laura S. Hamilton, Daniel F. McCaffrey, and Brian M. Stecher. "What Do Test Scores in Texas Tell Us?" *Education Policy Analysis Archives* 8, no. 49 (2000).

Lazarin, Melissa. "Testing Overload in America's Schools." Center for American Progress Report, 2014: https://cdn.americanprogress.org/wp-content/uploads/2014/10/LazarinOvertestingReport.pdf.

Lazear, Edward P. "Speeding, Terrorism, and Teaching to the Test." *Quarterly Journal of Economics* 121, no. 3 (2006): 1029–61.

National Commission on Excellence in Education. *A Nation at Risk: The Imperative for Education Reform.* United States Department of Education: Washington, DC, 1983.

Neal, Derek, and Diane Whitmore Schanzenbach. "Left Behind by Design: Proficiency Counts and Test-Based Accountability." *Review of Economics and Statistics* 92, no. 2 (2010): 263–83.

Papay, John P., Richard J. Murnane, and John B. Willett. "The Consequences of High School Exit Examinations for Low-Performing Urban Students: Evidence From Massachusetts." *Education Evaluation and Policy Analysis* 32, no. 1 (2010): 5–23.

Peterson, Paul E., and Carlos Xabel Lastra-Anadon. "State Standards Rise in Reading, Fall in Math." *Education Next* 10, no. 4 (2010): 12–6.

Reback, Randall. "Teaching to the Rating: School Accountability and the Distribution of Student Achievement." *Journal of Public Economics* 92 (2008): 1394–415.

Reback, Randall, Jonah Rockoff, and Heather Schwartz. "Under Pressure: Job Security, Resource Allocation, and Productivity in Schools Under NCLB." *American Economic Journal: Economic Policy* 6, no. 3 (2014): 207–41.

Rockoff, Jonah, and Lesley J. Turner. "Short-Run Impacts of Accountability on School Quality." *American Economic Journal: Economic Policy* 2, no. 4 (2010): 119–47.

Rouse, Cecilia E., Jane Hannaway, Dan Goldhaber, and David Figlio. "Feeling the Florida Heat? How Low-Performing Schools Respond to Voucher and Accountability Pressure." *American Economic Journal: Economic Policy* 5, no. 2 (2013): 251–81.

Chapter 12

Aaronson, Daniel, Lisa Barrow, and William Sander. "Teachers and Student Achievement in the Chicago Public High Schools." *Journal of Labor Economics* 25, no. 1 (2007): 95–135.

American Federation of Teachers. 2014. *AFT History.* http://www.aft.org/about/history/.

Ballou, Dale. "Pay for Performance in Public and Private Schools." *Economics of Education Review* 20, no. 1 (2001): 51–61.

Baugh, William H., and Joe A. Stone. "Teachers, Unions, and Wages in the 1970s: Unionism Now Pays." *Industrial and Labor Relations Review* 35, no. 3 (1982): 368–76.

Becker, Howard S. "The Teacher in the Authority System of the Public School." *Journal of Educational Sociology* 27, no. 3 (1953): 128–41.

Borjas, George. "Self-Selection and the Earnings of Immigrants." *American Economic Review* 77, no. 4 (1987): 531–53.

Chetty, Raj, John N. Friedman, and Jonah E. Rockoff. "Measuring the Impacts of Teachers II: Teacher Value-Added and Student Outcomes in Adulthood." *American Economic Review.* 104, no. 9 (2014): 2633–679.

Chubb, John E., and Terry M. Moe. "Politics, Markets and the Organization of Public Schools." *American Political Science Review* 82, no. 4 (1988): 1065–087.

Clotfelter, Charles T., Helen F. Ladd, and Jacob L. Vigdor. "Teacher Credentials and Student Achievement: Longitudinal Analysis with Student Fixed Effects." *Economics of Education Review* 26, no. 6 (2007): 673–82.

Clotfelter, Charles T., Helen F. Ladd, and Jacob L. Vigdor. "Teacher Credentials and Student Achievement in High School: A Cross-Subject Analysis with Student Fixed Effects." *Journal of Human Resources* 45, no. 13 (2010): 655–81.

Corcoran, Sean P., William M. Evans, and Robert M. Schwab. "Changing Labor-Market Opportunities for Women and the Quality of Teachers, 1957–2000." *American Economic Review* 94, no. 2 (2004): 230–35.

Eberts, Randall W., and Joe A. Stone. "Teacher Unions and the Cost of Public Education." *Economic Inquiry* 24, no. 4 (1986): 631–43.

Ehrenberg, Ronald G., and Dominic J. Brewer. "Did Teachers' Verbal Ability and Race Matter in the 1960s? Coleman Revisited." *Economics of Education Review* 14, no. 1 (1995): 1–21.

Eide, Eric, Dan Goldhaber, and Dominic Brewer. "The Teacher Labour Market and Teacher Quality." *Oxford Review of Economic Policy* 20, no. 5 (2004): 230–44.

Ferguson, Ronald F., and Helen F. Ladd. "How and Why Money Matters: An Analysis of Alabama Schools." In *Holding Schools Accountable: Performance-Based Reform in Education,* Helen F. Ladd (Ed.). Washington, DC: Brookings Institution Press, 1996.

Frandsen, Brigham R. "The Effects of Collective Bargaining Rights on Public Employee Compensation: Evidence from Teachers, Fire Fighters, and Police." *Industrial and Labor Relations Review* 69, no. 1 (2016): 84–112.

Freeman, Richard B. "Unionism Comes to the Public Sector. *Journal of Economic Literature* 24, no. 1 (1986): 41–86.

Freeman, Richard B., and Robert Valletta. "Appendix B: The NBER Public Sector Collective Bargaining Law Data Set." In *When Public Sector Workers Unionize,* Richard Freeman and Casey Ichniowski (Eds.). Chicago: University of Chicago Press, 1988.

Fryer, Roland G. "Teacher Incentives and Student Achievement: Evidence from New York City Public Schools." *Journal of Labor Economics* 31, no. 2 (2013): 373–407.

Goldhaber, Dan D. and Dominic J. Brewer. "Does Teacher Certification Matter? High School Teacher Certification Status and Student Achievement." *Education Evaluation and Policy Analysis* 22, no. 2 (2000): 129–45.

Goldhaber, Dan D., and Albert Yung-Hsu Liu. "Occupational Choices and the Academic Proficiency of the Teacher Workforce." In *Developments in School Finance 2001–02,* William Fowler (Ed.). Washington, DC: NCES, 2003. pp. 53–75.

Goldhaber, Dan, Betheny Gross, and Daniel Player. "Teacher Career Paths, Teacher Quality, and Persistence in the Classroom: Are Public Schools Keeping Their

Best?" *Journal of Policy Analysis and Management* 30, no. 1 (2011): 57–87.

Goodman, Serena F., and Lesley J. Turner. "The Design of Teacher Incentive Pay and Educational Outcomes: Evidence from the New York City Bonus Program." *Journal of Labor Economics* 31, no. 2 (2013): 409–20.

Hanushek, Eric A., and Richard R. Pace. "Who Chooses to Teach (and Why)?" *Economics of Education Review* 14, no. 2 (1995): 101–17.

Hanushek, Eric A., John F. Kain, and Steven G. Rivkin. "Why Public Schools Lose Teachers." *Journal of Human Resources* 39, no. 2 (2004): 326–54.

Holmstrom, Bengt, and Paul Milgrom. "Multitask Principal-Agent Analyses: Incentive Contracts, Asset Ownership, and Job Design." *Journal of Law, Economics & Organization* 7 (1991): 24–52.

Hoxby, Caroline M. "How Teachers' Unions Affect Education Production." *Quarterly Journal of Economics* 111, no. 3 (1996): 671–718.

Hoxby, Caroline M., and Andrew Leigh. "Pulled Away or Pushed Out? Explaining the Decline of Teacher Aptitude in the United States." *American Economic Review* 94, no. 2 (2004): 236–40.

Imberman, Scott A., and Michael F. Lovenheim. "Incentive Strength and Teacher Productivity: Evidence from a Group-Based Teacher Incentive Pay System." *Review of Economics and Statistics* 97, no. 2 (2015): 364–86.

Jepsen, Christopher, and Steven Rivkin. "Class Size Reduction and Student Achievement: The Potential Tradeoff between Teacher Quality and Class Size." *Journal of Human Resources* 44, no. 1 (2009): 223–50.

Kandel, Eugene, and Edward P. Lazear. "Peer Pressure and Partnerships." *Journal of Political Economy* 100, no. 4 (1992): 801–17.

Kane, Thomas J., Jonah E. Rockoff, and Douglas O. Staiger. "What Does Certification Tell Us About Teacher Effectiveness? Evidence from New York City." *Economics of Education Review* 27, no. 6 (2008): 615–31.

Kleiner, Morris M., and Daniel Petree. "Unionism and Licensing of Public School Teachers: Impact on Wages and Educational Output." In *When Public Sector Workers Unionize*, Richard Freeman and Casey Ichniowski (Ed.). Chicago: University of Chicago Press, 1988.

Krieg, John M. "Teacher Quality and Attrition." *Economics of Education Review* 25, no. 1 (2006): 13–27.

Lankford, Hamilton, Susanna Loeb, and James Wyckoff. "Teacher Sorting and the Plight of Urban Schools: A Descriptive Analysis." *Education Evaluation and Policy Analysis* 24, no. 1 (2002): 37–62.

Lavy, Victor. "Performance Pay and Teachers' Effort, Productivity, and Grading Ethics." *American Economic Review* 99, no. 5 (2009): 1979–2011.

Loeb, Susanna, and Marianne E. Page. "Examining the Link between Teacher Wages and Student Outcomes: The Importance of Alternative Labor Market Opportunities and Non-Pecuniary Variation." *Review of Economics and Statistics* 82, no. 3 (2000): 393–408.

Lott, Jonathan, and Lawrence W. Kenny. "State Teacher Union Strength and Student Achievement." *Economics of Education Review* 35 (2013): 93–103.

Lovenheim, Michael F. "The Effect of Teachers' Unions on Education Production: Evidence from Union Election Certifications in Three Midwestern States." *Journal of Labor Economics* 27, no. 4 (2009): 525–87.

Manski, Charles F. "Academic Ability, Earnings, and the Decision to Become a Teacher: Evidence from the National Longitudinal Study of the High School Class of 1972." In *Public Sector Payrolls*, David A. Wise (Ed.). Chicago: University of Chicago Press, 1987.

Moe, Terry M. "Collective Bargaining and the Performance of Public Schools." *American Journal of Political Science* 53, no. 1 (2009): 156–74.

Moe, Terry M. *Special Interest: Teachers Unions and America's Public Schools.* Washington, DC: The Brookings Institution, 2011.

Moore, William J., and John Raisian. "Union–Nonunion Wage Differentials in the Public Administration, Educational, and Private Sectors, 1970–1983." *Review of Economics and Statistics* 69, no. 4 (1987): 608–16.

Motoko, Rich. "Teacher Shortages Spur a Nationwide Hiring Scramble (Credentials Optional)." *New York Times,* August 10, 2015, national edition.

Murnane, Richard J., Judith D. Singer, John B. Willett, James J. Kemple, and Randall J. Olsen. *Who Will Teach? Policies that Matter.* Cambridge, MA: Harvard University Press, 1991.

Murphy, Marjorie. *Blackboard Unions: The AFT & the NEA 1900–1980.* Ithaca, NY: Cornell University Press, 1990.

Neal, Derek, and Diane Whitmore Schanzenbach. "Left Behind by Design: Proficiency Counts and Test-Based Accountability." *Review of Economics and Statistics* 92, no. 2 (2010): 263–83.

Podgursky, Michael, Ryan Monroe, and Donald Watson. "The Academic Quality of Public School Teachers: An Analysis of Entry and Exit Behavior." *Economics of Education Review* 23, no. 5 (2004): 507–18.

Raymond, Margaret, and Stephen Fletcher. "The Teach for America Evaluation." *Education Next* 2, no. 1 (2002): 62–8.

Rivkin, Steven G., Eric A. Hanushek, and John F. Kain. "Teachers, Schools, and Academic Achievement." *Econometrica* 73, no. 2 (2005): 417–58.

Rockoff, Jonah E. "The Impact of Individual Teachers on Student Achievement: Evidence from Panel Data." *American Economic Review* 94, no. 2 (2004): 247–52.

Rockoff, Jonah E., Brian A. Jacob, Thomas J. Kane, and Douglas O. Staiger. "Can You Recognize an Effective Teacher When You Recruit One?" *Education Finance and Policy* 6, no. 1 (2011): 43–74.

Roy, Andrew D. "Some Thoughts on the Distribution of Earnings." *Oxford Economic Papers* 3, no. 2 (1951): 125–56.

Sass, Tim R., Jane Hannaway, Zeyu Xu, David N. Figlio, and Li Feng. "Value Added of Teachers in High-Poverty Schools and Lower Poverty Schools." *Journal of Urban Economics* 72, no. 2–3 (2012): 104–122.

Springer, Matthew G., Dale Ballou, Laura Hamilton, Vi-Nhuan Le, J. R. Lockwood, Daniel F. McCaffrey, Matthew Pepper, and Brian M. Stecher, "Teacher Pay For Performance: Experimental Evidence from the Project on Incentives in Teaching." National Center on Performance Incentives, 2010: http://www.performanceincentives.org/data/files/pages/POINT%20REPORT 9.21.10.pdf.

Strunk, Katharine O. "Are Teachers' Unions Really to Blame? Collective Bargaining Agreements and Their Relationships with District Resource Allocation and Student Performance in California." *Education Finance and Policy* 6, no. 3 (2011): 354–98.

West, Kristine. "Teachers' Unions, Compensation and Tenure." *Industrial Relations: A Journal of Economy and Society* 54, no. 2 (2015): 294–320.

Wiswall, Matthew. "The Dynamics of Teacher Quality." *Journal of Public Economics* 100 (2013): 61–78.

Chapter 13

Aghion, Philippe, Leah Boustan, Caroline Hoxby, and Jerome Vandenbussche. "Exploiting States' Mistakes to Identify the Causal Impact of Higher Education on Growth." Mimeo, 2005.

Baumol, William J., and William G. Bowen. *Performing Arts: The Economic Dilemma.* New York: The Twentieth Century Fund, 1966.

Bishop, Morris. *A History of Cornell.* Ithaca, NY: Cornell University Press, 1962.

Bound, John, Michael F. Lovenheim, and Sarah E. Turner. "Why Have College Completion Rates Declined? An Analysis of Changing Student Preparation and Collegiate Resources." *American Economic Journal: Applied Economics* 2, no. 3 (2010): 129–157.

Bound, John, and Sarah E. Turner. "Cohort Crowding: How Resources Affect Collegiate Attainment." *Journal of Public Economics* 91, no. 5–6 (2007): 877–899.

Bowen, William G. *The Economics of Major Private Universities.* Bloomington, IN: Carnegie Commission on Higher Education, 1968.

Bowen, William G. "The 'Cost Disease' in Higher Education: Is Technology the Answer?" 2012. http:www.ithaka.org/sites/default/files/files/ITHAKA-TheCostDiseaseinHigherEducation.pdf.

Bowen, William G., and David W. Brenerman. "Student Aid: Price Discount or Educational Investment?" *College Review Board* 167, no. 35–36 (1963): 2–6.

Bowen, William G., Martin A. Kurzweil, and Eugene M. Tobin. *Equity and Excellence in American Higher Education.* Charlottesville, VA: University of Virginia Press, 2005.

Bowen, William G., and Michael S. McPherson. *Lesson Plan: An Agenda for Change in American Higher Education.* Princeton, NJ: Princeton University Press, 2016.

Campos, Paul F. "The Real Reason College Tuition Costs So Much." *New York Times,* April 4, 2015.

DeLong, Bradford J., Claudia Goldin, and Lawrence F. Katz. "Sustaining U.S. Economic Growth." In H. J. Aaron, J. M. Lindsay, and P. S. Nivola (Eds.) *Agenda for the Nation.* Washington, D.C.: The Brookings Institution, 2003.

Digest of Education Statistics (Various years.) https://nces.ed.gov/programs/digest.

Frank, Robert. "The Prestige Chase Is Raising College Costs." *New York Times*, March 10, 2012.

Goldin, Claudia, and Stephanie Riegg Cellini. "Does Federal Student Aid Raise Tuition? New Evidence on For-Profit Colleges." *American Economic Journal: Economic Policy* 6, no. 4 (2014): 174–206.

Goldin, Claudia, and Lawrence F. Katz. "The Shaping of Higher Education: The Formative Years in the United States, 1890 to 1940." *Journal of Economic Perspectives* 13, no. 1 (1999): 37–62.

Goldin, Claudia, and Lawrence F. Katz. *The Race Between Education and Technology.* Cambridge, MA: Harvard University Press, 2008.

Goldin, Claudia, Lawrence F. Katz, and Ilyana Kuziemko. "The Homecoming of American College Women." *Journal of Economic Perspectives* 20, no. 4 (2006): 133–156.

Hoxby, Caroline M. "The Changing Selectivity of American Colleges." *Journal of Economic Perspectives* 23, no. 4 (2009): 95–118.

Hoxby, Caroline M. "The Economics of Online Postsecondary Education: MOOCs, Nonselective Education, and Highly Selective Education." *American Economic Review* 104, no. 5 (2014): 528–533.

Hoxby, Caroline M. "Endowment Management Based on a Positive Model of the University." In Jeffrey R. Brown and Caroline M. Hoxby (Eds.). *How the Financial Crisis and Great Recession Affected Higher Education.* Chicago: University of Chicago Press, 2015.

Kane, Thomas J. and Cecilia Elena Rouse. "The Community College: Educating Students at the Margin between College and Work." *Journal of Economic Perspectives* 13, no. 1 (1999): 63–84.

Lemann, Nicholas. *The Big Test: The Secret History of the American Meritocracy.* New York: Farrar, Straus and Giroux, 1999.

Lovenheim, Michael F., and C. Lockwood Reynolds. "Changes in Postsecondary Choices by Ability and Income: Evidence from the National Longitudinal Surveys of Youth." *Journal of Human Capital* 5, no. 1 (2011): 70–109.

Moretti, Enrico. "Workers' Education, Spillovers, and Productivity: Evidence from Plant-Level Production Functions." *American Economic Review* 94, no. 3 (2004): 656–90.

Rhodes, Frank H. T. "The University and Its Critics." In *Universities and Their Leadership*, William G. Bowen and Harold T. Shapiro (Eds.). Princeton, NJ: Princeton University Press, 1998.

Rivard, Ry. "Discount Escalation." *Inside Higher Ed.*, July 2, 2014.

Sallee, James M., Alexandra M. Resch, and Paul N. Courant. "On the Optimal Allocation of Students and Resources in a System of Higher Education." *The B.E. Journal of Economic Analysis & Policy* 8, no. 1 (2008), Advances, Article 11.

Stange, Kevin. "Ability Sorting and the Importance of College Quality to Student Achievement: Evidence from Community Colleges." *Education Finance and Policy* 7, no. 1 (2012): 74–105.

"Trends in College Pricing." New York, NY: College Board, 2015. https://trends.collegeboard.org/sites/default/files/2016-trends-college-pricing-web_0.pdf.

Turner, Lesley. "The Road to Pell Is Paved with Good Intentions: The Economic Incidence of Federal Student Grant Aid." University of Maryland Working Paper, 2014. Accessed July 19, 2016. http://econweb.umd.edu/~turner/Turner_FedAidIncidence.pdf.

Vandenbussche, Jerome, Philippe Aghion, and Costas Meghir. "Growth, Distance to Frontier and Composition of Human Capital." *Journal of Human Capital* 11, no. 2 (2006): 97–127.

Winston, Gordon. "Part Church, Part Car Dealer." *New England Board of Higher Education*. Winter 2003, 42–43.

Chapter 14

Akers, Beth, and Matthew W. Chingos. "Student Loan Safety Nets: Estimating the Costs and Benefits of Income-Based Repayment." Brown Center on Education at Brookings Report, April 2014.

Andrews, Rodney J. "The Promise of 'Promise' Programs." In *Reinventing Financial Aid Charting a New Course to College Affordability*, Andrew P. Kelly and Sara Goldrick-Rab (Eds.). Cambridge, MA: Harvard Education Press, 2014, 55–74.

Andrews, Rodney J., Stephen DesJardins, and Vimal Ranchhod. "The Effects of the Kalamazoo Promise on College Choice." *Economics of Education Review* 29, no. 5 (2010): 722–37.

Bailey, Martha J., and Susan M. Dynarski. 2011. "Inequality in Postsecondary Education." *Whither Opportunity? Rising Inequality, Schools, and Children's Life Chances*, G. J. Duncan and R. J. Murnane (Eds.). New York, NY: Russell Sage, 2011.

Barr, Andrew. "From the Battlefield to the Schoolyard: The Short-Term Impact of the Post-9/11 GI Bill." *Journal of Human Resources* 50, no. 3 (2015): 580–613.

Belley, Philippe, and Lance Lochner. "The Changing Role of Family Income and Ability in Determining Educational Achievement." *Journal of Human Capital* 1, no. 1 (2007): 37–89.

Bettinger, Eric P., Bridget T. Long, Philip Oreopoulos, and Lisa Sonbonmatsu. "The Role of Application Assistance and Information in College Decisions: Results from the H&R Block FAFSA Experiment." *Quarterly Journal of Economics* 127, no. 3 (2012): 1205–242.

Bound, John, and Sarah E. Turner. "Going to War and Going to College: Did World War II and the G.I. Bill Increase Educational Attainment for Returning Veterans?" *Journal of Labor Economics* 20, no. 4 (2002): 784–815.

Bowen, William G., and Michael S. McPherson. *Lesson Plan: An Agenda for Change in American Higher Education.* Princeton, NJ: Princeton University Press, 2016.

Bowen, William G., Martin A. Kurzweil, and Eugene M. Tobin. *Equity and Excellence in American Higher Education.* Charlottesville, VA: University of Virginia Press, 2005.

Carneiro, Pedro, and James J. Heckman. "The Evidence on Credit Constraints in Post-Secondary Schooling." *The Economic Journal* 122, no. 482 (2002): 705–32.

Cohodes, Sarah, and Joshua Goodman. "Merit Aid, College Quality, and College Completion: Massachusetts' Adams Scholarship as an In-Kind Subsidy." *American Economic Journal: Applied Economics* 6, no. 4 (2014): 251–85.

Cornwell, Christopher, David B. Mustard, and Deepa J. Sridhar. "The Enrollment Effects of Merit-Based Financial Aid: Evidence from Georgia's HOPE Program." *Journal of Labor Economics* 24, no. 4 (2006): 761–86.

Cunha, Flavio, and James Heckman. "The Technology of Skill Formation." *The American Economic Review* 97, no. 2 (2007): 31–47.

Dynarski, Susan. "Hope for Whom? Financial Aid for the Middle Class and Its Impact on College Attendance." *National Tax Journal* 53, no. 3 (2000): 629–61.

Dynarski, Susan. "Does Aid Matter? Measuring the Effect of Student Aid on College Attendance and Completion." *American Economic Review* 93, no. 1 (2003): 279–88.

Dynarski, Susan M., and Judith E. Scott-Clayton. "The Cost of Complexity in Federal Student Aid: Lessons from Optimal Tax Theory and Behavioral Economics." *National Tax Journal* 59, no. 2 (2006): 319–56.

Dynarski, Susan M., and Judith E. Scott-Clayton. "The Feasibility of Streamlining Aid for College Using the Tax System." *National Tax Association Papers and Proceedings* 99 (2007): 250–62.

Ellwood, David, and Thomas Kane. "Who Is Getting a College Education? Family Background and the Growing

Gap in Enrollment." In *Securing the Future*, Sheldon Danziger and Joel Waldfogel (Eds.). New York, NY: Russell Sage, 2000.

Fitzpatrick, Maria D., and Damon Jones. "Higher Education, Merit-Based Scholarships and Post-Baccalaureate Migration." National Bureau of Economic Research Working Paper No. 18530, 2012.

Hansen, W. Lee. "Impact of Student Financial Aid on Access." *Proceedings of the Academy of Political Science* 35, no. 2 (1983): 84–96.

Hoxby, Caroline, and Christopher Avery. 2013. "The Missing 'One-Offs': The Hidden Supply of High-Achieving, Low-Income Students." *Brookings Papers on Economic Activity* 1: 1–65.

Kane, Thomas J. "College Entry by Blacks Since 1970: The Role of College Costs, Family Background, and the Returns to Education." *Journal of Political Economy*, 102, no. 5 (1994): 878–911.

Looney, Adam, and Constantine Yannelis. "A Crisis in Student Loans? How Changes in the Characteristics of Borrowers and in the Institutions they Attended Contributed to Rising Loan Defaults." *Brookings Papers on Economic Activity* Fall, 2015 1–68.

Lovenheim, Michael F. "The Effect of Liquid Housing Wealth on College Enrollment." *Journal of Labor Economics* 29, no. 4 (2011): 741–71.

Lovenheim, Michael F., and C. Lockwood Reynolds. "The Effect of Housing Wealth on College Choice: Evidence from the Housing Boom." *Journal of Human Resources* 48, no. 1 (2013): 1–35.

Scott-Clayton, Judith. "On Money and Motivation: A Quasi-Experimental Analysis of Financial Incentives for College Achievement." *Journal of Human Resources* 46, no. 3 (2011): 614–46.

Seftor, Neil S., and Sarah E. Turner. "Back to School: Federal Student Aid Policy and Adult College Enrollment." *Journal of Human Resources* 37, no. 2 (2002): 336–52.

"Trends in Student Aid." New York, NY: College Board, 2013. http://trends.collegeboard.org/sites/default/files/student-aid-2013-full-report.pdf.

"Trends in Student Aid." New York, NY: College Board, 2015. http://trends.collegeboard.org/sites/default/files/trends-student-aid-web-final-508-2.pdf.

Chapter 15

Altonji, Joseph G., Erica Blom, and Costas Meghir. "Heterogeneity in Human Capital Investments: High School Curriculum, College Major, and Careers." NBER Working Paper No. 17985, 2012.

Andrews, Rodney, Jing Li, and Michael F. Lovenheim. "Quantile Treatment Effects of College Quality on Earnings." *Journal of Human Resources* 51, no. 1 (2016): 200–38.

Arcidiacono, Peter, and Michael Lovenheim. "Affirmative Action and the Quality-Fit Tradeoff." *Journal of Economic Literature* 54, no. 1 (2016): 3–51.

Avery, Christopher, Andrew Fairbanks, and Richard J. Zeckhauser. *The Early Admissions Game: Joining the Elite.* Cambridge, MA: Harvard University Press, 2003.

Babcock, Philip, and Mindy Marks. "The Falling Time Cost of College: Evidence from Half a Century of Time Use Data." *Review of Economics and Statistics* 93, no. 2 (2011): 468–78.

Bettinger, Eric. "How Financial Aid Affects Persistence." In *College Choices: The Economics of Where to Go, When to Go, and How to Pay For It*, Caroline M. Hoxby (Ed.). Chicago, IL: University of Chicago Press, 2004.

Bettinger, Eric, and Bridget Terry Long. "Addressing the Needs of Underprepared Students in Higher Education: Does College Remediation Work?" *Journal of Human Resources* 44, no. 3 (2009): 736–71.

Bound, John, Michael F. Lovenheim, and Sarah Turner. "Why Have College Completion Rates Declined? An Analysis of Changing Student Preparation and Collegiate Resources." *American Economic Journal: Applied Economic* 2, no. 3 (2010): 129–57.

Bound, John, Michael F. Lovenheim, and Sarah Turner. "Increasing Time to Baccalaureate Degree in the United States." *Education Finance and Policy* 7, no. 4 (2012): 375–424.

Bowen, William G., and Derek Bok. *The Shape of the River: Long-Term Consequences of Considering Race in College and University Admissions.* Princeton, NJ: Princeton University Press, 1998.

Bowen, William G., Matthew M. Chingos, and Michael S. McPherson. *Crossing the Finish Line: Completing College at America's Public Universities.* Princeton, NJ: Princeton University Press, 2009.

Bowen, William G., Martin A. Kurzweil, and Eugene M. Tobin. *Equity and Excellence in American Higher Education.* Charlottesville, VA: University of Virginia Press, 2005.

Calcagno, Juan Carlos, and Bridget T. Long. "The Impact of Postsecondary Remediation Using a Regression Discontinuity Approach: Addressing Endogenous Sorting and Noncompliance." NBER Working Paper No. 14194, 2008.

Carnevale, Anthony P., and Ben Cheah. "Hard Times: College Majors, Unemployment and Earnings." Report. Washington, DC: Georgetown University Center on Education and the Workforce, 2013.

Carnevale, Anthony P., Stephen J. Rose, and Ben Cheah. "Executive Summary: The College Payoff: Education, Occupations, Lifetime Earnings." Washington, DC: Georgetown University Center on Education and the Workforce, 2014.

Carrell, Scott E., Richard L. Fullerton, and James E. West. "Does Your Cohort Matter? Measuring Peer Effects in College Achievement." *Journal of Labor Economics* 27, no. 3 (2009): 439–64.

Carrell, Scott E., Bruce I. Sacerdote, and James E. West. "From Natural Variation to Optimal Policy? The Importance of Endogenous Peer Group Formation." *Econometrica* 81, no. 3 (2013): 855–82.

Chade, Hector, and Lones Smith. "Simultaneous Search." *Econometrica* 74, no. 5 (2006): 1293–307.

Chade, Hector, Gregory Lewis, and Lones Smith. "Student Portfolios and the College Admissions Problem." *Review of Economic Studies* 81, no. 3 (2014): 971–1002.

Eisenberg, Daniel, Ezra Golberstein, and Janis L. Whitlock. "Peer Effects on Risky Behaviors: New Evidence from College Roommate Assignments." *Journal of Health Economics* 33 (2014): 126–38.

Fryer, Roland G., Jr., Glenn C. Loury, and Tolga Yuret. "An Economic Analysis of Color-Blind Affirmative Action." *The Journal of Law, Economics, & Organization* 24, no. 2 (2007): 319–55.

Gneezy, Uri, Muriel Niederle, and Aldo Rustichini. "Performance in Competitive Environments: Gender Differences." *Quarterly Journal of Economics* 118, no. 3 (2003): 1049–74.

Goldin, Claudia, Lawrence F. Katz, and Ilyana Kuziemko. "The Homecoming of American College Women." *Journal of Economic Perspectives* 20, no. 4 (2006): 133–56.

Hoxby, Caroline, and Christopher Avery. "The Missing 'One-Offs': The Hidden Supply of High-Achieving, Low-Income Students." *Brookings Papers on Economics Activity* Spring 2013: 1–65.

Hoxby, Caroline, and Sarah Turner. "Expanding College Opportunities for High-Achieving, Low-Income Students." SIEPR Discussion Paper No. 12-014, 2013.

Kane, Thomas J. "Racial and Ethnic Preferences in College Admissions." In *The Black-White Test Score Gap*, Christopher Jencks and Meredith Phillips (Eds.), 1998.

Kremer, Michael, and Dan Levy. 2008. "Peer Effects and Alcohol Use among College Students." *Journal of Economic Perspectives*, 22, no. 3 (2008): 189–206.

Long, Mark C. "Race and College Admission: An Alternative to Affirmative Action?" *Review of Economics and Statistics* 86, no. 4 (2004): 1020–033.

Long, Mark C. "Is There a 'Workable' Race-Neutral Alternative to Affirmative Action in College Admissions?" *Journal of Policy Analysis and Management* 34, no. 1 (2015): 162–83.

Manski, Charles F. "Schooling as Experimentation: A Reappraisal of the Postsecondary Dropout Phenomenon." *Economics of Education Review* 8, no. 4 (1989): 305–12.

Manski, Charles F. "Identification of Endogenous Social Effects: The Reflection Problem." *Review of Economic Studies* 60, no. 3 (1993): 531–42.

Martorell, Paco, and Isaac McFarlin, Jr. "Help or Hindrance? The Effects of College Remediation on Academic and Labor Market Outcomes." *Review of Economics and Statistics* 93, no. 2 (2011): 436–54.

Niederle, Muriel, and Lisa Vesterlund. "Do Women Shy Away from Competition? Do Men Compete Too Much?" *Quarterly Journal of Economics* 122, no. 3 (2007): 1067–101.

Pallais Amanda. Small Differences That Matter: Mistakes in Applying to College. *Journal of Labor Economics* 33, no. 2 (2015): 493–520.

Rothschild, Michael, and Lawrence J. White. "The Analytics of the Pricing of Higher Education and Other Services in Which the Customers Are Inputs." *Journal of Political Economy* 103, no. 3 (1995): 573–86.

Sacerdote, Bruce. "Peer Effects with Random Assignment: Results for Dartmouth Roommates." *Quarterly Journal of Economics* 116, no. 2 (2001): 681–704.

Sallee, James M., Alexandra A. Resch, and Paul N. Courant. "On the Optimal Allocation of Students and Resources in a System of Higher Education." *The B.E. Journal of Economic Analysis & Policy* 8, no. 1 (2008), Advances, Article 11.

Scott-Clayton, Judith. "What Explains Trends in Labor Supply among U.S. Undergraduates?" *National Tax Journal* 65, no. 1 (2012): 181–210.

Scott-Clayton, Judith, and Olga Rodriguez. "Development, Discouragement, or Diversion? New Evidence on the Effects of College Remediation." NBER Working Paper No. 18328, 2012.

Shulman, James L., and William G. Bowen. *The Game of Life: College Sports and Educational Values.* Princeton: Princeton University Press, 2002.

Stange, Kevin M. "An Empirical Investigation of the Option Value of College Enrollment." *American Economic Journal: Applied Economics* 4, no. 1 (2012): 49–84.

Stinebrickner, Ralph, and Todd R. Stinebrickner. "Working during School and Academic Performance." *Journal of Labor Economics* 21, no. 2 (2003): 473–91.

Stinebrickner, Ralph, and Todd R. Stinebrickner. "What Can be Learned about Peer Effects Using College Roommates? Evidence from New Survey Data and Students from Disadvantaged Backgrounds." *Journal of Public Economics* 90, no. 8–9 (2006): 1435–454.

Stinebrickner, Ralph, and Todd R. Stinebrickner. "The Effect of Credit Constraints on the College Drop-Out Decision: A Direct Approach Using a New Panel Study." *American Economic Review* 98, no. 5 (2008): 2163–184.

Turner, Sarah E., and William G. Bowen. "Choice of Major: The Changing (Unchanging) Gender Gap." *Industrial and Labor Relations Review* 52, no. 2 (1999): 289–313.

Wiswall, Matthew, and Basit Zafar. "Determinants of College Major Choice: Identification Using an Information Experiment." *Review of Economic Studies* 82, no. 2 (2015): 791–824.

Zimmerman, David J. "Peer Effects in Academic Outcomes: Evidence from a Natural Experiment." *Review of Economics and Statistics* 85, no. 1 (2003): 9–23.

Appendix A

Heckman, James J., and Paul A. LaFontaine. "The American High School Graduation Rate: Trends and Levels." *Review of Economics and Statistics* 92, no. 2 (2010): 244–62.

Jaeger, David A. "Reconciling the Old and New Census Bureau Education Questions: Recommendations for Researchers." *Journal of Business and Economic Statistics* 15, no. 3 (1997): 300–09.

Jaeger, David A. "Estimating the Returns to Education Using the Newest Current Population Survey Education Questions." *Economics Letters* 76, no. 3 (2003): 385–94.

Jaeger, David A., and Marianne E. Page. "Degrees Matter: New Evidence on Sheepskin Effects in the Returns to Education." *Review of Economics and Statistics* 78, no. 4 (1996): 733–40.

Mishel, Lawrence, and Joydeep Roy. *Rethinking High School Graduation Rates and Trends.* Washington, DC: Economic Policy Institute, 2006.

Name Index

Subject Index

Note: Page numbers followed by f, n, and t indicate figures, footnotes, and tables, respectively.